NEWBERY AND CALDECOTT MEDAL AND HONOR BOOKS

an annotated bibliography

The Newbery and Caldecott Medals. Reprinted by permission of the Association of Library Service to Children of the American Library Association.

NEWBERY AND CALDECOTT MEDAL AND HONOR BOOKS
an annotated bibliography

Linda Kauffman Peterson

and

Marilyn Leathers Solt

G. K. HALL & CO., 70 LINCOLN STREET, BOSTON, MASS., 1982

Copyright © 1982 by Marilyn Solt and Linda Peterson

Library of Congress Cataloging in Publication Data
Peterson, Linda Kauffman.

  Newbery and Caldecott Medal and Honor books.

  Bibliography
  Includes index.
  1. Children--Books and reading--Bibliography.
2. Children's literature--Bibliography. 3.Literary
prizes. I. Solt, Marilyn Leathers. II. Title.
Z1037.P45   [PN1009.A1]   011'.62'079   82-2880
ISBN 0-8161-8448-8   AACR2

This publication is printed on permanent/durable acid-free paper
MANUFACTURED IN THE UNITED STATES OF AMERICA

To Virginia Everett Leland--teacher and friend

Contents

The Authors

Linda Kauffman Peterson, author of the Caldecott section, is currently instructor of children's literature in the Department of English at Bowling Green State University, Bowling Green, Ohio. She has taught first grade and has given art instruction to children in kindergarten through sixth grade. She served on the committee to revise the Art Curriculum for the Franklin County Schools (Ohio) in 1976, and continues to work with children in classrooms and libraries, using literature to stimulate artistic creativity, literary appreciation, and verbal and written skills. She is also a contributor to and coeditor, with Marilyn Solt, of the <u>Children's Literature Association Quarterly</u> Special Section on the Newbery and Caldecott Medal and Honor Books, Fall 1981.

Marilyn Leathers Solt, author of the Newbery portion, teaches children's literature at Bowling Green State University, where she is associate professor in the Department of English. She has presented papers on children's literature at professional conferences and has had articles published in the <u>English Association of Northwestern Ohio Bulletin,</u> <u>Illinois English Bulletin</u>, and the <u>Ohio Media Spectrum.</u> She wrote the section on Ohio for <u>The Great Lakes Region in Children's Books</u> (Brighton, Mich.: Green Oak Press, 1980), and coedited, with Linda Peterson, the Fall 1981 Special Section of the <u>Children's Literature Association Quarterly</u> on the Newbery and Caldecott Medal and Honor Books.

Foreword

It has been an exciting 60 years! In 1922, the year of the first
Newbery award, I would just have been finishing fourth grade. I was
young, no question, for Van Loon's Story of Mankind, a book rated
"Gr. 7 and up," but nobody in our household stood on ceremony about
such things, and soon everybody was competing for a look--me, my
father, my mother, and even my sister, Nancy, in first grade.

Yes, I know that any first grader's "readiness" for the Story of
Mankind might have been questioned, but Nancy really had less trouble
than anyone--she'd simply find who had the book and have that person
read aloud! I made sure to do my share of the reading aloud, too.
After all it was something that grown-ups did.

Reading aloud was fun, and there was a "togetherness" about it
that transcended subject and underscored the irrelevance of grades
and word counts. From my father we might get A. A. Milne, but the
nice thing was that he wasn't reading down to us; he liked Milne,
too. He also read us Robert Frost. Our home reading circle might,
after all, have a 30-year age span, and stuff that wasn't good enough
for everybody wasn't good enough for anybody.

Reading aloud had a music and a magic that quite by-passed mere
communication. It wasn't just something you did for the benefit of
those who couldn't have done it for themselves. It was a way to com-
mune rather than communicate. We early learned the difference. Reading silently went much faster. We could start on our own. We could
race ahead, or refer back. But the big bonus was choice. We could
start anywhere and anytime. We could quit anywhere and anytime.

The past 60 years of Newbery/Caldecott as told here may just
memorialize the whole magic matter of choice and interest in print.
Reading is only one aspect of language. There are people who can
talk but not read, and even people who can read but not talk. The
difference, though, between free reading and assigned reading invites
analysis. I have seen situations where a child was denied a book
that he wanted on the ground that he wasn't ready for it. So have
you. I have heard it argued that any reading that a child isn't

ix

ready for could be dangerous, and could put him off reading entirely. The same people, though, seem braced for resistance to their choices, too, that is, to reading for self-improvement. What a dismal choice! Waste your time or lose your patience!

From the beginning, the definition of the books to be honored by Newbery and Caldecott awards seemed clear enough. They were to be "distinguished contributions" to "American literature for children," and exactly how "literature" might differ from other kinds of writing got no further attention. It was swiftly agreed that recognition of more than fiction or "belles lettres" was to be allowed for, and on the average every sixth book has been in areas of biography and information. We know that these were books of distinction. However, not everybody will be interested in every one. What counts will be helping readers discover what's for them. What makes a book interesting, anyway? The authors have a real feel for it.

Writing for children surely isn't so much a matter of diluting a subject until a child can take it without pain; it is more a matter of refining a presentation until it comes across without boredom or confusion. There are books and better books and the best are good enough for children. They don't have to be assigned, they just "provoke interest."

It is worth noting the degree to which our selection committees have here homed in on books that were "interesting" without worrying too much about age level, word count, etc. These were "distinguished" books, all right, but their qualifications were something to sense more than define.

Some choices tend toward the romantic, as if work delivering sheep would (or should?) excite more interest than, say, work delivering newspapers; but we can hardly hope to have selections "right" for many readers except as the range is wide. How define a "children's book" anyhow? How far can you accept that common school book assumption that ages of "reading readiness" are anything more than ages of interest? Just what sorts of subjects warrant the attention of children as distinct from adults? Is it fair to children to expect them to be interested in childish things? Don't they really have a life-long bias in favor of learning how the adult world operates?

Surely growing up doesn't so much hinge on getting older, but on gaining experience! We send them out "to play" when they'd really rather peel potatoes, or change light bulbs, or operate adding machines, or work typewriters, or wash windows, or lay fires.

Nothing in the "play" world can compare for "interest" to real-world activities like changing a fuse, or using a sewing machine, or telephoning grandma, or fixing a running toilet. If kids seem to watch

too much TV isn't it because their elders do, too, instead of coming
up with less tedious alternatives like reading?

What makes good books interesting may be hard to define, but in
the choices given here it comes clear enough. Distinction is its own
best definition.

It is the same with defining "literature" as here honored.
Limits were not set between fiction and nonfiction, between history
and contemporary affairs. Here, however, are 451 judgments out of
six decades not only identified but described. It isn't just praise,
it isn't just evaluation, it is description--and refreshing description it is.

Just as these selections form their own best definition of
"distinction," so may they also be taken as self-defining when it
comes to "grade level."

Over the years many new writers have taken to writing for children and made it a profession of its own. However, they have tended
to stay with the distinction of aiming to interest rather than instruct. They have respected grade levels but only of the most general kind, and interest levels rather than reading readiness. (Of
these 561 medal and honor books over half have an indicated grade
span of five years or more.)

Some of the excitement underscoring these choices surely is due
to the fact that they aren't narrowly graded. They aren't textbooks.
They may be tightly organized, they may move sure-footedly from A to
B, or from the simple to the more advanced, but Goal No. 1 is to reward the reader's interest.

Grading is meaningless if taken as limiting, but it provides
great guidance. There were risks in even suggesting more than minimal correlation between grade and subject, but here is where librarians have priceless advantages over teachers. Helping a child to
find a book that is right for him is challenging, certainly, but at
least it isn't impossible. It isn't like trying to make one textbook
right for 30 children, and it quite avoids the all-too-common approach of trying to make many children right for one textbook by
leaving some behind.

It is interesting that the first award went to a book graded "7
and up." Van Loon wasn't so much writing for children as just writing! He didn't write to instruct, he wrote to share. You could open
him whatever your age and find him hard to close. Some of the same
secret must have permeated most of the 561 choices described here, to
judge from the way even the descriptions can catch your interest and
open new vistas.

Foreword

A helpful feature of this 60-year review is the showing of the
O.P. status of the books. Presumably books in demand stay in print.
Libraries can probably have whatever they want, if enough people
"want." It could be interesting to study how the winning books differ as regards endurance, that is, which need recurring replacement
and which go less appreciated or exploited.

The factors determining the books to be kept in print are many
and can change. It can cost a lot to make ready for a reprint, but
comparatively little to run extras at the same time. Reprinting
color can be costly, but perhaps decreasingly so where anticipated
and allowed for.

Are there many OP books here that we would buy if we could get
them? Perhaps not. The publishers have every reason to print anything that will sell.

On average, a third of the books here honored are also OP, the
older more than the recent, but clearly subject to other kinds of ups
and downs. Over the thirty years from '42 to '71, three publishers
had 15 or more choices each. All have been keeping all their Medal
winners in print. As regards their Honor books, however, things are
different. One publisher keeps 12 of 15 in print, and one keeps 8 of
10 in print, but a third keeps only 4 of 14 in print.

How shall we interpret this? Does one of the publishers simply
do shorter-lived stuff, or does he do books that deserve better but
get retired to OP status every time some figure man's formulae pro-
nounce their rate of sale unacceptable?

If these business school types knew the books we read as well as
the books they balance, they'd know that books that sell themselves
don't have a cost-of-sales as large as average. If they could find
a place in their calculations for things like public service and
author relations they could come up with some values overriding mere
percentages.

This overview of which books go OP could be trying to tell us
something. Do we need a scheme for pooling library purchasing power
so as better to reward the deserving? Might we, in passing, get
feedback of interest to future selection committees?

Concern is being voiced about whether textbooks and teachers can
long compete against "more interesting" latter-day teaching tech-
nologies--audio and visual, tape and disk, data processing and word
processing. Real readers, on the other hand, wonder who would willingly work with words on cathode ray tubes if they could have them
on paper.

Might books and reading be made obsolete, too, by later develop-
ments in communication? Don't you believe it! Textbooks and teachers

may be on trial (where key concepts include regimentation, indoctrination, insemination, and programming), but books as such never had it better.

Each year sees us writing more books, printing more books, and moving more books through bookstores, libraries, newsstands, and mail order. There have been changes in the ways we set the type and get the ink onto the paper—but the "page" survives and thrives.

We must be doing something right—and nowhere does it show more clearly than in this factor of interest that librarians seem here to know so well to recognize and stimulate.

Daniel Melcher
Charlottesville, VA

Acknowledgments

We gratefully acknowledge the assistance of Mary Jane Anderson, Executive Director of the Association for Library Service to Children of the American Library Association, who supplied information for and read the essay on the history of the Newbery and Caldecott Medals.

Our grateful acknowledgment also goes to the Association for Library Service to Children of the American Library Association for granting us permission to reprint the Terms, Definitions, and Criteria for the Newbery and Caldecott Medals and for permission to use the photographs of the medals.

Our sincere thanks to those who helped make this work possible-- those who typed for us, located books for us, and offered us criticism and encouragement.

Preface

The Newbery and Caldecott Medals, bestowed by the American Library Association (ALA) each year since 1922 and 1938, respectively, remain the most esteemed awards in the realm of American books for children. For the pages within we have written annotations of these noted Medal and Honor Books so that they may be further utilized, appreciated, studied, and circulated. Although there is no real substitute for having these books in hand to peruse and evaluate, these annotations will at least provide an introduction to the stories, characters, and illustrations of these works. With this we might hope to supply enough information to allow the reader to determine whether the books in question have relevance to his or her particular needs.

PURPOSE

This bibliography is intended as a reference handbook for those who work with children's literature--librarians, teachers, instructors and students of children's literature, and parents. The purpose of the information contained within the following pages is (1) to provide a brief summary of each of the Newbery and Caldecott Medal and Honor Books since 1922 and 1938, respectively; (2) to provide critical commentary on the texts of the Newbery books and on the illustrations in the Caldecott books; (3) to provide a tool for quick reference to those familiar stories and characters of the Medal and Honor Books, as well as to help revive some of the excellent early works which remain obscure and often overlooked; and (4) to provide a commentary on the trends apparent in the Medal and Honor Books.

We have chosen to include the Honor Books in this survey to offer a more complete presentation of the books that have been considered by the ALA to be of literary and artistic merit. Because choices for the medals are only made from books published in a particular year, it is possible, in a year producing several superior books, that the Honor Books may be of as much literary or artistic merit as the medal winners of other years. Since critical tastes in books do not always agree, the overemphasis of concentration on one Medal book per year, ignoring others nearly as good, or even better, unnecessarily limits the original intent of both these esteemed awards--to recognize the creators, and their creations, of quality literature for children.

Preface

SCOPE

The annotations of this bibliography cover all the Medal and Honor Books since the inception of the Newbery (1922) and Caldecott (1938) Medals through 1981. The entries are arranged chronologically; for each year the Medal books are followed by the Honor Books, listed, since 1964, alphabetically by author in the case of the Newbery books and by illustrator for the Caldecott works. Honor Books prior to 1964 are listed according to the number of votes received, the books with the highest number of points listed first.

ARRANGEMENT

The bibliography is divided into the Newbery section, prefaced with the essay "The Newbery Medal and Honor Books: Characteristics and Trends," and the Caldecott section, which is accompanied by a similar essay, "The Caldecott Trends: 1938-1981." Following these major segments appear Appendices, which include a complete list of the Newbery and Caldecott Medal and Honor Books to 1981 (Appendix A); the Terms, Definitions, and Criteria (Appendix B) utilized by the Newbery and Caldecott committees to determine medal recipients; and charts categorizing the types of literature which have comprised the Medal and Honor Books (Appendices C and D). An author, illustrator, and title index and a subject index complete the bibliography.

ANNOTATIONS

The initial portion of each annotation contains a story/plot summary; the second segment of the Newbery entries provides critical commentary on the text, while the illustrations remain the focus of the latter portion of the Caldecott annotations.

The bibliographic information included in each citation provides author, title, illustrator, city of publication, publisher, date, and number of pages. If there is no illustrator indicated in the Caldecott citations, it can be assumed that the author is also the illustrator. Those works that are unpaginated have the number of pages enclosed within brackets. Books that no longer remain in print are noted with (OP) after the bibliographic citation. Where possible, first editions were utilized for the bibliography; though circumstances relegated some editions unavailable, the citations remain to first editions. Since many of the Medal and Honor Books only remain in print in paperback or revised editions, it is advisable to check the current volume of R. R. Bowker's Children's Books in Print for more specific information regarding the form in which a work is available.

Since the visual element is integral to the Caldecott works, the citations for these books also include detailed information on the illustrations in the text. The total number of illustrations included in the body of the text is noted and categorized according to whether they are black and white or color. The amount of illustration preceding and following the body of the text is indicated, as is the medium or media utilized by the illustrator. The trim size of the pages is also included, as the book's physical format often reflects a particular theme, shape, or size which may be of importance to the story within.

The final component of the information included prior to the annotations is a distinction as to the type of literature the work represents, as well as an indication of the intended grade level of the book's audience. The types of literature according to which these books are categorized fall into the following classifications:

Folk literature. Most of the traditional literature represented in the Newbery-Caldecott works falls under the division of folk literature, which includes both folk and fairy tales. The broad categorization of traditional literature also includes those titles classified as Mother Goose or nursery rhymes, fables, legends, epics, hero tales, and biblical stories or verses. These works are considered traditional by virtue of the fact that they originated in the oral tradition, spoken or sung, and have no known author. Much of traditional literature comes to us in recorded form--collected or compiled at some point by such people as the Grimm Brothers, Charles Perrault, Joseph Jacobs--but its origins are oral and aural, the stories transmitted from generation to generation, from culture to culture, by word of mouth.

Fantasy. Books of fantasy include some element beyond the realm of possibility in terms of reality--talking animals, inanimate objects brought to life, magical dwarfs and elves, new creatures and settings unknown in the "real" world, or imaginings of the mind are all conventions used in books of fantasy. Only authored fantasy, including those literary fairy tales of such people as Hans Christian Andersen, fall under the classification of fantasy in this bibliography. Though much of traditional literature is fantasy, it is unauthored fantasy and is not included under this category.

Biography. Biographies are considered those books that portray a significant portion of the life of an actual person or group of people. This type of literature takes on different forms in children's books. Collective biographies of specific groups of interest, partial biographies covering a limited span of the subject's life, or complete biographies from the subject's birth to death all fall within the realm of biography for the child audience. The subjects of biographies represented in the Newbery-Caldecott titles, for the most part, remain prominent figures from American history; but because the story or plot supersedes the relay of information and facts, the biographies are, to a large extent, fictionalized, providing a more consumable product for the audience.

Books of information. Informational books included in the Newbery-Caldecott works reflect the variety of nonfiction available to children and include those books whose prime function it is to communicate facts or concepts. Alphabet and counting books, science and geography works, and books that foster aesthetic appreciation or an understanding of different cultures and times are represented. As in biography, these books of nonfiction are closely tied together with the threads of an overriding plot. Woven into the fabric of the story, creating the patterns and designs, are the facts and information the author wishes to communicate to the audience.

Historical fiction. A book of historical fiction is one in which the setting is a time period earlier than that in which the author is writing and which incorporates authentic historical information into its text. This definition excludes novels that, when they were written, were contemporary, but, with the passage of time, seem historically oriented. This definition does include novels written today that are set in an earlier frame of historical reference.

Fiction. Those stories that are well within the realm of possibility, whose intent is realism, constitute the category of fiction. Fiction set in other lands, realistic animal stories, works about regions and minorities, and other settings within the United States comprise the divisions of fiction utilized in the introductory essays and in the appendices.

SUGGESTIONS FOR USE

The categorization, by literary type, of the Newbery and Caldecott Medal and Honor Books, discussed more fully in the essays preceding the major sections and charted in Appendices C and D, offers enormous possibilities for using this bibliography as a resource instrument as well. The information contained within this compilation is of historical, sociological, and comparative importance.

The chronological arrangement makes research in the trends of decades, the prevalence of works by specific authors, or the popularity of particular illustrators recognizable at a glance. These obvious facts and others can be discerned by noting the relationships of the books published in a given year or time span, by observing the subject matter or type of literature that predominates, or by tracing an author's or illustrator's career.

Much is also apparent by noticing the juxtaposition of Medal and Honor Books published within the same year--some years bursting with quality Honor Books, others lining up a scant one or two. In some years, too, the Honor Books have far outlived the Medal Books in popularity. The effects of economic and political climates in the country are also obvious after a closer look at these books as a whole.

It is our ultimate concern that this reference work will bring more quality children's literature to the eyes and ears of the audience for which it was intended. The Subject Index is included as a tool for locating books on specific topics, places, people, and times. Used in conjunction with the grade levels included in the annotations, the Subject Index serves as a valuable aid for teachers (in supplementing classroom activities in the subject areas), for parents (by helping them meet the special needs and reading interests of their children), and for librarians (by providing information on unfamiliar Newbery and Caldecott titles in specific areas).

The books that made this reference work possible indicate that the decision-making and selection processes that go hand in hand with the Newbery and Caldecott Medals are not simple procedures, nor are these methods infallible. Though many of the books included here remain popular and in demand, others have not withstood the test of time and remain unused, a further indication of the enormous task of determining what actually constitutes "the best." Are the best books those read most often by or to children? Are those books that present a bit of insight into life and ourselves "the best"? Or is it those books that sustain three or four readings and remain as meaningful, that, recalled from childhood, are subsequently passed on from generation to generation, that meet and fulfill the literary and artistic criteria for quality? Whatever the answer, it will be obvious, after using this handbook, that none of these works was an accident. None came about without much thought and effort. Likewise, the selection of these books by the American Library Association committees is not an easy task. The variety of books contained within this bibliography is a reflection of the people who have made them come to life; the value of the books is dependent upon the use to which they may be put. It is our hope that this work will help bring more quality literature to the hands and eyes and ears of children so that they, too, will grow capable of discerning and judging quality literature, whatever their age.

Introduction:
A History of the Newbery and Caldecott Medals

The most prestigious of the many awards given in the United States for children's books are the Newbery and Caldecott Medals. The Newbery Medal has been given annually since 1922 to the author of the "most distinguished contribution to American literature for children," and the Caldecott Medal has been given annually since 1938 to the illustrator of the "most distinguished American picture book for children." During these years an additional 200 books have been named Newbery Honor Books and approximately 140 have been designated as Caldecott Honor Books.

ORIGIN AND TERMS OF THE NEWBERY AWARD

The Newbery Award resulted from a spontaneous proposal made by Frederic Melcher, coeditor of Publishers Weekly, in a speech to the Children's Librarians' Section of the American Library Association at Swampscott, Massachusetts, in 1921. He recalled the occasion in an article published in the Saturday Review of Literature in 1933:

> I had been asked to give a talk . . . about Children's
> Book Week. . . . I remember looking down from the plat-
> form at all those enthusiastic people from every part of
> the Union and wondering whether they could not, as a
> group take one more job, by helping to assure a greater
> literature for children as well as a wider reading of the
> then available literature. . . . These people knew the
> audience of boys and girls, knew them intimately, knew
> what boys and girls really wanted. They could help build
> a greater literature by giving authoritative recognition
> to those who wrote well. I conceived the plan of an
> annual award and offered it on the spot with the sugges-
> tion that good old John Newbery's name be attached to the
> medal.[1]

His idea was promptly approved by vote and the incoming officers were charged to put it into effect the following year.

In November of 1922, after the first Medal had already been given, Mr. Melcher wrote a formal statement outlining origin, method, and purpose of the award. This was approved by the American Library

Association and has been the guiding document in administering the award. Among the terms stated were these:

> The medal is to be awarded annually to the author of the
> "most distinguished contribution to American literature
> for children," the award being made to cover books whose
> publication in book form falls in the calendar year last
> elapsed. The author is restricted to authors who are
> citizens or residents of the United States. Reprints
> and compilations are not eligible for consideration.
> There are no limitations as to the character of the book
> considered except that it be original work. It need not
> be written solely for children, the judgment of the librar-
> ians voting shall decide whether a book be a "contribution
> to the literature for children." The award considers only
> the books of one calendar year and does not pass judgment
> on the author's previous works or other work during that
> year outside the volume that may be named.[2]

In the summer of 1932, the stipulation that the book be original was further defined to include books traditional in origin that are "the result of individual research, the retelling and reinterpretation being the writer's own."[3] At this same conference a resolution was passed that aimed at fulfilling the purpose of the award as stated by Mr. Melcher in the 1922 agreement. To aid in encouraging "original and creative work" it was decided that "the book of a previous recip- ient of the Newbery Medal shall receive the award only upon the unan- imous vote of the Newbery Committee."[4] This resolution remained in effect until January 1958, when it was rescinded by the Children's Services Division Board since the need to encourage new authors and illustrators no longer existed.

ORIGIN AND TERMS OF THE CALDECOTT AWARD

The Caldecott Medal was established in 1937 for several reasons. A great variety and number of picture books distinguished in illustra- tion had been produced in the United States during the preceding dec- ade. Since most of the Newbery books had been written for older children, few of these outstanding picture books had received recog- nition. Two notable exceptions were Millions of Cats and ABC Bunny, both by Wanda Gág, which were named Newbery Honor Books in 1929 and 1934. Consequently, when Mr. Melcher suggested that a special award honoring the illustrator be given, the suggestion was enthusiastically received. The resolution that was passed stated:

> The name of this medal shall be the Caldecott Medal.
> This medal shall be awarded to the artist of the most
> distinguished American Picture Book for Children pub-
> lished in the United States during the preceding year.
> The award shall go to the artist, who must be a citizen
> or resident of the United States, whether or not he be

the author of the text. Members of the Newbery Medal
Committee will serve as judges.[5]

This resolution also stated that if a book is nominated for both the
Newbery and Caldecott Awards, the Committee shall decide the award
for which it shall be voted "so that the same title shall not be considered on both ballots."[6] In the late 1970s, this procedure was
changed to allow any eligible book to be considered for either or
both awards.

Additional qualifications for the Caldecott Medal added over the
years specify that, even though the pictures are of first importance,
the text must be worthy of the book. There are no limitations on the
character of the illustrations or on the age level of the book, although it is recognized that most picture books are intended for young
children.

NAMING THE AWARDS

It is a happy circumstance that we have Mr. Melcher's own words
for his choice of names. He wrote that he connected the name John
Newbery with the first award because "this lovable book-seller and
publisher of the eighteenth century, London, was perhaps the first
bookman to appreciate that the reading interests of children were
worthy of especial and individual attention."[7] He gave three reasons for naming the illustrators' medal for Randolph Caldecott, a
great nineteenth century English illustrator of children's books,
including "This is the House that Jack Built" and other nursery
rhymes. First, he felt that it would not be proper to use the name
of a living person. Second, he pointed out that "in the history of
the picture book, Caldecott has an important place."[8] And finally,
he stated, Caldecott "supplies us with a name that has pleasant
memories--memories connected with the joyousness of picture books as
well as with their beauty."[9]

THE MEDALS

When Mr. Melcher, as the donor of the Newbery Medal, engaged the
services of a young, but already noted, sculptor, René Chambellan, he
suggested to him that a medal in keeping with the intent of the award
might show "genius giving of its best to the child."[10] The medal
Mr. Chambellan designed does just this. On the face are three figures: the central one, a man holding a book, represents the author;
a boy and girl on each side have hands outstretched to him as if to
receive his creative talents. The reverse of the medal shows an open
book and the words: "For the most distinguished contribution to
American literature for children." Around the edge, the words "John
Newbery Medal" and "Given annually by the Children's Librarians' Section of the American Library Association" appear.

Introduction

When it came time to consider a design for the Caldecott Medal, Mr. Melcher again turned to Chambellan. Wishing the sculptor to understand the spirit of Caldecott, Mr. Melcher gave him a collection of Caldecott's books. He related that "Mr. Chambellan became so delighted with Caldecott's draftsmanship that he immediately said he could do nothing better than put a few of the typical scenes on the medal."[11] Circling an engraving of John Gilpin's famous ride, the legend "The Caldecott Medal" identifies the award. The reverse, displaying another of Caldecott's illustrations, portrays "four and twenty blackbirds baked in a pie" and bears the words "For the most distinguished American picture book for Children" and "Awarded annually by the Children's and School Librarians' Sections of the American Library Association."

Both medals are struck in bronze. In 1956, it was decided that gold facsimile seals of the medals may be placed on the award-winning books and, since 1971, silver facsimile seals with the designation "Newbery Honor Book" or "Caldecott Honor Book" may be placed on the Honor Books. The seals are available from the Association for Library Service to Children of the American Library Association. From the beginning all profits from seal sales have gone to the Frederic G. Melcher Scholarship fund. At present two $4,000 scholarships are given annually.

THE COMMITTEES

Excepting the first three years, when the selections were made by popular vote of the Children's Librarians' Section, the books have been chosen by committee. The verdict for the first winner was indisputable. By March 8, 1922, the Chairman of the Newbery jury had received 212 votes from librarians responding to the invitation to help nominate the first Newbery Medal Book. Of these votes, 163 were for Hendrik Willem Van Loon's The Story of Mankind. The remaining 49 votes were divided among 14 titles.

A special award committee was formed in 1924 after the Book Evaluation Committee of the Children's Librarians' Section reported that its members believed that a popular vote could not be depended upon to choose the most distinguished contribution of the year. By 1929, the committee, which had been slightly smaller the first few years of its existence, had been enlarged to fifteen. While the practice of asking section members to submit suggestions for the most deserving books has continued, choosing the winning books had become and remains a committee activity.

By 1934, the point system had been introduced, with committee members sending first, second, and third preferences to the chairman. In 1937, when the Caldecott Award was established, the School Librarians' Section was invited to name five of its members to the Awards Committee each year. This practice continued until 1958. Then, during a reorganization of the American Library Association, the Children's Library Association became the Children's Services Division and sections ceased to exist. From 1937 on, the committee was made up of twenty-three members, a number unaltered until 1978.

The composition of the committee changed from time to time, moving toward greater control by section members. In 1957, three members-at-large were chosen by membership vote; by 1966 this number had increased to eight, and by 1973 to twelve, plus the chair (who prior to that time had been the section's vice-president, president-elect). In 1978, the membership of the Association for Library Service to Children--which for the preceding twenty years had been named the Children's Services Division--adopted a change in the bylaws creating separate committees of fifteen members each for the Newbery and Caldecott Awards. This 1978 amendment states: "The Newbery Award Committee shall consist of the following fifteen (15) members: seven (7) members to be elected annually from a slate of no fewer than fourteen (14), a Chairperson elected annually from a slate of two (2), and seven (7) members appointed by the vice-president (pres-ident-elect)."[12] The structure for the Caldecott Award Committee is identical. The first election to separate committees took place in 1979; the two committees considered the books published in 1980, choosing the 1981 winners from them in January 1981.

The 1975 Awards Committee was the first to be entirely selected (by ballot and appointment) before the beginning of the calendar year in which the books it was to consider were published. Previous committees had been formed midway through the year of publication of the books they judged. In addition to choosing the winning books, the Awards Committee may make recommendations to the Board of the Association for Library Service to Children. At times these recommendations have effected major changes in procedure and additional definitions.

THE VOTING

For many years the committee balloted principally by mail. Since 1958-1959, however, all voting has been done at the American Library Association Midwinter Conference. Through 1933, the number of votes each book received on the final ballot was made public. Since that time the number of ballots, the tallies on ballots, and the discussions of the books have been kept secret.

This constraint does not extend to the procedures the committees follow. Former committee members have written interesting articles describing the process that takes place behind the committees' closed doors. Since 1978, manuals of procedures approved by the Board of the Association for Library Service to Children have provided direction also. The committee members come to their task fully prepared. For an entire year they have been reading, rereading, and evaluating the new books of the year including those nominated by committee members and the membership of the Association for Library Service to Children. In committee, before a vote is taken, the nominated books, one by one, are discussed. Usually general consensus indicates that the time has arrived for the first ballot. Each person votes for three books. First choices receive 4 points, second choices 3 points, and third choices 2 points. With a fifteen-person committee voting, a book needs at least eight first-place rankings to win either award, and must have an 8-point lead over the book receiving the next-highest number of points. After the results of the ballot are announced, if there is not a winner, the discussion begins again. Books on the list that received no votes are eliminated. Discussion and balloting continue until there is a winner.

THE HONOR BOOKS

From the first year of the award, the juries or committees listed the "runners-up," the books that remained longest in the voting. In 1971, the term "runners-up" was changed to "Honor Books," with the new terminology made retroactive so that all runners-up are now officially Newbery or Caldecott Honor Books.

There is no predetermined number of Honor Books. The Committee decides on the number, but there has been at least one Newbery and Caldecott Honor Book every year for which there are records. No records of Newbery Honor Books exist for 1923, 1924, and 1927. The trend has been to name fewer Honor Books, especially among the Newbery Awards. In the second decade (1932-1941) there were 46 Newbery Honor Books while in the sixth decade (1972-1981) there were only 23 Newbery Honor Books. In the period 1942-1951, 43 books were named Caldecott Honor Books; in 1972-1981, there were 28 Caldecott Honor Books. (See Appendices C and D for number of books named in each decade.)

Previous to 1977, Honor Books were named on the basis of the number of votes received on the final ballot. Persons who have served on the committees state that there was usually an obvious breaking point between the Honor Books and general contenders. The very first year the Newbery Medal was given provides an interesting exception. The winner received an overwhelming majority of 163 votes. Operating without precedent, the Newbery jury declared the next five runners-up to be Honor Books. They had received 22, 7, 5, 4, and 2 votes, respectively. The general contenders included nine other titles that received one vote each.

In 1977, the Board of the Association for Library Service to Children gave the Committees an expanded procedure for choosing Honor Books: "Following the selection of the Caldecott or the Newbery Medal winner, the Committee, if it chooses to name Honor Books, may ballot once again among the books that appeared on the final medal-winning ballot. The Committee may elect to name one or more

of the books that are highest in this balloting as Honor Books."[13]
This procedure gives the Committee a choice between balloting again
and choosing as Honor Books the next-highest books on the winning
ballot. If the Committee decides to use the award-winning ballot,
then it must decide how many of the titles to name Honor Books. "If
it chooses to ballot again, the only books which may be on this ballot are those that received points on the award-winning ballot."[14]
Following this balloting, the Committee decides how many of these
books will be named Honor Books. In either case "in determining
'how many,' the operative phrases from the 1977 policy governing the
decision are 'There is no set number . . .' and 'The Committee may
name as many or as few as it chooses . . . keeping in mind that the
books should be truly distinguished, not merely general contenders.'"[15]

   Since 1964, the Honor Books have been announced in alphabetical
order by author for the Newbery books and by illustrator for the
Caldecott books, to confer equal honor on all.

ANNOUNCEMENT

   For the first twenty-seven years the Medals were given, the results of the voting, which had taken place several months earlier,
were kept secret until the presentations of the Medals at the summer
conference of the American Library Association. This suspense-
building practice was discontinued for a number of reasons, but
chiefly because the news frequently leaked out so that the announcement came as an anticlimax to many. Beginning in 1949, soon after
the voting was completed in March, the Medals were presented--tempo-
rarily--to the winning author and artist in Mr. Frederic Melcher's
New York office. Public announcements were made at that time with
the official presentations and the acceptance speeches occurring, as
before, at the summer meeting. After Mr. Melcher's death in 1963,
his son, Daniel Melcher, presented the awards in his father's place.
Later the announcement time was changed to the midwinter meeting.

THE CELEBRATION

   For many of the years of the awards' existence, a highlight of
the summer conference was a gala dinner honoring the winning author
and, later, the winning illustrator. Judging from the accounts that
exist of these affairs, many were memorable. In 1937, First Lady
Mrs. Eleanor Roosevelt was the guest speaker. She wrote in her newspaper column the following day that the "crowning event of the evening was the Irish story told by Miss Sawyer,"[16] a famous storyteller
as well as the award recipient that year for Roller Skates. One
cherished tradition that continued for many years was Mr. Melcher's
annual reading of A. A. Milne's "The King's Breakfast." In recent
years especially, the evening banquet has received much criticism
for being expensive and overly elaborate. In response to these

concerns the Association for Library Service to Children Board, in 1980, approved experimenting with other celebratory patterns for the presentation of the Newbery and Caldecott Medals in 1981 and 1982, with an evaluation to occur prior to the planning for 1983 events.

THE AUTHORS AND ILLUSTRATORS

The types of books and trends are discussed in the essays that precede the separate annotations of the Newbery and Caldecott books. It seems appropriate, however, to make one or two observations here that pertain to both groups. It is not surprising to find that Caldecott book artists have illustrated Newbery books and several Newbery authors have written the texts of Caldecott books. It is rather astonishing, however, to note the number of people who were versatile enough to win recognition both for their writing and for their illustrating. At present Robert Lawson is the only person to have won both Newbery and Caldecott Medals, but a number of persons have a Medal-winning book in one division and one or more Honor Books in the other division, while others have Honor Books in both groups. Lawson received the Caldecott in 1941 for They Were Strong and Good and the Newbery in 1945 for Rabbit Hill. Others who have been cited for both Caldecott and Newbery Medal and/or Honor Books are Ludwigary Bemelmans, Mary and Conrad Buff, James Daugherty, Marguerite de Angeli, William Pène du Bois, Wanda Gág, Holling C. Holling, Dorothy Lathrop, Arnold Lobel, Kate Seredy, and William Steig.

While the stipulation that a book by a previous award winner must be the unanimous choice of the Committee was in effect, there were no repeat winners. The Newbery Committee apparently made the recommendation that led to this requirement because one of the books considered for the 1932 Medal was written by the 1930 Medal winner. (The book, Calico Bush by Rachel Field, became a 1932 Honor Book.) At this time the question of eligibility arose and the restriction was made since the original purpose of the award was to encourage an increasing number of authors to devote their best efforts to creating children's literature.

In the fall of 1957, Newbery-Caldecott chairperson Elizabeth Nesbitt, perhaps thinking that books of distinction were not being considered because their authors had already received one Medal, wrote that members of the Children's Services Division, in making nominations, should remember that the award is for the book, not the author. She suggested that "the rule . . . may have acquired too much weight."[17]

It is likely that this opinion influenced the sequence of events that occurred at the January 1958 meeting. In the course of its deliberations, the Newbery-Caldecott Committee adjourned to recommend to the Children's Services Division Board that the requirement for the unanimous choice be removed.[18] "The Board approved the recommendation during a special executive session. The Committee was informed of the decision and returned to its deliberations. . . ."[19] The 1958 Caldecott winner was Time of Wonder, by Robert McCloskey, who became the first person to win the same Medal twice. His first Medal was for Make Way for Ducklings in 1942.

It is interesting to speculate that some of the following Honor Books might have been winners if the requirement had not been in effect. Between his two winners Mr. McCloskey had three Honor Books: Blueberries for Sal, 1949; One Morning in Maine, 1953; and Journey Cake, Ho!, 1954. Virginia Lee Burton received the Caldecott for The Little House in 1943; her Song of Robin Hood was a 1948 Honor Book. The Newbery books that may have been affected by this ruling include The Singing Tree in 1940 by Kate Seredy (The White Stag won in 1938); The House of Sixty Fathers by Meindert De Jong in 1957 (The Wheel on the School had won in 1955); and The Black Fox of Lorne by Marguerite de Angeli in 1957 (The Door in the Wall was the 1950 winner).

Since the removal of this requirement, two authors have won the Newbery Medal twice: Elizabeth George Speare in 1959 and 1962 and Katherine Paterson in 1978 and 1981. A third repeat winner, Joseph Krumgold, whose And Now Miguel was the 1954 winner, received a second medal in 1960 after the restriction was rescinded. Illustrator Marcia Brown also won her first medal, in 1955, while the limitation was in effect, and her second one in 1962, after it had been lifted. Besides Marcia Brown and Robert McCloskey, three other illustrators have won twice: Nonny Nogrogian in 1966 and 1972, Leo and Diane Dillon in 1976 and 1977, and Barbara Cooney in 1959 and 1980.

INFLUENCES OF THE MEDALS

The basic purpose as suggested by Mr. Melcher to "help build a greater literature by giving authoritative recognition"[20] to outstanding authors and illustrators has not changed. That the awards have been positive influences is evident in several respects: the publication of good books for children has been stimulated; the books have been brought to the attention of parents, teachers, and librarians as well as children; and the standards by which these books are judged continue to serve as guidelines in evaluating all literature for children.

NOTES

[1] Frederic G. Melcher, "Newbery Medal No. 12," Saturday Review 10 (1933):277.

[2] Irene Smith, A History of the Newbery and Caldecott Medals (New York: Viking, 1957), p. 49. Smith is the source of the following quotations: terms of Mr. Melcher's statement (2, 7); resolutions

of the American Library·Association Executive Board (3, 4, 5, 6); reasons set down by Mr. Melcher (11); observations from Mrs. Roosevelt's column (16).

[3], [4] Ibid., p. 57.

[5], [6] Ibid., pp. 64-65.

[7] Ibid., p. 50.

[8], [9] Ibid., p. 65.

[10] Ibid., p. 41.

[11] Ibid., p. 65.

[12] Bette J. Peltola, "Choosing the Newbery and Caldecott Medal Winners," Top of the News 36, no. 1 (1979):44.

[13] "Detroit Conference Highlights," Top of the News 34, no. 1 (1977):4.

[14], [15] From information provided by Mary Jane Anderson, Executive Director of the Association for Library Service to Children.

[16] Smith, p. 60.

[17] Elizabeth Nesbitt, "Your Opinion is Important," Top of the News 14, no. 1 (1957):53.

[18], [19] From information provided by Mary Jane Anderson, Executive Director of the Association for Library Service to Children.

[20] Melcher, p. 277.

FURTHER INFORMATION ABOUT THE NEWBERY AND CALDECOTT AWARDS

The terms, definitions, and criteria for the Newbery and Caldecott Awards adopted in 1978 by the Association for Library Service to Children's Board of Directors are reprinted in Appendix B.

Top of the News is published quarterly by the Association for Library Service to Children of the American Library Association, the organization that administers the awards. This publication is the official source for information about the Newbery and Caldecott Awards.

Smith, Irene. A History of the Newbery and Caldecott Medals. New York: Viking, 1957. Provides good profiles of Mr. Melcher, John Newbery, and Randolph Caldecott. Describes the

literary climate of children's books in 1921 when Mr. Melcher pro-
posed the Newbery Award, covers in detail the early years of the
Newbery Award and the establishment of the Caldecott Award, and continues the history of both awards to the middle 1950s. The author is
especially successful in evoking the past and in recreating the excitement and festivities that attended the awarding of the medals.
The personality of Frederic Melcher is made evident through the many
quotations from Mr. Melcher's letters and other writing. There is an
error in Appendix 3 among the Newbery Honor Books. The books listed
under 1932 (the year of publication) were not the 1933 Honor Books.
These titles were the "also rans" for that year. The list also omits
some of the Honor Books for 1930, 1931, and 1934. Although at present
out of print, this book is still available in many libraries.

Miller, Bertha Mahony, and Field, Elinor Whitney, eds. Newbery
Medal Books: 1922-1955. Boston: Horn Book, 1955. Contains acceptance papers, biographies of the award winners, an evaluative essay,
and essays about John Newbery and Frederic G. Melcher.

Miller, Bertha Mahony, and Field, Elinor Whitney, eds. Caldecott
Medal Books: 1938-1957. Boston: Horn Book, 1957. Includes accept-
ance papers, biographical material, a biographical sketch of Randolph
Caldecott, and an evaluative essay.

Kingman, Lee, ed. Newbery and Caldecott Medal Books: 1956-1965.
Boston: Horn Book, 1965. Comprises acceptance papers, biographical
materials, an essay by F. G. Melcher relating the origin of the Medals,
three evaluative essays, illustrations in black and white from the
1956-1965 Caldecott Medal Books, lists of the Newbery and Caldecott
Winners and Honor Books, 1922-1965 and 1938-1965.

Kingman, Lee, ed. Newbery and Caldecott Medal Books: 1966-1975.
Boston: Horn Book, 1975. Contains acceptance papers, biographical
materials, pictures of the 1966-1975 authors and illustrators, pictures in color from the 1966-1975 Caldecott Medal Books, three evaluative essays (one about the 1966-1975 Honor Books), and lists of the
1966-1975 Newbery and Caldecott Honor Books.

The Newbery Medal and Honor Books: Characteristics and Trends

On June 29, 1981, in San Francisco, California, for the sixtieth time the Newbery Medal was presented "for the most distinguished contribution to American Literature for Children." The recipient was Katherine Paterson for her novel Jacob Have I Loved (N263). The first Medal was given on June 27, 1922, in Detroit, Michigan, to Dr. Hendrik Van Loon for his history, The Story of Mankind (N1). With growing prestige, in each of the years between, the award has been made for the book that was considered the "most distinguished" of that year. All types of fiction and nonfiction have brought the Medal to the various authors. Over the years an additional 205 books have been named Honor Books, a considerable distinction in itself. This essay reviews by genre the characteristics and trends of the Newbery Medal and Honor Books chosen from 1922 through 1981. While the decades run 1922 through 1931, 1932 through 1941, etc., the first decade is referred to as the 1920s, the second decade as the 1930s, and so forth.

TRADITIONAL LITERATURE

This category includes the titles classified as folk tales, fables, legends, epics, and hero stories.

Traditional literature has had fewer representatives among the Newbery books than most of the other genres. More than half the titles in this category appeared in the first two decades.

Folk tales make up one of the major divisions of traditional literature considered particularly suitable for children, and half of the Newbery titles classed as traditional literature appear in this group. Beginning with the collections of the Grimm brothers early in the nineteenth century, scholar after scholar recorded the folklore of his own region. It might seem that a hundred years later there would be none left to take directly from the oral tradition. Surprisingly, this is not true. Parts or all of most of these collections came from oral sources. Often the tales recorded were told to the reteller when he or she was a child in another country. For example, Padraic Colum related tales he heard in his native Ireland in The Big Tree of Bunlahy (N58, 1934), and Isaac B. Singer retold tales

1

he heard as a boy in Poland in <u>Zlateh the Goat</u> (N215, 1967) and <u>When Shlemiel Went to Warsaw</u> (N224, 1969). The most recent title in this group, <u>Anpao</u> (N258, 1978) is a folk history of the Indians of America by a Native American. [1]

FANTASY

The books of fantasy make up a smaller group than the biography and other books of information. Although fantasy has been represented in every decade, it has the largest number of titles in the first, fifth, and sixth decades. Six of the ten books appearing in the first decade are out of print, but most of the books from the 1930s on remain in print.

Animal fantasies, comprising nearly one-third of all the books of fantasy, appear in every decade. Among them is <u>Charlotte's Web</u> (N155, 1953), perhaps the best-loved book of the twentieth century. The animal subjects range from such small, commonplace, and multitudinous creatures as spiders and crickets to such fanciful creatures as a yellow and blue striped baby dragon and a 70,000-year-old Great Glass Sea Snail. While some stories have fairy-tale-like settings and events, all inspire belief by being closely linked to reality. All show originality of invention, humor, and lighthearted moments. They are well written. In addition, all demonstrate small universal truths with several, including <u>Charlotte's Web</u> and <u>Rabbit Hill</u> (N110, 1945), conveying larger themes.

The two types of fantasy that predominated in the first decade have appeared infrequently since. These were literary fairy tales, stories that followed the pattern of the traditional folktale; and stories in which history was blended with fantasy. Most of the former, and all but one, <u>Hitty</u> (N25, 1930), of the latter, are out of print.

In the 1960s and 1970s the Newbery authors of fantasy began to employ different elements of traditional literature. Utilizing components found in old hero tales, Lloyd Alexander (N210, 1966 and N222, 1969), Susan Cooper (N244, 1974 and N250, 1976), and others, in the manner of J. R. R. Tolkien, created original, believable worlds. In these, as in Tolkien's books, there is a great conflict between the forces of good and the forces of evil.

While the earlier fantasies--<u>Mr. Popper's Penguins</u> (N83, 1939), for instance--were often written for entertainment only, almost all the recent titles, including those portraying the battle between good and evil, deal with issues faced in real life. On the first level they are enjoyable adventure stories, but on the second level they comment on society or demonstrate certain unchangeable truths. In contrast to earlier decades when themes were usually explicitly stated, these are implicit in the stories.

In the past two decades there has been some movement toward science fiction. Written in the Jules Verne tradition, The Twenty-One Balloons (N126, 1948) was the first book in this area. A Wrinkle in Time (N201, 1963), Enchantress from the Stars (N231, 1971), and Mrs. Frisby and the Rats of NIMH (N233, 1972), all containing elements of science fiction, followed in the 1960s and 1970s.

Looking back over the group as a whole, one observes changes in subjects from dolls, brownies, and fairies to characters with whom young readers can more easily identify.

BIOGRAPHIES AND OTHER BOOKS OF INFORMATION

More biographies and books of information have been honored than any genre except historical fiction. One Newbery book in nine has been a biography; among these is one autobiography. And one in seventeen is another type of informational book.

Nearly three-quarters of the biographies appear in the two decades from 1931-1951; about two-thirds of these books are out of print. During this period biographies were being produced in quantity, some of them in response to curricular needs for older boys and girls. In the decades 1962-1981, the number of biographies named as Newbery books declined sharply. Interestingly, two of the five (out of twenty-six) biographies with women as subjects appeared in the most recent decade. Both The Upstairs Room (N241, 1973) and The Road from Home (N262, 1980) are partial biographies detailing the persecution of members of minority groups. Well-known male leaders like Washington (N85, 1939; N99, 1942; N141, 1950) and Lincoln (N113, 1945; N146, 1951) have been subjects most often, but less well-known men have also been written about: Johnny Appleseed (N144, 1951) and Amos Fortune (N143, 1951), who spent most of his life as a slave, to name two.

Most of the Newbery biographers have taken a middle position between history and fiction in an effort to balance readability and accuracy. They fictionalize by using invented conversations, and by supplying thoughts for historical personages. They do this against a true background, utilizing known facts. None of these writers uses a debunking approach and none attempts a psychological probe of his subject. Neither do they go to the opposite extreme of hagiography, although usually the author has admired the person and thus has a natural bias toward him. In some instances subjects may have been chosen as suitable for school libraries, or because the person had qualities that were considered worthy of emulation. Whatever the reasons for their choices, the biographers who have attained excellence have combined knowledge of the subject with an imaginative approach that vitalizes the person. Overall, the Newbery biographies are well written. A few of them--Elizabeth Janet Gray's books (N68, 1936 and N86, 1939), James Daugherty's Daniel Boone (N87, 1940), the books of Constance Rourke (N63, 1935 and N75, 1937), Jean Lee Latham's Carry On, Mr. Bowditch (N169, 1956)--are outstanding examples of the biographer's art.

Among the informational books, which are distributed through all decades except the sixth, histories are predominant, with histories of the United States being the most plentiful. Among the latter are two volumes of a trilogy written by a grandfather for his grandson: America Is Born (N191, 1960) and America Moves Forward (N194, 1961). Only three titles pertain to science. A few reflect contemporary interests such as art and black history. Almost without exception these books are intended for the upper elementary years and for junior and senior high school students. As a group they measure up to the canons for good books of knowledge: they are consistently accurate, provide clear explanations, and are competently written.

HISTORICAL FICTION

Several trends are discernible in historical fiction, the genre that has been more often honored than any other. Historical fiction dominated the Newbery Awards in the 1930s more than at any other time; by the 1960s there were only one-fourth as many titles. Two-thirds of those honored through 1951 are now out of print.

The typical historical novel of the 1920s was a romantic adventure story. History provided the background for a series of adventurous exploits that often took place over a long time and large space. While Charles B. Hawes took care to maintain historical authenticity in The Great Quest (N2, 1922) and The Dark Frigate (N8, 1924), many authors did not, although some sought to make the story seem true by using what was in actuality a pseudodiction. The British Isles or Europe appeared most frequently as a setting; the time was likely to be the twelfth through the seventeenth centuries. Plots moved rapidly, but the action and suspense often arose from implausible circumstances. Characters, usually boys, were treated as little more than puppets manipulated by the plots. Many actual historical personages were portrayed as characters in these books. Cedric the Forester (N3, 1922) exemplifies the typical historical novel of the 1920s.

The books of the 1930s retained many of the elements found in those of the 1920s. One change occurred in the settings, with American backgrounds now being used more frequently. The chief difference, however, was that there was a much greater emphasis on historical accuracy. Characteristically, books of this decade contained a great deal of information, often interesting of itself, but seldom integral to the plots. Armstrong Sperry's All Sail Set (N69, 1936) and Lois Lenski's Phebe Fairchild (N71, 1937) reflect these changes and, like many of the historical novels of this time, were used as supplementary reading for high school history courses.

Period stories, many with girls as protagonists, were written all through the six decades, but some of the best, including Caddie Wood-lawn (N65, 1936) and three of Laura Ingalls Wilder's "Little House" books (N80, 1938; N90, 1940; N95, 1941), won Newbery honors in the second decade. In these stories characterization rather than plot is of first importance. Since well-realized characters have universal and lasting appeal, that may account for most of these titles remaining in print.

Character, we have noted, is the focus of durable period stories, but character was long of secondary importance in adventure stories. Even the characters created by such good writers of the 1920s and 1930s as Agnes Danforth Hewes (N37, 1931; N59, 1934; N76, 1937) and Cornelia Meigs (N22, 1929; N49, 1933) were often little more than marionettes whose chief function was to keep the action moving. But that changed with the publication of Johnny Tremain (N105) in 1943. Although Johnny Tremain has an exciting plot, it is the characterization of Johnny that captures and holds the reader's attention. In the nearly forty years that have elapsed since the publication of Johnny Tremain, novels of historical fiction have much more frequently related people and events in such a way that the characters develop by means of their experiences, becoming different and more mature than they were in the beginning.

The fifth and sixth decades saw the development of a trend less in evidence earlier. In these years, historical fiction more frequently reflected the contemporary society. Themes that concerned adults became prominent: for example, ethnic concerns are explored in a number of stories including Sing Down the Moon (N232, 1971), Dragonwings (N252, 1976), and Roll of Thunder, Hear My Cry (N253, 1977).

Overall, the historical novel of today is different from the historical novel of sixty years ago in several respects. First, historical fiction written today usually focuses on shorter periods of time. There has been a movement from the panoramic and picturesque to more closely knit plots in which character is more fully developed. Second, today's writers take much more care to maintain authenticity, not only in details, but also in honesty of portrayal so that all viewpoints are presented. Third, there has been a definite movement away from archaic language to natural modern speech. Finally, the entire tone of historical fiction has modified from the romantic to a more realistic presentation.

LIFE IN OTHER LANDS

There have been more Newbery books in the category Realistic Fiction Set in Other Lands than in either the category Fiction about Regions and Minority Groups or the category Other Realistic Fiction Set in the United States. More than two-thirds of these books are now out of print. This genre was very well represented through the 1950s, but in the period 1962-1971 there were only two books, and none between 1972 and 1981. Many of the books about life in other lands written in the post-World War I period resulted from the belief that harmony and world peace would result if the peoples of the world knew more about each other as persons. Pran of Albania (N27, 1930) and Kate Seredy's two books, The Good Master (N67, 1936) and The Singing Tree (N88, 1940), appear to have been written with that thought in mind. Miss Seredy's books, as well as several others, recreate childhoods lived in other countries.

The decline of Newbery books in this category is primarily a reflection of the fact that fewer books about life in other lands are being written today. Several factors have contributed to this decline. Immigration has been greatly restricted since the early years of the century, and the number of first or second generation Americans who feel close to life in the "old country" has markedly decreased. Ease of travel has made it possible for greater numbers of people to visit other lands and learn first hand about their culture. In addition, there is a trend toward writing books of information rather than books of fact and fiction intermingled, a method used in many of the earlier books. Today, television travel programs supply information formerly available only in books. Finally, many more books originating in other countries are translated into English today than formerly, so that there is less need for Americans to write about other lands.

The two principal purposes for writing stories set in other lands are to increase a reader's knowledge of a different way of life and to demonstrate that all people are alike in many respects. Good stories about life in other lands fulfill both purposes, and such stories can be found over the first fifty years in which the genre is represented.

Typically, the early books had rural settings, were long, included picturesque customs of the country, and often contained inserted legends and tales. The best among these books--like Dobry (N61, 1935) and The Good Master (N67, 1936)--had three-dimensional characters, portrayed universal human problems, and were written in a style that was well suited to the author's concept of the story. In the best-written of the more recent books, the setting, as well as the customs, serves a far more functional role, important only in relation to the characters and story as a whole. These books tend to be shorter, cover briefer periods of time, and contain less description. The stories within the story have practically disappeared. Emphasis is on characterization and theme, and although the stories take place in a definite country, they deal with problems common to children everywhere. Titles with these characteristics are Shadrach (N162, 1954) and Wheel on the School (N166, 1955) by Meindert De Jong and Shadow of a Bull (N207, 1965) by Maia Wojciechowska.

REALISTIC ANIMAL STORIES

Although realistic animal stories appear in every decade, the largest number found in any one decade is four, with one or two being more typical. Five of the eleven stories were authored by Marguerite Henry or Meindert De Jong. Mrs. Henry's titles include Justin Morgan Had a Horse (N116, 1946), Misty of Chincoteague (N131, 1948), and King of the Wind (N132, 1949). Mr. De Jong's titles are Hurry Home, Candy (N163, 1954) and Along Came a Dog (N186, 1959). While there is great variety among the stories, which range from the humorous, such as Phil Stong's Honk: The Moose (N66, 1936), to the sad, such as Incident at Hawk's Hill (N234, 1972), the group as a whole shares several characteristics in common. All the stories have appealing animal characters and strong human and animal relationships. Each author has avoided over-humanizing his animal hero and has kept it true to the nature and ways of its species. Each has also avoided moralizing and sentimentality. Only one book in this group is out of print, perhaps proof that well-written animal stories have a remarkable lasting quality. Few noticeable contrasts have occurred between early and later prize-winning animal stories.

FICTION ABOUT REGIONS AND MINORITIES

Regions and minorities are represented in about 10 percent of the Newbery books; of these, one-third appear in the first three decades and two-thirds in the second three decades. Minorities represented in one book each include Swedish-American, Polish-American, Japanese-American, Jewish, and Eskimo. The remaining books are divided almost equally among regions, Native Americans, and blacks. Included among the regional stories are four that show boys growing up as they learn about sheep-raising.

One significant observation can be made about the books dealing with Native Americans. In the books out of print including two from the first decade--Runaway Papoose (N23, 1929) and Queer Person (N35, 1931)--there was strong emphasis on showing how people lived. The others are ultimately based on universal themes as is The Horse-catcher (N180, 1958) by Mari Sandoz. Girls are protagonists in the three most recently published: Island of the Blue Dolphins (N193, 1961), Sing Down the Moon (N232, 1971), and Annie and the Old One (N237, 1972).

The most notable trends for the group are in the books about blacks. There were no books showing blacks as chief characters in the first four decades. In the 1960s two stories, The Jazz Man (N216, 1967) and Sounder (N225, 1970), showed black protagonists in disadvantaged positions. In the four books winning honors from 1972 through 1981, the authors depict black persons in a positive manner. While portraying the black experience, these stories express universal meaning as well. Three of these are by black writers including two by Virginia Hamilton: <u>The Planet of Junior Brown</u> (N235, 1972) and <u>M. C. Higgins, the Great</u> (N245, 1975).

OTHER REALISTIC FICTION SET IN THE UNITED STATES

Unexpectedly, Newbery books with contemporary American children as principal characters barely outnumber biographies. Even including those books categorized as regional or minority fiction, the total is still a dozen fewer than for historical fiction. Nearly half of all the books in this group appear in the period 1962-1981. In contrast to most of the other genres, girls have been leading characters more often than boys; in several of the stories both boys and girls have important roles. With the exception of <u>The Westing Game</u> (N259, 1979), the books in this group are stories about preadolescent children on their own; families with preadolescent children; and boys and girls growing up.

Over the years significant changes have occurred in setting, characters, and point of view. Most of the stories written in this category in the first four decades were set in small towns and the country. Examples include Elizabeth Enright's <u>Thimble Summer</u> (N81, 1939) and Eleanor Estes's stories of the Moffats, <u>The Middle Moffat</u> (N103, 1943) and <u>Rufus M.</u> (N108, 1944). Those stories written in the 1960s and 1970s reflect the fact that the United States has become an urban and suburban country. <u>From the Mixed-up Files of Mrs. Basil E. Frankweiler</u> (N217, 1968) and <u>Jennifer, Hecate, Macbeth, William McKinley, and Me, Elizabeth</u> (N218, 1968) by E. L. Konigsburg represent this trend.

Characters in books written in the past two decades manifest concerns different from those of characters in the initial books. In such books, <u>Roller Skates</u> (N70, 1937), for example, the characters accept themselves as they are and the accent is most often on outward actions, while the characters in recent books frequently search for identity or have problems in personal relationships, as does April in <u>The Egypt Game</u> (N221, 1968).

One great change in realistic novels set in the United States is in the role played by adults. In the books written through the 1950s, the adults are often on the edge of the action. When they are present, they usually are model parents like those in <u>Gone-Away Lake</u> (N181, 1958). Beginning in the 1960s, parents are frequently shown with faults and are often an integral part of the story. <u>The Noonday Friends</u> (N212, 1966) and <u>Ramona and Her Father</u> (N257, 1978) are two titles in which very real, but imperfect, parents are depicted. Parents, as well as other adults, including a great-aunt and great-uncle in <u>Jennifer, Hecate, Macbeth, William McKinley, and Me, Elizabeth</u> are treated with less respect than in earlier years. This valid portrayal of parents and other adults increases the substantial reality of the stories.

The Newbery Books: Characteristics and Trends

In recent years many more characters tell their own stories, a change from the Newbery realistic fiction set in other lands in which all the stories are related in the third person. This may be an indication that authors are trying to deal with problems from their youthful characters' points of view rather than from their own adult perspectives.

OVERALL TRENDS IN THE NEWBERY BOOKS

If we include time as well as place as part of the setting, we find that the typical setting of the earlier Newbery books was frequently long ago and invariably far away. In more recent years, our own country has been the setting much more often and the time has been closer to the present day. In the earlier years those stories set in the United States were typically in the country or in a small town. Recently, the books reflect the population shift from rural areas to cities and suburbs. The panoramic setting was often used earlier, particularly in historical fiction.

The young heroes and heroines of the earlier books most often lived in a country other than the United States, frequently in an earlier century. Recent books are more likely to be about contemporary American boys and girls. Even more significant has been the movement from overt action of the adventure type to psychological action. This is true for fantasy, historical fiction, and fiction set in other lands as well as stories showing contemporary life in the United States. Although there still may be excitement and action, there is something more, with problems of identity and social problems often engaging the characters.

Before 1960, the complexities of the adult world were often ignored. The stories were set in a world of wonder and innocence. This movement from the sheltered childhood to one of involvement brings the whole society into these books. Recent Newbery books include alcoholics and the mentally retarded among their characters. This honesty extends to the depiction of parents—in these books we often find frustrated and ineffectual parents as well as the kind, firm ones who appeared in such books as the "Little House" series. In the early books, blacks rarely appeared except in minor stereotyped roles. Such discriminatory writing about minorities is no longer acceptable and has been avoided in recent children's books.

In sixty years there has been much modification in subject matter and theme. Although conservative, the trend manifested by the Newbery books has been toward the inclusion of hitherto taboo subjects, especially in fiction set in the contemporary United States. Race relations, violence, and war have all been dealt with in some measure in the various genres of the Newbery books. Recently, greater emphasis has been placed on cultural and humanistic values, while formerly the virtues of courage, patriotism, and devotion to duty were more frequently stressed.

The Newbery Books: Characteristics and Trends

There have been, in the course of sixty years, changes in form, style, and technique. Today's Newbery book is apt to be shorter and more unified. The practice of interpolating stories within the story prevailed for the first twenty-five years and contributed to the length of the books, as did a generally more ornate style. In the early years of the award, a few authors used obtrusive rhetoric. The omniscient point of view has been less used in recent Newbery books. A number of books have been written in the first person, although a limited third person viewpoint is most often used. Recent authors present characters by dramatic rather than expository means. Techniques established in mainstream literature--such as flashbacks, stream of consciousness, or use of symbolism--are now employed. The whole trend in vocabulary and diction has been from the formal--in the case of historical fiction, the archaic--to colloquial speech.

Through the decades, the authors have consciously and perhaps sometimes unconsciously, revealed the concerns, manners, and attitudes of the society in which they lived. This is true not only of realistic fiction, but of other genres as well, especially historical fiction and fantasy. As a consequence the books are interesting as documents of social history as well as literature for children.

The Newbery Award has continued for sixty years to fulfill the objectives of its originator, Frederic Melcher. Books of enduring value, written with artistic skill, have been honored, and their authors have been encouraged to contribute to a literature for children which is a part of the universal literature of humankind.

Note

[1] Dates in parentheses indicate the years in which the books received the Newbery Medal or were named Honor Books.

From *Gay-Neck: The Story of a Pigeon* by Dhan Gopal Mukerji, illustrations by
Artzybasheff. Copyright 1927 by E. P. Dutton & Co., Inc. Renewal, 1955, by Mrs.
Dhan Gopal Mukerji. Reprinted by permission of the publisher, E. P. Dutton.

Illustration from *Millions of Cats*, written and illustrated by Wanda Gag. Copyright 1928 by Wanda Gag. By permission of Coward, McCann & Geoghegan, Inc.

Mr. Popper's Penguins by Richard and Florence Atwater, illustrated by Robert Lawson. Copyright 1938, © 1966 by Florence Atwater, Doris Atwater, and Carroll Atwater Bishop. By permission of Little, Brown and Company.

Illustration from *Indian Captive: The Story of Mary Jemison,* written and illustrated by Lois Lenski. Copyright 1941 by Lois Lenski. By permission of The Lois Lenski Covey Foundation.

COAT OF ARMS OF KRAKATOA

Diamond-shaped emblem in tropical setting representing frying pan heated over volcano, symbolic of the Island's *Gourmet Government*. Motto: *"Non Nova, sed Nove"*—"Not New Things, but New Ways."

Illustration from *Minn of the Mississippi,* written and illustrated by Holling C. Holling. Copyright 1951 by Holling C. Holling. By permission of Houghton Mifflin Co.

Illustration from *Charlotte's Web*, written by E. B. White and illustrated by Garth Williams.
Copyright 1952 by E. B. White. Illustrations copyright renewed © 1980 by Garth Williams. By
permission of Harper & Row, Publishers, Inc.

From *Gone-Away Lake*, copyright 1957 by Elizabeth Enright. Illustrated by Beth and Joe Krush. Reproduced by permission of Harcourt Brace Jovanovich, Inc.

Illustration from *Zlateh the Goat*, written by Isaac Bashevis Singer and illustrated by Maurice Sendak. Translated from the Yiddish by the author and
Elizabeth Shubb. Pictures copyright © 1966 by Maurice Sendak. By permission
of Harper & Row, Publishers, Inc.

Illustration by Donna Diamond from *Bridge to Terabithia* by Katherine Paterson. A Newbery Award winner. Copyright © 1977 by Katherine Paterson. By permission of Thomas Y. Crowell, Publishers.

The Newbery Medal and Honor Books, 1922-1981

<u>1922</u>

N1   VAN LOON, HENDRIK WILLEM. <u>The Story of Mankind</u>. Illustrated
        by the author. New York: Boni & Liveright, 1921, 548 pp.
        Information: history   Gr. 7 up
    "History is the mighty tower of Experience," Van Loon wrote in
his foreword, "which Time has built amidst the endless fields of
bygone ages." By text and picture he shows the building of the
tower, tracing the important steps in the development of the human race from prehistoric days to his own time. Van Loon deals
primarily with movements and ideas, with less emphasis on dates
and picturesque incidents than had been usual in histories for
children. His rule in selection from the great quantity of information was this: "Did the country or persons in question produce a new idea or perform an original act without which the
entire human race would have been different?" Accordingly, he
includes chapters on Alexander, Charlemagne, Napoleon, Jesus,
Mohammed, Buddha, and Confucius, as well as a chapter on the arts.
He elucidates the characteristics of different peoples and the
distinctive quality of civilization in each period. His style
is clear, somewhat colloquial--that of a storyteller completely
engrossed with the story he has to tell.
    Nearly fifty years after its publication, Ruth Hill Viguers
judged the book to be "a revolutionary approach to history" (<u>A
Critical History of Children's Literature</u>, ed. Cornelia Meigs
[Toronto: Macmillan, 1969], p. 532). This is not a new opinion.
Its merit was recognized at the time it was written. Famed children's literature critic Anne Carroll Moore called it "the most
invigorating, and I venture to predict, the most influential children's book for many years to come" (<u>Bookman</u> 54 [1922]:468). His-
torian Charles A. Beard praised its comprehensiveness, its taste
and humor, and concluded his appraisal with the statement: "He
has written a great book, one that will endure" (<u>New Republic</u> 29
[1921]:105). In 1944, as it approached the quarter-century mark,
Frances Clarke Sayers reexamined it and evaluated its influence
on books for children. She credited it for being "largely responsible for the great regeneration which has taken place among
the books of information," noted that it had given "a whole

11

generation of writers in the field of non-fiction the courage to
be learned and gay at the same time," and commented that it had
been written without condescension and with "the excitement which
should be inherent in all processes of learning" ("Of Memory and
Muchness," Horn Book 20 [1944]:157).

The very first Newbery winner remains the only book of information to bring its author the Medal; however, other books of information written in ensuing years have been named Honor Books.
The author's son, in 1951, wrote a supplement which continued the
history through the Second World War and the postwar period. The
book was again brought up to date in 1972.

N2   HAWES, CHARLES B. The Great Quest. Illustrated by George
        Varian. Boston: Little, Brown, 1921 (OP), 359 pp.
        Fiction: historical   Gr. 6-11
The author subtitled this story "A Romance of 1826, wherein
are recorded the experiences of Josiah Woods of Topham, Massachusetts, and of those with whom he sailed for Cuba and the Gulf of
Guinea." When the story opens, twenty-year-old Josiah, the narrator, is living a quiet life and working as a clerk in the general store of his uncle, Seth Upham, a staid and parsimonious
middle-aged bachelor. Their quiet life abruptly ends with the
return to town of Neil Gleazen, who had been a wild companion of
Uncle Seth's youth and had to leave town in a hurry. Gleazen
now appears to the townspeople to be well off and respectable,
but he has no intention of settling down soberly in Topham. He
spends much time with Uncle Seth and, in a short while, persuades
Seth to sell the store and buy a brig, the Adventure. Josiah,
Seth, and Gleazen, with others, set off in quest of treasure--
gold, Seth and his companions believe. When they do not find
gold, they learn that all along Gleazen and his associates intended to engage in the slave trade. Subsequently there are two
opposed groups, much action, suspense, and real physical danger.
Some of these episodes are very exciting: the siege in the fort,
the eerie wailing of a witch doctor in Africa, and the escape
with the aroused blacks in pursuit. Only Josiah returns to Topham, accompanied by his wife, a missionary's daughter he met in
Africa.

Hawes took care to keep his story authentic. Having steeped
himself in the life of the period, he actually put words and
phrases taken from old books into the mouths of his characters
and shaped and used true incidents. As a result, the story has
immediacy. His diction rings true. But the solid historical
background does not crowd out human interest. It is the characters and their actions that remain in the reader's mind after
the book is closed.

N3   MARSHALL, BERNARD G. Cedric the Forester. New York:
        D. Appleton, 1921 (OP), 279 pp.
        Fiction: historical   Gr. 6-11

Early in the story, sixteen-year-old Cedric, the low-born son of a thirteenth-century English forester, saves the life of and becomes squire and companion to Dickon, the high-born son of Sir Richard Mountjoy. After going to live with the Mountjoys, Cedric fights in many a battle and gains fame as the best crossbowman in the country. In addition, he learns to read and, in a suprisingly short time, wins recognition as a Latin scholar as well as a soldier. Both he and Dickon are knighted after fighting bravely at the Battle of the Eagles and Cedric is rewarded with the manor house and lands of a knight who perished in battle.

An outstanding characteristic of this type of story is bold action and Cedric contains its share. There are numerous scenes featuring slashing sword play. Thousands of bolts are discharged from crossbows and numerous arrows from longbows on every occasion from a festival to a military expedition. The castle is besieged and relief arrives through a secret tunnel. There is warfare with robber barons and with bands of forest outlaws, as well as fighting in Scotland and Wales where Cedric proves to be a military strategist. Suspense is helped along with the free use of disguise and kidnapping.

Cedric also takes liberties with history. The last chapter deals with the drafting of the Magna Carta. Cedric, now Sir Cedric, argues eloquently for the inclusion of articles that would guarantee to the common people some of the privileges and immunities the aristocracy is seeking. Argument is not enough. To gain the support needed, he disguises himself and a couple of dozen lusty swordsmen as palmers and they ride off to kidnap an Abbot. The story assures us, however, that the articles were included, although historians agree that the ordinary Englishman gained little from the Magna Carta.

Even though historical accuracy is not maintained, the author sought to make the story seem true by his use of language. Doubtless in an attempt to suggest the vocabulary of the Middle Ages, he sprinkled the novel liberally with a pseudoarchaic diction. "Gadzooks!" is followed with "methinks, methought, in good sooth, forsooth, tush, mayhap, gainsaid, gainsay, sirrah, I trow, alackaday, and welladay" among others. Many present day readers will find these expressions distracting. Perhaps this book was honored because as critic Anne C. Moore wrote at the time it was published, "the historical period represented is one for which little story writing has been done" (Bookman 54 [1921]:246).

N4   BOWEN, WILLIAM. The Old Tobacco Shop: A True Account of What Befell a Little Boy in Search of Adventure. Illustrated by Reginald Birch. New York: Macmillan, 1921 (OP), 236 pp. Fantasy   Gr. 4-7

Toby Littleback, a hunchback, owns the little old tobacco shop where Freddie, a quite small boy, goes to buy pipe tobacco for his father. One day, when no one is watching, Freddie puffs a bit of tobacco that he has been told is magic. Immediately, Freddie, Toby, and several of their adult friends are aboard a ship, the Sieve, and off on a fantastic voyage to Correction Island on the Spanish Main. There they are captured by pirates who would be at home in a comic operetta and confined first in the fortress Low Dudgeon, then in the more formidable High Dudgeon. The church warden, one of Freddie's band, induces the pirates to breathe from the phial of Odour of Sanctity which he carries and they simply melt away. There are further adventures before the final scene. This shows Freddie in his own home recovering from a long illness and the reader assumes the adventures were feverish fantasies of his illness.

The story is well written and often amusing, but it does not involve the reader's emotions. One always feels like an observer, never a participant. The light-hearted tone of the first half seems more appropriate than the more serious tone of the second part. Now the adventurers pass through the White Fire of the Preserver, enter an enchanted state, and eventually receive corrections. The concept of the corrections is didactic and seems a difficult one for a child of Freddie's age to comprehend. It would have been a better book if the adventures had ended after the encounter with the pirates.

N5   COLUM, PADRAIC. The Golden Fleece and the Heroes Who Lived before Achilles. Illustrated by Willy Pogany. New York: Macmillan, 1921, 289 pp.
Hero Tale   Gr. 4-8

In The Golden Fleece and the Heroes Who Lived before Achilles, Mr. Colum has woven into a continuous narrative practically all the old Greek tales outside of Homer, using Jason and his quest of the Golden Fleece as a central unifying theme. Many of the stories introduced into the chronicle of Jason (such as "Demeter and Persephone," "Prometheus," and "The Story of Perseus") are told or sung by the master musician, Orpheus, while the Argonauts row their vessel across the open sea.

This convention of a story within a story, often used in the 1920s and 1930s, works well in this book because the characters appear and reappear throughout the narratives and the included tales often contain characters present in the central story. It seems, moreover, a natural device because stories would have been told on the long journey. The rhythmic language filled with poetic images captures the wonder inherent in the stories. The dramatic relationship between Jason and Medea is presented with discernment. Willy Pogany's many illustrations are in the spirit of the Greek stories.

N6   MEIGS, CORNELIA. The Windy Hill. New York: Macmillan, 1921
        (OP), 210 pp.
        Fiction   Gr. 4-7
     Fifteen-year-old Oliver and thirteen-year-old Janet go to spend
the summer with their mother's Cousin Jasper at his luxurious country estate in Medford Valley. Almost immediately they notice that
Cousin Jasper is not his usual cheerful self: he is preoccupied
and anxious and, in fact, pays little attention to his young guests.
Oliver has almost decided to go home when, on nearby Windy Hill,
they meet the beeman and his daughter, Polly, a winsome girl of
fourteen. They also meet Anthony Crawford, a disagreeable neighbor, who, they soon realize, is the one responsible for the sad
change in Cousin Jasper. Shortly, they find out that Crawford
is also Jasper's cousin and has recently returned to the valley
after a long absence to try to establish a claim to Jasper's extensive holdings. On the night the river swells and a portion
of the dike gives way--Crawford had neglected to keep his portion
in repair--the children learn that the affable beeman is also a
cousin and that in their youth the three were boon companions.
The three cousins put aside present differences and work through
the night with the men of the neighborhood to save the valley
from flooding. In the morning, Anthony Crawford renounces his
claim and departs hastily.
     Many present-day readers will find the characters unconvincing
and the plot contrived. Worrying Cousin Jasper, the villainous
Anthony Crawford, the wise beeman--all possess the qualities they
have simply for the sake of the plot. As an absolute scoundrel,
Anthony Crawford is unbelievable, but he is even less believable
in his repentant state. The children are not lifelike, either.
They are on the edge of the action, although the author tries to
make Oliver significant by having Anthony Crawford confess to his
cousins the morning after the break in the dike, "It was Oliver
who saw through me, saw that I had not a shade of honor or honesty
behind my claim and told me what I was." Seventy-five of the 210
pages of the book are filled with stories which the beeman relates
to the children when they meet on Windy Hill. They are interesting tales about the children's ancestors and so relate to the
story, but they impede the progress of the plot. This title, one
of the few books this prolific author wrote that was set in con--
temporary times, is inferior to her many volumes of historical
fiction.

N7   LOFTING, HUGH. The Voyages of Dr. Dolittle. Illustrated by
        the author. New York: Frederick A. Stokes, 1922, 364 pp.
        Fantasy   Gr. 3-7

1923

Dr. John Dolittle, an M.D. who became a naturalist and learned
to talk the languages of the birds and animals; Tommy Stubbins,
his nine-and-one-half-year-old assistant, who tells the story;
and an African, Prince Bumpo, the Crown Prince of Jolliginki,
sail from Puddleby, England, for Spidermonkey Island, a floating
island off the coast of Brazil. They hope to find there Long
Arrow, the great Indian naturalist who has disappeared. Enroute
Dr. Dolittle intends to study shellfish language. They are accompanied by Polynesia, a wise two-hundred-year-old parrot; Chee-
Chee, the monkey; and Jip, the dog.

On the way they stop at a Spanish island to replace provisions
and put a stowaway ashore. There, Dr. Dolittle, his pudgy body
stuffed into a sky-blue velvet matador's suit, gets into the bullfight ring with five fierce bulls at one time. He has talked to
the bulls previously and they cooperate to put on a great show.
As a consequence, Dr. Dolittle wins a wager whereby bull-fighting
is banished from the island. About one hundred miles from their
destination, their ship is wrecked during a violent storm. Dolphins come to their rescue and push the remnants of the ship to
Spidermonkey Island.

With the aid of picture language and a three-inch long beetle,
the Jabizri, Dr. Dolittle and his friends find and rescue Long
Arrow. They introduce fire to the natives, the Popsipetel people, and Dr. Dolittle calls on whales to push the island back
north from cold Antartica where it has drifted. Peace-loving
John Dolittle leads the Popsipetels to victory in the battle
against the other tribe on the island, the Bag-jagderags. Then,
much against his desire, Dr. Dolittle is made king of the two
tribes which unite. The Hanging Stone falls on the day of his
coronation setting up a reaction that causes the island to become permanently anchored in the warm climate.

It looks as if the great naturalist will spend the remainder
of his life as King Jong Thinkalot, but Polynesia is able to get
him away. They are transported back to England by the 70,000-
year-old Great Glass Sea Snail. On the way Dr. Dolittle studies
the bottom of the ocean. The story closes as the returned travelers walk home along the fog-bound river bank and talk of the tea
they expect Dab-Dab, the duck, will have ready.

The story is filled with originality and humor. Dr. Dolittle
is a genuinely kind and lovable character. The author's funny
and fanciful illustrations keep the spirit of the story. In
spite of its many merits, the book has been less praised in
recent years because of the depiction of Bumpo. After reading the initial description of him, the reader is certain the
author intends to make him a buffoon: He "was dressed in a fash-
ionable frock coat with an enormous red cravat. On his head was
a straw hat with a gay band; and over this he held a large green
umbrella. . . . He was very smart in every respect except his

16

feet. He wore no shoes or sox." The idea of his being made into a clown is reinforced when one observes that his speech is filled with long words, frequently incorrectly used. However, one soon learns of Bumpo's worth. Dr. Dolittle is genuinely glad to see him and is in no way condescending. On the voyage, Bumpo is treated as an equal in every respect and proves to be very well endowed with both intelligence and common sense. Polynesia, who has a keen mind but a rather vulgar way of speaking, uses the term "Nigger" a time or two but she does not mean it derogatorily. She relies on Bumpo to help her carry out practical matters that the kindly, but improvident, doctor would never think of. Although it is not likely the author intended to malign blacks, it is well that the offensive terms have been deleted from recent printings.

1924

N8   HAWES, CHARLES B. The Dark Frigate. Illustrated by Anton
        Otto Fischer. Boston: Atlantic Monthly, 1923, 247 pp.
        Fiction: historical   Gr. 5-11
    At nineteen Phil Marsham has already sailed on many vessels with his father, now dead, when he signs papers to voyage with Captain Candle on the Rose of Devon. Charles I is king. They have not been long at sea when the ship is captured by pirates captained by the Old One, Tom Jordan. Phil has no choice but to serve with them. After many months, when the ship is anchored close to land, Phil escapes. Later, he is able to warn Captain Winterton of His Majesty's ship Sybil that an attack by the pirates is imminent. Captain Winterton foils the pirates' plans and brings them to justice in England. Subsequently, Phil inherits a fortune left him by his father's father, the Reverend Dr. Marsham of Little Grimsby. He fights for the king against Cromwell, loses his inheritance in the war, and sails for Barbados, by chance, in the Rose of Devon, the dark frigate.
    Intrigue, action, and excitement combine with historical accuracy, authentic nautical background, and boisterous sailor talk to make an engrossing story. The adventures with the pirates make up most of the narrative. Hawes succeeds in making the reader feel the buccaneering spirit, and the boldness of the way of life led by seafaring men of the seventeenth century. Although young Phil is opposed to the "gentlemen of fortune" with whom he is forced to serve, he can still admire the cool courage and intelligence of the pirate leader, Tom Jordan, who had the "mark and pattern of a scoundrel" and "the courage and spirit of a hero." The author succeeds in arousing this same feeling in the reader. This is a pirate story worthy to sit on the shelf with Treasure Island.

1925

N9   FINGER, CHARLES. Tales from Silver Lands. Illustrated by
        Paul Honoré. Garden City, N. Y.: Doubleday, Page, 1924,
        207 pp.
     Folk Tales   Gr. 4-9
     Adventuring the length and breadth of South America at the
turn of the century brought Charles Finger into contact with a
variety of people. From them he took down at first hand the
nineteen tales recorded in this volume. Several of the stories
are prefaced by vivid descriptions of the place in which he heard
the story and of the storyteller. A number of the tales explain
beginnings: one learns the origin of seals and monkeys and how
the hummingbird got its colors and why the flamingo's breast is
crimson. Magic is important to many of the tales: a boy is able
to fly by means of a magic feather dropped by a condor; an old
witch has a magic powder which will turn plants into animals,
leaves into ants, and vines into serpents. The heroes overcome
evil in various forms including strong but stupid giants and powerful witches. For all the magic, the stories are firmly rooted
in reality. Birds and animals abound in every story: there are
jaguars, armadillos, and huanacos; albatrosses and ostriches; and
great butterflies. The stars of the Southern Cross guide travelers. Magic and reality blend in such unlikely feats as building
a house of feathers from every kind of bird all in a day. One
hero flies through the air more swiftly than a condor, on a mat
of feathers from the night owl and the hair of the skunk. Several of the stories contain elements found in European folk tales.
One features a race similar to that run by the hare and the hedge-
hog; in the South American version an identical pair of boys race
with a great evil cat. In "The Hungry Old Witch"--one of the
most exciting stories--a hag with a voracious appetite swallows
great turtles whole, the weight of which causes her to drown in
a lake, an ending reminiscent of the fate suffered by the wolf
in the German tale, "The Wolf and the Seven Little Kids." The
battle fought by the valiant South American boy, Na-Ha, at the
bottom of the sea has similarities to Beowulf's fight.
     Mr. Finger's telling is elemental, preserving the flavor and
atmosphere of the country. The illustrations share these qualities. Readers today will continue to find this book engrossing.

N10 MOORE, ANNE CARROLL. Nicholas: A Manhattan Christmas Story.
        Illustrated by Jay Van Everen. New York: G. P. Putnam's
        Sons, 1924 (OP), 331 pp.
     Fantasy   Gr. 3-6
     Nicholas is a little boy eight inches high who arrives in New
York City from Holland on Christmas Eve and stays until the Saturday before Easter. Except for his size, there is nothing out of

the ordinary about him. His hostess is Ann Caraway, who is an
alter ego for the author. On his very first evening in New York
he attends a party in the children's room of the public library
where the hosts, a brownie and a troll, introduce him to all of
the characters from storybook land who have come out of their
books for the party. This party is the first of many frolics
which Nicholas attends. Besides going to parties, Nicholas
spends time sightseeing and at the zoo, the theater, and the
circus. From stories related to him by his new friends, he
learns much of the Dutch history of the city and of Washington's
Revolutionary experiences in the New York area.

Nearly sixty years have elapsed since <u>Nicholas</u> was written,
with a setting of the New York at that time. Now one of the
chief interests of the book is that it provides a picture of New
York City in the early 1920s. Although it has charming moments,
overall it is crowded with events. There are too many parties
and too many inserted stories. The stories appear to be a pre-
text for including material not closely related to the main narrative. Although contemporary reviewers praised the story, it
now seems dated in subject matter and narrative style. At the
time the book was written Miss Moore was herself a well-known
critic of children's literature.

N11   PARRISH, ANNE and PARRISH, DILLWYN. <u>The Dream Coach</u>. Illus-
       trated by the authors. New York: Macmillan, 1924 (OP),
       143 pp.
       Fantasy   Gr. 2-6
In the dream coach drawn by a hundred misty horses, dreams are
brought to four different children: the King's little daughter;
Goram, a Norwegian boy; the young Emperor of China; and Philippe,
a French lad. All the stories begin in reality followed by the
fantastic dreams. The King's little daughter receives seven
white dreams; in each she is something white: once she is a
white cloud; another time a white lamb; and a third time a white
butterfly. On the day Goram's grandmother goes to the village
for winter supplies, the first snowstorm of the season comes and
Goram makes a snowman. In Goram's dream, the snowman comes alive
as does the teapot and the Queen of the playing cards. The little Chinese emperor's caged bird will not sing. The dream angels
send him dreams in which he is a captive of the birds. From the
dreams he learns that he must release the bird. In Philippe's
dream, his grandmother becomes Grandmother Rain, his Uncle
Pablôt, who has a tendency to blow a little, becomes Uncle Wind,
and his white-headed, white-bearded Grandfather becomes Grandfather Snow.

Two of these literary fairy tales remind the reader of Hans
Christian Andersen. In Goram's dream inanimate objects come to
life as they do in Andersen's stories. Reminiscent of Andersen's

1925

"The Nightingale" is the theme of the little Chinese emperor's
dream. The authors see things in terms of beauty and the writing
contains a number of poetic images: the King's little daughter,
in her spreading gown, looked like "a little white hollyhock out
for a walk." Such distinctive use of language does much to make
these simple stories exceptional.

1926

N12 CHRISMAN, ARTHUR BOWIE. Shen of the Sea. Illustrated by
     Else Hasselriis. New York: E. P. Dutton, 1925, 252 pp.
     Fantasy   Gr. 4-7
     This volume contains sixteen literary fairy tales told in tra-
ditional patterns. Among them are several which, like Kipling's
Just-So Stories, explain beginnings. Humorously and convincingly,
Mr. Chrisman relates the origins of chopsticks, printing, tea,
kites, gunpowder, and china dishes. He tells his readers that
mud pies baked by the princess Chin Uor became the first china
ware. The "shen of the sea" of the title story are six water
demons imprisoned in a jade bottle "buried deep . . . perhaps
under this very garden." That is why the city of Kua Hai is
never invaded by the sea even though it is below sea level. Virtue is rewarded in "Buy a Father." The emperor, disguised as a
beggar, is bought for a father by the orphan, Ah Tzu. After proving his worth, Ah Tzu is made heir to the emperor. Hai Low, in
the amusing "As Hai Low Kept House," also becomes a ruler, not because of merit but as a result of numskull behavior. Two stories
show women in a positive way. The story "Many Wives" tells how
the beautiful Radiant Blossom escapes becoming wife to either the
old king or the young barbarian, Wolf Hunt. The Rain King's
daughter, in a story with that title, tricks the enemy and with
the aid of the other women of the city saves the country from invasion. The book is decorated with more than fifty silhouettes
recreating the people of ancient China.
     Before writing these tales, Mr. Chrisman had studied the his-
tory of China for several years. He had also heard Chinese folk
tales and customs from an acquaintance, a Chinese shopkeeper. So
well do these tales reflect Chinese life and thought that it was
assumed at first that they were direct translations of traditional
Chinese folk tales.

N13 COLUM, PADRAIC. The Voyagers: Being Legends and Romances of
     Atlantic Discovery. Illustrated by Wilfred Jones. New
     York: Macmillan, 1925 (OP), 188 pp.
     Legend and History   Gr. 5-10
     On the coast of southwest Portugal Prince Henry the Navigator
built a high tower that looked out over the Atlantic. He called

to him there learned men from all over the world. They told him stories of the Atlantic and those who sailed it: the legend of Atlantis; the voyage of an Irishman, Maelduin; the voyages of Saint Brendan; and the Saga of Leif the Lucky and other children of Eric the Red. The second part of the book relates discoveries of history and includes accounts of Columbus, Ponce de Leon, and the early settlers of Virginia. The book ends with "The Naming of the Land." In Prince Henry's tower, years after his death, two students, Matthias Ringmann and Martin Waldseemuller, encounter Amerigo Vespucci. After Vespucci has left them, Ringmann suggests that Waldseemuller--on the world map he is making--use the name "America" for the part of the world Vespucci had described, which was actually South America.

Although several critics praised this book highly when it was published, today, in spite of the fact that it is well written, it seems contrived and lifeless.

1927

N14   JAMES, WILL.   Smoky the Cowhorse.   Illustrated by the author. New York: Charles Scribner's Sons, 1926, 310 pp.
Fiction   Gr. 4-10

Smoky's biography begins with his birth on the open range. After four years of freedom there, in which he learns to live according to the laws of nature, the smoke-colored horse is gentled by the cowboy Clint, who makes a first class cow pony of him. When Smoky is stolen and shamefully treated by a half-breed, the theme of a horse controlled by a bad man is developed. Smoky kills his captor and becomes an outlaw. After being recaptured he is entered in the rodeos and for several years unseats all who attempt to ride him. He suffers further poor treatment until Clint finds him. Finally, during his last years he roams happily and peacefully on the high mountain range where he had been a colt.

Author Will James gained his knowledge of and respect for horses from firsthand experience. From the age of thirteen he worked as a cowboy, performing with a rodeo for a number of years. Largely self-educated, he wrote in the western vernacular, which adds authenticity and local color to the story. Although the book gives many of the details of the life of the cowboy, Will James never lets his knowledge become mere descriptive tedium. In his depiction of Smoky, James does not use anthropomorphism in the usual sense of the word, but he does transfer some human intelligence and emotion to the horse, thereby heightening the dramatic impact of the story. The skillful use of this device is shown in the description of Smoky's feelings when he becamee an outlaw horse: "The breed [half-breed] he hated more than anything in the world, but Smoky, with that new heart of his, wasn't for showing them feelings much. He'd got wise in ways of how and when to do his fighting, and where it'd do the most good;--he'd wait for a chance." The many black and white illustrations capture Smoky at every age, in every mood, and most often in action.

1928

N15   MUKERJI, DHAN GOPAL. <u>Gay-Neck: The Story of a Pigeon</u>.
        Illustrated by Boris Artzybasheff. New York: E. P. Dutton,
        1927, 197 pp.
        Fiction   Gr. 4 up
      The master of Gay-Neck, who is Mukerji himself as a youth in India, tells most of the pigeon's story, interrupting his narrative at intervals to let Chitra-Griva, the Iridescent-Throated, tell his own story. Gay-Neck's story begins with his parents from whom he inherits wisdom, alertness, and bravery. When Gay-Neck is only a few weeks old his master begins to train him to a sense of direction. He takes Gay-Neck and his parents from their home in Calcutta on a trip down the Ganges. While the birds are flying home in a terrible storm, Gay-Neck's father loses his life.

      When Mukerji's family moves to Dentam, a village in the Himalayas, for the summer, Mukerji continues the pigeon's training in direction. He is assisted by his friend Radja, at sixteen already a Brahmin priest, and old Ghond, the boys' teacher in jungle lore. In the homeland of the Himalayan eagles, Gay-Neck's mother, trying to defend her son, is killed by a hawk and the frightened Gay-Neck leaves the humans. When they seek him in a Lamasery of Buddhist monks where they have been previously, Mukerji is told that the pigeon had been there and has been healed of fear. They find Gay-Neck in Dentam, but he leaves the following morning. They trace him to the Lamasery again where they learn that the previous afternoon Gay-Neck and the swifts who nested under the eaves of the monastery flew southward. Gay-Neck's recitation of the odyssey of his flight back to Calcutta concludes Part I.

      In Part II Gay-Neck fights to establish his leadership of Mukerji's flock. Then he leads all the flocks of the city to become truly a leader among leaders. After he is mated, Gay-Neck and another of Mukerji's pigeons are sent with Ghond to Europe to be trained to carry messages for the Indian army in France during World War I. Gay-Neck tells of twice carrying messages from the front lines back to headquarters. Next he is taken behind the German lines by Ghond who seeks an enormous ammunition dump. When he finds it, he draws a map, which he attaches to Gay-Neck's leg. Gay-Neck relates his flight back to the Allies, pursued part of the way by an aeroplane. He reaches his own line injured by bullets shot from the plane. Ghond, too, is injured.

After his broken wing is mended, Gay-Neck refuses to fly. Both he and Ghond are invalided home. In the Lamasery in the mountains both are healed of the fear that has possessed them since their last near-fatal war experience.

Mukerji stated that most of Gay-Neck is a record of his experiences with pigeons, although he had to use those of the army trainers of carrier pigeons to reconstruct the part Gay-Neck played in France. He said, too, that behind each of his books is a moral. The message implicit in Gay-Neck is that man and the birds are brothers. This message is especially strong when Gay-Neck tells his own story. From Gay-Neck one gains also a great deal of information about the raising and training of pigeons, learns what life was like for an Indian boy of high caste in the second decade of the twentieth century, and vicariously experiences the sublimity of the Himalayas and the dangers that abound in the deep jungles in India. The final two chapters "Healing of Hate and Fear" and "The Wisdom of the Lama" contain a distillation of the Indian philosophy.

N16   YOUNG, ELLA. The Wondersmith and His Son: A Tale from the
      Golden Childhood of the World. Illustrated by Boris
      Artzybasheff. New York: Longmans, Green, 1927 (OP),
      189 pp.
      Hero Tale   Gr. 5-10
The tales concerning the Wonder Smith come from an early mythology of Ireland. Also known as the Gubbaun Saor, the Wonder Smith is a god, the world maker, the creator, and possessor of the wisdom of all crafts. The skill and qualities of the Wonder Smith, his son Lugh, and his daughter Aunya, are set forth in the opening chapters. Aunya, who was not reared in her father's house, comes to it as his daughter-in-law. She alone displays the mental quickness of her father. The most exciting chapters are those set in the realm of Balor, the god of death and darkness. His country, a bleak and desolate wilderness, provides a striking contrast to beautiful Ireland. Balor summons the Wonder Smith there to build him a house more magnificent than any that has ever been built since the beginning of time. The Gubbaun says that he can erect such a structure. Once it is completed, Balor plans to kill the Smith and his son, who has accompanied him, so that they cannot build a similar one for another. Lugh learns of the plot but it is Aunya who saves them by out-guessing and out-tricking Balor's emissaries.

Ella Young gathered these stories from Irish peasant storytellers in remote regions of Ireland. She says that some of the stories are written nearly as recounted to her while others are pieced together from gathered fragments. Artzybasheff imaginatively portrays the characters of the story. He is at his best creating the terrible creatures of Balor's country.

1928

N17   SNEDEKER, CAROLINE DALE. <u>Downright Dencey</u>. Illustrated by
        Maginel Wright Barney. Garden City, N.Y.: Doubleday, Page,
        1927 (OP), 314 pp.
        Fiction: historical   Gr. 4-8

Dencey is a Quaker girl who grows up on Nantucket Island in
the years immediately before, during, and after the War of 1812.
During the War, Dencey's father, Captain Tom Coffyn does not
take his ship to sea. Those are two happy years for Dencey who
is very close to her father, but not to her mother. Dencey's
story begins on a spring afternoon when she and her cousin Hope-
still are walking home from school. In response to a taunt
Dencey throws a stone at Sammie Jetsam, a boy saved when a baby
from a shipwreck and now cared for by often-drunk Indian Jill.
From that day on Dencey's life becomes interwoven with Sammie's.
At the close, when both children are about fifteen, Sammie goes
to sea. The reader assumes that when he returns home in four
years he and Dencey will marry.

Mrs. Snedeker not only recreated authentically the Quaker community of Nantucket, but also succeeded in showing in her characters how the Quaker faith permeated the whole fabric of life.
Dencey is motivated and behaves as she does because she is a
child of Quakerism: it is the Quaker sense of responsibility
that causes her to tell lies to her mother so that she can sneak
off and teach the outcast, Sammie Jetsam; and it is her strong
Quaker feeling of being "under concern" for Sammie that drives
her out into the snowstorm seeking him. In Lydia, Dencey's
mother, the spirit of Quakerism abides so that she can live her
life with poise and clear purpose. The beloved Aunt Lovesta is
a Quaker preacher who goes "upon religious journeys . . . where-
ever the Spirit leads . . . to speak the word of life." Many
books deal with discord between father and son, but this is one
of few that shows friction between mother and daughter.

<u>1929</u>

N18   KELLY, ERIC P. <u>The Trumpeter of Krakow</u>. Illustrated by
        Angela Pruszynska. New York: Macmillan, 1928, 218 pp.
        Fiction: historical   Gr. 6-11

The story is set in fifteenth-century Poland. For two hundred
years the Great Tarnov Crystal, a fabulous gem of great beauty
and value, has been secretly guarded by the Charnetski family.
During that time, tales have been told about the crystal so that
its existence at the opening of the story is regarded as legendary. Then a Tartar servant of Andrew Charnetski sees his master
concealing it in a pumpkin. From him the knowledge of its existence spreads until it reaches Ivan of Russia who covets it and
sends Bogdan the Terrible, also known as Peter of the Button Face,

to get it. Pan Andrew, his wife and fifteen-year-old son, Joseph, escape with the crystal to Krakow where Pan Andrew intends to deliver it into the hands of the king. It is many months before he is able to accomplish this.

In Krakow, the Charnetskis procure an apartment directly under the lodgings of an alchemist, Pan Kreutz, and his niece, Elzbietka. Pan Andrew becomes a trumpeter in the Church of our Lady Mary, sounding the Heynal--a hymn to Our Lady--each hour of the night from a little balcony high up in the tower of the church. One night while Pan Andrew is at the church, Button-Face Peter overpowers Joseph and his mother and ransacks their home. Pan Kreutz drives him away, but the crystal is gone, too. Pan Andrew assumes that Peter has taken it. He learns this is not so a few months later when Peter and his men attack the church and demand the crystal. Joseph, who sometimes plays the trumpet, is with his father that night. Ordered by Peter to play the Heynal, Joseph plays the music in a slightly different way. Elzbietka notes the change and, certain that something is wrong, she summons help.

One night a few weeks after Peter's unsuccessful attack on the tower, it is revealed that Pan Kreutz has the crystal. Put into a trance that evening by a conniving associate, Johann Tring, Pan Kreutz, while gazing into the crystal, sees the formula by which he believes brass can be converted to gold. When he and Tring attempt to carry out the procedure, they start a fire that destroys a large portion of the city. Pan Kreutz escapes with the crystal and is found wandering the streets not in his right senses. The next day Pan Andrew, Joseph, the scholar-priest Jan Kanty, and Pan Kreutz take the crystal to the king who has returned to the city after a long absence. In the final moment before leaving the king's presence, the alchemist snatches the crystal from the king and hurls it into the rushing waters of the Vistula River. In spite of its beauty, because it had brought so much suffering and misfortune, the king decides to let it lie in the river bed.

The author, who was thoroughly familiar with Krakow, took care to make the setting, Krakow in the Middle Ages, accurate. Life is precarious, superstition is a powerful motivating force in the way people behave, and the science of alchemy comes close to being black magic. All of this is effectively woven into the background of the story, but, in addition, some material is included simply because it was interesting, not because it had a bearing on the story. Except for the alchemist, Pan Kreutz, who is influenced by the evil Tring and later by the Great Tarnov Crystal, the characters are flat, the Charnetskis and Elzbietka exemplifying good and Tring and Bogdan villainy. A good storyteller, the author keeps the story moving with ample action and suspense. The illustrations first published with the book were made in Krakow. Three colored plates depict events from the story; nine others, copied from fifteenth and sixteenth-century models, show buildings of the city. In 1966, the book was issued with new illustrations by Janina Domanska. Resembling medieval woodcuts, these half-page illustrations, one at the beginning of each chapter, depict a scene from the chapter.

N19   BENNETT, JOHN. The Pigtail of Ah Lee Ben Loo. Illustrated
          by the author. New York: Longmans, Green, 1928 (OP),
          298 pp.
          Fantasy   Gr. 3-8

Humor and robustness characterize the narrative poems and prose tales that comprise The Pigtail of Ah Lee Ben Loo, a book which the author illustrated with 200 "comical" (the author's term) silhouettes. The title story relates in verse how the romance between the rich banker's daughter and Ah Lee Ben Loo, "a poor laundry man, worthy and wise" is saved by his pigtail. With impunity, the author draws on traditional literary sources and utilizes them in new ways. Irreverently he converts King Arthur's mighty knight into "Sir Launcelot de Id-i-otte." Even his dragons are not traditional since "some sort of blight" has got in among them. As a consequence "they had withered away, turned sickly in color, and shrunken to shameful dimensions. Few now spat fire, or breathed noxious vapors or smoke; and so timid and rickety were those that remained that a good knight was ashamed to attack such as lurked in remote townships." Mr. Bennett uses pseudo-old-time speech and spelling and much play on words as in his tale of "The Merry Pieman and the Don's Daughter." The pieman with "no patent on nobility," but with a "patent on a pie, known as The Hot Hottentot" wins the beautiful daughter of the "narrow, violent, arbitrary, arrogant, unscrupulous" Don by trickery and battle using for a weapon a "broad, strong baker's paddle of ashwood." The exceptionally well done silhouettes, many of which caricature the subjects, add much to the rollicking action of the tales.

N20   GÁG, WANDA. Millions of Cats. Illustrated by the author.
          New York: Coward-McCann, 1928, [32] pp.
          Fantasy   Gr. Ps-2

In 1929, when Wanda Gág's Millions of Cats was named a Newbery Honor Book, the Caldecott Award had yet to be established. The author/illustrator's perfect unity of word and picture would unquestionably make it a worthy Caldecott recipient today. Told in folk tale style, the story has a simple plot, repetitive verse, and moralistic overtones, all of which account for its popularity.

When a little old man cannot decide which one of "hundreds of cats, thousands of cats, millions and billions and trillions of cats" to take to his lonely wife, he leads them all in procession back to his humble home. To decide which feline is most beautiful is a task left up to the animals themselves, which results in an enormous, and noisy, row. All that remains alive after the battle is a scraggly, homely kitten, which is adopted by the couple and fed until it grows into a plump and beautiful pet.

The humble pet is richly rewarded with a loving family, and Gág's rounded, curving compositions reflect the security of the kitten's new home. The characteristic repetition of shapes in the illustrator's style neatly reinforces the recurring verse in the text, as well as the numerous shapes in the group of cats.

The book's format and horizontal compositions, where appropriate, reflect the old man's journey over the hills, while the variety in the placement of the other illustrations on the pages helps avoid monotony. The hand-lettered text is integral to the book, and in harmony with the illustrations. The story continues to be a favorite of old and young alike, more than a half-century after it first appeared.

N21 HALLOCK, GRACE T. The Boy Who Was. Illustrated by Harrie
      Wood. New York: E. P. Dutton, 1928 (OP), 153 pp.
      Fiction: historical   Gr. 5-9
On Corpus Christi Day in 1927, Nino, a young Italian goatherd, leads an artist friend to a high place from which they view the Mediterranean. There he confides to him, "It's dull here now . . . nothing much happens and I like to think about all the people who once made the coast an exciting place to be. So I carved their pictures in wood." As Nino tells the artist the stories of the carved figures—whose history spans 3,000 years—he gives himself a part, too—he is always a boy with goats. Past times which he recreates include the visit of Odysseus to Capri; an incident from the Children's Crusade; and the organization of the Carbonari in the early 1800s. One of the best stories recounts the destruction of Pompeii—Miriam, a Jewish slave girl, runs away from the city on the day it was destroyed.

Readers not familiar with Italian history may find some of the episodes difficult to follow. The author has embellished her telling with a great deal of personification. Almost any page will yield an example: the little town of Amalfi is described as "sitting like a bather on the shore of the Mediterranean dabbling her white feet in the transparent water." The artist sees the island of Capri "kneeling like a two-humped camel on a desert of blue." Some readers will admire these figures, while others will find them ostentatious.

N22 MEIGS, CORNELIA. Clearing Weather. Illustrated by Frank
      Dobias. Boston: Little, Brown, 1928 (OP), 312 pp.
      Fiction: historical   Gr. 6-11
In the post-Revolutionary years 1787-1788, when commerce faltered and it seemed as if the colonies were not going to hang together, the Drury fortune, much of which had gone toward

financing the Revolution, was almost exhausted. Old Thomas's
former friend now incited the community against him and endeav-
ored to take over his property. When his uncle becomes incapac-
itated, young Nicholas Drury and Nicholas's friend, Michael
Slade, assume the management of the family's shipbuilding industry. They construct the Jocasta, in design a forerunner of
the clipper ship, and Michael sails it to China. With a successful trip accomplished, the Drury's financial situation improves and, figuratively, there is clearing weather.

Cornelia Meigs is a careful researcher and an adept writer.
The story moves rapidly, but the action and suspense sometimes
arise from circumstances that seem implausible. For example,
one of the most harrowing episodes occurs when the Jocasta is
imprisoned behind a great sand bar at the mouth of a river and
it appears that she and the crew are at the mercy of the hostile
Indians. Then, in their extremity, help arrives: an Indian,
whom one of the sailors had helped to fashion a canoe, paddles
out to the ship and, by means of sign language, indicates that,
on this one night, on the high tide of the full moon, a narrow
channel leading past an island to the sea will be deep enough to
navigate. Later, there is another unbelievable chain of events
in which the "little pirate" from the marauding Chinese junk
turns out to be the respected merchant they intended to seek out
in Canton. Such incidents caused a contemporary critic to call
it a "yarn well spiced with excitement and intrigue" (D. C. Lunt,
New York Herald Tribune Books, 28 Oct. 1928, p. 8).

N23   MOON, GRACE. The Runaway Papoose. Illustrated by Carl Moon.
         Garden City, N.Y.: Doubleday, Doran, 1928 (OP), 264 pp.
         Fiction   Gr. 3-6
       When outlaw Indians attack the camp of Nah-tee's band, small
Nah-tee runs out of the camp and is lost. After searching fu-
tilely for her, Nah-tee's parents continue their trip across the
desert to a new home. Nah-tee soon finds Moyo, an Indian shepherd boy a little older than she, and he tells her he will take
her on his pony to the great mesa, the destination of her parents
and other members of the tribe of which her father is chief. On
the way they are caught in a storm, spend a night in a cave that
is sometimes used by mountain lions, and tarry several days with
an old man who lives alone in an abandoned pueblo village.

Mrs. Moon and her husband, who illustrated her books, lived
for a long time in the desert regions of the Southwest and studied the Indian life and character that they portrayed with accuracy in their books. The Runaway Papoose is interesting for the
presentation of Indian life of the 1920s. It is less satisfactory, however, when examined as a piece of literature. The plot
often depends on coincidence and contrivance. For instance, it
is difficult to believe that the parents would go on without

finding Nah-tee. Later, there is another unreal episode in which the children are abducted by the outlaw Indian who attacked the camp at the beginning of the narrative. The story loses unity when the point of view moves for several chapters from Nah-tee and Moyo to Chi-Wee, a girl of about Nah-tee's age, who lives in the pueblo to which they are traveling. Chi-Wee's activities have little relationship to Nah-tee's story and seem included merely to show more of the way of life. This was one of the first stories portraying the life of contemporary American Indian children. This may have been a factor in its choice as an Honor Book.

N24   WHITNEY, ELINOR. <u>Tod of the Fens</u>. Illustrated by Warwick
      Goble. New York: Macmillan, 1928 (OP), 237 pp.
      Fiction: historical   Gr. 6-11
   As the title suggests, the story is about Tod, who is a stalwart and jolly youth of perhaps twenty living with a band of twelve in the fens near the town of Boston, England, early in the fifteenth century. Although the story is primarily his, it encompasses a great deal more than Tod's activities. It records, also, life in the town when English commerce was just beginning. Besides Tod, other important characters are Johanna, fourteen-year-old daughter of Sir Frederick Tilney who is a councilman and Mayor of the Staple, and Gilbert Branche, whose father is a merchant adventurer at a time when there were "few good English ships" to be found on the sea "so monopolized by the odious Easterling." Prince Hal, the future Henry V, in disguise and calling himself Dismas, interacts with both groups. While living a life of outdoor pleasure in the fens with Tod and the other "merry rogues," he goes into the city five times, disguised differently each time, and--a bit improbably--obtains the five keys to the town coffer. Tod, who is unusually astute, has recognized the disguised prince immediately, but he keeps his knowledge to himself. After some boisterous good times, a kidnapping, the unmasking of the Prince, and the restoration of the keys, Tod goes to sea as captain of the ship Sir Frederick Tilney has had built for trade.
   In an acknowledgment the author states that "a real effort has been made to have the details of the story accurate as far as the period setting is concerned." A criticism of the story is that she has included historical data that is extraneous.

<u>1930</u>

N25   FIELD, RACHEL. <u>Hitty: Her First Hundred Years</u>. Illustrated
      by Dorothy Lathrop. New York: Macmillan, 1929, 207 pp.
      Fantasy   Gr. 4-8

1930

Hitty was in fact a real doll, owned jointly by her author and illustrator. Made of mountain ash wood and only six and one-half inches tall, she was at least one hundred years old when they acquired her and decided to record her life by letting her write her memoirs. The story relates Hitty's personal adventures with a panoramic view of life in nineteenth- and early twentieth-century America as background. She was taken to sea by her first owner, Phebe Preble, the daughter of a Maine sea captain, was shipwrecked and had adventures in the South Seas and India before being returned to the United States--to Philadelphia--with the daughter of a missionary. She lived in Philadelphia through the Civil War, a part of the time in a Quaker household, where she sat for her daguerreotype and met the Quaker poet, John Greenleaf Whittier. Her adventures next took her to New York City. There she literally fell at the feet of Mr. Charles Dickens, who picked her up and returned her to her owner, Isabella Van Rensselaer. Later she traveled to Rhode Island in the new steam cars and, as an artist's model, went down the Mississippi to New Orleans in a boat with a big paddle wheel. She spent time on a plantation and in a dead letter box. She was even made into a doll pincushion. Finally, by coincidence, she lived awhile again in the farm house in Maine where Old Peddler had carved her. She was taken from there to an antique shop on Eighth Street in New York where she brought her memoirs to a close, but expressed the feeling that further adventures await her.

Miss Field's careful assimilation of history, her characterization of Hitty and her many owners, and her attention to style combine to make this a notable book. Dorothy Lathrop's meticulous illustrations, showing Hitty in many costumes and circumstances, but always with the same pleasant expression, are in complete harmony with the text.

N26   EATON, JEANETTE. A Daughter of the Seine: The Life of Madame
         Roland. New York: Harper & Brothers, 1929 (OP), 320 pp.
         Biography   Gr. 7 up
    When she was a young girl, Marie-Jeanne Philipon, known in history as Madame Roland, told her grandmother, "I'll call myself the daughter of the Seine." When she was grown she said of the river, "I grew up beside it. It is a part of me." Against this background, Jeanette Eaton has told the story of the woman who became a political adviser and hostess to the Girondist group during the French Revolution. Miss Eaton tells the whole story of her life-- from the time she was a schoolgirl until her death on the guillotine. Madame Roland had a conventional middle class upbringing, but even when young she showed the remarkable intellect and self-control that were dominant traits in her adult character, and stayed with her to the end. During the months she spent in prison previous to her execution she studied English, repeated poems,

kept up a correspondence with her friends, and wrote her memoirs. Jeanette Eaton successfully brings to life a person and times long vanished.

N27   MILLER, ELIZABETH CLEVELAND. Pran of Albania. Illustrated by
       Maud and Miska Petersham. Garden City, N.Y.: Doubleday,
       Doran, 1929 (OP), 257 pp.
       Fiction   Gr. 6-11
    Fourteen-year-old Pran lives with her father, Ndrek; her mother, Lukja; and her eight-year-old twin brothers, Nik and Gjon, in a little mountain town in Albania. The period is post-World War I, a time the author worked with the Red Cross in Albania. Early in the story while she and her brothers are out gathering green branches for winter fodder for the sheep and goats, Pran meets Nush, a boy about her own age. He keeps turning up--on the feast day with a gold piece to give to a designated person; when she walks to market at Skodra; to show her the signal fires in the north--and she grows to care for him so much that rather than acquiesce to an arranged wedding, she takes the virgin's vow. After that, although she is called a nun, she wears men's clothing, bears a rifle, eats, talks, and sits in council with the men. In the council, Pran and the old women, who also are permitted to attend the council meetings, persuade the chiefs to renew the truce that for several years had stopped the blood feuds between the tribes during which time they united to repel the Slavs. With the renewal of the truce, Pran learns that her betrothed is Nush, whose real name she has never heard because he was in hiding from one who would kill him because of the feud. The story ends gaily with prosperity for Pran's family and a traditional wedding celebration for Nush and Pran.
    The author, with her firsthand knowledge of the country, was doubtless accurate in her portrayal of it. The plot is somewhat too complicated and occasionally contrived. The abundance of details--as when she describes each person's attire minutely--tends to impede the progress of the action. Still the story, overall, is readable and interesting.

N28   McNEELY, MARIAN HURD. The Jumping-Off Place. Illustrabed by
       William Siegel. New York: Longmans, Green, 1929 (OP),
       308 pp.
       Fiction   Gr. 5-9
    After the death of their Uncle Jim, who had cared for them since their parents' death eight years earlier, the four Linville children leave Wisconsin and go to South Dakota to live on the land on which Uncle Jim had filed a claim. Becky, seventeen, and Dick, fifteen, assume adult responsibilities, but Phil and Joan, who are younger, do their part, too. They must deal not only with problems that arise from the environment, but also with

1930

squatters on their land. However, with the notes which Uncle Jim
had left them and the help and encouragement of Mr. and Mrs.
Cleaver who live in the nearest town eleven miles away, the children stay on the claim for the fourteen months needed to make it
valid.

In 1910, Marian Hurd married Lee McNeely and they homesteaded
for two years on the South Dakota prairies nineteen miles from a
railway station. She used this locale and some of the experiences as background material for The Jumping-Off Place. The
setting is well-realized and there are some realistic episodes--
a neighbor's child dies from the effects of a rattlesnake bite--
but the story suffers when compared to those Wilder chronicles
that are also set in South Dakota. The whole idea of the children going off by themselves to homestead is rather unbelievable,
that they would meet such helpful people as the Cleavers is unlikely, and that Uncle Jim would have left such complete instructions is improbable. Written in a time when many stories took
place long ago or far away, this one about contemporary Americans
may have had special appeal to the Award Committee.

N29   YOUNG, ELLA. The Tangle-Coated Horse and Other Tales: Epi-
          sodes from the Fionn Saga. Illustrated by Vera Brock.
          New York: Longmans, Green, 1929 (OP), 186 pp.
          Hero Tale   Gr. 5 up
     These fourteen tales, episodes from the saga of Fionn McCool,
the Gaelic hero, tell of his life and of the lives of his comrades. Fionn spent his earliest years in the forest with a wise
old woman, Bovemall, who taught him woodcraft and of his heritage.
When he was but a lad, he ate the Salmon of Knowledge. After he
became a young man, with a magical spear that had belonged to his
dead father, he slew Allyn, the High King's foe. For this deed
the King rewarded him with the Lordship of the Fianna of Ireland,
which his father had held. For many years Fionn headed this companionship of warriors and hunters and lived with open-handedness
in the beautiful Palace of Aloon, built by the Shining Folk for
Moorna, his mother. For a few happy months his lovely wife Saba
lived there with him until the Dark Shadowy One cast a spell over
her, and by trickery took her away. In the title story, a shaggy,
tangle-coated horse carried seventeen of the warriors of the
Fianna to the Land-Under-Wave. In the final story, "Three Hundred Years After," Fionn's son, Usheen, returns, after having
spent three centuries in the Country of the Ever-Young, to live
in a monastery with Patrick, who has brought Christianity to
Ireland.

Ella Young's vigorous, poetic prose does justice to the magical stories. The black and white illustrations are epic in style
matching the spirit of the book.

N30   ADAMS, JULIA DAVIS. <u>Vaino: A Boy of New Finland</u>. Illustrated
      by Lempi Ostman. New York: E. P. Dutton, 1929 (OP),
      271 pp.
      Fiction: historical   Gr. 6-11
   In the foreword, the author wrote that, as a result of a series
of visits she made to Finland between 1923 and 1926, she developed
a deep appreciation of the Finnish people and of their spirit
which enabled them in a few years to adapt to a democratic republic after centuries of domination by foreign powers. She imbued
young Vaino and his older brother, Sven, and older sister, Annika,
with this spirit and gave them a part in the Finnish Revolution
of 1917 when Finland declared its independence from Russia.
Annika and Sven are both actively engaged in the White forces,
and Vaino and his mother are more than mere bystanders. They
conceal a Russian officer in their country home; Vaino goes out
with his brother in a boat into the bay to procure arms and am-
munition from a German U boat; and Vaino, on skis, carries a
package to his brother in hiding with other members of the Civil
Guard. At the conclusion, he sees his hero Mannerheim enter
Helsingfors at the head of the victorious army. The author notes
that a number of the war experiences are based on the experiences
of Finnish friends.
   Because the author believed the imaginative legends of Finland
are important to the understanding of the Finnish people, she
introduced them into the story. They are told to Vaino by his
mother, Fru Lundberg, as she sits knitting before the great
stove. With their atmosphere of ancient lore and adventure,
these make a quite different contribution to the story of the
Finnish Revolution.

N31   SWIFT, HILDEGARDE HOYT. <u>Little Blacknose</u>. Illustrated by
      Lynd Ward. New York: Harcourt, 1929 (OP), 149 pp.
      Fantasy   Gr. 4-7
   Hildegarde Hoyt Swift subtitled her book "the story of a pioneer" and wrote that it was "the true and honest story of the
DeWitt Clinton engine, and of all he saw and did." Little Blacknose, the first engine ever built for the New York Central Railway, was a hundred years old at the time the book was written,
so his life story covers many years of railroading.
   In the nineteen twenties, those years when hundreds of thousands of Model-T Fords made the horse and buggy obsolete, it was
perhaps natural for writers to experiment with fanciful tales of
airplanes and buses and other mechanical wonders. These inanimate objects were personified just as the elements of nature had
been earlier by Thornton Burgess and others. <u>Little Blacknose</u>
was among the earlier stories of this genre which included the
still popular picture story book <u>Little Toot</u>. Probably <u>Little
Blacknose</u> has gone out of print because of the false emotionalism

that is present on nearly every page. One time after traveling quite a distance the engine is "horribly dizzy as well as horribly hot"; another time he is "horribly hungry" and happy to get chunks of wood in his "poor, starving little firebox"; he liked wood best finding coal "hard to chew." Attributing human emotions to him is overdone to the point of absurdity as when "he . . . shrieked with pain when they . . . hammered the rivets into his side." The first time he went backward, it was with "gasping and coughing and trembling" and "with great hot drops of fear standing out all over his black boiler." The same writing which made a reviewer in 1929 call Little Blacknose a "charming person" (J. Farrar, Booklist 26 [1929]:126) palls on many present-day readers.

1931

N32 COATSWORTH, ELIZABETH. The Cat Who Went to Heaven. Illustrated by Lynd Ward. New York: Macmillan, 1930, 63 pp.
Fable   Gr. 3-8

Shortly after his old housekeeper brings home Good Fortune, a little cat of three colors, a poor young Japanese artist is commissioned by the priest to make a painting of the death of the Buddha for the temple. Before beginning, for three days the artist meditates, reviewing the Lord Buddha's life in his mind. After meditation, he knows that the Buddha's countenance must impart "the look of one who has been gently brought up and unquestioningly obeyed; . . . and he must have the look of one who has suffered greatly and sacrificed himself; . . . and he must have the look of one who has found peace and given it to others." Having thus depicted the Holy One, the artist turns to drawing the gods, men, and animals who came to bid him farewell. As he paints each animal, the legendary tale linking the animal to Buddha is told. Good Fortune looks long at the painting each time an animal is put into the picture. The artist paints an elephant, a horse, a buffalo, a swan, a dog, and even a tiger, but no cat. Good Fortune becomes sad. The artist gently explains to her that among the animals only the cat refused to accept the teachings of Buddha; she did not receive his blessing and, as a consequence, cannot enter Heaven. The little cat becomes even sadder. Finally, the artist can stand it no longer. He takes up his brush and draws his cat. Good Fortune is so happy she dies. The next morning the priest comes to see the finished picture. He gazes at it long and with admiration. Then he sees the cat. Immediately, he informs the artist he will take the painting to the temple and burn it the following morning. All day and all night the artist sits and thinks, finally concluding that he has no regret because his action has

brought great happiness to Good Fortune. Early the following
morning the priests of the temple come and bid the artist to
hasten to the temple. He sees his picture, but it is different.
Now the tiny cat kneels with bowed head before the holy man,
whose hand rests in blessing on his head.

Elizabeth Coatsworth's style is such that the reader is deeply
moved by the fate of Good Fortune and made conscious of the compassion of a religion that has a place for even the lowliest of
creatures. Eight short, beautiful poems, songs of the housekeeper,
are spaced at intervals throughout the story. Lynd Ward's illustrations show noble animals, animals in whom the spirit of Buddha
seems to dwell.

N33   PARRISH, ANNE. Floating Island. Illustrated by the author.
       New York: Harper & Brothers, 1930 (OP), 265 pp.
       Fantasy   Gr. 3-6
This survival-adventure story told from a doll's-eye view begins with a shipwreck. Cast ashore at various points around
Floating Island, a desert isle in the tropics, are a Doll House
and a family of Dolls: Mr. and Mrs. Doll; their children:
William, Annabel, and Baby; Dinah the cook; and Lobby, Chicky,
Finny, and Pudding. Even though the last four are plaster food-
stuffs, they are really like members of the family. And, since
the dolls' food is always air, they are never eaten, although
each in turn sits on the table at mealtime. The story relates
the Dolls' adventures on the island, especially their efforts to
get back together. At the close of the story they are rescued.

Although these dolls are real personalities, one never forgets
that they are dolls: their movement is restricted because of
stiff joints; Mr. Doll cracks his china hair on a rock and Mrs.
Doll loses her glued-on wig. Just as Rumer Godden's The Dolls'
House clarifies and brings into perspective fundamental questions
of human life by treating them in a miniature way, so does Floating Island, because of the smallness of scale, give special insight. Here the reader's awareness of natural beauty is increased
by seeing it from a doll's viewpoint. Typically, Miss Parrish
uses colorful, descriptive words and the book is bright with word-
pictures of tropical flowers, fish, and birds. Although her descriptions seem to cry for color, the many pictures are in black
and white: the large pictures are drawn by the author; the small
ones are said to be by Mr. Doll; both are admirable artists who
often see the humor in a situation. A stylistic trait of Anne
Parrish is to speak directly in a confiding or intimate tone to
the reader. Many of these remarks occur in footnotes concerning
the flora and fauna on Floating Island. Although at the time the
story was written most critics approved of these notes, present-
day readers may find them distracting. Today's readers will also
observe considerable stereotyping--in both text and illustra-
tions--of the Negro cook Dinah.

1931

N34   MALKUS, ALIDA SIMS. The Dark Star of Itza: The Story of a
          Pagan Princess. Illustrated by Lowell Houser. New York:
          Harcourt, 1930 (OP), 217 pp.
          Fiction: historical   Gr. 6-11
       The Dark Star of Itza portrays life in Yucatán when the
Mayan cities were in their prime. The story revolves around
beautiful seventeen-year-old Nicte, who is the daughter, as well
as a pupil, of the chief priest. Ignoring Nicte's prophecy
that his actions will bring ruin on his own great city, Chac Zib
Chac, khan of Chichen Itza, kidnaps the intended bride of another
powerful chieftan, Hunac Ceel. In the war that ensues, Hunac
allies himself with the Toltecs who use long range bows and
obsidian-tipped barbs. In return for his aid, he promises
Pantemit, the chief of the Toltecs, the city of Chichen Itza and
Nicte, whom the Toltec chief had met when he visited her city in
the guise of a traveler. The city falls, as prophesied, but
Nicte's story ends happily although disaster is close when she
offers herself as the bride of the rain god of the well if the
Pantemit will cease making blood sacrifices. Nicte's father
arranges that Itzam Pish, the young nobleman Nicte loves, will
be waiting in the well. He saves her and they succeed in escaping from the doomed city.
       This interesting story, well-told, makes a long ago civiliza-
tion live. Before writing the book, the author visited the ruins
and studied the civilization which she depicts with authenticity.

N35   HUBBARD, RALPH. Queer Person. Illustrated by Harold von
          Schmidt. Garden City, N.Y.: Doubleday, Doran, 1930 (OP),
          336 pp.
          Fiction: historical   Gr. 4-9
       On a cold winter day when he was about four, Queer Person
wandered into the camp of a band of Pikuni Indians and was finally taken in by Granny, an old woman. The name was given him
because he was a deaf mute. Most of the tribe regarded him as
an idiot, also. When he was sixteen, Queer Person experienced
terrible pains in his head and something that looked like a hard
dried worm came out of each ear. After that he could hear, but
Granny makes him play the deaf-mute role for another four years.
Then his time to prove himself as a warrior comes. Queer Person
goes on the "old-time war trail, alone and without horses" to
hunt for the chief's lost seven-year-old son, Sun Pipe. He finds
him in the camp of the Crows which he has entered in disguise.
He rescues Sun Pipe, but is caught and made to do the Porcupine
Dance. Bearing Little Pipe on his back, Queer Person accomplishes the difficult feat. After having killed an old Crow
chief in single combat, he returns to his tribe in triumph. It
is revealed that the old chief was his father. Now that it is
proved that the blood of chieftans is in his veins, he is worthy
of Singing Moon, the chief's daughter.

For several years before writing this book, Mr. Hubbard was a special instructor in Indian lore to the Boy Scouts of America. Some of the early chapters seem to have been included so that the author could share some of that lore: he goes into detail about many aspects of daily life. The later chapters also contain information, but it is now more integral to Queer Person's story, as when he observes the Crows holding the ceremonial sun dance, or when the Porcupine Dance is described in detail.

N36   ADAMS, JULIA DAVIS. <u>Mountains Are Free</u>. Illustrated by
       Theodore Nadejen. New York: E. P. Dutton, 1930 (OP),
       246 pp.
       Fiction: historical   Gr. 6-11
The mountains are in Switzerland and William Tell is a character in the story. The incident in which Tell shoots an apple from his son Walter's head is an incident but not the climax of the story. The chief Swiss character is Bruno, a thirteen-year-old orphan boy the Tells have taken to rear. Because he wants to make his own way, Bruno goes to Austria to be a page for the harsh and autocratic Sir Rupprecht von Lowenhoke. There he meets the other two principal characters: the Lady Zellina, a wealthy heiress a year younger than he and a ward of the Duke of Valberg; and Kyo, a minstrel jester who came to the Duke's court with her. When Zellina is betrothed in the evening to Rupprecht and is to be married to him at dawn before he rides out to war, Kyo and Bruno succeed in getting her away from the Duke's castle. Eventually they make their way to Switzerland. Zellina adapts quickly to the life and is treated as a daughter in a Swiss home. But trouble with the ruling Austrian Habsburgs is not over. After the Swiss rise up against the resident Austrian rulers and take over the governing of their cantons, Austria sends a magnificently accoutred, splendidly equipped army to put down thee insurgents. Fighting in their own mountains, the Swiss are invincible. Among the slain Austrians are Rupprecht and the Duke of Valberg. Zellina remains in Switzerland and marries Bruno. After that, more than a century passed before anyone again attacked the Swiss bear in his mountains.
The historical material is authentic. The William Tell incident, placed in a larger framework, gains freshness. The story brings out well the contrast between the democratic spirit stirring in Switzerland and the autocratic feudal regime of Austria. The narrative moves quickly and is not impeded by the insertion of foreign words. Today's readers may find some of the episodes of plot contrived and the characters stereotyped. At the time the book was published, critics did not comment on these shortcomings.

1931

N37   HEWES, AGNES D. Spice and the Devil's Cave. Illustrated by
        Lynd Ward. New York: A. A. Knopf, 1930 (OP), 331 pp.
        Fiction: historical   Gr. 6-10
   Bartholomew Diaz, Vasco da Gama, and the young Ferdinand
Magellan are characters in this story set in the late 1400s in
Lisbon, Portugal. Da Gama makes the first sea voyage to India,
for spices, around the Cape of Good Hope, called the Devil's
Cave. Woven into the historical narrative is the story of beautiful Nejmi, the daughter of a European father and Arab mother.
After her parents' death in the middle east, Nejmi is kidnapped
by Abdul, placed in a cage, and narrowly avoids being sold as a
wife to a sultan. Saved by Scander, a Portuguese sailor, she
eventually arrives in Lisbon as a stowaway. These characters,
and Abel and Ruth Zabuto, who become Nejmi's foster parents in
Portugal, and Nicolo Conti, a young Venetian who falls in love
with Nejmi, are all involved in an exciting plot of international
intrigue and piracy involving the theft of the only maps showing
the "way of the spices." The historical discrimination against
Jews and the competition between Portugal and Venice also enter
into the story.
   The historical material is well integrated into this readable
story. The illustrations add atmosphere and interest.

N38   GRAY, ELIZABETH JANET. Meggy MacIntosh. Illustrated by
        Marguerite de Angeli. Garden City, N.Y.: Doubleday,
        Doran, 1930 (OP), 274 pp.
        Fiction: historical   Gr. 5-10
   Meggy MacIntosh begins in Edinburgh, Scotland, January 5, 1775,
and ends a little more than a year later in the backwoods of North
Carolina. Orphaned fifteen-year-old Meggy slips away from her
uncle's home in Edinburgh to go to the colony of North Carolina.
She is determined to reach Flora MacDonald who, when she was young,
had helped Bonny Prince Charlie escape after he unsuccessfully
tried to gain the Scottish crown. She does reach Flora, but does
not stay with her long. Flora is as warm and attractive as tradition had it but she is a Loyalist and Meggy finds herself increas-
ingly sympathetic toward the rebelling colonists. When she falls
in love with a Scots colonist who desires liberty, her future is
decided.
   Meggy is a well-realized character. Although she is a girl
with whom present-day girls can identify, yet she seems truly a
girl of the eighteenth century. The historical settings are
authentic with the author supplying sufficient details to recreate life in Scotland and Carolina. Like many of her contemporary authors, Miss Gray employs dialect to evoke a sense of time
and place. Meggy's Scottish dialect rings true and contributes
to the atmosphere of the story, but the Carolina Negro dialect,
which might not have been questioned by readers at the time the

story was written, now causes the Negro characters to seem stereotyped. But beyond their speech, the Blacks are made to seem too
irresponsible to be anything but servants requiring constant su-
pervision. Cuffey, one of the little black servants, is addressed
at various times as a "little black monkey," "a little black imp,"
and a "good-for-nothing nigger." This derogatory language aims
at historic representation, but it is doubtful that Miss Gray
would use it if she were writing the book today.

N39   BEST, HERBERT. <u>Garram the Hunter: A Boy of the Hill Tribes</u>.
       Illustrated by Allena Best [Erick Berry]. Garden City,
       N.Y.: Doubleday, Doran, 1930 (OP), 332 pp.
       Fiction   Gr. 4-8
     Garram lives in the hills of Africa; his father Warok is
chief of the tribe. To the west in a walled city, Yelwa, ruled
by an emir, live the Fulani of the West, Mohammedan in faith.
To the east live the traditional enemies of the hillsmen, the
Fulani of the East, also followers of Mohammed. From time to
time the Fulani of the East sweep down upon the hillsmen to capture and sell them into slavery. Both of these tribes enter into
Garram's story, but we first see him in his native hills on the
hunt with his great dog, Kon. Shortly, he departs for the West.
Even though few tribesmen from the hills go to Yelwa he is accepted there. His keen observation enables him to do the Emir
a great service and this deed, coupled with Garram's love of
joking, makes him a favorite of the potentate. When some of the
Mohammedan faithful become jealous of him, Garram leaves the city
and returns home. There he finds that his father's brother and
nephew, Sura and Menud, are trying to assume leadership of the
tribe and have his father imprisoned. Garram succeeds in rescuing him. As the elders sit in council deliberating the fate of
Sura and Menud, word comes that the tribes from the east are
approaching. All efforts turn to plans for repulsing the enemy.
Warok shows himself mighty in planning battle, but it is the
Rainmaker, the spiritual leader of the tribe, and the women who
are responsible for the final victory after Menud turns traitor.
Both Sura and Menud die in the battle. Emissaries arrive from
the Emir of the West, and the peace is restored.
     Doubtless the author wished to show the country and culture of
the people of whom he wrote and he was well qualified to do this,
having spent many years among them in the English civil service.
He does not do this, however, at the expense of the story or characters. We see the wide spaces of Africa, the round huts with
thatched roofs, the walled city, the wild life, not as pieces of
information, but as they relate to Garram and his exciting story.
Erick Berry's illustrations add to the atmosphere.

N40   LIDE, ALICE ALISON, and JOHANSEN, MARGARET ALISON.   Ood-le-uk,
      the Wanderer.   Illustrated by Raymond Lufkin.   Boston:
      Little, Brown, 1930 (OP), 265 pp.
      Fiction   Gr. 6-9
   For hundreds of years there was no contact between the small
fur-clad Eskimos of America and the fierce, fur-clad Tschuktschi
tribesmen of the Siberian Arctic.   Ood-le-uk, an Alaskan Eskimo
boy of a shore tribe, by accident gets across the Bering Strait.
After three years of wandering in Asia, he returns to his own
tribe and is instrumental in establishing trade between his tribe
and the Siberian tribesmen, who, in turn, trade with the Russians
each year at a great fair.
   Against a background in which hazards are common even in
everyday life, the theme of boy becoming a man is worked out.
Ood-le-uk, the weakling, develops into Ood-le-uk, the leader of
men.   He survives being cast out to sea on drift ice and slash-
ings by a bear and walrus.   His strength and cunning save the
reindeer herd from the wolves and he and Etel, his Siberian
tribesman friend, in the time of great famine, go to the much-
feared land of the Spirits to obtain food, mammoths frozen ages
earlier.   The narrative moves rapidly through many exciting episodes in which the reader incidentally learns much about the polar
world and the way of life of the people who adapted to it.

1932

N41   ARMER, LAURA ADAMS.   Waterless Mountain.   Illustrated by
      Sidney Armer and Laura Armer.   New York: Longmans, Green,
      1931, 212 pp.
      Fiction   Gr. 4-8
   Younger Brother, an eight-year-old Navajo boy of the 1920s,
lives with his parents, and Elder Brother and Baby Sister close
to Waterless Mountain.   Mother weaves rugs, Father works in turquoise and silver, Elder Brother hunts, and Younger Brother tends
his mother's sheep.   One special day his mother takes him to the
trading post for the first time.   There he meets the Big Man, who
is the trader at the post and the first white man Younger Brother
has ever seen.   The man treats him kindly and Younger Brother
knows he is his friend.
   These events make up only a part of Younger Brother's life.
His vocation is to be a medicine man and already he is learning
from his medicine man uncle.   As Younger Brother watches the
sheep, he meditates on the mysteries of the earth.   He reflects
that he is a child of the wind, the clouds, and the rainbow.   He
is a friend of the bees--they eat jam from his lips.   When he
sees the deer people dancing he makes a song, and Uncle gives him
a sacred name, Little Singer, which must be kept a secret until

he is a man. From Uncle he learns the stories of his people:
of the First Man and the First Woman and of Spider Woman who
taught the first woman to weave as all Navajo women have since.
He learns the stories of the Coyote and of the Pack Rats; and
stories of the Turquoise Woman of the Western Sea and of her
husband, the Sun Bearer. Uncle tells him, too, of the ancient
Holy People who lived in the land before the Navajos came.

By the time he is twelve, Younger Brother has his own pony to
ride while he herds the sheep. As he watches the sheep, he
practices the many songs a medicine man must know. He observes
the birds because he wishes to fly. His wish is granted when he
flies with the Big Man in a giant "dragon fly." Even though he
is happy with his family and can now help Uncle prepare for ceremonies, Younger Brother is restless. He believes the Turquoise
Woman is calling him and he must ride to the west. Part of the
way he travels alone on his pony; some of the time he travels
with a white boy. When he comes to the western mountains he
places a prayer stick there and prays that he may find the trail
of beauty to the west and reach the wide waters. Again, he is
assisted by the Big Man who takes Younger Brother, his parents,
and Little Sister in the train behind the "fire horse" to the
wide waters of the west. There, in a museum, his mother demonstrates Navajo weaving. As Younger Brother looks out over the
ocean, he sees in the distance the peak of an island that is
surely where the Turquoise Woman lives in her turquoise house.
Younger Brother sends her an offering of a turquoise bead, and
he fills a wicker jar with water to take back to Uncle. After
he returns home, Younger Brother and Uncle climb Waterless Mountain. A short while later, he is instrumental in finding the
twenty deerskin masks that were hidden in a cave in four jars
at the time of the Long March in 1863. Younger Brother helps his
uncle carry out the ceremonies that celebrate the finding of the
masks. On the sixth day they make a sacred sand painting illustrating the story of the Whirling Logs. The all-night dance of
the Yays concludes the ceremonies.

By living and working among them for years, Mrs. Armer gained
the friendship and trust of the Navajo Indians. With fidelity
she portrays their everyday life. In addition, through the eyes
of Younger Brother, who is essentially a poet and a mystic, she
reveals the Indians' religious beliefs and traditions. The point
of view presented seems truly Navajo rather than that of an outsider. This successful depiction is evidently a result of her
serious study of Navajo mythology and her extraordinary understanding of the Indians. The mysticism and introspection that
inform the book are important to understanding Younger Brother,
but they tend to impede the flow of the narrative. In addition,
because of the many incidents recounted, the story lacks unity
and becomes episodic. The beautifully done illustrations harmonize with the text.

1932

N42   LATHROP, DOROTHY P. <u>The Fairy Circus</u>. Illustrated by the
       author. New York: Macmillan, 1931 (OP), 66 pp.
       Fantasy   Gr. 1-4
    After having seen a circus, the fairies decide to put on a
circus performance. They use the animals of the field and wood
as circus animals: the red squirrels wrap their tails around
their necks for manes and become lions; the chipmunks are tigers;
the turtles are elephants; and the fairies themselves do the
juggling act, using dandelion puffs for juggling balls.
    The delicate black and white drawings and colored illustra-
tions are in harmony with and essential to the text. Dorothy
Lathrop's fairies are very slim children with pointed ears and
long gauzy wings. Toadstools make comfortable chairs for them.
The idea is original, the story well written, and the illustrations charming. A possible reason for the story's decline in
favor may be that gauzy-winged fairies appeal to fewer tastes
today. An additional cause may be that present-day children,
not having the opportunity to see the dazzling Barnum and Bailey
Circus that was in its heydey at the time the book was written,
feel less interest in circuses.

N43   FIELD, RACHEL. <u>Calico Bush</u>. Illustrated by Allen Lewis.
       New York: Macmillan, 1931, 213 pp.
       Fiction: historical   Gr. 4-8
    In 1743, when she is nearly thirteen, orphaned French-born
Marguerite Ledoux, called Maggie, goes as a Bound-Out girl with
the Joel Sargent family into the Maine wilderness. The story
chronicles their journey from Massachusetts and their first year
there, a time of hardship and worry about Indians. Treated as a
servant by Mr. and Mrs. Sargent, Maggie's life is made happier by
the children, who love her, and by a neighbor, Aunt Hepsa, who,
though past eighty, is young enough to jig, to doctor, and to
piece beautiful quilts. It is she who tells Maggie that the
thriving low-growing bush with the deep pink flowers that grows
out of rocky ledges is called "Calico Bush." As the calico bush
has adapted to the rough terrain, Marguerite adjusts to the difficult life, becoming hardy and resourceful. In the spring, when a
band of Indians comes, Maggie's quick actions save the Sargent family, including the father, who is confined to his bed with a broken leg. She passes food to them and then constructs a makeshift
Maypole around which she, the children, and the Indians dance. A
short while later, when a boat bound for Canada stops, Joel
Sargent offers to cancel Maggie's papers and send her to a French
convent near Quebec. By this time Maggie thinks of the family as
her own and chooses to stay.
    Maggie is a memorable character whose story comes alive against
a well-realized Maine background, country the author knew well.
Especially exciting is the chapter about the Maypole. Yet it is

not presented as a separate episode unrelated to earlier events. The author has prepared for it: late Christmas Eve afternoon Maggie had met one of the band of Indians in the woods. She had given him a gift--a gilt button from her dead uncle's coat--and they had exchanged greetings in French. The few wood engravings strengthen the emotional identification the reader feels with Maggie. The book is at once entertaining and historically accurate, and continues to appeal to new readers.

N44   TIETJENS, EUNICE. Boy of the South Seas. Illustrated by
        Myrtle Sheldon. New York: Coward-McCann, 1931 (OP),
        193 pp.
        Fiction   Gr. 4-7
      Teiki, ten, goes to sleep on an English trading schooner while it is in the harbor of his home island, one of the Marquesas. When he wakens, it is night and he is at sea. He swims ashore at the island of Moorea, the setting for most of the story, which extends over several years. Although Teiki can survive simply by gathering the food that grows everywhere in abundance, he soon goes to live with a family. He attends school and is an apt pupil. But after awhile he comes to dislike the lazy life the people on Moorea live--lazier than on his native island. At this point he has the good fortune to find an old hermit who, years earlier, had come from Teiki's native island. The hermit is a master carver, using as his subjects the old legends which the Mooreans have almost forgotten. He trains Teiki who shows marked artistic ability. At the close of the story Teiki finds a place for himself as a helper in a Hawaiian museum interested in the old customs, chants, stories, and art.
      The author took a trip to the South Seas before writing the book. She has included interesting folklore and customs and has effectively depicted the influence which the white man has had on the way of life of the natives. Her portrayal of Teiki is less successful. He does not develop as a character, and the plot serves merely as a vehicle to describe the surroundings. It seems likely the book appears among the Newbery books because of its sympathetic presentation of the South Sea islanders' culture.

N45   LOWNSBERY, ELOISE. Out of the Flame. Illustrated by
        Elizabeth Tyler Wolcott. New York: Longmans, Green,
        1931 (OP), 352 pp.
        Fiction: historical   Gr. 5-10
      Pierre de Bayard, nephew and namesake of a great knight, and ward of the King, lives in the sixteenth century in Renaissance France. Pierre serves as page and later as squire at the court of François I, but, since he is a ward of the Crown, he is given many of the advantages that the King's own five children receive. At the opening of the story François, the Dauphin, and Prince

Henri, Pierre's age, return home after three years imprisonment in a Spanish donjon. Henri is changed since the imprisonment. He is jealous of Pierre, who has a generous, outgoing nature, and often makes life difficult for him. Pierre usually bears up under Henri's ill-nature and abuse, remembering that he is a page in the service of the King. Although François I was a lover of fetes and tournaments--and the book is filled with them--he also had a keen intelligence and quick wit, and gathered about him the great minds of his age. The children benefit by these associations: Fabri is their tutor; Rabelais visits, as does Sir Thomas More and Erasmus. The children learn much about Leonardo da Vinci when they visit the small villa in which he spent his last days and look through his great sketchbook.

They examine paintings by Italian masters, musical instruments from Germany, and trees and seeds from all parts of the world. They gypsy for two years in a huge caravan and explore all parts of France and meet real gypsies. They become friends with the explorer Cartier. On a vacation in Navarre, Prince Henri is kidnapped by pirates. Pierre is responsible for his release. Later Pierre is abducted by the same pirates. He is rescued by twelve Canadian Indians who have returned to France with Cartier. At the close, Pierre who has always preferred lessons in books to lessons in arms, decides that he will become a scholar-knight.

Although the book received very favorable reviews at the time it was written, most readers today will find it filled with irrelevant details and contrived happenings. The characters seem little more than puppets manipulated by the plot.

N46   ALLEE, MARJORIE HILL. <u>Jane's Island</u>. Illustrated by Maitland de Gorgoza. Boston: Houghton Mifflin, 1931 (OP), 236 pp.
      Fiction   Gr. 4-8

An island off the coast of Maine is the setting for the summer adventures of twelve-year-old Jane and her companion, Ellen, who has just finished her first year of college. Jane's father is a famous scientist engaged in research at the Wood's Hole marine laboratory and Jane, too, is enthusiastic about collecting fish and crabs. But there is time, also, for swimming, picnicking, and boating.

Written for the growing-up girl, this pleasant story concerns itself with external events rather than the problems of adolescence that have been the focus of more recent books such as Betsy Byars's <u>Summer of the Swans</u>. It is interesting to read for the picture it draws of the life of the times, and it is gratifying to find a normal and attractive girl of that period interested and competent in science.

N47   DAVIS, MARY GOULD.   The Truce of the Wolf and Other Tales of
        Old Italy.   Illustrated by Jan Van Everen.   New York:
        Harcourt, Brace, 1931 (OP), 125 pp.
        Folk Tales   Gr. 3-8
   Six of the seven stories are retold from old Italian tales and
legends.   The author retells the introductory part of the title
story in her own way, but has faithfully followed the Fioretti of
St. Francis of Assisi in the dialogue between St. Francis and the
Wolf.   She adapted from Legends of Florence by Charles Godfrey
Leland "The Boar Who Was a Man," "The Goblin and the Rose," and
"The Enchanted Cow."   In the first, the boar appears as a man at
night to his beautiful young wife until she reveals this fact to
her mother.   He then must remain always a boar and she is changed
into a little frog who repeats and repeats the thing about which
she should have kept silence.   In the second story, the monk obtains the goblin's gold to use for decorations in the church as
payment for delivering to the goblins in January, without magic,
a fresh, full-blown rose.   "The Enchanted Cow" tells how a street
in Florence, the Street of the Cow, got its name.   "The Calandrino
and the Pig," taken from the Decameron, tells how poor Calandrino
is duped and cheated out of his pig by two rogues, and, in addition, provides a feast for the men of the village.   The story of
"The Signora Lupa and the Fig Tree" was told to the author by a
Tuscan peasant woman.   In this tale, two old peasants enjoy the
best Risotto they have ever had and also, thanks to Signora Lupa,
the choicest figs from the fig tree that grows in the garden of
the Padrome next door.   "The Tale of Nanni" is Miss Gould's own
creation.   Nanni is a beautifully formed, wise, and obstinate
donkey who turns out to be a hero.
   Contemporary reviewers praised these stories for so well capturing the atmosphere of Italy.   Present-day readers will find
them interesting still.

1933

N48   LEWIS, ELIZABETH FOREMAN.   Young Fu of the Upper Yangtze.
        Illustrated by Kurt Wiese.   Philadelphia: John C. Winston,
        1932, 265 pp.
        Fiction   Gr. 5-9
   In the 1920s, Young Fu, thirteen, and his widowed mother, Fu
Be Be, move from their village home to Chungking so that Young Fu
can take up an apprenticeship with Tang, a master coppersmith.
The story covers the three years of his apprenticeship and the
next two years spent as a journeyman in Tang's shop.   Naturally
ambitious, Fu is pleased when Wang Scholar, who lives in the room
above his mother and him, offers to teach him to read and write.
He profits from this instruction, but learns from unfortunate

experiences, too. When he has been in the city only a short while, unwittingly, he becomes indebted to an unscrupulous shop-keeper, but exercises ingenuity to pay the debt at the New Year. Later, he matures after a disastrous experience gambling with the dominoes. However, Fu's adventures usually turn out well. The night the foreign hospital burns, he assists a foreign lady who becomes his friend and brings her trade to Tang's shop. Once he travels with his master down the river to deliver some fine bras-ses. On the return journey, Fu's quick thinking prevents the river bandits from robbing Tang of the silver received for the brasses. He further gains Tang's gratitude by apprehending a burglar and by solving the mystery of the theft of brasses from the shop. At the close of the story Tang discloses his intention of making Fu his adopted son.

The author lived in China for a number of years before she wrote this book. To aid the reader, she provided a glossary giv-ing the pronunciations and definitions of Chinese words and notes for each chapter. Although the book remains worthwhile, in some respects it does not measure up to the highest literary standards. While the adventures themselves make exciting reading, yet they simply seem to happen to Young Fu rather than to arise out of his character. Too much of his success is a result of good luck. A further criticism is that even though the reader is told that Fu has become a skillful coppersmith with a talent for design, few pages depict him learning the craft. Finally, the author some-times includes information not essential to Fu's story. For example, much of the first chapter describes Chungking as it was when Fu and his mother moved there. While this detracts from its literary excellence, it does contribute to the very good background the author provides of that time. China is shown in turmoil with the centuries old culture, represented by Young Fu's mother with her tiny bound feet and Wang Scholar with his proverbs, coming in contact with the new. The unstable political condition of that era is made a part of the story, too. It is often dis-cussed in Tang's shop. The Nationalists are in control, but, in a tea shop, Fu hears arguments for communism. During the time of unrest, the military were in control and often ruthless. Once Fu is forced to carry supplies for some soldiers; he sees a coolie shot for refusing. As Pearl Buck wrote in an introduction for the 1972 edition: "To understand the vast, complex China of today, one must try to learn about its past. The story of Young Fu of the Upper Yangtze is a prologue to modern China."

N49   MEIGS, CORNELIA. Swift Rivers. Illustrated by Forrest W. Orr.
          Boston: Little, Brown, 1932 (OP), 234 pp.
          Fiction: historical   Gr. 5-8
     Chris Dahlbert lives on Goose Wing River in Minnesota in 1835
when that region is populated only by a scattered colony of

Swedish farmers. To augment his grandfather's small income,
Chris determines to float logs from his grandfather's vast timber
tract down the river to the St. Louis market, hundreds of miles
away. A number of exciting episodes grow naturally from this
situation: running the rapids, having the raft break up on a
sand bar. There is also a less convincing encounter with the
Indians. Besides the adventure, Chris's knowledge of human
nature is increased by his association with Pierre, the half-
Indian, half-French pilot of the great log raft, and Joe,
Pierre's estranged friend.

The story maintains suspense and moves rapidly, but often it
is by means of contrived episodes. The author's authentic historical background is well integrated into the story.

N50   SWIFT, HILDEGARDE HOYT. <u>The Railroad to Freedom: A Story
       of the Civil War</u>. Illustrated by James Daugherty. New
       York: Harcourt, Brace, 1932, 364 pp.
       Biography   Gr. 5-9

This is a fictionalized account of Harriet Tubman's life from
her birth into slavery in 1821 on Broadacres, a plantation in
Maryland, until the close of the Civil War. Harriet's mother,
Old Rit, was the plantation cook, but the strong Harriet became
a field hand. After being hit in the head by a rock when she
was sixteen, she occasionally lapsed into a queer lethargy that
left her suspended in time for two or three minutes; during this
interval she sometimes had visions. Following the death of the
kind old master, Harriet worried she would be sold South by young
Marse George who hated her independent ways. Although her chance
of escaping was small, she felt she must run away. She left in
1849 and, by chance, stumbled onto the underground railroad. She
returned in 1850 and led to freedom her brother, Benjamin, his
wife Lily and their baby, and her friend, Mame, whose husband had
been sold away from the plantation. Although she made numerous
other raids (in all she led more than three hundred people to
freedom), she did not dare to return to Broadacres until 1857
when she succeeded in getting her old parents away. By this time,
Harriet had influential northern friends including abolitionist
Dr. Theodore Parker of Boston. In a short time, her daring deeds
had become legendary and there was a high reward offered for her
capture. When war broke out Harriet served: as a nurse, a river-
boat pilot, and a scout.

The author, who grew up in Auburn, New York, Harriet's home
after the Civil War until her death in 1913, called her book "not
a biography . . . but a story based in authentic history." She
hoped to bring back to reality Harriet's "courage, vitality and
unselfish devotion." She has succeeded in doing that in this
fast-moving, dramatic narrative. Harriet--and all the blacks--
speak in dialect which may make the reading difficult for young

readers. Although the charge would not have been made at the
time the book was written, the dialect today may be regarded as
derogatory. Since the likelihood of Harriet's shooting young
Marse George in the war seems remote, a note regarding the authenticity of this incident would be fitting. A prologue in the form
of a dialogue between two anonymous voices states the best known
arguments for and against slavery. A six page bibliography and a
page of acknowledgments suggest the author engaged in careful
research.

N51 BURGLON, NORA. Children of the Soil: A Story of Scandinavia.
         Illustrated by E[dgar] Parin d'Aulaire. New York:
         Doubleday, Doran, 1932 (OP), 272 pp.
         Fiction   Gr. 4-7
    The story is set in Sweden early in the twentieth century.
Nicolina, a fourth grader, and Guldklumpen, a second grader, live
with their mother, Olina, the educated daughter of a wealthy
farmer, on a few acres of rented land. Two years earlier, the
father, who was from a lower social class than Olina, went to
sea. They have not heard from him since and never talk about
him. They are very poor, but ambitious and industrious. Finally,
they acquire chickens and a cow in addition to their two goats and
ducks. Although it is largely through their own efforts, they
give credit to the little tomte, which they are sure lives in a
small house filled with straw which Guldklumpen made for him.
    The setting is doubtless authentic. The author visited this
part of Sweden from which her father came before writing the
story. The children, however, seem a bit too good to be true.
Although the poorest children in school, they are the brightest,
and, in addition, are athletically talented and artistically
gifted. Guldklumpen wins the ski leap in competition with much
older boys and carves wooden figures that can be sold to tourists;
Nicolina wins first prize for her tapestry. At the time it was
published, Children of the Soil received enthusiastic notices:
one reviewer compared it favorably with Heidi; and another predicted that it would still remain good reading in fifty years.
One can only conclude that tastes and standards of excellence
have changed.

1934

N52 MEIGS, CORNELIA. Invincible Louisa: The Story of the Author
         of "Little Women". Boston: Little, Brown, 1933, 246 pp.
         Biography.
    A nonfictionalized biography of Louisa May Alcott, the author
of Little Women. Louisa and Anna, her older sister, were born
in Germantown, Pennsylvania, where her father, Bronson Alcott,

taught for two years. He then moved his family back to New England where both he and Mrs. Alcott had been born and reared. They lived in Boston and Concord and adjacent areas, moving frequently. In the first twenty-eight years of her life, Louisa moved twenty-nine times. Although Bronson Alcott was a brilliant man, he was seldom able to provide an adequate living for his family. From the time she was sixteen, Louisa worked to help support the family. She taught, sewed, served as a companion, and wrote. Little Women, published in 1868, when Louisa was thirty-six, was immediately popular. Written in response to a publisher's suggestion that she write "a story for girls," it was about her own family and detailed trials and struggles as well as the many happy times of her childhood. The royalties from Little Women and her subsequent publications, several of which were also based on her own experiences, enabled her to provide the financial security she so wished for her beloved family.

All aspects of Louisa's personality--faults as well as virtues--are revealed and she is indeed portrayed as invincible. Miss Meigs has selected anecdotes that reveal her indomitability and through them the reader comes to understand Louisa and to see that the qualities that sometimes made it difficult for her to live with herself are those that put iron into her character. The period and places--homes and communities--Louisa lived in are recreated, as is the temper of the times. Besides seeing Louisa as a person, the reader observes also the other luminaries of Boston and Concord--the Hawthornes, Thoreau, and especially Emerson--as friends of the Alcotts. The humanity and humor that pervaded the lives of the Alcotts permeate the book, so that the members of the Alcott family ultimately become as real as the characters in Little Women. The author's list of acknowledgments indicates she prepared herself thoroughly. The book is not footnoted, but sources of quotations are given in the text. A chronology, an index, and nineteen photographs of Louisa and members of her family and the houses they lived in add usefulness and interest.

N53   SNEDEKER, CAROLINE DALE. The Forgotten Daughter. Illustrated
        by Dorothy Lathrop. Garden City, N.Y.: Doubleday, Doran,
        1933 (OP), 309 pp.
        Fiction: historical   Gr. 6-11
     Rome and a remote country villa in the second century B.C.
provide the settings for this dramatic story. Chloé, the forgotten daughter, progresses in status from an abused slave girl to the daughter of a Roman patrician and the promised wife of another. Chloé's mother, a Greek girl, was taken prisoner in a military raid on her native Lesbos. Her captor, Laevinus, a young Roman centurion, fell in love with her, married her, and installed her as mistress of his villa. Later, while Laevinus was in Rome, Chloé

was born and her mother died. Told that neither his wife nor
child survived, Laevinus remarried and never returned to the
villa. Treated as a slave, Chloé was sometimes cruelly whipped
by the overseer, Davus, but knew of her heritage from a friend
of her mother, Melissa, with whom she lived in a hut on the hillside. When she is seventeen, she and the young Roman, Aulus,
whose estate adjoins the villa of Laevinus, fall in love. After
a plague in Rome kills his wife and children, Laevinus takes refuge in the country and is united with the daughter he has never
seen.

The Forgotten Daughter was written with an intensity of emotion and a certain conviction that surely arises from the fact
that Mrs. Snedeker had so fully imbued herself with the customs,
history, religion, and the spirit of the times that she was able
to write as though she were a contemporary. The treatment of
slaves, the influence of the Greek civilization on Rome, and the
weaknesses and strengths of Rome are all integrated into the plot,
which moves toward an inevitably happy conclusion in which interest is maintained to the very end. In those chapters that introduce Aulus, Chloé's beloved, and follow Tiberius Gracchus through
his brief career as tribune, Roman history comes alive as it does
in Julius Caesar. A stylistic trait of this author is to make
occasional comments in her own person. Reviewers of the 1930s
were pleased with the pictures drawn by artist Dorothy Lathrop
for the book.

N54   SINGMASTER, ELSIE. Swords of Steel. Illustrated by David
        Hendrickson. Boston: Houghton Mifflin, 1933 (OP), 262 pp.
        Fiction: historical   Gr. 6-11
       In 1859, twelve-year-old John Deane of Gettysburg, Pennsylvania,
becomes acutely aware of the division between the North and the
South when Nicholas, a free Negro and a special friend of his, is
captured by a slave-catching gang. Later that year, John travels
south with his father, an agent for a carriage company, and is in
Harper's Ferry when John Brown makes his raid. On that trip John
learns that his father's journeys involve more than soliciting
orders for the Acme Carriage Company: he is also a conductor on
the underground railroad. In 1860, John's father and his grandfather are jubilant when Lincoln is elected. National events
shape the Deanes' lives for the next five years. When war comes,
Father goes with the cavalry and the sweethearts of Sue and Sally,
John's twin sisters, enlist. Those at home follow the newspaper
accounts of the war eagerly. In 1863, the war comes to them.
John, now sixteen, stays in their home, which is used during the
battle of Gettysburg as a Confederate hospital, and helps care for
the wounded. A few months later John and his family attend the
dedication of the Gettysburg cemetery and shake hands with President Lincoln. Late in 1864, Father is sent home as an invalid

from Andersonville Prison. On January 1, 1865, his eighteenth birthday, John goes to enlist in his father's old unit. He is with Grant before Petersburg and at Appomattox Court House when the surrender terms are arranged. John reaches home on July 4 in time for the annual Fourth of July celebration and on the second anniversary of the Battle of Gettysburg.

The author, having grown up in Gettysburg, succeeds in investing the reader with her familiarity with the whole area. In addition, in this well-written story, she brings out the issues of the war as well as the everyday life of the time.

N55   GÁG, WANDA. The ABC Bunny. Illustrated by the author. New
          York: Coward-McCann, 1933. [38] pp.
          Fantasy   Gr. Ps-2
       Wanda Gág's 1934 Honor Book recounts the adventures in the day of a bunny in the rhyming format of an alphabet book. The bunny's day-long excursion begins when an apple falls from a tree, startling the hare on his way, and after he explores the marvels of nature--from frog, gale, hail, and insects to quail, porcupine, and squirrel--he completes his trek by disappearing into his burrow. The story and its natural flow best find expression when read aloud, and the inclusion of the letter in the reading is integral to the text's effect. The lyrical qualities are captured, as well, in a song, at the book's end, in which the words are put to music.

The rhythmic text progresses from letter to letter, page to page, to the accompaniment of lithographs of the black and white contrasts so characteristic of Gág's style. Large red upper-case letters are the only elements of color in the work, but Gág's compositions never rely on color for their impact. Though each page has its own illustration, the side-by-side pictures actually function simultaneously, complementing one another. The patterns of light and dark lead the eye from left to right in the same gentle curves and repetition of shapes that makes Millions of Cats (1929 Honor Book) such a popular work.

N56   BEST, ALLENA [Erick Berry]. The Winged Girl of Knossos.
          Illustrated by the author. New York: D. Appleton-Century,
          1933 (OP), 253 pp.
          Fiction: historical   Gr. 5-10
       Beautiful Inas, the Daughter of Daidalos, the architect and sculptor in Greek mythology, is the heroine of this story set on Crete in the time of King Minos. She is a fearless athlete and takes part in the Cretan sport of bull-vaulting, but she also takes a keen interest in her father's invention--the glider. Because of her friendship with Ariadne, she becomes involved in the escape of Ariadne and Theseus. In an exciting close, when she and Kadmos, her betrothed, must leave Crete in a hurry, they depart on gliders built by her father.

1934

At the time the story was written, Inas must have seemed a refreshingly different heroine. She remained feminine yet had the courage to break out of the conventional role assigned girls. One day while driving Kadmos's horses, she tells him, "I'm not so sure I want to marry you, or anyone. Why should I forego all adventures? See, I am as strong as any boy." The author's illustrations are redrawn from murals and decorations of Knossos and other Minoan cities. In a foreword, Miss Berry relates the status of the Cretan civilization at the time the story begins; in an afterword she tells of the events that followed.

N57   SCHMIDT, SARAH L. New Land. Illustrated by Frank Dobias.
       New York: R. M. McBride, 1933 (OP), 317 pp.
       Fiction   Gr. 5-9
       Sayre and Charley Morgan, seventeen-year-old twins, their father, and little sister arrive in Upham, Wyoming, in the Rattleshake, a Model T Ford, looking for an unproved homestead claim known as Parson's Eighty. A former associate of Mr. Morgan has assigned the claim to him. The time is the early 1930s, when the story was written. Dad Morgan is a gentle visionary who has failed at everything. Sayre vows that this time the Morgans will not quit. And it is largely through her efforts that in two years the family is established and has worked out a satisfactory life. Although Sayre is the stabilizing force, it is her twin, Charley, around whom much of the action centers. Throughout most of the story Charley is in competition with Frank Hoskins, Jr., whose father is the big man in the whole Pawaukee Irrigation Project. The rivalry begins in football, but extends to the vocational agriculture projects in which both of the twins are soon immersed. Vocational agriculture is a new subject at the time and Sayre is the only girl in the program.
       Sayre is a well-developed character, but the others are less so: Charley and Frank are rather shadowy figures engaged in many conflicts that seem devised for the sake of action; Frank's father seems too much of a villain. New Land does give an interesting picture of what life was like in a particular region of the country in the 1930s.

N58   COLUM, PADRAIC. The Big Tree of Bunlahy: Stories of My Own
       Countryside. Illustrated by Jack Yeats. New York:
       Macmillan, 1933 (OP), 166 pp.
       Folk Tales   Gr. 3 up
       As a youth, Padraic Colum heard twelve of these thirteen tales told in the Irish village in which he grew up. The thirteenth one is an original creation. Under the Big Tree of Bunlahy--"a great elm tree . . . there in my father's time and my grandfather's time, and . . . when my great-grandfather was a whistling boy"--those who came into the village on errands

rested and heard and told stories. Late nineteenth-century
Bunlahy comes to life for the reader as the author, in inter-
ludes between the tales, describes the next storyteller and the
occasion of the tale. Included in the collection are realistic
stories such as "Nannie's Shoes"; animal stories like the original "Our Hen" and "The Three Companions"; a story of the little
people, "When the Leprechauns Came to Ireland," and tales of
heroic times, "King Cormac's Cup," "The Story That Shattered
King Cormac's Cup," and "The Story That Put it Together Again."
 The rhythm and drama of these lovely stories are best conveyed by a skilled storyteller.

N59   HEWES, AGNES D. Glory of the Seas. Illustrated by N. C.
      Wyeth. New York: A. A. Knopf, 1933, 315 pp.
      Fiction: historical   Gr. 6-11
 The story opens in the early 1850s in the Boston counting
house of Pinckney and Fay, where young John Seagrave is employed
as a clerk. News has just reached Boston that the clipper ship,
the Flying Cloud, built in the Boston shipyard of Donald McKay,
has made the passage from New York around Cape Horn to San
Francisco in a record eighty-nine days. John, like many others,
is infected with California fever and almost everyone except the
senior partner, Mr. Pinckney, is enthusiastic about the new clipper ships. These slim, tall-masted vessels are the Glory of the
Seas and part of the story concerns them. John goes to the shipyard to see Sovereign of the Seas being built; he sees the Great
Republic launched, and, at the close of the book, takes passage
on her for California. The other part of the story concerns the
resistance, and, to a lesser degree, the support given to the
Fugitive Slave Law in Boston. The Compromise of 1850, which permitted California to enter the union as a free state, strengthened
this law imposing heavy penalties on those who aided in a slave's
escape or interfered with his recovery. The uncle with whom John
makes his home, Federal Judge Asa Wentworth, an abolitionist, re-
signs his judgeship because he feels he cannot uphold the law in
court. Suspense is generated as various characters--including
Uncle Asa, John, and Mr. Pinckney's nephew--play a role in trying
to help Jasper, a runaway slave, to escape. Mr. George Fay, the
junior partner of the firm of Pinckney and Fay, works with equal
diligence to recapture the slave. Sue Fay, George's beautiful
daughter, and John's fiancée at the close of the story, is caught
between two loyalties.
 The historical background is authentic and well integrated.
Although the plot is complicated and rather improbable, the action keeps the story moving at a fast pace. None of the characters is fully delineated; Jasper, the escaped slave, is stereotyped.
Two historical personages, shipbuilder Donald McKay and U.S. naval
officer and scientist Matthew Maury, appear briefly. The timeless

1934

theme of civil disobedience is worked out with care in relation
to the Fugitive Slave Law. The dilemma the individual faces is
well stated by Uncle Asa: "Which way is one to turn? Disobey
this law, and you're a traitor to your country. Obey it, and
you're a still worse traitor--to yourself!"

N60   KYLE, ANNE. The Apprentice of Florence. Illustrated by
         Allena Best [Erick Berry]. Boston: Houghton Mifflin, 1933
         (OP), 276 pp.
         Fiction: historical   Gr. 6-10
    When Nemo's father had been absent from home for four years
and is presumed dead in a shipwreck, sixteen-year-old Nemo becomes an apprentice. His master is Messer Bardo, a wealthy
bachelor and a silk merchant in fifteenth-century Florence, the
time when Florence led the world in luxury and culture as well
as wealth and commerce. Because Nemo shows unusual business
ability, Messer Bardo sends him to Constantinople with his nephew,
Everardo, the company agent, as an aide. Everardo, a few years
older than Nemo, is not really interested in the silk trade, but
for reasons of his own, he is happy to get out of Florence. One
dark night in the street, when both were drunk, he drew his sword
in self-defense and killed Corso Corsi, a young nobleman. Unknown to Everardo, Nemo and Clarice, Everardo's sister, witnessed
the killing. Clarice, who is a year or two younger than Nemo,
dons men's clothes and with her nurse takes passage to Constantinople, also. Everardo is ill for many weeks after their arrival,
so Nemo looks after Messer Bardo's interests. Nemo learns from
the Grand Vizier himself that many years earlier his father saved
the life of the Grand Vizier's son. The year is 1453 and Constantinople is besieged by the Turks. Both Nemo and Everardo fight on
the walls in defense of the city. Everardo is wounded and he and
Clarice board an Italian ship in the harbor shortly before the
city falls. In the final fighting, Nemo is injured. His life is
spared, however, because he wears a ring the Grand Vizier had
given him. After recuperating, Nemo returns to Italy on a ship
from Genoa. There, from Christopher Columbus, at that time still
a boy, he learns that his father is alive, but very ill. Nemo
finds his stricken father who, before he dies, tells of his wanderings and of being on New Land--apparently Central or South
America. Following his father's death, Nemo returns to Florence
where he is immediately arrested for the murder of the Corsi.
Clarice persuades her brother to write out a confession and ban-
ish himself to Venice. She carries the confession to Cosimo de
Medici who orders Nemo's release. Messer Bardo asks Nemo to be
in place of a son to him, and, the reader assumes that Nemo and
Clarice will be married.
    Although the story has many exciting incidents, from the
above summary it is apparent that the plot is over complicated,
dependent on coincidence, and crowded with events and people.

In addition to the several story strands, the author also introduces the art of the period through Vanni, Nemo's artist friend,
and brings out the fact that Constantinople was a repository of
learning. Nemo accomplishes too much and fills too many roles
successfully to make him seem like a real person. The book received both favorable and unfavorable reviews at the time it
was published.

1935

N61　SHANNON, MONICA. <u>Dobry</u>. Illustrated by Atanas Katchamakoff.
　　　New York: Viking, 1934 (OP), 176 pp.
　　　Fiction   Gr. 4-8
　　Dobry, a Bulgarian peasant boy, lives in a small village with
his mother and grandfather. His father had died fighting in
World War I. Dobry's daily life of work and play is good and
he revels in it. But, as he grows older, he desires something
more: he wishes to be an artist. Grandfather, who shares some
of the same feelings, is convinced that this is right for Dobry,
but his mother, Roda, is unable to understand that her handsome
peasant son would want to do anything other than till the fertile
fields that have been in the family for generations. Then, early
one Christmas morning in a corner of the courtyard, Dobry carves
from packed snow a Nativity scene: the stable, the Holy Family,
and animals of the village. So well executed is the sculpture
that all who see it kneel and pray. Roda knows now that Grandfather has been right in saying that Dobry's talents are God-
given and that she must not resist his wishes. At the conclusion
of the book Dobry is about sixteen and ready to depart for Sofia
where he will study art.
　　The characters are well realized. The mother, Roda, strong
and beautiful, passionately devoted to the soil and able to make
it produce, suggests an earth goddess. We often see Dobry's and
Grandfather's physical natures as well as their artistic, spiritual sides. Dobry gorges himself on the cold, crisp tomatoes
that he digs out of the snow and has a colossal stomachache that
his mother cures by applying to it a hot, fresh-baked loaf of
bread. Grandfather eagerly awaits the coming of the gypsies with
their massaging bear: in the fall he is anxious for a massage;
in the spring he wants his spring bath--he will take it in the
river as soon as the bear has gone in and found it a comfortable
temperature. Besides helping to characterize, such incidents
disclose the customs of the country. The powerful illustrations
are by an artist of Bulgarian heritage.

N62　SEEGER, ELIZABETH. <u>The Pageant of Chinese History</u>. Illus-
　　　trated by Bernard Watkins. New York: Longmans, Green,
　　　1934 (OP), 386 pp.

1935

Information: history   Gr. 6-10
This comprehensive record of Chinese history begins thousands
of years before Christ and extends to the founding of the Chinese
Republic in 1912. In addition to tracing political and military
events and characterizing the leaders, the chronicle also con-
siders the Chinese culture. There are sections on the family,
religion, literature, and the arts.

Even though the author did extensive research (two pages of
acknowledgments and sources are listed) and wrote with enthusiasm, the rambling, conversational style is not distinguished.
Useful maps are printed on the endpapers, but the illustrations
within the book add little. Though there were some unfavorable
comments at the time of publication, the book received mostly
good reviews. It would please fewer critics today. Three reasons may account for its being among the Newbery Award books.
First, it was the earliest substantial book of Chinese history
written for children. Second, it told of a faraway land, a
popular subject in the 1930s. Third, it was, like the first
Newbery winner, The Story of Mankind, a history book. In the
years since 1922, additional history books had not been named.
The judges may have thought that another historical account was
overdue.

N63   ROURKE, CONSTANCE. Davy Crockett. Illustrated by James
         MacDonald. New York: Harcourt, Brace, 1934 (OP), 276 pp.
         Biography   Gr. 7 up
Merging legends with known facts, the author recounts the life
of David Crockett (1786-1836) in a direct, informal style, neglect-
ing no part of his adventurous life. She depicts him as the great
pioneer hunter who, according to popular conception, charmed even
the forest creatures, but she shows him also as an intrepid soldier and scout in the war against the Creek Indians, and as a
serious frontier Congressman who had the temerity to oppose fel-
low Tennessean, President Andrew Jackson. She portrays him as an
author and a teller of tall tales and funny stories, and as a
brave defender of the Alamo. She represents him as a devoted
husband and father, even though he often went off leaving his
capable wife to manage the children and farm.

Miss Rourke does not fictionalize. She enlivens the narrative with many vivid and descriptive details, quoting generously
from the writings of Crockett and his contemporaries. A map on
the endpapers shows some of Davy Crockett's travels in early
America. Eight full-page illustrations in black and white and
additional smaller ones complement the text. The author closes
the book with a critical essay in which she discusses the nature
and authenticity of her sources. The reviewers, including notable
authors Mark Van Doren and Henry Steele Commager, wrote words of
high praise. Nearly fifty years later these judgments still remain valid.

N64   VAN STOCKUM, HILDA. <u>A Day on Skates: The Story of a Dutch</u>
       <u>Picnic</u>. Illustrations by the author. New York: Harper,
       1934 (OP), 40 pp.
       Fiction   Gr. 1-3
    One day, when the canals of Holland are solidly frozen, the
teacher of Evert and Afke, nine-year-old twins, takes his class
of boys and girls on a day long skating picnic. They start at
dawn and skate all day with stops for good things to eat: cocoa,
spicy korstjes, and snow pancakes. They have exciting moments,
too: Evert falls through a fishing hole, and he and three other
boys accidentally become locked in the tower of a beautiful old
church they have stopped to visit. As night falls, they are glad
for a ride home in a big sledge.
    The detailed illustrations--seven full pages in color and
numerous black and white ones--contribute a great deal to this
simple story of fun on the icebound canals of the Holland of
fifty years ago. They show the action, the costumes, the architecture, and the countryside of Mrs. Stockum's native land. It
is likely that this picture story book, after the institution of
the Caldecott Medal in 1938, would have been considered for that
award rather than the Newbery.

<u>1936</u>

N65   BRINK, CAROL RYRIE. <u>Caddie Woodlawn</u>. Illustrated by Kate
       Seredy. New York: Macmillan, 1935, 270 pp.
       Fiction: historical   Gr. 4-7
    In 1864, when her story begins, Caddie is eleven and "as wild
a little tomboy as ever ran the woods of western Wisconsin." She
and her brothers Warren and Tom "got in and out of more scrapes
and adventures than any of them could have managed alone. And in
those pioneer days Wisconsin offered plenty of opportunities for
adventure to three wide-eyed, red-headed youngsters." Among their
friends is a band of Indians that lives directly across the river
from the white community. In the most exciting episode, during
an Indian alarm, Caddie forestalls a massacre of the Indians by
the whites. Most of the events that occur during the year the
story covers are less frightening, however, and of the type that
might come to a family that has been comfortably settled for seven
years. Often the incidents are served up with humor. Even such
a grim object as a scalp belt is regarded more with curiosity than
horror. When Indian John leaves his scalp belt with Caddie while
he travels west, she and her brothers give a "show" and exhibit
it. At the close of the story, the family decides unanimously
that they will not migrate to England to claim an estate that
Mr. Woodlawn has inherited.
    Most of Caddie's adventures actually happened to the grand-
mother of the author. In a note she states that even the father's

1936

story of his English ancestry is as Caddie remembers it. The
lively illustrations substantiate the characters and incidents.

N66   STONG, PHIL. <u>Honk: The Moose</u>.   Illustrated by Kurt Wiese.
      New York: Dodd, Mead, 1935, 80 pp.
      Fiction   Gr. 2-6
   Waino and Ivar, both ten, live in the mining town of Birora,
Minnesota, in the early 1900s. On this particular winter's day,
the boys have been out hunting on skis and with an air gun--even
though the ground is covered with seven feet of snow and ice,
and the thermometer registers thirty degrees below zero. On
their way home, they stop at Ivar's father's livery stable to
oil their skis and plan tomorrow's hunting expedition. Alone in
the stable they warm themselves at the hot stove in the office
and talk about how exciting it would be to shoot a big moose.
Just then they hear a sad sound: "Haawwnnk-hawnk-hawnk-
haawwnnkk." In one of the stalls they discover Honk, a huge
moose with great spreading antlers, filling himself up on expensive hay. Bravely, Ivar tells him to get out. Honk pays no
attention. When Ivar's father returns he has no better successs
in getting the uninvited guest to leave. Nor does Mr. Ryan, the
town policeman. The moose lies down and goes to sleep. They
call the Mayor, Nils Olavsson, who summons the town council. No
one wants to shoot Honk, but no one can think of a way to get him
out. In the night, Honk leaves on his own. But, to the delight
of the boys, he turns up that evening and every evening thereafter until the Mayor decides the town will pay for his room and
board for the winter.
   Honk, a huge wild animal in his role of a docile pet, provides
the kind of incongruity from which humor arises. Mr. Stong exploits the humor inherent in the unlikely situation and still
manages to tell a believable tale. Although he does show a certain consciousness, Honk is not anthropomorphized. The vivid
descriptions of the Finnish-American residents of the town help
to authenticate the tale, as do Kurt Wiese's robust good-humored
illustrations in both black and white and color.

N67   SEREDY, KATE. <u>The Good Master</u>. Illustrated by the author.
      New York: Viking, 1935, 210 pp.
      Fiction   Gr. 4-6
   This is the story Kate Seredy wrote in response to her editor's
instructions that she go home and write a book about her childhood
in Hungary. The time is a few years before World War I. Because
she needs fresh country air after being very sick with the measles,
Kate is sent by her father, a widower, from Budapest, where he is
a teacher, to the ranch of his brother, Márton Nagy. But nine-
year-old Kate needs more than fresh air. In a letter he sends
with her, Kate's father says "she needs a strong hand! . . . She

is the most impossible, incredible, disobedient, headstrong little imp!" Because his brother has always been good with young things, Kate's father hopes he can modify the behavior of his spoiled young daughter. Kate arrives in April and is met at the railroad station by Uncle Márton and Cousin Jansci, who is ten. Jansci teaches Kate to ride and they become inseparable companions. Life on the Hungarian plains is disclosed as the theme of the gentling of Kate by her uncle, the Good Master, is carried out in a number of lively episodes. At Christmas, Kate's father arrives to find his daughter stronger in body and more mature emotionally. Kate and the others prevail upon him to stay permanently and become the schoolmaster in the village.

Kate is a fully realized character. Because she is a daredevil she has some exciting adventures: she disobeys instructions when she and Jansci turn aside stampeding horses during a roundup; she goes away with the gypsies to try to save the livestock and grain they have stolen from the farm; she also exposes a fraudulent freak at the fair. All of these incidents--and others--are in accord with her character and contribute humor and drama. Beautiful traditions are observed by the dyeing of Easter eggs and the filling of shoes by Mikulas on the night of December sixth. Inserted stories--told by Jansci's mother, the shepherds, and the miller--relate the folklore of the country. The theme of the superiority of life in the country over life in the city and of handcrafted articles over machine made ones is brought out. Kate Seredy's many graceful illustrations of the characters and horses contribute to the romantic interpretation that the text gives of a way of life.

N68 GRAY, ELIZABETH JANET. Young Walter Scott. New York: Viking (OP), 1935, 239 pp.
Biography Gr. 6-10

This pleasingly written fictionalized biography of Scott covers the years in Walter's life from age ten to seventeen, beginning with his return to Edinburgh from the home of his grandmother in the country, and closing with his apprenticeship to his father as a lawyer. In those years Walter develops from a shy, lame lad into a physically strong, extroverted young man.

A biographer who knew her subject less well might have overemphasized Walter's lameness. Miss Gray never moralizes about it and always keeps it in proportion. We see young Walter Scott as a person, not as a stereotype of a sickly boy who in a set number of pages will overcome his handicap. The conversation contains enough Scottish phrases and words to make the reader feel that he is participating in "bickers" with the laddies of the Square or savoring Percy's ballads with Walter and his friends; yet, the dialect is not an impediment to the reading. In addition to the Scott family, Miss Gray succeeded in recreating the atmosphere of late eighteenth-century Scotland. An

1936

admirer of Scott since childhood, Miss Gray visited the country
and home of her hero before writing his story.

N69   SPERRY, ARMSTRONG. All Sail Set: A Romance of the Flying
       Cloud. Illustrated by the author. Philadelphia: John C.
       Winston, 1935 (OP), 175 pp.
       Fiction: historical   Gr. 5-8
    Following the death of his father, Enoch finds employment in
the shipyard of the master shipbuilder, Donald McKay. He becomes
absorbed in the construction of the clipper ship, the Flying
Cloud, and when the ship sails for California in April 1851,
fifteen-year-old Enoch is aboard, one of four apprentice seamen.
The main part of the story concerns the passage to California
which is accomplished in a record 89 days and 21 hours. For
Enoch, who writes his story when he is an old man, it was a
never-to-be-forgotten voyage. Highlights vividly recorded include: his first time aloft among the high sails; his fight with
trouble-maker Jeeter Sneed, who later leads a mutiny; Neptune ini-
tiations for those who had never crossed the Equator; and doubling
Cape Horn in a furious storm.
    Although Sperry loved and understood sea-faring life and was
accurate in his descriptions, many readers today may find that
the book contains information and nautical terminology that are
nonessential to the story. The characters do not go beyond stereotypes and the situations, although frequently exciting, do not
ring true. Twice Enoch fights and beats Jeeter Sneed, a grown
man. He becomes a hero when he quells a fire apparently started
by Sneed, who perishes in it. The book is essentially a book of
information with a thin veneer of fiction. Many books were written in this mode in the 1930s. This one received acclaim. Many
excellent illustrations supplement the information given about
clipper ships.

                              1937

N70   SAWYER, RUTH. Roller Skates. Illustrated by Valenti Angelo.
       New York: Viking, 1936, 186 pp.
       Fiction   Gr. 4-7
    The story recounts a year in the life of ten-year-old Lucinda
Wyman, who lives in New York City in the 1890s. While her high
society parents are in Europe, she stays in a boardinghouse with
Miss Peters, a teacher in the school she attends, and her sister,
Miss Nettie. The only girl in the family and considerably younger
than her four brothers, Lucinda has always been regarded by everyone but her nurse, Johanna, as a difficult child, "to be disciplined and endured." Lucinda has hoped vaguely that sometime
she will find people who will like her for herself. That year

she finds such people. Freed from the nonsensical restrictions
of her French governess, and nurtured by the love, understanding,
and freedom the Misses Peters give her, Lucinda has an opportunity
to be herself. On her roller skates she skates to school and over
much of the city, making friends everywhere.

Among the many who make the year memorable for her are Mr.
Gilligan from Ireland, a hansom cab driver whose wife makes grid-
dle cake with currants. She also makes friends with artistic
Tony Coppino, the son of a fruit vendor. They skate together on
the city's sidewalks, picnic in empty lots, and on Twelfth Night
give a production of The Tempest in Lucinda's toy theater. Uncle
Earle, domineering Aunt Emily's second husband, makes her Saturday afternoons at Aunt Emily's a time to be anticipated with
pleasure rather than dread. To Lucinda's delight, he reads
Shakespeare with her in the library, after Aunt Emily banishes
her from sewing in the parlor with her docile, ladylike cousins.
And, at the boardinghouse, is little Trinket, four, the daughter
of a very talented but impoverished young violinist and his wife.
Lucinda "borrows" Trinket often, grows to love her as a sister
and has a Christmas tree for her on Christmas morning--the first
Trinket has ever had.

Although Roller Skates is an enchanting period story, it is
the character of Lucinda that makes it memorable. Lucinda is
an extrovert with a talent for making friends. She does not
have to force herself to be friendly--it is her natural disposition to be sincerely interested in others. She is consequently
able to develop warm relationships with people outside her immediate family, and often outside her social class--people accept
her because they know she is genuine. To this real interest is
added an ability to organize, and abundant energy to carry out
plans. Instead of merely offering sympathy when Tony's fruit
cart is overturned by the rowdies, Lucinda thinks the situation
through and comes up with a workable plan for remedying matters.
Lucinda is the antithesis of the passive, submissive heroine
that feminists have deplored in so many children's books. The
story is based on the author's own childhood. The illustrations
do justice to Lucinda and to the New York she discovered on roller skates.

N71   LENSKI, LOIS.   Phebe Fairchild: Her Book.   Illustrated by
        the author.   New York: Frederick A. Stokes, 1936 (OP),
        312 pp.
        Fiction: historical   Gr. 4-7
   In March 1828, when Phebe Fairchild is ten, her mother voyages
with her father, a sea captain, to England while Phebe travels by
stagecoach from their home in New Haven, Connecticut, to visit
relatives "inland" and learn what life on a farm is like. The
large family in the country includes Uncle Jotham and Aunt Betsy

Fairchild, their five children, Grandmother Fairchild, and Aunt Hannah, her father's older sister, a spinster. Phebe stays until after Thanksgiving, observing and participating in many aspects of farm life. Phebe's book, a copy of Mother Goose, is responsible for Aunt Hannah's modifying some of her Puritanical notions about the proper reading matter for children.

In her foreword, Lois Lenski states that she has attempted to picture a cross-section of New England life in 1830, a time of transition between the home industry period and the beginning of the small factory. Her research was thorough and included not only numerous reference books, but also "contemporary newspapers, store invoices, account books and church records." Her authenticity was praised over and over by contemporary reviewers. But, today, with careful research the rule, the reader is perhaps more inclined to observe and be critical of other elements. It appears that the author, absorbed in the study of her period, simply could not bring herself to omit interesting data, with the result that there is a plethora of facts, submerging the imaginative content of the story in an accumulation of irrelevant details. This may be the reason the author failed to create the living and memorable characters that appear in some of her later books. None of the children, not even Phebe, is a very real child. The adults are more memorable than the children, perhaps because they live for us in relation to their eccentricities.

N72   JONES, IDWAL. Whistler's Van. Illustrated by Zhenya Gay.
       New York: Viking, 1936 (OP), 235 pp.
       Fiction   Gr. 4-8
Gypsies are minor characters in many books with European settings, but they are the principal characters in this story set in Wales a few years after World War I. The story opens with a mystery. Thomas Anwyl, fourteen-year-old Gwilyn's grandfather and a wealthy farmer and scholar, has left in the night with pony and cart without a word. Gwilyn, too, has often longed to roam in the spring and this year the desire is satisfied. Almost immediately after Grandfather's departure, a family of gypsies, the Ringos, driving a horse-drawn van, stop at Grandfather's farm and, as they do every year, whistle. Gwilyn responds to the whistle and goes with them. He lives with the gypsies for a month and watches them at their crafts, enjoys their music, and appreciates their cunning. Perhaps best of all he learns about horses, for the Ringos are very knowledgeable about them. From hints that are dropped from time to time, the reader begins to suspect that Grandfather was a gypsy many years ago and that he is a Ringo. Gwilyn and his grandfather meet on the day of the great race at Sirnihatch. Gwilyn, true to his heritage, rides the horse that wins the race. After this triumph, Grandfather and Gwilyn set off for home, but it is settled that Gwilyn, for the next few years, will spend half a year in school and the other half with the gypsies.

This readable story evokes the atmosphere of the Welsh moorlands and presents the gypsy way of life with appreciation and humor. Often, as in Kate Seredy's The Good Master, gypsies are villains. It is pleasant to have one book in which the whole story is presented from the point of view of astute and fun-loving gypsies.

N73   BEMELMANS, LUDWIG. The Golden Basket. Illustrated by the
        author. New York: Viking, 1936 (OP), 96 pp.
        Fiction   Gr. 1-4
    Celeste and Melisande, two little English girls, and their
father stay at the Sign of the Golden Basket while visiting in
Bruges. The girls make friends with Jan, the proprietor's son.
They also watch the hotel's famous French chef at work, go for
a memorable boat ride on the canal, and visit the museum and
famous churches. The book contains many illustrations, both
black and white and colored.
    To present-day readers these children seem like paper dolls.
Much of the information included would interest adults more than
children. For example, the author gives a detailed history of
one of the great church towers they visit. The illustrations,
done in the same exuberant manner as those of the Madeline stories, are far more distinguished than the text. It would seem
that it was the intention of the Newbery Committee to honor the
illustrations. The Caldecott Award for outstanding picture books
had not been established at the time this book was written.

N74   BIANCO, MARGERY. Winterbound. New York: Viking, 1936
        (OP), 234 pp.
        Fiction   Gr. 6-11
    Written and set during the Great Depression of the 1930s,
Winterbound chronicles several months in the life of the Ellis
family. The father is away on an archaeological expedition and
is not a part of the story. Because the family income is down,
the remainder of the family moves to the country where rent is
cheaper. The mother, Penny, is soon called away to accompany a
niece, who has a spot on her lung, to Arizona. The two older
girls, nineteen-year-old Kay, an artist, and sixteen-year-old
Gerry, a lover of growing things, are left to manage and to look
after the two younger children, Martin and Caroline. They not
only manage their finances well, but have a good time, too. They
make friends with close neighbors, and, to augment their income,
take a winter boarder. The boarder, a writer, turns out to be
the aunt of their landlord, whom they had never seen. When Mother
returns in the spring, Gerry has a part-time job in a greenhouse,
and Kay's story for children has been accepted for publication.
She has also become friendly with the landlord who proves to be
young and wealthy.

1937

   Interest centers in the characters, but there is sufficient
action to keep the story moving. The setting of the small house
in the country is important and well done. The reader visualizes
the interior through the eyes of Kay, who does much to make it
comfortable and attractive. The exterior surroundings are seen
through the eyes of Gerry, the skillful gardener. This story has
reality and is a contrast to the sentimental, extremely unrealistic adult novels girls commonly turned to before books such as
this were written.

N75   ROURKE, CONSTANCE. Audubon. Illustrated by James MacDonald.
          New York: Harcourt, Brace, 1936 (OP), 342 pp.
          Biography   Gr. 6 up
          John James Audubon, a contemporary of Davy Crockett whose
biography Constance Rourke wrote earlier, was, like Crockett, a
versatile, interesting character who spent much of his adventure-
filled life on the American frontier. His entire life is recorded
in this volume, beginning with his childhood in France at which
time his passion for living creatures was already showing itself.
He spent much time in the woods, fields, and orchards watching
birds, imitating their songs, and sketching them. When he was
eighteen, his father sent him to a farm he owned in Pennsylvania.
There he continued to draw birds. He also fell in love, with Lucy
Bakewell, to whom he was married in 1808. The young couple journeyed by stage and flatboat to the small river town of Louisville
in which a polite society was already flourishing even though the
wilderness was close. Audubon kept store but his real interest
was finding and drawing birds, which abounded in the area that
was until a few years earlier the home of buffalo and Indians.
    In 1820, after Audubon's business failed, he and Lucy and their
two young sons moved to Louisiana where Lucy found employment as a
governess and John occasionally taught music and drawing and
painted portraits. He continued to draw birds in their natural
surroundings and now conceived the idea of publishing a collection of paintings of American birds. In 1826, in quest of a
publisher, he went to Scotland and then England where he remained
for much of the time until 1838, supervising the publication of
Birds of America which consisted of 435 life-sized colored engravings made from his watercolors. After returning to America,
the Audobons settled in "Minnie's Land" on the Hudson. Audubon
continued to go on collecting trips, to paint and write. He died
in 1851.
    The talented Audubon--lighthearted, sometimes impractical,
hardworking, and charming--comes alive in this readable book.
Equally well shown is the period in which he lived, a time when
America was as filled with life and color as the birds Audubon
painted. An element of mystery enters the story when the author
explores the possibility that Audubon may have been the Young

Dauphin, the son of Louis XVI and Marie Antoinette. A long note
explains the research that went into the book. Twelve colored
plates taken from original Audubon prints provide a sample of
the artist's work.

N76   HEWES, AGNES D. <u>The Codfish Musket</u>. Illustrated by Armstrong
          Sperry. Garden City, N.Y.: Doubleday, Doran, 1936 (OP),
          390 pp.
          Fiction: historical   Gr. 6-11
    John Adams is president when the story opens on the day the
ship <u>Columbia</u> sails into Boston Harbor after an absence of three
years. Dan Boit and his grandfather are among those on the wharf
to meet her, the first American ship to sail around the world.
Moreover, she has carried a cargo from America that the Chinese
are eager to receive: sea otter from the northwest coast. This
new market is of vital importance because England has shut off
her former colonies from their old West Indian and European ports.
That night Dan hears his grandfather and a friend, merchant
Israel Cotton, discuss the implications of the China trade for
Boston merchants, and he also hears his grandfather tell of John
Ledyard who, years before, had advocated trading furs to the Chinese. Dan soon goes to work in Mr. Cotton's store. He becomes
knowledgeable about weapons and feels responsible when a handsome
lot of firearms marked with a codfish are stolen from the gun
room. It was his suggestion that they lay in the stock and he
feels that Tom Gentry, a young Englishman with whom Dan has been
friendly and who knew where the weapons were stored, had something to do with the theft. His suspicions are confirmed when
Dan finds Tom stealing weapons a second time. In the ensuing
scuffle, Tom escapes.
    Later Mr. Cotton sends Dan to Baltimore to purchase Kentucky
rifles and on to Washington to learn if war is likely. Through
a chain of circumstances Dan becomes President Jefferson's secretary. In the third section, the President sends Dan to the frontier to deliver a personal message to Meriwether Lewis. On the
journey Dan discovers that Gentry is the leader of a gang that
is selling guns--including the codfish muskets--to the British
fur traders. The British are arming the Indians who in turn are
helping to keep the colonizing Americans away from the lands in
which they trap. The Gentry gang is broken up--most are killed.
Dan delivers the message to Lewis in the spring of 1804, just as
Lewis starts up the Missouri, and then returns to the President
with shoots of wild plum and an Osage apple plant.
    This long book really attempts too much. The John Ledyard
portion complicates an already involved story and really does
little to advance the action. The reader does gain an excellent
picture of Boston, the raw new Washington, and the movement west.
Dan travels on horseback, by Conestoga wagon, with a pack train,

1937

and on a flatboat. Jefferson is presented as a versatile person
with numerous interests. There are many twists and turns which
help to maintain suspense; some are believable while others are
dependent on coincidence.

1938

N77   SEREDY, KATE. The White Stag. Illustrated by the author.
        New York: Viking, 1937, 95 pp.
          Epic   Gr. 5-9
      Kate Seredy recorded this legendary account of the founding
of her native Hungary from the oral tradition, putting it down
as she remembered her father telling it to her when she was a
child in Budapest. The story begins in Asia with Nimrod's prophecy: far to the west his people will find a promised land between
two great rivers. It ends generations later with the fulfillment
of the prophecy. After Nimrod's death, the leadership passes to
his two sons, Hunor and Magyar, who follow a miraculous White
Stag west to the edge of a misty blue lake. Because their lands
in the east have become dry and barren, they lead their people
there where they remain for a number of years. Hunor and Magyar
marry moonmaidens. To Hunor and his wife is born Bendeguz, des-
tined to become the White Eagle and father of Attila, the Red
Eagle. Many years later the tribe divides. Magyar's followers
remain on a protected strip of land in the far east of Europe
while the Huns, as the followers of Hunor are now called, move
on west. On this final thrust west the Huns grow wealthy and
cruel and seem to live to conquer and kill as much as to gain
their promised land. Attila's mother dies the night he is born
and his father raises him without love or tenderness. He becomes
ruthless and undefeatable in battle. At last, with Attila at
their head, the Huns gain the promised land following the White
Stag through a pass in the Carpathian Mountains during a savage
snowstorm.
      The story is written in epic style. The author's dramatic
and powerful illustrations emphasize the heroic qualities of the
leaders and tell the story as effectively as the text.

N78   BOWMAN, JAMES CLOYD. Pecos Bill. Illustrated by Laura
        Bannon. Boston: Little, Brown, 1937, 296 pp.
          Tall Tales   Gr. 4-8
      When he was four years old, Bill was bounced out of the back
of his parents' covered wagon in the vicinity of the Pecos River.
He struck his head and lay in a daze for awhile and, since he was
one of eighteen children tumbling around in the wagon, he was not
missed for hours. Left behind alone, Bill was adopted by a pack
of wild coyotes. He learned the ways and languages of the

animals, and grew up thinking he was a full-blooded coyote.

In young manhood he was found by his brother Chuck who persuaded him to become a cowboy like himself. Almost at once he became boss of his outfit. Soon he invented modern cowpunching including branding. He organized the first Wild West show so that the cowboy would have fun playing, too. Next, to take some of the work out of ranching, he invented the Perpetual Motion Ranch. Subsequently he courted Slue-Foot Sue, "busted" the cyclone, and broke up the biggest cattle rustling racket of all times. With the arrival of large numbers of Nesters and Homesteaders, Bill decided to quit the ranching business. He and his cowboys finally rounded up his herd of 39 million cattle and drove them to market in Kansas City. After teaching all the Bullies of Kansas City a lesson, Pecos Bill disappeared on his horse Widow Maker and hasn't been heard from since.

Although able to perform superhuman feats, through all his fabulous adventures Bill remains a gentleman. His personal traits would have been admired on the frontier: he works hard, is considerate of women, and generous to both friends and foes. Hyperbole and broad humor permeate both the telling and illustrations.

Until recent years such tall stories as these were considered genuine American folklore. In 1959 a contradictory viewpoint was developed by Richard Dorson in American Folklore (Chicago: University of Chicago Press, 1959). There he labels Pecos Bill, Paul Bunyan and other tall-tale heroes "fake heroes," not folk heroes. Dorson claims that Pecos Bill was invented by writer Edward O'Reilly for the pages of Century magazine (ibid., p. 215).

N79   ROBINSON, MABEL L. Bright Island. Illustrated by Lynd Ward.
       New York: Random House, 1937. 268 pp.
       Fiction   Gr. 6-10
    Bright Island covers a year in the life of sixteen-year-old Thankful Curtis, who goes from her home on a Maine island to attend the academy on the mainland. The situations Thankful faces are familiar to many girls: leaving home for the first time, being the new girl in school, having clothes which are different, admiring a boy who is attracted to another girl. After a painful beginning, Thankful, a superior student, makes the transition from the simple island life, where there is neither electricity nor plumbing, to the fashionable boarding school, where the students dress for dinner. She learns about people in the process, but her values do not change. At the close she returns to the beloved island, where she expects to live after marrying Dave, also a native of Maine and a friend since childhood.

    From a critical point of view the story is well written, has an interesting setting, attractive characters, and enough action

1938

to keep the plot moving. Present-day readers will also enjoy the
portrait it paints of boarding school life in the 1930s.

N80   WILDER, LAURA INGALLS. On the Banks of Plum Creek. Illus-
          trated by Helen Sewell and Mildred Boyle. New York:
          Harper & Brothers, 1937, 239 pp.
          Fiction: historical   Gr. 3-7
      This, the fourth of the "Little House" books published, was
the first to be named a Newbery book as were the four volumes
that followed: By the Shores of Silver Lake in 1940, The Long
Winter in 1941, Little Town on the Prairie in 1942, and These
Happy Golden Years in 1944. In these volumes and in two others
that were not Newbery books--Little House in the Big Woods (1932)
and Little House on the Prairie (1935)--Mrs. Wilder, Laura in
the story, told the story of her life from age five until her
marriage at eighteen to Almanzo Wilder. She told of his boyhood
in New York state in Farmer Boy (1933), and in a posthumous volume, The First Four Years (1971), chronicled the first four years
of their marriage. In the seven books about the Ingalls family,
Ma and Pa Ingalls and their children--Mary, Laura, Carrie, and
Grace--are pioneer settlers in Wisconsin, first, then in Kansas,
Minnesota, and South Dakota in the 1870s and 1880s.
      On the Banks of Plum Creek covers a little more than two years
of the time the Ingalls family spent in Minnesota. They arrive
there by covered wagon, having traveled east from Indian territory, across Kansas, Missouri, and Iowa. Mary is eight, Laura
seven, and Carrie two or three. Pa trades his horses for land
and they settle on the banks of Plum Creek. Pa intends to raise
wheat and the girls will be able to go to school. The first fall
and winter they live in a dugout close to the creek. In the
spring Pa builds a frame house, buying the lumber on credit, but
confident he will be able to pay for it with the first wheat crop.
Mary and Laura start to school, walking the two and one-half
miles into town. They go to a party at Nellie Oleson's and give
a party in the country for the girls from town. The whole family
attends church.
      The wheat grows tall and is almost ready to harvest when a
horde of grasshoppers comes from the east in a great glittering
cloud. They devour all the wheat and everything else that is
green. When they honeycomb the ground with their eggs Pa knows
there will be no crop the next year either. He walks east three
hundred miles and helps with the harvest there, working for a
dollar a day. The winter is mild. In the hot dry summer that
follows, the grasshoppers hatch. After again eating the prairie
bare, they leave as abruptly as they had arrived. For three days
they march west, swarming over everything in their way: the
house, the stable, the creek. On the fourth day they begin to
fly and depart in a cloud as they had come.

Pa again goes east to work in the harvest there. Cold weather comes early that fall. There are several blizzards--Pa is lost in one of them--before the story closes on Christmas Eve in the warm house with the delicious smell of Ma's cooking in the air and the happy sound of Pa's singing fiddle.

Evaluation of the books follows These Happy Golden Years (N106), 1944 Honor Book.

1939

N81   ENRIGHT, ELIZABETH. Thimble Summer. Illustrated by the
       author. New York: Rinehart, 1938, 124 pp.
       Fiction   Gr. 3-6

Set on a farm in Wisconsin contemporary with the time the book was published, the story begins with nine-year-old Garnet Linden's finding a thimble: "It's solid silver . . . and I think it must be magic, too!" she happily tells her brother, Jay. That very night the drought that has parched the crops for weeks is broken, and good and exciting things continue to happen all summer. Shortly after, her father receives a government loan to build a new barn. Then Garnet spends a night in the woods watching her father fire a kiln in which lime is being made for cement for the new barn. That night, Eric, an orphan, comes into their family. Garnet has adventures away from home, too. She and her friend, Citronella, get locked in the library and aren't found until the middle of the night. Hitchhiking part of the way, Garnet goes the eighteen miles to New Conniston alone, buys gifts at the dime store for her family, and arrives home before she is missed because everyone else has been busy threshing. She has a wonderful day at the fair where her pet pig wins a prize. The author, daughter of artists and interested in art before writing, has portrayed Garnet's summer in pen and ink sketches and in full-page illustrations in watercolor.

Most critics have tended to regard Thimble Summer as a family story which the author developed more successfully in her stories of the Melendy family. British critic Margery Fisher sees the story in a different way. She views it as a story about the solitary child "where everything and everybody else becomes background, to be seen through her eyes. We are concerned here with the poetry of living, a single private affair" (Intent Upon Reading [New York: Franklin Watts, 1961], p. 270). Not long enough to develop the summer activities of a family, the story is long enough to show Garnet's happiness and contentment, her moods and longings as an individual in a rural family. As in all of her writing, the abundant similes make Mrs. Enright's style lively and distinctive: To Garnet "the watermelons in their patch were little green whales in a sea of frothy leaves, and the corn

1939

on the hillside was like a parade advancing with plumes and ban-
ners." From this story, present-day readers gain an excellent
idea of farm life in the 1930s.

N82   ANGELO, VALENTI. <u>Nino</u>. Illustrated by the author. New York:
        Viking, 1938 (OP), 244 pp.
        Fiction   Gr. 4-6
    The story relates episodes of Nino's childhood in a small
Italian village where Nino lives with his mother and grandfather
during the first decade of the twentieth century. At the close,
the three of them bid their friends goodbye and set out for
America where Nino's father has lived since his son was a baby.
The story presents both daily life and festival days. Nino helps
pick and sort olives and accompanies his grandfather to the mill
for the olive crushing. He and his best friend, Julio, watch
Julio's father stomping grapes for wine with his bare feet.
They enjoy the fair where Julio's father is bested by the gypsies' wrestling bear and they feast on the delicious foods their
mothers prepare for Easter and Christmas.
    Based on the author's own childhood, <u>Nino</u> is the kind of
pleasant story a person might write for his grandchildren as
he reflected on his life in another country. The reader senses
the sincerity of the author and gains considerable information
about life in Italy. The presentation is picturesque rather
than dramatic, the narrative flowing from one event to another.
The green and white illustrations are decorative and supply details of the life presented.

N83   ATWATER, RICHARD and ATWATER, FLORENCE. <u>Mr. Popper's Penguins</u>.
        Illustrated by Robert Lawson. Boston: Little, Brown and
        Co., 1938, 139 pp.
        Fantasy   Gr. 2-6
    Mr. Popper, a house painter, spends his winters reading about
Arctic and Antarctic expeditions. One fall, in response to a
letter he had written to the polar explorer Admiral Drake, he
receives a gift: a penguin from Antarctica. Both Mr. and Mrs.
Popper and the children, Janie and Bill, soon love the playful
penguin which Mr. Popper names Captain Cook. But, after a few
happy weeks, he becomes ill. Recovery is almost immediate, however, when they acquire another penguin, Greta. Soon there are
penguin chicks and the Popper household is crowded with twelve
penguins. The Popper family usually has to eat beans when Papa
isn't working, but the same economy does not extend to the penguins. For them Mr. Popper orders live fish that have to be
brought from the coast in tank cars, and he has an ice-making
machine installed in the basement so that they will have a
proper environment. In a short time the Poppers' meager savings
are exhausted and they are in debt. Then Mr. Popper decides

that they will train the penguins--he reasons that if there can
be trained dogs and trained seals there can be trained penguins
as well. Soon they have an act perfected and a contract which
takes them to theaters all over the country. Everywhere the
performing penguins are a huge success. The Poppers regain
financial solvency. In the spring Mr. Popper with his penguins
and Admiral Drake leave for the North Pole where they hope to
establish a penguin colony.

After more than forty years this book remains funny and refreshing. Part of the humor arises from the Poppers' matter-
of-fact modification of their own lives to provide a suitable
environment for the penguins. For example, after Greta arrives,
Captain Cook's bachelor quarters in the refrigerator are too
small so Mr. Popper decides they will leave the living room door
and windows open so that it will be comfortable for the birds
there. The authors comment that the Poppers soon were accustomed to sitting around in their overcoats and "Greta and Captain Cook always occupied the chairs nearest the open windows."
The book contains many similar ridiculous situations. Robert
Lawson's excellent illustrations capture the mood of the text.

N84   CRAWFORD, PHYLLIS. "Hello, the Boat!" Illustrated by
        Edward Laning. New York: H. Holt, 1938 (OP), 227 pp.
        Fiction: historical   Gr. 4-8
      In March 1817, the Doak family--Mother, Father, sixteen-year-
old Susan, Steve, fourteen, and David, ten--leaves Pittsburgh in
a storeboat. Their intention is to sell goods all the way down
the Ohio River to Cincinnati where they plan to live. The storeboat does a thriving business and the family has an interesting
trip. At one of the stops Susan meets Simon Winthrop who tells
her he is coming to Cincinnati soon to read law with Judge
Burnet. Disaster strikes while they are docked at Maysville:
a large amount of money is stolen from the money box. Happily,
it is returned to them in Cincinnati. The story ends on the
Fourth of July on which day Father receives a good job offer
and Susan and Simon become engaged.

Although there is little emphasis on character development and
some of the incidents are contrived, still the book is pleasant
reading. Life in the outlying settlements and river towns, as
well as life on the river, is integrated into the story. The
history and geography of the region are rather naturally included,
the reader absorbing information with the young Doaks who learn
of the Indian mounds, settlement of Gallipolis, and the story of
Blennerhassett Island. The accomplishments of the fabulous keel-
boatman Mike Fink and the slangy talk of the riverboatmen also
fit into the story. The encounters with one real historic per-
sonage, General William Henry Harrison, help to establish the
time of the story.

1939

N85   EATON, JEANETTE. <u>Leader By Destiny: George Washington, Man
       and Patriot</u>. Illustrated by Jack Manley Rosé. New York:
       Harcourt, Brace, 1938, 386 pp.
       Biography   Gr. 6-11
       This fictionalized biography begins in 1747 when George is
fifteen and ends in 1799 with his death. It is a record of his
personal life, but it is also a record of fifty years of his
country's history as seen from the viewpoint of Washington. In
addition to placing events in relation to Washington, the author
also provides very good pictures of the many great men whose
lives Washington touched. There are deft portraits of many
Virginians: George Mason, John Randolph, the Harrisons, the
Carters, the Carys, the Lees, and various members of the Washington family. Also depicted are leaders of the Revolution and
the Constitutional Convention and his associates as President:
Patrick Henry, John Adams, Nathanael Greene, Alexander Hamilton,
and Thomas Jefferson. General Braddock, various colonial gover-
nors, and Lafayette are also shown. The recreated society and
the life of the wealthy and influential of colonial Virginia are
of particular interest. Twenty-seven full page drawings--of people and buildings--are interspersed in the text. There is an
index.
       <u>Leader by Destiny</u> has been cited as a biography constructed
around a unifying theme expressed in the title. After studying
Washington's life, Miss Eaton could see that he did not consciously seek the important roles he filled, but that he became
a leader by destiny. The author's basic facts are authentic.
She quotes frequently from Washington's journals and letters.
She also enlivens the narrative with imagined conversation.
Besides putting words into the mouths of many characters, she
puts thoughts into Washington's mind. This device is overused
in relation to Sally Fairfax, his neighbor's wife who, according to the author, was the great love of Washington's life. The
text states that George "often found himself thinking of Mrs.
George Fairfax." Another time we read that "every nerve and
every drop of blood told him that she [Sally] would fill his
heart forever." When she and her husband left for England in
the early 1770s, Washington watched them board the ship: "Folded
over his broad chest, his arms crushed down the cry of his heart
'Sally! Sally! Darling of my life--goodbye!'" There are several similar entries. Reviewers of the 1930s did not criticize
this, but readers of today find it overly sentimental.

N86   GRAY, ELIZABETH JANET. <u>Penn</u>. Illustrated by George Gillett
       Whitney. New York: Viking, 1938, 298 pp.
       Biography   Gr. 6 up
       This biography gives a complete account of the public and
private life of William Penn (1644-1718), the famous Quaker who

founded the colony of Pennsylvania. Part I, titled "Son William," tells of his boyhood in England and Ireland, his time at Oxford and on the Grand Tour of Europe, and his conversion to Quakerism. This brought not only opposition from his father, Admiral Penn, but imprisonment and persecution at a time when religious toleration did not exist in England. The section closes with the death of his father. The second part, "Onas," tells of Penn's decision to found the colony in the new world as a refuge for all religious nonconformers. It details his fair treatment of the Indians whose name for him was "Onas," the Indian word for quill or pen; the early years of the colony; his relationship with King James II; and the years that followed the King's deposition.

Descended from Quakers, Elizabeth Janet Gray had heard of Penn all her life, but before writing his biography she visited England and his homes. She also read extensively in Penn's works and in books about him and his era. Filled with rich and vivid details of his life and of the times, the book also provides portraits of the many people whose lives touched his. His parents are seen as real people as also are the two women he loved and his children. Also revealed are George Fox, the founder of Quakerism; Samuel Pepys, the diarist and a neighbor of the Penns; and the most important men of England including the rulers. Penn was a forceful and prolific writer. The author uses quotations from his writings to reveal both events and the personality of the man.

In writing of Penn, Miss Gray not only chose incidents which provide insight into his character, but also she is successful in recording sufficient changes from chapter to chapter so that the reader sees the hero maturing and growing older. She brings out the drama of Penn's life by producing in her narrative the element of uncertainty as in the thrilling chapter "The Trial," one of the few fictionalized scenes in the book, where the reader reads with bated breath as the suspense increases. Miss Gray's fine craftsmanship is evident not only in her seemingly effortless style, but also in the way in which she organizes and unifies her materials, as at the close of the first brief chapter when the major themes and conflicts of Penn's life are foreshadowed. The overall accomplishment is a very good book about an admirable man.

1940

N87   DAUGHERTY, JAMES. Daniel Boone. Illustrated by the author.
       New York: Viking, 1939 (OP), 95 pp.
       Biography   Gr. 5-11
    In a nonfictionalized text and bold illustrations, the author
not only portrays the famous American trailblazer, but also

1940

provides an authentic picture of pioneer life at the beginning
of the great Westward movement. The biography begins with
Boone's youth in Pennsylvania and closes on the day he died in
Missouri at age eighty-six.

Appropriate emphasis is put on Boone's important role in the
opening up and settlement of Kentucky. Boone proved to be the
ideal man for this time: in addition to being a superb woods-
man, he was also a natural leader who inspired respect and confidence. Quotations from contemporaries affirm Daugherty's
opinions. The author's style, vigorous and simple like the
subject's life, conveys the pioneer spirit and suggests the
frontier speech without reproducing the idiom in tedious detail.
The lithographs of pioneers and Indians--done in black, brown,
and forest green--enhance the epic proportions of the narrative.

N88   SEREDY, KATE. The Singing Tree. Illustrated by the author.
       New York: Viking, 1939 (OP), 247 pp.
       Fiction   Gr. 4-7
    Kate is twelve and Jansci is thirteen when the sequel to The
Good Master opens shortly before World War I. Life on the ranch
is progressing very happily before the war which changes everything. Rabbi Joseph Mandelbaum, son of Aunt Sarah and Uncle
Moses, an altruistic Jewish merchant of the village, is killed
in the first battle on the Russian front. Soon Kate's father
leaves, and, a little while later, Jansci's father goes, too.
Word arrives that Kate's father is a prisoner of war in Russia.
At about the same time six Russian prisoners are brought in to
help with the harvest. Then, for months, they hear nothing from
Jansci's father.

    In the summer of 1916, Jansci, Kate, and a friend go to bring
Jansci's mother's parents to the ranch, from their home close to
the border where there is fighting. On the trip they find
Jansci's father, a victim of amnesia, in an army hospital. He
recovers his memory when Kate sees him and screams his name. He
goes home with the children and grandparents. Next they give a
home to six German children, aged six to twelve. The story comes
to an end with the close of the war. In the last chapter Jansci's
father tells the story of the singing tree: it was a live apple
tree filled with singing birds that he and his comrades saw at
dawn after having followed retreating Russians all night through
devastated country.

    The themes of brotherhood and world peace are strongly empha-
sized. Aunt Sarah and Uncle Moses are initially the focus for
the concept of brotherhood which is greatly expanded with the
arrival of the six Russian prisoners of war and the six little
Germans. Grigori, one of the big helpful Russians, states this
theme, "All same, Jansci . . . l'il Russian, l'il German, l'il
Hungarian, all men are brothers." A rounding out of this theme

comes at the end of the book when it is hinted that Kate's father
will be bringing home a Russian bride. Many references are made
through the characters to the evil of war: Father explains it
to Jansci as being a "stampede," a "mad whirlwind that sucks in
men . . . and spits out crippled wrecks." After the armistice
has been signed, Uncle Moses, speaking to Jansci's father, expresses the feeling that pervaded the whole world that a new day
is coming for all nations, when there will be no more wars, nor
persecution, nor intolerance. These words were published in
1939, when the nations were on the brink of another holocaust.
Although possible, Kate's finding Uncle Márton in the army hospital and his miraculous recovery from amnesia seems contrived.
The plentiful illustrations convey the vitality of the text.

N89   ROBINSON, MABEL L. Runner of the Mountain Tops: The Life
        of Louis Agassiz. Illustrated by Lynd Ward. New York:
        Random House, 1939 (OP), 264 pp.
        Biography   Gr. 6 up
    The runner of the mountain tops is the nineteenth-century
naturalist Louis Agassiz, who was born in Switzerland in 1807
and died in the United States in 1873. As a lad Louis showed
the attributes which he possessed all his life: great intelligence matched with tremendous vitality and personal charm. By
the age of twenty-three (1830), Louis had studied in the uni-
versities of Zurich, Heidelberg, and Munich, acquiring both a
Ph.D. and, at the insistence of his family, an M.D. At this
time he already had a reputation among naturalists and had published in Latin a book on Brazilian fishes.
    Four fourteen of the next sixteen years, Agassiz was an
inspiring--and underpaid--teacher at Neuchatel in his native
country. At the same time he continued with his other work.
His great volumes on fossil fishes appeared and won him world-
wide recognition. Characteristically, even before finishing
this work, he turned with enthusiasm to a different field: the
exploration of glaciers. The records he published as a result
of that study established the concept of the ice age.
    In 1846, Agassiz's wife and three children traveled to Ger-
many to stay with her family and he sailed for America to deliver lectures at the Lowell Institute. The lectures were
extremely popular and Louis was soon making new collections and
new friends. His wife's death in Europe in 1848 and the offer
of a professorship in zoology and geology at Harvard were two
determining factors in his decision to remain in America. His
son, Alexander, thirteen, joined him in 1849 and his two daughters in 1850 after his marriage to Elizabeth Cary. To the very
end of his life he continued to lecture and teach and to do research and writing. One of the great dreams of his life came
true with the establishment of the Agassiz Museum at Harvard.

1940

In the foreword the author states that "Louis Agassiz was the
only person whose biography I ever intended to write. I seem
always to have known him." She had lived in a house in which
he had often visited and had heard a multitude of stories about
him. She did not permit this special regard to lessen her objectivity: she includes his faults and weaknesses as well as
his strong points and accomplishments. She presents a complete
account of his life in relation to the people whose lives he
touched and to the milieu in which he lived and worked. Well-
chosen incidents recreated with concrete detail make the man
and his era real. A bibliography, chronology of Louis Agassiz's
life, and eight full-page colored plates add to the worth of
this well-written biography.

N90   WILDER, LAURA INGALLS. <u>By the Shores of Silver Lake</u>. Illus-
       trated by Helen Sewell and Mildred Boyle. New York:
       Harper & Brothers, 1939, 260 pp.
       Fiction: historical   Gr. 4-8
Approximately two years have elapsed from the close of <u>On the
Banks of Plum Creek</u>. In that time Grace was born. At the opening of this story, Mary has recently lost her sight as a result
of scarlet fever. Pa has harvested only two very poor wheat
crops since the departure of the grasshoppers and wishes to go
west to take a homestead. One spring morning, Pa's sister, Aunt
Docia, whom they have not seen since they lived in Wisconsin,
drives up in a buggy enroute to Dakota territory where her husband, Hi, is a contractor working on the new railroad. She asks
Pa to go with her and be storekeeper, bookkeeper, and timekeeper
for Hi. The pay is good--$50 a month--and Pa sees it as an op-
portunity to homestead. Although Ma would prefer to stay in more
settled country, she consents and Pa promises that this will be
the family's last move.
    Pa drives the wagon and team out with Aunt Docia. Ma and the
girls follow as soon as Mary is well enough, traveling by railroad to the end of the line. During the summer they live in a
little shanty close to the railroad camp and Silver Lake. Laura,
now twelve, loves the prairie from which the buffalo are only
recently gone.
    In the fall everyone goes back east except the Ingalls family.
In return for being responsible for the tools, they are permitted
to stay in the surveyor's house which has been stocked with food
and fuel. They have a good winter. Pa finds the homestead he
wants. On Christmas Eve young Mr. and Mrs. Boast arrive from
Iowa and the two families have a merry Christmas. The Boasts
move into the surveyor's office for the remainder of the winter
and the two families spend many happy winter days and evenings
together.

Beginning the first of March it seems as if the whole country is moving west. Because there is no other place for them to stay, every night there are strangers bedded down in front of the Ingalls's fire. Ma and Laura cook for them, charging a quarter a meal. They put all the money into a fund designated to send Mary to a college for the blind in Iowa.

Close to the surveyor's cottage a townsite, De Smet, is laid out and soon a town is taking shape on the open prairie. Pa goes back east to Brookins and files his homestead claim. He returns with lumber and builds a store in which the family lives for a few weeks before moving into a shanty on their claim a mile out of town. The day they move to the claim Laura sees her future husband, Almanzo Wilder, for the first time. He is driving a fine team of horses and Laura thinks how much she would like to have such horses. The year is 1880. Laura will soon be thirteen. See N106.

N91   MEADER, STEPHEN W. Boy with a Pack. Illustrated by Edward
        Shenton. New York: Harcourt, Brace, 1939 (OP), 297 pp.
        Fiction: historical   Gr. 4-8
    In the spring of 1837, seventeen-year-old Bill Crawford sets out from his New Hampshire home with a peddler's pack of "Yankee notions" on his back. His destination is Ohio. As he travels along selling his notions, he has several exciting adventures. He encounters horse thieves in Vermont, works as a teamster on the Erie Canal in New York, and forwards a slave two stations on the Underground Railroad in Ohio. After his merchandise is sold, he finds work in a gristmill and decides to stay in Ohio.

    Although the adventures seem somewhat designed and luck is a large factor in Bill's success, the story is continuously readable. Some incidents seem to have been included because they are true and interesting in themselves rather than integral to the story. The black and white illustrations are attractive and descriptive. Endpaper maps show the journey in detail.

1941

N92   SPERRY, ARMSTRONG. Call It Courage. Illustrated by the
        author. New York: Macmillan, 1940, 95 pp.
        Fiction   Gr. 4-8
    A Polynesian chief's son, Mafatu, meaning Stout Heart, fears the sea from which his tribe draws its living. His fear has existed since he was three; then he nearly drowned when his mother's canoe was destroyed in a storm at sea. Ostracized by the tribe, who rename him the Boy Who Was Afraid, he vows, in his fifteenth year to conquer his fear. Accompanied by his pets, a dog and an albatross, Mafatu sails from his island in an outrigger canoe.

1941

It is the season of storms and in a hurricane his canoe is disabled and he is tossed about the sea for four days before being cast ashore on a deserted island. There he finds food and fashions a shelter. While exploring the island, he discovers an idol with piles of charred human bones at its base. Mafatu realizes he is on a Forbidden Island where cannibals come periodically to make sacrifices. He knows he must leave as soon as he can make another canoe. In the days that follow, he works diligently at the canoe and also proves his courage. To save his dog, he kills a tiger shark with a knife carved from a whale's rib; he slays a wild boar and an octopus. Early in the morning of the day he had planned to leave, Mafatu is awakened by the booming of drums. Hastily he pushes off in his canoe and eventually outsails the pursuing cannibals. After days of desultory sailing and paddling over now quiet seas, he arrives home to be greeted by a proud father: "Here is my son come home from the sea. Mafatu, Stout Heart. A brave name for a brave boy!"

The author wandered through the South Seas for two years before he began writing stories set there. He writes that the story retold in Call It Courage occurred many years ago, before the traders and missionaries first ventured into the South Seas, while the Polynesians were still numerous and brave-hearted. But even today, he says, the people sing this story in their chants and tell it over the evening fires. Mr. Sperry's dramatic illustrations are appropriate to the story.

N93   GATES, DORIS. Blue Willow. Illustrated by Paul Lantz. New
      York: Viking, 1940, 172 pp.
      Fiction   Gr. 4-6
For five years, since their farm in a Dust Bowl region would no longer produce, the Larkin family--Janey, ten, her stepmother, and dad--have been migrant workers following the crops. The blue willow plate, the only item they have from their old home, is Janey's one beautiful possession. Because Janey's mom has said they will not set the plate up until they have a real home again, it has become for Janey a symbol of the permanent home for which she longs.

On a hot September day the Larkins move into an abandoned shack in the San Joaquin Valley and Janey's dad begins work picking cotton. The first day Janey makes a friend, Lupe Romero, who lives nearby. Soon Janey is wishing more fervently than ever before that they can stay here. Because of the dishonesty of Bounce Rayburn, the hired man of Mr. Anderson, owner of the land on which the shack is located, and through Janey's own actions, the Larkins's wanderings come to an end. Janey's dad replaces Bounce, and Janey at last has a real home in which to exhibit the blue willow plate.

Interpersonal relationships are convincingly portrayed: there
is genuine affection between Janey and her stepmother, and, in
the friendship that develops between Janey and Lupe, there is
regard for each other as individuals. Janey is a warmly human
little girl who remains in one's mind, and her father is also
memorable. Adversity has not made him bitter or warped. He
has remained a whole person who is still able to tease Janey in
the evening after a long day in the field. Bounce Rayburn is a
perfect foil for Mr. Larkin, but as a character he is the stereotype of the villain. The scenes in which he appears seem planned
while the others all develop naturally from the circumstances of
the Larkins's life. The book uses no condescension in depicting
underprivileged children but seeks to increase understanding of
the conditions under which the drifting worker's child must live.
The story grew out of the author's experiences as a children's
librarian working with the children of migrant workers. Appealing illustrations depict Janey in the various situations in which
the author places her.

N94   CARR, MARY JANE. <u>Young Mac of Fort Vancouver</u>. Illustrated
          by Richard Holberg. New York: Thomas Y. Crowell, 1940
          (OP), 238 pp.
          Fiction: historical   Gr. 5-9
       Donald McDermott, Young Mac, is the son of a white fur trader
and White Cloud, whose father was French and whose mother was
Cree. He lives with the Indians until he is thirteen when he is
taken, as his dead father had instructed, to Dr. John McLoughlin,
governor and doctor of Fort Vancouver, a principal trading post
for the Hudson Bay Company. Although he is three-quarters white,
Young Mac is certain at first that he wishes to live the Indian
way of life rather than that of the white man. Gradually he
changes his mind and at length goes to Edinburgh to study medicine. His mother dies while he is away. The closing chapter
takes place ten years later when he returns as a doctor from
Edinburgh. In the home of his grandfather, a judge in Quebec,
he is reunited with Mia, whom he had rescued from slavery while
at Fort Vancouver. After eight years at the Ursuline Convent,
Mia is now an educated and refined young lady.
       Although some of the incidents seem rather devised, the story
moves at a good pace. The reader absorbs with the story knowledge of the fur trade and learns the ways and traditions of both
the settlers and Indians. The struggle between the United States
and Canada over the Oregon territory is foreshadowed.

N95   WILDER, LAURA INGALLS. <u>The Long Winter</u>. Illustrated by
          Helen Sewell and Mildred Boyle. New York: Harper &
          Brothers, 1940. 325 pp.
          Fiction: historical   Gr. 4-8

1941

This narrative follows immediately after <u>By the Shores of</u> <u>Silver Lake</u>. In the hot sun out on the claim Laura helps Pa make hay, first on the upland, then in the slough. Almanzo Wilder and his brother Royal are also making hay there. Pleasant weather continues through September, but in October the first blizzard comes, lasting three days. The wind whistles through the cracks of the flimsy claim shanty. After observing warnings in nature and hearing the prediction of an old Indian that this will be the worst winter in twenty-one years, Pa decides he will move the family into the tight store building in town for the winter. Not only will it be warmer than the claim shanty, but also they will be closer to the railroad, their only source of supplies. The Wilder brothers also move in and live in the back of Royal's feed store.

Laura and Mary start to school, but almost immediately the blizzards begin. At first they can go to school about one day a week, but the storms become more frequent. The train from the east is cut off by snow. Soon the supply of coal and kerosene for school and homes is gone. The Ingalls family begins to burn twisted hay. They have no flour and only a little wheat. All day they twist hay for the fire; they grind the wheat for bread in a coffee grinder. During the height of a blizzard they cannot even see a light across the street. Several times the men nearly succeed in getting the railroad cuts free of snow, but, before a supply train can get through, another storm blows them closed. There is no meat: the Ingalls family subsists on coarse bread, potatoes, and tea in a blizzard that never ends.

When supplies are nearly exhausted, Almanzo Wilder and young Cap Garland, on a fair day between storms, drive sleds and horses out onto the prairie southeast of town and find and buy wheat raised there the preceding summer. Without that wheat some of the seventy-five or eighty inhabitants of the town would have starved.

The trains begin running again in May. The second train brings a Christmas parcel for the Ingalls family from a church in Minnesota. Packed at the bottom of the clothes are a turkey, still solidly frozen, and cranberries. With other groceries now available, Ma and Laura prepare a delicious Christmas dinner which they share with their friends, Mr. and Mrs. Boast. (See N106.)

N96   HALL, ANNA GERTRUDE. <u>Nansen</u>. Illustrated by Boris Artzybasheff. New York: Viking, 1940 (OP), 168 pp.
Biography   Gr. 6 up

Fridtjof Nansen was a famous Norwegian scientist, Arctic explorer, and statesman. This biography begins with his youthful days as a ski champion and tells the entire story of his life. The years he spent as an explorer are perhaps the most exciting. In the summer of 1888 he and five other men crossed Greenland from east to west, a feat that experts had declared impossible.

A few years later he and one other man traveled over the ice nearer to the North Pole than anyone before them and spent nine months in a hut ten feet long, six feet wide, and barely six feet high. Following his years of exploration he worked for many years as a scientist. In the last decade of his life he was a statesman and humanitarian who worked to prove his belief that "hatred could be overcome by brotherliness."

Mrs. Hall's biography is factual. Nansen left speeches, papers, books, and a diary for the last fifty years of his life. Quotations from his own writings help to bring the man to life. The illustrations by Artzybasheff add distinction to the story.

1942

N97   EDMONDS, WALTER D. The Matchlock Gun. Illustrated by Paul
           Lantz. New York: Dodd, Mead, 1941, 50 pp.
           Fiction: historical   Gr. 3-6
In November of 1757, the settlers of Guilderland, just outside Albany City, are on the alert for a raid by the French and
Indians. As his father, Captain Teunis Van Alstyne, prepares
for militia duty, ten-year-old Edward asks him why he doesn't
take the great Spanish Gun that hangs over the fireplace rather
than his musket. His father tells him it is a matchlock and
shows him it does not fire itself like a musket but has to have
the priming touched with fire. Before Teunis goes, he reassures
his wife, Gertrude, that there is no chance the Indians will get
as far south as their farm. Soon after her husband's departure,
Gertrude sends Edward and six-year-old Trudy to bed.

The next day about noon they receive word from Teunis: he is
safe, but may not get home that night; the Indians are burning
the upper settlements and a company of soldiers has been sent
out from Albany. Later that afternoon, Gertrude takes the children outside. From a knoll beyond the garden they see smoke in
the north. When they go inside Gertrude tells Edward she thinks
the Indians are quite near. Their only weapon is the ancient
matchlock gun. Together they load it and prop it on a table,
pointing it through a window straight at the steps of the stoop.
His mother tells Edward she is going outside to watch for Indians. He is to touch the lighted candle to the priming if he
hears her call his name.

Five Indians come. They sight Gertrude and chase her as she
dashes toward the house. She runs up the steps calling Edward's
name. They she feels a pain in her shoulder and knows she has
been hit by a tomahawk. Before she falls unconscious against
the door she hears the gun discharge and sees three of the Indians fall. Knocked to the floor by the recoil of the gun, Edward
lies stunned. When he rouses, he realizes the house is burning.

He and Trudy save themselves and the gun. Teunis, riding in later, finds his family in the yard. Gertrude is still unconscious, Trudy is asleep, and Edward has the gun across his lap pointed at the bodies of the three dead Indians.

This fast-moving, dramatic story is based on an incident that actually occurred. By identifying with Gertrude and the children, the reader experiences the mounting terror they felt from the time they saw smoke in the north. The story succeeds as literature, although, because of the nature of the material, it gives only one side of the relationship between the whites and the Indians. The illustrations, like the narrative, may evoke shock and horror in present-day viewers. Nevertheless, this is the way things were for some early Americans.

N98   WILDER, LAURA INGALLS. <u>Little Town on the Prairie</u>. Illustrated by Helen Sewell and Mildred Boyle. New York: Harper & Brothers, 1941, 288 pp.
       Fiction: historical   Gr. 5-9

This narrative begins at the conclusion of the long winter, in the spring of 1881, and closes in December of 1882 when Laura is nearly sixteen. Back on the claim, Laura is perfectly content to help with chores and the garden and to enjoy the beautiful prairie in springtime, but when the opportunity comes to work in town sewing for twenty-five cents a day, she accepts it. The nine dollars she earns for six weeks' work goes into Mary's college fund. That summer Laura and Mary enjoy long walks on the prairie and become real friends. In August, Ma and Pa take Mary to Vinton, Iowa, to the College for the Blind.

In the fall the family again moves from the claim to Pa's store building in town. Laura and Carrie start to school. The teacher is Miss Wilder, Almanzo's sister. The first day of school Laura is surprised when Nellie Oleson appears. Because of financial reverses, the Olesons have come to Dakota Territory to homestead. Nellie is now a tall, willowy blonde, but she is still as disagreeable as she was in Minnesota. She becomes a special friend of Miss Wilder's. For some reason—perhaps because of Nellie's insinuations—Miss Wilder picks on Carrie and Laura. Miss Wilder's classroom order becomes so bad that Pa Ingalls and the other two members of the schoolboard visit. They restore order and Miss Wilder returns to Minnesota at the end of the term.

That winter there are no severe storms and the little town is lively with activities. Mr. Clewett, the new schoolteacher, Pa, and some other men organize Friday-night "literaries." On successive Friday evenings they have a spelldown, charades, a musical program, a waxworks program, and even a minstrel. The new church building is roofed and on Sunday there are two church services and Sunday school. The minister's adopted daughter,

Ida, becomes Laura's close friend. The Ladies' Aid gives a New
England supper on Thanksgiving. Ben Woodworth has a birthday
party at the depot in January for the young people his age including Laura.

The Ingalls family moves back to the claim in April. Laura
helps Ma with the house and garden and Pa with chores and haying,
but she studies her textbooks, too. She hopes to get her teacher's certificate the following spring when she is sixteen. The
money she earns teaching will help keep Mary in school.

The family returns to town in the fall for the third winter.
Laura's teacher, Mr. Owen, is excellent. In November revival
meetings are held at the church. Each evening after the service,
Almanzo Wilder walks home with Laura.

In December the church is filled for the School Exhibition.
Laura and the seven other older boys and girls recite geography,
parse long sentences, and do mental arithmetic. Laura reviews
without a mistake the history of the United States from its discovery through the administration of John Quincy Adams. The
following day she is offered a two-months school. The pay will
be twenty dollars a month and board. Mr. Williams, the County
Superintendent, comes to the house and gives Laura the teachers'
examination, which she passes. Although Laura dreads going among
strangers to teach, she is happy that she will be earning money
for Mary's education. (See N106.)

N99   FOSTER, GENEVIEVE. George Washington's World. Illustrated
         by the author. New York: Charles Scribner's Sons, 1941
         (OP), 348 pp.
         Information: history and biography   Gr. 5-10
    The author explains in her introduction that the book tells,
not only the story of George Washington's life, but "of the people who were living when he was, both in America, and all over
the world, of what they did when they were children, how later
on the pattern of their lives fitted together, and what part
each one played in that greatest of all adventure stories, the
History of the World." The six sections cover the period when
Washington was a boy, a soldier, a farmer, the commander, a private citizen, and president. Preceding each section are two
pages of captioned illustrations of the people and events to
be discussed after Washington's life is related. For example,
these pictures show that when George Washington was young, the
future King George III was also a boy; Daniel Boone was a hunter;
farmer boy John Adams worked in the fields; Benjamin Franklin
experimented with electricity; Bach played for Frederick II,
King of Prussia; Voltaire wrote against injustice; and Ch'ien
Lung became Emperor of China.

The author's excellent organization, lively, clear writing,
interesting black and white illustrations, maps, charts, and
indexes combine to make a very readable book.

1942

N100   LENSKI, LOIS.   Indian Captive: The Story of Mary Jemison.
           Illustrated by the author.   New York: Frederick A. Stokes,
           1941, 270 pages.
           Biography   Gr. 3-7
       This narrative recounts the first two years of Mary Jemison's
captivity among the Seneca Indians.   Taken from her home in eastern Pennsylvania in 1758 when she was twelve, she journeyed with
her captors first to Fort Duquesne, then to Seneca Town in southern Ohio, and finally to Genesee Town in present-day New York
state.   At the close of the story, when the opportunity comes
for her to return to the white people, Mary decides that since
her own family are all dead she will remain with the Indians
who have adopted her.
       Although the biography is fictionalized and reads like an
exciting adventure story, it is based on fact.   At age eighty
Mary Jemison told her memories of her experiences to a doctor
who made a book from them.   Lois Lenski provides an authentic
background, integrating many details of Seneca Indian life into
her readable text and her many attractive, informative
illustrations.

N101   GAGGIN, EVA ROE.   Down Ryton Water.   Illustrated by Elmer
           Hader.   New York: Viking, 1941 (OP), 369 pp.
           Fiction: historical   Gr. 7-11
       This saga of Pilgrim life, told in first person by Matt Over,
begins in June 1608, on the day before his fifth birthday.   On
that day, into his mother's garden on Ryton Water in Scrooby,
England, comes one of the king's men, looking for Elder Brewster.
He is not found that day, but the Separatists of Scrooby, unwill-
ing to worship as the king dictates, know that it is no longer
safe for them to stay there.   They depart in two days.   The women
and children are carried in small boats down Ryton Water to Boston strand and the men walk.   Off Boston strand they board a
ship procured by Matt's seafaring uncle, Samuel Brode, and sail
to the Low Country.   Besides Matt and his parents, his immediate
family includes a baby, 'Memby; Winover, seven, an adopted
daughter; and Uncle John Brode, Goodwife Orris Over's eight-
year-old brother.   Although most of their possessions are left
behind to be sent on later, Goodwife Over takes a huge metal
bowl filled with simples from her garden.   The Pilgrims remain
in the Low Country for twelve years.   The Overs are happy there:
they find good friends among the Dutch, Father becomes a citizen
of Leyden, and Nicolas is born.   But when Elder Brewster decides
the Pilgrims must leave Leyden, the Overs and Orris's bowl of
simples go, too.   The final section takes place on the Speedwell,
the Mayflower, and in Plymouth Colony.   The children grow up and
marry, and except for Matt, who remains with his wife and family
at Plymouth, spread out into the new world.   John Brode and

Winover marry and move to the Puritan colony in Boston. 'Memby
and Nicolas marry into a Dutch family--their friends from Leyden
have emigrated to New Amsterdam--and become Dutch patroons on
the Hudson. The story closes when Matt is twenty-five.

The first two sections showing life in England and the Netherlands are especially good. The third section is less satisfying,
perhaps because a great deal has been written about Plymouth
Colony. The first terrible winter is described perfunctorily.
The adoption of the Indian lad, Wisset, seems to have been included to give an opportunity to introduce details of Indian
life. The migration of the Corts from Holland, while possible,
is unlikely. The author sometimes includes details that will
interest some readers, but do little to advance the story as
when she gives the uses of the great variety of herbs Orris
grows. Commendably, she has the characters speak modern English,
but she uses, without defining, a number of words no longer in use,
including poll, coif, besom, and mattock. Among the historic figures, Elder Brewster is well developed, and the reader gains a
good understanding of the young William Bradford, who is eighteen
when they leave England and governor of the colony at the close.
A contemporary reviewer found <u>Down Ryton Water</u> a novel of "scope
and richness" (E. L. Buell, review in the <u>New York Times</u>, 18
January 1942, p. 10), a judgment that is still valid in spite of
some weaknesses.

<u>1943</u>

N102   GRAY, ELIZABETH JANET. <u>Adam of the Road</u>. Illustrated by
       Robert Lawson. New York: Viking, 1942, 317 pp.
       Fiction: historical   Gr. 4-7
   Eleven-year-old Adam and his father, Roger Quartermayne, a
minstrel, leave St. Alban's Abbey, where Adam has been attending
school, in June of 1294. The adventures, which take Adam through
southeastern England, come to a close in Oxford in April of 1295.
Because Roger is now minstrel to Sir Edmund de Lisle they go
first to the de Lisle town house outside London. There they remain until after the August wedding of Emily de Lisle. Then,
since they will not be needed by Sir Edmund until Christmas,
they take to the road. The night before they leave, in a dice
game, Roger loses all his money and his horse, Bayard, to another
minstrel, Jankin. Roger, Adam, and Adam's dog, Nick, a silky red
spaniel who can do tricks, are obliged to go on foot carrying
their instruments and a change of clothes.

   They visit London first. There they happen to meet Jankin,
who admires Nick and suggests matching pennies for him. Roger
curtly refuses. They start west for Winchester, where St. Giles

1943

Fair, the greatest in England, is held each September. On the
way, while they are asleep in an inn one night, Jankin takes
Nick, leaving Bayard who is now lame. Adam and his father start
out after Jankin. During the pursuit, they become separated and,
although each keeps looking for the other, in a time when most
travel was by foot and most communication by word of mouth, it
is not surprising that they are not reunited for months.

Adam recovers Nick shortly before he finds his father again.
While away from his father, Adam makes his way by singing and
telling tales for meals and a place to sleep. He encounters
and is treated kindly by all sorts of people: a ferryman and
his wife, a parish vicar and his sister, and a plowman and his
family. He has some frightening times, too: a merchant with
whom he is traveling to Winchester is robbed by an outlaw knight.
Adam escapes and brings the sheriff to his rescue.

In beautiful prose, by means of hundreds of carefully chosen
details, Miss Gray recaptures the atmosphere and flavor of life
in thirteenth-century England for both the great and humble.
She elicits a real appreciation of the important role of min-
strels in an age when books were both scarce and expensive and
few could read. In addition, she deftly places the period in
the larger framework of history. An old man Adam meets recalls
King John's signing the Magna Charta in 1215; at Oxford, he sees
King Edward I's messenger bring word that for the first time the
Commons will sit in Parliament with the Lords. The part of the
plot involving Jankin and the dog seems a weakness, a small flaw
in an otherwise well done book. Robert Lawson's illustrations--
of castles, cottages, abbey buildings, inns, the countryside,
and people in their characteristic costumes--have the same living
quality as the text.

N103   ESTES, ELEANOR. The Middle Moffat. Illustrated by Louis
        Slobodkin. New York: Harcourt, Brace, 1942, 317 pp.
        Fiction   Gr. 3-6
     Ten-year-old Jane, the middle Moffat, lives with her widowed
dressmaker mother, her sixteen-year-old sister, Silvie, and her
brothers--Joey, thirteen, and Rufus, six--in Cranbury, Connecticut. The United States has entered World War I, but the only
time the war is important to the story is when Santa Claus writes
Rufus a letter to tell him he cannot bring him a pony because all
the ponies are needed for the army. Most of the episodes focus
on Jane, in this, the second book about the Moffats.

     Jane and her family have just moved to the street on which
Cranbury's oldest inhabitant, ninety-nine-year-old Mr. Buckle,
lives with his daughter. When Mr. Buckle sees Janey sitting in
the yard, he stops to make her acquaintance. He becomes her
special friend and Jane vows she will do everything she can to
be certain he reaches his hundredth birthday. He attends an

organ recital she gives and she visits him to see the furniture
he has carved out of chicken bones. On the day of his one hundredth birthday, Jane and the other Moffats ride home from the
celebration with him. It is Janey's fourth auto ride and
Rufus's first.

When she is not with the oldest inhabitant, Janey is frequently with her best friend, Nancy Stokes, who lives in the
house behind her. She does things with her family, too. In
the performance of "The Three Bears" at the Town Hall, Sylvie
is Goldilocks, Joey is the big bear, Rufus the little bear, and
Janey the middle bear.

Janey is a real little girl: imaginative, resolute, and
likable. The story is told from her viewpoint and the reader
often knows her thoughts. Mrs. Estes has a flair for humor and
some of the episodes are very funny, as when Jane cannot find
her middle bear's head and the show has to go on without it.
Although the Moffats never have much money, they manage and are
a happy, loving family. The illustrations give an excellent
portrayal of both the characters and the times: oil lamps, a
coal-burning kitchen range, the girls' basketball team in middy
blouses and bloomers. The author has said that her books are
autobiographical. Some of the incidents involving Jane had
their origin in her own childhood.

N104   HUNT, MABEL LEIGH. "Have You Seen Tom Thumb?" Illustrated
        by Fritz Eichenberg. Philadelphia: Frederick A. Stokes,
        1942 (OP), 260 pp.
        Biography   Gr. 5-9
        This is a sprightly fictionalized biography of the American
"man in miniature," Charles Sherwood Stratton, presented to New
York in 1842 by showman P. T. Barnum as General Tom Thumb. At
age five (Barnum said he was eleven), Charlie was twenty-five
inches tall and weighed fifteen pounds. His parents and siblings
were of normal size. He was intelligent and proved to be a naturally talented entertainer and actor, performing with skill and
aplomb the routines and acts Barnum contrived for him. The following year Barnum took him to Europe where he was received by
Queen Victoria.

This trip, which also included a visit to the continent, extended over three years and was the first of four tours of Great
Britain, France, and Belgium. The fourth visit came at the conclusion of a world tour that began by crossing the width of the
United States from east to west. At this time the General was
thirty-four and at his full height of thirty-one inches. He was
accompanied on this trip by his wife, Lavinia, also a midget,
and two other small people. Charles became wealthy and built
in his native city, Bridgeport, Connecticut, a large home which
contained an apartment beautifully furnished with furniture

1943

scaled especially to his size. Even though there was no financial need, he continued to make appearances until almost the end
of his life.

The author states that the biography is a blending of fact
and fancy based on stories in contemporary newspapers, eyewitness
accounts, and statements attributed to P. T. Barnum. The full-
page black and white illustrations are as delightful as the text.

1944

N105   FORBES, ESTHER. Johnny Tremain. Illustrated by Lynd Ward.
        Boston: Houghton Mifflin, 1943, 256 pp.
        Fiction: historical   Gr. 7-10

The setting is Boston and its environs in the years 1773-1775.
Fourteen-year-old Johnny Tremain, an orphan, is an apprentice to
old Mr. Lapham, a silversmith who no longer takes much interest
in his shop. Talented and intelligent, Johnny virtually manages
the shop, ordering the other apprentices about and enjoying favored treatment from Mrs. Lapham, Mr. Lapham's daughter-in-law,
who runs the household.

An accident changes everything. Johnny's right hand is severely burned on molten silver. When the wound heals, his thumb
has grown to his palm in the position the midwife bandaged it.
Johnny can no longer work as a silversmith. After weeks of
searching for a job he can do, Johnny, in desperation, goes to
wealthy merchant Lyte, who, his mother told him before she died,
is a relative. Merchant Lyte rejects him as an imposter.

At length Johnny obtains a job as a horse boy riding and
delivering the Boston Observer, a weekly newspaper sympathetic
to the cause of liberty for the colonies. He lives in the attic
room over the print shop with Rab, who is a couple of years older
than Johnny and an apprentice of the editor, his uncle. Rab is
a Son of Liberty, and the newspaper subscribers include such
patriots as Sam Adams, Paul Revere, James Otis, and John Hancock.
From time to time these and others meet in Johnny and Rab's room.
It is there they plan the Boston tea party, enlisting Rab, Johnny,
and other apprentice boys to dress up as Indians and dump the tea
into the harbor.

In retaliation Britain closes the harbor of Boston and quarters
troops in the town. Johnny comes to know and like some of the
British officers who have him exercise their horses and carry
messages for them. Rab begins to drill with the minutemen of his
home town, Lexington. The Lyte family, who are Tories, take ship
for London. Before they leave, Lavinia Lyte, merchant Lyte's
beautiful daughter, tells Johnny that her father is actually
Johnny's great-uncle.

The story closes on the day after the battles of Lexington and Concord. Rab dies that day, from wounds received at Lexington. Doctor Warren examines Johnny's hand and tells him he can free his thumb by cutting through the scar tissue. Although he cannot promise that he will be able to work with silver again, his hand will be good enough to hold a gun.

It has been suggested that, because of the depth of research she had done for her Pulitzer Award-winning biography, <u>Paul Revere and the World He Lived In</u>, when she came to write this book, Esther Forbes was able to forget the period as history and intuitively live within the times. With a deft hand she evokes both the physical environment and the spirit and feelings of revolutionary Boston. Historical events and characters, viewed in the context of their time, seem very real.

While not distorting or belittling the Tory point of view, the author has brought out clearly the reason for the rebellion, put into words by James Otis at a meeting of the patriots: "We give all we have, lives, property, safety, skills . . . we fight, we die, for a single thing. Only that a man can stand up."

Although setting, plot, and theme are executed admirably, still it is the characterization of Johnny that captures and holds the reader's attention. In the beginning he is bright and gifted, but also tends to be inconsiderate and overbearing. He puts down the other apprentices. He insults and teases his master's granddaughters, but is also eager to teach them to read and pleased when he has money to buy gifts for them. And he is willing to break the Sabbath by working because he is proud of his ability. For a while after the accident, he becomes depressed, self-pitying, and embittered, although he remains arrogant. He even hopes to find an easy way out--he will claim relationship and be taken in by the wealthy Lytes. And then gradually, after he goes to live with the mature Rab, acquires the job of delivering the <u>Observer</u>, and becomes caught up in a cause larger than himself, he regains his self-confidence and overcomes his bitterness. By the end he has become less impulsive, has greater humility, and is more understanding of others. This book remains a landmark of historical fiction for children.

N106   WILDER, LAURA INGALLS. <u>These Happy Golden Years</u>. Illustrated
       by Helen Sewell and Mildred Boyle. New York: Harper &
       Brothers, 1943, 300 pp.
       Fiction: historical   Gr. 5-10
This is the last of the seven books in which Laura Ingalls Wilder recorded fictionally her childhood and young adulthood. It follows immediately after <u>Little Town on the Prairie</u> and covers the period from January 1883 to September 1885, Laura's schoolteaching days and Laura and Almanzo's courting years.

In January and February of 1883, while she is still fifteen, Laura teaches the first of her three terms of school before her marriage. Laura and her five pupils, three of whom are older than she, attend school in an abandoned claim shanty. Because the school is twelve miles out from town, Laura boards with the Brewsters during the week. Mrs. Brewster, close to being psychotic, is so unpleasant that Laura is extremely happy that Almanzo Wilder drives out and takes her home every Friday for the weekend.

In March, after Laura is back home attending school again herself, she sews on Saturdays for fifty cents a day and goes sleigh-riding every Sunday afternoon with Almanzo. The pattern of attending school, sewing for the dressmaker on Saturdays and in the summer, teaching, and going places with Almanzo is followed for the next two years. Both of Laura's other teaching experiences are in new one-room schoolhouses and are pleasant. She earns thirty dollars a month in the last school for a three-month school. Some of the money Laura earns goes to buy an organ for Mary to play when she is home on vacation from the School for the Blind. Laura and Almanzo take long buggy rides in the summer and sleigh rides in the winter. Almanzo pays for their tuitions to a singing school which they attend together.

Pa enlarges and sides the claim shanty in the fall of 1884, and the family stays in the country, only a mile out from town, for the winter. Almanzo gives Laura a garnet and pearl engagement ring and they make plans to marry the following year.

The next summer Pa buys a sewing machine, and Ma and Laura sew Laura's trousseau. Then one morning in September, Laura and Almanzo drive to Reverend Brown's and are married. The last night Laura is home, Pa plays all the old tunes on the fiddle. The next afternoon after their wedding dinner with Ma, Pa, Carrie, and Grace, Laura and Almanzo drive to their own little gray home set in Almanzo's tree claim.

Each of the volumes of the Ingalls family saga contributes to the picture of a growing country. One finishes reading the series feeling that through the Ingalls family he has truly experienced pioneer days. The steadfast family love that permeates the chronicles provides a theme not only for that time but for all eras. Mrs. Wilder evokes the past through the perceptions of the characters, and it is from Laura's realization of life, that of a child secure in a loving relationship with parents and sisters, that we view the stories. Life is often hard, but Ma and Pa are courageous and resourceful. They have the ability to cope and so do their children: it never occurs to Laura that she will not be able to manage pupils who misbehave. At the same time they live rich lives, savoring the little things: the fresh lettuce and radishes from their own garden, a new bonnet, or Pa's fiddle music.

The "Little House" books contain much "how-to-do-it" information. While such factual material is often unsuitable in a novel,

it is an integral part of the narrative in these books. The
reader would be disappointed if Ma did not give Reverend Stuart
her "receipt" for fried salt pork. The explanation of how the
button lamp is made is not only necessary so that the reader can
visualize this unfamiliar object, but also it incites admiration
for the ingenuity of those who managed so well with so little.

While authentically recreating a period in America's past,
Mrs. Wilder has given us, in Laura, a well-rounded, memorable
character. Although she is usually obedient, hardworking, andd
self-disciplined, Laura is also independent and spunky, as demonstrated by many incidents throughout the series.

Before drawing the illustrations that have appeared in the
books since 1953, Garth Williams visited the various homesites
of the Ingalls family. These historically authentic illustrations harmonize with the author's simple, direct style.

N107   SAUER, JULIA L. Fog Magic. Illustrated by Lynd Ward.
       New York: Viking, 1943, 107 pp.
       Fantasy   Gr. 4-7
On days when the fog rolls in densely from the sea, eleven-
year-old Greta, whose home is a little Nova Scotian fishing village, goes over the mountain to find and visit Blue Cove, a
village of long ago that materializes from the fog. On sunny
days she finds only the ruined foundations of the houses. Old
legends become an integral part of the story as Greta fantasizes
that she takes part in some of the old tales and hears others
from the lips of those who were the principal actors. On her
twelfth birthday, the mother of her Blue Cove friend, Retha,
sends a kitten home with her. Greta realizes that since she is
growing up the village will no longer appear to her, although
her encounters there--and the kitten--will remain as vivid
childhood memories forever.

The obvious, common sense explanation for Greta's experiences
is that imagination spans time with the aid of the atmosphere-
producing fog. As the real world is obscured, fantasy becomes
reality. The story has also been regarded as a time story with
a ghost theme. Lynd Ward's portrait of Greta and the kitten
opposite the first page of text, his endpapers showing Blue Cove
shrouded in fog, and his cover design of gulls flying over the
sea are appropriate accents for this quiet, well-written story,
imbued with a strong sense of place.

N108   ESTES, ELEANOR. Rufus M.. Illustrated by Louis Slobodkin.
       New York: Harcourt, Brace, 1943, 320 pp.
       Fiction   Gr. 3-6
Rufus M., the youngest of the four Moffat children, is seven
in this book and at the center of most of these episodes. He,
his brother, Joey, and sisters, Sylvie and Jane, live with their

1944

widowed mother, who is a seamstress, in Cranbury, Connecticut, during World War I. Several chapters relate how Rufus helps in the war effort. He and all of his class knit washcloths for the soldiers, but Rufus, alone, manages to hand his directly to a soldier on a train leaving for camp. He raises a bumper crop of beans in a Victory Garden; and, in a popcorn partnership with Janey, earns enough money to become a Victory Boy. He is happily mystified by the invisible piano player who lives at the Saybolts' house, but loses interest when he learns that it is a player piano that works by machinery. With only his cardboard boy for company, he pedals his tricycle all the way to Plum Beach and rides Jimmy, his favorite horse on the merry-go-round. He takes up magic, practices ventriloquism at school, and has to stand in the cloakroom. The story closes with World War I coming to an end on Armistice Day.

Rufus, a dynamo of energy and less of a daydreamer than Jane, is an engaging, believable character. Again, as in the earlier two Moffat books, the characters and times live as vividly in the illustrations as in the text.

N109 YATES, ELIZABETH. <u>Mountain Born</u>. Illustrated by Nora S.
Unwin. New York: Coward-McCann, 1943 (OP), 118 pp.
Fiction Gr. 4-6

This rather quiet story about a boy growing up, a family, sheep raising, and a particular sheep begins on a March day during lambing season. Andrew brings into the house a little black lamb that is dead, he tells his wife Martha. Because she does not want their six-year-old son, Peter, to see death at so young an age, Martha tries to revive the lamb. With instructions from their old shepherd, Benj, she succeeds. Peter names the lamb Biddy and raises her by hand. That year he is with his father and Benj for many of the activities of sheep-raising: docking the tails, shearing, dipping, pasturing, and culling. By the next year he can also be of some help at lambing time. That year Biddy is sheared for the first time. From the wool, Mary's Granny makes a coat for Peter and a woolen dress for Mary.

Part II takes place five years later. Peter has worn his coat for five years and becomes a proficient shepherd. Biddy, now a leader in the flock, has had three white ram lambs. The following spring she has a black ewe lamb like herself. That year again her fleece goes for a new coat for Peter which Granny promises to have ready by the end of summer. The day Peter gets his new coat, an unseasonably early snow comes. Biddy breaks a path all the way down the mountain through deep snow and brings most of the flock in. But, as a result of the exposure, she dies. Her ewe lamb remains to comfort Peter.

The author of <u>Mountain Born</u> universalizes its setting by leaving time and place deliberately vague. Precise identification

is not really important for, as Benj tells Peter, sheep and
tending sheep have not changed much since the days when David
watched over his sheep in ancient Israel. The continuity of
life is suggested by the portrayal of the cycle of the seasons
and the generations of man. Besides the theme of a boy's growing up, there is also a general underlying theme that contentment and often wisdom abound in men who live simply and close
to nature as does Benj. This implicit comment on life is reflected in the general tone of serenity characteristic of the
book. Good black and white illustrations picture events of the
story.

1945

N110   LAWSON, ROBERT. <u>Rabbit Hill</u>. Illustrated by the author. New
        York: Viking, 1944, 127 pp.
        Fantasy   Gr. 1-4
    Rabbit Hill is the name the Lawsons gave to their country
home in Connecticut, the setting for this story. The important
characters are the woodland animals that live on the hill:
Father Rabbit, a cultivated gentleman from the Bluegrass region
of Kentucky; Mother Rabbit, a worrier; Little Georgie, irrepressible and a great jumper; Uncle Analdas Rabbit; Porkey the wood-
chuck; Phewie the skunk; Willie Fieldmouse and his relatives;
the Red Buck; and the Mole.
    The small animals have had lean times since no one has lived
in the big house to plant a garden. Then the new Folks come and
there is excitement over whether or not they will be planting
folks. Not only do they plant a huge garden, but they prohibit
the gardener's using guns, traps, or poison. Further acts of
kindness to the animals include putting up a sign instructing
motorists to drive carefully on account of small animals; rescuing Willie Fieldmouse when he falls into the rainwater barrel
outside the living-room window; and nursing little Georgie back
to health after he is run over by a car. Finally, on Midsummer's
Eve, the new Folks unveil a stone statue of St. Francis of Assisi
with Little Animals around his feet. There is also a pool of
water and a feeding ledge by the Good Saint. An inscription on
the statue reads, "There is enough for all." The bountiful feast
set out for the animals that evening is repeated every evening.
In gratitude the animals leave the garden undisturbed. Good
times have indeed returned to the hill.
    Inherent in this humorous and exciting story is a plea for the
preservation of wildlife. A multitude of beautiful sepia illustrations and the pictorial maps used as endpapers add reality to
the story. Although it may have been little noticed at the time
the book was published, the Negro cook is stereotyped. Recent
printings omit these references.

1945

N111   ESTES, ELEANOR. <u>The Hundred Dresses</u>. Illustrated by Louis
           Slobodkin. New York: Harcourt, Brace, 1944, 80 pp.
           Fiction   Gr. 3-6
     Motherless Wanda Petronski wears the same faded blue dress to
school day after day. One day she rather casually tells one of
her fifth-grade classmates that she has one hundred dresses all
lined up in her closet. After that the girls tease her everyday about them. Then the Petronskis move away to the city where
Wanda's father writes in a note to the teacher, "No more holler
Polack. No more ask why funny name. Plenty of funny names in
big city." Wanda has left before the winner of the drawing and
coloring contest is revealed. The winner is Wanda, who has
drawn one hundred dress designs "all different and beautiful."
     Mrs. Estes might have ended the story at that point, but she
did not; nearly half of the pages of this slim book record what
happens after Wanda leaves. Working through the consciousness
of Maddie, who just stood by while Peggy, her best friend, pried
at Wanda each day, she does more than make this a story in which
the reader feels compassion for Wanda. After carefully examining her part in the affair, Maddie decides her conduct was more
shameful than Peggy's even though Peggy had tormented Wanda more.
As a result of her soul-searching, Maddie decides that she will
never again stand by and say nothing when she sees another person mistreated. The author, without moralizing, allows the
reader to share Maddie's remorse and her thoughts, and lets the
moral decision Maddie reaches come as a revelation to the
reader as well.

N112   DALGLIESH, ALICE. <u>The Silver Pencil</u>. Illustrated by
           Katherine Milhous. New York: Charles Scribner's Sons,
           1944 (OP), 235 pp.
           Fiction   Gr. 5-10
     This story, recording the growing up years of Janet Laidlaw,
is partly autobiographical. It begins in Trinidad in the early
1900s when Janet is nine, and ends in the early 1920s in New
York City. In Trinidad, in the house on the hill Janet lives
a pleasant life with several servants, her brother Lawrence, ten
years her senior, her often ailing English mother, and her humorous and loving Scottish father. Following the unexpected death
of her father, Janet's mother suffers a breakdown, but regains
control of her life. When she is twelve, Janet and her mother
go to England and Janet attends school there. She had hoped to
attend college in England, which she has grown to love, but because her mother cannot stand the cold, damp English winters,
after four years, they return to Trinidad. In a short while,
Janet goes to New York City to take training as a kindergarten
teacher. The days of her training period, her first days of
teaching, and her first love are recorded. Subsequently, she

discovers Nova Scotia, has her first book published, becomes an American citizen, and meets a man the reader believes she will marry. When she was young, she had written numerous stories with the silver pencil, a Christmas gift from her father. But it was not until she was bedfast for a number of months with arthritis that she began to write as an adult, using her silver pencil.

Even though there is little action and no dramatic climax, this well-written story is interesting both for the portrayal of Janet's character and as social history. Janet's problems are those that young people still face, even though outward circumstances have changed.

N113   FOSTER, GENEVIEVE. <u>Abraham Lincoln's World</u>. Illustrated by the author. New York: Charles Scribner's Sons, 1944, 347 pp.

Information: biography and history   Gr. 5-10

Like its counterparts, <u>George Washington's World</u> and the others in the series, this book blends history and biography in an original way to show what was happening to various people around the world during the years of Abraham Lincoln's life. This book actually continues <u>George Washington's World</u> (a Newbery Honor Book, 1942). Washington died in December 1799 and the first section of this volume, "When Abraham Lincoln Was Born in Kentucky," covers the years 1800 to 1815. Among the people making history then was Napoleon who had been born when George Washington was a farmer. Baby Victoria was born in England when Abraham Lincoln was a boy in Indiana. In that section, old Daniel Boone, who learned to hunt when George Washington was a boy and led pioneers into Kentucky when Washington was a gentleman farmer, was crowded out by pioneers. The subjects include scientists, musicians, and artists as well as statesmen, generals, and rulers.

In an acknowledgment the author states she consulted several hundred books, including autobiographies, letters, and diaries. She brings immediacy to the chronicle by quoting from primary sources such as a letter Harriet Beecher Stowe wrote to her husband describing a riot over slavery that occurred in pre-Civil War days in Cincinnati. The author's many illustrations and maps add information and interest to the text. Two indexes, one of characters, and the other of nations, places, and events, are valuable for reference.

N114   EATON, JEANETTE. <u>Lone Journey: The Life of Roger Williams</u>. Illustrated by Woodi Ishmael. New York: Harcourt, Brace, 1944, 266 pp.

Biography   Gr. 8-11

This is a fictionalized account of the life of Roger Williams (1604-1683). By the age of sixteen, Roger, a thoughtful boy,

1945

had adopted Puritanism at a time when Puritans were being har-
assed in his native England. A keenly intelligent student, he
received a Master of Arts degree from Cambridge University and
became a Puritan minister who spoke out for religious freedom
and separation of church and state. When word reached him that
Archbishop Laud of the Church of England was taking steps to
have him brought before the King's Council for trial, he and
his wife, Mary, sailed for the new Puritan settlement of Boston.
There, and in Plymouth and Salem, the only other New England
settlements, he found the same intermingling of church and state.
He spoke against this type of government saying it was contrary
to the teachings of Jesus Christ for the civil state to impose
religion upon the people. He also protested the treatment of
the Indians, insisting they were the true owners of the land.

   In January 1636, when he was banished from Massachusetts,
Williams fled into the wilderness. Canonicus, a sachem of the
Narragansett Indians, sold him land near Narragansett Bay upon
which Williams established a settlement, New Providence. The
covenant he framed provided that the laws which the settlers
would draw up and abide by would pertain "only in civil things."
There would be freedom of worship. The years that followed saw
the slow working out of Williams's cherished dream.

   The character of Roger Williams, who first stood for the liberty of conscience that came to characterize America, is well
portrayed and his beliefs are clearly explained, but the book
less successfully evokes the period than does the author's Leader
by Destiny. The large print and the illustrations suggest a book
suitable for junior high students, but the content, which includes
much political history of both England and New England, seems too
advanced for most students of that level. Since the book is fictionalized and without footnotes, it is sometimes difficult to
determine whether a speech is a direct quotation or imaginary
conversation. Although the editorializing in the last chapter
has no place in a biography, it is gratifying to find a book
from the 1940s in which the leading character does not consider
Indians inferior to whites.

1946

N115   LENSKI, LOIS. Strawberry Girl. Illustrated by the author.
           Philadelphia: J. B. Lippincott, 1945, 193 pp.
           Fiction   Gr. 4-6
   The Boyer family and the Slater family are the principals in
this story, which concerns the life of the Florida "Crackers" in
the early 1900s. The children around whom much of the action
revolves are Birdie Boyer, the strawberry girl, and Shoestring
Slater, who is twelve, a couple of years older than Birdie.

Strawberry Girl shows two ways of life that developed in this particular environment. The Slaters follow the older pattern: Mrs. Slater tells her new neighbor, Mrs. Boyer, that they make their living by "messin' with cows and sellin' 'em for beef." Mrs. Boyer informs her neighbor that they are "studyin' to sell oranges and strawberries and sweet 'taters and sich and make us a good livin'." Conflict develops between the families over their different ways of making a living. The Slaters let their cattle forage for themselves, insisting that this country has always been open range and that the Boyers have no right to fence it to keep the stock out. Mr. Boyer says he will fence in what he paid for, a practice other farmers are also following. The reader's interest in the controversy is sustained by a series of dramatic incidents. The conflict is resolved as a result of Mr. Slater's conversion at a Camp Meeting. He stops drinking, sells his cattle, and takes a job as dynamiter with the phosphate company. His wife and children plan to put out strawberries and a grove of seedless grapefruit.

Miss Lenski has stated that she takes her books from life, and that most of her characters are real. She says that Birdie Boyer is a real little girl she saw plowing in a sandy field in Florida and that the incidents she uses are true as well. She stated that because her books were true-to-life stories she included certain characters like drunken fathers and malicious neighbors which had not often been used in children's books. She notes that after some of the worst fights, the quarreling neighbors would get together for a frolic; so she wrote it that way. The chapters that relate a merry making, cane-grinding with a candy-pulling and dance in the evening, for example, show the happier side of these people's lives, and they also provide relief from the tension that is built up in the other chapters.

The author's authenticity extends to reproducing with fidelity the peculiar speech of the Florida backwoods which has been handed down from Anglo-Saxon origins. In her illustrations, Miss Lenski does not glamorize Birdie and her friends, but draws them as she saw them at home and in the fields. Her illustrations, as well as her use of the native speech, strengthen the feeling of locality.

Although Lois Lenski began to write regional books because she wanted children to know the various areas of their own country better, she also wanted them to observe the ways in which people are alike as well as the ways in which they are different. Even though she had a definite purpose, she has avoided preaching and teaching while retaining her enthusiasm for her material. Strawberry Girl is regional literature at its best.

N116   HENRY, MARGUERITE. Justin Morgan Had a Horse. Illustrated
        by Wesley Dennis. Chicago: Wilcox & Follett, 1945, 89 pp.
        Fiction   Gr. 4-6

1946

In the late 1700s, schoolteacher-singing master Justin Morgan and a boy, Joel Goss, walk from Randolph, Vermont, to West Spring-field, Massachusetts, to collect a debt owed to Justin Morgan. In payment, he receives a large colt and a little one, Bub. He decides not to take the little one, but, to Joel's delight, Bub tags along. Joel gentles the little horse and Little Bub turns out to be both stronger and faster than any other horse in the county. The boy and the horse are parted when Joel is appren-ticed to a miller and Little Bub is rented out by the year. Justin Morgan races Bub, too, and his winnings are enough that he can pay all his debts. When Justin Morgan moves from the com-munity, he takes his horse with him and wills Little Bub to the family who cares for him in his last illness. Over the years it is Joel's dream to find again the little horse to which he was so strongly attached. He searches everywhere, even at the Battle of Lundy's Lane in 1814. He finally finds him in 1817 and pur-chases him. Under Joel's care, Little Bub, now called Justin Morgan, becomes almost young again and carries President Monroe in a parade.

In an introductory note, Marguerite Henry states, "This is the story of a common ordinary little work horse which turned out to be the father of a famous family of American horses . . . the Morgan horses." She writes that as part of her research she consulted Justin Morgan's great-grandson and Joel Goss's grand-daughter. Mrs. Henry fits her story into an accurate, but briefly drawn, historical background. The story has a number of dramatic moments, some of which are recorded in Wesley Dennis's beautiful sepia illustrations.

N117   MEANS, FLORENCE CRANNELL. <u>The Moved-Outers</u>. Illustrated by
        Helen Blair. Boston: Houghton Mifflin, 1945 (OP), 154 pp.
        Fiction   Gr. 4-9
The Oharas are the only Japanese-American family living in Cordova, California, on Pearl Harbor Day, December 7, 1941. Both parents were born in Hawaii of Japanese ancestry, but they have lived in Cordova, where Mr. Ohara is a successful nursery-man, for twenty-five years. Tad, the older son, is in the army; Amy, the older daughter, is in the east in college; and Sue and her brother, Kim, are happy and popular high school seniors. On the day of the attack on Pearl Harbor, the father is taken away and is separated from the family for nearly a year. The other three at home are moved out in February, first to a camp only a couple hours' drive from home and later inland to a camp in Colorado. Both camps are behind barbed wire. Sue adjusts better than Kim does. Her being interned is made easier because the Ito family, farmers who lived outside the town, are with them in both camps. Jiro Ito, twenty, and Sue fall in love in spite of parental disapproval from both sides. While in the camp, the Oharas

receive word that Tad was killed in action. The story closes in February 1943 with Sue and Tomi, Jiro's sister, leaving the camp to enter college. Kim and Jiro enlist in the unit for Japanese-American soldiers.

The story was motivated buy what actually happened to Japanese-American citizens on the Pacific Coast in the tense months following Pearl Harbor. Although she wrote out of strong emotion, the author managed to maintain objectivity. It was not necessary to editorialize; the implication of unfair treatment of these American citizens is present in the dramatic, natural presentation. Sue, from whose viewpoint the story is told, is a well-developed character in a shameful chapter of American history.

N118 WESTON, CHRISTINE. <u>Bhimsa, the Dancing Bear</u>. Illustrated by Roger Duvoisin. New York: Charles Scribner's Sons, 1945 (OP), 120 pp.
Fiction   Gr. 3-5

One spring evening Gopala, an Indian boy, accompanied by his tame bear Bhimsa, wanders into David's garden. David runs away with Gopala and his bear, and the three roam over India having fantastic adventures before returning to their homes.

The narrative unfolds against an authentic background of contemporary India in 1945. The pace is lively with variety in the adventures. In one chapter, the boys escape from the town of the Prince, a spoiled tyrant no older than they, in a cart of uncured hides. In another, they ride an elephant to a Haunted Village. Bhimsa frequently dances for money and once fights a tiger. Roger Duvoisin's sepia and green illustrations evoke the atmosphere of India and accentuate the humor inherent in the story.

N119 SHIPPEN, KATHERINE B. <u>New Found World</u>. Illustrated by C. B. Falls. New York: Viking, 1945 (OP), 262 pp.
Information: history   Gr. 5-10

The "new found world" is Latin America. The first chapter describes the topography and the native animals and birds. The next several chapters are devoted to the civilizations and ways of life of the native tribes: the Arawaks, Caribs, Aztecs, Mayans, and Incas. Subsequent chapters record the white man's conquest of these tribes. The following chapters chronicle the voyages of Columbus, Cortes's conquest of Mexico, Pizarro's plundering of Peru, and the search for El Dorado. Chapters are also devoted to the bringing of Christianity to the new world. The final chapters describe the breaking away of the South American colonies from Spain and Portugal. A concluding chapter deals with the art, literature, and music of Latin America. There is a full-page black and white drawing at the beginning of each of the twenty-seven chapters, as well as smaller drawings within some chapters. Maps show the voyages of Columbus and the routes followed by the conquistadors. A chart titled "Six Centuries in America" begins with 1400 and progresses through 1942, listing in three columns events that occurred simultaneously in Latin America, the United States, and Canada.

This well-written and readable book is complete enough to be used as a textbook on Latin America.

1947

N120 BAILEY, CAROLYN SHERWIN. Miss Hickory. Illustrated by Ruth Gannett. New York: Viking, 1946, 123 pp.
Fantasy   Gr. 3-6
With a hickory-nut head and an apple-wood twig body, Miss Hickory is a unique doll, although her being a doll is of little significance to the story. No one plays with her nor does she particularly miss not belonging to someone. Rather she is a self-sufficient, strong-minded spinster, a New Hampshire country woman. Left in her corncob house under the lilac bush when the family moves to town for the winter, Miss Hickory makes the best of the situation, enjoying the changing seasons of the New England countryside and the company of the birds and small woodland animals. The chapter in which the animals hasten to the barn to experience the wonder of the Nativity, and the original, albeit nearly catastrophic, ending are highlights of the book. The carefully done lithographs help to make this fanciful story believable.

N121 BARNES, NANCY. The Wonderful Year. Illustrated by Kate Seredy. New York: J. Messner, 1946 (OP), 185 pp.
Fiction   Gr. 4-7
Eleven-year-old Ellen Martin is dismayed when her parents tell her they are going to move from their comfortable home in Kansas to an undeveloped ranch in western Colorado. The doctor has told Dad that he needs to get away from his law practice, to work outside and relax to relieve the painful nerve tension at the back of his neck.

Although she had worried that she wouldn't like it, Ellen soon finds herself caught up in the new life: it is fun living in a floored tent while Dad and the carpenter from Fruitvale build a small pine house which Mother makes homelike with her velvet carpet with roses in it and Ellen's little carved piano. Their closest neighbors, the Erringtons, help them plant their apple orchard. Ronnie Errington, fifteen, treats Ellen like a sister. They fish and ride their bicycles on the Ditchrider's path along the irrigation canals; both families go camping over the Fourth of July.

After the cantaloupe crop is harvested in September, Father, now in restored health, decides they will move into nearby Mesa where he will resume his law practice and Ellen will go to school.

School has been in session for several weeks when Ellen arrives and, for awhile, she feels like an outsider. She knows the other eighth graders think she is stiff and stuck-up. Then, all at once, she does belong. When Ronnie comes to stay with them and attend the new agricultural school in Mesa and her father says they will move out to the ranch again for the summer, Ellen concludes this has turned out to be a wonderful year.

In contrast to many stories written in this time, the parents are not in the background, but are an integral part of the story. They respect Ellen's individuality but expect her to behave responsibly and to show consideration for others. Although the time is not designated, the text, reinforced by the illustrations, suggests the early 1900s. Horse and buggy and trains are the modes of transportation. The dedication to the author's parents "in remembrance of those happy years when all of us were young" causes the reader to assume the story is autobiographical.

N122   BUFF, MARY and BUFF, CONRAD. The Big Tree. Illustrated by the authors. New York: Viking, 1946 (OP), 80 pp.
Information: science   Gr. 4-8

This is the story of the first five thousand years in the life of Wawona, a great sequoia tree. His antiquity is made believable by references to events occurring in other parts of the world during his lifetime: he was nearly eight hundred years old when the pyramids were being built in Egypt and three thousand years old when Jesus was born. Besides recounting the life history of the tree, the story also tells of the large and small animals and the birds that lived close to him. In latter years a gold prospector made his home in the fire hole of Wawona's trunk, lumbermen felled the trees around him, and men came who rejoiced that Wawona and others like him would be preserved in a National Park.

More than a dozen full-page duotone drawings communicate a sense of wonder at the majesty of the sequoia trees. Numerous smaller sketches of the animals and birds--skunks and squirrels, deer and bears, owls and eagles--add interest. These illustrations are lovely, and, like the redwoods themselves, are timeless. The writing style, however, no longer seems appropriate. At the time the book was published it was praised for having been written without undue personalization. Today, the authors' description of Wawona's panic and fear of fire, like many similar passages, seems overpersonalized and sentimental.

N123   MAXWELL, WILLIAM. The Heavenly Tenants. Illustrated by Ilonka Karasz. New York: Harper & Brothers, 1946 (OP), 57 pp.
Fantasy   Gr. 5-9

The April evening before the Marvell family leaves their Wisconsin farm for their annual visit to Grandmother in Virginia is a fine night for stars. In the alfalfa field, Mr. Marvell identifies constellations of the zodiac for his children: Roger, eleven; Heather, eight; and the five-year-old twins, Tim and Tom. They leave the next morning after chores not knowing that August, the man hired to look after the livestock in their absence, is laid up with rheumatism in his little shack across the marsh. The next night is a fine night for stars in Virginia and father brings down from the attic the telescope he had used as a boy. He sets it up and after peering through it for several minutes exclaims, "That's the queerest thing I ever heard of! . . . I can't find the Crab . . . it just isn't there."

That same night back in Wisconsin a neighbor of the Marvells is awakened by a bright light. He thinks his barn must be on fire, but the barn is safe. The light is coming from somewhere beyond the edge of his farm--"the Marvells' place," he concludes. He starts for the Marvells--he has no need to turn the car lights on; the closer he comes to the Marvells' farm the brighter everything grows: "The light was not white like daylight, nor red like firelight. It was like an unusually clear starlite night only ever so much brighter." When he arrives there he finds the house is shining as are the barn and crib. The light "a pure constant bluish silver" did not change, but persisted every night during the three weeks' absence of the Marvells. The night they return Mr. Marvell finds the Crab back in the sky again and remarks to his wife: "All the time we were in Virginia I couldn't find a single one of the constellations of the zodiac."

Where had the stars of the zodiac been for three weeks? Apparently looking after the Marvells' house and animals. Without realizing who they were, Old August had glimpsed them when he finally felt well enough to go to the farm. He saw a golden lion on top of the silo and thought it was a new weather vane; he saw two fish larger than a man; a boy with a silver arrow; a milk white bull and a ram and a goat in the pasture--he knew that none of these belonged to the Marvells. Mystified but reassured that things were being cared for, August had returned home.

The morning after their return, each of the Marvells finds something unusual. Mr. Marvell finds two shiny new pails in the barn with the mark of the Water Carrier on them; Roger finds a silver arrow; and the twins find their sand buckets filled with what looks like "sparks from father's emery wheel, or like the smallest stars in the sky." When they pour water over the sparks they turn to ashes. And soon everything is back to normal.

Although the story is based on a novel idea, it is not very convincing. Still, as a contemporary critic wrote, one is "left with a sense of the nearness of the heavens to earth" (A. C. Moore, Horn Book 22 [1946]:455).

N124   TEILHET, DARWIN [Cyrus Fisher]. The Avion My Uncle Flew. Illustrated by Richard Floethe. New York: Appleton-Century, 1946 (OP), 244 pp.

1947

Fiction   Gr. 5-8
    Jean Littlehorn, a thirteen-year-old boy from Wyoming, visits
his mother's old home in rural France a few months after the close
of World War II. While Jean's young Uncle Paul is working on a
glider invention, Jean plans to climb mountains to strengthen his
leg, which was injured in an accident, and learn his mother's native language. The summer turns out to be less quiet than anticipated. Jean makes friends with Charles and Suzanne Neilhac, who
know even fewer English words than Jean knows French. In spite
of the difficulty in communication, the three work together to
play an important role in apprehending a Nazi agent who is still
in the country masquerading as a Frenchman.
    The story has a tightly woven plot with each new incident aris-
ing naturally out of the preceding one and moving as the suspense
increases toward a natural and satisfying conclusion. The pace
is fast and some of the incidents are wildly funny. The mayor
hunting truffles with his trained pig affords a welcome respite
from more sinister events. Reinforcing the careful plotting is
the background. The author had firsthand knowledge of the country, and this knowledge has contributed to making the story believable. Cyrus Fisher actually took off in a glider from the
same mountain that his hero Jean did. Criticism might be directed
toward the author's use of such trite conventions of mystery stories as a buried treasure and a graveyard scene reminiscent of
Huck and Tom's visit to the graveyard. And perhaps the villain,
Monsieur Simonis, is too easily disposed of. When Jean takes off
in the Avion, Monsieur Simonis pursues him on foot, and, because
he is shouting and shooting at Jean, he does not observe that he
has come to the edge of a high cliff. In the main, however, the
author has succeeded in writing a mystery-adventure-spy story and
teaching French at the same time.

N125   JEWETT, ELEANORE M. The Hidden Treasure of Glaston. Illus-
          trated by Frederick T. Chapman. New York: Viking, 1946
          (OP), 307 pp.
          Fiction: historical   Gr. 5-8
    The setting is an English monastery, Glaston; the time is
1171-1172. The principal characters are two thirteen-year-old
boys, Hugh and Dickon. Dickon, who has lived at the monastery
since infancy, longs to go adventuring in the outside world.
Hugh is the only son of Sir Hugh de Morville, one of the four
knights who rode at Henry II's bidding to slay Thomas à Becket,
a deed that has occurred shortly before the story begins. When
Sir Hugh is forced to flee the country, he leaves his son at the
monastery.
    The two boys become fast friends and continue the exploration
begun by Dickon of old passages and caverns beneath the abbey
grounds. Among the treasures discovered in the underground

1947

chambers by the boys and also by Bleheris, a mad old hermit, is
the sword of King Arthur.

Bleheris's great desire is to find the Holy Grail which legends
have placed in the area of the monastery. At the climax, Bleheris,
good Brother John, and Hugh see the Grail. From that time Hugh
is cured of a limp.

At the end Sir Hugh, who is now a Knight-Templar at the Holy
Sepulcher in Jerusalem, returns for his son. But it is Dickon,
not Hugh, who goes with him as a squire. Hugh remains at the
monastery to rewrite The Book of the Holy Grail, Glaston's most
treasured book, destroyed recently in a Great Fire. As a scribe,
Hugh had read all the stories and is the only person who can write
the book again.

In a note the author states that the details of the setting
are "as authentic as a good deal of research can verify." She
has used these details to create a warmly human picture of life
in an English monastery during the Middle Ages. She has also
skillfully blended in the legends of the Holy Grail that have
persisted in tradition.

1948

N126   Du BOIS, WILLIAM PÈNE. The Twenty-One Balloons. Illustrated
        by the author. New York: Viking, 1947, 180 pp.
        Fantasy   Gr. 5-9
Professor William Waterman Sherman's incredible adventure began
in the fall of 1883 after his retirement from teaching mathematics
for forty years in a San Francisco boys' school. In The Globe, a
huge balloon, well-provisioned with food, he started out over the
Pacific with the idea of floating around wherever the wind blew
him for a year. The adventure ended three weeks later when he
was picked up by a freighter in the Atlantic, clinging to a
wrecked platform to which twenty deflated balloons were attached.
When he was rescued, he refused to reveal anything but his name,
saying he would disclose his unusual adventures first to the
Western American Explorers' Club of San Francisco of which he
was an honorary member.

The tale he told the club comprises most of the book. On the
seventh day aloft, a seagull punctured his balloon and he was
forced down on Krakatoa, a small volcanic island, presumably un-
occupied. He found the island not only inhabited, but by the rich-
est people in the world, twenty families consisting of parents
and a boy and girl, all originally from San Francisco. In the
few days he was on the island, the Professor learned of the
source of their wealth: fabulous diamond mines located at the
base of the volcanic mountain. He was fascinated by the Gourmet
Government the Krakatoans had developed and impressed with their
architectural accomplishments and ingenious inventions.

Then, on the fourth day, the earth began to tremble violently. Sensing that an explosion was imminent, the Krakatoans hastily evacuated the island on the giant balloon raft lifted by twenty balloons. As they passed over India nineteen of the families left the raft to float to earth in their family parachutes. Because Professor Sherman had no parachute, it was decided he should land the raft over a large body of water. One family remained with him until he found a suitable place to go down. For nine days they traveled--all the way across Europe--without seeing a large body of water. When they sighted the English Channel, the last family dropped to earth in Belgium. The Professor passed over England and Scotland to land in the Atlantic.

The story is built around an actual place and event: Krakatoa is a volcanic island in the Pacific, and, Mr. Du Bois states that it did blow up with the biggest explosion of all time. It is firmly rooted in reality in other ways as well. There are accurate and detailed descriptions of Professor Sherman's balloon and his flight to the island. A very human greedy desire for the diamonds was an obstacle to the establishment of the Utopia on the island. The boundaries needed to give a total conception of the utopian restaurant government are well-defined, and, combined with the mass of details concerning life on the island, inspire credibility. The mechanical inventions of the Krakatoans not only add to reality, but are the primary manifestation of Du Bois's playful fancy: the airy-go-round, the giant balloon life raft, and, best of all, the Moroccan house of marvels with its electrified couches and chairs, continuous sheets, and elevator beds. The whole story is told with a humor and gusto that is expressed also in the author's magnificent illustrations.

N127   BISHOP, CLAIRE HUCHET. Pancakes-Paris. Illustrated by
        Georges Schreiber. New York: Viking, 1947 (OP), 62 pp.
        Fiction   Gr. 3-6
        The story takes place in Paris a few months after World War
II has ended while there is still a meager supply of civilian goods. Two American soldiers in a jeep give ten-year-old Charles a box of pancake mix, in return for giving them directions. The pancake mix becomes the foundation of a gala Mardi Gras celebration.

In spite of a background of poverty and sadness, the celebration is genuine because that is the way children are--they make the most of whatever good thing comes along. Mrs. Bishop knows this; and although she has made the story gay and brave, it is never sentimental. The author is a native of France married to an American. She wrote Pancakes-Paris out of her knowledge and feeling for a France which had just endured seven years of war.

N128   TREFFINGER, CAROLYN. Li Lun, Lad of Courage. Illustrated by
        Kurt Wiese. Nashville: Abingdon-Cokesbury, 1947 (OP),
        96 pp.

1948

Fiction   Gr. 4-7
Li Lun, a Chinese boy, proves himself, not by going off to sea
alone, as Mafatu of <u>Call It Courage</u> did, but by going to the top
of an arid mountain and there raising rice. The task is given
him by his angry father when fearful Li Lun refused to go on the
"man-making" fishing trip with his father and the other boys of
his age and their fathers. Li Lun completes the task and, in the
temple ceremony at which his accomplishment is made known, the
Good One announces that Li Lun shall teach others to grow rice
so that they no longer need bring it across the sea from the mainland as they have done for many years.

The story is economically and dramatically told. Li Lun's
achievement may appear less heroic than Mafatu's, but it is in
some ways more difficult and certainly more realistic. Circumstances force Mafatu to become brave or die, but Li Lun carries
out his task in sight of home. He can see the village from the
mountain top. A less resolute lad would have gone home long
before the end of the 120 days needed for the maturing of the
rice. He shows patience and resourcefulness as he outwits the
gulls and rats, and finds the water that is essential to ensure
a crop. Interesting customs are revealed, but they are an integral part of the story as when Li Lun's mother gives him dragon
bones to take as an antidote for fear. The illustrations are excellent. Each of the twelve chapters has at least one full-page
picture--in black, white, and green--and several smaller ones.

N129   BESTERMAN, CATHERINE. <u>The Quaint and Curious Quest of Johnny</u>
       <u>Longfoot, the Shoe-King's Son</u>. Illustrated by Warren
       Chappell. Indianapolis: Bobbs Merrill, 1947 (OP), 147 pp.
       Folk Tale   Gr. 3-5
This vigorous and humorous tale, filled with marvelous events,
is an expansion of an old Polish folk tale. Johnny's quest takes
him to Coral Island to get the seven-league boots for Barnac the
cat. His side adventures include giving dancing lessons to bears,
stitching the shark's and whale's skins, and being blown across
the ocean on a giant kite.

Johnny is quick-witted, resourceful, and, above all, kind. On
the trip his miserly Uncle Lucas--so miserly at the beginning that
he saves tears and uses them as a substitute for salt--learns that
money does not always mean happiness, and that a kind and brave
heart is worth more than all the jewels in the world. The illustrations suit the imaginative story.

N130   COURLANDER, HAROLD, and HERZOG, GEORGE. <u>The Cow-tail Switch,</u>
       <u>and Other West African Stories</u>. Illustrated by Madye Lee
       Chastain. New York: H. Holt, 1947 (OP), 143 pp.
       Folk Tales   Gr. 3-8
These seventeen stories which had not previously appeared in
collections were gathered in West Africa where they have been

told by the inhabitants for generations. A section of notes
gives the source of each tale and explains its significance to
the Africans. Included are talking animal tales; realistic stories of kings, rich men, and simple people; and origin stories.
One of the latter explains why the frog has flattened hands; another relates how debt came to the Ashanti. There are two stories about the trickster figure, Anansi, who is portrayed as a
human character. Trickery combined with humor is present in
several of the animal tales as well.

The stories are told in simple, direct language. Decorative
black and white drawings are authentic in detail.

N131   HENRY, MARGUERITE. <u>Misty of Chincoteague</u>. Illustrated by
       Wesley Dennis. Chicago: Rand McNally, 1947, 173 pp.
       Fiction   Gr. 3-6

Maureen and Paul, about ten and eleven, live with Grandma and
Grandpa Beebe on Chincoteague Island off the coast of Virginia.
A short distance away on the sea side of Chincoteague lies
Assateague Island, a wildlife refuge for birds and wild ponies.
Each year, on Pony Penning Day, the Assateague pony herds are
rounded up and swum across to Chincoteague. There the foals are
separated from the mares and sold for funds to support the island's fire department. Selling some of the young ponies prevents overpopulation of the outer island.

Maureen and Paul do all kinds of work to earn enough money to
buy a pony. Their dream is to become the owners of the Phantom,
a wild, fast three-year-old pony that has always escaped the
roundup. On Pony Penning Day, Paul goes on the roundup for the
first time and finds the Phantom, with a young foal he names
Misty. After an initial disappointment, the children become the
owners of the Phantom and Misty. The colt becomes tame at once,
but, though the Phantom is responsive to the children, she remains somewhat wild. The children train Phantom and the following year she wins the great race. A short time later, while Paul
is riding her on the beach, the stallion, the Pied Piper, swims
across from Assateague. Paul gives Phantom her freedom and she
returns to the outer island with her mate.

Legend says that the wild ponies of Assateague are descendants
of a boatload of Spanish horses wrecked off the island during the
seventeenth century. The author states that the characters are
based on real-life inhabitants of Chincoteague Island and the
incidents reflect actual events. The roundup of the ponies and
swimming them across to Chincoteague, and the race won by the
Phantom are exciting episodes. Also dramatic and realistic is
the Pied Piper's coming to get the Phantom; Misty's staying with
the children is fitting, too. The story is strengthened by lively
illustrations full of movement.

1949

N132   HENRY, MARGUERITE. <u>King of the Wind</u>. Illustrated by Wesley
       Dennis. Chicago: Rand McNally, 1948, 175 pp.
       Fiction   Gr. 3-8

Agba, a mute horseboy in the stables of an eighteenth-century
sultan of Morocco, promises a motherless baby colt, Sham, that
multitudes will bow before him and he will be King of the Wind.
Agba is convinced this will be so because Sham was born with a
white spot, an emblem of swiftness. But he was born, too, with
a wheat ear, a symbol of misfortune. The prophecies of both
markings are fulfilled. When Sham is two years old, Agba is
sent with him and five other stallions and horseboys to France
as a gift to the boy king, Louis XV.

Even before they arrive, the bad luck begins to manifest itself. During the next two years both Agba and Sham are treated
badly, first in France and later in England. Finally, the two,
and a cat, Grimalkin, that has attached himself to them, are
given a home in the stables of the Earl of Godolphin. When Agba
permits Sham to mate with the Lady Roxana, intended mate of the
mighty stallion Hobgoblin, the three are banished to Wicken Fen.

After two years they are brought back when it is found that
Lath, Roxana's unwanted colt by Sham, can run faster than any of
the other two-year-olds in the stable. Sham, now known as the
Godolphin Arabian, becomes the favored stallion. The following
year his son Cade is born and, the year after, Regulus. When
Regulus is two, Sham's three sons, on successive days, win races
at Newmarket. On the third day, when Lath races for the Queen's
Plate, Sham with Agba on his back stands at a place of honor
directly opposite the King and Queen. That day Agba feels he
has kept his promise to Sham.

The story of the Godolphin Arabian, an ancestor of Man o' War
and of many other superior thoroughbreds, is exciting. Equally
memorable is the moving character of Agba, the intensely dramatic
incidents, the fully realized historical backgrounds, and the
beautiful illustrations entirely in sympathy with the story.

N133   HOLLING, HOLLING C. <u>Seabird</u>. Illustrated by the author.
       Boston: Houghton Mifflin, 1948, 63 pp.
       Information: geography and history   Gr. 4-7

Seabird is a gull carved by fourteen-year-old Ezra Brown in
1832 from two walrus tusks during his first trip aboard a New
Bedford whaler. This ivory gull becomes the mascot for the seafaring Brown family, whose experiences all over the globe are
recorded for four generations. Ezra attaches Seabird's body to
a limber stalk of whalebone and keeps it with him at sea until,
years later, his son, Nathaniel, is born. Then he fastens it
above Nate's cradle, where it appears to fly, as it later flies

over the cradles of his grandson and great-grandson. When Nate grows up, he and his father sail as captains of clipper ships to the fabled cities of the world. Seabird voyages, too. Nate's son, James, does not become a captain, but a great designer of steamships. In the year that Ezra is one hundred years old, James's son, Ken, is born. Ken grows up to fly an airship with Seabird soaring with him.

An attractive full-page, full-color illustration faces each page of text, which is itself edged with detailed marginal drawings. These illustrations give the book distinction and provide a panoramic record of change during a century in the lives of the Brown family.

N134   RANKIN, LOUISE. Daughter of the Mountains. Illustrated by
          Kurt Wiese. New York: Viking, 1948 (OP), 191 pp.
          Fiction   Gr. 4-6
   Momo, a little Tibetan girl, desires more than anything else in the world a red-gold Lhasa terrier. Over and over she prays to Buddha for it. At length her prayer is answered. The leader of one of the mule trains that stops at her mother's tea house in the Tibetan mountains gives her a puppy. Pempa, the name she gives her puppy, is a beautiful two-year-old when a trader steals him. As soon as Momo discovers he is gone, she goes after him on foot. Her quest takes her from the high mountains down the Great Trade Route to Calcutta. Stout of heart, she is confident that she will accomplish her mission because she is guided and cared for by Buddha, the Blessed One. In Calcutta, Lady Paton, Pempa's new owner, who did not know he was stolen, returns him to her. This kind lady also helps Momo's father obtain a better job, thus fulfilling the astrologer's prophecy that Momo and Pempa would go through many adventures and that the dog would bring fortune to all of Momo's family.

   Even though the author has included some information that is interesting in itself but not really essential to the story, and the circumstances under which she finds Pempa are somewhat too fortuitous, still the reader is so involved and concerned that Momo get her pet back that these seem too minor to dwell on. The rapidity with which events occur as Momo plunges down the mountains, the exotic setting, and the fully delineated character of Momo combine to make her story notable. There is an abundance of well-done black and white drawings.

N135   GANNETT, RUTH STILES. My Father's Dragon. Illustrated by
          Ruth Chrisman Gannett. New York: Random House, 1948,
          87 pp.
          Fantasy   Gr. 1-4
   Young Elmer Elevator, supposedly the author's father, meets a well-traveled alley cat who tells him about a baby dragon held in

1949

captivity on Wild Island. Mean jungle animals force him to provide flying ferry service across the river there. Resolving to
rescue the dragon who, he is told, has blue and yellow stripes
and gold-covered wings, Elmer stows away in the hold of a grain
boat and sails to Tangerina Island, which is connected to Wild
Island by a long line of ocean rocks. It takes Elmer seven hours
to cross the rocks. On the island, while searching for the dragon,
Elmer encounters in turn seven tigers, a rhinoceros, a lion, and
a gorilla. Each one threatens to eat him, but Elmer's ingenuity
saves him: for instance, he placates the fierce rhinoceros, who
impales him by the seat of his pants on his tusk, by giving him
a toothbrush and paste to use on his yellow-gray tusk, which was
formerly pearly white. With the inducement of lollipops Elmer
persuades the crocodiles to form themselves into a bridge over
the river. On the other side he finds the baby dragon, cuts the
rope that holds him, and they fly off to the safety of Tangerina
where they intend to spend the night before starting the long
journey home.
   The events of this fantastic story seem perfectly plausible.
Elmer has no trouble communicating with the animals because they
speak a common language. The illustrations bring out the humorous and original details of the story and the endpapers, containing maps of Tangerina and Wild Island, further promote belief.

N136   BONTEMPS, ARNA. The Story of the Negro. Illustrated by
          Raymond Lufkin. New York: A. A. Knopf, 1948, 239 pp.
          Information: history   Gr. 5 up
   Langston Hughes's beautiful, dignified, and moving poem "The
Negro Speaks of Rivers," printed immediately after the title page,
establishes the tone for this objective and absorbing history of
the Negro people. As the life of the Negro in the West Indies
and the United States is depicted--in the days of bondage and
since--both celebrated and less well-known leaders are introduced.
In background chapters, the author presents several African tribes,
noting that there are more kinds of people, with greater differences,
in Africa than in Europe. He relates the story of human slavery
in the world previous to modern times and describes the new people
that resulted from the introduction of the Africans into Latin
America, the Caribbean region, and the United States. A twenty
page chronology parallels events in the story of the Negro with
events in world history. There is also an index. Interesting
half-page black and white drawings at the beginning of each chapter portray a scene or person from the chapter.
   Mr. Bontemps's well-written book is considered the first important history of his people for young people. In the fifth edition
the chronicle was extended to 1970.

1950

N137   De ANGELI, MARGUERITE. The Door in the Wall. Illustrated by
        the author. Garden City, N.Y.: Doubleday, 1949, 121 pp.
        Fiction: historical   Gr. 3-6
    Young Robin, the son of Sir John de Bureford and Lady Maud, is
left in his London home in the care of servants when his father
goes with King Edward III on a campaign against the Scots and his
mother goes to the Queen as a lady-in-waiting. At the time of
their departure, Robin expects to leave soon to become a page to
Sir Peter de Lindsay, whose castle is close to the Welsh border.
Before the time of departure, he becomes ill with an unnamed dis-
ease and loses the use of his legs. When the servants sicken
with the plague, which is raging in London, Robin is taken by
Brother Luke to St. Marks, the hospice he serves.
    There, as he is advised by Brother Luke, Robin begins to find
doors in the wall: he learns to carve in wood, to read, to write,
and to swim, an activity he can do well even with his weakened
legs. When he is strong enough, Robin and Brother Luke, accompanied by a minstrel, John-go-in-the-Wynd, travel to Sir Peter's
castle. Sir Peter, like Brother Luke, talks of doors: "Each of
us has his place in the world. . . . If we cannot serve in one
way, there is always another. If we do what we are able, a door
always opens to something else."
    Although Robin longs to see his parents, he is happy with Sir
Peter and his family. In late autumn the Welsh lay siege to the
castle. Under the cover of fog, Robin, with his crutches strapped
to his back, swims the river and reaches John-go-in-the-Wynd who
summons aid from a neighboring lord and his men. On the afternoon of Christmas Eve day, the King, Queen, knights, and ladies,
including Robin's parents, arrive at the castle. During the
happy reunion festivities, Robin is knighted by the king.
    The theme is well developed, although the events through which
it is disclosed are somewhat predictable. Aspects of life in
fourteenth-century England are revealed in both text and illustrations in black and white and lavish color. The costumes and
castles are especially enchanting. Archaic language is used
sparingly.

N138   CAUDILL, REBECCA. Tree of Freedom. Illustrated by Dorothy B.
        Morse. New York: Viking, 1949 (OP), 279 pp.
        Fiction: historical   Gr. 5-9
    In the spring of 1780, Jonathan and Bertha Venable and their
children travel from North Carolina over the mountains to Harrod's
Fort, Kentucky, to homestead in the wilderness. Told from the
point of view of Stephanie, thirteen, the story recounts the
journey and the first three or four months in the new country.
In spite of the fear of Indian raids and the worry that the

111

1950

ownership of their land may be contested before it is verified
in December, the family builds a cabin and plants a small crop.
    The war with Britain extends even into the backwoods and
Jonathan Venable is sent as a courier to Governor Jefferson in
Williamsburg. Noel, seventeen, goes across the Ohio with Colonel
George Rogers Clark on an expedition against the Indians. While
they are gone, Mother, Stephanie, and the younger children busy
themselves with a variety of tasks--they girdle trees, make hominy, and chink the whole cabin, and Stephanie tends her tree of
freedom, a little apple tree that she has grown from the seed
she brought from her old home. At the end, the family is reunited, new neighbors come, and Stephanie and Noel make plans to
return to the east for schooling. Stephanie wants to master the
skills needed to become a schoolteacher in Kentucky and Noel
wants to study law.
    A native of Kentucky, the author knows well the setting of
which she writes. Many pioneer stories recreate the daily life
as does this one. In addition, it defines clearly, in terms of
the characters, the national issues of the times.

N139   COBLENTZ, CATHERINE CATE. The Blue Cat of Castle Town.
        Illustrated by Janice Holland. New York: Longmans, Green,
        1949, 123 pp.
        Legend   Gr. 4-9
    Based on true happenings in Castle Town, Vermont, the story is
fashioned around the theme of singing one's own song. All of
those craftsmen of early Vermont who sang their own song created
beauty in their work and gained peace and contentment: Ebenezer
Southmayd, the pewterer, in his pewterware; John Gilroy, the
weaver, in twin white linen tablecloths; Thomas Royal Dake, the
carpenter, in the pulpit that came to be known as the most beautiful in the state of Vermont; and Zeruah Guernsey, a girl, in
a carpet so beautiful and unusual that it now hangs in the Metropolitan Museum of Art. Among the designs on the carpet is a fascinating blue cat. According to legend, the cat enables Castle
Town to sing its own song.

N140   MONTGOMERY, RUTHERFORD. Kildee House. Illustrated by Barbara
        Cooney. Garden City, N.Y.: Doubleday, 1949 (OP), 209 pp.
        Fiction   Gr. 3-7
    Jerome Kildee, a diffident bachelor, retires to a hundred
acres of redwood forest, expecting to live out his days as a
hermit. In his small house, built so that a giant redwood makes
the back wall, he finds a fuller life than he has ever had before. The animals that move in with him: the raccoons--Old
Grouch, his slim wife, their offspring--and Papa and Mama Skunk
and their children, are not personified, but they delight with
their distinctive animal ways. Kildee's young friend, Emmy Lou

Eppy, one of the nine Eppys who have come from West Virginia, contributes to the humor and helps to keep the action lively. Although it is treated humorously, the problem of overpopulation · is touched on when Jerome and Emmy Lou compute how many skunks and raccoons Jerome will have in one year--and in two years--if they continue to reproduce at the present rate. Although this is essentially a cheerful book there are some incidents in which animals are the victims of other animals and also of man and his hunting dogs. The illustrations are amusing and appealing.

N141   FOSTER, GENEVIEVE. George Washington. Illustrated by the
        author. New York: Charles Scribner's Sons, 1949 (OP),
        93 pp.
        Biography   Gr. 3-6
    Described on the title page as an "initial biography," the book is intended as a child's first book about Washington. The story begins with George's birth and ends with his death which is very briefly described. Simply written, it covers all periods of his life: his childhood, the teen-age years spent with Lawrence at Mount Vernon, his surveying experiences as a young man, his participation in the French and Indian War, the years spent as a gentleman farmer at Mount Vernon before the Revolutionary War, and his great public roles as Commander-in-Chief and first president.

    Washington's youth is recounted in somewhat greater detail than the later years. While there is a small amount of fictionalizing, quotations from diaries and letters written by Washington and by his contemporaries reassure the reader as to authenticity. They also contribute immediacy and promote a sense of intimacy between the subject and the reader. For example, the journal George kept when he went as a surveyor into the western wilderness soon after his sixteenth birthday reveals that his bed in a settler's cabin was "nothing but a little straw matted together without sheets or anything else but one thread Bear blanket with double its weight of Lice and Fleas." The author's double-page illustrations in sepia and aqua explain and add to the text.

N142   HAVIGHURST, WALTER and HAVIGHURST, MARION. Song of the
        Pines: A Story of Norwegian Lumbering in Wisconsin.
        Illustrated by Richard Floethe. Philadelphia: J. C.
        Winston, 1949 (OP), 205 pp.
        Fiction: historical   Gr. 9-11
    In the 1850s, orphaned Nils Thorson, fifteen, boards a sailing vessel in his native Norway to work his way to America. He takes with him his only possession of value, a grindstone. On the same vessel are other Norwegian immigrants and Nils is virtually adopted by the Svendsen family: Mother; Father; Kristen, fifteen; Helvor, eleven; and Lisa, five. From New York City, Nils

1950

and the Svendsens travel up the Hudson River, through the Erie
Canal, and across Lakes Erie, Huron, and Michigan to the
Koshkonong Lake area in southern Wisconsin. There they take
up land, build a cabin, plant a crop, and soon, listening to
the wind sigh through the pines, feel more at home than Kristen
had ever believed possible. At times when he is not needed on
the farm, Nils takes his grindstone and goes out through Wisconsin
seeking his fortune. During the winter he goes into the newly
opened lumber camps. There he sees the men handling the logs
with crowbars and recalls that in Norway the lumber was handled
with cant hooks. He soon has a thriving trade making hooks for
the lumbermen. When he returns to the family to help with spring
plowing, he finds them happily awaiting the arrival of a set of
grandparents from Norway.

Song of the Pines is one of a series of junior historical
novels about people who emigrated to America. Each book tells
the story of a national group and the contributions it made.
This story does that well. It describes accurately the life of
the Norwegians, but the reader does not truly experience it. The
characters never come alive and the plot is contrived and full of
coincidence. Several of the episodes are almost stock for pioneer stories: someone tries to claim the land they have chosen,
and Nils is able to substantiate the Svendsens' claim; the mother
removes a locust thorn from the hand of the Indian, Red Otter,
who repays his debt by rescuing her lost child. Hardships are
implied, yet the family prospers and expects to pay for their
farm with their first year's crop. Although not every contemporary reviewer praised the book, most did. The Newbery Committee
also found it worthy of recognition.

1951

N143   YATES, ELIZABETH. Amos Fortune, Free Man. Illustrated by
         Nora S. Unwin. New York: Alladin, 1950, 181 pp.
         Biography   Gr. 4-8
    Born in Africa the son of a chief, Amos (At-mun) was brought
on a slave ship to Boston in 1725 when he was fifteen. His first
owner was Caleb Copeland, a Quaker, who treated him like one of
the family. In his household, Amos learned to work and read and
adopted Christianity. After several years Mr. Copeland spoke of
manumission, but Amos said he did not want it yet. When Amos was
about thirty, Mr. Copeland died leaving debts. Amos told Mrs.
Copeland that she should sell him. He was bought by Mr. Richard-
son, a tanner, of Woburn, Massachusetts. Amos learned leather-
tanning and finally in 1769, when he was nearly sixty, bought his
own freedom. Subsequently, he established a tanning business that
prospered. He lived until the age of ninety-one, becoming a

1951

respected man of property in New Hampshire and buying the freedom of others, including that of his three wives.

The author, a resident of the area in which Amos Fortune spent his last years, made good use of the few records available to her: the document Amos received when he bought the freedom of his second wife, Lydia; the notation in the church register in 1779 recording his marriage to his third wife, Violet; the inscriptions on his gravestone and Violet's. She immersed herself in the period and brought her characters to life against an authentic background.

N144   HUNT, MABEL LEIGH. Better Known as Johnny Appleseed. Illustrated by James Daugherty. Philadelphia: J. B. Lippincott, 1950, 212 pp.

Biography   Gr. 6 up

"In the rich beautiful country of Ohio and Indiana," writes Louis Bromfield in a foreword to the book, "there has been growing for more than a century a legend not very different from that of St. Francis of Assisi. It concerns a humble man regarded in his day as an eccentric, but a man who was universally loved in the frontier wilderness country by Indians and white settlers alike." Using both the known facts and legends--many based on personal reminiscences recorded in county histories--the author has recreated the life of that man, John Chapman, "better known as Johnny Appleseed."

The first section tells of his birth in Massachusetts in 1774, his boyhood there, and his setting forth for the west when he was eighteen. Shortly before 1800 he left western Pennsylvania where he had worked as an orchardist and entered the Ohio country with a bag of appleseeds. His intention was to plant the seeds in the new wild land so that the pioneers would have apples when they came. Besides his precious seeds he carried healing herbs, Swedenborgian tracts, and a bag of stories.

The second section, comprising more than half the book, contains nine stories that are based on fact and tradition. The first of these tales, titled like the others for an apple of Johnny's day, is set in western Pennsylvania; the next six are set in Ohio; the eighth in Indiana; and the last in Illinois. The final short section covers his latter years and death.

Johnny, the people he met, and the country with which he became so familiar all come alive in this pleasant, well-written book. A map of the Ohio country permits the reader to trace Johnny's travels.

N145   EATON, JEANETTE. Gandhi: Fighter without a Sword. Illustrated by Ralph Ray. New York: Morrow, 1950 (OP), 253 pp.

Biography   Gr. 6-11

1951

A swift-moving, fictionalized account of the life of Mohandas K. Gandhi (1869-1948), India's revered leader, called by his countrymen Mahatma, meaning "Great Soul." The story opens when he is a high school boy of fifteen but already married for two years. It covers his life from that time forward: his college years in England, the twenty-one years he spent in South Africa working to overcome prejudice against Indians there, and the more than thirty years he strove in India for the well-being of his people and for their political freedom from Britain. The book details many incidents showing his adherence to nonviolent resistance against oppression. Indian freedom, ending two hundred years of foreign rule, came in 1947. Even though one of the great goals of his life had been realized, Gandhi was saddened by the partition of India into the two nations of India and Pakistan. The following year, while walking to the evening prayer service, he was assassinated by a young Hindu fanatic.

Gandhi's character is vividly depicted in this biography and his beliefs are clearly explained. The book contains no footnotes, index, or bibliography. The author, in an acknowledgment, thanks a lecturer in history and world politics for reading and criticizing the manuscript. The black and white illustrations reflect the spirit of the book.

N146   JUDSON, CLARA INGRAM. Abraham Lincoln, Friend of the People. Illustrated with drawings by Robert Frankenberg and Kodachromes of the Chicago Historical Society Lincoln Dioramas. Chicago: Wilcox & Follett, 1950 (OP), 206 pp.
Biography   Gr. 4-8

Clara Judson's readable and satisfying biography of Lincoln opens in 1813, when Abe is a lad of four on the Knob Creek farm in Kentucky, and closes with his assassination. In preparation for writing the book Mrs. Judson read more than two hundred books and consulted many more to verify details; she also traveled to Lincoln's various homes in Kentucky, Indiana, and Illinois. She chronicles the events of his life against an accurate background of the times. To dramatize a situation, she occasionally uses invented dialogue, especially in the early sections of the book. Later, she makes good use of newspapers, telegrams, and Lincoln's speeches. The fourteen colored plates taken from the Lincoln dioramas add an extra dimension of reality to Lincoln's story. The subtitle, "Friend of the People," serves as the theme.

N147   PARRISH, ANNE. The Story of Appleby Capple. Illustrated by the author. New York: Harper, 1950 (OP), 84 pp.
Fantasy   Gr. 1-3

Five-year-old Appleby Capple's story is told in a complex and ingenious ABC book. The reader meets Appleby, Apple, for short, in the first chapter on his way to have tea with his Aunt Bella and celebrate his Cousin Clement's ninety-ninth birthday. Apple

is troubled because he does not yet have a birthday present for
Cousin Clement. What Cousin Clement likes best in the whole world
is painting butterflies in watercolors, and, although he has
painted dozens of varieties, he has never painted a Zebra, and
that has become the wish of his life. Young Apple hopes to find
a Zebra and give it to Cousin Clement for his birthday. He does,
eventually, but there are many complications on the way.

Each of the twenty-six chapters is devoted to a letter of the
alphabet. Chapter B, for example, introduces Aunt Bella and
uses the letter B over and over:

> Aunt Bella has baked a beautiful birthday
> cake. . . . Aunt Bella brings in the Birth-
> day Cake. Brioche, butter-balls, and a tea-
> pot painted with a Blue Chinaman are on the
> table. Aunt Bella's bulb is blooming, and
> her bird in his bird-cage bursts into song.

Miss Parrish's alliterative ability never flags, but the fact
that this is an alphabet book becomes secondary as the reader's
involvement in the story increases. Plot complications develop
quite naturally. Apple becomes lost and his zany relatives and
friends seek him: absent-minded Uncle Francis; Cousin Kate with
the tremendous voice and colorful wool wigs; Mr. Perkins, the
Postman; Squaw Prickly Pear and Pinkfeather; and others. To add
to the confusion, the elephant at the zoo escapes from his cage,
frees all the other animals, and they throng to the woods where
Apple is lost. As a culmination, on the day Apple gets back
with the Zebra butterfly, Great Uncle Thomas arrives home from
one of his voyages bringing, as is his custom, quantities of
souvenirs, plus a Terrible Turk and a Smiling Sultan. Detailed
Victorian drawings, on which the author spent a year, add to the
merriment of the story.

1952

N148   ESTES, ELEANOR. Ginger Pye. Illustrated by the author. New
        York: Harcourt, Brace, 1951, 250 pp.
        Fiction   Gr. 3-6
    Ten-year-old Jerry Pye and nine-year-old Rachel Pye live in
Cranbury, Connecticut, with their pretty young mother, their
father, a famous ornithologist with little money, and Gracie-the-
cat. Gramma, Grampa, and three-year-old Uncle Bennie live only
a few streets away. The time is around 1920.

    With the dollar he earns dusting the church pews, Jerry buys
a little brown and white puppy which they name Ginger. School
begins the next day, but Ginger is such a smart pup that before
long he follows Jerry's scent to school and climbs the fire escape with a pencil of Jerry's he has found on the way.

1952

Then, on Thanksgiving Day, Ginger disappears. Heartbroken, the children search everyplace. They remember seeing someone in a mustard-colored hat apparently running away from them the afternoon they got Ginger, and that very night mysterious footsteps followed them home. They recall these incidents and one or two other times when they glimpsed the yellow hat--once outside their back fence--and conclude Ginger has been stolen by the man in the yellow hat, whom they dub "Unsavory."

For months Jerry and Rachel follow up all likely and unlikely clues in their seemingly fruitless search for Ginger. When spring comes, they search in faraway and hard places--they climb the Giant Steps up East Rock and search the vicinity of Judge's Cave on West Rock. On May 29, Jerry's birthday, through the astuteness of Uncle Bennie, they get Ginger back. At the same time, the mystery linking the man in the yellow hat to Ginger's disappearance is solved.

Although the affection of the children for their pet and their pain at his loss are very real, the book as a whole is less interesting than the author's earlier stories about the Moffats, who are contemporaries of the Pyes, although not known to them personally. The whole mystery about Ginger seems contrived, especially as it involves Wally Bullwinkle, a boy in Jerry's class.

Although the story is well written and often amusing, the use of flashbacks of memory is excessive. For example, while Rachel is climbing East Rock and thinking that she is not in the least afraid, she recalls an instance when she was afraid while climbing. That time she and Jerry and Dick Badger had been climbing to the top of Dick's barn and jumping off into a pile of old hay. The details of the incident--including not only what Rachel did, but how she thought and felt--are related in full and cover a page and a half. While the flashbacks help to characterize, they have the disadvantage of slowing the pace of the story. Sometimes, as the character's mind bounces from one related subject to another, the immediate situation is nearly forgotten. Perhaps the author received the award for the book as recompense for not having received it for any of the Moffat books. The Middle Moffat and Rufus M were Honor Books.

N149   BAITY, ELIZABETH CHESLEY. Americans before Columbus. Illustrated by C. B. Falls and with photographs. New York: Viking, 1951, 256 pp.
Information: history   Gr. 5 up
Preceding the text of this interesting account of life in America before Columbus are maps of North America and South America showing the distribution of the principal pre-Columbian Indian cultures and thirty-nine photographs of Indian arts and architecture. The many drawings scattered throughout the text help to re-create the life described. A poem precedes each chapter. All

the Indian cultures, from that of the wandering ice-age Americans to those in existence when Columbus came, are included. In several chapters an imaginary scene or story describing life in the culture follows a discussion of the archaeological remains. One such story tells of the discovery of maize, the event which made possible the growth of the great Indian civilizations. Another portrays life as lived by the Mound builders in Central America in the eleventh century. Still another describes the Mayan city of Chichen Itza as it would have been at the time of William the Conqueror's conquest of England in 1066. The epilogue suggests the reasons why even the great Indian states of Central and South America fell to the handful of Spanish invaders. Glossary, suggested readings, and index add to the usefulness of this well-written, readable book. Among the many acknowledgments are several to anthropologists for help in choosing and authenticating anthropological materials.

N150   HOLLING, HOLLING C. Minn of the Mississippi. Illustrated by
       the author. Boston: Houghton Mifflin, 1951, 87 pp.
       Information: science, geography, history   Gr. 3-8
    Minn, a snapping turtle, hatches far up north in Minnesota where the Mississippi begins. In this fictionalized account, an Indian boy who finds her paints MINN on her back--for Minnesota and because Minn is Indian for water--and returns her to the headwaters of the Mississippi. The story follows Minn for twenty-five years as she is carried the 2,552 miles down the river to the Gulf of Mexico. Into Minn's story the author weaves the saga of the Mississippi River--its legends and history, geography, and natural science.
    Mr. Holling uses animated language in his clear and straightforward explanations. Minn is not personalized, but the reader feels as if he knows her well. Twenty brilliant full-page colored pictures (the book is folio-sized) and hundreds of marginal drawings of birds, prehistoric animals, boats, and maps provide additional information and beauty. Although there is no bibliography, two pages of acknowledgments and the author's reputation for accuracy and thoroughness attest that an enormous amount of research went into the book.

N151   KALASHNIKOFF, NICHOLAS. The Defender. Illustrated by Claire
       Louden and George Louden. New York: Charles Scribner's
       Sons, 1951 (OP), 136 pp.
       Fiction   Gr. 4-8
    The Lamut, Turgen, lives alone high in the hills of northeastern Siberia with only a herd of wild mountain rams for friends. A vigorous but lonely man of middle years, he is shunned by all his Yakut neighbors in the valley below except a poor widow, Marfa, and her two children, son Tim and daughter Aksa. In

1952

former times, before the Shamanist turned them against him,
Turgen had the liking and trust of his neighbors. Because the
Shamanist was jealous of Turgen's knowledge of medicine, he dis-
credited him by maintaining that Turgen's friendship for the rams
was evidence that Turgen had bound himself to the devil. As the
chronicle unfolds, the reader learns how the mountain rams had
become a part of Turgen's life and about the relationship with
Marfa and her family over a period of four years. At the end of
that time, the Great Spirit visits Turgen in a dream. In reply
to Turgen's question of who will look after the rams after his
death, the Great Spirit suggests he ask Marfa and her children
to share his yurta. Marfa accepts and his marriage to her, in
addition to the overt goodwill of a much-respected merchant, convince the people that Turgen is not a sorcerer as the Shamanist
has said. Tim, now Turgen's stepson, promises to defend the rams
after Turgen, the defender, is gone.

The life of these remote people is revealed, but not at the
expense of the characters or theme. Primary interest is in the
character of Turgen, who, like Karana in Island of the Blue Dolphins, chooses to be a protector rather than a hunter of the wild
creatures. The admiration of this simple man for the "strength
and grace and daring" of the rams constitutes a powerful plea for
endangered species of wild life. A number of fine black and white
drawings evoke the background and atmosphere.

N152   SAUER, JULIA L. The Light at Tern Rock. Illustrated by
        Georges Schreiber. New York: Viking, 1951 (OP), 62 pp.
        Fiction   Gr. 3-6
     Even though their holiday plans are completely altered, Aunt
Martha and Ronnie manage to find the spirit of Christmas. On
December 1 they go out to the lighthouse on Tern Rock for two
weeks while Mr. Flagg, the keeper, visits his niece and her family in New Brunswick. He fails to return on the fifteenth as he
had promised. Finally, on the twenty-third they have proof that
he does not intend to come back until after Christmas. That day
they find gifts he has left for them, ingredients for a Christmas
feast, and a letter. Aunt Martha sets out to make Christmas for
the two of them but Ronnie remains sullen until nearly Christmas
Eve, when the spirit of Christmas comes to him, a little at first,
then with a rush. The awakening spirit dawns when Ronnie looks at
the festive tea table his aunt has arranged from the supplies
Byron Flagg left. Then they go up to light the great light and
Ronnie feels Christmas growing in his heart. He tells Aunt
Martha, "All over the world, on Christmas Eve, people are putting
little candles in their windows, to light the Christ Child on His
way. . . . We've lighted a candle tonight too—a big one. We've
lighted the biggest candle we'll ever have a chance to light for
Him—to help Him on His way." And the peace and loveliness of
Christmas Eve descends on them.

The illustrations in brown and white contribute atmosphere to this well-told story of Christmas and life in a lighthouse.

N153   BUFF, MARY and BUFF, CONRAD. The Apple and the Arrow.
       Illustrated by the authors. Boston: Houghton Mifflin,
       1951 (OP), 75 pp.
       Biography   Gr. 3-5
       This fictionalized retelling of the William Tell legend is
related from the point of view of Walter, the son from whose
head the apple was shot. The apple incident is woven into the
winning of Swiss freedom from the Austrians in 1291. Although
the book does not relate the complete life of either father or
son, it does put into the context of the time the incident for
which both are remembered. The many illustrations--both in black
and white and color--show the mountains, interior and exterior
views of buildings, weapons and costumes, making a book of distinction from an oft-told legend.

                              1953

N154   CLARK, ANN NOLAN. Secret of the Andes. Illustrated by Jean
       Charlot. New York: Viking, 1952, 130 pp.
       Fiction   Gr. 5-8
       Cusi, a Peruvian boy of eleven or twelve, leaves the Hidden
Valley high up in the Andes, where he has lived with old Chuto
caring for a large herd of llamas, and goes down to the lowlands
in search of another way of life. After this experience he knows
that he wishes to remain with Chuto and carry on his work when he
is gone. As soon as he has reached the decision, Chuto reveals
Cusi's heritage to him: he is descended from the Inca nobility;
the golden earplugs he wears are proof. The llamas they tend
also have a special relationship to that earlier time. According
to the legend which Chuto quotes to Cusi, the Spanish captured
the "mighty Inca" and "The Indians sent ten thousand llamas,/
carrying bags of gold dust/ to ransom their King." But the
Spanish, fearing the wrath of the King if they set him free,
killed him. "And the ten thousand llamas/ marching down the
trails of the Andes/ vanished from the land,/ and with them van-
ished/ the gold dust, ransom for the King." The llamas they herd
are descended from those of long ago. Chuto then takes Cusi to
the Sunrise Rock and shows him the secret cave containing the
bags of gold dust. With his blood, Cusi vows to keep the secret
of the cave forever.
       The theme of Cusi's coming to know himself and his relation-
ship with his ancestors is carefully worked out. Ann Clark knew
many Indian children, having worked with them from Canada to Peru,
she states in her acceptance speech. She exhibits a fine sense

1953

of place and, in telling Cusi's story, conveys information about llamas and Indian life. Charlot's pictures portray the dignity and strength of the people.

N155   WHITE, E. B. Charlotte's Web. Illustrated by Garth Williams.
        New York: Harper, 1952, 184 pp.
        Fantasy   Gr. 3-6
    Yielding to the pleas of his daughter, Fern, Farmer Arable spares the life of a little runt pig, which must be bottle-fed to survive. Under Fern's tender care Wilbur, as she names him, thrives and grows plump. When Wilbur is six weeks old Fern sells him to her uncle, Homer Zuckerman, who lives on a farm nearby, where Fern can visit him every day. Sitting on an old milking stool in the sheepfold next to Wilbur's pen, she watches Wilbur and listens as he and the barnyard animals converse.

    Although he has a comfortable home, plenty to eat, and is surrounded by other animals, including Templeton, the greedy rat who lives under his trough, Wilbur is lonely. Then Charlotte, a large gray spider living in the barn, becomes his friend. The spring days pass pleasantly until the old sheep tells Wilbur that he is being fattened for a purpose--to be turned into ham and bacon when cold weather comes. Charlotte promises Wilbur that she will save him from that terrible fate.

    After several anxious weeks, she has a lucky idea. In the center of Charlotte's web one foggy morning Lurvy, the hired man, discovers the words, "Some Pig," displayed over Wilbur's pen. People from miles around flock in to see Zuckerman's pig. Charlotte's plan is working well. When she decides that a different word is needed, Charlotte spins a new web with the word "Terrific" in block letters in the center. Wilbur, sleek and handsome, stands under the web trying to look "terrific." Next Charlotte weaves "Radiant" into the web and Wilbur tries hard to glow. Proud Mr. Zuckerman decides to show his pig at the county fair in September. Fern continues to spend a great deal of time watching Wilbur and the other animals, reporting to her mother conversations the animals have with each other. Fern's worried mother is reassured by the family doctor that the little girl is quite normal and will soon develop other interests.

    As time for the Fair nears, Charlotte secretly fears that she may not be able to save her friend, Wilbur, after all. The summer is nearly over; soon she must spin a sac into which she will deposit her eggs, and then she will die. Lethargic as she is, Charlotte travels in Wilbur's crate to the Fair. Templeton, the rat, goes along and finds a new word in a newspaper for Charlotte. On the night before the pigs are to be judged, Charlotte spins her last web, with the word "Humble" woven into it. Again Wilbur becomes the center of attention, and wins a special award. Nothing would now induce Mr. Zuckerman to eat his famous pig.

Charlotte's work is done. She lacks the strength to climb into
the crate to return home, but Wilbur gently carries the peach-
colored sac containing her eggs back to the barn cellar, places
it in a safe corner, and, year after year, is a good friend to
Charlotte's children, grandchildren and great-grandchildren.

Fern has missed the presentation of the ribbon to Wilbur, because she is riding the Ferris wheel with a boy, Henry Fussy,
just as the good doctor predicted.

In the thirty years since its publication, Charlotte's Web has
become one of the best-loved books of all time, with critics
showing as much enthusiasm for it as children and their parents.
Its merits are many: believable and lovable characters, an exciting plot, a timeless theme, and a style that perfectly adapts
ideas to words. The key to the book's success lies in the
author's treatment of fantasy in juxtaposition with reality.
The setting—Zuckerman's barn—is real and ordinary. The usual
animals of a farmyard inhabit it. The ways and life cycle of
the gray spider are integral to the story. Friendship as a cure
for loneliness is a universal theme. The people are well-
realized farm folk. Only the animals are at once fantastic and
realistic: they talk, they share with humans the emotions of
fear, pride, greed, friendship, and loyalty. In brief, E. B.
White has written a classic fable, sad yet amusing, and satisfying in the values it presents.

N156   McGRAW, ELOISE. Moccasin Trail. Illustrated by Paul Galdone.
        New York: Coward-McCann, 1952, 247 pp.
        Fiction: historical   Gr. 6-11
    Oregon in the 1830s and the problem of choice between two ways
of life are presented in Moccasin Trail. From age eleven to
seventeen Jim Keath lives with the Crow Indians. He leaves them
after seeing a blonde scalp lock in camp. The next couple of
years he traps beaver, part of the time with Tom Rivers, one of
the mountain men. Then a letter reaches him from his younger
brother, Jonnie, who, with their sister, Sally, and little brother,
Daniel, is in a wagon train bound for the Willamette Valley. Their
father has died several years earlier and their mother recently on
the trail. The letter asks Jim to join them and sign the homestead
claim since Jonnie is not the required age, eighteen. Jim goes to
them, but it is a long time before he can accept the white man's
way of life.

    The story is so absorbing that the historical background and
details—authentic and interesting as they are—are distinctly
secondary to the interest the reader feels in the characters.
At the beginning of the story, Jim—with long braids and a scalp
lock—looks completely Indian; and he thinks, feels, and acts as
an Indian would. Although the reader's sympathies are with the
troubled Jim, he can see the situation as it appears to Sally and
Jonnie, too. Jim's difficult readjustment is convincingly
presented.

1953

N157   WEIL, ANN. <u>Red Sails to Capri</u>. Illustrated by C. B. Falls.
       New York: Viking, 1952 (OP), 156 pp.
       Fiction: historical   Gr. 4-5
       A historical event, the rediscovery of the famous Blue Grotto
of Capri, provides the climax of the story. This grotto is in a
cave in a cove, which has been surrounded by superstitions causing it to be given wide berth by the fearful islanders. Then, on
November 1, 1826, three questing foreigners arrive at the island
of Capri in a red-sailed boat. They go to stay in an inn operated by Michele Pogano's parents, where they learn about the
cove and cave. Herr Nordstrom, one of the foreigners, says they
will go explore them. Michele and his friend Pietro are included
in the expedition.
       The story moves quickly and suspense is effectively maintained.
Even though the quests of the foreigners seem a bit schematic--a
writer in search of adventure, a painter in search of beauty, and
a philosophy student in search of truth--these objectives, which
are fulfilled with the finding of the grotto, serve to heighten
the significance of the events. There is much delightful humor
in the story. Mama Pogano, a famous cook, supplies some of it
by talking to the food as she cooks it.

N158   DALGLIESH, ALICE. <u>The Bears on Hemlock Mountain</u>. Illustrated
       by Helen Sewell. New York: Charles Scribner's Sons, 1952,
       62 pp.
       Fiction: historical   Gr. 1-4
       Eight-year-old Jonathan is sent to his Aunt Emma's to borrow
a kettle--a large iron one. The way to his aunt's is up and over
a small mountain, and there could be bears there. His mother
says that's all nonsense--there are no bears on Hemlock Mountain.
But, Jonathan meets two on the way home. He hides under the
great iron kettle and before too long his father and others come
and find him.
       The brief story is both exciting and humorous. Although the
year is not specified, the many stylized blue, black and white
illustrations suggest Pennsylvania Dutch country during the 1800s.
In an acknowledgment, the author states that the outline of the
story was given to her by the State Archivist of Pennsylvania who
"collects tales told by the people."

N159   FOSTER, GENEVIEVE. <u>Birthdays of Freedom</u>. Illustrated
       by the author. New York: Charles Scribner's Sons, 1952,
       58 pp.
       Information: history and biography   Gr. 5-8
       This volume traces the steps in man's progress to freedom from
earliest man to the fall of Rome in A.D. 476. Introductory and
concluding sections tie these birthdays to America's own birthday
of freedom, July 4, 1776. The first birthday of freedom came
when early man learned to make and use fire. Other landmarks of

freedom cited include man's learning to write, the Babylonian Code of Laws, the beginning of democracy in Greece, and the Twelve Tables of Roman Law. A second volume, published in 1957, notes milestones of freedom that occurred during the Middle Ages, the Renaissance, and to July 4, 1776.

Mrs. Foster's abundant illustrations augment and explain the lucid, well-written text which encompasses a tremendous sweep of history and ideas.

1954

N160   KRUMGOLD, JOSEPH. <u>And Now Miguel</u>. Illustrated by Jean
       Charlot. New York: Thomas Y. Crowell, 1953, 245 pp.
       Fiction   Gr. 4-7
For many generations the family of Miguel Chavez has raised sheep in New Mexico. Each summer the men take the sheep to pasture in the beautiful Sangre de Cristo Mountains, visible in the distance from their home. For years Miguel has longed to go with the men--he even secretly prepares a bundle each year so he will be ready if he is called at the last minute--but he is always told that his time will come later.

In the spring of the year Miguel is twelve he promises himself that things will be different this year. He will show his father and grandfather and uncles how helpful he can be with the flock. At lambing time he paints the number on the ewe right after she gives birth and the same number on her lamb: 894 lambs are born that year. He works so diligently when the shearers are there that he is allowed to eat at the table with the men instead of being expected to wait to eat with his mother, older sisters, and younger children. He finds a dozen ewes and lambs that have strayed from the flock during a storm.

But, when he asks his father if he may go, his father tells him "no"; for him, it is not yet time. Miguel still does not give up. He prays to San Ysidro, the patron saint of his village, asking that his wish be granted by whatever means the saint can arrange. His prayer is answered. Two days before the men are to leave, Miguel is told that he is to go this year, too--because his beloved nineteen-year-old brother, Gabriel, is being drafted into the army sooner than expected. Convinced that it is his fault, he prays to the saint to get his wish back. Gabriel finds him and the brothers talk until Miguel is reconciled. Gabriel goes to the army and Miguel to the mountains, feeling that at last he is regarded as a man.

"Everything comes and goes. Except one thing. The sheep. For that is the work of our family, to raise sheep." Thus speaks Miguel and the story relates the occupation of sheepraising as seen through Miguel's eyes and in his words. The reader marvels

1954

with Miguel at the miracle of birth and experiences the other
emotions that come to him such as the humiliation he feels over
falling, just like a little boy, into the big long burlap sack
into which he was throwing the tied fleeces. There is much detail but none of it seems superfluous. The whole account has a
rhythm that conveys the speech pattern of a bilingual Spanish-
American. The simple drawings match the text. And Now Miguel
took form first as a documentary film.

N161   BISHOP, CLAIRE HUCHET. <u>All-Alone</u>. Illustrated by Feodor
        Rojankovsky. New York: Viking, 1953, 90 pp.
        Fiction   Gr. 3-6
    Sent up into the French Alps to graze the family's cows, ten-
year-old Marcel goes against his father's express instructions
that he is not to associate with any of the other boys on the
mountains. Because he is tending Pierre's cows which have
strayed, he is not in his meadow when it is buried by a landslide. As a consequence, the old sayings of the village--"Pay
no attention to your neighbor's business" and "Each man for himself"--are discarded and a new era of cooperation is begun.
    Cowbells, yodeling, high meadows, all contribute to the dis-
tinctive mountain atmosphere in which the conflict between father
and son is enacted. The many realistically detailed black and
white illustrations picturing the boys and their cows, the village and the mountains, help bring the story to life. France is
Mrs. Bishop's native land.

N162   De JONG, MEINDERT. <u>Shadrach</u>. Illustrated by Maurice Sendak.
        New York: Harper, 1953, 182 pp.
        Fiction   Gr. 3-5
    "There was this boy, Davie, and he was going to have a rabbit.
His grandfather had promised it. A real, live rabbit! A little
black rabbit, if possible. In a week, if possible. And this was
in the Netherlands." Thus begins <u>Shadrach</u>. The time is early in
the twentieth century when the author was himself a small boy in
Holland. After a week that takes an eternity to go by, Davie
gets the wonderful rabbit which he names Shadrach. But, in three
weeks, even though he has given him the best of care, Shadrach
has grown so thin that Davie is very worried. Then Shadrach gets
out of the cage and finds some oats, a necessary part of his diet.
He grows plump again and the story reaches a satisfying conclusion.
    De Jong succeeds in making everyday occurrences absorbing by
relating them from the child's point of view. The reader shares
Davie's anticipation, his joy in owning his pet, and his anxiety
over Shadrach's declining vigor. Although the book focuses on
Davie, there are well-realized adult characters as well. Davie
is seen in a maturing relation to the other members of his family:
his Mother and Dad and big brother Rem. With Grandma and Grandpa
he has a very special relationship. Maurice Sendak's pen-and-ink

drawings communicate the spirit of the people as well as their
appearance.

N163   De JONG, MEINDERT. <u>Hurry Home, Candy</u>. Illustrated by Maurice
       Sendak. New York: Harper, 1953, 244 pp.
       Fiction   Gr. 4-7
       For a year the little dog has been a stray. Afraid of people
he has kept himself hidden, staying in woodlots during the day
and making the rounds of a few scattered farmhouses by night.
All memory of his former life--except fear--has left him. In a
flashback, his early life is told. When still an unweaned, un-
trained puppy, he was taken from his mother and puppy brothers
and sisters to become the pet of two children, Catherine and
George. They named him Candy and loved him dearly. With them
Candy was happy. But, while the children were at school, Candy
was often miserable. When he made messes on the floor, their
mother, an immaculate housekeeper, punished him severely with a
broom. One spring day, on the way home from a drive in the country, Candy wandered off while the children's father was changing
a tire. Although the children and their father searched and
searched, they did not find him. Candy, scarcely more than a
puppy, was on his own.
       At the end of the year, a series of events lead to a new home
for Candy. Pursued by a pack of dogs, Candy runs under a horse-
drawn wagon driven by a fat old woman. After she discovers him,
she gives him food and talks to him. When the wagon overturns,
the woman is injured and loses consciousness, but Candy stays
with her until help arrives. Several days later, Candy is taken
to the hospital to see the woman. There he is again frightened
by brooms and escapes from the policeman who is carrying him. In
front of a store, another broom comes at him. He dashes into the
street and is saved by Captain Carlson, a retired sea captain,
who takes Candy home to his large house.
       There, for the first time since he was a beloved puppy, Candy
is happy. When Captain Carlson discovers Candy's fear of brooms,
he tosses his away. Out walking one night Captain Carlson and
Candy stumble on some bank robbers immediately before the police
close in on them. In the confusion Candy is lost again, at the
very same bridge where he was lost as a puppy. In an exciting,
happy conclusion in which Catherine and George--no longer interested in the dog, but anxious to collect the reward offered by
Captain Carlson--assist, Candy is lured home to the good man.
       The portrait of Candy is so sensitively drawn it almost seems
as if the little dog is telling his own story. The plot gains
suspense from the author's non-chronological record of events.
The characterization of the adults is very good--the obsessively
clean mother, the grandmother, and Captain Carlson who relates
Candy's fear of brooms to similar fears in his own life. The

1954

title suggests that the plot will be like those in <u>Lassie Come
Home</u> and <u>The Incredible Journey,</u> in which animals travel great
distances to be reunited with their masters. The outcome of
this story reflects a more realistic turn of events, however,
as lost pets frequently are not returned to their owners.

N164   JUDSON, CLARA INGRAM. <u>Theodore Roosevelt, Fighting Patriot</u>.
        Illustrated by Lorence F. Bjorklund. Chicago: Follett,
        1953 (OP), 218 pp.
        Biography   Gr. 4-6
    This biography opens in 1866 in New York City when Theodore
Roosevelt is a boy of eight. Clearly written and based on exact
but unobtrusive research, it gives a balanced treatment of his
whole life, describing his personal relationships, his enthusiasm
for the outdoors and the strenuous life, and his discovery of
politics. The tone is admiring, but not adulatory, and the author
gives a vivid impression of T. R. at the various stages of his
life. We see all of this against a background of America from
the Civil War to the post-World War I days. In her foreword,
Mrs. Judson says that we always need "fighting patriots." As
she has portrayed him, Theodore Roosevelt is the archetype. The
pencil drawings complement the text well.

N165   BUFF, MARY and BUFF, CONRAD. <u>Magic Maize</u>. Illustrated by
        the authors. Boston: Houghton Mifflin, 1953, 76 pp.
        Fiction   Gr. 3-6
    Fabian, a young Guatemalan boy of the mid-1900s, lives in the
country with his parents, two sisters, and a baby brother. His
beloved elder brother, Quin, impatient with the old ways and customs to which his folks adhere rigidly, has left home to become
a peddler. On one of his visits he gives Fabian twenty kernels
of a new variety of corn that will, he promises, produce so much
better than the old that it is really "magic" maize. Because
Quin received the seed from "gringos," all of whom their father
distrusts, Fabian must plant the kernels in a secret place. He
plants them in the CITY UP YONDER, an ancient Mayan ruin. At
length when Father sees the plants, he is convinced of the superiority of the new seed. Father also alters his opinion of
gringos because of the fine and fair treatment they show his
sons. Besides the wonder of the maize, Fabian, at the close of
the story, has additional cause for rejoicing. The gringos have
convinced his father that Fabian should be allowed to go to
school; they have also paid his father well for the valuable
jade earplug Fabian found in the ruins of the ancients.
    Although character development is slight, the story reveals
elements of both the old and new ways of life, and includes
Guatemalan history and folklore. Conrad Buff's illustrations
enhance the story. Numerous muted brown and white pictures--

many full-page--depict the life and country more effectively than many words would. Endpapers and cover done in vibrant colors convey the beauty of the sea, land, and the people.

1955

N166   De JONG, MEINDERT. The Wheel on the School. Illustrated by
        Maurice Sendak. New York: Harper, 1954, 298 pp.
        Fiction   Gr. 3-6

The six school children in Shora, a small fishing village in Holland, decide to put a wagon wheel on the school roof in an attempt to attract luck-bringing storks to their village. Lina, the only girl in the school, begins it all on a Friday when she writes an essay about storks. On Saturday afternoon, their half-day from school, Lina and the five boys--big Jella; fat, steady Eelka; the twins, Pier and Dirk; and friendly Auka--scour Shora and the surrounding countryside looking for a wagon wheel.

An omniscient point of view moves the reader from one to another of the children as each is involved in an exciting adventure. Pier and Dirk, following their teacher's instruction to "look everywhere, where a wheel could be and where it couldn't possibly be," sneak over the fence and into the yard of wheelchair-bound, legless Janus, regarded by the children as the meanest man in Shora. He does not have a wheel but comes to play a part second in importance to that of the children.

Lina also looks where a wheel could not possibly be, through a hole in an old, overturned boat which lies half-buried in sand far out from the dike. In that impossible place she sees a wheel. The owner of the boat, hardy ninety-three-year-old Douwa, happens along at that moment. That very afternoon, just before high tide covers the boat, Lina and Douwa, aided by all the boys, the teacher, and Janus, as well as the tin man, his wagon and horse, procure the wheel.

During the night, the men of the fishing fleet--the children's dads--arrive home just ahead of a severe storm that rages all day Sunday. Even though the storm continues on Monday, the fathers, under Janus's direction, mount the wheel on the roof. The storm rages three days more. The children now fear that even though they have a wheel they will have no storks because many will have perished in the storm.

On the morning the fishermen return to sea, Linda, Lina's little sister, and Jan, Auka's little brother, finding the door to the village tower open, wander in. They climb until they reach the clock loft and then go on up to the bell loft. From there, through little slits, they can see far out in every direction. They see two storks standing on a sandbar close to the lighthouse.

As soon as they are rescued from the tower and have told of the storks, Janus, the teacher, and Jella--the three strongest

to row--with Lina and Pier--the two lightest to hold the storks--
go out in the dinghy and get them. Douwa and the boys on shore
have a fire going to dry out the storks and ladders in place on
the school. Before long, for the first time in many, many years,
there are storks on a roof in Shora.

It is difficult to imagine a more exciting and creative treatment of a simple idea, yet all the incidents develop in perfectly
logical and believable fashion from the decision to try to bring
storks to Shora. One reads the book the first time wondering
what will happen next, yet the second and third readings are
equally pleasurable. One observes then the good characterization, the skillful development of theme, and the effective style.
Each of the six school children is well delineated. We know them
better than the adults because, while the thoughts of the adults
are never given, those of the children are expressed in almost a
stream of consciousness manner. It is appropriate that a theme
that demonstrates the effectiveness of cooperation should have
characters from the whole community--from the youngest to the
oldest and including the handicapped.

By avoiding the picturesque, De Jong, in contrast to many who
have written of other lands, avoids giving the impression that
the novel was written to impart information. The reader's conception of life in the Netherlands at the time the story takes
place is built up from the observations the children make as they
move about in a world they have known all their lives. The reader
is made aware of the setting only as it is important to or exists
for the children. In another respect De Jong is almost alone
among writers of foreign lands; he uses no foreign words other
than names of people and places. His Dutch children wear wooden
shoes; but they speak in colloquial American: "All right for
you, Eelka"; "Boy, if the teacher finds out"; they call their
fathers "Dad." Yet one always thinks of them as Dutch, not American, children. The fact is that the author has given us the
universal child, and, by having his children speak as the American boys and girls of his reading audiences speak, he has removed
a barrier to complete identification. Wheel on the School is
worthy to be used as a touchstone for writing of life in other
lands.

N167   DALGLIESH, ALICE. The Courage of Sarah Noble. Illustrated
        by Leonard Weisgard. New York: Charles Scribner's Sons,
        1954, 52 pp.
        Fiction: historical   Gr. 2-5
    Sarah Noble is eight years old in 1707 when she travels with
her father from the Massachusetts Colony into the wilderness of
Connecticut to cook for him while he builds a new home for the
family. "Keep up your courage, Sarah Noble," her mother tells
her as she wraps her daughter's cloak closely about her before

she and her father set off. These words form themselves into a
refrain and with her warm cloak give her the comfort and strength
she needs to face the new life bravely. When her father goes to
bring the rest of the family, Sarah stays with Tall John, his
Indian wife, and their children.

This brief pioneer story, based on a true incident in Connecticut history, has literary quality and depth of feeling even
though it is easy reading. One of the few historical fiction
books written for younger readers, it emphasizes faith and friendship in a way that can be meaningful to them. Leonard Weisgard's
pictures in earthtone colors are a pleasing accompaniment to the
text and visually support the wilderness setting.

N168   ULLMAN, JAMES RAMSEY. Banner in the Sky. Philadelphia:
        J. B. Lippincott, 1954, 252 pp.
           Fiction: historical   Gr. 5-11
This is a fictionalized account of the first ascent of the
Matterhorn, the last summit of the Alps to be conquered; it is
called the Citadel in the story. The year is 1865, when the
Matterhorn was climbed for the first time; but the main events
of the story could have occurred many years before or in any
year since that time. Sixteen-year-old Rudi Matt, whose father
has died fifteen years before the story opens in an unsuccessful
attempt to scale the Citadel, practices climbing secretly since
his mother cannot bear the idea of his becoming a guide like his
father. He has reconnoitered on the Citadel many times and
finally has the opportunity to make his dream, and his father's
dream, come true. At the close of the book his father's red
woolen shirt is waving from the top of the mountain, like a
banner in the sky.

The narrative moves quickly and the author maintains suspense
by the skillful use of foreshadowing and flashbacks. Although
the reader is most emotionally involved with Rudi, the author's
use of the omniscient point of view helps to keep tension high,
as the action shifts from group to group on the mountain and
back to people in the village. The ending is particularly appropriate. Within reach of the summit, Rudi must make a moral decision: to climb for glory or to help another person in trouble.
In helping Saxo he proves himself to be truly his father's son
and takes a long step toward becoming a responsible adult. The
author, himself an Alpinist, demonstrates that great physical
courage is required to climb the Alps, but he brings out, also,
the courageous spirit that keeps the great climbers going, at
times on sheer will. This is a thrilling and satisfying adventure story.

N169   LATHAM, JEAN LEE. Carry On, Mr. Bowditch. Illustrated by
        John O'Hara Cosgrave, II. Boston: Houghton Mifflin,
        1955, 251 pp.
        Biography   Gr. 5-10
    From the time he was very young, Nathaniel Bowditch (1773-
1838) of Salem was brilliant in mathematics. Even though he
longed with all his being to prepare for Harvard, at the age of
twelve, he was indentured for nine years to a Salem firm of ship
chandlers. In spite of this denial of formal schooling, Nat,
encouraged by several educated men in the town who loaned him
books, studied astronomy, mathematics, navigation, algebra, Latin,
and French. In his twenties he went to sea. A mathematician and
linguist (he learned Spanish, too, when they sailed to Manila),
Nat was not the usual second mate. He thought the common sailors
could learn navigation if it were explained clearly enough, and
he proceeded to teach them. The astonished captain, when he became aware of Nat's success, exclaimed: "Carry on, Mr. Bowditch."
After Nat discovered many wrong figures in the tables in Moore's
Navigator, supposedly the best book of its kind in the world, he
set about writing a book without errors. Published before he was
thirty, his book, New American Practical Navigator, remains
"the seaman's Bible." The story ends a year or two later at the
conclusion of Nat's fifth voyage.
    The natural, lively dialogue makes the book, which the author
calls fictionalized biography, read like a novel. In her acceptance speech, Jean Latham explains her definition of the term and
her method of work. She states that the facts of her subject's
life, insofar as they were known, were accurate. So little was
known, however, that the author found it necessary to invent
characters, conversations, and incidents. She relates that,
although she imagined a dozen characters, she included four
dozen historical characters whose lives touched the life of
Nathaniel Bowditch, with fidelity to personalities and the historical period (acceptance paper for Carry On, Mr. Bowditch in
Newbery and Caldecott Medal Books: 1956-1965, ed. Lee Kingman
[Boston: Horn Book, 1965], pp. 18-19). Besides bringing alive
the subject, the author explains clearly mathematical and navigation terms and sketches the times authentically. Neat realistic
black and white drawings add interest.

N170   RAWLINGS, MARJORIE KINNAN. The Secret River. Illustrated by
        Leonard Weisgard. New York: Charles Scribner's Sons, 1955,
        57 pp.
        Fantasy   Gr. 1-4
    Calpurnia, a little girl, and Buggy-horse, her dog, live with
Calpurnia's parents in a dark green forest in Florida. One day

at breakfast Calpurnia's father says that, because there are no
fish, hard times have come to the forest. Calpurnia takes her
fishing pole and goes to Mother Albirtha, the wisest person in
the forest, and asks her where she can catch some big fish "so
that hard times will be soft times." Mother Albirtha tells her
that there are big fish in the secret river which Calpurnia can
reach by simply following her nose.

Heeding this instruction, Calpurnia and Buggy-horse reach the
beautiful secret river where Calpurnia catches many large catfish.
In late afternoon, as the shadows begin to fall, Calpurnia, laden
with fish, sets out for home. On the way back she encounters a
hoot-owl, a bear, and a panther. To each she gives catfish as
well as to Mother Albirtha. In the morning Calpurnia's father
takes the remaining catfish to his market and, because of the succession of events they set in motion, the hard times in the forest
turn into "soft times."

Later, Calpurnia searches for but cannot find the river again.
Mother Albirtha tells her that she will not find it again: "I
told you once, and I tell you twice, there is not any secret
river. . . . The secret river is in your mind." This explanation delights Calpurnia, who skips home, sits down under the
magnolia tree, closes her eyes, and sees the river "as beautiful
as she remembered it." Still, she thinks, when she opens her
eyes, she will truly find it again someday.

The story is highlighted with little poems made up by Calpurnia,
and enhanced by harmonious illustrations by Leonard Weisgard. Although basic to the story, a greater significance can be attached
to the river and to the bear and panther that Calpurnia meets.
This simple story can be interpreted on more than one level depending upon the reader's age and imagination.

N171 LINDQUIST, JENNIE. The Golden Name Day. Illustrated by Garth
      Williams. New York: Harper, 1955, 248 pp.
      Fiction   Gr. 3-6
      Nancy Bruce, just nine, goes to spend the year with her Swedish-
American grandparents, Grandma and Grandpa Benson. Theodore
Roosevelt is president, and Grandpa has named his cat "Teddy" for
him; he calls his horse Karl XII for a Swedish king. These names
and others are happy choices in a book that is largely concerned
with names and which gives a picture of American life enriched by
the flavor of another country. The slight plot is built around
finding a name day for Nancy, whose name is not in the Swedish
almanac. There are some attractive characters and some pleasant
scenes, especially the parties at which Swedish customs are observed. The book grew out of the childhood memories of the
author.

1956

N172   SHIPPEN, KATHERINE B.   Men, Microscopes, and Living Things.
          Illustrated by Anthony Ravielli. New York: Viking, 1955
          (OP), 183 pp.
          Information: science   Gr. 5 up
       This volume, one of the books on the history of science writ-
    ten by Miss Shippen, explains the succession of theories and ex-
    periments relating to living things and characterizes the great
    biologists who were responsible for them. After the microscope
    was invented, many theories long in vogue could be either sub-
    stantiated or disproved. The author begins with Aristotle who
    she calls the first biologist. Others included are William
    Harvey, Francis Bacon, Charles Darwin, and Gregor Mendel. She
    concludes by saying that even though great work has been done,
    there is still much in the living world that we cannot yet ex-
    plain. We are, therefore, "still at the beginning."
       The text is enjoyable reading as well as informative and the
    illustrations by Anthony Ravielli arouse interest. There is an
    index.

                                1957

N173   SORENSEN, VIRGINIA. Miracles on Maple Hill. Illustrated by
          Beth and Joe Krush. New York: Harcourt, Brace, 1956,
          180 pp.
          Fiction   Gr. 4-6
       In Miracles on Maple Hill movement from one locality to an-
    other provides impetus for the subsequent action. Marly, ten,
    and Joe, twelve, and their parents move from Pittsburgh to a
    farm in the northwestern corner of Pennsylvania. The story
    opens with the first miracle, the rising of the sap in the maple
    trees, and ends with the same miracle repeated a year later. In
    the interim, each season brings miracles of nature, and there is
    a special miracle for the family: by the time the year is com-
    pleted, Father, who has gone to the farm physically and mentally
    exhausted as a result of internment in a World War II prison
    camp, has regained his health.
       Told from the point of view of Marly, who is sensitive to
    nature and tender toward all living things, the story includes
    much information about wild animals and flowers of the woods and
    fields. Marly is entranced with all she sees, and the reader,
    through Marly, feels a corresponding appreciation. Besides the
    parents, the auxiliary characters--Mr. and Mrs. Chris, Harry the
    Hermit, and the truant officer Annie-Get-Your-Gun--are well-
    imagined persons. Realistic illustrations capture the mood of
    the story.

1957

N174 GIPSON, FRED. Old Yeller. Illustrated by Carl Burger. New
      York: Harper, 1956, 158 pp.
      Fiction: historical   Gr. 4-9
   Travis, the fourteen-year-old hero, is left at home with his
mother to look after the farm when his father departs to drive
cattle to market in Abilene, Kansas. Home for Travis and his
family is the Texas hill country, and the time is the 1860s.
Old Yeller is the name of the stray dog who wanders in. Travis
at first rejects him, but Old Yeller sticks around and wins the
affection and gratitude of the family: he saves little Arliss
from a bear, Travis from wild hogs, and Mother and the little
neighbor girl Lizbeth from a rabid wolf. Following this episode,
Travis makes a decision that raises him from the world of childhood to manhood: he has to shoot Old Yeller, who has been bitten
by the rabid wolf.
   In this exciting and believable story, the universal theme of
a boy's love for his dog is developed without sentimentality.
The authentic pioneer background properly assumes a secondary
place to the absorbing story.

N175 De JONG, MEINDERT. The House of Sixty Fathers. Illustrated
      by Maurice Sendak. New York: Harper, 1956, 189 pp.
      Fiction: historical   Gr. 4-8
   This suspense-filled story is set in China during World War II.
Small Tien Pao, alone in the family's sampan with his pet pig,
Glory-of-the-Republic, is swept by a storm from the city of
Hengyang deep into Japanese-occupied territory. When the storm
is over and Tien is able to leave the sampan, he starts on foot
with his pig back through the mountains toward Hengyang and his
family. On the way he gives aid to a wounded American airman whom
he sees shot down by the Japanese. After a terrible day and night,
they are found by Chinese guerrillas who carry the airman out of
the mountains and take Tien well on his way back to Hengyang.
When he enters the city he finds that the Japanese have now advanced this far and are fighting for the city.
   In the railroad station, which is packed with people clamoring
to leave the city, Tien is pulled aboard a freight car by a Chinese soldier who tells him to get into the deep basket in which
he is carrying Glory-of-the-Republic. During the night, when the
soldier relaxes his hold on the basket, it rolls out the open
door and down the incline by the railroad. Unhurt, Tien climbs
up onto a large rock where, late the following day, two American
soldiers find him sleeping. They take the nearly starved boy and
his pig to the barracks where sixty men who belong to a bomber
squadron live.
   Tien tells his story to the Chinese interpreter and, from him,
learns that this is the base of Lieutenant Hamsun, the airman
Tien helped. The interpreter tells Tien that the sixty men of

this squadron wish to adopt him if he cannot find his parents.
Tien is certain he will find them among the thousands of refugees
who have left Hengyang on foot. He watches from the rock all the
following day but does not see them. Late that afternoon, the
doctor brings Lieutenant Hamsun from the hospital to visit Tien.

In a small plane, Lieutenant Hamsun flies Tien and the interpreter along the railroad track and the two dirt roads leading
from Hengyang for as far as there are refugees in either direction. His family is not among them. Before they return to the
House of Sixty Fathers, to divert him, Lieutenant Hamsun flies
farther west to show him a new airfield that is being built.
There Tien finds his family and is dramatically reunited with
them.

De Jong handles with restraint and fidelity the emotions, ter-
rors, and suspense that are a part of Tien Pao's odyssey. Rather
than diminishing the perils through which he passes, the restraint
serves to augment them. The terse, tense narrative operates in
conjunction with meticulous plotting.

Glory-of-the-Republic, portrayed with the typical skill De Jong
exhibits with animal characters, is as real as Tien. He is a continuous comfort to Tien and his antics provide some humorous moments. Through Tien Pao the author has exposed the grimness of
war and children as victims of it. De Jong writes from firsthand
knowledge having served in China in the airforce during World War
II. Maurice Sendak's illustrations of the sampan, of the characters Tien encounters, and of Tien and his pig evoke an emotional
response from the reader.

N176   JUDSON, CLARA INGRAM. <u>Mr. Justice Holmes</u>. Illustrated by
          Robert Todd. Chicago: Follett, 1956 (OP), 192 pp.
          Biography   Gr. 4-8
     In a foreword, Mrs. Judson wrote that she wished to contribute
in some way to a wider understanding and respect for law. It
seemed to her as if "the complex subject of law might become simple and human if viewed through the life and work of some great
man in the legal profession." She chose to write about Holmes
because he was "above all, a courageous man who believed that
law was for all the people. . . . His outstanding contribution
was in showing that law is not a dull, static thing, but experi-
mental, fluid, and realistic."

With careful attention to detail, the author paints a vivid
picture of nineteenth-century Boston and Cambridge, of the
Holmeses' family life on Beacon Hill, and of young Wendell's
relationship with his father. His part in the Civil War is made
real by excerpts from letters to his family, and well-chosen quotations from his later writings reveal him as a great man and
jurist.

N177   RHOADS, DOROTHY. <u>The Corn Grows Ripe</u>. Illustrated by Jean
         Charlot. New York: Viking, 1956 (OP), 88 pp.
         Fiction   Gr. 4-6
    Tigre, a high-spirited contemporary twelve-year-old Central
American boy, shunned responsibility until his father is injured.
On the night of the accident Tigre walks for hours through the
brush in the dark to get the bonesetter. This is a brave act
since Tigre believes that witches and demons roam at night in
the form of animals. In the days that follow, Tigre becomes a
man. He can no longer go to school but must prepare the land
and plant the corn that is so important to his family. Tigre
labors day after day to clear the thick growth of brush. Next,
in accord with his father's instructions, he burns the fields and
plants the seed. Tigre's beautiful crop saves his family from
want. Blended into Tigre's story is the story of the meaning of
corn to these people and explanations of Mayan religion and
festivals.
    This simple tale not only sets forth the way of life of a
primitive Indian culture of the mid-1900s, but it also deals
with the universal theme of a boy becoming a man. Jean Charlot's
green, black and white illustrations complement the text.

N178   De ANGELI, MARGUERITE. <u>The Black Fox of Lorne</u>. Illustrated
         by the author. Garden City, N.Y.: Doubleday, 1956 (OP),
         191 pp.
         Fiction: historical   Gr. 4-7
    Fair-haired Jan and Brus, identical twins, are thirteen when
their father, Harald Redbeard, decides that his family and followers will leave Norway and go to Britain where Danish relatives
have already settled. These tenth-century boys are delighted to
go a-Viking. In high spirits, the party sets out in three ships.
But disaster soon overtakes them. In a fierce storm, the vessels
become separated, and the ship in which the boys are sailing with
their father is wrecked off the northern coast of Scotland. The
father and those men who survive the shipwreck are murdered by
wild clansman. Brus hides, but Jan is captured and made the personal slave of the avaricious and cruel Black Fox of Lorne. When
the Black Fox and his retainers move south, Brus follows close
behind and the boys are sometimes able to meet and even change
places for a while. The Black Fox ostensibly is going to join
King Malcolm in a campaign against the British, but he actually
intends treason. The twins assist in foiling his plans, are
awarded the lands of one of those who slew their father, and are
reunited with their mother.
    The text portrays the historical period accurately and the
illustrations supplement the text splendidly. Nevertheless, the
book is not without weaknesses. Characterization does not go
much beyond establishing persons as either good or bad. The ease

with which these Scandinavian boys get around Scotland with no
language difficulty seems unrealistic. The explanation offered
is that they had learned the language from their nurse, who had
been captured in a raid in Scotland earlier. Finding their
mother is a happy event, but the reader is not really prepared
for it--she just seems to materialize as a lady-in-waiting to
the queen. The boys and their mother rather quickly take up
Christianity and forget the old gods. Material success comes
with little effort on the part of the boys. The author's reputation and the superb illustrations were probable factors in
causing the committee to choose this as an Honor Book.

1958

N179   KEITH, HAROLD. Rifles for Watie. New York: Thomas Y. Crowell,
       1957, 332 pp.
       Fiction: historical   Gr. 5-11
    Rifles for Watie recounts the Civil War experiences of Jeff
Bussey, a Kansas farm boy, who enlists in the Union Army in 1861.
The setting of the novel is what the author terms the "seldom-
publicized, Far-Western theater" of the War--Kansas, Missouri,
Arkansas, and the Indian territories which now compose Oklahoma.
    On one level, the book is a novel of education; it shows Jeff's
increasing development against the background of war. As the
novel progresses, he moves from a glamorized concept of war and
from an overly simplified view of the people and politics which
the war involves to a more realistic view of both. Though not
excessively naturalistic, the novel does show the sordid side of
war: the drudgery and deprivation of the troops, infested with
lice and subsisting on skimpy rations; the brutal authoritarian-
ism of military discipline; the impact on the civilian population,
looted and displaced by the ebb and flow of the rival armies; and,
in addition, the horrors of combat, the fear, the crippling injuries, the despair, and the sudden death. The evils of the war
are mitigated by the comradeship of the troops and by Jeff's
growing awareness of the essential humanity of those on the other
side of the conflict. Harold Keith, in his Newbery acceptance
speech, said that he "tried to change Jeff from a carefree country
boy who saw only the Union side and was anxious to get into battle, into a mature young man who was capable of understanding the
enemy even if he didn't agree with what they were fighting for"
(Newbery and Caldecott Medal Books: 1956-1965, ed. Lee Kingman
[Boston: Horn Book, 1965], p. 59). The element which ties the
book's numerous incidents into a coherent whole is this continuing development.
    The central incident of the novel involves an attempt by Con-
federate General Stand Watie, a Cherokee Indian, to obtain modern

repeating rifles for his cavalry. Jeff becomes involved in these
events when he is captured by some of Watie's men while on a
scouting expedition behind the Confederate lines. To prevent
himself from being branded as a Union spy, he pretends to join
Watie's forces. Jeff's stint among the rebels allows Keith to
show the war as it appeared from the Confederate side, and leads
directly to the novel's climax: Jeff's discovery of the plot by
a Union officer to sell Watie rifles and his escape and subsequent desperate flight on foot back to the Union fort.

Successful both as a novel of action and as a novel of character, the book also appears to authentically depict its historic
period. The author relied on original sources: both the diaries
of Union veterans and the reminiscences of twenty-two Confederate
veterans who Keith interviewed in 1940 and 1941 (Newbery Award
Acceptance for Rifles for Watie, in Newbery and Caldecott Medal
Books: 1956-1965, p. 56). The details of day-to-day life are
recounted with convincing precision, the characters are believable, and the scenes of battle are in particular described with
compelling vividness.

N180   SANDOZ, MARI. The Horsecatcher. Philadelphia: Westminster,
         1957, 192 pp.
         Fiction   Gr. 6-11
      Herds of buffalo still roamed the western plains at the time
this story takes place. There are no white characters although
references are made to trading posts and white settlements in
Texas. Young Elk, son of a chief of a southern Cheyenne tribe,
has a gentling hand and a way with horses. While he wishes to
be a horsecatcher and capture wild horses, his father expects him
to become a warrior like his brother, Two Wolves. But Young Elk
hates killing. Even after Two Wolves is killed by Comanches,
Young Elk refuses to go on the warpath to avenge him. Instead,
he travels by himself deep into enemy country and, in a period
of two months, catches and tames a herd of fifteen horses including six highly prized dun-colored ones.

After that, the Old Horsecatcher of the village takes him as a
son and offers to teach him. Young Elk spends a winter with the
northern Cheyennes and their friends the Sioux and brings home a
Pelousy, a breed of horse seldom captured.

Soon, in the company of peaceloving Arapahoes who are neutral
in the wars between the Comanches and Cheyennes, he departs for
Comanche country hoping to see two Comanche sisters who are ex-
pert horsecatchers. He hopes also to glimpse the White One, the
ghost stallion that no one can catch. He sees the famous sisters
and not only glimpses but captures the White One. On the way
home he comes upon a large war party heading toward the Cheyenne
villages. So that he can ride swiftly to give warning he releases the hobbled stallion and the nineteen other horses he is
taking home. His horsecatching feat becomes known, however, and

1958

Young Elk receives the recognition due a warrior. His father and
Old Horsecatcher give him their names together: Elk River, the
Horsecatcher.
Excitement and suspense abound in this story of Young Elk's
long struggle to be himself. For much of the time he is out
alone catching horses. The reader shares the long, lonely, dangerous days when he not only must be constantly thinking of his
quarry but also must be wary of enemy tribes. There is in addition a fine sense of place and good integration into the story
of the complex Indian cultures. Young Elk's devotion to peace
and reverence for life are themes not often developed in stories
about Indians.

N181   ENRIGHT, ELIZABETH. Gone-Away Lake. Illustrated by Beth and
        Joe Krush. New York: Harcourt, Brace, 1957, 192 pp.
        Fiction   Gr. 3-6
    In June, Portia and Foster Blake, eleven and six-and-a-half,
go to the country to spend the summer with Uncle Jake and Aunt
Hilda Jarman and their twelve-year-old son, Julian. Portia and
Foster's parents are in Europe, but plan to join them in August.
The Jarmans have just moved to the country and Julian has not
yet explored the surrounding area.
    The very next morning he and Portia, equipped with a bird
guide, field glasses, butterfly net, collecting jar, and lunch,
set off through the woods at the back of the house. In the afternoon they come on a large swamp filled with tall reeds and rushes.
Along one edge is a row of big, shabby old houses, apparently all
empty. Then they hear a radio commercial and know that one is
occupied. Even though they feel apprehensive, they go up to the
door. Their knock is answered by a small, elderly lady dressed
in old-fashioned clothes. She greets them warmly and invites
them in. Her name is, she tells them, Minnehaha Cheever, Mrs.
Lionel Alexis Cheever. Before they leave that day they have also
met her brother, Mr. Pindar Payton, who lives in a house at the
other end of the settlement. Portia and Julian learn that, in
the 1890s when Minnehaha and Pindar were young, the swamp was
beautiful Tarrigo Lake. The houses belonged to the families who
vacationed there. After a dam was constructed in 1903, the lake
drained away and became known as Gone-Away Lake. Years later,
after experiencing hard times, the brother and sister decided to
return to Gone-Away.
    On their way home, Portia and Julian decide to keep their dis-
covery to themselves for awhile. They return the following day
and almost every day thereafter. They have a wonderful time fixing up one of the old houses as a clubhouse and hearing from
Minnehaha and Pindar about Gone-Away days of long ago.
    One day Foster follows them, sinks in quicksand in the swamp,
and is rescued by Pindar. When Minnehaha and Pindar take Foster
home in their antique car, the secret is out. The fun does not

come to an end, however. Foster and his friend, Davy, become
members of the club and Portia invites another girl and Julian
two other boys.
    At the very end of the summer, the Blake and Jarman families
and Minnehaha and Pindar explore the Villa Caprice, the one house
built away from the lake in the woods and better preserved than
the others. Because the owner has been dead for over fifty years,
it now belongs to the state. Portia and Foster are jubilant when
their father promises to try to buy it for a summer home.
    Gone-Away Lake has much to recommend it: an original setting;
a plot filled with excitement and expectancy; a fine appreciation
of nature; and interesting, attractive characters. Minnehaha and
Pindar are far from being mere eccentrics introduced for the sake
of the plot. The author's characteristic ability to see by analogy adds a patina of charm to whatever is being observed: for
example, the puppies "had little dark flat faces like pansies,
and ears that felt like pieces of silk, and claws like the tips
of knitting needles." This descriptive ability aids also in
making precise characterizations and when Aunt Minnehaha remembers
Mrs. Brace-Gideon, owner of the Villa Caprice, as being like "a
battleship just going forward and going forward while everything
else gets out of the way: all the little boats and the fishes
and the people in swimming. Everything." The reader enjoys the
book for the first time for its appealing story. On second reading, he savors the style. Line drawings portray faithfully the
details of the story.

N182   LAWSON, ROBERT. The Great Wheel. Illustrated by the author.
       New York: Viking, 1957 (OP), 188 pp.
       Fiction: historical   Gr. 4-7
    The Great Wheel is the first Ferris wheel, and certainly the
largest of all Ferris wheels. Higher than a twenty-story building, the wheel carried thirty-six enclosed plush-seated cars and
it was possible for 2,160 people to ride at once. Designed by
G. W. G. Ferris, it was built for the Chicago World's Columbian
Exposition of 1893. After having helped with its construction,
Conn (Cornelius Terence Kilroy), recently of Ireland, works as a
guard on the number one car. He thus fulfills the fortune Aunt
Honora told for him before he left Ireland--he would follow his
star to the west and ride on the biggest wheel in the world. The
gay tone is appropriate, for Robert Lawson's story portrays
America of the 1890s as a land of unlimited opportunity. Conn's
Uncle Michael has made a fortune building curbs and sewers in New
York City and the German family into which Conn marries in Chicago
are pork magnates. The author's lively black and white drawings
help in his portrayal of the wheel and the period.

1958

N183   GURKO, LEO. <u>Tom Paine: Freedom's Apostle</u>. Illustrated by
       Fritz Kredel. New York: Thomas Y. Crowell, 1957 (OP),
       213 pp.
       Biography   Gr. 6-12
     This biography vividly brings to life the fiery pamphleteer
whose <u>Common Sense</u> and <u>Crisis</u> papers greatly influenced political
thinking in America during the Revolutionary War. Born in England into a poor family, Paine received little schooling and
worked at a variety of low-paying jobs for the first thirty-seven
years of his life. After meeting Benjamin Franklin, he decided
to go to America. The pamphlets, written soon after his arrival,
brought him fame.
     In 1787, at age fifty, after thirteen years in America, Paine
sailed for visits to France and England. In England he was
courted by Edmund Burke and other Whigs who hoped through Paine
to reestablish good relations with America. He lost their favor
with his publication of <u>The Rights of Man</u>, a reply to Burke's
denunciation of the French Revolution which had begun.
     Paine left England for France in 1792, barely escaping the
King's constables with a warrant for his arrest. Received in
Calais as a hero, Paine was made a French citizen and a member
of the National Convention. When the moderates with whom he
affiliated himself lost power and later--in the Reign of Terror--
their lives, Paine was imprisoned for ten months, but was saved
from the guillotine because of his standing and reputation in
America.
     He finished the first part of the <u>Age of Reason</u> before his im-
prisonment and he wrote the second part in prison. This work,
stating his views on religion, disagreed with many orthodox church
teachings and was strongly condemned in America. This disapproval
continued after Paine's return to America in 1802 where he spent
the last seven years of his life.
     The biography presents the character defects and failures as
well as the high ideals and successes of this complex and contro-
versial figure. Excerpts from Paine's writings, placed against
the background of the times in which they were first received,
become fresh and new. Events and ideas in America, England, and
France in the last quarter of the eighteenth century and these
countries' famous men--from George Washington to Napoleon--are
cogently presented. Paine's whole life is depicted, although not
chronologically. The opening chapter, one of few fictionalized
scenes in the book, shows Paine traveling with Washington's retreating army in 1776. Although this chronology is confusing,
the book remains a major work.

1959

N184   SPEARE, ELIZABETH GEORGE. The Witch of Blackbird Pond.
        Boston: Houghton Mifflin, 1958, 249 pp.
        Fiction: historical   Gr. 5-11
    In 1687, spirited Kit Tyler, sixteen, raised in luxury in the
West Indies, is left alone and destitute upon the death of her
grandfather. Impulsively she decides to go make her home with
her only relatives: the Matthew Wood family, who live in Puritan
Connecticut. The story opens as Kit completes the last few miles
of the sea voyage to Wethersfield where the remainder of the
action occurs. Kit's Aunt Rachel and her lame cousin Mercy--a
little older than she--welcome her warmly. Her other cousin,
beautiful Judith, who is slightly younger, soon treats her like
one of the family, but Kit finds her Uncle Matthew stern and for-
bidding. In addition, everything about the new life is so different from the old one that Kit finds it very difficult to adjust.
    In her loneliness, Kit makes friends with gentle old Hannah
Tupper, an outcast Quaker, known as the witch of Blackbird Pond.
This association, along with Kit's other nonconforming ways,
leads to her being accused of practicing witchcraft. In the
pretrial inquiry, Prudence Cruff, the daughter of Kit's accusers,
and Nat Eaton, the son of the captain whose ship carried her to
Connecticut, are responsible for the charges being withdrawn.
The story concludes satisfactorily a year following Kit's arrival with the engagement of the three girls: Mercy to John
Holbrook, a ministerial student; Judith to wealthy young William
Ashby who courted Kit for months; and Kit to Nat.
    At the time Mrs. Speare wrote the book, Wethersfield, one of
the oldest towns in New England, had been her home for twenty
years. She found the historical research fascinating but took
care to include historical detail only as it was of importance
to the characters. She chose the year 1687 arbitrarily because
she wanted to include the hiding of the Connecticut Charter, a
vignette showing that already America was moving toward independence. Essentially she recreated a Puritan community as viewed
through the eyes of an outsider, Kit. Against this well-realized
background, she introduces a number of interesting characters.
Although Kit develops the most, there are observable changes in
several other characters, too. Uncle Matthew alters his opinion
of Kit, and John Holbrook becomes his own man. Through her experiences and the examples set by Cousin Mercy and Hannah, Kit
changes: she learns more self-control, becomes less selfish, and
realizes that all people's lives are not like hers had been in
tropical Barbados. The witchcraft theme is well developed through
the plot which moves quickly. The situation that will develop is
foreshadowed early in the story when Goodwife Cruff suspects Kit
of being a witch because she can swim. Except for Hannah's Quaker
use of "thee" and "thy," the characters speak present-day English.

1959

N185   CARLSON, NATALIE. The Family under the Bridge. Illustrated
       by Garth Williams. New York: Harper, 1958, 97 pp.
       Fiction   Gr. 2-6
       In post-World War II Paris, high-priced housing forces the
mother of red-headed Suzy, Paul, and Evelyne to set up housekeeping in a sheltered nook under a bridge. This spot happens to be
the chosen home of Armand, a happy hobo. Although he is determined not to take on responsibilities, in a short time the "star-
lings"--his term for the children--capture his heart, and at the
end "Grandpa" Armand secures a job for himself and a home for the
little ones. The gypsies that were a part of the pastoral life
in earlier Newbery books, including Dobry and The Good Master,
appear in Paris still mending pots and pans, but now traveling by
car and truck. Armand and his adopted family live with the gypsies briefly. For an unusual Christmas Eve celebration Armand
takes his family to the party given by the Ladies of Notre Dame
for the hobos of Paris. These events are typical of the happy,
out-of-the-ordinary experiences the children have with Armand.
       Natalie Carlson handles her materials with a light touch.
Garth Williams's black and white pictures--one or two full-page
ones for each of the nine chapters--capture the charm of the
debonair Armand and the three appealing children.

N186   De JONG, MEINDERT. Along Came a Dog. Illustrated by Maurice
       Sendak. New York: Harper, 1958, 172 pp.
       Fiction   Gr. 4-10
       Along Came a Dog tells of the friendship that develops between
a little red hen, the only red hen in a white flock, and a large
black dog that comes along in the first chapter; on the periphery
is a man, Joe, who talks to animals. For a year, since the rest
of the red flock was destroyed by a pack of dogs, the little red
hen has been the man's special pet. On the day in early spring
that he turns the chickens loose in the barnyard for the first
time, the little hen's toes, frozen during the winter and now
dead, fall off. At that moment the dog arrives, obviously looking for a home.
       Remembering what the dogs did to his chickens causes Joe to
decide that he will take the dog for a ride and let him out. He
takes the hen, too, because, with her toes gone, she is crippled
and may be harmed by the flock. During the ride, the little hen
looks at the dog inquisitively and the dog fixes his eyes on her.
The man and the little hen come back from the ride. Later the
dog turns up again, too. When the man sees him he takes him away
a second time. This time the dog sneaks back and stays hidden
when the man is around, but, when he is away working at the big
farm, he becomes the little hen's protector.
       Then the little red hen disappears. Unknown to Joe, she has
made a nest under the willow at the edge of the swamp, laid some

eggs, and become broody. The dog sleeps by the nest to guard her.
When the man finally sees the dog again, once more he packs him
off, pushing him out in the middle of a busy town.

This time the dog does not find his way back for two weeks.
During that time, his lingering scent about the little hen's
nest protects her at night, but in the daytime, the watching
hawks prevent her from going for food. By the time the dog
returns she is nearly starved. That day the chicks hatch. The
big black dog leads the little hen and her five chicks home.
The man sees them coming. There will be no more rides for the
dog. Now, he, too, has a home.

Plot, style, and characterization all contribute to making
this simple, moving story memorable. Extraordinary suspense is
attained as the author transfers the hen, the dog, and the man
from one happening to another to reach a desirable, but logical,
outcome. The author's diction, particularly his use of verbs,
enhances the telling as do Maurice Sendak's pictures. The little
red hen, running about on her knucklebones after her toes are
frozen off, with her clucks and pecks of tenderness for the man
and her tyranny toward the dog when she becomes broody, seems
almost human although she is ever true to her species. Perhaps
De Jong's naturalistic animals seem human because he so subtly
interprets their instincts that the reader comes to regard them
with the concern ordinarily felt only for human beings. The
author avoids sentimentality and keeps the large scene in perspective: the hawks are the natural enemies of the chickens and
the reader is glad the dog is near to protect the hen and her
chicks from them; still the story is not diminished by De Jong's
showing that it is the hawks' need that causes them to prey on
domestic animal life, and that they, too, are, as Joe observes,
"splendid." Even though he appears to take no particular pains
to describe, De Jong has recreated here a typical small farm of
the 1920s or 1930s--probably similar to the one on which he lived
during the Depression years and where, his brother wrote, he came
"face to face and soul to soul with all the animals he had always
loved" (David Cornel de Jong, Biographical Note, "My Brother
Meindert," in Newbery Medal Books: 1922-1955, p. 430).

N187   KALNAY, FRANCIS. Chucaro: Wild Pony of the Pampa. Illus-
        trated by Julian de Miskey. New York: Harcourt, Brace,
        1958 (OP), 127 pp.
        Fiction   Gr. 4-8

Twelve-year-old Pedrito lives with his drunken father, the
old Vaquero, on a large cattle and horse ranch in the Argentine
pampas. The time is approximately contemporary with the writing
of the story. One day in the open field, Pedrito finds a beautiful pony "the color of the pink geraniums in the owner's patio"
which his friend, Juan, a most excellent gaucho, lassos for him.

1959

They name him Chucaro. When the ranch owner asks his manager for a pony for his spoiled son, Armando, the manager thinks of Chucaro. Because they will not give up the pony, Juan is fired and told to leave the ranch and take Chucaro with him. Juan on his horse, Gitana, and Pedrito on Chucaro leave the next day, striking off in the direction of the Waterfalls of Iguazá, which Juan has long desired to visit.

The story reveals a strong sense of place, moves briskly, and is gay in tone. Even Juan's being fired is not treated as a major calamity. The life and activity of the Argentinian estancia are well described, including the differences in modes of living between the patron and his gauchos and other ranch people. The owner lives in a house with sixty-five windows; the gauchos live in windowless little adobe casitas made from mud mixed with either cornstalks or horse dung. Yet the gauchos are happy working, dancing, drinking, and eating huge quantities of meat roasted over an open fire. The narrative is informal--the author at times speaks directly to the reader--yet the story is integrated and the easy conversational style matches the way of life being shown. Vigorous black and white drawings catch the expressions and personalities of the people and the spirit of the handsome pony Chucaro.

N188   STEELE, WILLIAM O. The Perilous Road. Illustrated by Paul
           Caldone. New York: Harcourt, Brace, 1958, 191 pp.
           Fiction: historical   Gr. 4-8
    This is a Civil War story for younger readers. Eleven-year-old Tennessee mountain boy, Chris Brabson, hates the Yankees and cannot understand why his older brother has joined the Northern Army. When he sees a Federal wagon-train making camp for the night, he gets the word to his squirrel-hunting companion, Silas Agee, believed by Chris to be a Confederate spy. Later, after he learns that his brother may be with the wagon-train, he goes to the camp to warn him. While looking for his brother, Chris talks to and is treated kindly by a number of Yankee soldiers. He is in the camp when the Confederate Cavalry attacks. He sees the battle at close range and is sickened as he reflects on what he is certain are the consequences of his action. Through this painful experience he comes to realize the meaning of his father's words: "War is the worst thing that can happen to folks," and hatred is "a big knife cutting folks off from each other."

Authentic background and good characterization combine with a strong theme and compelling action to make this a memorable story. Customs of the mountain people, their speech, and appropriate similes all contribute to the realism of the story. We see them snaking up logs for firewood, making cornhusk mattresses, singing ballads, and telling ghost stories to make "setting down" tasks pleasant in the accomplishment. On the Brabson's mountain top "on a still night you could most nigh hear a frog swallowing bugs"; in the dark Chris "floundered around like a three-legged cow." Good black and white illustrations depict the characters, the country, and the events of the story.

1960

N189   KRUMGOLD, JOSEPH. <u>Onion John</u>. Illustrated by Symeon Shimin.
       New York: Thomas Y. Crowell, 1959, 248 pp.
       Fiction   Gr. 5-8
       Twelve-year-old Andy Rusch, Jr., becomes friends with European-born Onion John, who lives in a little hut close to the dump and does odd jobs. The setting is a small town in New Jersey during the 1950s. Andy's friendship with Onion John brings into focus a conflict that has been developing between the boy and his father, a hardware store owner who had wanted to be an engineer and now plans that Andy shall follow this profession. Onion John believes in old superstitions and practices old customs that Andy finds fascinating but which his father rejects as unscientific. One day Mr. Rusch visits Onion John's home with Andy and decides that the Rotary Club, as a project, should build John a new house. Nearly the whole community participates in building the house which burns the day after it is completed. When it appears that the club is determined to rebuild it even though John does not want a new house, John leaves town. But before his departure, John causes Andy's father to realize that he cannot choose his son's career. Overjoyed, Andy looks forward to becoming a hardware merchant like his father, as he had always wished.
       The characters of Andy, his father, and Onion John are well-drawn and believable as are the relationships between Andy and the two men. Amusing incidents lighten the tone of the story which is told by Andy. Well-intentioned do-gooders are humorously satirized and the theme that children should be permitted to make their own decisions is developed without didacticism.

N190   GEORGE, JEAN. <u>My Side of the Mountain</u>. Illustrated by the
       author. New York: E. P. Dutton, 1959, 178 pp.
       Fiction   Gr. 4-8
       Sam Gribley, about fourteen, runs away from his home in New York City, not because he is estranged from his parents, but because he is tired of living with ten other persons in four crowded rooms. He goes to the Catskills to a specific destination: the farm abandoned by his great-grandfather Gribley nearly a hundred years earlier but still in the family's name.
       In his own words Sam records his year on the mountain living off the land. Sam fashions himself a house in the hollow trunk of a huge old hemlock, furnishing it with a bed made from ash

1960

slats, a small fireplace of stones and clay, and a deerskin door.
He hunts, traps, and fishes, prepares his own salt, and learns to
eat all kinds of wild plants. In the winter he keeps warm in
rabbit underwear and a deerskin suit. He makes friends with a
weasel and raccoon and tames a falcon which he teaches to hunt
for him. Sam loves the primitive life, but he misses his family.
When his parents, brothers, and sisters arrive with plans to build
a house and reestablish themselves on the land, Sam is delighted.

The author writes from firsthand knowledge of her subject; yet
the information never overpowers the story nor seems to be offered
as explanation, since it is so closely related to Sam. The style
is slightly more formal than conversational, but it seems natural
for an intelligent, observant boy recording his experiment in survival. From time to time, Sam inserts into his narrative passages
from notes he made during the course of his experiment, as when
he gives his instructions for making snowshoes or his recipe for
possum soup. These notes increase the realism and make the story
more credible, as do the author's many sketches of plants and the
useful articles Sam devises.

N191   JOHNSON, GERALD. America Is Born: A History for Peter.
        Illustrated by Leonard Everett Fisher. New York:
        Morrow, 1959, 254 pp.
        Information: history   Gr. 4-8
    This is the first of a three-volume history of America written
by the author for his grandson. The third volume, America Moves
Forward, was a Newbery Honor Book in 1961. The first book tells
of the following: the discovery of the New World by Columbus; the
other voyages of discovery and exploration; the founding of the
thirteen British colonies and the settling of colonies by other
nations; the conflict between Britain and France over control of
the country culminating in the French and Indian War; events leading to the Revolutionary War; and the war itself.

    The swift-moving narrative places the events of three hundred
years of American history in perspective. The author avoids making explanations too involved but relates causes and effects in
enough detail to be meaningful. He selects significant incidents
and gives them color and reality as when he recreates the settlement of Jamestown. He also highlights a few historical personages:
Queen Elizabeth I, Captain John Smith, and George Washington.
Johnson uses clear, vigorous language and a personal style appropriate for a grandfather addressing his grandson and for making
the familiar events seem fresh. Large print aids readability.
The many authentically detailed illustrations in black and white
add information and impart the spirit of the text. There is an
index.

1960

N192   KENDALL, CAROL. The Gammage Cup. Illustrated by Erik Blegvad.
        New York: Harcourt, Brace, 1959, 221 pp.
        Fantasy   Gr. 4-7
    The setting is the inaccessible and verdant Land Between the
Mountains. There, for 880 years, a colony of small people, the
Minnipins, have lived in peace in twelve nearly identical villages. Nearly all of the inhabitants of Slipper-on-the-Water,
one of the villages, are conformists who wear green cloaks,
paint their front doors green, and revere tradition. Their first
family are the Periods, one of whom, Ltd., is the mayor. One of
the nonconformists, Curley Green, an artist, has a red front door.
Another, Muggles, sometimes wears an orange sash, rather than the
usual brown one. The two others referred to derisively as "Oh,
Them" spend their time in thoroughly impractical ways: Walter
the Earl studies ancient parchments and searches for early scrolls
and treasure; and Gummy idles his time away exploring the countryside and mountains and writing nonsense rhymes, called "scribbles."
    When a contest for the best village is announced, the Minnipins
of Slipper-on-the Water decide that if they are to have a chance
to win the prize all houses and all dress must be identical. The
prize is the country's most precious object, the Gammage Cup,
brought to the Land Between the Mountains by its founder, Gammage.
Because they will not conform, the four are exiled to the mountains. One other, Mingy, the keeper of the town's money box,
chooses to go with the nonconformists.
    In the mountains, the outlaws, under the leadership of Muggles,
establish a home for themselves and discover that the ancient
enemy of the Minnipins, the hairless Mushroom people, have tun-
neled through a mountain and are preparing to attack. The five
outlaws rouse the village and lead the army that repulses the
attack by the Mushrooms. In a happy ending, Slipper-on-the-Water
wins the Gammage Cup--because of the five exiles.
    Many intricate details, a map of the country, and pictures of
the small people work together to create an original, believable
world. There are traditional elements, also: battle is waged
with ancient magical swords that, as in Tolkien's books, glow
and become warm at the approach of an enemy. The theme of daring to be oneself develops naturally in the clashes between the
individualists and the tyrannical, aristocratic Periods. At the
time the book was published, it was a novel twist to place a girl,
Muggles, in the role of leader. The delightful play on words,
noticeable especially in the names, contributes humor as do
Gummy's scribbles and Muggles's maxims.

1961

N193   O'DELL, SCOTT. <u>Island of the Blue Dolphins</u>. Boston:
        Houghton Mifflin, 1960, 184 pp.
        Fiction   Gr. 4-8
     The setting for this story is the island of San Nicolas
(called Island of the Blue Dolphins in the story), seventy-five
miles southwest of Los Angeles, where, from 1835 to 1853, an
Indian woman lived alone. Like Defoe, who based <u>Robinson Crusoe</u>
on an actual incident, the survival of a man alone on an island
for many years, Scott O'Dell chose a similar historical event and
embellished it to give the reader a believable and memorable experience. Twelve-year-old Karana and her six-year-old brother
Ramo are left behind when their people are being removed by ship
from their home island after many of the men have been slain by
Aleutian hunters. Ramo is soon killed by wild dogs and the remainder of the book is Karana's story of survival, completely
alone, for eighteen years.
     There is so much conflict and the details of Karana's everyday
life are so interestingly presented that the story is noteworthy
as a survival story, but it is a great deal more than that. On
the second level, the author is dealing with man's basic need to
love and be loved. On a still deeper level he weaves into the
structure of the story and shows us through the action that the
way we react to disaster is of more importance than the disaster
itself. Scott O'Dell states in his Newbery acceptance speech
that through Karana he "wanted to say to children and to all
those who will listen that we have a chance to come into a new
relationship to the things around us." He goes on to say that
in her time alone on the island Karana made the change from a
world "where everything lived only to be exploited, to a new and
more meaningful world. She learned first that we each must be an
island secure unto ourselves. Then, that we must 'transgress our
limits' in reverence for all life." O'Dell extends this idea of
a new relationship to forgiveness of our enemies. It is first
seen in Karana's saving the life of and adopting the dog that had
killed her brother. This forgiving "lies in the heart of the
episode of Karana and her enemy, the Aleut girl." So strongly
does O'Dell feel about this that he can say: "I believe that
the hopes of civilization, unique and obscure as they are, really
exist in the act of identification with our enemies" (<u>Newbery
and Caldecott Medal Books: 1956-1965</u>, ed. Lee Kingman [Boston:
Horn Book, 1965], pp. 102-104).
     Part of the power of the book comes from the emotional response
it elicits from the reader. Since Karana tells her own story, we
know what her thoughts and emotions are. Although few people have
experienced the extreme isolation and loneliness that Karana does,
almost everyone knows what it is like to be lonely and can identify
with her need to love and be needed.

In this, as in his other books, Scott O'Dell's style adds distinction to the narrative. Since Karana is telling the story, it reads much like a diary or journal. The sentence structure is basically short and simple. She tells her story with stoicism, dignity, and a certain restraint. The natural world provides the subject for the metaphorical language throughout: "The sea . . . is a flat stone without any scratches"; the sea elephants "like gray boulders . . . sat on the pebbly slope." The style is particularly suitable to the concept of the book considering the setting and Karana's cultural background.

N194   JOHNSON, GERALD. <u>America Moves Forward: A History For Peter</u>.
        Illustrated by Leonard Everett Fisher. New York: Morrow,
        1960 (OP), 256 pp.
        Information: history   Gr. 4-8
The third volume of the history of America which the author addressed to his grandson covers United States participation in World War I, President Wilson's unsuccessful battle for the League of Nations, the Russian Revolution, the Depression, the rise of Fascism and Nazism, World War II, the United Nations, the Cold War, and the War in Korea. In April 1917, when the United States entered World War I, the course of America changed for the third time since the colonists landed at Jamestown in 1607. World War I thrust upon the United States the duties of a Great Power. The events most emphasized in this work are those showing the United States in that role.
    As in the earlier books of his trilogy (<u>America Is Born</u> was a Newbery Honor Book in 1960), the author deals with underlying causes and explains complex issues clearly. He provides good word portraits of Woodrow Wilson, Franklin D. Roosevelt, Adolf Hitler, and others. As in the other books he points out weaknesses and mistakes as well as courage and triumphs. Leonard Everett Fisher's illustrations of events and people are in accord with the text. There is an index.

N195   SCHAEFER, JACK. <u>Old Ramon</u>. Illustrated by Harold West.
        Boston: Houghton Mifflin, 1960, 102 pp.
        Fiction   Gr. 5-9
The boy in the story, whose name is not given, is the son of Ramon's patron. His father has sent him to spend the summer in the mountains with Old Ramon, to watch and listen to him, and to learn the care of sheep. The boy tells Ramon, "You are my book about sheep." The brief narrative covers the few days required to drive the sheep to the grazing grounds. Even in that short time the boy learns much. He sees Old Ramon deal with such commonplace situations as getting the balky sheep across a stream to such dangerous ones as saving the flock in a sandstorm. Ramon tells him stories, too--stories that are interesting but teach of

1961

life and living. He tells how he and the boy's grandfather in
their youth drove a big flock of sheep across the Mojave desert
to California, and how his dog Pedro saved his life when he was
attacked by a bear. After the boy's dog, Sancho, is killed
fighting a wolf, Ramon promises him a pup from a litter fathered
by Pedro, the very best dog Old Ramon has ever had.
    The writing enhances the simple story which is told with dig-
nity in cadenced prose.

N196   THOMPSON, GEORGE [George Selden]. <u>The Cricket in Times Square</u>.
       Illustrated by Garth Williams. New York: Farrar, Straus,
       1960, 151 pp.
       Fantasy   Gr. 2-6
    Chester Cricket arrives in New York City's Times Square Subway
Station one June in a picnic basket he entered while the owner
was picnicking in Chester's native Connecticut. Mario Bellini,
whose parents operate an unprofitable newsstand in the station,
finds him and puts him in the newsstand for a pet. Tucker Mouse
and Harry Cat, who share a home in a nearby drainpipe, become his
good friends. Chester has a satisfying summer with these two
friends and with Mario who plays games with him and buys him a
cricket cage in Chinatown.
    In August Chester begins to chirp. One night while he, Tucker,
and Harry are having a dinner party complete with background music
from the Bellinis' small radio, the three friends make a startling
discovery: Chester has the ability to imitate perfectly any music
he hears once on the radio. The next day the Bellinis overhear
him playing an Italian folksong he had heard the previous evening.
Chester, his cage atop a stack of magazines, is soon giving con-
certs twice a day and business is booming for the Bellinis. As
fall approaches, Chester becomes so homesick for Connecticut that
he feels he must return. Harry Cat carries him on his back to
Grand Central Station where he catches a train for home. When
he cannot find him, Mario is convinced he has gone home. Harry
and Tucker make plans to visit Chester in the country the following summer.
    A cricket with Chester's unusual talent seems far from reality,
yet so successfully does the author evoke the subway station and
the New York City atmosphere that the reader accepts it. Garth
Williams's twenty-five full-page illustrations in black and white
provide enriching detail for everything from the interior of Sai
Fong's novelty shop to Chester in concert before an enraptured
audience.

1962

N197   SPEARE, ELIZABETH GEORGE.   The Bronze Bow.   Boston: Houghton
        Mifflin, 1961, 255 pp.
        Fiction: historical   Gr. 5-10

For ten years, since the death of his father at the hands of
the Romans and his mother's death as a result a few weeks later,
eighteen-year-old Daniel bar Jamin of ancient Galilee has lived
only to avenge their deaths. The first years he was with his
grandmother and younger sister, Leah. Then he was apprenticed
to Amalek, the village blacksmith, who treated him so badly he
ran away to the mountains. There, for five years, he lived with
and did the blacksmithing for Rosh and his band. Rosh is building an army and although Daniel regards him as the Messiah who
will one day free the country from the Romans, some people say
he is nothing but a bandit concerned only with his own welfare.

After Amalek and then his grandmother die, Daniel goes back
to the village to look after Leah. Jesus has begun to preach
and Simon the Zealot, like Daniel a blacksmith, longs to follow
him. He offers his home and attached smithy to Daniel and Leah.
Daniel works in the shop, but also, with a friend, Joel, the son
of a wealthy rabbi, recruits young men who meet in secret and
anticipate the time they can become a part of Rosh's liberating
army. They take as their symbol and password a bronze bow from
the Song of David: "He trains my hands for war, so that my arms
can bend a bow of bronze." Only he who is strong enough to bend
a bow of bronze would be strong enough to vanquish the Romans.

Daniel, Joel, and Joel's sister, Malthace, go to hear Jesus
several times. They are very much drawn to him, but since he
does not speak of raising an army, Daniel thinks he cannot be
the Messiah. While spying for Rosh, Joel is caught by the Romans.
When Rosh refuses to attempt to rescue him, Daniel and eighteen
other boys decide they will try the rescue themselves. They succeed, but would have failed had not Samson, a huge black-skinned
man who was devoted to Daniel, followed them and assisted.

Samson is killed in the skirmish. Daniel now feels he must
avenge Samson as well as his parents. When he tells Jesus this,
Jesus replies that Samson gave him love, not vengeance, and He
asks him if he can repay such love with hate. Daniel listens
but he cannot yet give up the hate for which he has lived so long.
In the final chapter when Leah lies near death, Jesus heals her.
Daniel's first act showing his acceptance of Jesus is to invite
a Roman soldier who has been a friend to Leah in to see her.

Mrs. Speare spent three years in research and this is reflected
in the atmosphere of reality created by her careful choice of historical details. Daniel is a well-developed, believable character, as is his sister, Leah. In her Newbery acceptance speech,
Mrs. Speare states that she felt she failed in her portrait of

1962

Jesus. Many will not agree with her but with the reviewer who
wrote, "The introduction of Jesus is done with such skill that
he is neither diminished nor sentimentalized . . ." (M. S. Libby,
New York Herald Tribune Books, 12 Nov. 1961, Sec. 12, p. 4).
Certainly she did accomplish what she set out to do: "I would
show the change wrought in just one boy who came to know the
teacher in Galilee" (Newbery and Caldecott Medal Books: 1956-
1965, ed. Lee Kingman [Boston: Horn Book, 1965], p. 114).

N198   TUNIS, EDWIN. Frontier Living. Illustrated by the author.
       Cleveland: World, 1961, 167 pp.
       Information: history   Gr. 5 up
     This large, beautifully designed book, similar in format to
several other books of American history by Mr. Tunis, is both an
authentic reference source and a book for pleasurable browsing.
In nineteen sections the author describes the frontiers of America
beginning with the "Deepwater Frontier" of the seventeenth century,
followed by "The Piedmont" of the early eighteenth, and ending with
"The Sodbusters and the Cattle Drivers" of the late nineteenth
century. Between chapters he provides a brief historical transition in italic type and a map of the section that follows. Within
the chapters he discusses the conditions of daily living primarily as they existed for the common people. He describes their
everyday work, recreation, religion, means of transportation,
and government.
     The writing is lively and candid. The author is neither
patronizing nor sentimental in discussing the Indians, taking
the side of the Indians against the pioneers where the rights
of Indians were clearly violated. More than 200 black and white
meticulously accurate drawings illuminate the text. There are
drawings of all kinds of tools, utensils, and modes of transportation, including simple items such as a log cradle and a hominy
block, and complex equipment such as the mechanism of a gristmill.
He even portrays the whole town of Independence, Missouri, in its
heyday. A table of contents and an index facilitate finding
information.

N199   McGRAW, ELOISE JARVIS. The Golden Goblet. New York: Coward-
       McCann, 1961 (OP), 248 pp.
       Fiction: historical   Gr. 5-10
     Ranofer, a boy of twelve or thirteen, son of the recently
deceased goldsmith Thutra, lives in ancient Egypt in the city
of Thebes with his half-brother Gebu. Ranofer did not know of
Gebu, who is much older than he, until the day of his father's
funeral when Gebu arrived and claimed all the father possessed,
including his young son. Gebu, a burly, bad-tempered man, mis-
treats his young brother and ignores his dead father's wish that
Ranofer, who has already shown aptitude for the work, be placed

as a pupil of Zau, the greatest goldsmith in Thebes. Instead, he places him as a porter in a lesser goldsmith's shop and later makes him an apprentice in his own stonecutting shop.

A sequence of events causes Ranofer to suspect that his brother is a thief. But, until he happens to find the magnificent golden goblet concealed in clothing in Gebu's chest, he has no idea that Gebu is robbing the tombs of kings. On the day of the High Nile Festival, while all Thebes is occupied with feasting, Ranofer follows Gebu and his partner-in-crime into the Valley of the Tombs and succeeds, with the help of friends--a boy his age and an old man--in imprisoning the robbers in the tomb they have entered to plunder. The pair is captured and Ranofer is rewarded by the queen. At the close he is to become a pupil of Zau.

Many details of the enormous business that flourished around the preparations made for the dead are smoothly incorporated into this action-filled, suspenseful story.

N200   STOLZ, MARY. Belling the Tiger. Illustrated by Beni
       Montresor. New York: Harper, 1961 (OP), 64 pp.
       Fantasy   Gr. 2-4

The story arises from the old fable in which the mice endeavor to bell the cat. Asa and Rambo, two small, timid mice, are appointed by Portman, the bossy leader, to bell Siri, the cat. Reluctantly they go to the hardware store and get a collar with a bell. While crossing the docks on the way home they escape a menacing cat by running along a great rope that attaches a ship to shore. The gangplank goes up before the cat can cross it and the ship sets sail for a tropical land with the mice aboard.

There they go ashore and find a sleeping cat, one hundred, maybe two hundred times larger than Siri. In a moment of daring they decide to bell this great cat by placing the collar over its tail. Before they can release the collar, the cat raises its tail and Asa and Rambo go up with it. Expecting to die, they soon find themselves in interesting conversation with the cat which tells them it is really a tiger. They feel like heroes when, while riding on the tiger's back, they frighten an elephant.

Soon they return to the ship and sail home. In the meeting Portman holds to deal with their running away, Asa and Rambo do not tell of their adventures because they know they will not be believed, but they learn they are no longer intimidated by Portman. In fact they ask for a promotion from the basement to the pantry. The other mice are delighted with their bravery in standing up to their tyrannical chief, who is obliged to acquiesce.

The good diction and sprightly dialogue make this old story with a new twist excellent for reading aloud. The mice's adventure is interesting of itself, but it also contains subtle satire.

1962

The animals are appealingly portrayed in Beni Montresor's illustrations.

<u>1963</u>

N201   L'ENGLE, MADELEINE. <u>A Wrinkle in Time</u>. New York: Farrar,
        Straus, 1962, 211 pp.
        Science Fantasy   Gr. 5-9
   In <u>A Wrinkle in Time</u>, Madeleine L'Engle combines elements of
fantasy and science fiction with social criticism to create a
novel concerned with themes of universal good and evil. The
book's primary science fiction device is the tesseract, an in-
stantaneous, faster-than-the-speed-of-light method of space and
time travel involving the fifth dimension. By means of the
tesseract, Meg Murry, a high-school freshman; her precocious
five-year-old brother, Charles Wallace; and Calvin O'Keefe, a
high-school friend, embark on an intergalactic journey in search
of the Murry children's father, a scientist who disappeared
while conducting his own space/time experiments. While engaged
in their travels they discover that the entire universe is involved in a battle between the forces of good and the "Black
Thing," a force of cosmic annihilation. They are brought eventually to Camazotz, a planet in many ways similar to Earth, but
which is totally dominated by the forces of cosmic evil. Camazotz
is a planet of complete conformity, with those who deviate in the
least from the most rigid behavioral norms being subject to the
horrors of "reprocessing." Camazotz is under the central control
of "It," a large, disembodied brain which seems to be L'Engle's
symbol of rigid and emotionless intellect. The book describes
the children's struggles with "It," the rescue of Mr. Murry, and
their subsequent escape.
   While on one level an exciting excursion in fantastic adventure, the book functions at another level as an exercise in
social criticism. Camazotz constitutes an anti-Utopia exemplifying the evils of conformity and patternless intellect. "It" expresses in an extreme form some of the evils of contemporary
society, particularly those of the America of the 1950s, the age
of conformity. The society of Camazotz also finds analogy in the
totalitarian practices of the Soviet Union and Nazi Germany. The
novel upholds the ideal of individualism versus rigid conformity
and the powers of love and emotion as opposed to emotionless intelligence. While these themes are clearly present, the story is
not obtrusively didactic; its "message" is well integrated into
the fictional structure of plot and character. The novel moves
convincingly from the mundane to the fantastic and provides a
compelling image of very human characters engaging themselves in
a conflict of universal proportions.

N202   ALGER, LECLAIRE [Sorche Nic Leodhas].   Thistle and Thyme:
        Tales and Legends from Scotland. Illustrated by Evaline
        Ness. New York: Holt, Rinehart & Winston, 1962 (OP),
        143 pp.
        Folk Tales   Gr. 4-10
      The author has recorded ten Scottish stories not found in
earlier collections for children as she remembered hearing them
told in her own childhood. Included are legends, cottage stories,
seanachie stories, and sgeulachdan. Each of these types is explained in the introduction where the tales are classified as to
type and origin.
      One of the three legends is "St. Cuddy and the Gray Geese," a
medieval legend originating in the Lowlands. It tells how St.
Cuddy changed a greedy old woman and her flock of twelve fat
geese into great gray stones. "The Lass Who Went Out at the Cry
of Dawn" is a seanachie, a story told by a wandering storyteller.
The lass who went out at the cry of dawn never came home again.
Eventually her younger sister found her in a wizard's castle and
rescued her. "The Changeling and the Fond Young Mother" is a
cottage tale, which the author calls a true folk tale because it
was made up by a common person and repeated around the fires on
winter evenings. The fairies are usually present in this type of
tale. In this one a wild fairy woman steals the fond young
mother's bonny babe. One of the five sgeulachdan--a story
created by a master storyteller for a particular occasion--is
"The Bride Who Out-Talked the Water Kelpie." This story was
told at the wedding of a cousin of the author's grandfather who
brought the story to America. A good old woman with second sight
helps the soldier's young bride to undo the spell put upon her by
a malicious water kelpie.
      Gaelic phrases and intonations establish native character and
environment as do Evaline Ness's striking woodcuts.

N203   COOLIDGE, OLIVIA. Men of Athens. Illustrated by Milton
        Johnson. Boston: Houghton Mifflin, 1962, 244 pp.
        Biography   Gr. 6-10
      This collective biography consists of thirteen separate bio-
graphical stories covering the three portions of the "century of
Athens" between 500 and 400 B.C. Presented as fiction, these
biographies provide intimate glimpses into the lives of the subjects. At the same time, the author, who received a classical
education at Oxford, has maintained historical accuracy, an accuracy that may be more intuitive than literal, akin perhaps to
Carlyle's interpretation of the French Revolution. Such a presentation is possible only when an author has complete mastery of
the materials.
      Men of Athens offers memorable portraits of such great Athen-
ians as Pericles, Euripides, and Socrates. Equally well done are

1963

fictitious portraits of less illustrious Athenians. Through
these men--a small businessman who serves on the Athenian Council
of five hundred, an athlete who twice wins the pentathlon in the
games at Olympia, and one of the jurors for the trial of Socrates--
the author clearly shows the operation of the democracy and its
importance to all Athenians. Miss Coolidge also focuses on women
of Athens: on Aspasia, Pericles's gifted mistress; on Socrates's
complaining wife, Xanthippe, as well as the wives of the less
notable. Although the book presents Athenian life panoramically,
it does more than pictorially represent the times: it allows the
reader to experience the emotional and intellectual climate of
that great period.

1964

N204   NEVILLE, EMILY. It's Like This, Cat. Illustrated by Emil
        Weiss. New York: Harper & Row, 1963, 180 pp.
        Fiction   Gr. 5-9
    In It's Like This, Cat, Dave Mitchell, fourteen, relates epi-
sodes that reveal the life of a typical middle-class boy of the
1960s. Dave lives in an apartment in Manhattan with his mother,
his cat, and his lawyer father, who is frequently exasperated
with his son. Dave is just as frequently impatient and irritated
with his father: "My father is always talking about how a dog
can be very educational for a boy. That is one reason I got a
cat."
    Although there is a generation gap between Dave and his dad,
it is a gap that is not unbridgeable. Cat is a focal point for
some of the clashes that occur between Dave and his father and
precipitates encounters between Dave and Tom, a college-age boy,
and Mary, a girl of his own age. Tom has also had difficulties
with his father, and Mary's parents think only of her mental
development and concern themselves very little about her emotional and physical welfare. As Dave observes the contrast between his family life and that of Tom or of Mary, he begins to
appreciate his own father more.
    Some of the most pleasing chapters are those touching on the
boy-girl relationship. Two or three times Dave and Mary meet and
spend several hours together: they go to see West Side Story and
ride the ferry to Staten Island on a cold, wet, blowy day. Emily
Neville succeeds in giving a wonderful sense of modern New York
City: its sights, sounds, smells, and even its motion as Dave
gets about on bus or subway. The modern teenage conversation
sets the pace and establishes the tone. Overall, It's Like This,
Cat emphasizes the positive rather than the negative aspects of
growing up: there are difficult times, but the buoyancy and
enthusiasm of childhood are still much in evidence, also. By

the 1960s, when this book was written, this attitude was less prevalent in children's books than it had been in earlier decades.

N205   NORTH, STERLING. <u>Rascal: A Memoir of a Better Era</u>. Illustrated by John Schoenherr. New York: E. P. Dutton, 1963, 189 pp.

Fiction   Gr. 4-7

A strong emotional link between child and animal is manifested in <u>Rascal</u>. Based on the author's boyhood, <u>Rascal</u> recreates a year in the life of a twelve-year-old boy and his pet raccoon. Sterling acquires Rascal when he is an unweaned baby that has to be given warm milk through a wheat straw. As Sterling delightedly relives the satisfying hours spent with his raccoon, the reader learns of its habits. Since the story is told in the first person, Sterling's animals are not given thoughts except as he guesses at them. As in <u>The Biggest Bear</u> and <u>The Yearling</u>, a problem develops when the pet grows larger and causes damage: Rascal discovers the delicious sweet corn, and at night raids the gardens in the neighborhood; later he is caught in a hen house. Because Rascal now must be kept penned, Sterling decides to free him, if he wishes to go. It is mating season and Rascal chooses to return to his kind.

For several years before he found Rascal, Sterling had earned Christmas money by trapping muskrats and selling the pelts. That fall Rascal accompanied the boy as he oiled his traps, sniffing and examining them. As he watched his pet with its "sensitive, questing hands," Sterling became repelled at the idea of killing. He burned his fur catalogues and hung his traps in the loft of the barn never to use them again. Learning to understand and love the ways of wild creatures had led him to want to preserve them.

Subtitled "a memoir of a better era," <u>Rascal</u> is also a period story showing what life was like for a boy in a small Wisconsin town during World War I. There no one locked doors; woods and unpolluted streams were close to the town. Automobiles were just becoming common--at the Irish picnic a race is run between a spirited horse and a Model-T roadster. Traveling in the days before superhighways was perforce more leisurely. The great influenza epidemic of 1918 swept through the town killing more of its citizens than died in the War, but the War casts a gloomy shadow over bright days when Sterling thinks of his brother and others fighting in France. All of this is appreciated by an adult reading the book. For a child, it is simply a good story of a boy and his fascinating and lovable pet.

N206   WIER, ESTER. <u>The Loner</u>. Illustrated by Christine Price. New York: D. McKay, 1963, 153 pp.

Fiction   Gr. 4-8

1964

The loner is an orphan boy who knows neither his name nor age. For as long as he can remember he has fended for himself and earned his living as a migrant by harvesting crops. After seeing the one person who has been kind to him killed in a horrible farm accident, the boy leaves the fields and finally is taken in by Boss, a Montana sheep woman who is spending the winter with her sheep on the range. The story relates his adjustment to the new life and his transformation from a loner to one who cares and is cared for. As Tex, one of Boss's men, tells the boy: "Somebody will care if you just give 'em a chance. . . . There's always people who need you as much as you need them. . . ."

The Loner has a faster-moving plot than the other Newbery books concerned with sheepraising. That may be because a sheep station in winter is a place where something is likely to happen, especially to an inexperienced boy. The exciting incidents develop from natural situations: protecting the sheep from storms and wild animals.

The author tells a story that grips the heart yet avoids sentimentality. It would be easy to be sentimental about a forlorn waif like David, who gains his name when Boss has him open the Bible at random and from it take a name. He is believable as a boy who has always looked out for himself. He has not even been friendly with animals and at first is wary of the sheep dogs; the only dogs he had known before had been snarling, half-starved strays that hung around the pickers' camps stealing food. His first attachment is to Cluny, the one sheep in the nine hundred with a mind of her own: "I like her because she's a loner," he thought, "and because I know how she feels."

Boss is a memorable character, too. She is six feet two inches tall, and, at the beginning, almost obsessed with the memory of her dead son, Ben, and almost irrational in her desire to get the grizzly that killed him. The scene close to the end in which David shoots the bear and Boss sees him do it is thrilling. David has behaved like a man and even attained a measure of heroism. Boss tells Tex that the slaying reminds her of "David in the Bible, facing up to that giant Goliath with only a stone in his slingshot." The scene is a satisfying climax to all that has gone before, in David's slow but convincing growth from a desperately lonely boy to a courageous young man, capable of giving and receiving devotion.

1965

N207   WOJCIECHOWSKA, MAIA.   Shadow of a Bull.   Illustrated by Alvin
       Smith.   New York: Atheneum, 1964, 165 pp.
       Fiction   Gr. 5-9
       When he is nine, Manolo Olivar becomes aware that everyone in
his hometown of Arcangel, Spain, expects him to become a famous

bullfighter like his dead father. But Manolo feels he is a coward; moreover, he does not have a strong desire to become a matador. Because his father fought and killed his first bull at the age of twelve without ever having practiced, it is decided that Manolo also will fight at the same age under the same circumstances.

Six self-appointed mentors undertake his education for bullfighting. In order not to disgrace his mother, Manolo practices in secret the passes the bullfighter makes with the cape. While he is doing this, a friend, Juan Garcia, poor but with great desire, is sneaking out to play with bulls in the pasture. Once Manolo goes with him and recognizes that Juan has all the qualities that he lacks. He asks to take Juan with him on the day he is to fight his first bull.

By the time he enters the ring, Manolo has overcome fear so that he is able to perform the cape work creditably. He becomes less effective after he picks up the muleta, used in the last part of the bullfight. Having previously decided that he will let his performance in the ring govern his future, at this point Manolo announces that he does not wish to become a bullfighter. He requests that Juan be permitted to take his place in the ring.

As Juan begins a brilliant performance, Manolo goes to sit by the old doctor, because medicine is the vocation he wishes to follow.

The author lived in Spain for awhile and has studied the subject of bullfighting extensively. Once she even fought a bull. Although there is a fair amount of information given about the country and so much information about bullfighting that the book is practically a manual of bullfighting, complete with glossary of terms, it is all in very close relationship to Manolo. All incidents in the story contribute to the growing tension and expectation. The universal themes dealing with courage and of a boy's becoming a man are well developed. Shortly before Manolo is to meet his first bull, he sees a painting that he has never seen before. It is of his father and the first bull he fought. As Manolo studies it, he knows it to be "the face of a boy . . . becoming a man," and he realizes that perhaps that day he, too, will become a man. In addition to giving information about bullfighting, the author emphasizes the art, the grace, and the beauty of the sport. Precise diction and strong black and white illustrations contribute to the artistic whole of the story.

N208   HUNT, IRENE. <u>Across Five Aprils</u>. Chicago: Follett, 1964,
        223 pp.
           Fiction: historical   Gr. 6-10
      For this story set at the time of the Civil War, Irene Hunt
used fresh sources: family letters and records and the stories
she remembered hearing her grandfather tell when she was a child.

1965

Her grandfather was nine at the beginning of the Civil War, the
age of Jethro Creighton, a southern Illinois farm lad and the
character through whom the reader views the story. Possibly because much of what she was writing was her own family's history,
the members of the family stand out as individuals about whom
the reader experiences the concern felt by the family. Although
the primary interest is in the characters, and although the story
relates only the incidents and news that reach the home front,
the author has carefully plotted the story so that the war is
seen in its entirety. A nephew of Mrs. Creighton from Kentucky
visits the family early in the narrative before the firing on
Fort Sumter and expresses the Southern viewpoint and also antic-
ipates some of the problems that will arise from freeing the
slaves. Jethro's brothers are divided, and his favorite brother
Bill fights for the Confederacy. Brothers Tom and John and
cousin Eb serve in the Western theater; and Shad, the schoolmaster loved by fifteen-year-old Jenny Creighton, is in the East.
After the war begins, the hard life is unrelieved by the dances
and other festivities that had previously lessened the daily monotony. But Jethro and Jenny are young and resilient and, even
though often overworked and anxious, still capable of responding
to small pleasures: eating delicious ripe peaches or enjoying a
beautiful spring day. A high point in the story comes when
Jethro, not knowing what to do about Eb, who has deserted and
returned home to hide out in the woods, writes a letter to the
President. Irene Hunt does not state that the letter that comes
to Jethro from the President was really written by Lincoln, but
it is in Lincoln's style, shows his compassion, and reveals his
decision that deserters could return to their regiments without
punishment. The reader closes the book with the feeling he has
lived through the Civil War with the Creighton family.

1966

N209   De TREVIÑO, ELIZABETH BORTON. <u>I, Juan de Pareja</u>. New York:
       Farrar, Straus & Giroux, 1965, 180 pp.
          Biography   Gr. 5-8
       The son of a black slave and a Spaniard, Juan de Pareja was
born in Seville early in the seventeenth century. Upon his
master's death when he was about twelve, Juan became the property
of her nephew, the painter Don Diego Rodriguez de Silva y
Velasquez of Madrid. Juan was treated kindly by Velasquez who
instructed him in grinding and mixing colors and in all matters
relating to painting except painting itself: slaves were not
permitted to practice any of the arts. But Juan longed to paint
and taught himself by observing the Master. Many years later
when Velasquez learned his slave's secret, he gave Juan his

freedom and made him his assistant. While still quite a young
man, Velasquez was made the court painter. In time, he and the
king, Philip IV, became devoted friends. Because of these circumstances, aspects of Spanish court life are introduced naturally into the story.

The records available to Elizabeth de Treviño were scant. In
an afterword she states that "very little, for certain" is known
of the lives of Velasquez and Pareja. She used their paintings
as a supplement to the few known facts. Since the written records
are so few, permitting de Pareja to tell his own story, even
though it is fictionalized, is acceptable.

N210   ALEXANDER, LLOYD. The Black Cauldron. New York: Holt,
       Rinehart & Winston, 1965, 224 pp.
       Fantasy   Gr. 6-9

At Caer Dallben, home of Dallben, the greatest enchanter in
Prydain, Prince Gwydion holds a Council of War. Arawn, Lord of
Annuvin, the Land of Death, poses a new threat to the land. He
has long had among his warriors the mute and deathless Cauldron-
Born, "the stolen bodies of the slain, steeped in Arawn's Cauldron
to give them life again." Now to swell his ranks Arawn has begun
to strike down living men to place in his cauldron. Gwydion plans
to march to Annuvin, seize the cauldron, and destroy it.

Taran, the young assistant Pig-Keeper to Dallben's oracular
pig, Hen Wen, is named to the band whose task is to guard the
pack animals. The leader of this group is the brave and wise
Adaon. Also in Adaon's group is an immensely strong, boastful
young man, Prince Ellidyr. Although Taran and Ellidyr do not get
along well, Adaon keeps peace between them as they ride to Annuvin.
While they stand holding the animals near Arawn's castle, Princess
Eilonwy of the red-gold hair and the creature Gurgi appear unexpectedly; they have followed to have a part in the quest. Shortly,
the bard Fflewddur Fflam, and Doli, a dwarf with the power to make
himself invisible, arrive with disturbing news: the cauldron is
no longer in Annuvin. Gwydion's forces are to ride to King
Smoit's castle for the making of new plans.

Before Adaon's group can start, they are attacked by Arawn's
vicious Huntsmen. After fighting free, they find refuge in a
way post of the Fair Folk kept by the mournful Gwystyl. From him
they learn that the cauldron is in the hands of Orddu, Orwen, and
Orgoch who live in the marshes of Morva. They decide to seek it
there. When they stop to sleep, Ellidyr steals off; his trail
indicates he is going toward the marshes. The Huntsmen attack
again, but Fflewddur and Doli are able to lead them off. Adaon
is mortally wounded, however. Before he dies, he gives Taran his
magic brooch. As soon as he begins to wear the brooch, Taran is
wiser and has greater vision. The following day Taran, Eilonwy,
and Gurgi are reunited with Fflewddur, but not Doli, and proceed
to the marshes.

1966

Orddu, Orwen, and Orgoch prove to be three enchantresses who most often appear as short plump women. They have the cauldron, but the price Taran and his companions have to pay for it is Adaon's brooch. As soon as the cauldron is theirs, they seize iron bars and sledges and attempt to smash it, but their blows do not damage it in the least. Then Orddu tells them that it will cost a life to destroy it: the cauldron will shatter only if someone willingly gives up his life to it.

Taran and his companions know then that they must get the heavy cauldron to Dallben because he alone will know what to do with it. Slowly, and with great effort, they move it across the moorlands, through the Forest of Idris, and across the River Tevvyn. At the far edge, Fflewddur slips on a rock and falls, breaking his arm. The cauldron sinks in the muddy shallows. At this point, Ellidyr turns up. He dictates conditions under which he will lend his great strength to the raising of the cauldron: he is to receive all the credit for finding and winning it. After it is raised, he leaves, taking the three horses to move it.

Next day when Taran sights an ally, King Morgant, he thinks they are safe. But Morgant has turned traitor. They soon find themselves fettered and in a tent with a battered and bound Ellidyr. Morgant announces his intention to use the cauldron in the same way Arawn did. He gives Taran a choice of becoming a war leader for him or becoming, at dawn, the first of the Cauldron-Born.

Just before dawn, Doli, who has made himself invisible, enters the tent. He frees them. Ellidyr, who has told Taran he is sorry for the ill he has done them, plunges from the tent to fling himself into the cauldron. As the cauldron splits, King Smoit and Gwydion burst from the woods. Morgant is killed in the battle. The dead are buried and Taran, Eilonwy, and the other companions ride back to Caer Dallben.

This is the second of the five volumes comprising the Chronicles of Prydain. Evaluation of the series follows The High King, the fifth volume and Newbery Medal Book for 1969 (N222).

N211   JARRELL, RANDALL. The Animal Family. Illustrated by Maurice
       Sendak. New York: Pantheon, 1965, 179 pp.
       Fantasy   Gr. 4 up
    The Animal Family is not a story about animals exclusively, although a bear cub and a lynx kitten become a part of the family. The other members are a hunter, who had lived alone in a log house by the sea, and a mermaid, who joined him after he had won her confidence. The last to join the family is a little boy, washed ashore from a shipwreck and brought home by the lynx and bear.

    Written in a poetic style and adorned with illustrations that complement, this fable for all ages suggests that even persons

who are very different can live together contentedly, even joyously, in a family.

N212   STOLZ, MARY. The Noonday Friends. Illustrated by Louis S.
        Glanzman. New York: Harper & Row, 1965, 182 pp.
        Fiction   Gr. 4-7
    The setting is Greenwich Village during the 1960s. The noon-
day friends are Franny Davis, eleven, and Simone Orgella. Because her mother works away from home, Franny has to take care
of her four-year-old brother, Marshall, after school every day.
Simone often has to watch the current baby, so that the noon
hour is almost the only time for developing friendships. Besides the girls, Francisco, Simone's cousin recently arrived
from Puerto Rico, and all the members of the Davis family are
well-realized characters. In addition to Marshall, Franny has
a twin brother, Jim. Mama, who had come from Ireland fifteen
years earlier, is hard put to be always patient with Papa who is
an artist. But since he cannot provide a living for his family
from his art, he works at any job he can find. Usually it is
uninteresting to him and poorly paid. Mama's job in a laundry
does not bring in much money, either. The story covers the time
Papa Davis has a job, loses it, and finally gets one he says he
can stand. In the same time period, Franny and Simone quarrel
and share good times together.
    The story concerns Franny particularly and the point of view
is most often hers, although not limited to her perceptions only.
At times events unfold through the eyes of the other characters:
Simone, Franny's brothers, Franny's father. Although characterization is exceedingly good for several of the characters, it is
Franny who develops most. The friendship theme, explicitly
stated by Francisco, is related directly to Franny's maturing.
By the close, Franny not only understands friendship in relation
to Simone, but she is better able to understand Lila, a third
girl. She has gained confidence and seems to be leaving her
world of mermaids and opening her eyes to the world around her.
Besides the friendship theme, the author presents a particular
view of life which operates in the story as the general theme
even though it is never specifically stated. Through the Davis
family, the author shows that good family relations and love and
happiness in the home can exist even though the family has very
limited material resources. Working with this theme, it would
be easy to moralize or to allow sentimentality to permeate the
story. Mrs. Stolz does neither and her story is memorable.

<u>1967</u>

N213   HUNT, IRENE. <u>Up a Road Slowly</u>. Chicago: Follett, 1966,
          192 pp.
          Fiction   Gr. 5-10
     <u>Up a Road Slowly</u> covers ten years in the life of Julie
Trelling, from the time she is seven--the year her mother dies
and she goes to live in the country with her strict, but kind,
spinster Aunt Cordelia--until she graduates from high school at
age seventeen. Julie attends the one-room country school Aunt
Cordelia teaches through the eighth grade. The summer before
she enters high school, her father remarries. Her attractive
stepmother, Alicia, an English teacher at the high school, and
her father redecorate her old room and ask her to stay in town
with them. But Julie chooses to remain with Aunt Cordelia and
commutes to high school with a neighbor boy, Dan Trevort. When
she is a junior she falls in love with a handsome transfer student, Brett Kingsman, who professes to love her, too; but Julie
learns that he merely uses this as an excuse to persuade her to
write his English compositions. The next year she and Dan Trevort
discover their love for each other and plan to marry after they
finish college.
     Internal references indicate that the action takes place in
the 1930s, or possibly even earlier. Cars are in common use,
but roads are not improved. Bus transportation to high school
is not provided: the boys commonly commute, but the girls sometimes take a room in town. Schools are being consolidated and
one-room schools are being abandoned. There are no cities or
states named to help in establishing the place and no reference
to national events to establish the time. By keeping both the
time and place indefinite, Miss Hunt has increased the universality of her novel.
     Julie tells her own story; the first person point of view is
a happy choice for this book since Julie is the major participant, and maturing is closely related to one's personal reactions
to the external events of life. Julie aspires to be a writer,
and this is reflected in her beautifully recorded narrative.
She is conscious of beauty: poems by Edna St. Vincent Millay
and Sara Teasdale often express her feelings, and their view of
life affects hers and is reflected in her style. But since she
grows up in Aunt Cordelia's home, she is aware of the realistic
as well as the romantic view of life. Both Aunt Cordelia and
Julie are believable characters.
     Two characters who have a part in Julie's maturing would not
frequently have been included in children's books before the
1960s. One of these is mentally retarded Aggie Kilpin, who goes
to the one-room school Julie attends and Aunt Cordelia teaches.
Aggie comes from a home in which personal cleanliness is ignored;

she is a repulsive figure who does not realize that she is offensive. Her death causes remorse in Julie, who, like the other
girls, has often avoided playing with her. The second character
who would formerly have been considered inappropriate for a
children's book is Julie's Uncle Haskell, an alcoholic and a
pathological liar. It is he who temporarily plays the role of
the "good gray uncle" and offers counsel that helps Julie to cope
with her guilt in relation to Aggie. One of the minor characters, Katy Eltwing, is insane. Insanity, like drunkenness and
mental retardation, was until recently a taboo subject in children's literature. These characters are perceptively and sym-
pathetically presented by Julie as narrator.

N214   O'DELL, SCOTT. The King's Fifth. Illustrated by Samuel
        Bryant. Boston: Houghton Mifflin, 1966, 264 pp.
        Fiction: historical   Gr. 6-11
    The story opens with seventeen-year-old Esteban de Sandoval a
prisoner in a fortress in Vera Cruz in New Spain. He awaits
trial for not having paid the King's Fifth of the gold gained
on a quest for the golden cities of Cibola. In his cell each
night Esteban writes the narrative of the quest and at intervals
interrupts the tale to record the progress of the trial.
    Seven set out from Coronado's camp in search of the fabled
cities: Captain Mendoza and his three soldiers went because of
their greed for the treasure; Father Francisco to save the souls
of the Indians; Esteban, a cartographer, to draw maps of territories yet uncharted; and Zia, a Zuni girl, to guide and interpret. After Esteban held a large nugget in his hands he, too,
for awhile became infected with the desire for gold. The death
of Captain Mendoza and other occurrences put Esteban in possession of a vast quantity of gold dust carried in deerhide bags on
eight mules and four horses. Following Zia's departure with a
band of Indians and Father Francisco's death in the Inferno,
Esteban reached the decision that the gold was evil, as Father
Francisco had said. To rid himself of it he dropped the bags
into a crater--one of many--filled with poisonous-looking hot
water giving off a sulfurous stench. He was arrested as soon
as he reached the city of Culiacán where he told his story. The
tale closes with his receiving a sentence of three years in jail
for withholding the King's Fifth.
    By relating what happens on the quest after the adventure is
over, the events themselves become less important than how and
why things happened as they did. Although Esteban declares himself to be a map-maker, not a scrivener, he is articulate enough
to make the reader feel the immensity and beauty of the land,
the charm of Zia, the dedication of Father Francisco, as well
as his own temporary surrender to the lust for gold. The history
is enacted in relation to the characters. O'Dell writes of a

1967

particular situation; yet his theme, the greed for gold, is made
to seem part of the universal lure of wealth.

N215   SINGER, ISAAC BASHEVIS. Zlateh the Goat and Other Stories.
        Translated by the author and Elizabeth Shub. Illustrated
        by Maurice Sendak. New York: Harper & Row, 1966, 90 pp.
        Folk Tales   Gr. 4 up

Well-known as a writer for adults when he began writing for
children, Isaac Bashevis Singer, in two Honor Books, Zlateh the
Goat and Other Stories and When Shlemiel Went to Warsaw and Other
Stories (1968), recorded tales from the middle-European Jewish
folklore he heard from his mother and grandmother as a boy in
Poland in the early years of this century. Four of the fifteen
stories he tells in these two volumes are not folk tales, but
products of his own imagination. Like his book-length fantasy
The Fearsome Inn (1967), also an Honor Book, these invented stories utilize many elements found in the traditional tales.

In the first book, the moving realistic story Zlateh the Goat
seems to have grown from the author's experience and imagination
rather than folklore. Just before Hanukkah, Zlateh and her young
master, Aaron, become lost in a fierce blizzard. They find shelter in a haystack where they stay for three days. Zlateh's milk
and animal warmth save Aaron's life. Two devil stories show the
devil making mischief and provide a contrast to the four stories
about sillies or numskulls. One of the latter shows the renowned
seven Elders of Chelm attempting to preserve the pearls and diamonds they see by the light of the moon on new-fallen snow. Another tells of the day the first shlemiel ate a pot of jam
thinking it was a pot of poison. "The Mixed-up Feet and the
Silly Bridegroom" shows a girl as silly as her bridegroom. In
"Fool's Paradise" Atzel imagines himself dead. To cure him of
this delusion, a great doctor instructs the family to lead him
blindfolded by a circuitous route to a room prepared to look like
paradise. After spending eight days there in monotonous same-
ness--he is even served the same food day after day--Atzel is
glad to learn that a mistake has been made and he is not really
dead.

Singer is a master stylist and it is likely that these tales
have never been better told. Besides providing good stories,
they reflect the environment, customs, and attitudes of the
country from which they came. The seventeen full-page black
and white illustrations by Maurice Sendak, whose ancestors, like
the author, lived in Poland, depict events of the story and convey atmosphere and humor.

N216   WEIK, MARY HAYS. The Jazz Man. Illustrated by Ann
        Grifalconi. New York: Atheneum, 1966, 42 pp.
        Fiction   Gr. 4-7

Zeke, a lame nine-year-old Negro boy, lives with his parents in Harlem on the topmost floor of an old brownstone house. Because of his physical handicap, he does not play with other children or attend school. He is alone during the day while his parents work. One day a jazz pianist moves into the apartment across the court. All summer long the Jazz Man plays and his music stimulates Zeke's imagination and makes him almost ecstatically happy. The music of the Jazz Man and his friends is so good it even plays the worries out of his Mama's head and his Daddy out of his no-job blues. But that is only temporary. Zeke's parents quarrel and one night his Mama does not come home. Soon Zeke's father is not coming home until late. When he does arrive he has a bottle tucked under his arm. Zeke has very little to eat. Then one night he dreams that he goes to a tavern where the Jazz Man is playing a gold piano. He wakens from this happy dream to find his father home and his mother with him.

As one reviews Zeke's situation it seems one of the saddest presented in books for children. A grim determinism seems to have shaped his destiny: he has a physical handicap; his father is often out of a job and drinks; his parents have little education; Zeke does not go to school; for a time his parents abandon him. Even the ending is not reassuring. With the return of his parents, Zeke's world is right for the moment; but, with none of their problems solved, the future remains as bleak as the present. Though the author shows that even in this hopeless situation, the spirit is capable of being lifted, still it is the problem rather than Zeke's response to the music that remains to haunt the reader. Both the author's understatement and economy of words and the artist's woodcuts suit the quiet, somber mood that envelops the story.

1968

N217   KONIGSBURG, ELAINE. From the Mixed-up Files of Mrs. Basil E. Frankweiler. Illustrated by the author. New York: Atheneum, 1967, 162 pp.
Fiction   Gr. 3-6
Bored with the same old routine at home and at school and tired of not being properly appreciated by her parents, eleven-year-old Claudia Kincaid of Greenwich, Connecticut, decides to run away for awhile. She chooses as a hideout the Metropolitan Museum of Art in New York City. For a companion she selects Jamie, nine, the middle one of her three younger brothers, because he has money saved from his allowance. The children are gone from home for just a week and the happenings of that week constitute most of the story.

1968

The running-away-from-home theme becomes less important after they see Angel, an exquisite small statue and the museum's newest important acquisition. Is it by Michelangelo? Neither the museum officials nor the Michelangelo experts know for certain. Finally, in an attempt to find out, Claudia and Jamie use their last money for train tickets to go see Mrs. Frankweiler, an immensely rich eighty-two-year-old woman, the previous owner of Angel. In return for taping their entire adventure in detail for her, Mrs. Frankweiler permits them to search her mixed-up files to learn the identity of the sculptor of Angel. After that search, Claudia has a secret and finds that appreciation is no longer so essential to her. The knowledge of the secret makes her "different on the inside where it counts" and Claudia can go home happy. Jamie is happy, too, because Mrs. Frankweiler has her chauffeur drive them home in her Rolls-Royce.

Mrs. Frankweiler not only plays a role in the story, but also writes the narrative of the children's adventure from the tape they made. She sends it with a letter to her longtime lawyer, Saxonberg, who just happens to be the children's devoted grandfather. Mrs. Frankweiler does not tell the children that she knows their grandfather so she has a secret, too.

Claudia and Jamie are well-rounded characters who complement each other, Claudia being cautious and a careful planner in everything but money matters and Jamie adventurous in spirit but a skinflint. Both have faults to balance their virtues: Claudia is fussy and rather bossy. It is revealed that Jamie regularly cheats his best friend at cards. Besides the growth in self-knowledge which Claudia experiences, both children grow somewhat in appreciation of each other. The venerable Metropolitan Museum provides an unusual setting for a realistic story of runaways. The Museum, as adapted to the uses of two youngsters who make it their home, provides some of the best and most humorous reading in the book. The realistic illustrations reinforce the text.

N213   KONIGSBURG, ELAINE. Jennifer, Hecate, Macbeth, William McKinley, and Me, Elizabeth. Illustrated by the author. New York: Atheneum, 1967, 117 pp.
Fiction   Gr. 3-6
Set in a present-day New York City suburb, this is the story of two ten-year-old girls, who, after months of playing an elaborate and secret game of witchcraft, finally learn to be friends. The girls meet for the first time on Halloween while returning from lunch to William McKinley School, where both are fifth graders but in different classes. Elizabeth, who tells the story, and her parents have lived in the community only since September and Elizabeth does not yet have any good friend. Jennifer tells Elizabeth she is a master witch--even though she, like Elizabeth, is wearing a pilgrim's costume--and will take Elizabeth as her apprentice.

Suddenly life becomes exciting for Elizabeth. The master and her apprentice meet in the park every Saturday where Jennifer draws in chalk a magic circle, within which they perform their mystic ceremonies. During the week they write notes back and forth and plan for Saturday. As an apprentice witch, Elizabeth not only studies about witches and witchcraft, but is required to eat a different special food each week--one week the food is a raw egg each day, another week it is a raw onion. These special foods and the taboos which she later has to observe as a journeyman witch often cause Elizabeth trouble, but the reader, while appreciating Elizabeth's predicament, is invariably entertained.

The witchcraft game comes to an end in April, on the day they meet in the park to make the flying ointment. All goes well until Jennifer dangles their pet toad, Hilary Ezra, over the cauldron in which the ointment is cooking. Toads, according to Jennifer, who got it from <u>Macbeth</u>, are a proper ingredient. Convinced that Jennifer intends to sacrifice the toad, Elizabeth grabs her hand and shakes it until she drops him on the ground. The game ends abruptly and Jennifer dismisses Elizabeth, telling her that she will never make a proper witch. Happily, the end of the game proves to be the prologue to something even better . . . friendship.

The plot is fresh and original and both girls are convincing. In telling their story, Elizabeth uses the vocabulary an articulate ten-year-old would possess. Her description of events is often amusing: as an example she describes Jennifer's unique way of getting treats on trick or treat night, or her own behavior at "two-faced" Cynthia's birthday party.

The author demonstrates that children, uninfluenced by adult prejudice, pay little attention to differences in skin color. From the very good illustrations, the reader knows that Jennifer is black and Elizabeth white, but the text refers to her color only once. The night the fifth grade gives a play for the parents, Elizabeth sees Jennifer's mother sitting in the audience and makes this matter-of-fact comment: "I knew it was Jennifer's mother because she was the only Negro mother there." The reason for making that observation is that the mother does not look in the least like a witch; Elizabeth concludes: "Maybe Jennifer inherited being a witch from her father. Maybe Jennifer's father was a wizard, which is a boy witch." It may not concern the child reader, but an adult will ponder how much of Jennifer's pose of aloofness is due to her being the only black child in a white community. Perhaps Jennifer pretends to be a witch, because, through her make-believe power to do evil, she has a chance to get back at a world in which no one, until Elizabeth, has been her friend.

1968

N219   O'DELL, SCOTT. The Black Pearl. Illustrated by Milton
        Johnson. Boston: Houghton Mifflin, 1967, 140 pp.
        Fiction   Gr. 6-10
        Ramon Salazar, son of a pearl dealer of La Paz, a town located
on a Mexican peninsula, becomes a partner in his father's business on his sixteenth birthday. A short time later, on his first
diving expedition, Ramon finds the black pearl, so large it fills
a man's hand, perfect in shape and of a rare quality. When the
other pearl dealers in the city refuse to pay him the price he
asks for the pearl, Ramon's father, Blas, gives it to the Madonna.
In a great celebration, the Madonna is carried from the church
down to the water to bless the Salazar fleet of five pearl boats.
The next time the fleet goes out, Blas Salazar and all but one
of the thirty-two men with him are lost in a storm at sea. The
survivor is Gaspar Ruiz, who is envious of Ramon.
        Ramon believes that the bad luck befell his father because of
the wrath of the Manta Diablo about which much superstition clus-
ters. According to the old Indian who taught Ramon to dive, the
Manta, a great raylike fish, is the rightful owner of the fabulous pearl. Ramon steals the pearl from the Madonna with the
intention of throwing it back into the sea close to the Manta's
cave where he found it. He is thwarted by Ruiz who forces him
at knife point to begin rowing in the direction of the city of
Guaymas where Ruiz expects to sell the pearl. The Manta Diablo
pursues them. While trying to harpoon it, Ruiz becomes enroped
to the Manta and dies as Captain Ahab did in Moby Dick. Ramon
returns the pearl to the Madonna as a gift of love.
        The terse narrative is told in first person by Ramon. Because
nothing extraneous is included, the story moves rapidly. As a
consequence of the physical danger and mental stress he experiences, Ramon matures, with the story ending on "the beginning day
of manhood." Symbolic significance can be attached to both the
black pearl and the Manta Diablo. The information given about
diving for pearls and dealing in them is integrated into the
story. Impressionistic black and white illustrations, black endpapers, and a black cover decorated with a large gray pearl accent
the atmosphere created by the text.

N220   SINGER, ISAAC BASHEVIS. The Fearsome Inn. Translated by the
        author and Elizabeth Shub. Illustrated by Nonny Hogrogian.
        New York: Charles Scribner's Sons, 1967 (OP), [48] pp.
        Fantasy   Gr. 5-9
        Doboshova, a witch, and her half-devil husband, Lapitut,
operate an inn in Poland a long time ago, plying their witchcraft on the travelers who stop. Their servants are three captive girls: Reitze, with black hair and black eyes; Leitze, with
blonde hair and blue eyes; and Neitze, with red hair and green
eyes.

1968

One winter morning three young men seek shelter in the inn:
Herschel, a university student; Velvel, a merchant; and Leibel,
a student of the Cabala, "the ancient Hebrew books that reveal
the mysteries of heaven and earth." With him he carries a piece
of chalk with magical properties. The master told him that if
he drew a circle around either man or beast it would imprison
him. Not only would he be unable to escape but no one would be
able to get into the magic ring.

Leibel soon suspects the true nature of Doboshova and Lapitut.
He tricks them and imprisons them in a magic circle. Then, by
drawing a chalk line around all the openings in the house including the chimney, he makes the inn impregnable to the Evil Host
summoned by Doboshova and Lapitut to rescue them. Late that
night, having stood without food all day within the magic bound-
ary, the witch and devil realize they have no choice but to sign
in blood an oath that they will leave the inn forever and return
to the Lower Regions.

It is dawn until the pledge is written and signed. The moment
the wicked ones depart, the inn seems a cozy, wholesome place.
In the time that Doboshova and Lapitut have been held captive
the young people have fallen in love. Using as a wedding canopy
a large embroidered shawl, in turn, and according to the law of
the Talmud, Herschel is wed to Reitze, Velvel to Leitze, and
Leibel to Neitze. The three couples live happily, have many children and grandchildren, and once a year gather with their families at the inn.

The story is expertly told in Singer's distinguished style.
Nonny Hogrogian's delicate pastel illustrations render atmosphere
and interpret the text with integrity.

N221   SNYDER, ZILPHA K. The Egypt Game. Illustrated by Alton
       Raible. New York: Atheneum, 1967, 215 pp.
       Fiction   Gr. 4-7
The setting is a California city in the late 1960s. The participants in the game are six children, from five different families. April, Melanie, Ken, and Toby are sixth graders; Elizabeth
is in fourth; and Marshall, Melanie's brother, is only four. In
the unused fenced-in storage yard at the back of a shabby antique-
and-used-furniture shop owned by an old man called the Professor,
the children build a make-believe Egypt of the pharaohs. They
adopt Egyptian names and assume the roles of ancient Egyptian
generals, wise men, priestesses, and queens. For example, April
names herself Bastet after a famous cat goddess, and Marshall
becomes Marshamosis, a boy pharaoh whose life and throne are continuously threatened by enemies. In their temple they carry out
ceremonies and rituals. After a neighborhood child is abducted
and killed, the playing of the game is almost halted because the
children are not permitted to play outside. Several weeks later,

173

1968

even though the murder remains unsolved, they gradually resume play in Egypt. At the climax of the story, the game becomes linked to the solution of the murder.

Against a well-realized background, using an imaginative game as a framework, the author has constructed an exciting, unified plot. Episodes in the game arouse interest, provide action, and create suspense. Motivation is provided for the characters' actions so that events move logically and inevitably to the climax. Because of the game, the real-life situation of two of the characters is greatly improved. In the playing of the game, April has gained good friends, for the first time in her life. She has been searching for her identity and for improved personal relationships as well. Through the game she has gained both. Because of his involvement in the game, the Professor is drawn from his shell back into the world.

The fact that the children are white, black, and Oriental seems not a device but the natural intermingling that exists in the university section of a large western city. Even the murder, though sinister, does not seem out of keeping with this neighborhood. Melanie and Marshall's parents are engaged in occupations that are not stereotyped for blacks: their mother is an elemen--tary school teacher and their father is a graduate student at the university. The dialogue is lively. The illustrations capture both the mood of the Egypt Game and the personalities of the children who play it.

1969

N222   ALEXANDER, LLOYD. The High King. New York: Holt, Rinehart
        & Winston, 1968, 285 pp.
        Fantasy   Gr. 6-9
        This is the fifth and final volume of the Chronicles of
Prydain. The Black Cauldron, the second volume, was a 1966
Newbery Honor Book.

Taran and Eilonwy, now young adults, and the other companions set off with Prince Gwydion of the House of Don to try to regain the magical black sword, Drynwyn, the mightiest weapon in Prydain, which has been stolen from Gwydion by Arawn, Lord of Annuvin, Land of Death. When they discover that Arawn is gathering his forces, including troops of vicious Huntsmen and battalions of the deathless Cauldron-Born, they abandon their search for the sword to rally their own forces.

At Caeth Dathyl, the golden castle, and home of the High King, Math, they await the arrival of King Pryderi and his mighty army. Pryderi arrives with a host greater than any ever raised in Prydain, but, instead of joining Gwydion, he demands his surren-der. He has allied himself with Arawn! In a dreadful battle,

Gwydion's forces are defeated by Pryderi's legions which have been augmented with regiments of the Cauldron-Born. In the storming of Caer Dathyl, King Math is killed. Gwydion becomes High King. He gathers his warlords together and explains his plan.

With the Cauldron-Born away, Annuvin is unprotected. Gwydion will take troops north to the sea and sail to the western shore of Prydain, which is close to Annuvin. Taran, with a smaller force, will pursue the Cauldron-Born and seek to slow their return to Annuvin so that Gwydion may arrive there ahead of them.

It is now winter and mishap after mishap plagues Taran and his followers as they pick their way through the mountains. Once the Cauldron-Born, captained by Huntsmen attack and slay one-third of his band. After a troop of dwarves led by Doli joins them, they attempt to take a shortcut through an abandoned mine of the dwarves. When they have traveled half a day, a cave-in forces them to retrace their steps.

Although progress remains slow and painful, their fortunes improve. A huge number of Huntsmen are destroyed when Taran's band and the dwarves pile a veritable mountain of brush on a frozen waterfall and light it with the dwarves' hot-burning tinder. The heat thaws the waterfall which pours down on the Huntsmen drowning them in their camp in the gorge below.

At last Taran's tired group reaches the summit of Mount Dragon, one of the approaches to Annuvin. From there Taran can see that Gwydion and his warriors have reached the stronghold. But the Cauldron-Born, who have completed the final portion of the march by a lower route, are streaming into Annuvin, too. At that moment some of the Cauldron-Born see Taran and start up the mountain toward him. When they are nearly upon him, Taran manages to loosen a tall stone which he sends crashing among them. Then he looks down. In the socket in which the rock had rested lies the sword, Drynwyn. As Taran snatches it, it begins to blaze. He drives it into the Cauldron-Born warrior who is almost upon him. The indestructible warrior shrieks and falls as do the whole host of Cauldron warriors. Annuvin is taken and Arawn is killed.

Home again in Caer Dallben, Gwydion announces that now that the Lord of Annuvin and his minions have been destroyed, the Sons of Don, and their kinsmen and kinswomen must board the Golden Ship and set sail for the Summer Country of neverending life from which they came. With their departure all magic will pass from Prydain and men will guide their own destiny without aid. As a reward Taran is told that he may journey with them. But he chooses to remain in Prydain--as High King. Eilonwy renounces her powers of enchantment to stay with him as Queen.

Like Tolkien, Alexander was inspired by the ancient heroic tales and legends; the folklore of Wales especially intrigued him. When he began his stories he set them in the Welsh countryside, but Prydain soon grew in his mind until it became a distinct country--a believable secondary world, not unlike the Middle Ages. As in Tolkien's trilogy, a great conflict between the forces of good and the forces of evil takes place.

Among the characters there is a great range. Some stem from traditional figures taken directly by Alexander from the Welsh Mabinogion--the wizard Dallben, and Prince Gwydion, for example-- while others appear to be original. Two characters who lighten the predominantly serious tone are Fflewddur Fflam, the owner of a truthful harp, a string of which snaps each time he stretches the truth, and the grotesque Gurgi with his rhyming verbals: "seekings and peekings," "smackings and whackings," "whiffings and sniffings," etc. Taran, the young hero, is a believable character whose maturation is an important theme running through- out the series. Although Alexander uses many traditional conven- tions, it has been shown that Taran does not operate within the traditional myth of the hero (Marion Carr, "Classic Hero in a New Mythology," Horn Book 47 [1971]:508-14). Even less does Eilonwy seem the traditional heroine. Indeed, her royalty and beauty are the chief qualities she has in common with the hero- ines of the old tales. In other respects she is a high-spirited girl with whom present-day readers can identify.

Although Alexander's fantasy recalls the old days, it is also contemporary: in its values, its emphasis on the common man, and in the concept of the hero it develops. His use of simple strong Anglo-Saxon words, in contrast to the elevated language of the epics, also contributes to the contemporaneity of the stories. Overall, the Chronicles of the land of Prydain provide heroic fantasy on a magnificent, epic scale.

N223   LESTER, JULIUS. To Be a Slave. Illustrated by Tom Feelings.
        New York: Dial, 1968, 156 pp.
        Information: history   Gr. 5 up
    "If you want Negro history, you will have to get it from some- body who wore the shoe, and by and by from one to the other, you will get a book," said an ex-slave of Tennessee. Most of the words in Julius Lester's moving book are, like the above, direct quotations from those who wore the shoe. The slave narratives from which the quotations were obtained were recorded a hundred years apart: the first group was taken down during the first half of the nineteenth century by the American Anti-Slavery So- ciety and other northern abolition groups who recorded the sto- ries of thousands of blacks who escaped from the South. The second group was put into writing during the 1930s when partici- pants in the Federal Writers' Project interviewed those ex-slaves still alive. In many instances the nineteenth-century slave nar- ratives were rewritten to conform to the literary standards of

the time. By contrast the collectors for the Federal Writers'
Project took great care to record the narratives in the speech
patterns and language of the ex-slaves. "Together," the author
writes, "the two [narratives] present a vivid picture of how the
slaves felt about slavery."

Lester has organized the quotations into chapters which cover
all aspects of the life of the Negro as slave in North America
beginning with their abduction in Africa, through their labor on
the plantations, and closing with their experiences with the Ku
Klux Klan and segregation in the early post-Civil War years.
The quotations are connected by factual, unemotional commentary
by the author. Tom Feelings's full-page charcoal illustrations
reflect the same strength shown by the slaves in their narratives.
The author lists sources consulted in a bibliography.

N224   SINGER, ISAAC BASHEVIS. When Shlemiel Went to Warsaw and
        Other Stories. Translated by the author and Elizabeth
        Shub. Illustrated by Margot Zemach. New York: Farrar,
        Straus & Giroux, 1968, 116 pp.
        Folk Tales   Gr. 4 up
In a note at the beginning of the book, the author states that
five of the eight tales he has retold here were told him in
Poland by his mother who heard them from her mother and grandmother. The other three are products of the author's imagination.
In one of the latter, a friendship exists between a cricket and
an imp; in the second, Rabbi Leib outwits the witch Cunegunde
and banishes her to a wasteland close to where Lot's wife was
turned into a pillar of salt; in the third, an orphan, Menaseh,
in a dream visits a castle with a crystal tower and a roof of
silver. There he sees everything and everyone that have been a
part of his past life as well as mist-shrouded, transparent figures that he will meet in his future. Although these stories
are well conceived and very well told, they lack the wit and
appeal of the five folk tales.

Two of the folk tales involve Schlemiel: one records his mis-
adventures in the business world and the second, the title story,
relates what happened when he started out for Warsaw but ended up
in a village identical to his hometown of Chelm and containing a
house, wife, and children exactly like his. One story concerns
the seven Elders of Chelm, all fools. In another, Utzel and his
daughter, Poverty, overcome their natural laziness to become respected members of their community. "Shrewd Todie and Lyzer the
Miser" tells how Todie gets the best of Lyzer. Silver soup spoons
give birth to silver teaspoons and a pair of silver candlesticks
that die are a part of Todie's cunning. The full-page soft line
drawings for every story capture the flavor of the text.

1970

N225   ARMSTRONG, WILLIAM. Sounder. Illustrated by James Barkley.
        New York: Harper & Row, 1969, 116 pp.
        Fiction   Gr. 5-8
      The father, a poor black sharecropper, is arrested in his
cabin for stealing meat from a white man's smokehouse to feed
his hungry family. As he is taken away, Sounder, his great
mellow-voiced coon dog, pulls away from his son who is holding
him and leaps at the wagon in which his master is chained. One
of the sheriff's deputies shoots the dog. His terrible injuries
leave him crippled and disfigured. His spirit is maimed, too,
for he never barks. The man receives a long sentence and is sent
away to the work gang. His patient wife endures; but his son,
each year after the crops are off, goes looking for his father.
      One year, while searching, he meets an old Negro man, who
becomes his teacher and friend. After six years, the father comes
home--paralyzed and deformed as a result of being caught in a
dynamite blast in the prison quarry. Long before his family
realizes that it is he dragging himself along the road, Sounder
has bayed a melodious welcome. The man dies in a couple of
months and the dog soon after. The boy gets wood in for his
mother and the younger children and goes back to his teacher
for the winter.
      The story was told to the author when he was a child by a
gray-haired teacher. It is the history of this man's youth, but
it must be an inhumanity that happened over and over. For this
reason it seems appropriate that the people in the story do not
have names: because they are simply "the boy," "the mother,"
and "the father," in the reader's mind they become every man,
woman, or child who has had comparable experiences. There is
universality in the setting, also. It is apparent that it takes
place in the South but no towns or states are named. Although
Sounder contains cruelty and tragedy, it also shows courage,
human dignity, and love. The writing is simple and cadenced.
Good images vivify the story: "The white man who owned the vast
endless fields had scattered the cabins of his Negro sharecrop-
pers far apart, like flyspecks on a whitewashed ceiling." The
black and white illustrations evoke the mood of the text.

N226   ISH-KISHOR, SULAMITH. Our Eddie. New York: Pantheon, 1969,
        183 pp.
        Fiction   Gr. 6-11
      Eddie's tragic story, covering the years of his life from
about thirteen to seventeen, is told in three parts: Hal Kent
relates the beginning and the ending, framing the bulk of the
narrative told by Sybil Raphel, Eddie's sister. The story begins
in London, perhaps around 1910, where the Raphels, a Jewish

1970

family, have always lived and where Hal, an American boy, resides for a short time. Hal becomes friendly with all the family except Mr. Raphel, a Hebrew scholar. Greatly loved by the poor children he teaches, the father is cold, insensitive, and selfish toward his own family and unconcerned that because he earns so little they must live isolated from their own kind in poverty. The relationship between the father and Eddie, who is the older son, is particularly strained.

About halfway through the book, the family emigrates to the United States, but neither the tensions within the family nor their economic situation improves; the estrangement between Eddie and his father deepens. The mother develops a crippling illness, apparently multiple sclerosis. Shortly, Eddie manifests some of the same symptoms. Following an operation, Eddie dies without having reached a reconciliation with his father. After Eddie's death, Papa Raphel is considerably changed, but the reader is left with the feeling that Eddie's life was indeed futile.

The characters are sensitively portrayed. The book is concerned with family rather than ethnic problems, although part of the family problem develops from the fact that the father is such a fanatical Zionist that he neglects his own family. In its somber view of life, Our Eddie is unlike most of the Newbery books preceding it, which never depicted incurable illness in the central character nor a severely maladjusted parent.

N227   MOORE, JANET GAYLORD. The Many Ways of Seeing: An Introduction to the Pleasure of Art. Illustrated with black and white and color reproductions and photographs. Cleveland: World, 1969 (OP), 141 pp.

Information: art   Gr. 5 up

Hendrik Van Loon, in his The Story of Mankind, the first Newbery Medal winner, concluded his chapter on art with the statement that "slowly the arts are coming back into their own." This interesting and attractive book is one indication that his words were prophetic. The author's stated purpose is "to suggest ways of sharpening visual awareness and of cultivating perception in the visual arts." This she aims to do by discussing techniques and media, art movements, and the relationship of art to nature and to the society in which it exists. She intersperses her comments with pencil exercises, passages of poetry, and prose quotations. The text is illustrated with eighty black and white plates and thirty full-color plates which are well-chosen and advantageously placed. Miss Moore is enthusiastic about her subject and writes with insight, but without pedantry. An index, a list of the paintings reproduced in the book and the museums in which they are located, and an extensive bibliography further increase the book's usefulness.

1970

This book, the only one of its kind in sixty years of Newbery awards, may be considered as a reflection of contemporary interests. By 1969, more people had time for art than previously, and with a repudiation of the materialistic, there came an emphasis on the aesthetic. When the book was written, the author was an artist and staff member of the Cleveland Museum of Art.

N228   STEELE, MARY Q. Journey Outside. Illustrated by Rocco Negri.
         New York: Viking, 1969, 143 pp.
         Fantasy   Gr. 5-9
Dilar is a boy of the Raft People, who, since his grandfather's grandfather's time, have lived on twenty-three rafts linked together on a subterranean river. Although all his life he has heard that they are traveling to a Better Place, Dilar is convinced that they are actually traveling in a great circle. In the dim light of his underground world he is sure he recognizes the same caves and cliffs time after time.

To prove that they are going around and around Dilar, taking only a fishnet and a torch, leaves the raft at a narrow place in the tunnel where a small ledge extends into the water. He intends to live on the ledge until the rafts come that way again. Soon he finds he is not alone: the ledge and a cave behind it are inhabited by thousands of furry creatures with blazing eyes. They crowd in on him, but he finally escapes by climbing up a wide crack in the rock. He finds himself in the beautiful green upper world--in the "day" and "green" about which grandfather had heard when he was a child from his grandfather.

Dilar sets out hoping to find a wise man who can answer his questions and tell him something about his people. He lives for awhile with Dorna and her mother, Norna, a physician who heals with simple herbs. These people are happy today but make no provision for the next day, a direct contrast to the Raft People who dried fish endlessly and thought only of the future. Dilar travels to the mountains and spends the winter with a hermit named Wingo, whose kindness to the birds he feeds really leads to cruelty. He learns no answers here. Nor does he learn from the Desert People, who live on the other side of the mountains. They escape the problems of life by wanting nothing. Finally, from Vigan, a wise old goatherd, he learns some answers.

Vigan tells him he should have learned from the people among whom he lived because "all men are wise about one thing or another--and all men are stupid about an equal number of things." He learns the background of his own people, too. At one time the Raft People lived along the sea where they were fishermen. After a particularly savage winter, they went to live on the underground river. With this knowledge and a map given him by Vigan, Dilar begins to retrace his steps. He intends to find his people and lead them out into "the light of day and the loveliness of green growing things."

While all the strange worlds Dilar visits are well imagined, the world of the Raft People is the most original. With nothing but fish to sustain them, they make ingenious uses of them: fish-oil torches illuminate their rafts; Dilar wears fishskin pants and eats his fish stew with a fishbone spoon. Such a mass of detail inspires belief in their way of life. The story can be read as a pure adventure story, but it is also an allegory commenting on life. Striking double-page woodcuts depict Dilar's adventures.

1971

N229   BYARS, BETSY.   Summer of the Swans.   Illustrated by Ted
       CoConis.   New York: Viking, 1970, 142 pp.
       Fiction   Gr. 4-9
   Summer of the Swans sensitively presents the pain of growing up and the tragedy of mental retardation in the story of thirteen-year-old Sara Godfrey and her brain-damaged younger brother, Charlie. A small town in West Virginia, similar to thousands of small towns in America, provides a particular setting. The action of the story is compressed into less than twenty-four hours, a period that becomes for Sara a culmination of all that has gone wrong before in the summer. The events of that time consist of Charlie's wandering from home in the night to find the swans and becoming lost in the woods, and Sara's finding him after a day's search in which many members of the community participate.
   This is essentially Sara's story, but it is Charlie's, too. The reader is with Charlie for a part of the time he is lost. Charlie's limited thoughts and perceptions give a concept of the world in which the mentally retarded child dwells. We learn more of this world from his actions and from the conversations the other characters have about him. Mute Charlie provides a contrast to voluble Sara. There is little narration by the author; most of the story is gained from the natural-sounding dialogue. Sara's conversations with her sister Wanda, Aunt Willie, her friends Mary and Joe, and Charlie help to characterize her as do her thoughts. We see all sides of her personality. Even in her misery and anger with herself she can still manage a little humor as she tells Wanda, "I'd like to know who would call me Little One except the Jolly Green Giant." Sara is a convincing character who speaks and acts as a real girl might in the circumstances in which the author places her.
   The title has literal significance and it also reflects the theme, as well as a pattern of imagery that appears throughout the book. The family and neighbors will remember the summer when Charlie became lost for that was the year the swans left their

1971

home pond at the university and settled for a little while on the
pond close to the Godfreys' home. Sara will remember that, and
more, too. At the end of her long day of searching, when she
finds Charlie, she knows that she has found more than a frightened, lost boy; in some way she has also found herself. Images
of swans and ducks call to mind Hans Christian Andersen's story
of the ugly duckling. At the beginning of the story, Sara is an
ugly duckling: she feels clumsy, too tall, hopelessly unattractive. Her large feet in their orange sneakers remind her of
Donald Duck's. At the close, as she dresses for the party, Sara
is beginning to feel a bit swanlike. Her discontent is gone and
she no longer wants "to fly away from everything, like the swans
to a new lake."

N230   BABBITT, NATALIE. <u>Kneeknock Rise</u>.   Illustrated by the author.
       New York: Farrar, Straus & Giroux, 1970, 118 pp.
       Fantasy   Gr. 4-8
       The people of Instep, a little village at the foot of Knee-
knock Rise, derive pride and satisfaction from the Megrimum,
their name for a strange and fearful creature that no one has
ever seen, who is reputed to live at the top of the Rise. Although no one has ever climbed to see, they know he is there because they hear him on stormy nights when he lifts his great
voice and moans "like a lonely demon, like a mad despairing
animal, like a huge and anguished something chained forever to
its own great tragic disappointments." Because of the Megrimum,
the village is a mecca for tourists, who especially love to come
in the fall during fair time when storms are frequent.
       One fall, young Egan goes to Instep for the first time. He
rides the forty miles from home in a mule-drawn cart with his
father's friend, a chandler. As they approach the town and Rise,
the chandler whispers to Egan that he has seen it fifty times,
but it always makes him shiver. Egan stays in Instep with relatives: Aunt Gertrude, Uncle Anson, and Cousin Ada, a little
younger than he. Uncle Ott, the fourth member of the family,
who has never done anything except read books and write verses,
and who is often sick with colds and wheezing, has disappeared
again. Aunt Gertrude worries he may have gone to the top of the
Rise, a foolish thing to do. Egan sleeps in Uncle Ott's room
with Uncle Ott's fat, old dog Annabelle for a companion. That
night during a thunderstorm Egan hears the Megrimum.
       Two days later Egan has a wonderful time at the fair. Late
in the afternoon clouds gather and the fairgoers excitedly anticipate hearing the Megrimum. For no clear reason--except that
Ada dares him--Egan decides to climb the Rise. Annabelle goes
with him. At the top he finds moist, warm air and Uncle Ott
breathing comfortably. He tells Egan that there isn't any
Megrimum and he shows him that the moaning is due to a natural
phenomenon.

Uncle Ott and Annabelle set off down the other side of the mountain and Egan, anxious to reveal his discovery, returns to Instep. He is not believed. As he leaves for home the following day, his climb is already becoming part of the legend of the Megrimum. The chandler, not knowing Egan was the boy who climbed, tells Egan: "He [the boy] got down all right, I understand. . . . But they say he lost his dog to the Megrimum."

The ironic conclusion that most people prefer fantasy to facts is presented with subtlety. The moments of humor and the freshness of the story are made more enjoyable by a smooth and lively writing style and good illustrations.

N231 ENGDAHL, SYLVIA. <u>Enchantress from the Stars</u>. Illustrated by
      Rodney Shackell. New York: Atheneum, 1970, 275 pp.
      Science Fiction   Gr. 6-12

Three peoples, representing three different levels of advancement, are brought together on Andrecia, a planet resembling medieval Europe in both topography and culture. The Andrecians, who believe in magic and have no knowledge of machinery, regard the giant earth-moving machine of the Imperials as a dragon. The Imperials, who have come to Andrecia to colonize, are technologically advanced but have no knowledge of psychic powers. All except Jarel, the expedition's young doctor, look upon the Andrecians as "humanoid animals." They use stunners on those who venture into camp brandishing swords in the direction of the "dragon" and lock them up.

The third group of people, those of the Federation, are the most advanced people in the universe: they communicate by mental telepathy and have mental control over matter. A Federation team composed of Elana; her fiancé, Evrek; and her father come to the planet hoping to save the Andrecians. Their task is to persuade the Imperials to leave Andrecia of their own free will without the least idea that more advanced people have had a hand in it. For this reason the Federation must operate through the Andrecians. A way is presented because the Imperials know nothing of the concept of controlling objects by conscious mental effort. Elana poses as an enchantress, her father as a wizard who understands magic, and Evrek as an evil one. They undertake to teach Georyn, an intelligent young Andrecian who longs to slay the dragon, how to release his latent psychic powers. At length they believe he is ready. They have trained him in psychokinesis, and taught him how to "cast a spell," and given him a "magic" stone.

Unknown to her father and Evrek, Elana decides to accompany Georyn on his quest. In the "enchanted" forest they are captured by Andrecians who bind them to a tree close to the dragon, hoping it will accept them as a propitiating sacrifice. When the Imperials find them, they stun them and take them to Jarel. Although he is sure she cannot understand, Jarel talks to Elana. When he tells her that he'd "give anything to fix it so that our glorious Empire would simply pull out and leave the place as we found it," Elana decides to confide in him. The morning the spaceship is scheduled for a flight back to the Imperials' world carrying Elana, Georyn, and others as "specimens," Jarel, complying with Elana's request, releases Georyn, declaring that he has a bad heart.

Georyn finally has an opportunity to use his "magic" stone and cast a spell. So amazing is his exhibition--he is able to arrest in midair a huge load of rocks and stones spewed forth by the "dragon"--that the Imperials decide on an immediate mass exodus. None of them wants to stay on a planet where the natives have such power. Shortly, Elana, her father, and Evrek depart in their spaceship, too. Before they leave, Georyn returns his stone to Elana. To his brothers and father he gives most of the wealth bestowed on him by the grateful king. Then he sets off on his steed to learn the wisdom of his world.

Action and drama result naturally from a situation in which such diverse groups are juxtaposed. The absorbing story--a blend of scientific possibility and philosophy combined with interesting characters--achieves emotional tension through the heroine's alternating first- and third-person narration.

N232   O'DELL, SCOTT. Sing Down e Moon. Boston: Houghton
        Mifflin, 1970, 137 pp.
        Fiction: historical   Gr. 5-11
        Set in the 1860s, this story of the Navajos reveals the shameful treatment the Indians were receiving at the hands of white men. Like Karana of the author's earlier book, Island of the Blue Dolphins (1961), the heroine, Bright Morning, relates her own story. In Part I she and her friend, Running Bird, while grazing their sheep, are captured by two Spaniards. They are taken south and sold into slavery. In a short while they succeed in escaping and return home. The second part of the story is based on two years, 1863-1865, in the history of the tribe. During this time United States soldiers destroyed the hogans, crops, and peach trees of the Navajos and marched the then destitute Indians three hundred miles to Fort Summer. Again Bright Morning escapes, this time with Tall Boy, her recently-married husband. Eventually they find their way back to the old canyon and take up their former way of life, which the Navajos were still following at the time of Waterless Mountain (1931) sixty-five years later.

Like Karana, Bright Morning is a courageous girl, but while Karana must make her life alone, Bright Morning's life is closely bound up with her family's life and later with her husband's. More far-seeing and capable of planning than he is, she takes the initiative and plans their escape from Fort Summer. And

when Tall Boy wants to rush from concealment and fall on the soldiers on the trail, Bright Morning deters him. Tall Boy's urge
for vengeance and Bright Morning's hope for peace somewhat parallel desires that were experienced in succession by Karana in the
earlier book. As in Island of the Blue Dolphins, the theme is
integrated into the plot, but it is a theme that extends beyond
the story itself to become not just a tribute to Bright Morning's
spirit, but a tribute to the human spirit. Mr. O'Dell's lucid
but unemotional style suggests the tragedy while understating it.

1972

N233   O'BRIEN, ROBERT C. Mrs. Frisby and the Rats of NIMH. Illus-
        trated by Zena Bernstein. New York: Atheneum, 1971,
        233 pp.
        Fantasy   Gr. 3-6
    Mrs. Frisby, a fieldmouse and widow of Jonathan Frisby, is
worried. Plowing time is near and Timothy, her youngest son,
is still too weak from pneumonia to move from their snug winter
cinder block home in Mr. Fitzgibbon's garden to their damp summer home along the brook. The owl advises her to go to the colony of rats that live under the large rosebush near the tractor
shed and ask them to move the house to a place out of the way of
the plow. Although she does not ask why, she is puzzled by the
owl's implying that the rats will help her because she is Mrs.
Jonathan Frisby.
    The moment she enters the rats' home she realizes these are
not ordinary rats. From their leader, Nicodemus, she hears a
strange story that also involves her husband. One night several
years earlier at the Farmers' Market, a number of rats and a few
mice, including her husband, were caught, placed in a truck with
NIMH lettered on the side, and taken to a laboratory. There they
were given injections of a substance that stopped the aging process almost completely. It also caused them to advance greatly
in intelligence. After they learned to read, they were able
to escape from the laboratory. They spent the winter in a
closed-up home with an extensive library, then found the Fitzgibbon farm where they established themselves in comfort. They
tapped Mr. Fitzgibbon's underground power cable for electricity,
and a water pipe for running water.
    At this point, the action returns to the present. Mrs. Frisby
takes a sleeping powder into the farmhouse and puts it into the
cat's food so that he will be asleep while the rats move her
house. On the way back to safety, she is captured by Billy
Fitzgibbon and put into a canary cage. Although rescued a few
hours later by one of the rats, she is there long enough to
learn that the scientist who conducted the experiments on the

1972

rats will be coming to the farm with an exterminator in two days. This news causes the rats to hasten a move they had been anticipating--to Thorn Valley, where they intend to build a rat civilization in which they produce their own food and live without stealing.

The story is original, suspenseful, and humorous. By carefully adhering to the laws of the created world and by supplying sufficient detail to inspire belief, Mr. O'Brien succeeds in making the superintelligent rats entirely believable. The theme of a back-to-basics life in preference to a gadget-filled one is suggested by the rats' move to Thorn Valley. Many good black and white drawings support the text.

N234   ECKERT, ALLAN W.   <u>Incident at Hawk's Hill</u>.   Illustrated by
        John Schoenherr.   Boston: Little, Brown, 1971, 173 pp.
        Fiction   Gr. 4-9
    An author's note states that the story is a "slightly fictionalized version of an incident which actually occurred at the time and place noted." The time is 1870. The setting is Hawk's Hill, the Canadian farm home of Esther and William MacDonald and their four children: John, sixteen; Beth, twelve; Carol, nine; and Benjamin, six. Ben, a small, shy child, spends hours watching, following, and mimicking the movements and sounds of the animals and birds around the farm. When he follows a big prairie chicken far out onto the prairie, he becomes lost. During a driving rainstorm he stumbles over the entrance to a badger burrow. Because he is so slight he is able to wriggle himself into it. When the badger returns, Ben's ability to act and talk as she does causes her to adopt him. She brings him eggs and small animals which he eats raw. In a short while he is behaving like a badger. He even hunts with her and helps her kill a vicious dog. After two months he is found by John. The family has looked for him continuously although the search party of thirty-two men gave up after two days and two nights, concluding, when no clues were found, that he had drowned in the river.

    The author's good choice of events and details and clear and fluid writing make Ben's story suspenseful, believable, and touching. It is also an engrossing and accurate realistic animal story in which inhumane trapping practices are observed. In addition, it is a good story of pioneer life in Manitoba. And, finally, it is a universal story of faith and love in a family. Nine full-page black and white illustrations of Ben and the badger echo the moving quality of the writing.

N235   HAMILTON, VIRGINIA.   <u>The Planet of Junior Brown</u>.   New York:
        Macmillan, 1971, 210 pp.
        Fiction   Gr. 5-10

The story begins one Friday afternoon and ends the following Friday. For two and one-half months, two bright New York eighth graders have not been attending classes although they have been in the school building. One is Junior Brown, a talented pianist and artist who weighs 262 pounds and has a neurotic, overprotective mother. The other is Junior's devoted friend, big Buddy Clark, who is brilliant in science and mathematics, employed part-time at a newsstand, and the leader of a group of boys without homes who live on a "planet" in the basement of an abandoned house. Junior and Buddy spend their days with Mr. Poole, formerly a teacher of mathematics and astronomy, but now a janitor, in a basement room behind a false wall in the broom closet. There Mr. Poole and Buddy have constructed for Junior, who has become depressed, a marvelous ten-planet solar system that is lighted and revolves. Much larger than earth, the tenth planet, "glazed in beige and black" and "shaped in the soft, round contours of Junior Brown's own face," is named Junior Brown.

After school, Junior goes to take his music lesson. Buddy goes along but remains outside the apartment building of Miss Peebs, the teacher. Today, as he has done for several weeks, Junior props his music up and beats it out on a chair. Miss Peebs will not let Junior play her grand piano because, she explains, a filthy, diseased relative who does not like music is visiting her. As the boys ride home on the bus, Junior fantasizes what the relative, whom he has not seen, is like.

The boys separate and do not see each other until Monday. The reader follows Buddy to his planet and sees him instructing the homeless boys in survival skills. Junior is shown in his comfortable apartment with his mother; he is disappointed that his father cannot get home for the weekend.

Buddy and Junior spend Monday, Tuesday, and Wednesday safely in the basement room. Wednesday evening Junior invites Buddy to his house for dinner. Before the meal, Junior plays his piano. The keys are soundless—all the wires needed to produce the music have been removed because the sound bothers Junior's mother. Just as they finish eating, Junella Brown, whose treatment of Buddy has been cold and patronizing, suffers a severe asthmatic attack. Junior administers the needed medication intravenously and Mrs. Brown sleeps.

After Buddy leaves, Junior, feeling "red inside," paints for most of the night, drawing one-inch-high figures of people living their lives into a huge figure of a Red Man. Thursday, the boys get caught and the assistant principal tells Junior he is to bring his mother the next morning. That night Junior's mother barely speaks to him and he does not tell her. She had found and destroyed the painting because it looked to her like "a terrible sick thing . . . full of people involved with one another in a way . . . any decent boy would never think to draw."

Friday morning Junior leaves early before his mother is up.
Again the boys spend the day in the basement room; Buddy and
Mr. Poole disassemble the solar system. After school Buddy
goes with Junior to take his lesson. This time he goes in with
him. The moment Miss Peebs opens the door, Buddy realizes she
is crazy. He finds no relative in Miss Peebs's heaped, untidy
apartment. Miss Peebs insists he is there and Junior agrees.
When they leave, Junior tells Miss Peebs he is taking the relative with him. While they ride the bus back to school, Junior
talks continuously to the imaginary relative. Mr. Poole takes
the planetary system, Buddy, Junior, and the relative to Buddy's
planet which Buddy names "the planet of Junior Brown."

The characterization, especially of Junior and his mother, is
convincing. Frustration follows frustration so that Junior's
slipping away from reality is absolutely believable. Both boys
exemplify themes relating to the "race that is yet to come,"
which is the way Mr. Poole often thinks of Buddy and Junior.
The race to come possesses two qualities: one is realized in
Junior, the artist; the other is seen in Buddy who tells the
boys of his planet including Junior: "We are together . . .
because we have to learn to live for each other." The boys are
black, but Miss Hamilton states that their humanity, not their
blackness, is the central theme. The humanity shows clearly
through the bizarre--the solar planets, the planet of boys, Miss
Peebs and her apartment. The story is original and compelling.

N236   LeGUIN, URSULA K. The Tombs of Atuan. Illustrated by Gail
        Garraty. New York: Atheneum, 1971, 163 pp.
        Fantasy   Gr. 5 up
   At age five, Tenar, born within the hour of the death of the
One Priestess of the Tombs of Atuan, and consequently presumed
to be the Reborn One, is taken from her family to the Place of
the Tombs to relearn everything she knew in her previous lives.
When she is six, in rituals that last all day, she becomes Arha,
the Eaten One, priestess to the Nameless Ones, who ruled the land
before men came and are buried under the tombs. After this initiation, Arha sleeps in the Small House by herself, guarded by
the eunuch Manan who stays on the porch. She continues to work
at spinning and weaving with the other girls, but also learns the
rites of the Nameless Ones. She learns, too, from the High Priestess Thar, of the treasure concealed in the vaults of the Labyrinth,
Arha's special domain which extends for miles under the place.
When Arha is fifteen, the other High Priestess, Kossil, who, in
contrast to Thar, is cruel, and whom Arha fears, takes her into
the Undertomb and the lesser maze. After that, and especially
after Thar's death, Arha explores alone both the lesser maze and
the Labyrinth.

Then, one day she finds a man there. It is Ged, the hero of The Wizard of Earthsea, who has come from the west to the tombs to hunt for half of the Ring of Erreth-Akbe--he possesses the other half. The whole ring with its power for peace is needed for the kings in his land to rule well. Although Arha knows he must die because he has come to rob, she cannot bear to let him die of starvation and thirst as Kossil insists she must. She takes food and drink to him secretly. He treats her with the humanity and compassion she has never known in this place and calls her by her name, Tenar. Then one day they are aware that Kossil is observing them through one of the spy holes. When Kossil blocks the only exit from the Labyrinth, it seems they will both die there. But, with Tenar's knowledge of the under-ground passages and Ged's skill in magic, they escape, taking the ring with them. As they leave, an earthquake topples the tombstones and the Hall of the Throne, burying Kossil. The two escape to the western lands, where, with Ged's first master, now an old man and a great Mage, Tenar will have a new life.

The book succeeds admirably as a piece of high fantasy. Tenar and Ged are well-drawn characters about whom the reader cares. Problems of adolescence are worked out through Tenar. As a re-sult of her contact with Ged she changes from the self-centered, revengeful person she had become because of her upbringing. The plot is exciting. The Place of the Tombs is made real both by description in the narrative and by two maps: one shows the above-ground buildings and the other the Labyrinth. Half-page, stylized illustrations at the beginning of each chapter depict characters and events. The author's choice of words produces a style fitting to the story.

N237   MILES, MISKA. Annie and the Old One. Illustrated by Peter
         Parnall. Boston: Little, Brown, 1971, 42 pp.
         Fiction   Gr. 4-8
Annie, a present-day Navajo girl of nine or ten, lives with her parents and her grandmother, the Old One, in a snug hogan near a low mesa. Annie's life is happy and secure: her mother weaves, her father makes jewelry, and Annie goes to school on the yellow school bus. At home she helps her grandmother with chores and listens to the stories the Old One tells of times long ago.

Then everything changes. One evening the grandmother speaks to her family: "My children, when the new rug is taken from the loom, I will go to Mother Earth." Annie's parents accept the inevitability of death but, because she cannot, Annie tries to delay the completion of the rug. After two plans fail, she stealthily unravels at night the weaving her mother has done during the day. On the third night her grandmother discovers her unraveling the rug.

1972

The following morning the Old One takes her granddaughter to
the small mesa and talks to her. She tells Annie that she has
tried to hold back time, but "this cannot be done. . . . The
sun comes up from the edge of earth in the morning. It returns
to the edge of earth in the evening. Earth, from which good
things come for the living creatures on it. Earth, to which all
creatures finally go." Annie begins to understand. When they
return to the hogan Annie picks up the weaving stick her grandmother had given her and tells her mother that she is ready to
learn to weave.

The author uses no unnecessary words. The understated style
and brief dialogue suit the simplicity of the story. The fine,
expressive illustrations—black and white with accents of gold
and rust—depict the characters and the Navajo world of the story.

N238   SNYDER, ZILPHA K. The Headless Cupid. Illustrated by
        Alton Raible. New York: Atheneum, 1971, 203 pp.
        Fiction   Gr. 4-7

The story is told from the point of view of eleven-year-old
David, the eldest of the four Stanley children. He; Janie, six;
the four-year-old twins, Blair and Tesser (Esther); Jeff, their
college professor father; and their stepmother, Mollie, have
recently moved into the old Westerly house, quite far out in the
country. As soon as they are settled, Mollie goes to bring her
daughter, twelve-year-old Amanda, who has been staying with her
own father during Mollie and Jeff's honeymoon and while the move
was taking place. Already the Stanley children are comfortable
with Mollie. Because they were so young when their own mother
died, the twins and Janie quickly accept her as their mother.
Amanda, whom the Stanley children have met only once, arrives
in an outlandish ceremonial costume, her hair braided into dozens of long tight braids some of which are looped around and
fastened to her head. She wears a triangle on her forehead
which she says is her center of power and she carries a cage
containing a large crow which she declares to be her familiar
spirit.

Amanda treats both her mother and stepfather with contempt
but gets along with the Stanley children because they become
her neophytes in the supernatural. They successfully pass all
the "ordeals" Amanda specifies, including going for a whole day
without letting anything made of metal touch their skin, carrying a reptile on their persons from sunup to sundown, and not
speaking for a whole day except for three-word replies to direct
questions. Later Amanda conducts rites of initiation and tells
her stepbrothers and sisters that they have been accepted into
the world of the occult.

Shortly, after Dad leaves with students on a three-week field
trip, Amanda and David learn some of the history of the house

190

from Rom Golanski, an old workman who comes to make electrical repairs. His father, a master woodcarver, fashioned the elaborate bannisters, including the wooden cupids on each side of the newels, when the house was built seventy-five years earlier. Soon after the house was completed it was haunted by a poltergeist. One night during that time, the head of one of the cupids was cut off. It was never found or replaced, although the poltergeist activities subsided after the Westerly girls, twelve and fourteen, were sent away to boarding school.

A short time after Mr. Golanski's call, poltergeist activities begin to manifest themselves again: a large potted plant crashes down the stairs, a picture falls from the wall, and pebbles and stones are tossed about everywhere. David suspects that Amanda may be responsible, but he does not know for certain until the evening Molly is delayed getting home. The younger children are in bed, Amanda is in the kitchen, and David is watching television in the parlor when they both hear what sounds like an avalanche of objects bouncing down the stairs. On the landing and stairs they find an old wooden box, rocks, pebbles, old toys, and the cupid's missing head. Amanda, terrified, admits responsibility for all the other activities, but not this one. The next day David learns a logical explanation for the occurrence. Blair had found the box of things in the window seat in his and David's room and fell while carrying it downstairs. Frightened by Amanda's scream, he had gone back to bed and soon fell asleep. Because Amanda's attitude toward the family is improved, David decides he and Blair will not tell the rest of the family for awhile.

The big "haunted" house provides an evocative setting. Natural characters, well-paced plot, and a lively, humorous style are all in evidence. The Stanley children are credible and likable. The behavior of the unhappy Amanda is perfectly believable. She is displeased with her mother and blames her for her parents' divorce even though the divorce was by mutual agreement. She acts as she does because she wants to get even with her mother. When she believes there is actually a poltergeist, she confesses the tricks she had played and she and her mother reach a better understanding. By the end she is feeling more secure in this new family. From the moment Amanda arrives there is action, with the atmosphere of excitement and suspense intensifying after the poltergeist activities commence. A part of the satisfying conclusion is that the possibility of psychic phenomena is not absolutely ruled out. From their conversation, David surmises that Blair, the truly psychic one, may have had contact with the earlier poltergeist.

1973

1973

N239   GEORGE, JEAN.   Julie of the Wolves.   Illustrated by John
         Schoenherr.   New York: Harper & Row, 1972, 170 pp.
         Fiction   Gr. 6-10
   Julie of the Wolves, like Island of the Blue Dolphins, is
another distinguished survival story featuring a girl.   The summer she is thirteen, Julie-Miyax, an Eskimo girl of the 1970s,
leaves her husband, Daniel, to whom she has been married by her
father's arrangement, and sets off across the tundra toward Point
Hope, where she expects to obtain passage to San Francisco and
her California pen pal, Amy.   Julie becomes lost and survives
only because of her knowledge of Eskimo lore and because she
makes friends with Amaroq, the leader of a wolf pack.
   As winter approaches she is able to set her course, first by
the migrating birds and then by the North Star.   At length, from
human beings she encounters, she hears word of her father,
Kapugen, a famous hunter, whom she thought had drowned in the
Bering Sea on a seal hunt.   With Tornait, a little bird she has
found, she makes her way to him.
   Disappointment accompanies the reunion because Kapugen--who
had told her to never forget that she was Eskimo--has married a
"gussak," a white woman from the lower states, and now hunts from
a plane for sport rather than for food.   Julie leaves his house
and walks a little way out of town where she pitches her tent in
the snow.   She resolves that, even though her father has abandoned
that way of life, she shall live as an Eskimo.   Only hours later,
but after her little bird has died, Julie changes her mind.   She
sings a song in English to the totem of Amaroq she had carved from
bone:
         My mind thinks because of you.   And it thinks,
            on this thundering night,
         That the hour of the wolf and the Eskimo is over.
And "Julie pointed her boots toward Kapugen."
   In Julie, "a classic Eskimo beauty, small of bone and deli-
cately wired with strong muscles . . . pupil at the Bureau of
Indian Affairs in Barrow, Alaska . . . citizen of the United
States," we see the coming together of two cultures.   The book
convincingly portrays Julie living in harmony with nature as the
traditional Eskimo did.   Also convincing and informative are the
scenes that show in fascinating detail the behavior of the wolves.
The author, a naturalist, gained this knowledge from studying the
ecology of the Arctic, reading scientific investigations of wolves,
and observing a pack of wild wolves in McKinley National Park.
Although likely realistic, the ending seems less convincing, perhaps because it was not sufficiently foreshadowed.   The artist's
illustrations bring both Julie and the wolves to life.

N240   LOBEL, ARNOLD. <u>Frog and Toad Together</u>. Illustrated by the
        author. New York: Harper & Row, 1972, 64 pp.
        Fantasy   Gr. Ps-2
    This, the second "I Can Read" book about Frog and Toad, con-
tains five stories, like the first book, <u>Frog and Toad Are</u>
<u>Friends</u> (1971 Caldecott Honor Book). As in the earlier book,
the subjects are those with which children can identify. In
"A List" Toad makes "a List of things to do today." While taking a walk with Frog, one of the items on the list, Toad's list
blows away. Toad (with Frog keeping him company) sits down and
does nothing all day until bedtime because the only item he remembers is "Go to Sleep." The flower seeds Toad plants in "The
Garden" finally sprout and come up after he has spent days reading to them, playing music for them, and singing songs to them.
In "Cookies" the two friends try to exercise will power and in
"Dragons and Giants" they learn about courage. In the final
story, "The Dream," Toad dreams he is the Greatest Toad in all
the World, and a great performer: he plays the piano, he walks
a high wire, he dances. Each time he performs he asks Frog, who
is seated in the audience, if he can do as well. Each time as
he answers "No" Frog becomes smaller until finally Toad cannot
see him at all. Just as he shouts for Frog to come back, Frog
walks into his house and awakens him. The two go outside to
spend another happy day together.
    The simple plots contain action, suspense, and humor. The two
friends are consistent, credible characters. Toad is more im-
petuous and childlike than kind, understanding Frog, yet both
behave in a manner children will find believable. The themes
are readily understandable but not trivial. Although Lobel did
not work from a standard word list, what he and his characters
had to say was best stated in easy words and short sentences.
Young readers can guess an occasional more difficult word--like
avalanche--from the context and the pictures.
    The illustrations, one on nearly every page, are integral to
the book--they make the adventures and characters real. Lobel
mostly uses shades of green and gold-brown, colors appropriate
for his characters and their environment. Frog is usually togged
out in brown-tone jackets and trousers and Toad is natty in green.
Each has a cozy home with flowers growing around the door and a
dining table beside an open window with a view--a delightful spot
for sharing cookies or tea with a friend. Both text and illustrations extol the simple life and friendship as they are idealized in <u>The Wind in the Willows</u>.

N241   REISS, JOHANNA. <u>The Upstairs Room</u>. New York: Thomas Y.
        Crowell, 1972, 196 pp.
        Fictionalized Autobiography   Gr. 4-8

1973

Annie de Leeuw was just six in 1938 when she first heard of Hitler and his persecution of the German Jews. But, even though she was Jewish, she did not worry because her home was in Holland. Her father, however, was very concerned and wanted to take his family to America. But his invalid wife refused to go. With the German invasion of Holland in 1940 came the collapse of the De Leeuws' comfortable, secure life.

In October 1942, after receiving a letter stating that his family must go to a Dutch work camp, Mr. de Leeuw made arrangements for their going into hiding. The mother was terminally ill in the hospital and could not be moved. Mr. de Leeuw was taken by one family; Rachel, twenty-five, by another; and Sini, twenty, and Annie, now ten, by a family of farmers, the warm-hearted Oostervelds: Opoe (Granny), her son Johan, and his wife, Dientje. Rachel managed to visit Annie and Sini once during the two years and seven months they were in hiding, but their father was too far away to come at all.

Even though danger of discovery was always present, much of the time their concerns centered on the day-to-day monotony and frustrations that came from staying upstairs in a room day in, day out, and month after month. Once in a great while, the shades were drawn and the girls ate a meal downstairs with the family. They also sneaked down at night to hear a Dutch broadcast from England of the War news over the radio Johan had not turned in as ordered. Because of lack of exercise, Annie almost lost the use of her legs. Once the house was searched, but the girls were not discovered in the hiding place Johan had made for them behind shelves in a closet. For awhile all the downstairs rooms except the kitchen were used by the Germans for their headquarters. The girls had to stay in bed then. The village was liberated by Canadian soldiers in April of 1945.

In a foreword the author writes:

> I have not tried to write a historical book, although it may have some historical value. What I did try to write was a simple, human book, in which my sister and I suffered and complained, and sometimes found fault with the Gentile family that took us in for a few years, in which the members of that family were not heroes but people, with strengths and weaknesses.

That describes precisely the book she wrote.

N242   SNYDER, ZILPHA K. The Witches of Worm. Illustrated by Alton
          Raible. New York: Atheneum, 1972, 183 pp.
          Fiction   Gr. 4-8
    Imaginative Jessica, twelve, who lives in an apartment building in a city on the west coast, spends much time alone. Her

young-looking, very pretty mother works every day as a secretary and often dates in the evening and on weekends. Jessica has no close school friends and for a year has scarcely spoken to Brandon, the only other child in the apartment building, and her best friend from the time they were five until the previous year. One chilly August day while Jessica sits at the entrance to a secret cave in the hill behind the apartment house reading a book called The Witches of Salem Town, she hears a little scraping sound behind her and finds an unusual-looking kitten, so young its eyes are not yet open. Even though Jessica has always said that she does not like cats she takes this one, which she names Worm, to raise. Old Mrs. Fortune, the owner of the apartment building, tells her how to care for it and suggests that Worm belongs to a rare breed descended from the cats of ancient Egypt. For weeks, Jessica must feed Worm at two- and then four-hour intervals. During those times, although she feels little affection for him, she talks to him and imagines his replies. They one day Worm, no longer a kitten, begins to talk. He tells Jessica he is a witch's cat. He also tells her to do things she ought not to do: she ruins her mother's expensive new "dry clean only" dress by washing it and she pushes Brandon's trumpet out a third story window. She does not tell about Worm, but accounts for her behavior by saying that, "Things get funny." She reads more about witches and becomes convinced that Worm possesses a demon. For a long time she tells no one, but she becomes afraid of the cat and treats him cruelly. Finally, after talking with Mrs. Fortune about witchcraft, she decides to exorcise Worm's devils. Immediately after the ritual Worm dashes out of the apartment house into a driving storm. Brandon helps Jessica look for him. They find him. At the close of the story, Jessica and Brandon are friends again and it appears that Jessica's behavior will change and she will begin to face her problems.

The story, told from Jessica's point of view, very well portrays her loneliness, frustrations, and anger. Her mother is also well depicted. Joy wants to be a good mother, but she wants, too, the good times she did not have after her husband abandoned her and Baby Jessica when Joy was only eighteen. Although she works to provide for her physical needs, she does not fulfill Jessica's emotional needs and offers little understanding and direction. Under these circumstances the idea of a witch cat and an exorcism that works seems believable for a child like Jessica. The story is fast-paced with good dialogue and black and white illustrations that reflect the eeriness that tinges the story.

1974

N243   FOX, PAULA. The Slave Dancer. Illustrated by Eros Keith.
        Scarsdale, N.Y.: Bradbury, 1973, 176 pp.
        Fiction: historical   Gr. 6-11
    The Slave Dancer explores the horrors of the slave trade
through the eyes of a thirteen-year-old white boy, Jesse Bollier,
who lives in New Orleans in 1840. One day while sitting on the
docks playing his fife, he is kidnapped and taken aboard The
Moonlight, which he soon learns is a slave ship bound for West
Africa. Although he is expected to make himself generally useful,
his principal job will be to play his fife for the captured Africans on the return voyage so that they will exercise themselves
by dancing. Of the ten in the crew only Purvis, one of his ab-
ductors, and Ben Stout pay much attention to Jesse. Ben Stout
treats him kindly, but Jesse soon realizes he is a treacherous
man. Purvis is rough-spoken, but it is he who Jesse likes and
trusts. As much as possible Jesse stays out of the way of
Captain Cawthorne who, Purvis tells him, "likes to eat well,
and likes to beat men."
    In Africa, the Captain, a man with a reputation for being a
"tight packer," trades his goods and packs ninety-eight slaves
into the holds of his small ship. The return voyage is a nightmare for Jesse. Daily he plays his fife and the shackled slaves
move about dispiritedly. Before long the slaves develop the
"bloody flux" and fight among themselves trying to reach the
latrine buckets. On the order of the Captain, Ben Stout throws
overboard a black woman ill with a fever said to be contagious.
Jesse is flogged for refusing to obey an order.
    At length they reach Cuban waters. The evening before the
day on which the cargo of slaves is to be unloaded, an American
patrol boat approaches. The Captain immediately gives the order
to throw the slaves over the side. Before all have been thrown
over, a terrible storm breaks and the ship is carried out to sea.
A day later the wrecked vessel sinks off the coast of Mississippi.
Only Jesse and one of the slave boys, Ras, survive the shipwreck.
They are cared for by an old Negro who arranges to send Ras north
on the underground railroad. Jesse walks home to New Orleans.
    Preceding the story is a page designated "History" on which
are listed the name of the ship, officers, crew, cargo, date of
shipwreck, and survivors. The author gives flesh to these bare
bones of fact. Through the words and actions of the characters
she makes life on a slave ship and the slave trade in Africa and
America very real. Since Jesse tells his own story the language
and sentence structure must be appropriate for an intelligent,
perceptive boy. The author uses ordinary, present-day English
rather than trying to reproduce the language of the time. Her
many similes bring vividness to the scene: "After a few days I

had stopped clinging to the hammock like a wounded crab clings
to a bit of weed." The tone of this powerful, well-written
novel is grim, a quality reinforced by the ten black and white
double-page illustrations showing characters and events.

N244   COOPER, SUSAN. <u>The Dark is Rising</u>. Illustrated by Alan E.
       Cober. New York: Atheneum, 1973, 216 pp.
       Fantasy   Gr. 4-10
   Life changes dramatically for Will Stanton, the youngest son
in a large, happy English family on the day before his eleventh
birthday which falls on Midwinter's Eve. That afternoon a neighbor, Farmer Dawson, gives him a curious ornament: a flat, black
iron circle quartered by a cross. He tells him he is to keep it
with him all the time looped through his belt. On the following
day, Will goes through the high, carved wooden doors of time that
appear on a snow-covered hill. In a great hall of the past, he
meets Merriman Lyon, a tall, vigorous man with white hair.
Merriman tells Will that he and Will, as well as Farmer Dawson,
are Old Ones, whose destiny is to devote themselves to the Light
in the long conflict between the Light and the Dark. Will is
the Sign-Seeker. Using his powers which are fully awakened now
that he is eleven, he will seek for the six great Signs of the
Light--the iron ornament is the first--which, when forged together, will be a potent force toward vanquishing the powers of
the Dark that are reaching out all over the world. Will is
warned that the Dark, at the height of its power between Christmas and Twelfth Night, will seek to deter him.
   The story chronicles Will's successful quest which is mostly
carried on in his own time, sometimes in the presence of his unaware family. He receives the second sign, the Sign of Bronze,
from the Walker, who had been Hawkins, Merriman's liege man, in
the thirteenth century. After betraying the Light, Hawkins was
sentenced to carry the Sign for six hundred years into the twentieth century. Will finds the third sign, the wooden Sign of
Learning, on Christmas Eve in the manor home of his neighbor,
Miss Greythorne, another Old One. He takes the fourth, the Sign
of Stone, on Christmas morning from an enchanted niche in the
church.
   On Christmas Day, the Dark's spells of the deep cold and snow
that have already caused freak storms over the south of England
become more intense. For over a week--until the eve of Twelfth
Night Day--snow falls and the cold becomes bitter. Many of the
villagers move into the manor of Miss Greythorne, where Merriman
is serving as butler while Miss Greythorne's butler is on holiday. But the Dark gains access there, let in by the treacherouss
Hawkins. Will knows he must find the next sign, the Sign of Fire.
With it he can break the Dark's spell of the cold and snow. This
is accomplished when Will and the other Old Ones in the manor

1974

seize the ice candles of winter which the Dark has summoned.
When Will places his candle in a candleholder of the Light, it
turns into a flower which soon produces a seed pod that opens to
yield a beautifully crafted gold sign. The moment the sign is
in Will's hand, the cold lessens.

Suddenly, there is thunder and the snow turns to rain which
runs off the frozen ground to swell the nearby Thames River. In
the floods that follow, the last part of the quest is carried
out. Will's greatest danger comes after he has obtained the
final sign, the Sign of Water, but before the signs are joined.
The Dark pursues him in a great tornado-cloud. Will is saved by
Herne the Hunter and his endless pack of hounds, who, Merriman
tells him, will hunt the Dark to the ends of the earth. There
the Lords of the Dark must skulk until they can recover their
losses. When the next attack comes, the Light will be stronger
because of the Six Signs procured by Will. The joining of the
Signs takes place in a bubble of time. On the morning of Twelfth
Night Day, Merriman walks Will home from the manor where his
family thinks he has spent the night sleeping.

This is the second of a five-book sequence called by the same
title as this book, The Dark is Rising. Evaluation follows The
Grey King (N250), the fourth book and the 1976 Newbery Medal Book.

1975

N245   HAMILTON, VIRGINIA. M. C. Higgins, the Great. New York:
        Macmillan, 1974, 278 pp.
        Fiction   Gr. 7 up
    On a hot, humid August morning, M. C. Higgins, the Great
(self-proclaimed), leaves his home on Sarah's Mountain close to
the Ohio River and goes to check his traps. He meets his friend,
Ben Killburn, child of a family shunned by neighbors as "witchies,"
and they talk and play awhile. On the way home he whistles at a
strange girl he encounters on the path. He later comes to know
her well, but at this moment Luhretta Outlaw ignores him. Back
home he climbs his forty-foot-high steel pole with a bicycle seat
fixed at the top and takes a ride. As the pole swings in a slow,
sweeping arc he glimpses wooded hills, the Ohio River, his younger
siblings swimming in a nearby lake, and the "dude" climbing toward
him.

    The "dude" is James K. Lewis, who, M. C. has heard, is travel-
ing through the hills recording folksongs on his tape recorder.
Because M. C.'s mother, Banina, has a beautiful voice, M. C. is
certain that once the "dude" hears it he will want to take her and
her family away to Nashville and make her a recording star. M. C.
loves the mountain, home to his family since 1854 when his great-
grandmother Sarah, a runaway slave, found refuge on it, but he

feels they must leave. Up the mountain, directly behind his
family's home, he can see an enormous spoil heap left by strip-
miners, which seems to be oozing slowly down the hillside to
engulf and demolish the Higginses' house. Since his father,
Jones, refuses to acknowledge the danger, M. C. thinks he must
save the family.

The events of that day and the following two days as M. C.
interacts with his family, Ben and his family, Luhretta, and
Mr. Lewis cause M. C. to change and mature. Finally, after M. C.
realizes that his father can never leave his threatened home,
M. C. sets to work building a wall of earth reinforced with
branches, old automobile fenders, and even his great-grandmother
Sarah's gravestone. The wall stands between the family's home
and the spoil heap, and, with all the family helping, M. C. will
make it strong enough to stop or divert the landslide.

Miss Hamilton is a dexterous writer; her writing is complex
yet graceful. Her empathy with the hill people is complete.
Like herself they are descendants of slaves who found safety and
freedom in Ohio before the Civil War. Until the coal companies
stripped soil and trees from the ridges to reach seams of coal
below, leaving huge mounds of debris and acid-bearing residues,
the people were self-sufficient. Now poverty-stricken but proud,
intelligent but uneducated, they face inevitable and painful dis-
ruption to their way of life.

While the author presents the black experience with distinctive style and viewpoint, her story is universal as well. This
is observable especially in M. C.'s relationship with his parents
and Luhretta. Characteristically, the author's choice of materials removed from reality helps to dramatize her themes. The
steel pole and the "witchy" Killburns, with six fingers on each
hand and six toes on each foot, living in their compound under
a gigantic web of vines, evoke singular images. Yet each has
great significance in M. C.'s development. At the beginning
M. C. is great because of his physical prowess: his father gave
him the pole as a prize for swimming the Ohio River; he propels
Luhretta, who cannot swim, through a water tunnel. At the close
his greatness is connected with taking positive action as Mr.
Lewis urged him to do to save their home from the spoil heap.
It is linked too to his open acknowledgment of Ben Killburn:
Luhretta has made him aware that external differences are of no
importance. In short, the author has proved that a boy with the
unconquerable spirit of M. C. Higgins, the Great, can overcome
great difficulties.

N246   COLLIER, JAMES LINCOLN and COLLIER, CHRISTOPHER. <u>My Brother
        Sam Is Dead</u>. New York: Four Winds, 1974, 246 pp.
        Fiction: historical   Gr. 6 up

1975

The story opens in Redding, Connecticut, the setting for most of the story, on the evening of April 20, 1775, one day after the battles of Lexington and Concord. Most of the residents of Redding are Tory in their sympathies but Eliphalet Meeker, who operates the tavern with his wife and thirteen-year-old son, Tim, the narrator of the story, is less interested in politics than in avoiding fighting and bloodshed.

That evening Sam Meeker, sixteen and a student at Yale, arrives home in uniform with word of the American victory and the announcement that he is going to fight the "Lobsterbacks." Sam informs his father: "I am an American, and I am going to fight to keep my country free." Mr. Meeker answers with equal vehemence: "We are Englishmen, we are subjects of the King, this rebellion is the talk of madmen." Father and son quarrel, and Mr. Meeker orders his son out; after Sam leaves, Tim, listening at the top of the stairs, hears his father crying.

Although it is soon hard to get supplies and prices are high, most of the time the war seems remote to Tim. After a long interval, a letter arrives from Sam. Father tells Mother she is not to answer it. In spite of her husband's objections, Mrs. Meeker answers the second letter that comes. Once rebels come to the village looking for weapons. Father receives a sword slash in the cheek for not giving them his Brown Bess--he tells them, truthfully, that Sam stole the gun when he left.

In November of 1776, Tim helps his father drive a few cattle to market in Verplancks on the Hudson River. On the return trip, Father is kidnapped by "cowboys," presumably because of his Tory leanings. Tim makes the trip home with the ox-team and wagonload of supplies by himself. From that day Tim assumes adult responsibilities.

In the spring of 1777, British troops move through Redding taking a few prisoners including Jerry Sanford, a boy Tim's age. They are followed by Continental soldiers under the command of General Benedict Arnold. Tim and his mother see Sam briefly and ask him to come home when his enlistment expires. He refuses. In June of that year they learn that Father is dead of cholera contracted while on a British prison ship in New York. Two days later they learn that Jerry Sanford, too, died on a prison ship. In December of 1778, Sam comes to Redding with General Israel Putnam's troops for winter encampment. One evening in January, when Sam is visiting Tim and his mother, they hear a disturbance outside. Sam rushes out and tries to apprehend two Continental soldiers who are driving their cattle away. The two turn on Sam, tie him up, and swear to their superiors that it was he who was stealing the cattle. Sam is court-martialed, found guilty, and sentenced to die before a firing squad. Appeals for clemency by Tim and his mother are denied. On February 16, 1779, Sam is executed.

History had a great deal to do with the shaping of the story. The authors state that the setting is authentic, many of the characters were real people, and events are portrayed as they happened. Although the Meekers are invented characters, their activities and actions are typical of people of Revolutionary times. The authors chose to have the characters speak modern language, partly to make the story easier to read, but also because it is not really known how people in those days talked. The story is a powerful indictment against war. Both Mother and Father Meeker make strong statements against it: "War turns men into beasts," Mother states on more than one occasion. In the closing words of the epilogue Tim comments: "But somehow, even fifty years later, I keep thinking there might have been another way, besides war, to achieve the same end." The injustice of the sentence that sent Sam Meeker to his death and the graphic description of the execution are perhaps the most compelling testimony against war.

N247   GREENE, BETTE. <u>Philip Hall Likes Me. I Reckon Maybe.</u>.
        Illustrated by Charles Lilly. New York: Dial, 1974,
        135 pp.
        Fiction   Gr. 4-6
    Elizabeth Lorraine Lambert, called Beth, age eleven, tells her mother in September, "Philip Hall likes me. I reckon maybe." Phil lives on the Hall dairy farm which adjoins the Lambert pig and poultry farm in Arkansas. He likes her so much in fact that every evening, after she has finished doing her chores, he lets her do his while he entertains her by playing his guitar. At school he is "number-one best" in everything: arithmetic, spelling, reading. Occasionally Beth wonders if he is number one only because she lets him be because she is afraid he would not like her if she were best. This dilemma concerns Beth off and on for a year. Between times she is growing up happily and having good times with her family, her four best friends (the five of them call themselves the Pretty Pennies), and the Tiger Hunters (Phil and his friends).
    In December, Beth, with Phil's help, is responsible for capturing thieves who have been stealing the Lamberts' turkeys. In February Beth discovers she has an allergy, decides she wants to be a veterinarian, and names her new baby brother Benjamin. April through June, Elizabeth L. Lambert and friend (Philip) tend their vegetable stand. In July and August the Pretty Pennies have fun each week while they sew. The Tiger Hunters join them in picketing the local store that sold the Pennies inferior merchandise and challenge them to a relay race at the Old Rugged Cross Picnic. In September, Madeline, Beth's calf, wins the 4-H calf-raising contest with Leonard, Phil's calf, coming in second. Later, after Phil gets used to the idea of being number

two, they team up to enter the square-dancing contest and he
tells her, "Sometimes I reckon I like you, Beth Lambert."

Beth is an engaging heroine with spirit and initiative. The
reader can sense the security she feels as part of a warm, loving, and real black family. Humor and characteristic speech add
charm to the everyday events that provide the subject of the
story. Although the time is indefinite, internal evidence suggests the 1940s or 1950s. The illustrations of Beth, her parents,
and Philip are in harmony with the text.

N248   POPE, ELIZABETH MARIE. The Perilous Gard. Illustrated by
        Richard Cuffari. Boston: Houghton Mifflin, 1974, 280 pp.
        Fiction: historical   Gr. 6-10
        In July of 1558, Kate Sutton, a plain but intelligent lady-in-
waiting to Princess Elizabeth, is banished by Queen Mary Tudor
because of a critical letter sent to the Queen by Alicia, Kate's
beautiful younger sister. The Queen sends Kate away--to Sir
Geoffrey's castle, Elvenwood Hall, in Derbyshire--because she
is certain that Kate, not Alicia, contrived the letter. Before
Kate leaves, Master Roger Ascham, Princess Elizabeth's tutor,
tells her that Sir Geoffrey is an honorable man. Elvenwood
passed to him several months earlier through his wife, Anne
Warden, to whom he was married for only a few years, all of
which were spent in Ireland. The house was formerly known as
the Perilous Gard and many curious tales are told of it.

Kate rides with Sir Geoffrey and his men for six days to
reach Elvenwood. Even before they arrive, Kate has reason to
remember the curious tales. The last day they ride in pouring
rain through dense primeval forest, which is, Kate learns, part
of the Elvenwood. They are met there by Randal, a half-witted
minstrel who comes singing an old ballad to Sir Geoffrey, his
protector. Once, Kate hears a laugh. Looking up, she sees, in
the trees up the bank from the road, a green-cloaked woman with
long dark hair.

Soon after they arrive, Sir Geoffrey is called away leaving
Kate in the care of Dorothy, his wife's old nurse, and Master
John, steward to the estate for many years. Christopher Heron,
Sir Geoffrey's younger brother, only two or three years older
than Kate, is also there, but he is withdrawn and stays by him-
self in a hut away from the house. Old Dorothy, a gossip, tells
Kate that she is sure that Christopher killed four-year-old
Cecily, Sir Geoffrey's only child, who disappeared while
Christopher was watching her.

From comments made by Dorothy before she is silenced by
Master John, Kate learns that, for hundreds of years, the Warden
family has provided food and protection for the People of the
Hill. Also known as Fairy Folk, they live in caves under the
hill and lurk in the Holy Well down behind the house to catch

the gold and precious stones pilgrims throw into the well. A story Kate hears from a woman she befriends in the village makes her believe the Fairy Folk have stolen Cecily. While Kate is telling Christopher this story, Randal appears singing "Tam Lin," a ballad about a young man taken by the Fairy Folk to be sacrificed to "pay a teind [tax] to Hell." Then Randal shows them a slipper given to him by a little yellow-haired girl who was dancing with the Fairy Folk. Christopher recognizes it as Cecily's. Randal says that in the old days the Fairy Folk took a man, sometimes the King himself, but now the best they can hope for is a child. Christopher arranges to substitute himself for Cecily.

When Master John spies Kate watching the exchange from behind a stone, he summons the lady in the green cloak, who is Queen of the Fairy Folk. She takes Kate below to be a scrubbing woman. Kate refuses the drug the other mortal women take every day so that they won't mind the wretched lives they lead. At length, in the labyrinth of caves, she locates Christopher and they manage to talk a little while every day.

Two months later, on All Hallows' Eve, when Christopher is taken out to be sacrificed, Kate saves him by laying claim to him as the lady did in the ballad, "Tam Lin." Because they have been bested, the Fairies have lost their power over their last stronghold in England. That very night Sir Geoffrey returns. A few days later Kate's father and Alicia arrive with the news that Mary Tudor is dead and Elizabeth is now the Queen. Kate and Christopher make plans to wed.

The setting and period are most convincingly presented. The pace of the story is brisk with the dialogue developing the plot. The use of ballads adds another dimension to the story. The author, a Shakespearean scholar who spent time in England doing research for the book, never suggests that the Fairy Folk are other than human beings still practicing a heathen religion. Full-page and double-page illustrations portray the characters and happenings.

N249   RASKIN, ELLEN. <u>Figgs and Phantoms</u>. Illustrated by the
        author. New York: E. P. Dutton, 1974, 153 pp.
        Fantasy   Gr. 4-8
    Mona Lisa Newton, a moody adolescent, lives with her father, Newt Newton, a likable used-car dealer who manages to lose money on almost every deal, and her mother, Sissie Figg Newton, an effervescent teacher of tap dancing, in the town of Pineapple. Her mother's family, the "Fabulous Figgs," had settled there after leaving show business. The actions of her parents and most of her Figg relatives embarrass Mona. Uncle Truman, "the human pretzel" is a "double-jointed idiot who bites his toenails." He makes his living painting signs filled with misspelled words. Uncle Romulus, "the walking book of knowledge," now inexpertly

1975

operates a travel business while his twin, Uncle Remus, "the
talking adding machine," advertises himself as the "world's greatest C.P.A." Uncle Kadota Figg, who had an act with dogs in the
show business days, practices veterinary medicine with a mail
order degree and operates a kennel. His only child, Fido II,
Mona's age, is allergic to dogs.

The one person Mona loves and admires without reservation is
her ailing Uncle Florence Italy Figg, Sissie's gentle oldest
brother. Uncle Florence, only four feet six inches tall and
formerly a dancing star, is now a respected dealer in rare color-
plate books. When her Uncle Florence dies, Mona cannot accept
his death and says she is going to find him in "Capri," the Figg
family's concept of paradise. Because he wrote "From books I
built my dream; in a book I found Capri," she goes through his
books seeking clues. She becomes very, very ill. In a surreal-
istic nightmare sequence she enters Capri. She sees but is not
recognized by her phantom uncle, now well and happy with his
dream love, Phoebe. And she is told by the phantom Pirate King
of Capri, who appears to her first as a leopard, that she is a
"selfish, stubborn, self-centered child." The sound of her
mother's tap dancing feet brings her back to reality. She returns with the realization that the members of her irrepressible
family are more highly regarded in Pineapple than she thought
and that they truly love her. Mona is suddenly happy that she
has "a lot of living and learning and loving to do."

The book is filled with delightful invention and easy-to-
understand humor. One example is the nine foot tall Figg-Newton
giant which strides about Pineapple. The giant consists of Mona
balancing on her Uncle Flo's shoulders; a long black cloak con-
ceals the giant's trunk and legs. The story is also intricate
and, at times, confusing. The enigmatic references made to
composers, artists, and authors in the Capri section would be
difficult for children to comprehend. Truman Figg's misspelled
signs contribute humor. Five of the seven black and white full-
page illustrations at the beginning of each chapter show Mona.
She is sullen and unattractive in the first four, serene and
pretty in the last. The other two illustrations show the
leopard and the pirate.

A problem remains in regard to the audience for which the
book was intended. The choice of names for characters borders
on slapstick comedy, which might be enjoyed by the younger child,
while numerous references to the details of the rare book business would be lost on children of any age.

1976

N250   COOPER, SUSAN.   The Grey King.   Illustrated by Michael
        Heslop.   New York: Atheneum, 1975, 208 pp.
        Fantasy   Gr. 4-10
        In this volume, the fourth of The Dark Is Rising Sequence, an
eleven-year-old English boy, Will Stanton, the youngest of the
Old Ones of the Light, with his magic powers and his own good
sense, goes to Wales.   His quest is to gain the harp of gold
whose song will waken the Sleepers who lie by the Pleasant Lake.
They shall ride forth to be a part of the host of the Light in
the last great battle between the Dark and the Light.
        Will is assisted in his quest by a Welsh boy his age, Bran
Davies, whose father, Owen, is a shepherd on the farm of David
Evans, Will's uncle.   Although dressed in the clothes of an
ordinary Welsh schoolboy, Bran's appearance is far from ordinary:
his hair and eyebrows are white, his skin pale, and his eyes are
golden "like the eyes of a cat or bird."   When Will meets Bran,
he learns that Merriman, the first of the Old Ones, has already
told Bran of the Dark and the Light and that he is to help Will.
Their opponent is one of the Great Lords of the Dark, the Brenin
Llwyd, the Grey King, whose stronghold is in the peaks of Cader
Idris, one of the highest mountains in Wales.
        Guided by verses that have been put into Will's head, Will
and Bran, accompanied by Bran's dog, Cafall, enter the oldest
hills through Bird Rock.   In an immense high-roofed chamber they
find three figures wearing long, hooded garments, each a different shade of blue.   They are the Lords of the High Magic.   After
the boys answer correctly three riddles as demanded by law, Will
is told to open a carved chest.   From it he lifts the golden
harp.   The first part of the quest is completed.
        But the Grey King is not easily defeated.   He sends his North
Wind in all its fury on the boys.   The song of the harp quells
it.   Then he sends the king of his great grey foxes--seen only
by Will and Bran--into the flock of a quarrelsome neighbor,
Caradog Prichard.   Cafall pursues the fox.   When the fox sinks
his teeth into the throat of a sheep, Caradog shoots Cafall.
Will's uncle and Bran's father, like Caradog, have seen only
Cafall.   The Grey King continues his harassment.   His fox, in
the form of Pen, another of the Evanses' sheep dogs, kills more
of Caradog Prichard's sheep.   Caradog vows to kill the dog.
        In the midst of the events that follow, a part of Bran's mind
he has never before been aware of awakens and he discovers that
he, like Will, has supernatural abilities.   Into the consciousness of both boys comes the realization of Bran's true identity:
Owen Davies is not his real father.   Bran is the son of King
Arthur and Queen Guinevere, brought forward into time when he
was a baby to grow up in the twentieth century.   Will understands

1976

now that his destiny is to aid and support Bran just as Merriman has always been at the side of Bran's father.

Will's final confrontation with the Grey King takes place at Llyn Mwyngil--Pleasant Lake in English--which lies below Cader Idris, the Grey King's stronghold. The Grey King attempts to best Will and at the same time shield himself by channeling his immense power through Caradog Prichard. Will eludes Caradog to play the harp and the lilting sweet notes awake the Sleepers. From the lowest slopes of Cader Idris six horsemen, in silver-grey on silver-grey mounts, ride over the Lake without touching the water. As they pass Bran, each salutes him by kissing the flat of his sword held upright before his face. They then spring into the sky and ride from the valley. Caradog Prichard snatches the harp from Will and flings it far out into the lake. As Prichard's mind snaps under the strain, the powers of the Dark vanish forever from Cader Idris and Will's quest is completed.

Fantasy and realism are deftly blended in compelling narratives set in landscapes the author knew well and recreates in detail. The Dark Is Rising (N244) takes place in Buckinghamshire where she grew up. Wakes, the setting of The Grey King, was her grand-mother's home when Ms. Cooper was a child and is her parents' home now. She moves her characters with ease from one world to another: from a real sheep farm in the green Welsh mountains and valleys or from a real English family's Christmas celebra-tion into a world of enchantments. Old tales and legends were a part of Ms. Cooper's young life and the Arthurian stories were important to her long before she began writing this sequence. The mythic elements are interwoven into the story to form a cohesive whole. A quick pace and suspense characterize both adventures. The cosmic struggle between good and evil provides a powerful and timeless theme. The author's prose is image-filled and rhythmic. The books are in the tradition of J. R. R. Tolkien and C. S. Lewis, whose lectures the author attended as an undergraduate at Oxford.

N251   MATHIS, SHARON BELL. The Hundred Penny Box. Illustrated by Leo Dillon and Diane Dillon. New York: Viking, 1975, 48 pp.
Fiction   Gr. 3-8
A very special relationship exists between young Michael John Jefferson and his great-great aunt, Dewbet Thomas, one hundred years old. Aunt Dew now lives with Michael and his parents in Michael's former room, but her thoughts often return to her home in Atlanta and her life there. She shares those times with Michael when they count the hundred pennies, one for each year of her life, in the hundred penny box. The box was given to her when she was thirty-one by her deceased husband Henry Thomas who died after putting in the fifty-sixth penny. Because the box is

big and ugly and has a broken top, Michael's mother wants to burn
it. Michael asks Aunt Dew where she'll put the pennies when she
loses her hundred penny box. "When I lose my hundred penny box,"
Aunt Dew answers, "I lose me." Then Michael knows he must save
it.

This quiet, poignant story is economically structured and
adeptly written. The love between Michael and Aunt Dew is evident. Leo and Diane Dillon's soft two-color pictures in shades
of brown and white show perfectly the strength and fragility of
Aunt Dew.

N252   YEP, LAURENCE. <u>Dragonwings</u>. New York: Harper & Row, 1975,
        248 pp.
        Fiction: historical   Gr. 6-11
Moon Shadow Lee, who tells his own story, is eight in 1903
when he leaves the Middle Kingdom, "or China as the white demons
call it" and joins his father, Windrider, whom he has never seen,
in San Francisco. They live in the town of the Tang people,
Chinatown, above the laundry where his father works. In his
leisure time, Windrider tinkers with mechanical inventions.

After two years, the two of them leave the Tang people's town.
Their new home is in the stable behind Miss Whitlaw's boarding
house on Polk Street. When father is not working as a janitor-
repairman, he studies aeronautical books and builds gliders, his
imagination having been stimulated by the flight of the Wright
brothers. "What some demon did," Windrider tells Moon Shadow,
"I can do."

Moon Shadow does the shopping and housekeeping. He becomes a
friend of Robin, Miss Whitlaw's niece. From the Whitlaws he
learns American customs; in turn he tells them of Chinese dragons.
Miss Whitlaw teaches him to read and write English and she helps
him write a letter to Wilbur and Orville Wright telling them that
his father would like to fly, too. They send him tables and
diagrams.

The earthquake in 1906 destroys Miss Whitlaw's house as well
as the laundry. Uncle Bright Star, the head of the company that
owns the laundry, urges Windrider and Moon Shadow to return to
the rebuilt laundry, but Father decides to turn all his energies
to building a flying machine. In the foothills above nearby
Oakland, he rents a barn, which serves both as a home and work-
shop. He and Moon Shadow earn their living doing odd jobs.

After three years, in the fall of 1909, the flying machine,
Dragonwings, is finished. For Windrider, it is the realization
of a dream he has had for many years going back to the time when,
in a dream, the Dragon King gave him wings. Members of the Company, Miss Whitlaw, and Robin are all present when Father makes
his short, but successful, flight. The flight ends after a few
minutes when the right propeller snaps off the frame. Dragonwings

1976

is destroyed and Father is injured in the crash. Father decides
that knowing he can fly is enough. When Uncle offers him a partnership in the company, he accepts. The following summer he
sails for the Middle Kingdom to bring back Mother.

Using the available facts of the Chinese-American experience,
the author, a native of San Francisco and a third generation
Chinese-American, recreated early twentieth-century San Francisco
and populated it with memorable characters. In vivid detail he
depicts the laundry operated by the bachelor society of the Company of the Peach Order Vow, the fraternal brotherhoods, the
opium dens, and the great earthquake. The confrontation between
two ethnic groups is well portrayed: references to the occasional harassment of the Chinese by the whites are balanced by
the account of the friendship that develops between the Whitlaws
and Lees. Love and trust grow naturally between father and son
as Moon Shadow supports his father in his desire to fly.

The flight itself was based on a true incident. On September
22, 1909, a young Chinese flier flew in the hills near Oakland
for twenty minutes. The motif of flying unifies the book. As a
young child in China, Moon Shadow flew the marvelous kites his
father had made before his departure from China prior to the
birth of his son. At the welcoming feast given for Moon Shadow,
Windrider gives him the most beautiful kite he has ever seen.
Although the members of the Company scoff, Moon Shadow believes
that Windrider truly encountered the Dragon King in his dream.
The Dragon King told Windrider he was once a dragon before he
was reborn "among the softskins." To increase his chances of
becoming a dragon again in his next life he must prove himself
worthy by passing tests that will be given him as a softskin.
Windrider is certain that flying is one proof of his dragon-ness.
There is frequent humor, much of it provided by the way America
looks to Moon Shadow.

1977

N253   TAYLOR, MILDRED D. Roll of Thunder, Hear My Cry. Frontis-
        piece by Jerry Pinkney. New York: Dial, 1976, 276 pp.
        Fiction: historical   Gr. 5-9
        The setting is Mississippi. The story extends from October
1933, the opening day of school for the black children, to
August 1934, the night after the closing of the annual revival
meeting. Although most blacks sharecrop, David and Mary Logan
and their four children--Stacey, twelve; Cassie, the narrator,
nine; Christopher John, seven; and Little Man, six--together with
Big Ma, David's mother, live on their own 400-acre farm. Part of
the land has been in the family since 1887 when Grandpa Logan,
Big Ma's husband, bought 200 acres. In 1918, after that was paid

for, he bought the second 200 acres. There is still a mortgage on the second acreage and taxes to pay on all the land. So that there will be enough money to make payments, since 1930, when the price of cotton dropped sharply, Papa has worked away from home laying railroad tracks in Louisiana. Uncle Hammer, unmarried and two years older than Papa, works in Chicago and also provides money for the mortgage payments and taxes.

The story concerns the Logans' struggle to make ends meet in this time of Depression. But it concerns, too, the discrimination, condescension, and persecution the Logans and other black families of the community suffer at the hands of whites. The white children ride to school in buses, but the black children walk; one of Stacey's friends has a three and one-half hour walk to school. Their few books already have been used by the students in the white school for ten years. Still, there are greater injustices than these. Three black men are burned by whites. All the blacks know that the Wallaces, who own the only store in the neighborhood, are guilty, but they feel powerless to do anything.

Then Mary and David Logan organize a boycott of the Wallace store. Harlan Granger, on whose land the store is located and who has long coveted the Logan land because, until after the Civil War, it was part of the Granger plantation, insinuates that if the boycott is not stopped, the bank that holds the Logans' mortgage may call it due. Pressure from the plantation owners makes most of those cooperating in the boycott back down, but the Logans do not.

Harlan Granger and two other members of the schoolboard visit Mama's class and fire her for teaching black history. While bringing supplies home from Vicksburg, Papa is shot and wounded by the Wallaces. He will not be able to return to his work on the railroad for months. Then the bank declares the mortgage due. By borrowing in Chicago and selling his sleek Packard—the same model and color as Harlan Granger's—Uncle Hammer raises enough money to pay the mortgage. A night or two later, to divert a mob bent on lynching young T. J. Avery, a boy a little older than Stacey who has been framed by two white boys, Papa sets fire to his cotton field adjoining Harlan Granger's land.

The story closes on a somber note. T. J. is in jail accused of the murder of a white storekeeper. With one-quarter of their cotton crop destroyed, the Logans still face very hard times economically. Nor is Harlan Granger likely to discontinue his campaign to get their land and put them in their place.

This is the second story about the Logan family, the first being the brief Song of the Trees. In her Newbery acceptance speech the author stated that she plans two more books about the Logans, which will carry the Logan children through adolescence into adulthood. The book is dedicated to the author's

1977

father who, she states in the introduction, "lived many of the adventures of the boy Stacey and who was in essence the man David."

The Logans are a strong black family, united in love. Even though times are hard and life is often cruelly unjust, they do not intend to let circumstances get the best of them. This attitude is expressed in a verse which precedes the last chapter and from which the title is taken. Although the family's problems are not solved by the book's end, spunky Cassie and her brothers have experienced some triumphs in the racist society in which they live. These bring both humor and satisfaction to a story that has many grim and frightening moments. It is suspenseful and well-told with good characterization and dialogue that seems to have been overheard and set down.

N254   BOND, NANCY. <u>A String in the Harp</u>. New York: Atheneum, 1976, 370 pp.
        Fantasy   Gr. 5-9
Almost as soon as Jen Morgan, fifteen, arrives at windy, wet Borth in northern Wales for her Christmas vacation, she notices the tension between her father and brother, twelve-year-old Peter. Father appears to be enjoying himself as a visiting professor at the University at Aberstwyth, and ten-year-old Becky has made friends in the little town between the bog and the sea. But Peter hates Borth and blames his father for bringing them here from their home in Massachusetts where Jen had been permitted to remain with relatives.

Peter's only small comfort is a secret he has so far told no one. Two weeks earlier, while walking on the beach, he picked up a peculiar looking metal object shaped like an old-fashioned roller-skate key. One day while he was holding it, without warning, it began to hum. And then Peter saw a picture: of water, sun, an island, and boys his age. On the Sunday after Jen's arrival, the key shows him a picture again: he sees one of the young boys, whose name is Taliesin, set off with an older man to learn to be a bard. After that, he begins to see pictures of Taliesin and his world more frequently. From a friend of his father, Dr. Rhys, a scholar of folklore and mythology, Peter learns that Taliesin was a famous sixth-century bard who lived in that part of Wales. When Peter tries to tell Jen about the pictures, she tells him he is imagining things.

After that, Peter keeps to himself and Father buries himself in work. Becky takes Jen around and introduces her to her friends, Gwilym Davies, who is a little younger than Jen, and Rhian Evans, a schoolmate. Gwilym takes them on hikes to observe birds and Rhian invites them to her family's sheep farm. One evening the family attends a harp concert and Peter sees an object like his being used to tune a harp. At the end of her

vacation Jen decides to stay in Wales because she feels they all
need to be together.

The story continues to alternate between the Morgans' everyday life and the world of the key. One day during a discussion
of unexplained lights in the bog, Rhian's father states that
there are things that cannot be explained. Troubled, Jen goes
to Dr. Rhys, who suggests, too, there may be forces we do not
understand. On a visit to the National Museum at Cardiff, the
children learn that the museum does not have a truly old harp
key. Peter knows he ought to give his, but he cannot bring himself to part with it. At length the story of Taliesin and his
times is all told. The key is dead. Still Peter cannot give up
the key. He doesn't think it belongs in a museum. Then Peter
finds Taliesin's burial cairn and takes the key there. He also
finds that he now likes Wales. In fact, they have all grown to
love the country so much that when Mr. Morgan is asked to stay
at the university for another year, all the children vote for
the idea.

The story has an excellent sense of place. The relationship
between Mr. Morgan and his children is well developed. The
Evans and Davies families and Dr. and Mrs. Rhys are also very
real. Because reality fades into fantasy without any warning
the story is sometimes hard to follow. All the episodes involving the fantasy appear believable so long as the fantasy is being
observed. But the episode in which Peter and Gwilym participate
to return the key is less credible. The title is a line of
poetry from the eighth book of Taliesin.

N255   STEIG, WILLIAM. <u>Abel's Island</u>. Illustrated by the author.
       New York: Farrar, Straus, & Giroux, 1976, 119 pp.
       Fantasy   Gr. 4-8
    <u>Abel's Island</u> is a refashioning of one of childhood's (and
mankind's) favorite stories--the survival of a lone castaway on
a desert isle. This time the castaway is a rodent, and a pretty
spoiled one at that. He is Abelard Hassam di Chirico Flint of
the Mossville Flints, and until the day he impetuously dashes
into a storm to retrieve his beloved Amanda's wind-tossed scarf,
he has only watched other people work and never struggled with
anything himself. Struggle and survival become synonymous for
the next year of his life. He first attempts to escape the
island to which he has been exiled by the storm's flood. Ingenious as his attempts are, they fail, so Abel prepares himself
for a long stay. He learns to forage for food, weave clothes
out of grass, make a secure winter shelter in a log, and fend
off a fierce owl. He never stops missing Amanda, however, and
his isolation comes close to driving him crazy. Art comes to his
rescue. He makes a statue of Amanda, and then makes statues of
his mother, sisters, brothers, and father. When spring rolls

1977

around again, he adds another statue to his collection. His subject is Gower, an elderly frog who is washed ashore by a May torrent. Before his stay on the island, Abel would have felt delicate about shaking hands with a frog, but the months on his own prompt him to greet Gower joyously. Now that he is rid of his social pretensions, has proven that he can manage on his own, and has found his vocation of artist, Abel is ready to go home. The river is at its most sluggish, and Abel is hardy enough to swim across, outwit a cat who lurks on the river bank, and make his way back to present the lost scarf to his loving wife. Abel is able indeed.

Abel's Island is satisfying on many levels. It can be read as an adventure story, as a fantasy about growing up, as a story about the growth of the artist, or even as a fable about marriage. Most importantly, Abel's Island can be read as a book which, like many other Newbery books, celebrates independence and self-reliance while at the same time showing the depth and needs of the heart's affections.

1978

N256   PATERSON, KATHERINE. The Bridge to Terabithia. Illustrated
        by Donna Diamond. New York: Thomas Y. Crowell, 1977,
        128 pp.
        Fiction   Gr. 4-7
    Jesse Aarons, ten, the middle child and the only boy, lives with his parents and four sisters in rural Virginia. His father, who leaves in his pickup truck early every day to do construction work, pays scant attention to his son and Jess knows that neither of his parents approves of his desire to become an artist. Jess has little to do with his two older sisters, Ellie and Brenda, or the baby, four-year-old Joyce Ann. He does pay some attention to six-year-old May Belle who worships him. Jesse milks Bessie the cow, helps Momma with the garden, and practices running every day. His immediate goal is to be the best runner in the fifth grade at Lark Creek Elementary School: that accomplishment would make his dad proud and win him respect at school where he is looked upon as that funny little kid who likes to draw.

    The week before school begins, Leslie Burke, who will also be in fifth grade, and her well-to-do parents, both writers, move into the old Perkins place on the adjoining farm. On the first day of school, Leslie--the only girl to run--wins the race and becomes the fastest runner in the fifth grade. All of the school except Jess reject her--she raced with the boys and came to school in faded cutoffs. By the end of the week she and Jess are friends.

In the woods beyond the creek, which they swing across on an old forgotten rope hung in a tree, they invent a secret magic world which they name Terabithia. They build a castle stronghold, take the roles of king and queen, and play out many adventures based on Leslie's extensive reading. Jess's life expands to become more exciting and fun than it has ever been. Their friendship makes school better for Jess, who has always been a loner, and it makes it bearable for Leslie. Together they grow in understanding of others. They get even with Janice Avery, a fat seventh-grade bully, who picks on May Belle. Later, influenced by Jess's natural empathy that lets him sense that even unattractive, mean people have human qualities, Leslie befriends her.

Jess's newfound happy world comes to an end during Easter vacation. He returns from a day away and learns that Leslie is dead. The rope to Terabithia broke as she was swinging across and she was killed when her head struck something when she fell. Jess's initial shock and disbelief at length give way to grief. His father comforts him and his mother is solicitous. Before they move away, Leslie's parents give Jess all of Leslie's books, and her paint set and real watercolor paper.

After they leave, Jess goes to the creek and crosses into Terabithia on a large branch. In the sacred grove he places a pine bough wreath intertwined with spring flowers as a memorial to Leslie. Then he hears May Belle calling. She has followed him and halfway across the branch bridge has become terrified. He rescues her. A week later, after he has constructed a plank bridge, he takes her across to Terabithia where "there's a rumor going around that the beautiful girl arriving today might be the queen they've been waiting for."

Not only Jess and Leslie, but the members of their families--exemplifying two very different ways of life--are well characterized. The two sets of parents, neither of them conventionally middle class, could hardly be less alike; yet both show love and concern for their children. Although Leslie's death brings sadness, the ending is hopeful. Jess's life will always be better than it was before his friendship with Leslie. He has become enough at home in the new world she helped him see that he can induct May Belle into it. Very good writing style, natural-sounding dialogue, and full-page pictures of Jess and Leslie contribute to the book's vitality.

N257   CLEARY, BEVERLY. <u>Ramona and Her Father</u>. Illustrated by Alan
        Tiegreen. New York: Morrow, 1977, 186 pp.
        Fiction   Gr. 2-5
    When Ramona is in second grade and Beezus in seventh, their father loses his job and almost immediately life becomes less pleasant for Ramona. Her mother begins to work full-time, is

1978

tired in the evenings, and has less time for Ramona. Father
looks after Ramona after school. Sometimes they have fun as
when they draw the longest picture in the world, but often he
appears worried and is irritable. In addition, Beezus has
reached a difficult age and is frequently grouchy. There is
less money for everything and small luxuries like eating out
on payday have to be omitted.

Then one evening, after a dispute over feeding the cat a
cheaper brand of cat food that he doesn't like, Beezus demands
to know how her father can afford cigarettes. When he becomes
angry, Beezus does not back down, but tells what she has learned
about cigarettes at school: "Cigarettes can kill you. Your
lungs will turn black and you'll die." Ramona is frightened,
but the next day resolves to save her father's life by getting
him to stop smoking. She begins a campaign which Beezus joins.
Father ignores their signs--big ones posted in conspicuous places
around the house and little ones in his shoes and pockets. He
appears not to notice Ramona holding her nose everytime he smokes
a cigarette. But, when the girls replace his cigarettes with
rolled pieces of paper, he explodes and tells them that enough
is enough. Shortly after they abandon the campaign, Father decides to try to give up smoking. A few days before Christmas
he gets a job that is to begin January 2. Beezus is Mary in the
Christmas pageant at church and Ramona is a sheep.

Ramona and her whole family are as believable as they were in
Ramona the Pest and Ramona the Brave. A working mother, an un-
employed father, and worry about a parent's smoking are concerns
of many children. Mrs. Cleary deals with the problems realistically, but in a reassuring, frequently humorous, way. The
dialogue is excellent and the writing style fluent.

N258   HIGHWATER, JAMAKE. Anpao: An American Indian Odyssey.
       Illustrated by Fritz Scholder. Philadelphia: J. B.
       Lippincott, 1977, 256 pp.
       Folk Literature   Gr. 6 up
    Ko-ko-mik-e-is, "more beautiful than flowers, more eloquent
than antelope, and very proud" refuses to marry any of the young
men of her village because the Sun has told her that she belongs
to him. But when scarred Anpao, a visitor in the village, asks
her she says that she will marry him if he obtains the Sun's
permission. As a sign, the Sun must remove the scar from his
face. The narrative, chronicling Anpao's long and arduous quest,
brings him to manhood. Skillfully interwoven into Anpao's story,
which is drawn from the Blackfeet legend of Scarface, are many
traditional North American Indian tales, some very old and others
so recent they reflect the Indian's experience with the white
man.

From the old swan woman Anpao learns of "the Dawn of the
World" and of his own origin: he is a son of the mighty Sun and
an earth woman; his name means "Dawn." As he journeys over prairies, mountains, and deserts he learns the "Lessons of Heaven and
Earth." The trail is long and he nearly dies.

After traversing the vast and terrible desert, Anpao comes at
last to the country of the Sun. He meets and becomes a friend of
handsome Morning Star, whose parents are the Sun and the Moon.
After Anpao saves Morning Star from the monster birds, the Sun
removes the scar. He then recognizes his lost son.

Laden with rich and beautiful gifts from the Sun, the Moon,
and Morning Star, Anpao departs for earth. On the desolate flat-
land adjacent to the mountain on which Ko-ko-mik-e-is and her
people live, Anpao encounters Smallpox who tells him that sooner
or later everyone will come to know him and that all the people
he visits die. Anpao hurries on to claim and save Ko-ko-mik-e-is.
They are married and go to live happily and forever in a village
below a great water.

In "The Storyteller's Farewell" the author, who is of Black-
feet/Cherokee heritage and a holder of degrees in anthropology
and comparative literature, explains that he created Anpao out
of many stories of the boyhood of early Indians, and from his
own experience in order to make an Indian 'Ulysses' who could
become the central dramatic character in the saga of Indian life
in North America. He notes that, although he fashioned these
stories as a writer would, he took care "to preserve the qualities unique to nonwritten folk history." His words are those a
present-day storyteller might use. Notes on sources and a bibliography are included. The book is decorated with four lithographs from stone which are nonliteral representations of the
owl, the buffalo, the bat, and death. They are appropriate for
a book which blends history and mysticism.

1979

N259   RASKIN, ELLEN. The Westing Game. New York: E. P. Dutton,
            1978, 185 pp.
            Fiction   Gr. 5-10
    The sixteen beneficiaries of the estate of millionaire
Samuel W. Westing, thirteen of whom are residents of a luxurious
Milwaukee apartment building erected on land adjoining the old
Westing house, gather in the south library of the Westing mansion
for the reading of the will. At the front of the room in "an
open coffin draped in bunting" lies Sam Westing's corpse "dressed
in the costume of Uncle Sam--including the tall hat."

    The sixteen assembled hear themselves designated in the will
as my "nearest and dearest, my sixteen nieces and nephews" and

1979

learn that Westing did not die of natural causes. "My life was taken from me," the will states, "by one of you." Declaring that "my soul shall roam restlessly until that one is found," the will specifies that the one making the discovery shall become his heir.

The will divides the sixteen into eight pairs, provides clues as well as $10,000 to each pair and exhorts, "You, too, may strike it rich who dares to play the Westing game." Thus the Westing Game begins.

As the plot progresses, it is disclosed that each of the heirs has had some connection with Westing who had disappeared from the country thirteen years earlier following recovery from an automobile accident in which he suffered severe facial injuries. One of the legatees, Grace Windsor Wexler, is, in fact, Westing's niece. She is certain that with her clues and those of her podiatrist husband, Jake; her beautiful, dutiful daughter, Angela; Angela's fiancé, an intern in plastic surgery; and her younger daughter, junior-high Turtle, she will soon solve the mystery. But they are paired with others and do not choose to help her.

The participants display ingenuity in their search for clues, a search that consumes all their thoughts and energy when they are housebound during a blizzard. It continues in spite of thefts and amateurish bombings in the apartment house. As the game continues both Grace and Jake Wexler discover their true vocations; Angela learns who she really is, and Judge J. J. Ford, the first black and the first woman to have been elected to the State Supreme Court, finds a way to repay Sam Westing for her education. But it is precocious Turtle with a long braid, a habit of kicking in the shins people she does not like, and an obsession for playing the stock market, who puts the bits and pieces together to solve the mystery.

The plot is clever and complicated; the pace is quick. The reader is likely to be as puzzled as the characters, although, as he rereads, he notices that the author has generously supplied hints for his benefit. The characters are varied and interesting. The author's wit and fascination with words manifest themselves in her lively style. Although it is highly improbable that this scenario would be found in real life, the story itself at the time of reading does not seem too incredible. The author calls it a puzzle-mystery; it is the only Newbery book that could be fit into that category.

N260   PATERSON, KATHERINE. The Great Gilly Hopkins. New York: Thomas Y. Crowell, 1978, 148 pp.
        Fiction   Gr. 6-9
    In the eight years since eleven-year-old Gilly has been away from her mother as a ward of the county welfare department, she

has lived in one foster home after another. On the way to her
new home, she reflects that her new foster mother, Maime Trotter,
like the others, will not want "to tangle with the great Galadriel
Hopkins . . . Gruesome Gilly . . . too clever and too hard to
manage." Mrs. Trotter, "a huge hippopotamus of a woman," turns
out to be uneducated and a careless housekeeper. Despite her
faults she is a kind and understanding person, and an excellent
cook. She has been a foster mother for over twenty years and
"has never met a kid she couldn't make friends with." Also a part
of the family are one other foster child, very shy William Ernest
Teague, seven, and Mr. Randolph, a blind black man who lives next
door and takes his meals with Mrs. Trotter.

At first Gilly finds the situation in her foster home impossible, and she hates school, where her teacher is Miss Harris,
a young black woman as astute as Gilly. For the millionth time
she wishes her mother, Courtney Rutherford Hopkins, would come
from California to Maryland and take her with her. The dream
seems closer to reality when Gilly receives a post card from her
saying: "The agency told me you had moved. I wish it were to
here." Gilly writes her mother a letter misrepresenting the circumstances of her life at Maime's. She asks her to send her
money for a bus ticket, promising that she will get a job and
pay her back as soon as possible. She does not receive an answer
from her mother.

Harassing Miss Harris at school backfires and, in spite of
herself, Gilly finds herself responding to W. E., Mr. Randolph,
and Maime, who love her for what she is. All at once Gilly
feels she must leave to avoid becoming soft: "I can't go soft--
not as long as I'm nobody's real kid--not while I'm just something to play musical chairs with. . . ." She steals money from
Maime's purse and from blind Mr. Randolph's house for the ticket
to California. Suspecting that she is running away, the ticket
agent calls the police. Maime refuses to press charges and, when
the social worker wishes to relocate Gilly, Maime refuses to give
her up. For the first time in many years Gilly feels secure and
loved.

Then, on Thanksgiving Day, her grandmother--Courtney's mother--
comes. Gilly's letter had been sufficiently disturbing to
Courtney to cause her, for the first time in thirteen years, to
contact her own mother, who lives in Virginia. Against her
wishes, Gilly has to go live with her grandmother. Gilly's
grandmother sends her daughter plane fare to come for Christmas.
Courtney arrives with only sufficient luggage to stay for two
days, not the two weeks her mother suggested. At the airport
Gilly realizes that her mother does not really want her. She
calls Maime Trotter who does not say she may run back to her.
She must remain where she is: "You're home, baby. Your grandma
is home."

The book is outstanding in characterization, theme, and style. The character of Gilly is believable and consistent and will remain in a reader's mind long after details of plot are forgotten. Although her actions, speech, and the comments of other characters reveal her, it is her thoughts that contribute most to the characterization. They reveal the reason for her tough exterior: it is her defense against being hurt, a pose adopted after the Dixon family whom she loved moved to Florida several years earlier leaving her behind. All the unused affection from that time on was lavished on the beautiful mother she created in her mind, "a goddess in perpetual perfection." The predictable ending to Gilly's story would have been finding happiness with Maime Trotter and becoming reconciled to the fact that her mother is not going to come for her. Gilly does find happiness with Maime but she has to leave it, as a result of her own actions—it was her letter that brought her grandmother. In a time when self-centered happiness has been an often expressed goal in both life and literature, it is noteworthy when the heroine—as Gilly does in the end—learns to do things she has to because it is her duty. The author does not rule out the idea that Gilly will be happy with her grandmother—in fact it is likely that she will be—but as the book ends she would rather be with Maime. Much lively dialogue, appropriate imagery, and humorous incidents—such as Gilly beating up six boys in one noon recess—save the story from pathos.

1980

N261   BLOS, JOAN. A Gathering of Days: A New England Girl's
        Journal, 1830-1832. New York: Charles Scribner's Sons,
        1979, 144 pp.
        Fiction: historical   Gr. 6-10
    Catherine Cabot Hall begins her book in October 1830 when she
is thirteen years and seven months old. The last entry is for
March 8, 1832, on which day she leaves her farm home in New
Hampshire to travel "hours and hours away" to help friends after
the birth of their child. At thirteen, since the death of her
mother four years earlier, she has been keeping house for her
father and sister, eight-year-old Mattie. Her dearest friend,
Cassie Shipman, lives on the adjoining farm.
    The title is taken from the entry for New Year's Day 1832:
"This year, more than others, has been a lengthy gathering of
days wherein we lived, we loved, were moved; learned how to
accept." As this entry suggests, Catherine records everything
that touches her life. Included among the day-by-day activities
and interests are the meals she cooks, recipes, precepts learned
at school, stories told by her father and Uncle Jack, the games

they play outside on summer evenings. She writes about the "breaking out" that takes place after a severe snowstorm, the Fourth of July celebration, and nutting in the fall.

The biggest personal changes come with the marriage of her father in May 1831 to Mistress Ann Higham, a widow of Boston with a son Catherine's age; and Cassie's death from fever a few months later. Issues of concern to the nation are also important in Catherine's life. Mr. Holt, the schoolteacher, brings William Lloyd Garrison's new newspaper advocating the abolition of slavery to school and she and Cassie provide food and a quilt for a runaway slave. Later, from Canada, they receive crocheted lace and the message, "Sisters Bless You. Free Now."

Two letters written in 1899 by Catherine to her namesake, a great-granddaughter, frame the narrative and add a note of authenticity. The author states that the house and barn where the story takes place still stand, both restored. Her intention was to "reconstruct life as it was when the house was new." She has accomplished this. Although the story moves along without a great deal of intensity, that is because it is filtered through Catherine's consciousness. The language has been chosen with precision to be in accord with Catherine's era, her education, and disposition.

N262   KHERDIAN, DAVID. The Road from Home: The Story of an
        Armenian Girl. New York: Morrow, 1979, 238 pp.
        Biography   Gr. 6 up
    This is the story of the life of the author's mother, Veron Dumehjian, from the time of her birth in Turkey in 1907 until the announcement of her engagement by her fiancé's family in Greece in 1924. Veron will go with his family to America to marry Melkon Kherdian, who has asked his family to bring him an Armenian bride.

    The first seven years of Veron's life, recounted in the opening chapters, were happy ones. In her eighth year--in 1915--the order for deportation of almost all the Armenians living in Turkey came. In only three days, Veron, her parents, sister, two brothers, grandfather, and two uncles travel east from their home in western Turkey by horse-drawn wagon. Grandma, two aunts, and their children are permitted to remain because two of Grandma's sons--the aunts' husbands--have been drafted into the Turkish army.

    In 1919, Veron returns by train with cousins whose home is in an adjoining town. Her own family is dead: all except her mother and father died from cholera in a camp in Syria; her mother died soon after from shock and grief; and her father died on his feet while unloading a wagon. Although the four-year exile was filled with frightening experiences, hardship, and sorrow, Veron, who had always tried to find good in everything, had happy memories,

1980

too. She enjoyed the scenery before they came to the desert and
she made friends everyplace, especially in the school for orphans
she attended in Aleppo.

    After her return home, Veron lives with her grandmother in
her old home from 1919 to 1921. Then the Greeks attack Turkey.
Injured in a bomb blast, Veron is hospitalized for several months
in a nearby town. She finally reaches her beloved Aunt Lousapere,
now widowed, and Cousin Hrpsime in the seaport city of Smyrna.
In September 1922, the Greeks evacuate the city taking with them
many Armenians who are treated as enemies by the Turks. The two
years Veron spends in Greece among other Armenian refugees are
happy ones.

    Told in first person, the story reads like an exciting novel.
But, except for the conversation, one assumes absolute veracity
since Veron Kherdian was still living at the time it was written.
Two quotations, an author's note, and a map showing Veron's journey precede the text. The first quotation, dated September 16,
1916, states that the Turkish government has decided "to destroy
completely all the Armenians living in Turkey. . . . An end must
be put to their existence, however criminal the measures taken
may be, and no regard must be paid to either age or sex nor to
conscientious scruples." The second quotation is from an order
given by Hitler in 1939 ordering the extermination "without
mercy or pity men, women, and children belonging to the Polish-
speaking race. . . . After all who remembers today the extermination of the Armenians?" Everyone who reads this dramatic,
well-written book will remember.

1981

N263   PATERSON, KATHERINE. Jacob Have I Loved. New York:
        Thomas Y. Crowell, 1980, 216 pp.
        Fiction: historical   Gr. 6-10
    In the summer of 1941, when tall, large-boned Louise Bradshaw--
called Wheeze--is thirteen, she and pudgy fourteen-year-old McCall
Purnell, Call for short, earn money by catching crabs in the
waters close to their Chesapeake Bay island home, small Rass
Island. Caroline, Wheeze's beautiful talented twin, practices
her music and goes to the mainland each Saturday for a voice lesson. Though their father, a waterman, earns enough for necessi-
ties by tonging for oysters and crabbing, there is little left
over for luxuries, and some of the money Wheeze earns goes for
Caroline and her mother's ferry and taxi fare on Saturdays.
Although Caroline has always been pampered because she was delicate and received more attention because of her talent, that
summer, before America's entry into World War II, Wheeze begins
to resent Caroline more than she has in the past.

The story records the tumultuous years of Louise's adolescence, which is made more difficult because of her relationship with Caroline. When they are fifteen, Captain Wallace, recently returned to the island after an absence of fifty years, provides money so that Caroline can attend a good boarding school on the mainland and continue her study of music. Later that year, Call, who has been helping their father on the oyster boat, joins the navy. Louise takes his place and becomes her father's helper for two years. When she is ashore, her mother, who was a teacher before her marriage, and Captain Wallace, one of the few islanders to have attended college, tutor her so that she is able to complete work for her high-school diploma.

Almost coincident with the ending of the war in Europe in May of 1945 comes news that Caroline has been accepted at the Juilliard School of Music in New York on a full scholarship. With the war rapidly coming to a close, Louise thinks of Call who will be home soon. When he comes, he is changed: he has become tall, slim, and handsome. The easy friendship is still there, but the promise of anything else is gone because Caroline and Call are engaged. After their marriage the following year, Louise leaves the island "to build myself a soul, separate from the long, long shadow of my twin." The closing pages reveal her finding a place in the world as a nurse midwife in western Virginia and married to a widower with children.

Louise tells her own story. She convincingly presents the pain of adolescence and the difficulties she experienced growing up as Caroline Bradshaw's twin sister. Besides being unlike in appearance and talent, the girls are unlike in disposition. Caroline is sunny and sensible, and knows exactly what she wants. Louise is moody and given to romantic fantasies. She wishes she had been a boy. For a short while she is passionately in love with Captain Wallace. But the crux of her problem is Caroline. Although they are never close, Louise takes pride in Caroline's musical abilities. Still, in her adolescent years she resents her bitterly. To Louise it seems that the few minutes before Caroline was born represent the only time in her life when she was the center of everyone's attention: "From the moment Caroline was born she snatched it all for herself." It is small comfort when her mother tells her that she never caused them a moment's worry. These words, "Jacob have I loved, but Esau have I hated," spoken by their meddlesome, Bible-quoting grandmother into Louise's ear in a hoarse whisper the day Captain Wallace offers to pay for Caroline's musical education, summarize the way Louise feels about her position for years. Caroline, like Jacob the younger twin, is loved while Louise, like Esau, the older, is hated. Louise often dreams that Caroline is dead. In the dream she feels exultation that she is free of her, but she also feels guilt. Like everyone on Rass Island she is a strict Methodist

and lives in fear and mercy of the Lord. She searches the
scriptures for evidence that she is not to be eternally damned
for hating her sister. The two brief final chapters and the
short prologue reveal that she was able to resolve her hate.
The closing scene in which she delivers a strong healthy twin
and a weak one that requires her attention for hours is a re-
enactment of her and Caroline's births. At last she fully
understands.

As Louise tells her story she recreates the life and times so
well that the reader feels as if he has experienced life on Rass
Island in the 1940s. Descriptive details add emotional coloring.
The writing style, which captures some of the island speech, is
appropriate to plot, theme, and characters. The jacket cover by
Kinuko Craft portrays the scene with fidelity: the two girls,
the white frame houses with snowball bushes in the yard and enclosed with picket fences, the tower of the Methodist church, the
coarse grass growing in the marshland, the docks, a stormy-
looking sky, and a choppy sea.

N264   LANGTON, JANE. The Fledgling. Illustrated by Erik Blegvad.
       New York: Harper & Row, 1980, 182 pp.
       Fantasy   Gr. 3-7
Even before eight-year-old Georgie Dorian, who is small and
light for her age, makes friends with a large Canada goose--the
Goose Prince she calls him--she longs to fly. As she watches
the geese fly over her home on Walden Street in Concord, Massachusetts, she thinks, "If only I could fly like that. . . . If
only I could do it again." She is certain that once, in the
middle of the night, she flew down the twelve steps of the front
hall stairs "in two great floating bounds." And another time,
when she jumped from the railing of the front porch she drifted
up to the top of the house before floating to the ground "like a
feather or a piece of milkweed down." So when the Goose Prince
hoots softly from the porch roof outside her window, Georgie is
ready.

In the predawn light, she climbs out her window and nestles on
his back. He asks her if she would like to fly around Walden
Pond. She would indeed. They circle the pond three times, skim-
ming the tops of the pine trees. The next time he takes her to
the pond, he teaches her to fly. Then night after night he comes
for her and carries her through the moonlit night to high above
the pond. There Georgie slips off his back and with outstretched
arms drifts downward in long gliding flights in the cool September
air. When she is just above the water the Goose Prince comes up
beneath her and she settles herself firmly on his back for the
flight home. Soon Georgie feels that she is no longer a
fledgling.

The wonderful flights and the companionable talks with the Goose Prince come to an end shortly after midnight on the opening day of the duck hunting season. While Georgie and the Goose Prince fly through "smooth billows of creamy air" a little way above the pond, Georgie is shot by near-sighted Ralph Preek who mistakes her for a goose. He aims for the larger goose, but his shot catches both: Georgie in the upper arm and the Goose Prince in the leg. The Goose Prince is able to carry Georgie home and awaken her mother by beating with his wings and clacking his bill against her window.

After Georgie's arm is healed, she sees the Goose Prince only once more. In the hour before midnight on the last day of the hunting season, he comes to her with a present he found in Walden Pond. On the walk in front of her house, they talk and laugh a little because Georgie is growing taller and will soon be too big to fly. She tells him goodbye and he promises to try to come again next year. As he takes off--awkwardly because his leg is still lame--Mr. Preek sees him and shoots him. It is his opinion that the goose is dangerous and will harm the child.

Uncle Fred and Georgie bury the Goose Prince by Walden Pond. Georgie mourns for a week then resolutely says that she is all right. The present, a small rubber ball with blue and white streaks, remains to remind her of its donor. Soon Georgie makes a discovery: in the dark, the ball becomes great and gleaming, lifts from Georgie's hand, and begins to turn slowly. The gift of the Goose Prince is an image of the earth. He had told her to take good care of it. Georgie renews the promise in her heart, "I will."

Excellent writing style, good plotting and characterization, well-realized setting, and themes from Thoreau are all in evidence in The Fledgling. Uncle Fred Hall, Georgie's stepfather and a world-renowned scholar of Thoreau and Emerson, conducts the Concord College of Transcendental Knowledge in their large nineteenth-century home. He quotes Thoreau daily and naturally patterns his life on the teachings of Thoreau and Emerson. Georgie herself is sure that Henry Thoreau is awake inside his white marble bust that stands in the hall. The story shows very good family relationships. Uncle Fred's orphaned niece and nephew, Eleanor and Eddie, fourteen and twelve, love and protect Georgie as if she were truly their little sister. Georgie's mother, in turn, is in the place of a mother to the two of them and is understanding of Eleanor's adolescent moods. Mr. Preek, who is the president of the local bank, and his secretary, Miss Prawn, who happens to be the Halls next door neighbor, are meddlers and in contrast to Georgie and her family. In addition, Miss Prawn with her flowerbed of plastic flowers and highflown rhetoric provides some moments of humor.

This is the fourth book in which magical adventures originate for the children in the old house in Concord.

N265   L'ENGLE, MADELEINE. <u>A Ring of Endless Light</u>. New York:
       Farrar, Straus & Giroux, 1980, 324 pp.
       Fiction   Gr. 5-10
       In the fourth novel about the Austin family, Vicky, the nar-
rator, now nearly sixteen, and her family go to Seven Bay Island
off the coast of New England to stay with her mother's father, a
retired clergyman, who is dying of leukemia. Her older brother
John has completed his first year of college at MIT and has a
summer job at the Marine Biology Station on the island. One of
his coworkers is another collegian his age, Adam Eddington, a
character from <u>The Arm of the Starfish</u>. Vicky helps Adam with
his summer project which pertains to dolphins. Although Vicky
does not think of herself as scientific she finds she has unusual
rapport with the dolphins and is able to communicate with them
telepathically. She also helps her mother with the housework,
reads to her grandfather, writes poetry, and dates Leo Rodney
and Zachary Gray, two young men just out of high school.
       The opening event of the story is Leo Rodney's father's fu-
neral. Commander Rodney dies of a heart attack after saving a
rich young man from drowning. The young man turns out to be
Zachary Gray whom the Austins had met the preceding summer while
on a camping trip. Zachary's mother has died recently and
Zachary reveals that he was trying to kill himself when Rodney's
father saved him. Both Leo and Zachary profess to like Vicky
very much but it is Adam of whom she dreams.
       As Grandfather's condition worsens, death seems to be every-
where. Adam tells Vicky that the preceding summer he was unwittingly responsible for the death of a friend. Then Dr. Nutteley,
Adam's superior at the laboratory, is struck by a motorcycle and
lies unconscious in the hospital for several days. While waiting
in the emergency room for her parents who are with her grandfather
in another part of the hospital, Vicky holds a child who has a
convulsion and dies in her arms. The darkness closes over Vicky
and she goes into shock. The following day Adam swims out with
her to the dolphins. Their sane and loving behavior causes her
to see events in perspective again.
       As the other stories about the Austins do, this one shows a
spectrum of pleasing family relationships. Vicky is shown inter-
acting with her parents and grandfather, as well as with John,
sensitive seven-year-old Rob, and her bright and beautiful
thirteen-year-old sister, Suzy, who wants to be a doctor like
their father. Mrs. Austin does not work outside her home. Her
primary interest is maintaining a happy home for her family, but
her special talent is bringing words and music to life: in the
evenings she reads aloud from Shakespeare and she sings to the
family accompanying herself on a guitar. The values of the family are not materialistic. Spending time together in conversation is important to them. Family love and understanding sustain
them in difficult times.

The author is adept at weaving into the story both philosoph-
ical and scientific ideas. The title comes from Henry Vaughan,
a seventeenth-century English poet and divine admired by Grandfather who quotes him: "I saw eternity the other night/ Like a
great ring of pure and endless light." Grandfather observes that
"we're out of touch with death." Because he believes that to
accept death as a friend is to affirm wholeness and life, he
speaks of it to his family and his words bring them comfort.
Although the dolphin theme appears incredible, we may be sure
it is based on scientific data. While providing many interesting episodes, Vicky's relationship with the three young men
seems devised. The emphasis on death may seem depressing to
some, yet the author's intention obviously is to stress the
beauty and naturalness of death, and not its pain.

The Caldecott Medal and Honor Books: Characteristics and Trends

The Caldecott Medal, first awarded in 1938 by the American Library Association, remains the most prestigious commendation for illustrators of picture books in the United States. In the past forty-three years, numerous artists have been honored for their excellence in illustrating these books for children. Books of traditional literature, fantasy, biography, fiction, and poetry have found representation in the Caldecott Medal and Honor Book titles, and the artistic interpretations of these one hundred eighty-six books are as varied as their literary types. These titles, when categorized by genre and decade, reveal some trends in the choices for the Medal and Honor Book recipients, and it is through this classification that the body of works will be discussed. The decades by which the literary types are classified correspond with those of the Newbery Medal and Honor Books and refer to the following time spans: Decade One, a partial decade, 1938-1941; Decade Two, 1942-1951; Decade Three, 1952-1961; Decade Four, 1962-1971; and Decade Five, 1972-1981. The types of literature represented in each decade are summarized in the chart in Appendix D, which can be referred to for further information regarding the literary types as discussed below.

TRADITIONAL LITERATURE

Traditional literature, including the titles classified as Bible, folk tales, fairy tales, folk sayings, fables, legends, epics, hero stories, and Mother Goose and nursery rhymes, has remained constantly represented throughout the years of the Caldecott Medal, and, unlike in the Newbery works, this category remains one of the major areas of concentration throughout the decades. The first Caldecott Medal recipient in the category of traditional literature was Animals of the Bible (C1, 1938), also the first book to receive the Medal in 1938. The Bible, in the early two decades of the Caldecott, offered material suitable for young readers, but in latter decades remains represented only by the more secular One Wide River to Cross (C132, 1967) and Noah's Ark (C172, 1978).[1]

The bulk of titles classified under traditional literature are single Mother Goose rhymes or collections and folk tales from all

227

corners of the world. The appeal of Mother Goose stories, the rhyme and rhythm, participation and narration, has continued to hold the attention of young audiences, and titles range from songs, in Sing Mother Goose (C37, 1946), to single rhymes, Three Jovial Huntsmen (C159, 1974), in addition to numerous collections interspersed throughout the years.

The surge of folk tales in the last two decades of the Medal and Honor Books may indicate the concern for fostering early apprecia- tion of cultures different from the backgrounds of the readers, as well as an increased interest in investigating the ancestry of diverse heritages. Though these folk tales originated in oral form, they have been revived again and again, given new life through the breath of inventive artistic creations by the winners of the Awards. Afri- can (A Story, A Story [C145]), American (Arrow to the Sun [C161]), Armenian (One Fine Day [C149]), English (Tom Tit Tot [C130]), German (Snow-White [C156]), Italian (Strega Nona [C164]), Japanese (The Wave [C125]), Jewish (It Could Always Be Worse [C174]), Russian (The Fool of the World and the Flying Ship [C137]), and Scottish (Always Room for One More [C127]), titles attest to the international inter- dependence of the world of children's literature. Children are sup- plied now with greater opportunities and materials that enable them to look beyond themselves and away from the sheltered world repre- sented in earlier books for children.

The trends in the traditional literature of the Caldecott titles, as with the works in all of children's literature, appear to be away from the didacticism of early books for children, and the Medal, through its recipients, has fostered and encouraged the child reader to broaden his or her understanding of other peoples through their literature.

FANTASY

Fantasy remains represented throughout all five decades of the Caldecott Medal, but the occurrence of fantasy in the second, third, and fourth decades is most frequent. Except for a few titles, this genre takes the form of animal fantasy; from lions (C9, C99), monkeys (C80), and bears (C73, C114), to dogs (C69), cats (C65, C86), rabbits (C118), and mice (C70, C97, C134, C141), the characters of animal fantasy arise. Even a few "wild things" and imaginary creatures make appearances in this category. The affinity small children have for animals of all sorts no doubt accounts for the popularity of these characters as subjects for books.

Fantasy, in the second (1942-1951) and third (1952-1961) decades, deals with the concerns of its animal characters. But in the last two decades the concerns of these animal characters have become more the voice of the needs and characteristics of the audience. Little

Bear's Visit (C114, 1962), Swimmy (C120, 1964), Frederick (C134, 1968), and Fables (C182, 1981) demonstrate the increasing complexity of to- day's audiences and the need for the literature to meet and recognize these demands. The sophistication of these more psychologically- tuned themes reflects the changing concerns of the audience, a prod- uct of a society preoccupied with television, mobility, and the early infusion and dissemination of information of all kinds.

There also remain, though infrequently, as in the Newbery selec- tions, those works of fantasy classified as literary fairy tales, those stories that follow the conventions of traditional literature but have known, identifiable authors. Among these works are Many Moons (C24, 1944), The Steadfast Tin Soldier (C84, 1954), The Emperor and the Kite (C136, 1968), The Judge: An Untrue Tale (C144, 1970), and Hildilid's Night (C152, 1972). The production of this form of fantasy has more recently been surpassed by the resurgence of tradi- tional literature, especially in the area of folk and fairy tales. Artists of Caldecott books are finding the traditional tales suitable material for their artistic expression, without the confines of de- veloping an original text.

BIOGRAPHY, BOOKS OF INFORMATION, ABC, 123

Biographies for children that have won Caldecott status remain about figures from American history, the people who built this coun- try. Abraham Lincoln (C10, 1940) and America's Ethan Allen (C58, 1950) are represented in biographies for the child reader, though they both could be more accurately classified as illustrated books rather than picture books. Other than historical fiction, this type of literature is least represented in the Caldecott titles.

Books of information in history, geography, the sciences, the arts, and languages are all represented by Caldecott recipients. This classification of nonfiction has shown the greatest development and improvement in the last decade. Though early books of informa- tion, such as Paddle-to-the-Sea (C19), You Can Write Chinese (C39), and Houses from the Sea (C108), still provide pertinent facts to their audiences, the quality of information, storyline, and illustra- tion in such books as When Clay Sings (C154, 1973), Cathedral (C160, 1974), Jambo Means Hello (C162, 1975), Ashanti to Zulu (C166, 1977), and The Way to Start a Day (C177, 1979), cannot be overlooked and serve as an indication of new standards for books of nonfiction. The demand and production of such quality books of nonfiction for chil- dren is an outgrowth of a society that spoonfeeds its children on television; the dissemination of information and an awareness of the world--regions, countries, peoples--outside the boundaries of cities, states, or countries make these books a logical answer to the ques- tions and curiosities of the young. What is heartening is the pre- dominance of books of nonfiction in the Caldecott titles that help reinforce the social sciences--and an appreciation of others.

229

The Caldecott Books: Characteristics and Trends

Alphabet and counting books will always remain in demand and the original and personal interpretations of these, represented by Moja Means One (C151, 1972) and Hosie's Alphabet (C155, 1973), demonstrate there is room for creativity and inventiveness with even the most common of subjects. These subjects will continue to offer the illustrator a forum for personal expression, though works such as those mentioned above often wander from the original purpose of these concept books.

HISTORICAL FICTION

Historical fiction and biography are the least represented types of literature among the winners of the Caldecott Medal and Honor Books. All three books of historical fiction, one in each of the last three decades, take place in northeastern United States and deal with life in colonial America. The Thanksgiving Story (C90, 1955) recounts the landing of the forefathers of the United States; Thy Friend, Obadiah (C143, 1970) paints a picture of early Nantucket Island; and Ox-Cart Man (C178, 1980) portrays the life-cycle of a farm family in New Hampshire. Since children of the picture-book age have little real perception of time and history, the minor representation of historical fiction does not seem unreasonable. It is the Newbery Medal and Honor Books that find this genre so appropriate for the audience of children, those readers who have a firmer grasp of the concept of time, past and present.

REALISTIC FICTION SET IN OTHER LANDS

After World War II, the number of books of realistic fiction set in other lands dropped and then regained a temporary representation in the third decade (1952-1961). Since that time, however, few books in this category have received Caldecott recognition. Mei Li (C4, 1939) was the first book of fiction set in other lands to win the Caldecott Medal. Ludwig Bemelmans (Madeline [C12, 1940] and Madeline's Rescue [C81, 1954]) and Taro Yashima (Crow Boy [C93, 1956] and Seashore Story [C135, 1968]) remain the major contributors to this classification.

At a glance, the last two decades perhaps provide an indication of less concern with countries outside our boundaries, as represented in the Caldecott choices, but the surge of folk tales from all nations most certainly fills the gap in this category. It is these folk tales, too, that often give the audience a better understanding, appreciation, and sensitivity for the culture than any work of fiction could possibly hope to accomplish.

The Caldecott Books: Characteristics and Trends

REALISTIC ANIMAL STORIES

Four of the ten realistic animal stories of the first two decades of the Caldecott Medal were produced by Clare Turlay Newberry: Barkis (C8), April's Kittens (C15), Marshmallow (C23), and T-Bone, the Baby-Sitter (C68). The teams of Elmer and Berta Hader (Cock-a-doodle-doo [C11] and The Big Snow [C52]) and Lavinia Riker Davis and Hildegard Woodward (Roger and the Fox [C50] and The Wild Birthday Cake [C59]) were responsible for another four of the books in these two decades. Several of the books in this category are now out of print, indicating that the quality and appeal of these works have not stood the test of time. After 1953 (The Biggest Bear [C75]), realistic animal stories have not been represented in Caldecott titles.

Fantasy seems to provide children most often with exposure to animal characters, and the growth of increased dissemination of information on animals, through television and books of nonfiction, and increased interest in the mechanical and computerized playmate have perhaps lessened the reception and audience for books of this type, though the category was never heavily represented by Caldecott titles. The stimulation of young imaginations in animal fantasy does much to hold the interest of the developing attention spans of the picture-book audience.

FICTION ABOUT REGIONS AND MINORITIES

This category was most represented by Caldecott titles in the second decade (1942-1951), half of the titles of which were done by Leo Politi: Pedro, the Angel of Olvera Street (C44), Juanita (C55), and Song of the Swallows (C57). Though this classification has never been heavily represented, the subjects of the books of this category have dealt with those groups or minorities within the culture of the United States. The latest titles, Hawk, I'm Your Brother (C170, 1977) and Ben's Trumpet (C179, 1980), deal with Native American and black children, respectively. The subjects of these books seem to be re-investigating the concerns of the society and reflecting them in the choices for the awards. Earlier books of this category reflected nothing but the self-contained existence of the children of minorities or groups within their cultures, but the latter works demonstrate how these groups reflect the values and needs of society as a whole, of peoples of all nationalities, races, and religions. This shift in perspective seems a healthy one, and one more constructive in fostering an understanding and appreciation of those different from ourselves.

OTHER REALISTIC FICTION SET IN THE UNITED STATES

This category is most commonly represented by everyday stories in the lives of children, girls and boys alike. From Blueberries

231

for Sal (C53, 1949), Play with Me (C92, 1956), and Sam, Bangs & Moonshine (C131, 1967) to Bambino, the Clown (C49, 1948), The Moon Jumpers (C109, 1960), and A Pocketful of Cricket (C126, 1965), the children of these stories reflect the concerns and preoccupations of the young. From berrypicking and seeking companionship to moonlight dancing and sharing crickets in school, these stories have remained relevant to today's audiences because they reflect the essence of childhood.

This classification also contains, within the last decade, two books that demonstrate the acceptance of a new interpretation for future recipients of the Caldecott Medal. The Grey Lady and the Strawberry Snatcher (C183, 1981) and Truck (C184, 1981) represent wordless picture books that have perhaps been influenced by Peter Spier's 1978 nearly wordless Noah's Ark (C172). The recognition of these books demonstrates the infinite range of possibilities open to illustrators of books for children. These artists, Molly Bang and Donald Crews, have offered a new interpretation of the picture book, and their acceptance indicates that the solution is a viable one. A far cry from many of the illustrated books of the early Caldecott years, these books have opened the door to a new and, assuredly, exciting decade for the Caldecott Medal in the 1980s.

OVERALL TRENDS IN THE CALDECOTT MEDAL AND HONOR BOOKS

Traditional literature, fantasy, and all categories of fiction combined contribute to the majority of titles from the Caldecott Medal and Honor Books. In the last decade, however, only traditional literature remains strongly represented, in contrast to its decline in the Newbery works. Fiction, in all classifications, has lost considerable representation in the last two decades, and Medal recipients for books of fantasy have been greatly reduced in the last ten years as well. The growth of books of nonfiction, specifically books of information, may be an indication of the trends of the future, for good books of nonfiction for children fulfill dual needs--they offer interesting storylines interwoven with fact and they provide the information necessary for research within the classroom and for recreational reading in areas of personal interest to children.

Many of the early Caldecott choices can most accurately be classified as illustrated books. The movement from this form of book is apparent in the more recent years of the Medal. The initiation of the wordless picture book into the ranks of the Caldecott Medal and Honor Books is a milestone in the development and growth of the realm of picture books. The Caldecott Medal is, in part, responsible for the maturation and growing prestige of this art form. Though increased and improved technology have allowed for the reproduction of books of better quality, the incentive and stimulation offered by this esteemed award are no doubt partially responsible for the enormouse growth in the quality and design of picture books.

The Caldecott Books: Characteristics and Trends

Artistic styles and creativity are reaching new heights in books for children. Earlier artistic styles and limited technology produced many books that seemed merely mechanical replications of a style dictated by the reproduction processes, with little attention devoted to the interaction of text and its visual counterpart. Such works as The Mighty Hunter (C27), The Christmas Anna Angel (C34), Rain Drop Splash (C41), All Around the Town (C54), The Wild Birthday Cake (C59) seem to suffer from a technical standpoint and provide an interesting contrast to the finely designed books now produced for the picture-book audience. The individuality of style in the illustrations of picture books of more recent years and the ability of printers to reproduce these works are making these creations the works of the art world itself. No longer do illustrators of children's books need to feel inferior to creators of other art forms.

Though forty-two of the one hundred eighty-six Caldecott Medal and Honor Books are currently out of print, the majority of the remaining titles are favorites of children today. Those books that are no longer circulated and read attest to changes in critical taste and in the needs and interests of the audience. Economic conditions, technological restrictions, and misguided artistic criticism, however, are perhaps the culprits more than changing audiences. The task of selection is not an easy one, but the Caldecott Medal has done much to encourage and foster growth and experimentation in the production of books for young readers. The drawbacks and inconsistencies of the selection processes are far outweighed by the wealth of quality books that bear the honor of having received a Caldecott Medal.

Note

[1] Dates in parentheses indicate the years in which the books received the Caldecott Medal or were named Honor Books.

Illustration from *Animals of the Bible: A Picture Book,* compiled by Helen Dean Fish and illustrated by Dorothy P. Lathrop. Copyright 1937 by Dorothy P. Lathrop. Copyright © renewed 1965 by Dorothy P. Lathrop and Emily P. Street. By permission of J.B. Lippincott, Publishers.

And when night falls they swim to their little island and go to sleep.

Illustration from *Make Way For Ducklings*, written and illustrated by Robert McCloskey. Copyright 1941 by Robert Mc-Closkey. By permission of Viking Penguin, Inc.

The Little House
was very sad and lonely.
Her paint was cracked and dirty . . .
Her windows were broken and her shutters hung crookedly.
She looked shabby . . . though she was just as good a house as ever underneath.

Illustration from *The Little House*, written and illustrated by Virginia Lee Burton. Copyright 1942 by Virginia Lee Demetrios. Copyright © renewed 1969 by George Demetrios. By permission of Houghton Mifflin Company.

Illustration from *Book of Nursery and Mother Goose Rhymes*, illustrated by Marguerite de Angeli. Copyright 1954 by Marguerite de Angeli. By permission of Doubleday & Company, Inc.

"In faith," the fox answered, "it shall be done." As soon as he spoke the words, the rooster nimbly broke away from his mouth and flew at once high into a tree.

Illustration by Barbara Cooney from *Chanticleer and the Fox*, adapted and illustrated by Barbara Cooney. Copyright © 1958 by Harper & Row Publishers, Inc. A Caldecott Award winner. Adapted from the translation by Robert Mayer Lumiansky of "The Nun's Priest's Tale" from *The Canterbury Tales* by Geoffrey Chaucer. Copyright 1948 by Simon & Schuster, Inc. By permission of Thomas Y. Crowell, Publishers.

From Marcia Brown, *Once a Mouse*. Copyright © 1961 by Marcia Brown. Reprinted with the permission of Charles Scribner's Sons

Illustration from *Where the Wild Things Are*, written and illustrated by Maurice Sendak. Copyright © 1963 by Maurice Sendak. By permission of Harper & Row, Publishers, Inc.

Illustration from *Sam, Bangs & Moonshine*, written and illustrated by Evaline Ness. Copyright © 1966 by Evaline Ness. By permission of Holt, Rinehart & Winston, Publishers.

Illustration from *Cathedral,* written and illustrated by David Macaulay. Copyright © 1973 by David Macaulay. By permission of Houghton Mifflin Co.

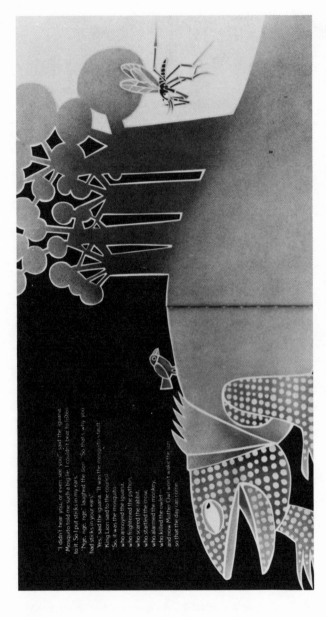

"I didn't hear you, or even see you," said the iguana.
"Mosquito told me such a big lie, I couldn't bear to listen
to it. So I put sticks in my ears."

"Nge, nge, nge," laughed the lion. "So, that's why you
had sticks in your ears."

"Yes," said the iguana. "It was the mosquito's fault."

King Lion said to the council:

"So, it was the mosquito
who annoyed the iguana,
who frightened the python,
who scared the rabbit,
who startled the crow,
who alarmed the monkey,
who killed the owlet—
and now Mother Owl won't wake the sun
so that the day can come."

Illustration from *Why Mosquitoes Buzz in People's Ears: A West African Tale*, written by Verna Aardema and illustrated by Leo and Diane Dillon. Illustrations copyright © 1975 by Leo and Diane Dillon. By permission of The Dial Press.

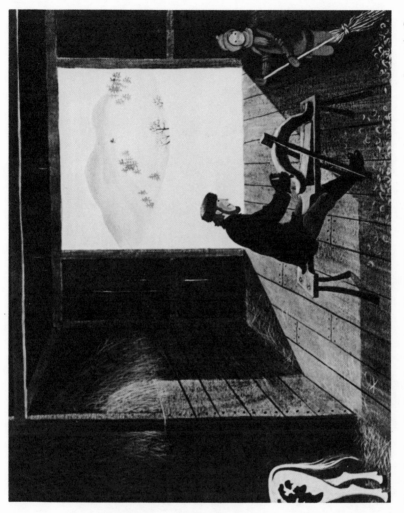

Illustration from *Fables*, written and illustrated by Arnold Lobel. Copyright © 1980 by Arnold Lobel. By permission of Harper & Row, Publishers, Inc. and Jonathan Cape Ltd.

The Caldecott Medal and Honor Books, 1938-1981

1938

C1   FISH, HELEN DEAN. Animals of the Bible. Illustrated by
        Dorothy Lathrop. New York: Frederick A. Stokes, 1937,
        66 pp. 30 illus.: black and white-30/illustrated title
        page/lithographs/24.8cm x 18.4cm
        Bible   Gr. Ps-3
     Dorothy Lathrop's black and white interpretations of Old and
New Testament Bible verses, which deal specifically with animals
and were selected by Helen Dean Fish, received the first Caldecott
Medal in 1938. The subject of this first Medal winner reflects
the trends of earlier books for children--their didacticism and
moralism--but it also establishes reverence and prestige for the
Caldecott Medal, a tradition that continues today. Lathrop's
anatomical studies of animals and her naturalistic approach to
the flora are in harmony with the text of the book. The settings,
not always realistic, help retain some of the mysticism of the
biblical verses and allow the artist to develop her compositions
with care.
     Lathrop's animals express the humanism of the Bible verses,
with each illustration rejoicing the splendor of the creations
of the animal kingdom. The animals, ironically, are so realistically handled that the introduction of the figures of Man, be
it Abraham, Elijah, Rebekah, or Noah, comes across awkwardly.
Either the artist is more comfortable in her execution of animals than Man, or she has focused upon the contrast between these
two kingdoms of Man and animal. Because of their stylization,
especially in the angel figures, the human figures often become
more interesting, when they are present, than the realism of the
animal figures. It is certainly not the illustrations that prevent the work from working as effectively as it could.
     The major weakness of the work lies in the book's design,
which prescribes large amounts of text to a single illustration
or sometimes no illustration at all. Increased effectiveness
could be gained by two methods--selection of passages of shorter
length, such as "The Foxes Have Holes" (Matthew 8:19, 20) or "As
a Hen Gathereth Her Chickens" (Matthew 23:27), or by allotting
more illustrations per selection. Lack of physical integration

of words and picture, not lack of quality text and pictures, is
the culprit here and continues to be a determining factor in
producing a picture book that is pleasing to look at, worthy of
reading, and easy to appreciate.

C2   ARTZYBASHEFF, BORIS. Seven Simeons: A Russian Tale. New
           York: Viking, 1937 (OP), [32 pp.] 26 illus.: color-26/
           illustrated endpapers and title page/line engravings/
           28.5cm x 22cm
           Folk Tale   Gr. 1-3

The illustrations in this Russian tale, retold by Boris
Artzybasheff, lend a medieval flair to the story of the seven
Simeon brothers. Each brother possesses a skill which becomes
instrumental in capturing the beautiful Princess Helena for
King Douda to marry.

As the brothers are sent to the Island of Boozan to capture
Helena from her tyrant Father, the Simeons' trades demonstrate
the virtue of hard work and skill, practical or magical. Their
virtue does, of course, pay off, as they all return to their
land to till and reap the rewards of what they have sown.

The ochre, red, and green line drawings give this book an
air of ancient medieval manuscripts, a characteristic reinforced
by the decorative items in the margins and interspersed throughout the text. Artzybasheff portrays the handsome King Douda,
ruler of a vast empire, as a stylized figure of nearly feminine
characteristics, which adds to the fantasy of the tale. The
architecture included, however, is very reminiscent of Eastern
structures and domed mosques, which helps reflect the origin of
the tale.

Of the books awarded honors in this year, Seven Simeons comes
the closest to actually functioning as an entire unit of cohesive
text and illustrations. Although the format becomes a bit monotonous, with the left side of each full-page spread bearing an
illustration, faced by an entire page of text, the artist does
much to extend and embellish this tale in his individual style,
supplying the subtle indicators of the tale's origin. The many
delicate linear patterns that Artzybasheff incorporates into his
illustrations help to extend the decorative sense of the artwork
of manuscripts, but these patterns also serve to reinforce the
image of the unreal and fantastic elements of this story of
kings, princesses, castles, and happily-ever-after endings.

C3   FISH, HELEN DEAN. Four and Twenty Blackbirds: Nursery Rhymes
           of Yesterday Recalled for Children of To-Day. Illustrated
           by Robert Lawson. New York: Frederick A. Stokes, 1937
           (OP), 104 pp. 59 illus.: black and white-37; teal and
           white-9; black, white, and teal-13/illustrated half title,
           front matter, title page, dedication, contents page, and
           Foreword pages/lithographs/24.8cm x 18cm

1939

Mother Goose/Nursery Rhymes   Gr. Ps-1
Over the years, several of the Caldecott Medal and Honor Books,
such as Helen Dean Fish's Four and Twenty Blackbirds, illustrated
by Robert Lawson, have been illustrated collections of one literary form or another. Mother Goose, biblical scriptures, as was
the first Caldecott Medal Book, or nursery rhymes have remained
favorite forms for compilations, and such collections appear from
time to time among the winners of Caldecott Medals.

Fish's compilation of twenty-four nursery rhymes has the distinction of coming from the oral tradition, passed on from generation to generation by word of mouth. Many of the rhymes had
never, before the book's publication, been recorded, and Robert
Lawson's reputation as an illustrator no doubt also enhanced the
reception of this early Caldecott Honor Book. Fish's "Foreword,"
as well, helps the reader develop an understanding of the book's
purpose and fosters an appreciation for these rhymes of childhood.

Lawson captures the essence of many of Randolph Caldecott's
illustrations and translates it into his own bold, sure style.
Lawson picks up on the humor of the situations which develop
within the rhymes, and his drawings take on an air lighter than
his heavy style normally dictates. The sheer joy and absurdity
of the rhymes and their rhythm momentarily infect Lawson as he
dresses Dr. Dog in trousers and comforter in "Old Mother Tabby-
skins," or as he portrays Joe Dobson's ineptitudes as he tries
to assume the household chores for a day. Lawson's illustrations
bring these rhymes to life and produce an enjoyable collection
that needs to be read aloud to gain full appreciation. The music
for thirteen of the rhymes, included at the end of the book, adds
another dimension to some of the selections and helps demand a
participation in the text, an interaction that the illustrations
have helped establish.

1939

C4   HANDFORTH, THOMAS. Mei Li. Garden City, N.Y.: Doubleday,
     Doran, 1938, [48 pp.] 44 illus.: black and white-44/
     illustrated endpapers, title page, and front matter/brush
     and lithographic pencil on copper plates/30.3cm x 22.5cm
     Fiction   Gr. 1-2
With this 1939 Caldecott Medal Book, the award for excellence
in picture books begins to truly establish its reputation.
Thomas Handforth's bold, black illustrations, reminiscent of
calligraphic brush strokes with ink, against the stark white of
the pages, demonstrate his intimate knowledge of Chinese life and
customs. Handforth's compositions reflect a clean, direct style
through which he imparts an enormous amount of authentic information on Chinese culture. Not only does he bring prestige to the

picture book by virtue of his artistic training, but he also
provides a text of adequate quality upon which the Caldecott
reputation might begin to build.

It is a Chinese custom that supplies the basis for this story
of Mei Li, a young Chinese girl, who sneaks off to the New Year's
Fair in a northern Chinese city, far from her home in the country. Mei Li gathers her three lucky pennies and her treasures,
three marbles--lapis blue, coral red, and jade green--and sets
out for the City, knowing she must return home before midnight,
at which time the kitchen God must be greeted, and instructions
for the coming year must be listened to with respect and reverence by the entire household.

Mei Li's adventures at the Fair enable Handforth to include a
great deal of his knowledge of Chinese culture, gathered during
years of residence in China. His minimal compositions account
for the lack of backgrounds in many of the illustrations, but
Handforth's intimate association with China allows him to filter
out the unnecessary, leaving the reader with a very condensed
impression of Chinese life. His figures, many actual studies
of live models, as Mei Li was, have a life and vitality that
add humor <u>and</u> dignity to the book. The figures tumble through
the story, which ends neatly with the kitchen God's reinforcement
of the fortune Mei Li had told in the city: the kingdom she
rules is her home, and in this palace all living things are her
subjects.

Handforth enriches this simple story with the elements of this
Eastern culture that intrigue the Western audience, and his illustrations and text have indeed become a symbol in themselves, a
symbolic union.

C5 ARMER, LAURA ADAMS. <u>The Forest Pool</u>. New York: Longmans,
Green, 1938 (OP), 40 pp. 28 illus.: color-8; rust and
white-8; dark green and white-6; teal and white-4; brown
and white-2/illustrated half title, title page, and dedica-
tion/ink and opaque paint/25.6cm x 19.2cm
Fiction   Gr. 1-2

This tale of a young Mexican boy, Diego, and his friend Popa
is portrayed in eight stylized, full-color illustrations. Since
Diego is convinced the iguana holds the answer to the secrets of
the world, he coaxes his father into catching the animal for his
personal zoo. It is on this excursion that Diego's father discovers some pearls hidden in the tree by the pool of the Plumed
Serpent. With the occurrence of these circumstances, the boys
remain convinced that the iguana bears the knowledge of the world
and imparts his knowledge to humans in secret and mysterious ways.

Though interspersed in the margins of this story are drawings
of various aspects of the flora, fauna, and culture of Mexican
life, Armer's illustrations do little to extend the text and

often reduce the book to merely an illustrated text, with little interaction between text and pictures. The stylized technique of the artist is reminiscent of that of Gaugin, though Armer's shapes are more clearly defined. The bright, gaudy colors of the full-page illustrations impart some of the colorful emotions of the South Seas paintings of Gaugin and do give the tale a flair that could have been capitalized on very effectively. The illustrations remain nearly decorative, with little attention given to the details of the large, flat shapes.

The cultural tidbits in the margins do not contribute to the unity of story and text but could serve a more definite purpose were the book approached from an informational standpoint. The realistic style of these one-color drawings is indicative of Armer's command of portraying the objects at hand, but the style is contradictory and incongruous to the freely interpreted style of the full-color illustrations. A conflict then arises between the two styles, a competition develops, rather than a balance and harmony.

C6   LEAF, MUNRO. <u>Wee Gillis</u>. Illustrated by Robert Lawson.
New York: Viking, 1938, [76 pp.] 33 illus.: black and white-33/illustrated front matter and title page/lithograph/ 25.4cm x 17.5cm
Fiction   Gr. K-2

Alastair Roderic Craigellachie Dalhousie Gowan Donnybristle MacMac, Wee Gillis for short, is the young Scottish boy in this 1939 Honor Book who has to make a decision between living with his mother's Lowland relatives or his father's Highland relatives. Robert Lawson's compositions of black and white emphasize the decision Wee Gillis has to make, as the artist utilizes the highs and lows of the Scottish terrain to illustrate the conflict in the text.

Wee Gillis resolves the situation diplomatically--he chooses to reside "half way up the side of a medium-sized hill," utilizing the attributes he acquired from each terrain. His strong lungs, a result of holding his breath in the Highlands, while stalking stags, and also of shouting for the long-haired cows of the Lowlands, give him the ability to play the "BIGGEST BAGPIPES IN ALL SCOTLAND," as he lives a life content, peaceful in his decision.

Lawson, in a style much like James Daugherty, demonstrates his skill as an artist in his renderings of Scottish geography and native dress. His illustrations offer a humorous and gentle interpretation of a boy faced with a dilemma. But the format of the book, a page of text faced with an illustration, does little to enhance or enliven the story; if the audience takes the time to look beyond the superficial monotony of the illustrations, they will quickly realize the skill of the artist, even though Lawson chooses to use only black and white. If anything is

amiss, it is the text that comes across as the weakness of this
Honor Book, and it seems the merits of the illustrator alone have
been the influencing criteria in the book's inclusion as an Honor
Book in this year.

C7   GRIMM, JACOB and GRIMM, WILHELM. Snow White and the Seven
     Dwarfs. Freely translated and illustrated by Wanda Gág.
     New York: Coward-McCann, 1938, 43 pp.   32 illus.:   black
     and white-32/lithograph/19.7cm x 15cm
     Folk Tale   Gr. Ps-1
Wanda Gág's translation and illustration of this ever-popular
fairy tale are embellished with her inimitable style of prose and
art. Black and white illustrations give body to the story, in
which, true to the Grimm Brothers' tale, Gág extends the drama
by allowing the wicked queen to return three times to the home
of the seven little men--first to tempt Snow White with bodice
laces that take her breath away; second to entrance Snow White
with a poisonous comb that renders her unconscious; and finally
to share a poison-filled apple with the innocent girl.
     Even a touch of the Three Bears' "who's been" pattern rein-
forces the repetitive quality of Gág's style; the structure of
this tale has built-in cues upon which Gág can capitalize. Recurring sevens in the text and in its visual interpretations give her
the perfect opportunity to display her repetitive, curving, and
secure style. At times the repetition in the visuals is directly
reminiscent of the style of Millions of Cats, a 1929 Newbery
Honor Book (N20), which emphasizes a repeated pattern within a
given space. The pages, though, are never stagnant; movement
and energy are continually present, from the twisting, spiraling
bark on the trees of the forest to the flowing, swirling lines
that soften the shape of the wicked queen as she prepares the
poison fruit.
     Gág's interpretation of this often-told tale reflects her
ability to handle some of the more violent aspects, often ob-
jected to by critics of fairy tales, with charm. The queen's
face is frequently hidden by a hat or a mask, or at times only
the queen's back is seen, obscuring her wickedness. The text,
which gives Snow White three chances before the inevitable happens, and the illustrations, which focus on the positive consequences of Snow White's naiveté, provide a balance between good
and evil appropriate for the book's audience.
     Gág's illustrations help break the chain of Disneyesque
stereotypes that imprisons the realm of much fairy-tale illustration, and her style naturally emphasizes the characteristics of
fairy lore that empower such tales to linger in memories long
after other childhood experiences are forgotten.

C8   NEWBERRY, CLARE TURLAY. Barkis. New York: Harper & Brothers,
     1938, 31 pp. 13 illus.:   brown, black, and white-9; brown

and white-4/illustrated half title, front matter, title
page, and dedication/pastel and charcoal/18.7cm x 22.4cm
Fiction   Gr. Ps-2

In the story of <u>Barkis</u>, Clare Newberry's 1939 Honor Book, a
lesson is to be learned, not only in the story, but in the handling of the illustrations as well. When James receives a cocker
spaniel pup for his ninth birthday, he and his sister, Nell Jean,
embark upon a feud rooted in jealousy and resentment. Nell Jean's
kitten, Edward, and James's pup, Barkis, lead the brother and
sister toward the moral of the story--selfishness and jealousy
is dangerous to everyone--humans and beloved pets alike. When
Barkis's life is endangered because Nell Jean vengefully lets the
pup traipse outside into the cold alone, both Nell Jean and James
realize that the compromise of sharing is less dangerous to them
all.

Although the story line of <u>Barkis</u> leads the reader to the obviously moralistic ending, the illustrations supply little extension of the text and in some ways hinder the effectiveness of the
honesty of feelings in this example of sibling rivalry. The soft
illustrations of the pup and cat, upon blank, white backgrounds,
are reminiscent of unfinished sketches from an artist's pad. The
compositions, therefore, are minimal in background, as are those
in <u>Mei Li</u> (C4), but Newberry's pages lack the extension and integration of text and pictures.

To lovers of puppies and kittens, the illustrations will no
doubt evoke emotional responses, for the pictures are delicate
and touching, sometimes with those surprising details of familiar
characteristics that endear a small, warm pup or kitten to its
owner. But these illustrations do little to strengthen or reinforce a text that could have had more impact on its audience and,
consequently, could have been remembered more as a picture book
than for the shallowness of the drawings and text. For the weaknesses in the drawings create an emphasis on the text, which then
appears more didactic than perhaps originally intended were the
artist to consider the book's function as a whole, as a work of
art.

C9   DAUGHERTY, JAMES. <u>Andy and the Lion: A Tale of Kindness
     Remembered or The Power of Gratitude</u>. New York: Viking,
     1938, [80 pp.] 42 illus.: black, white, and ochre-42/
     illustrated endpapers, front matter, title page, dedication,
     and half title/brush and ink/26.9cm x 19.6cm
     Fantasy   Gr. Ps-2

Ochre and black illustrations bring this 1939 Honor Book <u>Andy
and the Lion</u>, by James Daugherty, to life. Developed in three
parts, the tale of Andy's imaginary adventures begins as he takes
a book on lions home from the library. Part One finds Andy intrigued with tales of lions, an intrigue which continues into the

second section as the boy, on his way to school, discovers a
lion suffering from a thorn in his paw. It is, coincidently,
this very lion that escapes from a circus act in Part Three,
and Andy, recognizing his feline friend, protects the animal
from the angry crowd.

Daugherty's illustrations, of bold, black lines and shapes,
highlighted and given form by the ochre and white of the pages,
reflect a style similar to those of Lynd Ward and Robert Lawson.
The sweeping movement of Daugherty's lines creates a feeling of
constant motion, as do the figures, which are invariably engaged
in some exaggerated motion. Although some monotony develops from
the illustrations falling on the right-hand side of the pages,
the interruption of full-page spreads between the three sections
helps lessen the monotony. The action developed through the
compositions of the pages helps detract from the regularity with
which the text is always faced with an illustration.

The compositions, of exaggerated movement, deliberately executed, are the most striking characteristic of Daugherty's style.
The placement of a book swinging on a book strap in midair or the
curve of the lion's tail neatly holds the illustration within a
tight composition, directing the eye exactly where the artist
intends. Were Daugherty less skilled in his execution, this
Honor Book would hold little appeal, but his ability to inject
humor and expression into these tightly constructed compositions
produces a book which could have been much less effective.

1940

C10   d'AULAIRE, INGRI and d'AULAIRE, EDGAR. Abraham Lincoln.
        Garden City, N.Y.: Doubleday, Doran, 1939, [56 pp.]
        52 illus.: color-27; black and white-25/illustrated title
        page and front matter/lithographic pencil/29.9cm x 20.7cm
        Biography   Gr. 1-3
    In the year that Daniel Boone (N87) won the Newbery Medal,
Ingri and Edgar d'Aulaire received the Caldecott Medal for
Abraham Lincoln. Five-color stone lithographs alternate with
black and white illustrations of lithographic pencil on stone,
and all reflect the wholesome qualities for which Lincoln was
famous. The popular anecdotes of Lincoln's life--his footprints
on the cabin ceiling, his skill as a railsplitter, his reputation
as a wrestler, his honesty in returning money to an overcharged
customer--and the events of his presidency--the Civil War, the
Gettysburg Address, the Emancipation Proclamation of 1863--paint
the picture of this simple and honest President of the United
States.

    The crayonlike illustrations reveal much history regarding
the time period and geographical settings surrounding Lincoln's

life, and every page is filled with details revealing the life
and culture of this pioneer President. The lack of realism in
the style of the illustrations helps reinforce the brighter,
lighter side of Lincoln's life, but it is the style that also
prevents the audience from experiencing a true compassion for
the primitive and adverse conditions which gave rise to such an
important figure in the history of the United States. That
Abraham Lincoln rose above these obstacles was what truly made
him great; he was great in spite of them.

Subsequent reprints of this 1940 Medal Book include changes
in the illustrations; compositions of pages, inclusion of details,
features of faces, quality of color, and even the frontispiece
vary in later editions. These changes, however, are subtle and
do little to change the overall appearance or effect of the illustrations and the text. Slight discrepancies in the illustrations,
open cabin doors and windows in February, and stereotypes of
blacks and Indians, indicate that the d'Aulaires have taken some
liberties with some details of their interpretation, and as an
early biography, the book is subject to presenting so positive
a picture that it ends without explaining the death of Lincoln,
which, by its omission, evades some of the significance of
Lincoln's life.

C11   HADER, BERTA and HADER, ELMER. Cock-a-doodle-Doo: The Story
      of a Little Red Rooster. New York: Macmillan, 1939,
      [56 pp.] 50 illus.: color-25; black and white-25/
      illustrated title page and front matter/watercolor and
      pencil/25.2cm x 20.1cm
      Fiction   Gr. Ps-2

Little Red, a rooster hatched by a duck, runs away to a farm
on the hill to discover his true identity in Berta and Elmer
Hader's Cock-a-doodle-Doo. Alternating color and black and white
illustrations give life to the dangers Little Red encounters on
his journey to his real "home." The natural flora and fauna of
the woods through which Red travels offers the Haders the chance
to portray some of the baby chick's natural enemies--crow, owl,
skunk, raccoon, fox, and hawk. Throughout the light, airy watercolor illustrations, anatomical studies of natural history abound,
lending a reality to the "ugly duckling" motif of the story. With
the rhyme at the conclusion recounting Little Red's maturation
into a rooster, the saga of the little chick's life is complete.

The Haders, like many illustrators of children's books, choose
to portray their animal characters with a realism that no doubt
is interesting to a young audience. But the story line, with its
anticipated outcome, its familiar motif, has a deadening effect
upon the illustrations, strangling some of the life out of them.
The illustration that shows Little Red hiding from the skunk and
raccoon, during the night he spends in the woods, is a very

interesting combination of black and white on the left and color
on the right side of the spread. What the illustration fails
to do, however, is expand or embellish the text, and, consequently,
the picture loses its impact as the most unusual illustration of
the book.

To compare this work with <u>Madeline</u> (C12), of the same year,
is to recognize the difference in the vitality and strength that
comes from an original text. In <u>Madeline</u> the illustrations contribute to the text, as the text contributes to the illustrations,
in a cooperative effort. The use of realism in <u>Cock-a-doodle-Doo</u>
cannot substitute for originality, and a book that uses one to
offset the other often results in a less effective work.

C12   BEMELMANS, LUDWIG. <u>Madeline</u>. New York: Simon & Schuster,
      1939, [48 pp.] 44 illus.: yellow, black, and white-36;
      color-8/illustrated front matter and title page/watercolor
      and pen-and-ink/29.8cm x 22cm
      Fiction   Gr. K-2
Ludwig Bemelmans's 1940 Honor Book, <u>Madeline</u>, is one of the
first early Award Books to introduce a digression from the se-
date, low-keyed books that dominate the early years of the
Caldecott Medal. This rhyming text, about a young girl in a
Parisian boarding school who has an emergency appendectomy,
moves the story along with action, both in word and picture.
The repetition in the illustrations and the long and narrow
spatial feelings resulting from this repetition moves the eyes
up and down with the rhythmic verse of the text.

Too quickly comes the humorous ending of this book, when the
remainder of the girls covet the chance to "suffer" as Madeline
did among the toys and candy and flowers of her hospital room.
But as quickly as Miss Clavel "turned out the light--/and closed
the door," the story is over and nearly begs to be reread and
perused.

The illustrations, full of motion and life, expertly expand
the text and the artist's conception of such abstractions as
good, bad, and sad. Eight full-color illustrations are interspersed among pages of yellow, black, and white watercolor, pen,
and ink, adding variety and interest to the book's format. The
full-color pages contain much more detail than the others, but
the expressionism, present in all the illustrations, is an integral part of the book. As "Miss Clavel ran fast/and faster,"
the diagonal tilt of her body and of the hallway offers an abstract visualization of the motion present in the situation. It
is just this ability to express the essence of an idea in the
simplicity of a few lines, shapes, and words, that makes Bemelman's
work, text and illustrations, an integrated, cooperative unit that
does not lose its flavor, reading after reading.

C13   FORD, LAUREN. The Ageless Story. New York: Dodd, Mead,
       1939 (OP), [40 pp.] 24 illus.: color-24/illustrated
       front matter, title page, dedication, contents pages,
       and end matter/opaque paint/25.4cm x 26cm
       Bible   Gr. K-3

Lauren Ford's New England interpretation of the story of the
Christ Child, written for her goddaughter, is graced with Grego-
rian music of the Rhythmic Signs of Solesmes; the words of the
Holy Gospel according to St. Luke; and illustrations in the style
of the illuminated manuscripts of the ancients. Ford's letter to
her goddaughter helps bring her book into focus and explains the
reasons she had for presenting her subject as she does. The terrain, architecture, interiors, and clothing are strictly New England and are the means through which the artist gives the story
relevance and familiarity.

In twelve full-page spreads, Ford depicts significant events
leading up to the birth of Christ, concluding with the early
years of his life when he worked as a carpenter with Joseph.

The pages are edged with a New England version of the borders
of ancient manuscripts—swatches of calico, plaid, and bandana
prints outline the perimeter of each page. The figures of children, snuggled into the lower corners of the borders, remain the
same for each of the twelve presentations, so as not to detract
from the more important components—aural, verbal, and visual.
Accompanying the antiphons on the left leaf are children singing,
and, appropriately, on the right leaf, the figures enjoy the
visual and written impact of the book.

The major illustrations, all framed within gold, help carry
out an impression consistent with the book's historical emphasis.
Although the settings of the illustrations are incongruous with
the subject, Ford has adapted her style to that of the early
Italian Renaissance, especially in "Saint Anne in the Garden"
and "The Annunciation," and through her style has created a personal interpretation of the humanism that pervaded the early
Renaissance.

Ford tackles a very complex subject in this 1940 Honor Book,
and her solution is a complex one as well. Her work was met
with mixed reactions, especially to the regional settings, and
the book remains one that requires careful explanation to be
effective. This is a book that would undoubtedly be less offensive today, but to those who have training in the field of art
history, her portrayals in the style of some great masters are
more difficult to assimilate than are her New England settings.

1941

C14   LAWSON, ROBERT. <u>They Were Strong and Good</u>. New York:
          Viking, 1940, [66 pp.]   36 illus.:   black and white-36/
          illustrated title page/ink and brush/24.5cm x 20.4cm
          Biography   Gr. 1-2
<u>They Were Strong and Good</u>, the 1941 Medal Book, written and
illustrated by Robert Lawson, is an attempt to immortalize the
ancestry that has made the ideal of America so strong. Lawson
uses his own relatives as universal symbols of those who were
strong and good--those who built America with their own hands.
Lawson's artistic style is well suited to the theme of this book,
as his technique reflects the sturdy wholesomeness of his
characters.
     The story, unfortunately, remains a glorified, almost propa-
gandized, recounting of Lawson's ancestry. The simplistic,
glossy interpretation is sure to show through, even to a child,
and is probably the major weakness of the book. The illustrations extend the text in several ways--humorously, in the pictures of Lawson's maternal grandmother's dislike for the sea and
in the destruction of the Panama hat by the parrot; compassion-
ately, in the scenes of the Civil War; and romantically, in the
pictures that demonstrate the love the characters had for one
another. But the shallowness of the text, a far cry from his
later Newbery winner, <u>Rabbit Hill</u> (N110), cannot fully be compensated for by Lawson's expertise as an artist.

C15   NEWBERRY, CLARE TURLAY. <u>April's Kittens</u>. New York: Harper &
          Brothers, 1940, 32 pp.   15 illus.:   black, white, and pink-
          7; black and white-8/illustrated front matter, title page,
          dedication, and end matter/charcoal and pastel/26.5cm x
          22.5cm
          Fiction   Gr. Ps-1
     April and her parents live in a small New York apartment, "a
'one cat' apartment," and when Sheba, the family pet, gives
birth to three kittens, young April has to face the dilemma of
choosing which of the four she wants to keep.
     Four-year-old Geoffrey helps ease the situation when he de-
cides to adopt Butch, one of the tiger-striped kittens. When
Miss Elwell, a friend of the family, can no longer resist the
"little darlings," she gathers up Charcoal to take home with
her--a perfect match for her other two black cats. But April
is still left with an enormous decision--to keep Sheba, the
mother, or Brenda, the remaining kitten.
     Although April has grown to favor Brenda, the young child
makes the decision to keep Sheba, after overhearing her parents'
fears regarding giving away a grown cat. The decision quickly
becomes of little consequence when April's father decides the

family should move to a larger apartment--with enough room for April to sleep in a regular bed instead of a crib. But, of course, the apartment would be a "two-cat apartment" as well.

Like other of Newberry's Honor Books, the theme in this book plays on the emotional relationships between children and their pets and carries it even further in suggesting the trauma in having to part with one so beloved. No one will argue with Newberry's expertise in creating loveable studies of animals, especially cats and kittens, and their natural habits, but Newberry capitalizes on this excessively, and in doing so has created picture books that depend heavily on this emotional bond between pet and owner, at the expense of presenting a book of integrated word and picture.

It is not unusual for the text and illustrations to have little correlation, as in the spread of Charcoal playing with Miss Elwell's other cats. There is no reference in the text to the reaction of the cats to Charcoal nor to anything other than the fact that Miss Elwell took the kitten home. The presentation of the illustration and caption--"At first the big cats were afraid of little Charcoal!"--seems extraneous and confusing to the story line.

The book, and others by Newberry, remains popular with animal-loving children, and the black and white, and sometimes pink pastel illustrations will always play on the emotions. The picture of Butch, included for framing, has no doubt become a favorite of many young readers, but originality and creativity have worn a little thin.

1942

C16   McCLOSKEY, ROBERT. Make Way for Ducklings. New York:
          Viking, 1941, [72 pp.] 62 illus.: brown and white-62/
          illustrated endpapers and title page/lithographic crayon
          on stone/30.4cm x 22.8cm
          Fantasy   Gr. Ps-1

Robert McCloskey, author and illustrator of this early Caldecott Medal winner, relies on the intimate study of nature to draw his readers into the sensitive, secure world of Make Way for Ducklings. The relocation of Mr. and Mrs. Mallard to the city of Boston provides the background for this gentle story of their attempts to raise a family in this eastern metropolis.

Unfamiliar with the sights and dangers of the city's cars, buses, and bicycles, the Mallards leave the busy Public Garden to nest on an island in the Charles River. McCloskey's accurate geographical information, both in text and illustrations, lends credence to this tale, as do his anatomically accurate drawings

of ducks and ducklings in flight and on foot. But what these
illustrations, the gentle, soft drawings of the birds against
the backdrop of a thriving, harsher city, do is pull the reader
into the sensitivity of the story. The champion of humankind,
or birdkind, Michael, the policeman, protects these innocent
ducks and ducklings from the dispassionate, bustling city.

The graceful pictures, all in brown and white, often studies
of family interaction, childrearing, and natural history, encompass and reinforce the simple, yet touching, saga of the survival
of the Mallard family. McCloskey does not embellish his book
with elaborate colors (even the text is brown) or complex technique; his execution is a combination of clean lines and gentle
shading that helps tie together two incongruous entities: the
city and the Mallard family. The compromise is provided; once
their clan is of sufficient age to protect themselves, the
Mallards return to the Public Garden via the busy streets of
Boston. Only with the help of the symbolic heart of the city,
Michael, do the Mallards safely survive.

McCloskey's work remains a favorite with children as he offers
them the chance to identify with the triumph of small over big;
young over old; innocence and naiveté over experience and maturity.

C17   PETERSHAM, MAUD and PETERSHAM, MISKA. An American ABC. New
      York: Macmillan, 1941 (OP), [56 pp.] 44 illus.: blue,
      black, and white-16; color-13; red, black, and white-8;
      blue, red, black, and white-7/illustrated title page and
      front and end matter/3-color lithographs/25.4cm x 20.2cm
      Alphabet Book   Gr. Ps-1

Maud and Miska Petersham's An American ABC utilizes the alphabet to retell the history of the United States of America, from
"A is for America/The land I love." Each letter deals with an
individual or location of historical importance, the principles
upon which America was founded, or the symbols of American
freedom.

It is this spirit of patriotism, which the illustrations and
text espouse, that no doubt won it a 1942 Honor Book position.
The predominantly red and blue illustrations and the embellish-
ment of the alphabet reinforce the sense of pride the audience
should feel in the United States. Unfortunately, in retrospect,
the book's illustrations portray many stereotypical elements that
greatly affect the durability of the book over the years. American Indians, blacks, and South Americans are illustrated in ways
that today seem offensive. The presentation of "X is for Xmas"
might also be deemed a less than appropriate designation for the
letter and seems out of place, especially in a book dealing with
a country founded on diverse religious beliefs.

The strength and courage it took to mold the United States
into the nation it is shines through in the illustrations of

early heroes and explorers who risked their lives for freedom.
The detailed figures, in their historical clothes and settings,
reflect a compassion for the suffering the characters had to
endure. The Petershams' style helps make these characters more
real to the audience and brings both closer together.

C18   CLARK, ANN NOLAN. In My Mother's House. Illustrated by
         Velino Herrera. New York: Viking, 1941 (OP), 56 pp.
         51 illus.: black and white-41; color-10/illustrated end-
         papers and title page/lithographs in black and white and
         color/25.9cm x 21.3cm
         Information: geography   Gr. 1-3
    Pueblo Indian culture and world-view are portrayed in Ann
Nolan Clark's 1942 Honor Book through the symbolic and realistic
illustrations of Velino Herrera. The simple, direct text, containing repetition in word and beat, reinforces the style of
traditional Native American literature and seems adaptable to
singing or chanting, reflecting its evolution from the oral tradition. The more authentically and realistically presented style
of this early work does capture the essence and style of the
Pueblo world-view more closely than later works dealing with the
same concepts--it is not an attempt to "Americanize" the style,
but it does reflect a common attempt to "civilize" the Native
American in some portions of the text and illustrations.
    The illustrations, by this self-taught artist, which are
really the heart of this book, are the symbolic, traditional
black and white renderings that provide the most authentic segments. Scattered among other black and white and color illustrations, these abstract designs provide more information about the
Pueblo beliefs and world-view than all the illustrations combined.
The representations of lakes and of the growth of three stalks of
corn give more meaning to the text than do the pictures of the
Pueblo Fathers digging irrigation ditches or working the fields
with horse-drawn plows.
    Each segment the text deals with, be it Home, Council, Pasture,
pueblo, Pipeline, people, fire, wild plants, Birds, Mountains or
others, contributes to the whole picture of the young boy's life
as a Pueblo Indian. "I string them together/Like beads./They
make a chain,/A strong chain,/To hold me close/To home,/Where
I live/In my Mother's house."

C19   HOLLING, HOLLING CLANCY. Paddle-to-the-Sea. Boston:
         Houghton Mifflin, 1941 (OP), [64 pp.] 54 illus.: black
         and white-27; color-27/illustrated title page, dedication,
         contents page, and end matter/pencil and watercolor/27.8cm
         x 22cm
         Information: geography   Gr. 1-3
    The journey of a small, hand-carved Indian (Paddle-to-the-Sea)
and canoe, from Lake Nipigon, through the Great Lakes to the sea,

sets the stage for the presentation of an extraordinary amount
of technical and geographic information concerning the Great
Lakes region. From the iron-ore mines of Duluth through the
Soo Locks, on to Lake Erie via Detroit, and over Niagara Falls,
the journey of Paddle-to-the-Sea offers a setting conducive to
the informative text and illustrations that Holling creates.

The author takes advantage of the situations that arise to
include visual and written definitions in the margins, and above
and below the text of his book. Black and white maps of the
lakes, diagrams of a sawmill, canal locks, a breeches buoy, a
lake freighter, and tracings of Paddle-to-the-Sea's journey all
border the text of the story, and facing these pages are full-
color illustrations depicting scenes from Paddle's journey.

Because of the amount of detail and text included in this
1942 Honor Book, Holling's book drifts from the realms of the
picture book into the category of illustrated books of information. Although the creative invention of Paddle-to-the-Sea gives
the work the appearance of a storybook, the informational and
technical aspects remain of major importance, even though the
humanitarian efforts of the people who help the journey proceed
are touching. The complexity of the technical aspects and the
geographical information makes the book more useful to children
who are past the picture-book stage. The full-color illustrations, depicting segments of twenty-seven "chapters," though
authentically handled, seem an attempt to transform the work
into a picture book merely by their inclusion. What the book
becomes is an informative, detailed lesson in geography or
social studies, a book whose usefulness is apparent, but not
particularly on the picture book level.

C20   GÁG, WANDA. Nothing at All. New York: Coward-McCann, 1941,
      [32 pp.] 25 illus.: green, orange, black, and white-25/
      illustrated endpapers, title page, and dedication/litho-
      graphs/16.6cm x 24.2cm
      Fantasy   Gr. Ps-1
      Three orphan puppies, living on an old forgotten farm, are
the characters in Wanda Gág's tale of Nothing at All. Pointy
with the pointed ears, Curly with the curly ears, and Nothing-
at-all, the formless, invisible dog, are perfectly content until
a young boy and girl take the two visible puppies home.

Nothing-at-all follows the advice of a Jackdaw by rising nine
mornings at sunrise, to twirl around chanting "I'm busy/Getting
dizzy/I'm busy/Getting dizzy." Each day new form and shape is
given to the puppy, until on the ninth day he becomes a completely
visible dog, with spots, eyes, a nose, a mouth, ears, paws, a
tongue, and a black tip on his tail. When the canine, now named
Something-after-all, spies the young boy and girl returning for
the puppies' kennels, he jumps into his rounded kennel and travels home to a reunion with his siblings.

The orange and green illustrations of the characters, reminiscent of Gág's Newbery Award Book <u>Millions of Cats</u> (N20) when they pick up on the cues for repetition in the tale, do not blend together as cohesively with the text as the Newbery winner does or as well as her earlier Honor Book, <u>Snow White and the Seven Dwarfs</u> (C7). Gág does, however, frame many of her pictures in horizontal compositions which repeat the format of the pages and of the book. The addition of color, not present in <u>Millions of Cats</u> or <u>Snow White</u>, allows for a more realistic presentation of the figures in the story and does not require an extensive use of line, as is her usual style. The crayon effect of the colors in the illustrations allows Gág to model and shade her shapes more softly than in her predominantly line illustrations.

Though not an example of one of Gág's better texts or works of illustration, this book demonstrates her ability to incorporate different techniques into her style to reinforce the text with which she is working.

<u>1943</u>

C21   BURTON, VIRGINIA LEE. <u>The Little House</u>. Boston: Houghton
       Mifflin, 1942, 40 pp.   39 illus.:   color-39/illustrated
       endpapers, title page, and dedication/watercolor/22.7cm x
       24.6cm
       Fantasy   Gr. Ps-1

Colorful, circular compositions, entwining and doubling back upon themselves, dominate the illustrations of <u>The Little House</u> in its country setting, until progress overtakes the country and turns it into a hustling, bustling city. The closer the city creeps toward the Little House, the more pronounced the vertical emphasis becomes; the soft, curving lines turn to a hard, vertical and horizontal environment for the Little House.

Virginia Burton not only utilizes her lines to convey the alienation the Little House begins to feel in this 1943 Medal Book, but she also transforms the light, clean blues, yellows, greens, and oranges of the country into darker grays and browns, reflecting the Little House's gloom as the city overtakes her. Spring, summer, winter, and fall all lose their color in this city--there seems to be no distinction between the seasons in the Little House's new environment of subways, tenements, and masses of people.

But, finally, out of the hustle and bustle, the great-great-granddaughter of the building's original owner rescues the Little House and returns it to the country, where it can enjoy the quiet and serenity once again. The illustrations, too, return to the soft, curving compositions, full of the clear colors of the seasons.

1943

It is clearly evident that Burton's illustrations reinforce
and extend the text, and her skill in illustration enables her
to mold the elements--color, line, composition--into a work that
truly functions as a picture storybook. Burton's technique becomes
evident as the illustrations change with the mood and visually
reflect the impact of the city. Both the text and illustrations
grow dependent upon each other so that to separate them would be
to sever equally important facets of the book. It is work such as
this that help define the concept of a picture storybook and build
the reputation of the Caldecott Medal, rather than those books in
which the text or illustrations dominate or overpower the other.

C22   BUFF, MARY and BUFF, CONRAD. <u>Dash & Dart</u>. New York: Viking,
       1942 (OP), 75 pp. 54 illus.: brown and white-46; color-8/
       illustrated title page/brown and colored pencil/24.8cm x
       16.2cm
       Fiction   Gr. Ps-1
     Four full-page color spreads appear throughout the pages of
sepia and white illustrations of this 1943 Honor Book. The terrain in which Dash and Dart, the male and female fawns of this
story, grow up is depicted in full-color impressions of lush
vegetation, steep mountains, and clear lakes. The sepia studies
of the natural history of the flora and fauna of this unnamed
territory carry the story from the birth of the fawns to their
development into mature buck and doe.
     As the fawns grow they learn of their natural enemies--
weather, coyote, bear--the necessity of developing skill in
finding food, and their need to migrate to the valleys in the
winter. The text and illustrations impart a great deal of information concerning the maturation process of the young buck, Dash,
as his wish to grow antlers is answered when he recognizes himself in a reflection in a lake. The two knobs on his head eventually grow into antlers, "a great tree upon his head," and his
life as a fawn has ended.
     What is disappointing in the text, however, is the lack of
comparison or development of Dart, the doe. The inclusion of
Dart in the title would seem to indicate her importance in the
text, but this does not bear out in the reading; she seems superficial to the story, and this, in turn, has a weakening effect
upon the text. To consider this work a picture book, as with
many of the early Medal and Honor Books, would be misleading,
for it leans toward being an illustrated book of information,
enlightening its audience as to the process of animal maturation.
     The illustrations are reduced to mere studies of the animals
and vegetation of the terrain, with little extension or integration with the text; the drawings remain stagnant, often with no
backgrounds, and look almost incomplete in their compositions.
They add no life of their own to the text, which is set up in

verse format. All these conflicting segments create a confusion
in the total synthesis of the components of the book and prevent
the work from becoming as effective as it could be in relaying
the information it has to offer.

C23   NEWBERRY, CLARE TURLAY. Marshmallow. New York: Harper &
       Brothers, 1942 [32 pp.] 25 illus.: black, white, and pink-
       25/illustrated half title, title page, and dedication/char-
       coal and pastel/25.1cm x 29.5cm
       Fiction   Gr. Ps-1
    Clare Newberry's 1943 Honor Book, Marshmallow, is a work that
has emotional appeal to young children, much like Barkis (C8)
and April's Kittens (C15), her earlier Caldecott Honor Books.
This appeal, however, which draws upon the relationship of pets
and their owners, is not effectively capitalized on in text or
illustrations. The drawings of the animals of this story, of
Oliver, a cat, and Marshmallow, a bunny, are black and white
studies, with a tinge of soft pink, appear to come from pages
of a sketchbook, and are undoubtedly taken from live models, as
is Newberry's practice. But these simple studies of the characters do little to enhance or strengthen the story line.
    Oliver, living in Manhattan with his owner, Miss Tilly, is
shaken from his comfortable existence by the introduction of a
baby bunny. Never having seen another animal in his sheltered
existence creates some natural problems for the cat, so Oliver
and Marshmallow are given separate rooms, until Miss Tilly unexpectedly leaves them alone longer than usual. After Oliver manages to manipulate the door open to Marshmallow's room, the
animals become inseparable companions rather than the instinctual
enemies Miss Tilly expected.
    There is more variety to the format of this book than in
Newberry's earlier Honor Books. Working the type around some
illustrations, including some captions for the drawings, incorporating poems into the text, and including visual information on
right and left sides of the page introduce some interest to the
book that is missing in the others.
    The work suffers because of the weakness of the text, which
is not compensated for in the visual portions of the book. As
with Barkis, the text and illustrations do not reinforce and
complement each other to create a book that functions as an
entire work of art. But what this work does, and many others
like it do, is raise the question of the standards and qualifications used in determining the Caldecott winners. There are
those books of obvious artistic and literary creativity that for
some reason do not appeal to children, while those of less quality tap something in the spring of childhood and remain favorites
year after year.

1944

C24   THURBER, JAMES. Many Moons. Illustrated by Louis Slobodkin.
      New York: Harcourt Brace, 1943, [48 pp.] 37 illus.:
      blue, red, black, and white-17; 3-color-9; red, black, and
      white-4; blue and yellow-3; red, yellow, black, and
      white-2; blue, black, and white-2/illustrated endpapers
      and title page/3-color watercolor with pen and ink/24.7cm
      x 21.2cm
      Fantasy: folklike tale   Gr. K-2
      The only cure for Princess Lenore's overindulgence in rasp-
berry tarts is a simple prescription--she wants the moon. Louis
Slobodkin's illustrations, predominantly in pinks and blues, depict the futile efforts of the Lord High Chamberlain, the Royal
Wizard, and the Royal Mathematician to determine a way to appease
the King and fulfill his daughter's wish. Only the Court Jester
has common sense enough to ask the Princess how she perceives the
moon--it is, very simply, made of gold and the size of her
thumbnail. But as soon as the Princess is presented with the
golden moon on a chain, the King begins to worry about what
Lenore's reaction will be when she sees the moon the next
evening.
      Slobodkin's illustrations help preserve the humor and appeal
of this whimsical text by allowing his compositions to remain
loose and full of expression with a minimum of concentrated
detail. The sharp, suggestive black lines upon the washes of
blues, pinks, and grays assist the artist in maintaining the air
of fantasy. The quickness with which the lines appear to have
been laid down on paper gives considerable movement, life, and
shape to the areas of wash and leads the eye around and around
the pages.
      In this year of several Honor Books, Many Moons presents it-
self as the nearest example of a picture storybook in which text
and illustrations work together to complement and reinforce each
other. The Honor Books for 1944 all demonstrate less originality of text or an overemphasis on illustration, often detracting
from the books. The combination of Thurber's humorous style and
Slobodkin's expressiveness of line creates a work that meshes
more effectively than any of the Honor Books of this year and
seems the logical choice for the Medal. The humor of the text
is carried through to the end, right down to Lenore's childlike
explanation for the return of the moon--"When I lose a tooth, a
new one grows in its place, doesn't it?"

C25   JONES, JESSE ORTON. Small Rain: Verses from the Bible.
      Illustrated by Elizabeth Orton Jones. New York: Viking,
      1943, [40 pp.] 31 illus.: black and white-19; black,
      white, and ochre-12/illustrated half title and title page/
      lithograph/22.2cm x 25.2cm

Bible   Gr. Ps-2
Bible verses selected by Jessie Orton Jones and illustrated
by Elizabeth Jones in the 1944 Honor Book, Small Rain, offer an
approach quite different from the first Caldecott Medal Book,
Animals of the Bible (C1). The selections in Small Rain serve
as an effective presentation of these familiar verses particularly relevant to children. Jones's interpretation of these
verses on the child's level makes them more applicable to the
child's world than some of the verses Lathrop illustrates. The
Golden Rule (Matthew 7:12), for instance, comes to life in the
black and white illustrations as five young boys share the contents of a bag full of goodies.
This work appears to be a practice run for Jones, who, in the
following year, received the Caldecott Medal for her illustration
of a prayer for children. The soft golden and black and white
illustrations of Small Rain give meaning to words that are heard
but often not understood by small children. The meaning of "Make
a joyful noise unto the Lord" (Psalm 100), is clear, as the gathering of cherubic faces sings and plays their instruments, presumably in praise of the Lord. Their smiles indicate their joy
in performing as they are and give new meaning to the words.
Jones's interpretation of these verses is what makes it worthy
of recognition, and her ability to visualize and clarify some of
the wonder and mystery of the Bible for children has won her
this award.

C26   KINGMAN, LEE. Pierre Pidgeon. Illustrated by Arnold Edwin
        Bare. Boston: Houghton Mifflin, 1943 (OP), [46 pp.]
        43 illus.: gray, salmon, olive, black, and white-36; 2-
        colors, black, and white-2; 1 color, black and white-2;
        salmon, olive, and gray-2; olive, gray, and white-1/
        illustrated endpapers, front matter, title page, and end
        matter/lithographs/27.9cm x 23cm
        Fiction   Gr. 1-2
At the age of seven, Pierre Pidgeon only wanted an intriguing
boat-in-a-bottle for his eighth birthday, but one dollar was an
enormous amount for the son of a Canadian fisherman even to hope
for. But after Pierre rescues a woman from the frightening stare
of Henri, the family ox, the boy is rewarded with the exact sum
needed to purchase his delicate dream present. Thus is the setting for Lee Kingman's 1944 Honor Book, illustrated by Arnold
Bare.
As the story proceeds, the salmon, gray, and olive illustrations do little to add any life or zip to the story. In fact,
the compositions and colors of the illustrations are sometimes
so busy and distracting that they encourage a closing of the
book rather than continuing. The flat shapes of the figures
and backgrounds are juxtaposed with small, haphazard patterns

of grass and trees and curving lines that leave the eye chaotically hopping around the page from one corner to the next. The colors provide little other than an unusual and unappealing element that pulls the eye here and there in a tug of war. The cohesiveness that would hold the text and illustrations together cannot develop in an environment in which the illustrations create so much havoc themselves.

It is unfortunate that the style is not more consistent, as the ingenuity of Pierre's discovery of how to get his boat back into a new bottle, after his dog has caused it to shatter, becomes rather boring by the time the reader reaches this portion of the book. Were the large, broad areas of color and shape not competing against the smaller, distracting dots of color, the pictures and story could have held together more effectively. As it stands, the illustrations compete within themselves, and therefore the book is difficult to look at or to read.

C27 HADER, BERTA and HADER, ELMER. The Mighty Hunter. New York: Macmillan, 1943 (OP), [52 pp.] 43 illus.: black and white-22; color-21/illustrated endpapers, half title, title page, front matter, and dedication/pencil and watercolor/24.8cm x 20cm
    Fantasy   Gr. Ps-1

Instead of going to school, Little Brave Heart, a Native American boy, decides to go hunting. His first near victim, a wood rat, persuades him into bigger game and so the story snowballs. The illustrations of Berta and Elmer Hader, alternating spreads in color and black and white, follow Little Brave Heart's hunt, from a prairie dog right up to a bear, who chases him all the way to an obvious ending--school.

The illustrations of The Mighty Hunter bear the characteristics also evident in Cock-a-doodle-Doo (C11), a 1940 Honor Book; studies of natural history, flora and fauna, reveal the expertise of the artists. As in the earlier Honor Book as well, the illustrations of The Mighty Hunter alternate full spreads of color and black and white, but the black and white pages often become more interesting than the color. The textures and values created by the side of a pencil or piece of charcoal create more variety within the black and white drawings than in the color, which are sometimes distracting because of the wide variety of hues included. Most interest is generated from the fine studies of the parade of animals that Little Brave Heart stalks.

The human characters, however, show less realism in their portrayals and verge on the stereotypical. Facial features show little resemblance to those of the Native American and again demonstrate a perspective that changes over the years. The reputation of the Haders as competent illustrators of books for children remains established today in works still popular, but

their portrayal of the Native American, innocent as it was meant
to be, has changed over the years. The artists' reputations no
doubt overrode any concern there might have been, if any, over
the portrayal of a "typical" Native American boy upon which the
white man's standard of values has been imposed. In retrospect,
the book is weakened by time and does not withstand the concerns
of a new generation.

C28   BROWN, MARGARET WISE. A Child's Good Night Book. Illustrated
        by Jean Charlot. New York: W. R. Scott, 1943, [32 pp.]
        16 illus.: color-14; olive and white-2/illustrated front
        matter, title page, and end matter/colored pencil and ink/
        23.5cm x 19.8cm
        Fiction   Gr. Ps-1

Jean Charlot's illustrations of pastel textures add the hues
of reds, blues, and browns to Margaret Wise Brown's story of
what happens to animals, objects, and children when night comes
and sleep creeps upon them. From birds, fish, wild beasts, sailboats, cars, kangaroos, and bunnies, to children--all find their
appropriate niches to snuggle into when sleep overcomes.

Charlot's unusual and stylized figures, outlined and detailed
in bold, olive lines, give the book a unique appearance that is
intriguing to study. The bold, green type picks up the lines of
the shapes on the facing pages and visually helps unite the text
and pictures. The circular lines and compositions reflect the
security and simplicity of the text. Figures of a mother and
father bird complete a circular composition as they sleep over
their four babies, cuddling up in their nest just as securely as
the baby kangaroos cozily snooze in their mother's pouch.

The completion of the book, accompanied by a color change in
text, offers a religiously symbolic conclusion, as, presumably,
two guardian angels gather up all the small, sleeping things in
a blanket, protecting and blessing them in their innocence.
Charlot's artistic interpretation shows originality in visual
concept and provides an interesting contrast to the following
year's Medal Book, Prayer for a Child (C30).

C29   CHAN, CHIH-YI. Good Luck Horse. Illustrated by Plato Chan.
        London: Whittlesey, 1943 (OP), [52 pp.] 20 illus.:
        turquoise, orange, black, and white-10; black and white-10/
        illustrated endpapers and title page/pen and ink and
        color/14.1cm x 21.6cm
        Legend   Gr. 1-2

This adaptation of a Chinese legend, from long before the Hsia
Dynasty, is described in the words of Chih-Yi Chan and in the
pictures by her twelve-year-old son, Plato. The tale, a favorite
of Plato's, recounts the events that occur when Wah-Toong, the
lonely son of a rich merchant, cuts himself a paper horse, which

1944

is transformed into a live horse after a gust of wind snatches
it up and drops it in the garden of the Magician.

With Wah-Toong as his master, Good-Luck Horse embarks on some
disastrous adventures which earn him the name Bad-Luck Horse.
After damaging much of Wah-Toong's father's garden and scaring
off the family horses, Bad-Luck Horse, outcast, runs away to a
land beyond the Great Wall, falls in love with a beautiful mare,
and brings his Good-Luck Wife back to visit Wah-Toong. After
Wah-Toong nearly suffers a fatal fall from the back of Good-Luck
Wife, Good-Luck Horse again loses his confidence, until war breaks
out between the two countries bordering the Great Wall.

Good-Luck Horse, with Wah-Toong on his back, ventures off to
war, and after a bit of conversation with the enemy's horses, the
animals mingle with the opposition so that no battle ensues.
Peace is restored without a fight--Good-Luck Horse retains his
name and honor, and Wah-Toong's father realizes there is no distinction between good and bad luck: "There is only luck! and
that means that every day must be lived so that a man always
does his best."

Plato Chan's visual interpretations of this Chinese legend
are simple, clear line drawings of black and white, alternating
with color drawings of similar style, with the addition of turquoise and orange. Remarkable in terms of the artist's age, the
illustrations reflect the purity and ingenuousness of the child
artist and reinforce the concept of the innocence of childhood
that helps grown men divert a war.

The legend becomes a cultural and historical record of this
Eastern culture and remains more resilient than most fabricated
stories of Chinese background; the illustrations, however, at
the hands of a more mature artist, may have been able to complement the literary significance of the tale more effectively, for
it is the tale, much more than the illustrations, that leaves an
impact on the reader.

1945

C30   FIELD, RACHEL. Prayer for a Child. Illustrated by Elizabeth
        Orton Jones. New York: Macmillan, 1944, [32 pp.]
        26 illus.: ochre, black, and white-19; color-7/illustrated
        title page, dedication, and front matter/pencil and water-
        color/21.5cm x 17.7cm
        Fiction   Gr. Ps-1
      The entire poem, "Prayer for a Child," appears at the begin-
ning of the 1945 Medal Book by Rachel Field. The illustrations
of Elizabeth Orton Jones depict the lines of the prayer throughout the book, as she visually interprets the author's words.
The small figures that appear on the first page, facing the

entire poem, are a motif that is repeated in each segment of the poem. The wooden-like carved figures sit on, next to, and in front of the first letter of each new division.

The soft, warm illustrations depict all the important parts that make up a child's world--Mother, Father, family, friends, toys--and bring meaning to the words of the prayer. The color illustrations emanate the warmth of the words as the comforting golden tones envelop the scenes. A number of the illustrations are reproduced only in the golden tones, tones also dominant in many of the color illustrations, with black and white. These monochromatic drawings retain the gentle aura of the color illustrations in that they take on the softly modeled appearance of pencil drawings, highlighted and contrasted with sharp, clean lines and given shape by areas of smudged shading which highlight form and add dimensionality.

The illustrations reinforce the comforting concept of this prayer and skillfully reflect the security that the young child asks for through the prayer. With the ending of the poem, the spiritual peace that comes from the word of the text, "Amen," is reflected in the innocence of the young sleeping child, surrounded by those loving guardians of the night--teddy and elephant--who will ensure her safety until the morning's dawn.

C31   TUDOR, TASHA. <u>Mother Goose: Seventy-seven Verses with Pic-tures</u>. New York: Henry Z. Walck, 1944, 87 pp. 78 illus.: color-40; black and white-38/illustrated endpapers, title page, and dedication/pencil and watercolor/18.3cm x 16.4cm
Mother Goose/Nursery Rhymes   Gr. Ps-1

Mother Goose remains a favorite topic for children and illustrators alike, and these rhymes of childhood find frequent representation among the Caldecott titles. The characters in the color illustrations of this Honor Book, alternating with black and white, are softly and gently modeled figures, most with the cherubic curls, smiles, eyes, and cheeks of childhood. Only a few pages are missing the idealized forms of Tasha Tudor's children as they participate in the rhymes of Mother Goose. Old King Cole has two infants crawling about his feet, and in "Sing a Song of Sixpence," the interpretation includes two children in a serene, family-oriented setting, opening up a pie of very tame blackbirds.

This focus on the gentle, more positive aspects of the seventy-seven rhymes included is quite apparent in all but two of the illustrations--"Ding, dong, bell, Pussy's in the well!" and "Trip upon trenchers." There are other rhymes which deal with unfortunate circumstances, "Humpty-Dumpty," "Jack and Jill," and "Little Polly Flinders," but the artist has chosen to emphasize the action that usually takes place <u>before</u> the misfortunes occur. This form of artistic censorship seems to lessen the impact of the rhymes upon the audience.

1945

The deemphasis of the forcefulness of these nursery rhymes through the illustrations results in a visual impact which does not always reinforce the rhythmical beat of the verses themselves. Tudor's interpretation, though, would have the power to lull a child to sleep in the arms of an adult in a rocking chair. The pastel colors are used very conservatively, some pictures having little contrast and variation in values, which reinforces the calm in Tudor's interpretation. Tudor's choice has been uniformly adhered to in all but a few instances—notably "Hey diddle diddle," in which the smoky blue-gray darkness of the picture is interrupted by the stark, white moon partially shining behind a hill. Though the illustrations deny some of the colorful life and vigor of these childhood verses, Tudor creates some memorable scenes of Mother Goose in the process.

C32   ETS, MARIE HALL. <u>In the Forest</u>. New York: Viking, 1944,
       [44 pp.] 37 illus.: black and white-37/illustrated title
       page/charcoal/17.1cm x 22.7cm
       Fantasy   Gr. Ps-1
This 1945 Honor Book, by Marie Hall Ets, is filled with black and white illustrations depicting the story of a young boy's walk in the forest. As his walk progresses, the boy gathers a parade of animals strutting behind him, all of which disappear when the boy's father arrives upon the scene. The white figures of the small boy and the animals—a napping lion, baby elephants, brown bears, hopping kangaroos, an old stork, little monkeys, a silent rabbit—are a definite contrast to the dark backgrounds of the forest.

The effect of the drawings, which often take on the appearance of being done with the side of a piece of charcoal, is to draw the viewer's attention to the clean white figures, while the background remains fuzzy and indefinite. Because of the technique, the only sharp lines are those that define the outlines of the animals. This is achieved by surrounding the figures with solid areas of black, creating the greatest contrast between the figure and its immediate surroundings. Because of the technique, the figures are drawn with minimal detail, only including those lines which define the distinguishing characteristic of each species.

The cumulation of each of the types of animals through the text, which contains no obvious rhymes but flows with a definite beat, leads the entourage to a picnic area where a meal of peanuts, jam, ice cream, and cake is consumed before the games commence. As the congenial group find their secret places for Hide-and-Seek, Dad appears and animals disappear, ending the tale of a little boy's fantastic walk in the forest.

There is evidence in the illustrations to indicate the fictitious presentation of the walk, the events and the behavior of the characters in the story, but the transition from reality to fantasy is not made clear in the beginning and may cause some confusion for a young audience. The surprise ending does help clarify the imaginative journey, but it is handled so abruptly that the effect may not be as it was intended. There is no need for the move from reality to fantasy to be explicitly spelled out, but the "crossing over" requires a delicate balance and careful selection of text to make it effective and understand-able to the audience for which it was intended.

C33   De ANGELI, MARGUERITE. <u>Yonie Wondernose</u>. Garden City, N.Y.:
       Doubleday, Doran, 1944, [48 pp.] 32 illus.: black and
       white-25; color-7/illustrated endpapers and title page/
       pencil and watercolors/24.3cm x 22.5cm
       Fiction   Gr. 1-2

Marguerite de Angeli's 1945 Honor Book takes place in the heart of Pennsylvania Dutch country--Lancaster County. Yonie Wondernose, the nickname for a young, curious Amish boy, dis-covers what responsibility is all about when his parents leave him in charge of the farm for a day. With only a few minor mis-haps, including locking Granny in the chicken house, he completes the day's chores and falls asleep to the growl of rolling thunder.

Yonie is abruptly awakened by a flash of lightning that sets the barn afire and jolts him back to the reality of his responsi-bilities. The young boy's diligence, as he is prodded along by his father's voice remonstrating "Yonie Wondernose" for his curiosity and tendency to get sidetracked, pays off as he res-cues the animals from the barn, just as his father returns to the farm a bit early.

This involved story line makes for quite a bit of text in the book, though the action does carry the story along. The concen-tration upon Yonie's completion of the chores earlier in the day seems to detract from the important event--the barn fire. By the time the story reaches this point, the fire seems almost anticlimactic.

The illustrations, the majority of which are done in black and white, with a few full-color watercolors, do not emphasize the second portion of the story, and in fact only three of the seven color pictures appear in the second half of the book. The visual emphasis on the first portion seems to bear out the tex-tual concentration as well, and even though Yonie receives a pig, a calf, and the position of farm hand as a reward for his ef-forts, the theme seems to come across without force. All Yonie wanted was to be considered grown up enough to drive the work horse, a fact he had already proved prior to the fire.

It is unfortunate that the use of watercolor illustrations was not expanded in this book, for the scarcity with which they appear, so often juxtaposed with the stylistically different

1945

black and white illustrations, makes their absence more obvious and emphasized. Because of these incongruities in text and illustrations, much of the important social and cultural information may go unappreciated.

C34   SAWYER, RUTH. The Christmas Anna Angel. Illustrated by Kate
       Seredy. New York: Viking, 1944 (OP), 48 pp. 24 illus.:
       color-17; brown and white-7/illustrated front matter, half
       title, title page, dedication, and end matter/lithographs/
       21cm x 15.9cm
       Fantasy: folklike tale   Gr. 1-2
   A Hungarian family is the focus of this Christmas story in
which Anna, the young daughter, tells St. Nicholas that she wants
Christmas cakes for her gift. She realizes the impracticality
of her request, at a time of economic depression imposed by war,
and settles for a request of a white fur muff with a hot potato,
even though she still secretly holds onto the belief that she
will receive the Christmas cakes. With the miraculous visit of
her angel on Christmas Eve, Anna is granted her wish for the
tiny confections.
   Though the predominantly yellow, pink, and blue illustrations
provide glimpses of Hungarian life and the customs surrounding
the holiday, while smaller black and white illustrations appear
scattered among some of the pages not faced with color, the text
of this book dominates the entire work. The book is weighted
down by this abundance of print, and the pictures seem sluggish
and dominated by black, which imparts a sense of gloom. If the
illustrations were meant to reflect the severity of the economic hardships, a time when the military searched houses and
confiscated wheat and flour for the wartime effort, then this
feeling is definitely conveyed. There is no real change in
style or color of the illustrations when the miracle of the
angel's visit occurs, and it is difficult to sense the excitement when such a heavy, dark visual image is presented. In the
illustrations dealing with the liveliest and most exciting segments, when Anna's angel arrives late on Christmas Eve and has
Anna help her bake the cakes, the smiles on the faces of Anna
and her angel are the only clues to the excitement of the moment.
   Were the book closer to a picture storybook in concept, with
greater economy of text and a stronger, more intimate relationship between word and picture, it could function more effectively,
rather than merely as an illustrated work for children.

1946

C35   PETERSHAM, MAUD and PETERSHAM, MISKA. The Rooster Crows.
       New York: Macmillan, 1945, [64 pp.] 58 illus.: black,

white, and 1 color-34; color-12; black, white, and 2 colors-
12/illustrated title page and contents page/lithographic
pencil with color separations/25.9cm x 20.3cm
     Mother Goose/Nursery Rhymes   Gr. Ps-1
Rhymes and Jingles, Finger Games, Rope Skipping Rhymes,
Counting-Out Rhymes, Games, and Yankee Doodle make up the sections
of the 1946 Medal Book by Maud and Miska Petersham. This collection of American rhymes and jingles of childhood recounts many
familiar words of the forgotten days of youth. It is the nostal-
gia of these chants of youth and the Petershams' ability to capture the essence of these games in their illustrations that made
the book a popular choice for the Caldecott Medal.
     The fifty-eight illustrations, some in full color, others in
one or two colors with black and white, capture the humor, rhythm,
and all-around fun that are contained in the words. Nothing but
compassion can be felt for "Fuzzy Wuzzy," who loses his hair, as
he sits forlornly staring out from the page. The humor of "Engine, Engine, Number Nine," the locomotive so shiny a cow cannot
take her eyes off her own reflection (much to the dismay of the
train's conductor), brings a new meaning to those words of rote
so often recited in childhood.
     The illustrations of the Finger Games help guide the child
with the proper hand positions and give the book a kinesthetic
extension beyond its pages. The predominantly blue, brown, and
pink illustrations add variety to the book's format, and the
interjection of full-color pictures adds more interest. There
are only two pictures, since removed in a revised edition, that
detract from the book's illustrations, both of which negatively
depict blacks.
     But aside from these illustrations, the reception of which
has changed from the time of the book's publication, the work
would have interest for today's audience, especially were an
adult to demonstrate how some of these games were played "in
the olden days."

C36 BROWN, MARGARET WISE [Golden MacDonald]. Lost Little Lamb.
       Illustrated by Leonard Weisgard. Garden City, N.Y.:
       Doubleday, Doran, 1945 (OP), 48 pp. 19 illus.: color-11;
       black, white, and umber-8/illustrated endpapers, title page,
       and removable illustration/opaque color and washes/24.3cm
       x 22.5cm
       Fiction   Gr. Ps-1
Every day the little shepherd boy takes his flock of sheep to
the mountain meadows to graze. One early spring day he leads
his flock higher up the mountain than ever before, and the only
black lamb of the flock scampers off to romp in the lush grass
of the mountaintop valley. When the absence of the "little
black smudge" is finally noticed, a frantic search begins, but

the setting sun forces shepherd and herd back down to the lower valleys to safety from mountain lions, cold, lightning, and rain.

Concern for the lost lamb keeps the young shepherd from sleep, and he finally decides to creep back up the mountain. In the darkness the shepherd and his dog hear the shrill "scream of a mountain lion," who is scared off by the approaching rescuers. The little lamb is recovered, and all return to safety, the completion of the story paralleled in the text by Brown's repetition of the exact words with which she opens the tale (pp. 8, 44).

The initial eleven illustrations in this 1946 Honor Book, typical of Leonard Weisgard's work in The Little Island (C40), 1947 Medal Book, run the gamut of the artist's palette. The eight following illustrations, depicting the final events of the story, are all appropriately done in black, white, and a pink-toned umber, helping portray the darkness of nightfall as well as the darkness of the mood of the story--its danger, loss, fear. This change in mood and time is also noted by the shifting of the illustrations to the left-hand leaf, the text to the right. Where the contrast of light and dark serves to direct the movement of the eye in these latter illustrations, the vibrant hues of the initial ones perform the task.

Weisgard's expressionistic movement of colors and shapes, the obvious feeling of actual brush strokes, makes his work very lively. A few quick lines for detail can accent a shape or give definition to a form. The illustration included at the beginning of the book, which can be removed and framed, is an excellent example of the artist's ability to define his subject with a minimum of line. With the wide range of colors and shapes employed, though, the artist runs the risk of sacrificing a tight composition to an imbalance of competing colors and shapes, which does occasionally happen in this Honor Book.

C37   WHEELER, OPAL. Sing Mother Goose. Illustrated by Marjorie
       Torrey. New York: E. P. Dutton, 1945 (OP), 103 pp.
       84 illus.: black and white-37; color-28; black, white,
       and 1 color-19/illustrated endpapers, front matter, title
       page, and dedication/watercolor, pen and ink, and pencil/
       28cm x 20cm
       Mother Goose/Nursery Rhymes   Gr. Ps-1
Opal Wheeler's collection of fifty-two Mother Goose rhymes and original airs for piano, written by the author, won Honor Book status in 1946. The contents page lists some common, traditional rhymes, from "Three Little Kittens" and "Little Bo Peep" to "Simple Simon" and "Polly, Put the Kettle On," as well as some less familiar rhymes of the era. The collection alone, illustrated by Marjorie Torrey in black and white and full-color drawings, is a well-balanced presentation of visual and written elements, and the addition of tunes for the rhymes becomes

instrumental to the book's purpose, as well as to the composition
of the page.

Torrey's full-color illustrations, though, are serene and sometimes fail to reflect the action and rhythm of these childhood
chants; these pages take on an almost religious sense, perhaps
foreshadowing the style of her 1947 Honor Book of religious hymns
for children (C45). The black and white illustrations, or those
in black, white, and one color, are much more effective in relating the movement and beat of their accompanying rhymes. In
"There Was a Crooked Man," the eye travels across the full-page
spread, following the delicate, curving lines from the crooked
house on the left to the crooked figures of man, mouse, and cat
on the right.

In a similar fashion, the illustrations for "Seesaw, Margery
Daw" pick up on the textual cues as the eye travels from the
left to the teeter-totter and strong diagonal composition on
the right. The tune, rhymes, and black and white motif of a
group of singing children, which appears throughout the book,
provide a balance and contrast for the extreme movement indicated on the left, a visual impact heightened by the addition
of red to the black and white drawing.

Although not a picture book in the strict sense of the term,
this Wheeler-Torrey effort demands adult, as well as child,
participation to utilize it to its fullest potential and is perhaps still a useful tool for teachers of the very young.

C38   REHYER, BECKY. My Mother Is the Most Beautiful Woman
       in the World. Illustrated by Ruth Gannett. New York:
       Howell, Soskin, 1945, [44 pp.] 36 illus.: color-18;
       black and white-18/illustrated endpapers and title page/
       color separation/20.8cm x 17cm
       Folk Tale   Gr. K-2

The final gathering of wheat and preparation for the harvest
feast is the setting in which six-year-old Varya gets separated
from her mother in the fields of the Ukraine. So overcome with
fear at the consequences of her falling asleep in the fields,
Varya can only describe her mother to her rescuers by blurting
out, "My mother is the most beautiful woman in the world." The
search for Varya's mother drags on until the child is finally
claimed by her rounded, "almost toothless" mother, who is the
most beautiful woman in the eyes of her loving daughter.

The style of Ruth Gannett's illustrations, small dots of red,
yellow, blue, and black, creating the shapes of the compositions,
also translates well in the eighteen black and white illustrations of the book. The technique of pointilism, especially
effective in black and white, allows the shapes, at a distance,
to appear as solid values of black or color. At closer inspection, the interest is intriguing and effective in creating an

1946

appropriate atmosphere for the lively peasant feast day and its
exciting preparations.

The Russian flare, revealed in the turrets of the architecture
of the illustrations and in the tapestry designs that decorate
some pages, does not detract from the universal theme of the
Russian proverb upon which the story is based: We do not love
people because they are beautiful, but they seem beautiful because we love them. To demonstrate the universal sentiment even
further, a frame is provided at the end of the book with space
for a picture of the owner's Most Beautiful Woman in the World.
The wholesomeness of the story and illustration has made this
book a memorable one, in visual and written modes alike.

C39   WIESE, KURT. <u>You Can Write Chinese</u>. New York: Viking, 1945
         (OP), [64 pp.] 60 illus.: black, white, and red-30; black,
         white, and blue-28; black and white-2/illustrated front mat-
         ter and title page/india ink and pastel/19.5cm x 26cm
         Information: social studies   Gr. 1-3
    In a Chungking schoolroom in 1945, Peter Parrish, the only
American in the class, learns to read and write Chinese. The
teacher begins the day's lesson by explaining the Chinese language as a system of pictures represented by characters. Thirty-
four strokes comprise the entire system of the formation of these
characters, which are always made by beginning at the upper left
and finishing at the lower right. The skillful teacher and
artist, Kurt Wiese, takes the class, and reader, on a tour of
numbers, nouns, adjectives, and verbs, culminating in a symbolic
unity of China and the United States of America on the final
pages.

Kurt Wiese transforms this book, basically a book of information, into an intriguing intertwining of character, word, and
figure. Integrated into the black and white brush and ink figures, from which the Chinese characters are derived, is color
enough to define and clarify the shapes that the characters
mimic. Wiese utilizes minimal color, the red or blue of the
side of a pastel or soft crayon, to focus attention on the <u>shape</u>
of the character, and thus adds dimension to the teaching technique. It is only the pronunciation of the Chinese words that
is missing.

Wiese's expressive brush and ink drawings help the reader
visualize the Chinese characters, no doubt creating an impact
more influential than that which most teachers could ever hope
to accomplish. Wiese helps bridge the cultural gap between
China and the United States in this book and probably does more
to instill a curiosity and respect for these peoples than any of
his other books dealing with this Eastern culture have done.

1947

C40   BROWN, MARGARET WISE [Golden MacDonald]. The Little Island.
      Illustrated by Leonard Weisgard. Garden City, N.Y.:
      Doubleday, 1946 (OP), [48 pp.] 29 illus.: color-20;
      black and white-9/illustrated endpapers and title page/
      gouache/20.3cm x 25.2cm
      Fantasy   Gr. Ps-1
   The seasons come and go on the little island as it exists far
apart from the rest of the world, surrounded by miles and miles
of water. But a little kitten discovers that this island is
also part of the rest of the world, attached underwater to the
land that makes it part of the whole and, therefore, justifies
the island's existence.
   Leonard Weisgard's illustrations help make this book a meaningful experience, though the theme seems a sophisticated one for
the picture-book level. Weisgard's expressionistic colors bring
to life the seasons, animals, and terrain of the little island,
as this watery environment is particularly well suited to the
artist's free-flowing style and splashes of color. Even the
black and white studies that accompany the pages which hold the
text emit the feelings and essence of the creatures and vegetation of the island.
   The lobsters and seals, kingfishers and gulls are fine studies
and compositions which have minimal detail, but nonetheless are
complete and give the impression of being easily adapted to a
canvas two or three times the size of the book. The artist uses
his palette effectively to convey the moods associated with fog
and storm, spring and summer, morning and night, especially as
they affect the little island. Even the positioning of the black
and white studies helps draw the eye around the full-page spreads,
externally integrating text and illustration.
   The illustrations become a major consideration in the acceptance of this book as a Caldecott winner, but the sophistication
and handling of the theme, of finding the meaning of one's existence, may make the book less popular in future years, with
those of picture-book age.

C41   TRESSELT, ALVIN. Rain Drop Splash. Illustrated by Leonard
      Weisgard. New York: Lothrop, Lee & Shepard, 1946, [32 pp.]
      26 illus.: red, yellow, and umber-15; yellow and umber-5;
      umber and white-5; red and umber-1/illustrated title page/
      ink and 2-color separation/25cm x 21.1cm
      Information: science   Gr. K-2
   Rain Drop Splash is the saga of a rain drop as it journeys
from pond to brook, lake, river, and finally out to the expan-
sive sea. Leonard Weisgard's illustrations, the majority done
in yellow, red, and black, are mainly large silhouettes and

shapes of color, dominated by black, with little fine detail. This absence of fine detail, also characteristic of the illustrations in his Medal Book, <u>The Little Island</u> (C40), is simply an aspect of the medium with which he works, where subtle changes in value, resulting from the less rigid brush, allow for the detail.

Weisgard's use of color is very limited in comparison to his Medal Book, so color is employed deliberately, imposing a balance and cohesiveness to the compositions of the illustrations. The red of the roof and steeple of a church and the yellow of a house and schoolhouse balance perfectly with the black and white of the facing page, on which the text and a runaway umbrella skillfully lead the eye back to the color of the buildings. It is obvious that the placement of colors is deliberate, and the balance of the intensity of the hues is felt. The tilting and listing of the ships on the river give the viewer the sensation of having motion sickness, as the colors help reinforce the rocking motion of the water by leading the eye from color to line and back.

The originality of Tresselt's story and Weisgard's handling of the subject matter in his dramatic and flowing style account for the work's Honor Book status, but today it might seem outdated because of its simplistic portrayal of life and society seen via the journey of the rain drop.

C42   FLACK, MARJORIE. <u>Boats on the River</u>. Illustrated by Jay
        Hyde Barnum. New York: Viking, 1946 (OP), 32 pp. 28
        illus.: color-28/illustrated title page/watercolor, pen
        and ink, and brush/24.4cm x 30cm
        Information: science   Gr. 1-2

From ferryboats and tugboats to submarines and warships, Jay Hyde Barnum's illustrations depict the myriad of boats that have access to a river that flows into the nearby sea. The daily stream of tugboats, sailboats, rowboats, and barges is depicted in twenty-eight color illustrations that identify the types and uses of these nautical vessels. The sometimes rhythmic text and illustrations, all bursting with information, create a novel approach to what is, in essence, a book of information.

Barnum's watercolor and ink paintings present an abundance of information regarding the classifications and uses of the vessels discussed, and his illustrations help move along a text that sometimes gets bogged down by its technical aspects; even though the beat and repetition in the words flow along with the illustrations, there are spots where this rhythm weakens and creates an awkwardness in the text. Barnum's compositions travel left to right across the full-page spreads, circling around the text and bringing the eye back. The moods captured during the fog scenes and the river at night recreate the still and calm of these situations.

Other than in the diversion in the text when the sailors from
the warship enjoy their leave in the city, this picture book
could function quite well without a text. The illustrations
provide enough technical information and distinction between
the vessels to generate an interesting discussion with children
in which they could share their experiences without the help of
a text. With the text, however, there seems little excitement
or interest generated in what the words reveal, and, consequently,
the strength of the illustrations becomes incidental.

C43   GRAHAM, AL. Timothy Turtle. Illustrated by Tony Palazzo.
       Cambridge, Mass.: Robert Welch Pub. Co., 1946 (OP),
       [36 pp.] 25 illus.: black and brown-12; black and blue-
       13/illustrated endpapers and title page/black and white
       pen and ink over wash/30.2cm x 23cm
       Fantasy   Gr. Ps-1
     Timothy Turtle of Took-a-Look Lake, tiring of his lucrative,
but monotonous, ferry business, sets out to seek adventure and
fame, though he decides climbing steep hills and getting walloped
by a rock is not his idea of adventure. Fame, disguised in
Timothy's unnatural ability to turn a somersault, of sorts, to
get off his back, finally does come to the turtle once he returns
to the trail which takes him back to Took-a-Look Lake. Barnaby
Bee has witnessed Timothy's feat, so word of the turtle's fame
arrives ahead of the celebrated personality, who is welcomed
home with a gala party.
     Tony Palazzo's pen-and-ink illustrations, with backgrounds of
blue and brown (pastel) washes, capitalize on the humor of
Timothy's quest for fame and adventure and portray these human
emotions through the animal figures. Whether Timothy is "mer-
rily tripping along" or "agog with surprise," his feelings are
apparent in Palazzo's expressive portraits.
     Expression seems to be the key to Palazzo's drawings, as the
quick strokes of the pen give action and life to the pages, even
though there are often large amounts of empty white space on the
pages. Palazzo puts major emphasis on and detail into his animal creations and in doing so focuses upon the personal identity
struggle of Timothy. The rhyme and "Dr. Seuss" quality of word
choice and word invention seem appropriate to this light and airy
story, the disastrous circumstances of which end up to be as much
as, if not more than, Timothy had hoped. This turtle's lust for
fame and adventure certainly paid off, but Palazzo's illustrations
play down this aspect and concentrate on the humor and surprise
as Fate smiles upon the terrapin.

C44   POLITI, LEO. Pedro, the Angel of Olvera Street. New York:
       Charles Scribner's Sons, 1946, [32 pp.] 28 illus.:
       color-25; black and white-3/illustrated title page and

dedication/watercolor with white paint (opaque)/19.9cm x
16.5cm
Fiction   Gr. Ps-1
    Because Pedro, of Olvera Street, Los Angeles, California, has
a voice like that of an angel, he leads the Christmas parade,
La Posada, through the streets for the nine-day duration of this
customary celebration. After completing this honorable task on
Christmas Eve, Pedro recovers a music box from the party's
piñata; this making his evening complete, he falls asleep to
the soft tune of his prize and to the gentle voices of the angels.
    Leo Politi's visual presentation of this Mexican custom re-
flects the honest simplicity and deep regard for the values of
the culture. This authenticity is further extended by the use
of Spanish words in the text, which are parenthetically defined
and then used throughout. Some of the illustrations, dominated
by red, yellow, and blue, reflect the solemnity of the symbolic
parade, while others are merely decorative designs of Mexican
motifs which border the pages. This variety, coupled with the
inclusion of two traditional Mexican songs, and the primitive,
simple artistic style, prevents the format from stagnating.
    What is interesting about the illustrations in this predomi-
nantly color book is that the most striking pages are the three
black and white illustrations in the work. The long procession
of singing participants, with glowing candles in their hands,
creates a dramatic composition of contrasting lights and darks,
which evokes the same feelings of expressionism that Ludwig
Bemelmans captures in his 1940 Honor Book, Madeline (C12). The
juxtaposition of the color and black and white compositions
creates more emphasis on the latter, which appear only in the
second half of the book. Politi presents a sentimental story
of the Mexican culture and couples it with a visual image that
helps reinforce the solemnity of the occasion and the joy of its
celebration.

C45   WHEELER, OPAL. Sing in Praise: A Collection of the Best
       Loved Hymns. Illustrated by Marjorie Torrey. New York:
       E. P. Dutton, 1946 (OP), 95 pp. 44 illus.: black and
       white-24; color-16; black and white and 1 color-4/
       illustrated front matter and title page/watercolor, pen
       and ink, and pencil/26.9cm x 19.5cm
       Information: music   Gr. Ps-3
    The collaboration of Opal Wheeler and Marjorie Torrey again
results in the production of a Caldecott Honor Book, this time a
collection of hymns. Focusing on hymns of special relevance to
children, this compilation includes historical and biographical
information on the origins and creators of the words and melodies
of the songs and offers a basic history of hymnody and its father--
Isaac Watts. The contents pages, indicating the inclusion of

nineteen stories about the twenty-five hymns, reveal some of the most familiar of Christian tunes--"Onward, Christian Soldiers," "Rock of Ages," "Fairest Lord Jesus," and "Christ the Lord Is Risen To-day."

Accompanying these hymns are Marjorie Torrey's illustrations, which zero in on the relevance of the songs and help interpret their meaning on a child's level. The full-color illustrations reflect the solemnity and reverence seen in Torrey's Mother Goose collection, and these interpretations communicate the essence and importance of the songs' words. Although the major emphasis of the collection is aural, Torrey's gentle black and white drawings help embellish the text and provide interest in the variety of styles and media used. Some black and white illustrations possess the softness of pencil, some the sharp lines of pen and ink, and others a combination of both. These, in juxtaposition with the full-color pages, help break up the monotony of the large blocks of text needed to explain some of the hymns.

Although not a picture book in the strict sense, the work imparts valuable information and demands adult and child participation, as did the earlier Mother Goose collection produced by these women. Older children will find the information included in the stories of great interest, as many focus on the childhood days and family lives of the composers of the melodies and the authors of the verses. Today the appeal of the book may only be to church choir directors or Sunday-school teachers, but the understanding of the hymns remains its forte, and the illustrations help create a visual, as well as emotional, impact.

1948

C46   TRESSELT, ALVIN. White Snow, Bright Snow. Illustrated by
      Roger Duvoisin. New York: Lothrop, Lee & Shepard, 1947,
      32 pp. 23 illus.: color-22; black and white-1/illustrated
      endpapers and front matter/acetate color separations with
      black india ink/25.7cm x 21.6cm
      Fiction   Gr. Ps-1
      A three-stanza poem serves as the introduction to the 1948
Medal Book by Alvin Tresselt and illustrated by Roger Duvoisin.
Snow is in the air, and when it finally starts to fall, "one flake, two flakes, five, eight, ten," the people begin to react to the situation in a variety of ways. The postman, farmer, policeman, and children all prepare for the effects of winter, retrieving rubber boots, snow shovels, cough mixtures, and sleds from summer storage spots as the new season begins its visit. Just as quietly as the snow comes, it departs, leaving behind the signs of spring, including the first robin.

1948

The simplicity of Tresselt's text, like that of Rain Drop
Splash (C41), a 1947 Honor Book, speaks through the bold, solid
shapes of the red, yellow, black, and white illustrations. The
quick, expressive strokes that create the shapes help reflect
the movement of the text through the seasons. As the snow gradually accumulates, the visual images darken, until only the glow
of red and yellow light emanates from the windows of the house at
nightfall. When the snowfall is complete and morning dawns, the
reader is presented with the dramatic contrast of a full-page
spread of bright, blinding snow. The juxtaposition of these illustrations, with their grayness of night and intensity of the
bright snowfall, allows the viewer to experience the exact feeling of surprise and quiet calm that follows a heavy, overnight
snow.

Duvoisin recreates these authentic reactions and events skillfully for such a limited color scheme. His artistic expertise
and expression have combined with the text to demonstrate the
continuity of nature and man's adaptation to his environment.
Where Rain Drop Splash (C41) illustrates the continuity in the
cycles of nature, White Snow, Bright Snow brings the experience
one step closer--to man.

C47   BROWN, MARCIA. Stone Soup: An Old Tale. New York: Charles
        Scribner's Sons, 1947, [50 pp.] 42 illus.: brown and
        orange-42/illustrated front matter, title page, and dedica-
        tion/2-color separation/25.3cm x 20.1cm
        Folk Tale   Gr. 1-3
Marcia Brown's Honor Book is a story of three hungry soldiers
who outsmart a village of wary peasants. Hiding their food to
avoid sharing what little they have, the poor French peasants
find flimsy excuses for denying the soldiers food and shelter.
When the men decide to make their own dinner, stone soup, and
come up a few ingredients short, the peasants, in their curiosity
about this unique recipe, gladly contribute the missing items:
carrots, cabbage, beef, potatoes, barley, and milk. But for the
peasants, a dinner is not complete without a bountiful table of
roasts, bread, and cider; thus this magical "recipe" reaps the
clever soldiers a plentiful spread and, ironically, "the best
beds in the village."

The brown and orange illustrations accompanying this humorous
tale of human nature reflect the activity that surrounds the making of the soup. Areas of color and wash, given shape with quick,
expressive lines, move the eye across the page and back and forth,
creating an air of excitement as the soup is prepared. What could
easily become a demeaning portrait of peasant provincialism is
skillfully handled by the artist, and the sincerity and gullibility of the peasants result in an advantageous situation for them
all.

As in many tales of the oral tradition, the audience is left in the position of recognizing the scam, while the characters in the story remain ingenuously oblivious to the end. Because of this technique, the gullibility of the peasants remains more acceptable to the audience--no harm done. Brown retells this French tale of humor in the tradition of oral literature and allows her audience to share in the fun.

C48   GEISEL, THEODORE [Dr. Seuss]. McElligot's Pool. New York:
       Random House, 1947, [56 pp.]   51 illus.:   color-26; black
       and white-25/illustrated front matter, title page, and
       dedication/watercolor/27cm x 19.5cm
       Fantasy   Gr. Ps-1

Flowing, moving, and vibrant describe both text and illustration for McElligot's Pool, another 1948 Honor Book. When Marco begins imagining that McElligot's Pool is attached to bigger and better bodies of water, his chances of catching an exotic species of fish greatly increase with his imagination. Via a possible underground brook, these exotic inventions of Marco's gain access to the pool; from Dogfish and eels to Australian fish and Circus fish, the endless supply flows. Utilizing these imaginary possibilities, Marco justifies his activity to a skeptical farmer who happens by.

The text, typically in rhyme, is as lively and imaginative as the watercolor and black and white illustrations. Geisel creates a unique species on nearly every page, and though his word invention is kept to a minimum in this text, he does not avoid it completely: A "THING-A-MA-JIGGER!!" is quite some fish.

During this period of picturebook production, the imagination and frivolity of this book undoubtedly insured it a warm welcome from an audience that was predominantly presented with more serious themes. The sheer nonsense of McElligot's Pool and the sense of fun in the plethora of Geisel books that follow appeal to the lighter side of childhood and eventually become books that children themselves turn to read. The evolution into I-Can-Read-It-All-By-Myself books is an indication of the "readability," which is facilitated by the rhyming text and unforgettable illustrations of the artist's imagination. All this ensures a continual audience and popularity far beyond the picture-book age.

C49   SCHREIBER, GEORGES. Bambino, the Clown. New York: Viking,
       1947 (OP), 32 pp.   25 illus.:   color-25/illustrated end-
       papers and title page/watercolor, pen and ink/25.2cm x
       19.2cm
       Fiction   Gr. K-2

Being of small stature and a native of Italy, Bambino, Italian for child, makes his home in a stereotypical town, presumably of the United States, complete with Main Street and General Store.

1948

Here Bambino's occupation as a professional clown makes him a
favorite with the children of the town. One day he reveals the
secrets of his trade to a small, unhappy child who has had his
hat carried off by the wind. Bambino attempts to cheer the boy,
Peter, by presenting him with a new hat, as well as by introduc-
ing him to Flapper, Bambino's pet seal.

Peter's behind-the-scene introduction to this profession does
not end here: he is privilege and audience to the actual process
of Bambino's transformation from man to clown, as the entertainer
readies for a performance for the children of the town. Bambino's
comical routines with instruments and Flapper and a dangerous feat
of balance enthrall the audience and once again help accomplish
the simple goal of Bambino, the Clown: "To laugh and make everybody happy."

Schreiber accompanies his text with illustrations of watercolor
and pen and ink, using the contrast of sharp, expressive black
lines to give form to the shapes and areas of watercolor wash.
The predominantly blue and red illustrations, often appearing to
have been done on wet paper, a technique common to the watercolor
process, are as expressive and vibrant as Bambino's personality
and occupation. When the text dominates a page, the margins are
employed or the illustrations are woven in and around the text.

The text, in this instance, is the major drawback of the work
in that the abundance of extraneous detail and information leave
little to the imagination and little for the illustrations to extend. Only the full-page spread of Bambino's final balancing act
expands upon the pages without being directly verbalized in the
text.

It is unfortunate that Schreiber's artistic talent is over-
shadowed by the explicitness of the text, for his illustrations
alone are vibrant, expressive, and full of movement. The written
work weights down, numbs, the impact of the visual images of the
artist's skillful talents.

C50   DAVIS, LAVINIA RIKER. <u>Roger and the Fox</u>. Illustrated by
         Hildegard Woodward. Garden City, N.Y.: Doubleday, 1947
         (OP), [48 pp.] 37 illus.: color-37/illustrated endpapers
         and title page/wash and 2-color separation/20.3cm x 25.2cm
         Fiction   Gr. K-2

When Roger receives a pair of skis for his seventh birthday,
he is armed with the best device available for quietly spying on
an elusive fox down by the river. His earlier attempts in the
fall, thwarted by a noisy companion of a dog, cawing crows, and
rustling leaves, are put behind him as he tackles the problem
with his new gift and a fresh blanket of snow. But this young
"city boy," displaced in the countryside of Connecticut, finally
succeeds in spying the fox; even more surprising to Roger is his
discovery of not one fox, but two.

The color illustrations of Hildegard Woodward, creator of a 1950 Caldecott Honor Book (C59), appear to be black and white watercolor paintings with blue and rust overlays. Woodward's depiction of Lavinia Davis's text is dominated by the light and dark areas of these washes, with form and detail given by quick, descriptive lines that define the shapes. The woodland scenes are full of peering forest animals, which are capable of catching the eye of the discerning child and help remind the audience of the pressure Roger feels to complete his task.

Davis's text, a body much longer than that of most picture books, is aided by Woodward's drawings, but its ending seems abrupt, incomplete, and the transition from fall to winter in the middle of the story, via Roger's illness and convalescence, seems an unnecessary elaboration which could have been handled in a few words. But the theme of the text and that universal struggle between the world of the young and the adult, makes this book relevant to the picture-book audience.

The reproduction of Woodward's illustrations, however, reflects an awkwardness in the use of colors, hues which often do not seem to be an integral part of the picture. This appearance of laid-on, superficial color is distracting, and some pages would be more effective without this imposition. Woodward's illustrations help bring Roger's struggle to life, and were more attention given to the technical aspects of their reproduction, the subtle grace of the illustrations might be better appreciated.

C51   MALCOLMSON, ANNE. <u>Song of Robin Hood</u>. Illustrated by
        Virginia Lee Burton. Boston: Houghton Mifflin, 1947 (OP),
        123 pp. 107 illus.: black and white—107/illustrated front
        matter, title page, preface, and glossary/pen and india ink
        and scratchboard/27.6cm x 22.2cm
        Epic   Gr. 2 up

Anne Malcolmson has collected eighteen songs that portray the original concept of Robin Hood which prevailed in the 13th and 14th centuries. The ballads included demonstrate Robin Hood's reputation as a symbol of middle-class England and not the romanticized eighteenth-century image of the nobleman of the forest. In her Preface, Malcolmson makes note of the importance of including the airs to the collected ballads as a reminder of the true mode of transmission of the epic of Robin Hood. Grace Castagnetta is responsible for arranging the airs, which help convey the oral tradition so integral to the concept of Robin Hood.

Virginia Lee Burton's illustrations are also integral to the concept of this book, which was awarded Honor Book status, even though its function is hardly that of a picture book. Burton approaches the artistic handling of this book as she has any other work--with the strong conviction that word and picture be

1948

closely integrated. She accomplishes just that and more, for
the intricate, meticulous artwork is a visual statement of her
philosophy.

The delicate design of the pages and artwork were done pur-
posely, in order to prevent an overpowering of the reduced type
necessitated by the inclusion of so many verses. Each verse,
sometimes as many as forty-seven in "Robin Hood and the Prince
of Aragon," has an individual illustration woven into the tapestry of the carefully planned compositions, whose formats are
reminiscent of medieval manuscripts.

Even the glossary presents a unity of word and picture, as the
artist has woven the letters into the design of the page, as well
as incorporated miniature depictions of the definitions into the
illustrations. Though the techniques and effects of scratchboard,
pen, and ink create a very different visual image from those of
Burton's other works, the same careful compositions that encircle,
envelop, and create the security of The Little House (C21) are
evident here.

In her explanation of the handling of the Song of Robin Hood,
Burton's dedication to her craft is evident. The detailed illustrations, that entwine the words of the ballads and prevent the
reader's attention from wandering from the words, are no accident.
Her own words describe the reasoning behind every illustration,
even down to a list of flora and fauna contained in the illustrations of each ballad. This work is truly an integration of visual
and written communication and has, unfortunately, gone largely
unnoticed. Burton's philosophy regarding her illustrations is a
treasure trove and should be an enlightenment and lesson to those
interested in the art of illustration in children's books.

1949

C52   HADER, BERTA AND HADER, ELMER. The Big Snow. New York:
       Macmillan, 1948, [48 pp.] 43 illus.: black and white-28;
       color-15/illustrated endpapers, front matter, title page,
       and dedication/full-color watercolor and pencil and wash/
       25.2cm x 21.6cm
       Fiction   Gr. Ps-1

The rainbow around the moon on Christmas Eve meant snow was
coming--BIG snow--and the effects this snow has on the animal
kingdom is the subject of Berta and Elmer Hader's 1949 Medal Book.
From deer and pheasant to sparrows and field mice, nature's residents cope with the loss of their food supply with the help of a
benevolent couple who sets out seeds and nuts and bread crumbs,
until the arrival of spring.

The Haders' work offers an interesting contrast to the 1948
Medal Book, which deals with how the human element copes with the

snow until spring arrives. The books offer complementary perspectives, the human and the animal viewpoints, while both demonstrate the eternal struggle of man and animal against nature.

The Haders' skill in utilizing watercolor makes the full-color
illustrations well-controlled studies of their natural subjects.
The black and white illustrations of pencil, charcoal, and wash,
though, offer more interesting compositions and detail, which are
often not present in the full-color medium. Although humans appear in only two of the illustrations in the body of the text,
their presence is a reminder of the interdependence of the
universe.

The authors have created a story with a theme whose universality goes a step beyond that of their 1940 Honor Book, Cock-a-
doodle-Doo (C11). Finding one's place in the scheme of the
universe, being part of a greater scheme, comes across more
clearly in this Medal Book, as it well demonstrates the cooperative aspects of life, animal and human alike.

C53   McCLOSKEY, ROBERT. Blueberries for Sal. New York: Viking,
          1948, 56 pp.   50 illus.: navy blue and white-50/illus-
          trated endpapers and title page/lithograph/21.4cm x 27.8cm
          Fiction   Gr. Ps-1

When Little Sal wanders off from her Mother on a berry-picking
expedition to Blueberry Hill, she temporarily finds herself a
surrogate Mother to follow around--a Mother bear. On the opposite side of the hill, Little Bear tags along behind Sal's Mother,
until she discovers the mix-up and sets out to track down her
daughter. When both parents recover their respective charges,
they all head toward their homes, Little Bear and Mother full
of berries for their winter hibernation and Little Sal and her
Mother toting berries to put up for consumption during the
approaching winter.

Robert McCloskey's sure and confident hand brings the inquisi-
tive innocence of childhood to his pictures, all of which are
done in navy "blueberry" and white. Clean, sharp lines against
white create contrasts both subtle and dramatic. Areas of solid
color juxtaposed with areas of stark white and hatched, shaded
areas provide definite, bold patterns that move the eye across
the page and right onto the next. The sharply hatched areas and
the modeling of darks and lights soften with distance, which
serves to accentuate the value patterns.

McCloskey taps, with sentimental innocence, the sometimes
frightening independence of childhood and parallels Little Sal
and Little Bear in a tightly constructed, simple tale. Wandering
off from a parent is not an uncommon experience, for bear or
child.

1949

C54 McGINLEY, PHYLLIS. <u>All Around Town</u>. Illustrated by Helen
      Stone. New York: J. B. Lippincott, 1948 (OP), [64 pp.] 55
      illus.: color-28; black and white-27/illustrated title
      page and front matter/wash and 3-color separation with
      black/24.4cm x 19cm
      Alphabet Book   Gr. Ps-1
       An alphabet book full of sights and objects familiar to a
child living in the city, illustrated by Helen Stone, is one of
the Caldecott Honor Books for 1949. From airplane and kindergarten to subway and zoo, the rhyming text and red, blue, and
yellow illustrations whisk the reader along on a whirlwind tour
of city sights.
       The reproduction of Stone's illustrations does not do justice
to her expressionistic brush strokes, the effectiveness of which
is lessened by having the colors laid on over the black and white
pictures. The result is a garish appearance that does little to
attract the eye of the audience and in fact almost discourages
interaction.
       The elements of the text by Phyllis McGinley were no doubt of
interest and of common experience upon the book's publication,
but these elements now provide a base of experience common to a
limited audience. Good-Humor men, organ grinders, and vendors
are no longer as common as before but were once, no doubt, symbols of life in the city.
       The atmosphere of city life, its hustle and bustle, is condu-
cive to Stone's expressive, flowing lines, which swirl the merry-
go-round in circles and the ice skaters in figure eights. But it
is in the black and white illustrations that the artist's ability
is most fully recognized and appreciated.

C55 POLITI, LEO. <u>Juanita</u>. New York: Charles Scribner's Sons,
      1948 (OP), [32 pp.] 30 illus.: color-14; red, black, and
      white-14; black and white-2/illustrated title page/water-
      color with white paint (opaque)/25.4cm x 20.5cm
      Fiction   Gr. Ps-1
       <u>Juanita</u>, like Politi's Honor Book of 1947, takes place on
Olvera Street in Los Angeles and deals with traditional Mexican
custom and ceremony. The blessing of the Animals on Easter eve
and the customs associated with birthday celebrations are the
events which surround the main character, four-year-old Juanita,
daughter of Antonio and Maria Gonzales. Juanita's birthday gift,
a white dove, provides her with a pet that she can carry in the
Procession to the Church, where the padre blesses the animals and
pets belonging to the street's young inhabitants.
       The text incorporates many Spanish words and expressions, most
of which are followed by the English translation, in contrast to
<u>Pedro, the Angel of Olvera Street</u> (C44), in which Spanish words
are parenthetically defined. <u>Juanita</u>, too, includes songs

278

traditional to the events and ceremony--"Las Mañanitas," a birthday song; "La Paloma," the dove song; and "Duérmete, niña," a
Spanish lullaby, with which Juanita's mother sings her to sleep
on Easter eve.

Politi's illustrations, similar in style to those of Pedro,
reflect the simplicity and reverence that accompany the ceremonies of the story. The predominating reds, blues, and greens of
the illustrations, with figures and shapes outlined in black, reflect an atmosphere of the Mexican neighborhood and its inhabitants in their simplification of art forms. At times almost to
the point of abstraction, the illustrations convey the importance
of the events in a minimum of line, whether it be in the adobe-
like buildings--puestas, churches, plazas--or in the stylization
of natural shapes and forms--trees, flowers, animals. The two
pages with black and white illustrations demonstrate Politi's
style most effectively, as careful placement of lights and darks
creates a contrast and atmosphere of serenity and calm in a minimum of detail, in contrast to the excitement of the day.

Politi's text and illustrations portray a picture of Mexican
custom that may not be as prevalent today, but he does give the
reader a glimpse of a culture with deep roots, one that delights
in the joys of a simple existence.

C56   WIESE, KURT. Fish in the Air. New York: Viking, 1948 (OP),
      [36 pp.] 28 illus.: color-28/illustrated endpapers and
      title page/pen and ink and color separation/20.9cm x 25.5cm
      Fantasy   Gr. K-2

When a Chinese boy named Fish asks his father, Honorable Fish,
for the largest fish-shaped kite he can buy, the child learns a
lesson as a gust of wind carries him off into the air. Were it
not for a fish hawk, who attacks the kite, Fish might be up there
still; instead he ends up dripping wet after a quick descent and
rescue in Old Man Li's fishing net--a soggy "catch" that costs
Big Fish a silver dollar.

Wiese's authenticity in illustration is evident in every nook
and cranny of his predominantly violet, blue, and yellow pictures.
From furniture to Chinese festivals and customs, Wiese saturates
his colorful illustrations with Chinese detail. Large areas of
flat color, detailed with expressive black lines reminiscent of
Chinese calligraphic strokes, reflect the Chinese setting and the
moralistic and humorous ending of the tale: Boy who grows greedy
may end up all wet.

Wiese reassures the audience that Little Fish has learned a
lesson; obvious as it may seem, on the surface, the meaning runs
deeper than this overt, simple statement: "Honorable Fish, I want
you to buy me the smallest Fish Kite there is." Though the author
allows the adventure to focus on the humor of the story--"stepping
to the nose of the grouchy letter writer" and leaping to "the

snout of the fierce dragon" on a roof-top--a more serious message is communicated.

Wiese falls into the group of author-illustrators who help expand the horizon of the American picture book, as did Thomas Handforth, Leo Politi, and others, and provides the audience with a large amount of cultural information that is integrated into a story that children can enjoy and from which they can learn.

1950

C57   POLITI, LEO. Song of the Swallows. New York: Charles Scribner's Sons, 1949, [32 pp.] 29 illus.: color-29/ illustrated front matter and title page/watercolor with white paint (opaque)/25.3cm x 20.5cm

Fiction   Gr. Ps-1

On St. Joseph's Day, the swallows return to the Mission Church at Capistrano and signal the beginning of spring. Julian, keeper of the Mission, spends many hours telling Juan of the swallows and tending to the Mission garden, to which the swallows and their song return year after year. Juan's admiration for the birds prompts him to build a garden in front of his house after the swallows leave for the winter.

As winter passes, Juan looks forward to the swallows' return, and after their late arrival on St. Joseph's Day, the birds again fill the garden with their song and beauty. Juan rushes home to find his labors rewarded as a pair of swallows settle into his very own garden.

Politi's simple illustrations, mostly done in grays and pinks, reflect the simplicity and honesty of the art of the culture that Song of the Swallows presents. Politi's undetailed shapes take form through tonal and color changes and exhibit many of the same motifs found in Pedro, the Angel of Olvera Street (C44, 1947) and Juanita (C55, 1949), earlier Caldecott Honor Books. Swallows, too, contains the songs sung in the story, one titled "La Golondrina," the other untitled. Spanish words, as well, are incorporated into the text rather than separated by parentheses, as in the earlier books.

Politi's use of color is more vivid in this Medal Book than in his Honor Books, but the style is so similar in all three that it becomes monotonous when all are viewed in relation to one another. Politi's concentration on similar cultural motifs draws attention to the customs of the Spanish population, but his unchanging style makes this work less effective, a seeming replication of illustration with new text.

C58   HOLBROOK, STEWART. America's Ethan Allen. Illustrated by
       Lynd Ward. Boston: Houghton Mifflin, 1949, 96 pp. 94
       illus.: black and white-71; color-23/illustrated title
       page/watercolor and wash/22.5cm x 16.6cm
       Biography   Gr. 1-3
    1737 was the year in which Ethan Allen was born in Litchfield,
Connecticut. After the death of Ethan's father, which forces the
boy to sacrifice an education in order to care for his family,
Allen takes this responsibility upon himself. Eventually, though,
he turns the family farm over to his brothers so that he can join
the militia to fight against the French. This is his first taste
of war, but not his last.
    After selling the family iron-ore business, Allen moves to the
Green Mountains of New Hampshire. When he is forced to fight for
the New Hampshire land grants that had also been sold in New York
to different people, his reputation is established as the rebel-
lious and defiant leader of the Green Mountain Boys. Allen and
his men are called upon to capture Fort Ticonderoga from the
British, and this courage and devotion to the American cause
follow Allen throughout his life until his death in 1789, in the
state of Vermont.
    The heroism and bravery of Ethan Allen, early American patriot,
are easily conveyed by the bold, sure style of Lynd Ward. His
black and white and color illustrations depict the hardworking,
devoted temper of the times when, and where, Allen lived. Although the book is dominated by text, with little physical integration of word and picture, Ward's style of high art, in the
tradition of earlier illustrators such as N. C. Wyeth, indicates
a sense of the illustrations having once been full-sized paintings.
Even the partial black and white illustrations in the margins,
cropped and placed next to their specific references in the text,
appear to belong to larger compositions.
    The idealized Allen becomes a bit more believable through
Ward's illustration, and though the life of this patriot seems
glamorous at times, the illustrations give an inkling of just
how much stamina and courage the wilderness demanded. Allen is
perhaps a hero simply because he survived as long as he did.

C59   DAVIS, LAVINIA. The Wild Birthday Cake. Illustrated by
       Hildegard Woodward. Garden City, N.Y.: Doubleday, 1949
       (OP), [52 pp.] 44 illus.: color-44/illustrated endpapers
       and title page/color separation/19.6cm x 24.9cm
       Fiction   Gr. K-1
    Johnny departs from Broomstick Hill for a day of adventure and
is intent upon this purpose until the Professor reminds the boy
that he must come and help the Professor celebrate his birthday.
Since Johnny has no present for his good friend, his day of adventure turns into a mission to secure an appropriate gift. When

1950

Johnny ends up at Penton's Pond, he discovers an injured wild
duck and decides to take it home, unaware that this will eventually be the present for his friend. Coincidentally, Professor
receives three baby Mallards as a gift, and they need nothing
more than a mother duck to make them feel at home in the Professor's pond. When Johnny retrieves the duck from home and presents
her to the Professor, they both celebrate the perfect gift with a
cake and bestow an appropriate name upon the waterfowl--Birthday
Cake.

The Wild Birthday Cake, as did Roger and the Fox (C50, 1948),
an earlier Caldecott Honor Book, concentrates on the world of
nature--trees, ponds, and the creatures therein. Woodward's
skill in portraying the animals of the story and their habitats
cannot go unnoticed, but the yellow, green, and brown illustrations are not sufficient to overcome the heaviness and abundance
of the text they accompany. The illustrations' effectiveness
would have been better served were the yellow and green hues
eliminated from the drawings, leaving the soft, modeled figures
and backgrounds of brown. As in Roger and the Fox, the color
seems superfluous, and this particular combination of hues seems
odd.

An overabundance of text and detail, accompanied by illustrations that do not mesh with the text, results in a book that
seems disjointed, not integrated in a unity which makes for lasting quality and continued popularity.

C60   KRAUSS, RUTH. The Happy Day. Illustrated by Marc Simont.
       New York: Harper, 1949, [36 pp.] 28 illus.: black and
       white-27; color-1/illustrated front matter and title page/
       pencil in color separation/29.6cm x 21.6cm
       Fantasy   Gr. Ps-1

When something unusual arouses the sleeping mice, bears,
snails, squirrels, and ground hogs, they all sniff about to
determine what is different. Running from their trees, lairs,
and burrows, the inhabitants of the woodland come out of hibernation to discover and celebrate the blooming of a lone yellow
flower, pushing its way up from under a layer of soft white snow.
What a happy day for them; spring is finally near.

The simple sentences of Ruth Kraus's story offer an interesting contrast to the rich black and white illustrations of
Marc Simont. The soft grays and subtle value changes and modeling give shape to the animal forms of the story and create a
harmonious relationship between the creatures and their habitat.
Sturdy, protective trees rise out of a snow-covered ground; the
blending of the pencil and the smudging of lines soften the contrast of the values of lights, darks, and grays.

A few fuzzy lines contribute the details of paws, faces, and
shapes in the full-page spreads, and the only spot of color remains the blooming yellow flower at the end of the book. Simont's

compositions are dramatic in their range of value, but the soft-
ening of line and shape avoids the harshness that could develop
in strictly black and white illustrations.

The white of the falling snow, dots sprinkling over the compositions, is nearly the only pure white that appears on the
pages, and this absence of value creates miniature areas of
great contrast without detracting from or competing with the
whole composition. Simont gives sustenance to a simple text
and demonstrates the power the visual elements of a picture book
can wield in the hands of a skilled artist.

C61   GEISEL, THEODORE SEUSS [Dr. Seuss]. <u>Bartholomew and the</u>
       <u>Oobleck</u>. New York: Random House, 1949, [50 pp.]   45
       illus.: color-34; black and white-11/illustrated endpapers
       and title page/pen and ink and color separation/27.7cm x
       20.2cm
       Fantasy: folklike tale   Gr. K-2
When King Derwin, of the Kingdom of Didd, summons his royal
magicians and orders them to conjure up something new to fall
from the sky, he did not have in mind what he got--oobleck--
green, gooey, gluey oobleck. When the small globs of oobleck
begin to fall over the kingdom of Didd, no one knows what a
nuisance it will become--no one but Bartholomew Cubbins, the
court page. It is Bartholomew who finally stops the deluge of
green globs, which grow larger and larger every minute.

When Bartholomew discovers King Derwin sitting in all his
majesty on his throne--stuck fast in green oobleck--he prods the
King into admitting his haughty desire and apologizing for wanting anything so unusual as oobleck to fall from the sky. As the
King speaks these simple words, the goo begins to disappear,
until the Kingdom of Didd is free of green gloop.

Though more text is included in this tale than is customary
of Seuss's style, the illustrations remain characteristic. More
and more green is added to the black and white illustrations as
the oobleck continues to fall throughout the story, and Seuss's
expressive illustrations transform the imaginary tale into a
setting convincingly appropriate. The movement in the illustrations, within pages and across pages, keeps up with the pace of
the story, and the careful placement of green oobleck helps the
eye travel in a path as hectic as Bartholomew's wild attempts to
warn the people of the Kingdom of the oobleck's arrival.

Seuss's style of art and prose, unique and original as it is,
undoubtedly accounts for the wide appeal his work holds. The
silly, unimaginable events momentarily become real at his hand
and even possess a touch of moralism to balance the frivolity
of the story.

1950

C62   BROWN, MARCIA. Henry Fisherman. New York: Charles
         Scribner's Sons, 1949, [32 pp.] 17 illus.: color-9;
         blue, red, and white-8/illustrated title page/color
         separation/19.6cm x 25cm
         Fiction   Gr. K-2
      On St. Thomas Island in the Caribbean lives young Henry, who
only wants to be a fisherman like his father. But Henry, not
yet old enough to help out on the Ariadne, has other tasks with
which to occupy his days. Fetching water by the harbor, washing
clothes, marketing with his mother, tending the goats, or getting
coconuts for pudding keep Henry's days full of a variety of activities, though he never stops yearning to go to sea with his
father.
      When Henry's father finally decides his son is old enough to
help out on the Ariadne, the boy gets the chance to prove his
abilities. While unhooking a fishpot, Henry is surprised by a
shark but manages to outswim the creature and return safely to
the surface. With a boat full of fish, Henry and his father return
to shore, where the novice fisherman announces their good fortune by blowing on a conch shell.
      Native dialect, interspersed throughout the text, lends au-
thenticity to the pages of the story, as do the illustrations,
which reflect the primitive and native setting of the tale.
Coral, turquoise, brown, dark blue, and yellow create clean,
stylized shapes, often abstract in appearance.
      On alternating pages, dark blue, white, and red illustrations
provide a contrast to the color pages. Shapes appear in solid
forms, with little detail needed to explain or interpret the figures. Simplicity of life on the island is recreated in a visual
experience that presents a culture and lifestyle in which the
sea is the dominant force. Though the text is weak in its climax, man's interaction with nature and this ever-tenuous relationship remains the dominant theme in word and illustration alike.

                                 1951

C63   MILHOUS, KATHERINE. The Egg Tree. New York: Charles
         Scribner's Sons, 1950, [32 pp.] 29 illus.: color-24;
         black and white-5/illustrated front matter and title
         page/tempera/24.2cm x 19.4cm
         Fiction   Gr. Ps-1
      On Easter morning Katy and Carl can hardly wait for the egg
hunt to begin, but Katy does not find any eggs until she discovers a hat full of six hand-painted eggs that her Grandmom had
made years ago. Katy, Carl, and their cousins are so taken with
the traditional designs of the eggs that they beg Grandmom to
show them how to paint and decorate the fragile shells.

The next day a tradition begins--painting the eggs and hanging them on a small tree, the children resolve to decorate a
larger tree the following year. With hundreds of eggs hanging
from its branches, the tree becomes an annual attraction and is
visited by people from far and wide, who bear presents and toys.
Katy's discovery has materialized into a tradition that is enjoyed and appreciated by her family and others as well.

An appreciation for the culture of the characters in this
Pennsylvania Dutch-based story is visible in the illustrations,
as well as in the text. The flat, simple designs of the folk
art of the Pennsylvania Dutch are evident in the soft pink and
gray border designs and in the bold, simple shapes of the figures in their traditional attire. The bright yellows, reds, and
blues of the color illustrations are reminiscent of the vivid
hex symbols often seen painted on barns in Pennsylvania
communities.

The text and illustrations in this 1951 Medal Book are simple,
honest, and unembellished, a reflection of the culture; word and
picture seem in harmony with one another and remain a record of
tradition and art, simplified yet meaningful.

C64   BROWN, MARCIA. Dick Whittington and His Cat. New York:
       Charles Scribner's Sons, 1950, [32 pp.] 29 illus.:
       black, white, and ochre-29/illustrated title page and
       dedication/linoleum cuts/24.5cm x 19.1cm
       Folk Tale   Gr. 1-3
Dick is a poor orphan in England who goes to London to find
wealth and happiness, but nearly starves to death instead. He
is taken in by a local merchant, Mr. Fitzwarren, and is expected
to help the cook with her work. Living conditions are so horrid
that Dick has to spend his only penny to buy a cat to kill the
mice and rats in his garret room.

The day comes when one of Mr. Fitzwarren's ships sails, and
all the servants have a chance to contribute an item to be traded
abroad. Dick's cat, his only possession, becomes his contribution. Eventually the cat ends up on the Barbary Coast, ridding
the king's court of its pesty rats and mice, and the king rewards
the captain with rubies and diamonds. On the ship's return Dick
is a wealthy man, now worthy of marrying Mr. Fitzwarren's daughter, Alice. And, because Dick is so well liked and famous, he
becomes the Lord Mayor of London--his dream comes true, with the
help of a rat-chasing cat.

Marcia Brown's linoleum cuts, in black, white, and ochre, produce illustrations of prominently contrasting light and dark patterns. The outlines and textures create movement and vitality in
the illustrations, even though there is not much detail present.
The stylized and decorative designs capture the setting and mood
of the tale, as the patterns of the courtly palace floors and

the fabrics of the garments of the wealthy repeat the motifs
throughout.

The artist's medium is well suited to the setting of the tale,
lends a medieval flair to the proceedings, and demonstrates the
importance of choosing a visual means of expressing a text that
is compatible and conveys the desired message.

C65   LIPKIND, WILLIAM [Will]. The Two Reds. Illustrated by
        Nicolas Mordvinoff [Nicolas]. New York: Harcourt, 1950,
        [54 pp.] 44 illus.: color-44/illustrated endpapers and
        title page/acetate color separation for line reproduction/
        27.4cm x 21.2cm
        Fantasy   Gr. Ps-1
Red, a boy with blaze-colored hair, and Red, a rusty-colored
cat, find it difficult to be friends since Red, the cat, is so
fond of fish and Red, the boy, is afraid his goldfish might fall
into the paws of the hungry feline. One morning, though, the
two Reds' paths do cross, and the confrontation is an unavoidable
one.

Red, the boy, happens upon the initiation proceedings of a
neighborhood club, the Seventh Street Signal Senders. A chase
ensues for the "spy" who has witnessed the secret ceremony, and
Red takes flight over a nearby fence. Meanwhile another chase
is in progress, this one involving Red, the cat, who has just
snitched a tasty morsel from the fisherman. Both chases soon
come to a climax as both groups meet head on at a street corner--
the Signal Senders and the fisherman end up in a heap; Red and
Red escape to a nearby doorstep. With a handshake, they become
official friends, complete with a guarantee that goldfish are
off limits.

The expressive use of color in the red, yellow, and charcoal-
gray illustrations of The Two Reds helps guide the eye around and
across the pages, as do the lines of the simple drawings. The
figures and shapes often appear flat, dimensionless, with only
an occasional line or the addition of color lending some depth
to the objects.

As in the following year's Medal Book, Finders Keepers (C69),
by the same author and artist, the illustrations alternate--in
The Two Reds, yellow, red, black, and white illustrations alternate with red, black, and white drawings. Mordvinoff's unusual
style is almost childlike in its simplicity and may hold appeal
for children who can recognize and identify with this similarity.

C66   GEISEL, THEODORE SEUSS [Dr. Seuss]. If I Ran the Zoo. New
        York: Random House, 1950, [62 pp.] 44 illus.: color-44/
        illustrated endpapers and title page/pen, ink, brush, and
        color separation/27.8cm x 20.2cm
        Fantasy   Gr. Ps-1

The imagination of young Gerald M. McGrew grows and grows, as does the menagerie of animals, when the young boy pretends he runs the zoo. After freeing all the ordinary, mundane animals in the zoo, Gerald restocks the cages with the inventions of his own imagination. Not only does he capture the most outrageous animals of the imagination--a ten-footed lion, an elephant cat, a scraggle-footed Mulligatawny--but the places in and means by which he traps these unique species are just as inventive.

The Bad-Animal-Catching Machine helps protect the zookeeper from those dangerous and vicious inhabitants of the Jungles of Hippo-no-Hungus and the Desert of Zind. As is customary, Seuss's text demands the attention of the reader, for the words are an invention in and of themselves. The hyphenated words help produce such a rapid verbal pattern that it is often easy to wind up tongue-tied before the end of a page.

The rhythm of the twisting word patterns demands as much attention as do the red, yellow, blue, and black and white illustrations. If the text is outrageous, then Seuss's visual interpretation is equally so. The primary colors produce rapid, successive eye movements across and around the pages, and the use of black and white is just as integral to the illustrations as the color.

It is no surprise that Seuss's work remains so popular; he creates worlds where the impossible becomes ordinary and the underdog, child or animal, is for a time in command--the hero.

C67   McGINLEY, PHYLLIS. The Most Wonderful Doll in the World. Illustrated by Helen Stone. Philadelphia: J. B. Lippincott, 1950 (OP), 64 pp. 48 illus.: color-22; black and white-26/illustrated front matter and title page/watercolor wash and 3-color separation/19.7cm x 13cm
Fiction   Gr. 1-2

Dulcy is always wishing that everything were a little better or more unusual or more beautiful, especially when it comes to her collection of dolls. So when she loses an old doll and box of clothes given to her by an elderly neighbor, she has the perfect opportunity to fantasize and elaborate as much as she wants about poor lost Angela. The doll quickly accumulates a wardrobe beyond compare--patent-leather shoes with heels, tiny leather gloves, raincoat and umbrella. She can even walk by herself and wave her hand in the air. As Dulcy's imagination grows, so does Angela's wardrobe, but the young girl ostracizes her friends in the process and even grows dissatisfied with the rest of her collection.

In the spring, when Angela is uncovered in a pile of leaves, Dulcy is surprised to discover how plain and ordinary the doll really is. Dulcy's realization of her imaginary exaggerations brings her one step closer to growing up, for now she is aware of the difference between wishful thinking and reality.

1951

McGinley's text, more appropriate for Newbery than Caldecott recognition, dominates this Honor Book, and Helen Stone's illustrations are relegated a secondary role. Though the illustrations vary between black and white drawings, full-color watercolors, and black and white illustrations with up to three-color overlays, they do not seem an integral part of the book.

Dealing with a text of this length makes a balance between word and picture more difficult to attain. Full-page spreads of solid text, with only a decorative border, cornered with floral patterns, or illustrations scattered among the words of the story, create the impression often found in Newbery Medal Books, which contain illustrations that do little more than mirror the words of the text rather than visually embellish and reinforce. In a year that recorded few Honor Books for the Caldecott Award, it is an enigma as to why this text is even included within the realm of possibilities. The style is neither distinctive nor distinguished, and the book's popularity, if this be the reason for its initial consideration, has not withstood the years and remains an indication of the difficult decisions which govern the selection process.

C68   NEWBERRY, CLARE TURLAY. <u>T-Bone, the Baby-Sitter</u>. New York:
      Harper & Brothers, 1950 (OP), 36 pp. 21 illus.: black,
      white, and pink-21/illustrated endpapers, title page, and
      dedication/charcoal and color separation/17.1cm x 23.8cm
      Fiction   Gr. Ps-1

When T-Bone, the Pinnys' black and white cat, wakes up feeling full of mischief one day, Mrs. Pinny not only loses her best pink feather hat but also her babysitter. After T-Bone is quickly shipped off to the country with Aunt Mabel, Mrs. Pinny soon discovers how helpful the cat has been. With no one to entertain her daughter, Mrs. Pinny gets less and less accomplished each day, and eventually she even runs out of time to fix dinner.

T-Bone, meanwhile, cannot appreciate being chased by a rooster all day when he was far more accustomed to sitting in a playpen with the baby, and the cat is more than delighted when Mr. Pinny drives to the country to retrieve him. So T-Bone is welcomed home with a bear hug from the baby, a scrumptious lunch, and the baby's first word: kitty.

The sentimentality of Newberry's stories is evident here as it has been in her numerous Caldecott Honor Books, and her habit of playing on the emotions of animal lovers still persists. The black, white, and rose-pink illustrations in this book, however, come nearer to being better-structured compositions than her previous work. The addition of foreground and background objects takes the illustrations a step further in that they all no longer appear to be merely sketchbook studies of the characters at hand.

The charcoal renderings with a touch of pink added here and there on every illustrated page are evidence of Newberry's skill in portraying cats, but the most effective works are those that begin to depict the actions of the story--the events that make it all happen--not just the still poses of a family pet.

1952

C69   LIPKIND, WILLIAM [Will]. <u>Finders Keepers</u>. Illustrated by
      Nicolas Mordvinoff [Nicolas]. New York: Harcourt, 1951,
      [36 pp.] 28 illus.: color-28/illustrated endpapers, front
      matter, and title page/acetate color separations for line
      reproduction/27.5cm x 20.7cm
      Fantasy: folklike tale   Gr. Ps-1
When Nap and Winkle simultaneously uncover a bone buried in the barnyard, they seek advice on determining who should have possession of it. After unsatisfactory assistance with the problem from Mr. Haymaker, the farmer, and Mr. Tuftichin, the goat, the dogs decide to bury the bone and go looking for a mediator.
      Mr. Longshanks, a large dog, seemingly wants to help the two canines, but he needs to see the evidence to decide the question, so Nap and Winkle dig up the bone and are stunned to see the large dog pick it up and make for the gate. In a cooperative effort, the dogs wrestle Mr. Longshanks for the bone and come to the realization that they can both enjoy the bone--if they share.
      This obviously didactic tale, the 1952 Medal winner, possesses the elements of one of Aesop's Fables; the trek to find a moral-istic solution to a dilemma is a familiar one, but the illustra-tions of Nicolas Mordvinoff are very unusual. Large flat areas of color, red or ochre, and black lines and shapes present a visual impression of foreign flavor.
      Fine, minute detail is often missing from the illustrations, and the pictures often possess an abstract impression, a collage appearance. There is no modeling of shapes and forms; only line and shape are employed to indicate space and dimensionality.
      The unusual color scheme, the artist's technique, and the simplicity of the story present the reader with a unique and hauntingly unforgettable impression.

C70   ETS, MARIE HALL. <u>Mr. T.W. Anthony Woo: The Story of a Cat
      and a Dog and a Mouse</u>. New York: Viking, 1951 (OP),
      55 pp. 34 illus.: black and white-34/illustrated end-
      papers, front matter, and title page/paper batik/19.5cm x
      26.5cm
      Fantasy: folklike tale   Gr. Ps-1

1952

A 1952 Honor Book winner by Marie Hall Ets, whose full title reminds the reader this is The Story of a Cat and a Dog and a Mouse, Mr. T.W. Anthony Woo pits three natural enemies against an even deadlier adversary, Miss Dora, the sister of the cobbler of Shooshko. The cobbler and his pets, Meola, a cat, Rodigo, a dog, and Mr. T.W. Anthony Woo, a mouse, lead a rather competitive, but satisfactory, existence, until one rainy day when all the animals are left inside the shop alone.

As soon as the cobbler leaves for the city, Meola and Rodigo begin such a brawl that Miss Dora is notified of the disturbance and takes it upon herself to straighten the shop, put the animals outside where they belong, and move her belongings in so that her brother will have proper meals and a clean house. Since a clean house means no cats, dogs, or mice, the animals have to cooperate to conspire to drive Miss Dora, and her overzealous talking parrot, back to her own home. All it takes is a visit from T.W., who just happens to drop onto Miss Dora's neck while she is sleeping, and the cobbler and his pets once again enjoy the comfort of their own home--no more brawls, no more Miss Dora.

In a style that occasionally recalls the indistinct illustrations of In the Forest (C32), a 1945 Honor Book, Ets employs black and white illustrations, encased within rounded, rectangular shapes, to interpret the tale visually. The strong patterns of light and dark, of black and white, offer a bold presentation of this tale, which has a humorous twist that would undoubtedly amuse children who are lovers of pets of all kinds. At times, however, due to the length of the text, the illustrations are tiresome to look at and become hard and heavy, when sensitivity and levity seem more in demand.

C71   BROWN, MARCIA. Skipper John's Cook. New York: Charles
      Scribner's Sons, 1951 (OP), [36 pp.]   27 illus.: color-27/
      illustrated endpapers and title page/pen, ink, and color
      separation/25.2cm x 20.1cm
      Fiction   Gr. K-2

When Skipper John, captain of the Liberty Bell, tacks up a sign advertising for a cook on his ship, he is looking for someone who can cook a meal other than beans. So when Si applies for the job, he has his well-fed dog, George, with him as proof that he is indeed a good cook. George is proof enough to the skipper of Si's cooking ability, so the next morning the Liberty Bell sets sail with a new cook and his dog.

On their first day out, the men begin to smell the fish Si is cooking for George, and they are sure they will be content with the new chef, since all they'd ever had before was beans, beans, and beans. But now all the crew gets is fish, fish, fish, until Skipper John asks Si if he can cook anything else. For the rest of the trip, then, Si is happy to fix them something else--fish and beans, fish and beans, fish and beans. So upon the Liberty Bell's return to shore, Skipper John does not waste any time in putting up another sign--for a new cook.

Marcia Brown's red, blue, ochre, black, and white illustrations for this 1952 Honor Book seem a bit under par for her talents. The vitality so often present in her work is absent, and the colors do not work effectively enough to pull the book together. The compositions are filled with a variety of textures and techniques that fail to mesh together in any sort of harmony. Unfortunately, the book appears hastily done and does not represent the quality of which Brown is capable.

C72   ZION, GENE. All Falling Down. Illustrated by Margaret Bloy Graham. New York: Harper, 1951 (OP), [32 pp.] 26 illus.: color-26/illustrated title page and dedication/watercolor and wash/19.4cm x 27.1cm

        Information: science   Gr. Ps-1

Gene Zion's 1952 Honor Book is full of falling objects--petals, water, apples, leaves, nuts, snow, rain, shadows, night. Zion runs through a list of falling items familiar and common to most of the experiences of children but, in contrast, closes with one last object that does not fall--a young boy tossed gently in the air and caught by the hands of a loving father.

The full-page spreads, in soft hues of blue, green, red, and yellow, interpret the text by depicting experiences common to many young children, as well as their fascination with the effects gravity has on objects in their environment. Blocks falling from a teetering tower, sand castles washing out with the waves, snow drifting from a winter sky--Graham's illustrations offer a wide range of possible actions and behaviors surrounding the events, striving to make them relevant. On the seashore, some children build sand castles, another swims, and still another walks hand in hand with a parent. And with the final object, which does not fall to the ground but lands softly in Daddy's arms, the security and reassurance of these familiar events culminate the story.

The light, airy watercolors and wash, in which gray predominates, are soft and nonthreatening, and when night falls the warm glow of room interiors against the nocturnal darkness reinforce the idea of the security of home and family. With Zion's simple text, Graham has helped embellish and extend the words with her illustrations, and although the illustrations remain calm and serene, they also suffer from a monotony of value and lack of vitality so integral to the lives of children and the demands of their literature.

C73   Du BOIS, WILLIAM PÈNE. Bear Party. New York: Viking, 1951 (OP), 48 pp. 44 illus.: color-44/illustrated front matter, title page, and dedication/watercolor/20.2cm x 13.5cm

        Fantasy   Gr. Ps-2

1952

When the koala bears in Koala Park, Australia, become so angry that they just stare and make growling noises, the wise old bear decides something must be done to end this siege of silence. From high above the tallest eucalyptus tree, he proposes a costume ball as the solution--the bears will not recognize each other, will enjoy themselves, and will forget their differences.

All goes well until the bears remove their costumes at the end of the evening; then they cannot recognize each other at all, so to compromise, they continue to wear part of their costumes for identification. When they have had enough time to renew their friendships, the koalas eventually shed their partial costumes, and Koala Park once again returns to its days of happiness.

The variety of the compositions, the color, and the placement of illustrations in this Honor Book keep the story moving and interest high. Full-page spreads are juxtaposed with pages of nearly all text, these each sprinkled with the cuddly figures of du Bois's teddy bears.

The human characteristics that the bears possess--getting angry, dancing, making up--transform the characters and the story into a lesson in getting along with others. It is not surprising that the story would have great appeal to young children, as they can quickly identify with the feelings, actions, and reactions of the huggable creatures, not to mention their distinction of being the smallest of bears.

The colorful illustrations of the wild, uninhibited party and the following events contrast sharply with the almost stagnant illustrations that depict the terrible stalemate of the bears' earlier disagreements. As a koala sweeps up the remnants of the party on the final page, the story ends with the comfortable feeling that peace will reign in Koala Park for a long, long time.

C74 OLDS, ELIZABETH. <u>Feather Mountain</u>. Boston: Houghton Mifflin, 1951 (OP), 33 pp. 31 illus.: color-16; black and white-15/ illustrated endpapers, front matter, and title page/watercolor, wash, and color separation/21.7cm x 23.7cm
Fantasy: folklike tale   Gr. K-2

Long ago, when birds had no feathers, they asked the Great Spirit to give them plumage to cover their nakedness. On Feather Mountain, the Spirit tells them, they will find the trees of feathers they desired, so the turkey buzzard, a powerful and sensible bird, volunteers to make the long, cold journey.

Upon the buzzard's return, each species is able to obtain a suit of feathers appropriate to its habitat, and every year thereafter the birds grow a covering to protect and aid them in finding food, keeping warm, and hiding from their enemies.

This tale, explaining a phenomenon of nature, is accompanied by both black and white and color illustrations. The fifteen black and white illustrations work more effectively in handling and portraying the anatomies and actions of the birds. The quick, expressive lines of the black and white drawings, sometimes enhanced with areas of wash in varying values of gray, capture the essence of the animals more gracefully than do the color pages.

The spontaneity in these lines is overpowered by the haphazard use of color on sixteen of the book's pages, and the garishness of the hues detracts from the overall unity of the book. The content itself is reminiscent of those tales in Native American and African folklore that attempt to account for phenomena in the natural world, but the illustrations fall short of upholding a cultural tradition of such esteem and sensitivity.

1953

C75   WARD, LYND. The Biggest Bear. Boston: Houghton Mifflin, the Riverside Press, 1952, 85 pp. 43 illus.: sepia and white-43/illustrated title page/wash drawings in opaque sepia watercolor/25.6cm x 17.8cm
Fiction   Gr. Ps-2

Johnny Orchard is humiliated because his is the only barn never to have a bearskin tacked up to it; so he sets out to shoot the biggest bear he can find. And Johnny does come back with a bear--a bear cub, who eats the calves' and chickens' food, the neighbor's corn, ham, bacon, maple syrup, as well as apples, maple sugar, and pancakes.

It is evident that the bear, now very large from his copious diet, must return to the woods, so Johnny sets out, several times, to set the bear free. Each time, however, the creature returns to the farm, so Johnny is faced with the unpleasant task of shooting his bear. On the final walk to the woods, the creature bolts through the trees, dragging the boy with him, until they both end up in a trap set by men from the city zoo.

Such a fine specimen of a bear would well serve a zoo, so the boy's pet is toted to the zoo, where Johnny can visit him and feed him maple sugar whenever he wants.

Lynd Ward's black and white illustrations have won him the honor of the 1953 Caldecott Medal, and though he received recognition for his 1950 Honor Book, America's Ethan Allen (C58), this later work demonstrates his skill in picture book illustration at its best. Even though all the illustrations appear on the right-hand page, faced with text (with the exception of the first page), the format does not detract from the overall effectiveness of the book because the illustrations become the dominant and important focus. Ward's subtle words of humor find easy expression in his impressive style and careful compositions.

1953

Pathos flows from the illustrations when the friendship that develops between the lovable bear and his owner is jeopardized, the lumbering bear obediently following his owner, rifle over shoulder, to his death. The final solution of the story completes the unity of the text and illustrations, demonstrating the intimate relationship that can develop in picture and word, as well as between man and animal.

C76   PERRAULT, CHARLES. Puss in Boots. Translated and illustrated
       by Marcia Brown. New York: Charles Scribner's Sons, 1952
       (OP), [32 pp.] 28 illus.: color-28/illustrated front mat-
       ter and title page/crayon, pen, and ink/25.6cm x 20.4cm
       Folk Tale   Gr. K-2

Marcia Brown's free translation of Charles Perrault's Puss in Boots begins with the youngest of three sons inheriting only a cat from his father's meager estate. But this cat is to provide the young man with more than he ever could dream.

Dressed in a pair of boots, the clever feline makes a habit of trapping unsuspecting animals in his sack, carrying them off to the King, and pretending they came from his Master, the Marquis of Carabas. After the wily puss engineers a ride for his master with the King and his daughter in the royal carriage, he marches ahead and intimidates the local peasants into cooperating with his scheme.

After the cat tricks an ogre into transforming himself into a mouse, which the puss promptly consumes, the ogre's castle becomes that of the Marquis of Carabas. When the royal carriage arrives at the palace, the King is thoroughly impressed and hesitates not an instant to allow his daughter to marry the Marquis.

Marcia Brown's illustrations for this traditional French tale are lively and full of movement and color. Red, yellow, blue-gray, and green shapes are given definition by her quick, expressive lines that travel across page after page. The compositions are more controlled and cohesive than those of the earlier Skipper John's Cook (C71), a 1952 Honor Book; the confusion has lessened considerably, though the activity still remains.

Brown's looseness of style is perhaps a reaction to or deviation from the rigid and more controlled medium of linoleum cut, the technique of her 1951 Honor Book, Dick Whittington and His Cat (C64). Whatever her style, Marcia Brown's name remains synonymous with the quality inherent in her interpretations of the folk tales of traditional literature.

C77   McCLOSKEY, ROBERT. One Morning in Maine. New York: Viking,
       1952, 64 pp. 59 illus.: navy blue and white-59/illustrated
       title page/lithograph/50cm x 22cm
       Fiction   Gr. Ps-1

This morning is an important one because today Sal is going
across the bay to Buck's Harbor with her father and her sister,
Jane. It is also a memorable day because Sal loses her first
tooth while she is helping her father dig for clams for lunch.
Though she cannot find her tooth in the sand, Sal still makes
a secret wish on a gull's feather she finds on the beach.

Sal and her father return home to ready for their trip to
Buck's Harbor, but when the motor of their boat will not start,
the journey has to be made with oars. Once the outboard is re-
paired and the groceries safely packed, Sal unexpectedly gets
her wish--Mr. Condon scoops her up a big chocolate ice-cream
cone, and, of course, a vanilla one for little Jane.

Robert McCloskey's navy and white illustrations and sensitive
text reflect the familiarity the author/artist must have felt for
his subject. The everyday events of childhood and the routine of
a life spent near the water are both apparent in the illustration
of a father and daughter's interaction in this northeastern
environment.

The fuzzy, crayonlike illustrations, highlighted with and in
contrast to the sharp crisp lines used to accentuate or define a
shape, are of the style of Blueberries for Sal (C53), McCloskey's
1949 Honor Book. The same careful attention is given to the play
of lights and darks in each carefully arranged composition, and a
little distance gives the illustrations more definite patterns of
light and dark. It is McCloskey's own experiences, though, that
bring this story, its characters, and the illustrations to life.

C78   EICHENBERG, FRITZ. Ape in a Cape: An Alphabet of Odd Animals.
      New York: Harcourt, 1952, [32 pp.] 26 illus.: color-26/
      illustrated endpapers, half title, title page and dedica-
      tion/acetate color separations/27.5cm x 20.7cm
      Alphabet Book   Gr. Ps-1

The alphabet book, by Fritz Eichenberg, which won Honor Book
status in 1953, is full of animals that are not so odd in themselves but in the way in which the artist has portrayed them.
Many of the animals assume human characteristics and clothing to
advertise their respective letters of the alphabet.

The vulture, of letter "V", is depicted intently studying a
book so that he may assimilate some culture into his life, while
a mouse admires his blouse in a looking glass, for letter "M".
With the exception of "X" and "Z", each letter is represented by
an animal engaged in an activity and is accompanied by a short
rhyme.

Eichenberg's illustrations, full pages alternating the use of
red and blue and blue and ochre, and occasionally the colors produced by their combinations, are typical of many books of this
period, which have a limited range of hues. The work also bears
a stylistic resemblance to the first alphabet book to win a

1953

Caldecott Medal (<u>An American ABC</u> [C17]), Maud and Miska Petersham's 1942 Honor Book.
The popularity of <u>Ape in a Cape</u> most likely rests in its humorous approach to this common subject. The book utilizes the appeal of animals to stimulate the child's imagination and to
communicate its information.

C79   ZOLOTOW, CHARLOTTE.   <u>The Storm Book</u>.   Illustrated by Margaret
       Bloy Graham.   New York: Harper & Brothers, 1952 [32 pp.]
       14 illus.:   color-14/illustrated title page/pencil, black
       wash, and color separation in watercolor wash/18cm x 25.3cm
       Information: science   Gr. Ps-1
Charlotte Zolotow's 1953 Honor Book is a description of the
effects of a summer thunderstorm on a variety of settings.   The
contrast between the calm, before the storm darkens the country
sky, and the results of the meteorological event on the city,
seashore, mountains, and their inhabitants, are verbally and
visually felt.   With alternating full-page spreads of text and
illustration, this Zolotow-Graham production enables the reader
and/or listener to enjoy the verbal and visual effects through
this physical separation of word and drawings.   The water peaking
in waves at the seashore, the figures pressing against the pelt-
ing rain, and the rain lashing down on the mountainside depict
the effects of the water on each area's inhabitants.
The poetic flow of the text is interpreted in watercolor and
wash illustrations that depict the changes as they occur simultaneously in the different environments.   The sky darkens in the
country, in the city, in the mountains, and at sea, and after the
storm departs, a rainbow arcs over the countryside, where the
story began.   Graham's illustrations easily reflect the changing
events of the story, with the use of darker values and colors
during the storm and the use of light, airy hues before and after
the downpour.
Children should be quite interested in this natural phenomenon,
many even frightened by it.   The text is simple and straightforward and should provide some reassurance and proof that a
storm is a natural occurrence and the rainbow a welcomed, beautiful end to it all.

C80   KEPES, JULIET.   <u>Five Little Monkeys</u>.   Boston: Houghton
       Mifflin, 1952, 33 pp.   31 illus.:   color-15; black and
       white-16/illustrated endpapers, front matter, and title
       page/ink, watercolor, gouache, pen, and brush/24.6cm x
       21.5cm
       Fantasy   Gr. Ps-1
Buzzo, Binki, Bulu, Bibi, and Bali are notorious throughout
the jungle for playing tricks on any convenient target.   After
the five monkeys bombard Lion with coconuts, the other animals

1954

of the jungle conspire to lure the monkeys into a pit lined with bananas, with the intention of their being carted off to the zoo by hunters.

The trap is successful, but the animals are persuaded by Peccary, a wild pig, to help the monkeys out of the pit, under the condition that their mischief cease. The monkeys, surprisingly, keep their word and even come to the rescue of Peccary when Tiger the Terrible nearly consumes the wild prey. With the rescue, the animals, even Tiger, begin a peaceful cohabitation, free of practical jokes and the natural predatory dangers of the jungle.

The animals in this 1953 Honor Book appear as stylized, rather than realistic, representations, sometimes merely a contour drawing defining their shapes on the alternating spreads of color and black and white. The flow of line and the cohesiveness of composition are generally more effective in the black and white illustrations. On alternating pages the addition of color tends to add confusion rather than enhance the illustrations in which the primary colors predominate.

Children probably find the mischievous antics of the young monkeys humorous and their subsequent heroic acts redeeming, but the text seems unnecessarily lengthy in parts, sometimes slowing the pace of the story and its events.

1954

C81   BEMELMANS, LUDWIG. <u>Madeline's Rescue</u>. New York: Viking, 1953, 56 pp. 50 illus.: color-10; black, white, yellow-40/ illustrated endpapers and title page/brush, pen and ink, and watercolor/29.5cm x 21cm
         Fiction   Gr. Ps-1

The rescue of Madeline from the waters of a river in Paris sets the stage for the 1954 Medal Book by Ludwig Bemelmans. A quick-thinking dog becomes the pampered and beloved resident of a girls' school after she retrieves the soggy Madeline from certain death. Genevieve, the name bestowed upon the pet, leads a comfortable life until the annual trustees' inspection of the school on the first of May.

Lord Cucuface banishes Genevieve to the streets, and hours of searching cannot uncover her whereabouts. But late in the night, as is her habit, Miss Clavel senses something amiss and discovers a pathetic Genevieve sitting in the light of a street lamp. All settles down once again until a fight develops concerning in which bed Genevieve should sleep. The dilemma is soon settled, however, when the dog gives birth to puppies, enough for all to take one to bed.

1954

Bemelmans's rhyming text and expressive illustrations move the story of Madeline's Rescue along at a pace as feverish as that of the 1940 Honor Book Madeline (C12). In the style of Madeline, Bemelmans uses predominantly yellow, black, and white illustrations to represent his text. Ten full-color illustrations are interspersed throughout and, in Bemelmans's unique impressionistic style, help reflect the atmosphere of the French capital.

Although the story culminates in an event as similarly surprising as that of Madeline, this Medal Book and its creator receive the recognition which their creativity and originality are due.

C82   SAWYER, RUTH.   Journey Cake, Ho!   Illustrated by Robert
          McCloskey. New York: Viking, 1953, 45 pp.   40 illus.:
          blue, brown, white-40/illustrated front matter and title
          page/25.5cm x 19.6cm
          Folk Tale   Gr. K-2

Merry, Grumble, and Johnny live comfortably on Tip Top Mountain until the fox carries off the hens and sheep, the pig gets lost, and the cow breaks her leg. With hardly enough food for themselves, Merry and Grumble pack up Johnny's belongings and send him off to find a new home.

Johnny travels only halfway down Tip Top Mountain when the Journey Cake in his pack bounces out and rolls down the road. Yelling like the gingerbread man, the Journey Cake collects a procession behind him--a brindle cow, a white and black sheep, a spotted pig, red hens, and a gray donkey.

When the procession ends up back at Merry and Grumble's on Tip Top Mountain, the animals, tired from their chase, settle in, and Johnny does too. With the farm full of animals again, there is enough for everyone, and especially enough Journey Cakes, which Merry appropriately christens Johnny Cakes.

Robert McCloskey's brown and blue illustrations are full of the action and humor of Ruth Sawyer's words. The facial expressions of the characters reflect the simple pleasures of this American tale. The blue backgrounds give McCloskey the advantage of using white as if it were a color, and he utilizes it often in his characteristic patterning of light and dark in the compositions.

McCloskey demonstrates his flexibility of style and the suitability of his work to the text in this 1954 Honor Book, and his expressive, lively illustrations continue to uphold the dignity and excellence of children's book illustration, to which he began his Caldecott contributions with Make Way for Ducklings, in 1942.

C83   SCHLEIN, MIRIAM.   When Will the World Be Mine?   Illustrated
          by Jean Charlot. New York: W. R. Scott, 1953 (OP),
          [34 pp.] 31 illus.: color-31/illustrated endpapers and
          title page/opaque paint/24.3cm x 20.4cm

298

1954

Fantasy   Gr. Ps-1

A little snowshoe rabbit gradually discovers the world around
him, and once his ears have grown large enough, he begins to
understand what is important to his survival. The grass is
there for him to eat, the breeze to carry the scent of danger,
the thicket to hide in, the bark of trees to eat, and the stream
from which to drink.

When winter finally comes and snow covers the ground, Little
Snowshoe Rabbit learns the final lesson in survival before he
starts out on his own. He grows a coat of fur as white and pure
as the snow, and this is the last important discovery the young
hare makes; all his mother has taught him, coupled with his new
identity, enables him to hop out on his own into a world of nature with which he has learned to coexist.

The cooperation of the animals and nature in this 1954 Honor
Book is interpreted by Jean Charlot in forest green and rose
illustrations, with a text corresponding in hue to the rose of
the illustrations. The very stylized, simple illustrations
possess the abstract qualities of the illustrations in A Child's
Good Night Book (C28), a 1944 Honor Book, also illustrated by
Charlot.

The outlined shapes of the rabbits and the vegetation of their
environment are modeled with subtle value changes, produced by
the strokes of the artist's medium upon the paper. The illustrations, working around the text, which is set off in well-defined
white blocks of space, draw attention to this physical separation
and create an eerie distance between the words of the story and
the visual representation.

Charlot's style is very mature, as is Miriam Schlein's text,
and the abstract concepts in the words and pictures require an
appreciation of art not always demanded in picture books for
young children.

C84   ANDERSEN, HANS CHRISTIAN. The Steadfast Tin Soldier. Trans-
      lated by M. R. James. Illustrated by Marcia Brown. New
      York: Charles Scribner's Sons, 1953, [32 pp.] 27 illus.:
      color-27/illustrated front matter and title page/crayon,
      pen and ink/24.3cm x 18.6cm
      Fantasy: folklike tale   Gr. K-2

A set of twenty-five tin soldiers was one of several gifts a
young boy receives for his birthday in The Steadfast Tin Soldier.
One of those soldiers is a bit unique, for he has a single leg.
That does not stop him, however, from falling in love with a
ballerina, who also stands on one leg. The star-crossed lovers
find no happiness together because the tin soldier falls out the
window and sets sail in a paper boat, which travels through a
culvert and eventually sinks in a canal.

But the soldier, now consumed by a fish, remains steadfast
in his love for the ballerina and in his courage, and sees her
again after the fish is bought at the market and cut open by the
cook at the soldier's original home. The toy is returned to its
owner. Reunited at last with his beautiful ballerina, the tin
soldier's hopes of love vanish when one of the children throws
the toy into the stove and the Steadfast Tin Soldier melts into
a heart-shaped lump of tin. His steadfast love is rewarded, however when a draught sweeps the ballerina into the fire and the
lovers, symbolically, are finally united--all that remains is a
lump of tin and a coal-black spangle.

Marcia Brown's interpretation of this tale of steadfast love
comes to life in red, blue-gray, and yellow illustrations, which,
due to the solemn nature of the tale, reflect a mood less lively
than those of her lighter, traditional fairy tales. Shapes of
color, with brush strokes clearly visible, are given form by
sharp lines of black that create detail in large areas of unde-
fined color. Black and gray dominate the line and color illustrations and are a step on the way toward refining a style in
Caldecott winners that originated in Skipper John's Cook (C71),
a 1952 Honor Book, and culminates in her 1955 Medal Book
Cinderella (C87).

C85   KRAUSS, RUTH. A Very Special House. Illustrated by Maurice
          Sendak. New York: Harper & Brothers, 1953, [24 pp.] 20
          illus.: black, white, blue, ochre-13; black, ochre-7/
          illustrated front matter and title page/2-color separation
          and pen and ink/25.1cm x 19.6cm
          Fantasy   Gr. Ps-1

The illustrations of Maurice Sendak's 1954 Honor Book transform Ruth Krauss's story of a child's imaginary house into a
menagerie of domesticated and wild animals, crayoned walls, and
abused furniture. This is indeed a very "special" house in which
beds are made for jumping on; in which animals romp and wander,
freely munching on furniture; and in which all the action moves
to the musical rhythm of the words and pictures.

Sendak's line drawings expand upon the repetition of Krauss's
words and share in the mounting rhythm of the song of the story.
After the lion eats all the stuffing from the "chairs chairs
chairs" and keeps "going snore snore snore," the chorus chimes
in for "MORE MORE MORE," and no one ever says "stop stop stop."
The cumulative effect of this imaginary noise, outrageous destruction, and sheer delight of the participants is a very healthy release, especially as the young child admits that this very special
house exists only in the middle of his "head head head."

Sendak's attention to detail, even in this early work, helps
fuse the text and pictures, which reinforce each other as they
go. At the height of the melee, each animal engages in his own

version of eccentric behavior, only to leave the young child
alone in quietude at the close of the story. What makes the
book effective and worthy of Honor Book status is in part due
to Sendak's characteristic style. His attention to detail expands the text when the words do not, and he creates a sense of
his enjoyment and the characters' as well. What might have fallen
down as a weak text is strengthened by the artist, even though
the book employs only black line drawings, interspersed with the
blue and white figure of the young child, on ochre-toned
backgrounds.

Sendak's abilities as an artist of children's books manifest
themselves here, for his appeal is to the child, and all things
forbidden become possible in the hands of this artist.

C86   BIRNBAUM, A. <u>Green Eyes</u>. New York: Capitol, 1953, [40 pp.]
       38 illus.: color-38/illustrated title page/watercolor/
       25.6cm x 25cm
       Fantasy   Gr. Ps-1

Green Eyes, a white cat with emerald eyes, reminisces over its
first year as a kitten, recalling the initial experiences of exploring and discovering the world outside the cardboard box.
Grass, trees, flowers, farm animals, and the four seasons provided an everchanging environment for the kitten. Blowing leaves,
falling snow, and warm, sweet milk, fresh from the cow, provided
sensory experiences for the curious feline. After a year of such
events, the kitten, now a full-grown cat, prepares to enjoy the
changing seasons and their accompanying effects on nature and on
his life.

The text of this 1954 Honor Book, uneventful and less substantial in its theme than some, accompanies illustrations of splashy
color and expressionistic style. With the exception of the full-
page snow scene, a calming gray background, sprinkled with white
blotches of snow, and two black, barren silhouettes of trees
balancing each other on opposite sides of the spread, most of
the book's forty pages are filled with brush strokes of vibrant
greens, yellows, and reds.

Principal shapes are outlined with bold, black lines, which
give the figures an elementary, primitive appearance. The palette
evokes emotional responses to the scenes of the pages and attempts
to provide a visually sensual experience. Were the illustrations
accompanying a text of more body and substance, this work would
function more effectively, and the artistic style could, perhaps,
be more appreciated.

1955

1955

C87   PERRAULT, CHARLES.   Cinderella, or The Little Glass Slipper.
        Translated and illustrated by Marcia Brown.   New York:
        Charles Scribner's Sons, 1954, [32 pp.]   26 illus.:
        color-26/illustrated front matter and title page/water-
        color, ink, and crayon/24.8cm x 19.2cm
        Folk Tale   Gr. Ps-2
      In Marcia Brown's translation of Perrault's Cinderella,
Cinderseat, as she was originally called, spends her waking
hours waiting on her stepmother and two stepsisters. So when
the king's son decides to give a ball, Cinderella has even more
work to do to get her family ready for the festivities. When
they all finally drive off to the ball, a fairy godmother appears
and transforms Cinderella into a beautiful woman, complete with
coach, footmen, horses, and a jeweled gown, so that she, too,
may attend the ball.
      The first evening of the ball, Cinderella remembers to leave
before the stroke of midnight, but the second night she is so
entranced by the prince that she lets the time slip by, and,
rushing out at the last moment, she loses a glass slipper.
      When Cinderella's foot slips perfectly into the lost glass
shoe, she is instantly transformed into the beauty of before and
soon marries the wonderful prince. Her kindness never failing,
she even marries off her stepsisters to two respectable lords of
the court.
      The light, airy drawings of Marcia Brown seem very appropri-
ate for the mood and atmosphere of magic in this fairy tale.
Rose, blue, lavender, and gold shapes are defined with quick
active lines of black that give the open and loose illustrations
some bounds. Brown's style is very synthesized, and though the
lines seem spontaneous, they are much more controlled than those
in the illustrations for Skipper John's Cook (C71), 1952 Honor
Book, and Puss in Boots (C76), 1953 Honor Book. With fewer
lines and extraneous patterns and with a less competitive color
scheme, Brown has captured the essence of this fairy story, whose
words never become tiresome, reading after reading.

C88   de ANGELI, MARGUERITE.   Book of Nursery and Mother Goose
         Rhymes.   Garden City, N.Y.: Doubleday, 1954, 192 pp.
         183 illus.: color-30; black and white-153/illustrated
         front matter, title page, and dedication/watercolor and
         pencil/30.1cm x 21.7cm
         Mother Goose/Nursery Rhymes   Gr. Ps-1
      Marguerite de Angeli's collection of nursery and Mother Goose
rhymes represents one of the largest, most complete compilations
of this type. Over 300 rhymes, riddles, and childhood chants,
as well as 183 illustrated pages, combine to make this a volume

full of many potential hours of reading. Although there are no
titles given for the rhymes, an index of first lines and familiar
titles is included.

Small black and white drawings appear among the rhymes and
riddles, and occasionally a full-color picture is included.
Large, full-page illustrations, in color and in black and white,
provide some variation in format, but it is unfortunate that
more of the enjoyable watercolor illustrations are not present
to break the monotony of the large volume's format.

The full-color illustrations that are included are reminiscent
of those done in Yonie Wondernose (C33), de Angeli's 1945 Honor
Book. No harsh lines intrude upon the soft, gentle atmosphere
of these fifteen full-page color illustrations, while stronger
contrasts of darks and lights emerge in the full-page black and
white illustrations where there is no color to direct the eye.
Whatever the media, the pictures remain a serene and gentle contrast to the strong verbal patterns of these childhood rhymes.

Though the collection is honored for the excellence of its
illustrations and for the suitability of the illustrations to
the text, it is the physical presentation that is at fault.
De Angeli's work reflects the mood and heart of childhood in
the cherubic faces of her characters, and will undoubtedly continue to do so for some time.

C89   BROWN, MARGARET WISE. Wheel on the Chimney. Illustrated by
        Tibor Gergely. New York: J. B. Lippincott, 1954, [32 pp.]
        30 illus.: color-30/illustrated title page/opaque paint/
        27.9cm x 19cm
        Fiction   Gr. 1-2
The natural migratory cycle of the storks in Europe is the
subject of this 1955 Honor Book written by Margaret Wise Brown
and illustrated by Tibor Gergely. The superstition that it is
good luck to have a stork nest on a house is responsible for the
practice of binding cartwheels to chimneys to induce the birds
to settle.

The story opens in the spring, with one stork, then two,
building a nest on a wheel on a chimney. When it comes time to
migrate, the storks gather and fly south to Africa. When spring
returns to the North, the storks begin their journey once again,
and although one stork is lost in a storm, instinct guides him
back to the wheel on the chimney, where this cycle repeats itself.

Tibor Gergely mainly interprets this story in bright shades
of blue, green, violet, and fuchsia. The simple shapes of color
have little detail to them; they speak for themselves. The expressive qualities of the colors and shapes are especially evident in the four full-page spreads that contain no text. Here a
European flavor emerges through the emotional use of color so
common to the Expressionistic movement, a use which also reflects

1955

the colors' sensual qualities, qualities easily captured by this
self-taught artist.
    The simplicity of the shapes creates a primitive, unsophisti-
cated atmosphere that reflects the aura of the simple villages
where the storks choose to settle, where the simple pleasures of
life abound. And so this tale of nature's cycle ends as it begins, with one, then two storks building a nest atop a wheel on
a chimney.

C90   DALGLIESH, ALICE. The Thanksgiving Story. Illustrated by
          Helen Sewell. New York: Charles Scribner's Sons, 1954,
          [32 pp.] 18 illus.: color-10; red-8/illustrated front
          matter and title page/opaque paint and ink/25.3cm x 20cm
          Fiction: historical   Gr. K-2
    A trip across the ocean from England brings the Hopkins family
to America in the 1955 Honor Book by Alice Dalgliesh. Landing
first at Cape Cod in the winter, the Mayflower eventually sails
across the bay to Plymouth, where the Pilgrims make their
settlement.
    After suffering through the winter months, the Pilgrims greet
a green spring and receive several visits from the Indians in
the area. Samoset, Squanto, and Chief Massasoit meet with the
Pilgrims to insure a peaceful coexistence, and Squanto furthers
this friendship by teaching the settlers how to plant corn. By
harvest time there is enough corn and food to share with the
Indians in the first feast of Thanksgiving, a feast that lasted,
then, for three days.
    In ten color illustrations, alternating with pictures of a
brick-red hue, Helen Sewell holds to the simplicity of the Pilgrim life-style and produces unembellished, primitive images on
the pages. This is achieved largely through the use of flat
shapes of color which give the impression of a collage of cut
paper, of abstract and stylized objects.
    The red silhouettes reinforce this simplicity on alternating
pages, as they border or embellish the text. The solid shapes
of plants, animals, and tools of importance to the Pilgrims help
break the monotony of the pages of the five chapters which contain a good deal of text. The final illustration in the book,
a full-color spread, contains no text and portrays the Thanksgiving table, surrounded by Pilgrims and Indians. Though not
the most effective illustration in the book, these silent pages
allow for reflection on this solemn occasion.

1956

C91   LANGSTAFF, JOHN, ed. Frog Went A-Courtin'. Illustrated by
          Feodor Rojankovsky. New York: Harcourt, 1955, [32 pp.]

29 illus.: color-14; green, black, and white-15/illustrated front matter, title page, and dedication/brush, in, crayon, and color separation/26.7cm x 20.2cm
Mother Goose/Nursery Rhyme   Gr. Ps-2

The now traditional text of the marriage and wedding of Frog and Miss Mouse received the Caldecott Medal in 1956. Feodor Rojankovsky's illustrations become a procession of insects and animals that attend the wedding reception: a white moth, black bird, raccoon, spotted snake, bumblebee, flea, gray goose, two ants, a fly, and a chick. All dance across the pages until the festivities abruptly end.

When the tom cat pounces upon the party, the guests quickly disperse, and Frog and Mouse sail off to France to honeymoon. The rhyming text snaps to an end on the final page of text as the newlyweds are shown comfortably reclining in their deck chairs. The tune to this tale, whose origins lie in the oral tradition, is included as a reminder of the story's original function, and Rojankovsky's illustrations help reinforce the tempo of tune and text.

Alternating pages of color illustrations and black, white, and green reflect the rhythm of the text in the actions of the insects and animals attending the party. The predominantly red, yellow, and blue illustrations, as well as the monochromatic ones, humanize the tale's characters without stripping them of their dignity and natural traits. The light-footed flea flits across the leaf of a plant, and although little chick wears a bib, he scurries across the page in characteristically quick, darting movements.

Rojankovsky has recorded this tale so that it works well with the text and extends and synthesizes word and picture in a manner which retains the humor and fun of its original intent.

C92   ETS, MARIE HALL. <u>Play With Me</u>. New York: Viking, 1955,
        32 pp. 28 illus.: color-28/illustrated title page/pastel
        with 2-color separation/25.3cm x 19.3cm
        Fiction   Gr. Ps-1

When a little girl goes to the meadow to play, she scares off all her would-be playmates: a grasshopper, frog, turtle, chipmunk, bluejay, rabbit, and snake. Dejected, the young child sits down on a rock by a pond and quietly watches a waterbug. As she sits in silence, her playmates return, one by one, until her self-control is rewarded even more when a Fawn comes out of the bushes, cautiously approaches, and licks her on the cheek. Now she has all the companionship she wants.

The putty-colored backgrounds for the illustrations, by Marie Hall Ets, allow the artist to make use of white as a color, as well as offer a means to highlight and draw attention to the focal point--the little girl. In her simple white dress, the

1956

child's figure contrasts sharply with the neutral background;
the addition of two other colors--yellow and a flesh tone--helps
add interest and direct attention around the page, with light
sketchlike lines of black completing the compositions.

Although the white rays of the sun extend into the foregrounds
of illustrations, enveloping and containing the compositions, the
white-clad figure remains the center of attraction on each page.
The airiness of these compositions contrasts with the bold, heavy
black and white compositions of two earlier Ets Honor Books, In
the Forest (C32, 1945) and Mr. T.W. Anthony Woo (C70, 1952).
The diversification of style in these Caldecott works attests to
her skill as an artist and author of children's books, but in
Play With Me she is most successful in meshing word and picture.
The appropriateness of the style to the mood and character of the
text is highly important, but the style, in turn, does much to
shape the reception of the words. Ets touches upon a subject of
wide appeal and develops a visual interpretation which is just
as pleasing.

C93   YASHIMA, TARO. Crow Boy. New York: Viking, 1955, 37 pp.
      34 illus.: color-34/illustrated title page and dedication/
      colored pencil, brush, and ink/29.5cm x 21.6cm
      Fiction   Gr. K-2
      Chibi, meaning tiny boy, the main character of Taro Yashima's
1956 Honor Book, is always an outcast, in the schoolroom and on
the playground. When the other students in this school in Japan
attend to their work or listen to the teacher, Chibi occupies
himself observing more interesting objects--the ceiling, his
desktop, a patch of cloth, or nature via the classroom window.
Everyday the small boy walks miles to school and observes the
environment around him, carefully noting the subtle changes that
take place.

After six years of perfect attendance, Chibi is rewarded, for
his teacher, Mr. Isobe, recognizes the boy's knowledge of nature
and his hidden accomplishments. Chibi shares the voices of crows--
baby crows, mother crows, father crows, happy, and sad crows--with
his classmates in the talent show and for a moment transports the
audience to the countryside. Now Crow Boy, as he comes to be
called, is proud he has earned the respect of others and himself.
His familiar cry--the call of a happy crow--resonates from village to countryside.

The emotions of Crow Boy come to life in the expressive red,
blue, and yellow illustrations that create the impression of
calligraphic brush strokes. The quick black lines reinforce
this feeling of Eastern influence, especially as a few short
lines give form and expression to the colorful shapes of the
pages, be it the face of the young boy or the trees of the countryside in which he lives.

Though Yashima's text and illustrations present a story of a land far from the America of the Caldecott Medal, the universal qualities of the story make it an experience in artistic internationalism, as well as a lesson in human understanding and compassion.

1957

C94   UDRY, JANICE MAY. A Tree is Nice. Illustrated by Marc
          Simont. New York: Harper & Brothers, 1956, [32 pp.]
          29 illus.: color-15; black and white-14/illustrated front
          matter and title page/casein/27.9cm x 16cm
          Information: science   Gr. Ps-2
The virtues and versatility of trees are expounded upon in this 1957 Medal Book, illustrated by Marc Simont, and their contribution to man and nature helps demonstrate that book's theme of conservation. Besides beautifying the landscape, trees supply leaves in which to play, limbs to climb, apples to munch, sticks with which to draw, and shade to cool both man and beast.
In these days of energy conservation, the book strikes a familiar note as it explains the importance of trees in shading homes in the summer months and in warding off the frigid winds of the winter. The campaign for trees culminates with a constructive conclusion: a tree is so nice, why not plant one?
Simont visualizes these aspects of trees through the changing seasons in alternating spreads of black and white and color. The bright watercolors of spring, summer, fall, and winter do, indeed, demonstrate the beauty of trees. Large areas of verdant hues, touched here and there with a quick, black line, give the impression of the rich foliage of these tall, noble plants.
The verticality of the trees mimics the book's shape, of vertical emphasis, and relays the proportions and sense of height in the illustrations. The black and white and wash illustrations provide a pleasant contrast to the vibrancy of the color pages, with the increased use of line creating the emphasis and detail necessary with the absence of color. The subtle value changes in the wash produce the depth and modeling that the color supplies in the alternating illustrations, leaving a visual impression that only enhances this exquisite creation, the tree.

C95   ETS, MARIE HALL. Mister Penny's Race Horse. New York:
          Viking, 1956 (OP), 64 pp. 54 illus.: black and white-54/
          illustrated endpapers, front matter, half title, and title
          page/paper batik/25.3cm x 19.7cm
          Fantasy   Gr. K-2
When Mister Penny decides to take his produce, flowers, and animals to the fair, he does not realize the consequences of

promising the animals a Ferris wheel ride. Splop, the goat, and
Doody, the rooster, investigate the other entrants, to insure
their chances of winning enough money to finance their ride, but
their nighttime excursion around the fairgrounds results in the
expulsion of Mister Penny, animals and all, from the fair.

As the farmer prepares the cart and horse for their return to
the farm, Limpy, the horse, is overwhelmed by his desire to become a racehorse. As he watches the racehorses on the track with
envy, Splop grabs the reigns, and Limpy hits the track. After
an hilarious trip around the field, thrilling the spectators
with their antics, the animals are invited back to the fair by
the director. After their well-earned ride on the Ferris wheel,
Mister Penny and his animals look forward to their return to
next year's fair to once again entertain the crowds.

In black and white illustrations, Ets recreates the events of
the story within the rectangular borders which are characteristic
of her style. The black on white and white on black illustrations create some variation within the format, as do the full-
and single-page spreads, but the length of the text and the
monotony of the lights and darks in the illustrations both contribute to the overall impression of weightiness and lifelessness.

The compositions, in and of themselves, are interesting in
terms of their balance of lights and darks and the patterns
created, but they are not lively enough to compensate for the
lengthy text and short attention spans of young audiences. The
artist's style, so similar to those of previous Honor Books, In
the Forest (C32, 1945), and Mr. T. W. Anthony Woo (C70, 1952),
loses the creative and original impact of earlier works and
seems a mere reproduction of pictures accompanying a new text.

C96   TUDOR, TASHA. 1 Is One. New York: Henry Z. Walck, 1956,
          [48 pp.] 40 illus.: color-20; black and white-20/
          illustrated front matter, title page, and dedication/
          watercolor and pencil/17cm x 22.6cm
          Counting Book   Gr. Ps-1
In Tasha Tudor's counting book, from one to twenty, each number is clearly represented by an object or objects in alternating
illustrations of full color and black and white. Items of familiarity to young children, offering concrete representations of
the numbers, are easily visible in the compositions. Birds, animals, flowers, trees, fruits, candles, and children, themselves,
appear in the pictures, which are all bordered by garlands of
flowers and assorted vegetation.

The text is simple and straightforward, with the sentences of
odd numbers rhyming with those of the following even digit, lending a cohesiveness to the format often missing in books of this
nature. The left-hand sides of the full-page spreads consistently
bear a small illustration, while the right-hand side contains the
appropriate number of objects mentioned in the text.

The delicate watercolors and old-fashioned dress of the children endear the book in a manner similar to that of Kate Greenaway's works, and though more creative counting books have since reached the market, Tudor's contribution is representative of the unblemished innocence of childhood and childhood experiences that dominated the sheltered world of picture books for years.

Though undoubtedly still popular among children, especially young girls, the book is probably less read than it once was and has been joined by several very creative counting books that are found entertaining by the more demanding audiences of today's picture books.

C97 TITUS, EVE. Anatole. Illustrated by Paul Galdone. New York: Whittlesey, 1956 (OP), 32 pp. 27 illus.: color-13; black and white-14/illustrated front matter and title page/wash, ink, and 2-color separation/25cm x 18.1cm
Fantasy   Gr. K-2

Anatole, his wife, Doucette, and their six children live very comfortably in a mouse village near Paris. One evening, on his nightly excursion into Paris to collect food for his family, Anatole overhears some people discussing their low opinion of mice. His self-esteem and honor in question, Anatole resolves to leave the human beings something in return for the food he collects.

The next evening the ambitious mouse enters the Duval Cheese factory, samples the cheeses, evaluates their flavor, and leaves notes and directions for improving their taste. After heeding Anatole's advice, Duval becomes the most famous producer of cheese. Though Anatole prefers to remain unknown, he becomes a self-respecting business mouse and continues to earn every bite of cheese his family consumes.

Lively red and blue illustrations give this light tale the Parisian atmosphere it deserves, but the black and white pictures are as effective in their own right. The same expressive lines appear in all the illustrations and possess a mouselike quickness about them. At the hands of Paul Galdone, Anatole, complete with beret, scarf, and smock, has dignity, pride, and ingenuity. The gray washes and active lines of the black and white pages give the book a free-flowing looseness and informality that reflect the spirit of the book. Much akin to the spirit of Maurice Sendak's A Very Special House (C85, 1954 Honor Book) or Madeline (C12, 1940 Honor Book) of Ludwig Bemelmans, Anatole is a refreshing addition to the Caldecott Honor Books.

C98 ELKIN, BENJAMIN. Gillespie and the Guards. Illustrated by James Daugherty. New York: Viking, 1956 (OP), 63 pp. 58 illus.: brown, black, and white-58/illustrated title page/lithograph/27.1cm x 19.6cm

1957

Fiction   Gr. 1-2
Three brothers, who possess very keen eyesight, are invited
to join the Royal Guard in the 1957 Honor Book <u>Gillespie and the
Guards</u>. The King is so proud of the special powers of his guards
that he offers a diamond-studded gold medal to anyone who can
trick them.

After repeated attempts to fool the men fail, the guards become very smug and complacent, so Gillespie, a friend of the
young prince, devises a plan to fool the sentinels and rid them
of their haughtiness. Day after day Gillespie lugs a little red
wagonload of sand, stone, or leaves past the guards, who laugh
at the worthless cargo with which the boy toils.

Gillespie is, in fact, fooling the Royal Guards, for he soon
accumulates a garageful of little red wagons from the palace
storeroom. The medal is the boy's, and the guards soon realize
their pride had been their undoing.

The humor of the circumstances in having a young child teach
these adults a lesson is captured in James Daugherty's dramatic
brown, black, and white illustrations. Pointing fingers, sweeping
robes, and curving swords all deftly direct the eye exactly where
the artist wants. As in Daugherty's <u>Andy and the Lion</u> (C9), a
1939 Honor Book, the patterns of lights and darks help reflect
and reinforce the action of the story.

Often the illustrations contain no backgrounds; the figures
of the page are of principal interest--the setting is merely a
device from which the characters and story evolve. The exaggera-
tion of the movement of the characters is instrumental to the
point of the story. Extreme behavior is the guards' demise, but
through Daugherty's humorous style, the lesson they learn is a
valuable one for all.

C99   Du BOIS, WILLIAM PÈNE. <u>Lion</u>. New York: Viking, 1956, 36 pp.
        22 illus.: color-18, black and white-4/illustrated end-
        papers, front matter, half title, and title page/black line
        with color separation/25.3cm x 19cm
            Fantasy   Gr. K-2
When Artist Foreman, of The Animal Factory up in the sky,
decides to create a new animal, he finds he has lost some of the
skill it takes to be a successful inventor. With the advice of
several artists, he finally produces a satisfactory drawing of
his new animal: LION. As advised, changes made in size and
color, as well as in the beast's legs, haircut, and plumage, result in an acceptable rendering.

The Chief Designer gives his approval to the new creation, but
is curious as to the noise LION might make. Artist Foreman thinks
a modest "PEEP PEEP" would be appropriate, but he quickly follows
the Chief Designer's suggestion that the animal must certainly
roar like the thunder. And in this fashion LION joins the ranks
of the animal kingdom.

As LION slowly evolves, William Pène du Bois records the events of this story in illustrations of black line, interspersed with bright, colorful illustrations. Red, blue, and yellow provide the dominant colors and appear mainly in the drawings of the animal itself. Du Bois's clean, sharp line drawings, often with the addition of a small amount of color for emphasis, take on the intricacy and look of the line drawings of Leonardo da Vinci's inventions, especially in the front matter and first page of the text.

The winged figures of Artist Foreman, presumably an angel, and other artists of the factory give the story an extraterrestrial atmosphere, in keeping with the setting of the story. This unearthly setting is consistent with the notion of the creation of the animal kingdom by some higher being, in this case the artists of the factory and the Chief Designer. Du Bois creates an interesting interpretation and explanation for the inclusion of the lion in the animal kingdom, and his drawings help the story retain and explain a little of the mystery of this creation.

1958

C100   McCLOSKEY, ROBERT. <u>Time of Wonder</u>. New York: Viking, 1957, 64 pp. 58 illus.: color-58/illustrated title page/watercolor/30.6cm x 23.5cm

Fiction   Gr. 1-3

Summer vacation is a time to revel in nature and to enjoy the opportunities made available by living near the ocean. Penobscot Bay provides just such an experience in the 1958 Medal Book by Robert McCloskey. Commonplace activities fill the weeks of summer as the changes in land, water, plants, animals, and weather hurry the summer too soon to an end.

Endless days of boating, swimming, and exploring go by all too quickly; when a hurricane blows in, the storm signals the end of summer. McCloskey's style is full of language which mimics the storm and its ensuing calm. As fall approaches, the memories of the past months allow for reflection--reflection on the unanswerable secrets of nature.

Robert McCloskey records this nearly religious experience with nature in a predominantly blue and green palette. The watercolor illustrations, which lap over the center of the book, leaving the far left for the text, are conspicuously void of the expressive lines of other McCloskey books. The medium takes control and interprets the emotional responses appropriate to the text through the color and the natural characteristics of the paint.

The blues and greens are well suited to producing the visual effects of the water, fog, storm, and sunshine that are integral to the book's theme. The style, because of the manner in which

1958

McCloskey has used his medium, has less detail and is more expressionistic, demanding more from the viewer.

C101   FREEMAN, DON. <u>Fly High, Fly Low</u>. New York: Viking, 1957,
        58 pp. 52 illus.: color-52/illustrated endpapers, title
        page, and front matter/color pencil, brush, and ink/27.9cm
        x 20.1cm
        Fantasy   Gr. Ps-1
    A love affair develops between a pigeon named Sid and his fly-
ing companion, a white dove, Midge, high above the city of San
Francisco. The birds build their nest in part of an old sign,
the lower portion of a letter "B." One day before the pair's
eggs get a chance to hatch, while Sid is away collecting food,
a demolition team removes the letters.
    After he returns to an empty sign, Sid embards upon a search
for Midge and his nest. Fog, heavy rains, and a dunk in a flooded
gutter interrupt his search until Mr. Hi Lee, Sid's friend from
Union Square Park, rescues the soaked bird. Mr. Lee tucks Sid
safely inside his pocket and saunters off to a nearby bakery for
some nourishing crumbs to feed the bird.
    When Mr. Lee nears the shop, Sid recognizes a familiar coo;
there above the bakery, snuggled in the same letter "B," is
Midge and the two eggs. The pair is united just in time to welcome their babies into the world, and eventually the offspring
make their nest in the upper story of the letter.
    The red, yellow, and blue illustrations of this 1958 Honor
Book are defined by black lines and often have the effect of
those works by Taro Yashima. Though not as dark and heavy as
Yashima's, these illustrations also contain quick, expressive
lines which give minimal detail to the blended, blurred shapes
of color.
    The actual pencil strokes, at times, assimilate the strokes of
a brush and lend the pictures an Oriental style, which is also
evident in the architecture of the streets of San Francisco and
in the character of Mr. Hi Lee.
    Freeman's text, a bit melodramatic at times, is aided consider-
ably by his energetic illustrations which are full of diagonals
and eye-catching lines and color. The book stands as an example
of the wide variety of styles that are beginning to develop in
the late 1950s--a trend that will continue in full force into
the 1960s.

C102   TITUS, EVE. <u>Anatole and the Cat</u>. Illustrated by Paul Galdone.
        New York: Whittlesey, 1957, 32 pp. 28 illus.: color-14;
        black and white-14/illustrated title page and front matter/
        wash, ink, and two-color separation/24.5cm x 17.5cm
        Fantasy   Gr. Ps-1
    In this sequel to <u>Anatole</u> (C97), the self-respecting mouse
continues in his job as Cheese Taster for Duval Cheeses, until

one night when his work is interrupted by a cat. Anatole and Gaston, his assistant and friend, find the conditions impossible to work under, so that evening Anatole's evaluations of the cheeses are uncharacteristically poor in quality.

The next day M'sieu Duval finds it necessary to write a letter to Anatole, inquiring as to the problem, to which Anatole responds in so many words: the cat. The only solution, the Cheese Taster decides, is to attempt an age-old suggestion made by Gaston: bell the cat.

Anatole does just that, is able to resume his work, and helps reestablish the popularity of Duval Cheese. Though the popularity of the cheeses dropped temporarily, one good thing becomes of all this confusion. One variety of cheese that Anatole suggested--a concoction including chopped cucumber--becomes so popular that it is named Cheese Anatole.

Alternating black and white and red and blue illustrations, in the same style of Anatole, a 1957 Honor Book, project a similar, lively atmosphere in which Anatole's ingenuity rises to the occasion as he triumphs over another natural foe. The underlying suggestion of the triumphs of small over large, weak over strong, is a theme that is relevant and popular in the realm of literature for children. Though these illustrations may lose appeal, the text will undoubtedly remain meaningful as long as there remain small children struggling to exist in adult worlds.

1959

C103   CHAUCER, GEOFFREY. Chanticleer and the Fox. Translated by
        Robert Mayer Lumiansky. Adapted and illustrated by Barbara
        Cooney. New York: Thomas Y. Crowell, 1958, [36 pp.]
        31 illus.: color-16; red, black, and white-15/illustrated
        endpapers, half title, title page, and dedication/scratch-
        board, 4 colors in Dinobase/26cm x 19.8cm
        Fable   Gr. K-2
        An adaptation of the "Nun's Priest's Tale" from The Canterbury
Tales of Geoffrey Chaucer, Chanticleer and the Fox retells the
perils of frivolous flattery and how Mr. Chanticleer nearly
loses his life.

Owned by a widow and her two daughters, Chanticleer, a proud rooster, is tended to by seven hens. After an ominous dream one evening, Chanticleer's fears are realized when he is startled by a fox in the hedges. The fox flatters the rooster into crowing with his eyes closed, which gives the predator the perfect opportunity to snatch the fowl by the neck and carry him off to the woods.

The rooster, though scared for his life, tricks the fox into opening his mouth, just long enough to escape. Lacking

1959

self-control and putting faith in flattery show both animals to
be vulnerable because of their vanity, not unlike many people.

Barbara Cooney has interpreted this moralistic fable in wholesome, solid shapes of red, blue, green, and ochre. The design of
the book--the physical relationship of the text to the illustrations and the design of the objects within the illustrations--
reflects much thought and skill. Carefully selected vegetation,
common to the setting, complements the compositions, adding authenticity and interest to the visual presentation.

The black and ochre of the patterned plumage of the hens and
the rooster produce a dramatic design, yet the black and white
illustrations, with a touch of red, are equally interesting. The
careful placement of the color on the page--the red tongue and
eye of the fox or the ruby beaks of the ducks and dangling
cherries--serves to emphasize and entice movement of the eye in
the desired direction. Cooney has created a visual experience of
disciplined style and composition, which is reflective of the
traditional origins of the tale itself.

C104   FRASCONI, ANTONIO. The House That Jack Built ("La Maison que
        Jacques a Bâtie"): A Picture Book in Two Languages. New
        York: Harcourt, Brace, 1958, [32 pp.] 27 illus.: color-
        26; black and white-1/illustrated endpapers, title page,
        dedication, and front matter/woodcuts/26.2cm x 20.2cm
        Information: language arts   Gr. K-3
The nursery rhyme, "The House That Jack Built," comes to life
in two languages and woodcuts of green, yellow, and fuchsia. The
story follows the lines of the traditional tale in which a series
of events accumulates as a result of the malt "that lay in the
house that Jack built." The French and English text of this tale,
English preceding the French, is accompanied by full- and single-
page illustrations which capitalize upon the repetition of words
and the reinforcement of the pictures to create a tool for use
with children by parents or teachers.

The vibrant colors of the illustrations provide an interesting
contrast to the black and white textures and patterns of the
wood. Far from traditional representations of the rhyme,
Frasconi's style creates an interpretation heavy with symbolic
shapes and bold contrasts.

Because the book is, in part, a tool to develop language understanding in children, a question-and-answer section is included
at the book's close. Each question appears within a colorful
bordered area, arranged vertically on the page, and is accompanied
by a small black and white figure that indicates the correct answer. Not only are the answers presented visually, but they are
also given in French to reinforce the bilingual aspects of the
book. The original artistic concept and handling of this traditional rhyme make the work seem less an educational tool than an

enjoyable picture book, but in separating the tale from its traditional realm, a bit of its original rhythm and charm is lost.

C105   JOSLIN, SESYLE. <u>What Do You Say, Dear? A Book of Manners for All Occasions</u>. Illustrated by Maurice Sendak. New York: Young Scott, 1958, [48 pp.] 34 illus.: blue, black, and white–34/illustrated title page and front matter/ pen and ink with 2-color wash separation/17.3cm x 21.1cm
      Fantasy   Gr. Ps-1

    Sesyle Joslin has manufactured the most absurd situations to demonstrate the socially acceptable responses every child should know, even under the most ludicrous of circumstances. Everyone knows that bumping into a crocodile requires a sincere "Excuse me." But if a wild cowboy should inquire as to whether he should shoot a bullet through the head, a polite, "No, thank you," should convince him otherwise. And so the fabricated situations continue until an orchestra of bears wants to gobble everyone up; then it is definitely time to go!

    This humorous and nonsensical approach to the training of youngsters provides a hidden and effective reminder to the audience, and the repetitive format allows the child to guess or recall the appropriate responses. Maurice Sendak helps emphasize the absurdity of the situations by making his characters, human and animal alike, appear completely serious about what they are doing, and dignified as well. Tilted heads, uplifted noses, or closed eyes give the stilted appearance of those well trained in the amenities of proper etiquette.

    The blue of the monochromatic color scheme adds variety to the predominantly gray, black, and white illustrations, and this color allows the eye to focus on the more important events portrayed in the pictures. The simple, outlined figures retain their childlike faces, even though they are clothed in adult apparel and are expected to properly behave in these rather sophisticated situations.

    Sendak's visual interpretation, as with most of his work in children's books reaches the heart of what makes children laugh. He creates worlds where children, or their animal counterparts, are of primary concern, and he possesses the ability to focus his work on what is important to children in relation to the adult world. These relationships between the generations and Sendak's ability to visualize them, as in this 1959 Honor Book, gain for him continued respect as an artist, and author, of children's books.

C106   YASHIMA, TARO. <u>Umbrella</u>. New York: Viking, 1958, 33 pp. 32 illus.: color–32/illustrated front matter and title page/ink, pen, brush, and crayon/19.7cm x 23.1cm
      Fiction   Gr. Ps-1

1959

On Momo's third birthday, she receives a pair of red rubber boots and an umbrella, but the weather is not cooperative enough to warrant their use. Impatient to try out her precious gifts, Momo tries to convince her mother that the umbrella would be beneficial in keeping the sun and wind out of her yes. Her mother, unfortunately, does not agree, so Momo has to wait for the rain.

When it finally rains, the small child gets to use her treasured gifts on the walk to and from her nursery school. It is an exciting day for more than one reason, for it is the first time Momo walks to school without holding anyone's hand; she has grown up a little on that rainy day in New York City.

The text of this 1959 Honor Book is accompanied by predominantly red, yellow, and blue illustrations that lend a Japanese atmosphere to the book, especially in the quick lines of calligraphic quality. In addition, four pages contain Japanese characters and their pronunciations. Spring, summer, rain, and peach are the words that appear above the text in the left-hand corner of the pages.

As in his previous Honor Book, Crow Boy (C93, 1956), Yashima combines blended colors and fine lines to create the shapes and characters of his story. He is more concerned with creating the impression or essence of a shape or figure rather than with recording a detailed likeness of the object. This is widely evident in the faces and figures of his characters: two quick lines may represent the eyes, thereby establishing the dominant feature of the face and defining it as such. The artist's economic style adequately reflects the self-discipline associated with the culture which Momo and Yashima share.

1960

C107   ETS, MARIE HALL, and LABASTIDA, AURORA. Illustrated by
        Marie Hall Ets. Nine Days to Christmas. New York:
        Viking, 1959, 48 pp. 41 illus.: color-41/illustrated
        title page/pencil on Dinobase, four colors/27.9cm x 20.2cm
        Fiction   Gr. Ps-2

Though Ceci is only in kindergarten, she is going to have her own posada, one of the traditional Mexican Christmas parties that occur on the nine days before the holiday. With school over and little else to occupy her time, Ceci grows impatient waiting for the day of her posada; with each day her curiosity grows as she wonders whether or not she will have a piñata at her party.

The day before the celebration, Ceci's mother takes her to a market, and the little girl chooses her piñata. She picks a large golden star, which she takes home and fills with oranges, candies, and sugar canes. With the piñata hanging on the patio, the posada begins, but Ceci hides behind a tree when it is time to break open the golden star. As the shell of papier-mâché bursts, the shining star drifts into the dark night sky and shines for Ceci and her doll, Gabina--a reminder of the magical moments of the Christmas tradition.

Old and new, traditional and modern are juxtaposed in this story of the celebration of Christmas. Bright yellow, magenta, and orange are placed on gray backgrounds, lending the colors added vibrancy. The neutral background allows white to be effectively utilized as if it were a color, a technique Ets employs in Play With Me (C92), a 1956 Honor Book.

Though the text contains some lengthy portions not directly integral to the story, these segments help paint the culture from which the story rises. Ets fills her compositions, as well, with indicators of the story's culture, and her pencil backgrounds create a backdrop of markets, gardens, and parks that help convey an understanding of and appreciation for the culture and its traditions.

C108   GOUDEY, ALICE. Houses from the Sea. Illustrated by Adrienne
        Adams. New York: Charles Scribner's Sons, 1959, [32 pp.]
        27 illus.: color/27/illustrated title page/watercolor,
        wash, and pastels/25.3cm x 20.1cm
        Information: science   Gr. K-2

The Author's Note at the beginning of this 1960 Honor Book helps categorize this work as a book of information. Along with the section at the back of the book, entitled "How Shells Are Made," Alice Goudey explains and identifies a variety of shells found on East, West, and Gulf Coast shores. The lapping waves of the shore provide the setting in which a young brother and sister collect the relics which at one time housed small creatures of the ocean. From angel wings and moon shells to slipper shells and periwinkles, the children gather these specimens, which become the center of attention on rainy days.

Adrienne Adams helps identify the shells that the author describes by relating their shape to objects they resemble. The shape of scallop shells is akin to that of a fan, and tiny keyhole limpets bear a resemblance to Chinese hats. All these associations Adams portrays in the pastel watercolor and wash drawings that reflect the watery image of ocean and seashore.

Pink, blue, and yellow shapes are modeled and defined with lines and shadings of brown, eliminating the harshness sometimes achieved by the use of black. Sailboats and turrets emerge from watery blue backgrounds and help visually imprint on the memory the information in the text.

A full-page spread identifying the types of shells gathered by the children is included and serves as a condensed reference to the information in the book. The production of a picture book of information is a difficult undertaking, for a plot must be sufficient enough to carry the story, while at the same time avoiding a monotonous listing of detail and facts. Author and

1960

artist have been able to successfully synthesize their information, written and visual, into a balanced presentation of fact.

C109 UDRY, JANICE MAY. The Moon Jumpers. Illustrated by Maurice
      Sendak. New York: Harper & Brothers, 1959, [32 pp.]
      28 illus.: color-14; black and white-14/illustrated title
      page and front matter/tempera with black line and washes/
      25.3cm x 18.1cm
      Fiction   Gr. Ps-1

As shadows fall and darkness wraps its eerie arms around the
creatures of the night, children dance in the moonlight, along-
side the moonfish, frogs, moths, and moonbeams. Night transforms
the familiar sights of day into a new environment; here the children perform their playful rituals and dance in the summer darkness as the moon grows and rises in the sky.

When the time arrives to go to bed, the spell of the moon is
broken, and the "Moon Jumpers" become children once again. Their
reluctance to surrender the freedom of the spell of darkness is
evident, but tomorrow will bring the rays of the sun and, eventually, another nightfall.

The illumination of the moonbeams casts haunting shadows in the
seven full-page color spreads, which are devoid of text. Sporadic
glints of light create an unusual atmosphere for the twirling,
dancing, nymphlike figures as they try to capture the fleeting
moonbeams.

The alternating black and white illustrations are contained
within rectangular shapes, with an occasional plant or flower
creating a border around the text. Black lines define the gray
shapes on these pages and create a visual harmony in the pages'
compositions, with the lines of the text intervening.

The color pages of blues, greens, and violets, accentuated by
the eerie glow of the moon, relay the true sense of the atmosphere
and environment of the story. With no text to interfere, the hyp-
notic spell of the story takes over; the silence seems appropriate.

It is easy to identify the elements of Sendak's style that
will eventually evolve into the 1964 Medal Book, Where the Wild
Things Are (C119). Creative and unusual, Sendak has produced a
visual interpretation that is often more effective than the text
it accompanies.

1961

C110 ROBBINS, RUTH. Baboushka and the Three Kings. Illustrated
      by Nicolas Sidjakov. Berkeley, Calif.: Parnassus, 1960,
      [28 pp.] 15 illus.: color-15; illustrated endpapers and
      title page/tempera, dyes, felt pen, and liquitex/16.5cm x
      17.8cm
      Folk Tale   Gr. K-2

During a night of drifting snow and howling winds, a procession of travelers visits Baboushka in her modest hut. The travelers, trying to follow a bright star to a land where a Babe has been born, ask Baboushka to lead them through the snow, but she refuses, advising morning a safer time to travel. Not heeding the woman's advice, the three kings and their entourage continue their journey into the blizzard of the night.

Baboushka wakes the next morning intent on seeking out this wonderful Babe, so she, too, begins a journey. She travels miles and miles with her sack of meager gifts for the child, but no one knows where the Babe might be. Every year Baboushka renews her search, and, as the Russian tradition goes, children look forward to the small gifts she leaves behind each Christmas Eve.

This small book holds a treasure of words and art for children, as well as the tune and verses for the song of the story. Nicolas Sidjakov's illustrations give this Russian tale a distinctive, original look. Shapes of red-orange, royal blue, and iridescent yellow are added to the lines of illustrations--lines done in black marker. Gray backgrounds tone down the colors somewhat and give the illustrations an opaque appearance.

Stylized, flat shapes, perspectives and faces Cubistic in appearance, add to the unusual artistic style, and often the most effective illustrations are those of gray backgrounds, black lines, with only one or two small shapes of color. As the old woman searches through village after village, her red-orange figure and forest green sack direct the eye to the focal point of the story--Baboushka.

Stylized asterisks fill in the lines of the text so that no break occurs between sentences or paragraphs, and these decorative symbols, as well as the domed architecture of the villages through which Baboushka trudges, reflect the Russian origin of the tale. Individuality of style in this 1961 Medal Book has been justly rewarded; the book presents a visual experience worthy of the straightforward, simply worded text.

C111   LIONNI, LEO.   <u>Inch by Inch</u>.   New York: Obolensky, 1960, [28 pp.] 26 illus.: color-26/illustrated title page and front matter/multi-media: rice paper, cut paper, crayon, ink/27cm x 22.7cm
Fantasy   Gr. Ps-1

To save his life, an inchworm convinces a robin that he is very useful for measuring. After the worm calculates the length of the robin's tail, he flies off with robin to measure some other items. A flamingo's neck, a toucan's beak, the lion's legs, a pheasant's tail, and a hummingbird's body--all are inched off by the worm. When the nightingale threatens to eat the inchworm if he doesn't measure the bird's song, the ingenious little green worm begins to measure while the nightingale warbles. Inch by inch, he safely inches out of sight.

1961

As the little green worm travels across the pages of this book, his ingenuity and that of the artist become more and more apparent. The design of the compositions is creative and striking, and it becomes a challenge to locate the little green figure on each page. Cut shapes, torn shapes, corrugated cardboard, crayon and patterned paper give rise to a style and technique for which Lionni remains well known. The stark white backgrounds provide a perfect contrast for his creative designs. The curving neck of the flamingo loops across two pages, the beak of the bird curving back toward the inchworm, completing the composition.

The long legs of the heron lift the bird's body out of sight so that all that can be seen on the right is the graceful curve of the bird's neck, again leading the eye back toward the main character. As the worm inches across the pages at the close of the book, his progression through the tall blades of grass contrasts with his small size and emphasizes the triumph of the tiny crawler over his natural predator.

<u>1962</u>

C112   BROWN, MARCIA. <u>Once a Mouse . . .</u>. New York: Charles
          Scribner's Sons, 1961, [32 pp.] 29 illus.: color-29/
          illustrated endpapers and title page/woodcuts/24cm x 23.3cm
          Fable   Gr. K-2
    This tale from ancient India opens with a hermit contemplating the rhetorical question of big and little. As he ponders he is distracted from his meditation by a crow chasing a mouse. The hermit rescues the small mouse from its large predator, and, through a series of transformations to save the creature's life, eventually changes the mouse into a royal tiger.

The powerful tiger soon forgets his humble beginnings and decides to kill the hermit, who reprimands the beast for his ingratitude. But before the ungrateful animal has a chance to carry out his plans, the hermit returns the animal to his former status. Thus ends the tale of big and little; the hermit still ponders the mystery of his initial query.

Angular shapes of olive, red, and gold combine to define the characters and backgrounds in the woodcuts of this 1962 Medal Book. Alternating two- and three-color spreads are full of patterns created by the nature of the medium. Deep, clean cuts create sharp lines and contrasts, while shallow, broad cuts create less definite distinctions in backgrounds and foliage.

Overlapping shapes and areas of color help reflect the heavy undergrowth of the jungle setting of the tale. Though fine detail is absent from the illustrations, Brown indicates the essence of the shapes through stylized representations of objects. A

medium which is difficult to control, the woodcut relies heavily
on the absence of color to define its shape. The white of the
illustrations becomes as important as the hues of the unusual
color scheme. The age-old technique of woodcut helps convey the
mysticism and origin of this Asian tale and demonstrates the
creative talents and versatility of the artist.

C113   SPIER, PETER. The Fox Went Out on a Chilly Night: An Old
       Song. Garden City, N.Y.: Doubleday, 1961, [46 pp.]
       42 illus.: color-22; black and white-20/illustrated end-
       papers and title page/watercolor and pen and ink/20cm x
       26.2cm
       Mother Goose/Nursery Rhymes   Gr. Ps-1
     An old song, titled "The Fox," is the basis for the 1962 Honor
Book by Peter Spier, which includes the tune and seven verses at
the end of the story. With the moon high overhead, a fox sets
out on a trip to town. After many miles of travel, the animal
makes a visit to a farmer's bin, where the ducks and geese are
housed. With instinctual quickness and stealth the perpetrator
nabs a goose and a duck before Mother Giggle-Gaggle is awakened
by the ruckus.
     Though John, the farmer, sets out with horn and gun to pursue
the thief, the fleet-footed fox escapes with his catch and returns to his den. The fowl are quickly prepared as a feast for
the ten baby foxes; never such a dinner did they eat.
     The rhyming words of the song's lines and the repetition of
portions of lines and words keep pace with the fox's movements
across the full-page spreads. Alternating spreads of black and
white and full color provide some variety in format and allow for
a contrast of style. Though all the illustrations are packed
from corner to corner with infinite detail, the black and white
illustrations require closer scrutiny because of the lack of
color and contrast which emerges from the beautiful palette of
the color pages.
     The minute details of house interiors, barnyards, countryside
scenes, and town buildings contrast, as well, with the simple
words of the text. There is a cooperation of visual and aural
modes that makes the book effective and easy to enjoy. Spier's
style is easily recognized, but it never loses the element of
surprise contained within those fine, delicate lines.

C114   MINARIK, ELSE H. Little Bear's Visit. Illustrated by Maurice
       Sendak. New York: Harper & Brothers, 1961, 64 pp. 56
       illus.: color-42; brown-4; black and white-10/illustrated
       half title, title page, dedication, and contents page/pen
       and ink with 3-color wash separations/21.5cm x 14.7cm
       Fantasy   Gr. Ps-2
     Little Bear's visit to Grandmother and Grandfather Bear's
house is a full day of stories, good things to eat, and the

1962

company of two loving grandparents. Although Little Bear is not
supposed to tire Grandfather out, the old gentleman, clothed in
vest, suit, and tie, falls asleep, so Grandmother tells the young
cub the story of his mother's robin.

When Grandfather wakens from his snooze, Little Bear hears
another tale, "Goblin Story," before his parents come to take
him home. Though Little Bear professes to be perfectly wide
awake, not tired at all, he falls asleep in his father's arms
before they are out the door.

This "I-Can-Read" book is divided into four chapters, as noted
on the contents page, two of which are stories within the main
story; one story provides the opportunity to extend the childhood
experience, the other serves as an example of the humor young
bears, or even young humans, enjoy. Sendak's portrayal of the
bear family and the interaction of young and old could be a human
family. Grandmother, Grandfather, Father, and Mother all wear
clothing, sit in chairs, and live in houses.

This humanization is especially apparent in the childlike
qualities of Little Bear; he likes stories, eats cake and cookies,
and visits his grandparents' house, often dressing up in their
much-too-big clothing. Sendak's hatched and cross-hatched lines
over muted green and brown areas of color create illustrations
that build an atmosphere of safety and security around the young
child.

The text and pictures are contained within a border, each
corner embellished with a decorative, leafy motif, and this en-
closure helps safely contain the story and characters in an environment of warmth and love. The subtle use of brown, gray, and
green is instrumental in avoiding serious distraction of young
readers from the text. If a child can enjoy the simple sentences
of the text, he or she will get added enjoyment out of the lovable, huggable illustrations.

C115   GOUDEY, ALICE. The Day We Saw the Sun Come Up. Illustrated
        by Adrienne Adams. New York: Charles Scribner's Sons,
        1961, [32 pp.] 29 illus.: color-29/illustrated title
        page/watercolor, wash, and color separation/25.4cm x 20.4cm
        Information: science   Gr. K-2

A young boy and his sister rise early one morning, so they can
witness the dawning of day. From the eastern sky they watch the
changes that occur as the sun creeps over the hill. Throughout
the day they observe the long shadows of early morning and evening, and the short shadows of noon, and, as they prepare to re-
tire, their mother tells them more about the sun.

Explanations follow regarding the effects the sun has upon the
earth--the occurrence of night and day and those rainy days with
no sunshine. Before they take advantage of the darkness to drift
to sleep, the children even experiment with an apple and a flash-
light to better understand the daily cycle of night and day.

In addition to the Author's Note, which relates several basic facts regarding the sun and its location in the solar system, the text provides information about this star and its effects on the earth. The simple experiment, often used in elementary class-rooms in one form or another, provides some concrete means to visualize the concepts presented.

The illustrations, too, provide visual reinforcement of the concepts woven into the story--the changing shadows, daybreak, and sunset--and the soft watercolors easily communicate the hazy atmosphere that accompanies the sun's schedule.

As in the 1960 Honor Book, Houses from the Sea (C108), Goudey weaves her information into some semblance of a story in which a boy and a girl are the vehicle through which the author imparts the information. Because it is difficult to achieve a synthesis of fact and fiction within such a limited space, the book at times seems strictly informational, at others, merely a story.

The illustrations of Adrienne Adams, as in the 1960 Honor Book, help bridge this gap by incorporating the information into illustrations that are neither totally aesthetic nor scientific. This casual handling helps make the information more consumable and develops a book useful as a tool in elementary classrooms.

1963

C116   KEATS, EZRA JACK. The Snowy Day. New York: Viking, 1962, 32 pp. 27 illus.: color-27/illustrated endpapers and title page/collage: mixed media/20.2cm x 22.6cm
Fiction   Gr. Ps-1

When Peter wakes up to a snow-covered world, he is not long in donning his bright red snowsuit to embark upon a day of adventure. The freshly-fallen ground cover provides the young boy with innumerable opportunities for entertainment. Patterns develop across the pages from Peter's feet, a stick, and his entire body, activities which are interspersed with knocking snow off branches, building snowmen and sliding down hills.

When it is time to return to the warmth of his house, Peter carefully packs his pocket with a firm snowball and is disappointed to find it melted before he climbs into bed. After a night of dreams, in which he sees the snow melt away, Peter wakes to another day full of fresh snow--a day he spends, this time, with a friend.

Ezra Jack Keats has brought the simple, direct story of Peter to life in bright, sharply defined shapes of color, texture, and patterns. The collage of shapes, some cut from pieces of wall-paper and wrapping paper, creates compositions of abstract forms and colorful juxtapositions, which lead the eye across the page with artistic skill and with very little detail. Only Peter's face and that of the snowman contain an added touch of detail.

1963

The shape of Peter's red snowsuit in the compositions immediately catches the eye, as do the trail of footprints, the
tracks of dragged feet or stick, or the shape of piled hills of
snow. The large flat areas create a visual impression as striking as a new snowfall itself.

The introduction of this artistic style in picture books, like
the style of Leo Lionni, is a marked departure from the realism
of earlier works of children's literature; the proof of the effectiveness of the book lies in the originality with which the
story is visually expressed, as well as in what is expressed.
Keats's artistic style is indisputably successful in its creative
economy, and his text is as well.

C117   BELTING, NATALIA, ed.   The Sun Is a Golden Earring.   Illus-
         trated by Bernarda Bryson.   New York: Holt, Rinehart &
         Winston, 1962 (OP), [48 pp.]   38 illus.:   color-26; black
         and white-12/illustrated half title page, dedication, and
         front matter/pencil drawings/14.6cm x 22.7cm
         Folk Literature   Gr. 2-5

Natalia Belting has collected folk sayings from around the
world to include in this 1963 Honor Book, illustrated by Bernarda
Bryson. The theme of these twenty-five traditional quotes centers on the natural phenomena of the world and man's attempts to
explain them. Sun, moon, stars, clouds, sky, wind, thunder,
lightning, and the rainbow--all are touched upon in one or more
segments of the collection. Efforts to explain and describe the
occurrence of these elements provide some insight into the cultures
from which the sayings come; each selection reflects the perspective of the culture and usually includes references to items of
importance to inhabitants of the various regions of the world.
In a selection from India, references to elephants are utilized
to explain the occurrence of rain. A selection from the Society
Islands, a culture in which water is an integral part of their
life-style, makes reference to the Milky Way by comparing it to
a sail. The selections from the literature of the various American Indian tribes make constant references to the wind, an element important in their close association with the earth.

The book is full of beautiful associations and comparisons
and is striking in design; its pages contain a wide variety of
color combination within its limited color scheme of yellow,
blue, black, and white. The pencil drawings sometimes appear
on gray, yellow, blue or white backgrounds, often with white on
all blue or charcoal gray pages. White is effectively used on
the darker backgrounds, but when it occasionally appears on a
yellow background, either as the typeface or incorporated into
the illustration, it is difficult to distinguish because there
is such little contrast. The skillful illustrations are often
ephemeral, in a style that reflects the mysticism of the sayings

and their constant references to gods, goddesses, and extra-terrestrial beings.

The wide range of cultures from which this collection grew and the variety within the book's design are overwhelming at times and not always cohesive in the visual effect. Some pages work well in and of themselves, but the use of color and gray or white type from page to page, and often on the same page, some-times produces a disjointed impression.

C118 ZOLOTOW, CHARLOTTE. <u>Mr. Rabbit and the Lovely Present</u>.
Illustrated by Maurice Sendak. New York: Harper & Row, 1962, [32 pp.] 14 illus.: color-14/illustrated endpapers and title page/watercolor/17cm x 20cm
Fantasy   Gr. Ps-1

A little girl confides in Mr. Rabbit that she does not have a suitable gift for her mother's birthday. Mr. Rabbit offers his suggestions, none suitable, some highly impractical, but the little girl finally decides on an apple, since her mother does like red. But an apple just is not enough, so they also gather a banana from an abandoned picnic site, some Bartlett pears, and a bunch of blue grapes. After the red, yellow, green, and blue fruits are neatly arranged in a basket, the little girl finally has a very lovely present befitting her mother's birthday.

The casual conversations of Mr. Rabbit and the child through-out the book make Zolotow's text a useful tool in identifying colors; the repetitive events of the text, the sequence of naming various objects of one of the four colors, make it a book that can be successfully used with young children. The conversations between the characters seems perfectly natural, and Maurice Sendak's illustrations help make the book an enjoyable one for children.

The impressionistic illustrations, small dabs of color that create the foliage of the trees and the grass of the countryside, produce a cool blue and green environment in which the characters carry out their search for the perfect gift. The characteristic qualities of the watercolors are particularly suitable to the mottled effect achieved by dabbing the color on the paper.

There is little of the linear detail characteristic of Sendak's style in these illustrations, which appear solely on the right-hand side of the spreads. There is no physical integration of word and picture, but this separation is effective in making the audience spectators, as though viewing the relationship of rabbit and child from a distance. This perspective enhances Sendak's visual impact and also creates an atmosphere reflective of the elements of fantasy in the text.

<u>1964</u>

C119   SENDAK, MAURICE. <u>Where the Wild Things Are</u>. New York:
        Harper & Row, 1963, [40 pp.] 29 illus.: color-29/
        illustrated endpapers, title page, and front matter/india
        ink over full-color watercolor/22.8cm x 25cm
        Fantasy   Gr. Ps-2
        When Max, clad in his wolf suit, is confined to his room,
without supper, for making all sorts of mischief, his imagination
transports him to a world where he becomes king of the most wild
creatures of all. But gradually, as the wild things, and Max,
partake in a wild rumpus, the novelty of authority wears off,
and Max sentences the creatures to bed without <u>their</u> suppers.
Max quickly decides he would rather be where he is loved; he
travels back over the seas of his imagination to discover the
reassurance of a warm, aromatic supper awaiting him.
        Maurice Sendak's illustrations for his own text demonstrate
the integral relationship between word and picture. As the story
begins, the pictures specify Max's particular, ingenious acts of
mischief--pounding nails in walls and chasing a pet with a fork.
As Max's confinement irritates the active youth, his imagination
grows, as does the size of the illustrations. The extent of Max's
imagination reaches its limits with the climax of the wild rumpus,
which lasts three full-page spreads--all without text.
        Sendak's hatched and cross-hatched pen lines over watercolor
create the verdant surroundings of the jungle of the wild beasts.
The monsters' figures also take form from the pen lines placed
over their basic shapes. Impressionistic settings, similar to
those of <u>Mr. Rabbit and the Lovely Present</u> (C118), a 1963 Honor
Book, and the eerie casts of moonlight evident in <u>The Moon Jumpers</u>
(C109), a 1960 Honor Book, combine to communicate the physical and
mental states of uproar, which prevail in the book.
        Sendak synthesizes the efforts of his previous works into a
book whose text is as imaginative as his visual interpretation.
Max's rebellion and subsequent discovery are very much in tune
with the needs and occupations of his intended audience, and this
accuracy of emotion will continue to ensure the popular appeal of
Sendak's books.

C120   LIONNI, LEO. <u>Swimmy</u>. New York: Pantheon, 1963, [32 pp.]
        28 illus.: color-28/illustrated title page and front
        matter/watercolor wash, ink, rubber stamp, pencil, and
        stencil/27.1cm x 22.7cm
        Fantasy   Gr. Ps-1
        After a large tuna gobbles up a school of little red fish,
Swimmy, the only black fish and sole survivor of the massacre,
swims off through the sea. The beautiful marvels of this underwater setting--medusa, lobster, seaweed, eel, and anemone--restore

Swimmy's spirits. Hidden in the darkness of the ocean floor,
Swimmy discovers another school of little red fish, all of whom
refuse his offers to swim and play, for fear of being eaten.

The little black fish uses his ingenuity and instructs the
school to swim in a formation the shape of a fish. In a cooperative effort, with Swimmy serving as the eye, the school can
safely glide through the water, chasing the big fish away.

Individual differences can be very beneficial, as Lionni has
demonstrated in word and pictures. His own individual, creative
style brings the tale of Swimmy to life. Watery blues, grays,
greens, and violets combine with repeated pattersn and texture to
create Swimmy's underwater home. The repetition of the figures
in the school of fish gives the effect of block prints, and the
patterned doily motif appears throughout the book and provides
some unity.

When Swimmy's mood is lonely, sad, or troubled, the gray tones
of the water dominate the page. When his spirits are high, the
vibrant colors of the ocean floor predominate. Size remains an
important element in this Honor Book, where a tiny being triumphs
over larger, more dangerous foes. Physically, too, Swimmy remains a small black shape in contrast to the large pages of
colorful underwater inhabitants.

Though Lionni's text is simple and direct, the economy of
words makes the illustrations highly important in extending and
embellishing the story. The artist's inventive style remains a
popular one within the realm of picture books, and the underlying
themes have a relevancy that wears well with time.

C121   ALGER, LECLAIRE [Sorche Nic Leodhas]. All in the Morning
       Early. Illustrated by Evaline Ness. New York: Holt,
       Rinehart & Winston, 1963 (OP), [32 pp.] 28 illus.: color-
       14; raw sienna, black and white-14/illustrated endpapers,
       title page, and front matter/wash, line and color separation/
       20.2cm x 22.1cm
       Folk Tale   Gr. Ps-1
This cumulative tale, of Scottish origin, begins when a boy
named Sandy starts off one morning to take a sack of corn to
the old mill. On his journey he encounters one huntsman, two
ewes, three gypsies, four farmers, five lads, six hares, seven
geese, eight burnybees (ladybugs), nine larks, and ten lassies--
all of whom walk with him to the mill, early in the morning.

The alliteration and rhymed couplets in the text move the
repetition of the chorus along as each addition to the company tacks on another line. Though the rhythm and pairs of couplets in the book are a part of the traditional, oral literature
of Scotland, many of the original words have been changed. Those
that do remain help authenticate the text, and their definitions
are included in the Author's Note at the close of the book.

1964

Evaline Ness also helps place the story in its proper setting
through the Scottish nature of the clothing and countryside which
she creates in turquoise, olive, and raw sienna. The pages, each
edged in one of the three colors of the illustrations, alternate
with spreads of raw sienna, black, and white or all three colors
and black and white. The background of overlapping shapes of color
or wash provide the base from which the characters of the story
emerge. It is the shape and color of the background that direct
the eye around the page and hold the compositions together.

The black lines that sometimes refine and outline the shapes
are rough and uneven, often with the effect of a line made by
paint on the edge of a piece of cardboard. Those lines that
define the round, impish faces of the lads are a contrast to
the gaunt, weathered lines in the faces of the adults. The
artist demonstrates the varied effects possible from her unusual
color scheme, and her illustrations, striking and unique, help
embellish this tale, which needs a little beefing up.

C122   REED, PHILIP, ed. <u>Mother Goose and Nursery Rhymes</u>. New York:
       Atheneum, 1963, 54 illus.: color-54/illustrated title
       page/wood engravings/27.4cm x 19.7cm
       Mother Goose/Nursery Rhymes   Gr. Ps-1

Philip Reed is the artist responsible for producing the collection of sixty-six Mother Goose and nursery rhymes that received Honor Book status in 1964. The limited number of rhymes
included, in conjunction with the clean, well-defined illustrations, makes this a collection in which the reader is not overwhelmed by the amount of text or illustration. Though strictly
not a picture storybook, the work is more cohesive than many in
its uniformity of visual interpretation, but its omission of
several standard rhymes may limit its appeal.

A pleasing harmony is achieved in the book among the size of
type, the illustration, and the dimensions of the page. The work
does not succumb to the overcrowding of many collections of this
type, and the use of color illustrations throughout adds a continuity sometimes lacking in compilations in which both black and
white and color visuals are included.

Nearly every rhyme has some illustration to its words, some
humorous, some serious in intent. As the index of the first
lines reveals, many of the more common rhymes, such as "Mary Had
a Little Lamb," or "Baa, Baa Black Sheep," are not included.

The sharp, black lines of the wood engraving and the soft,
muted colors help reflect the traditional background of the
literature. This technique, rooted in the history of illustration, not only provides a visual impression in keeping with the
origins of the rhymes, but also produces illustrations which
hold their own upon the pages.

1965

C123   De REGNIERS, BEATRICE SCHENK. <u>May I Bring a Friend?</u>.
       Illustrated by Beni Montresor. New York: Atheneum, 1964,
       [48 pp.] 29 illus.: color-21; black and white-8/illus-
       trated title page, dedication page/drawings on board with
       solid overlays and screened overlays on acetate/24.1cm x
       19.5cm
       Fantasy   Gr. K-2
   When the King and Queen extend an invitation for tea to their
young friend, they have no qualms about the little boy's bringing
along a guest. So each day, with each invitation, the King and
Queen are in the company of animals of one sort or another. A
giraffe, a hippo, monkeys, an elephant, lions, and a seal all
take their turn accompanying their young friend to the royal
palace.
   As the week progresses and Saturday arrives, the animals in-
sist the King and Queen join them for tea--at the City Zoo, of
course. Just as comfortable as if sitting on their thrones, the
King and Queen join the animals in a cage to sip a bit of their
favorite beverage.
   Beni Montresor's illustrations which accompany the rhyming
text of this 1965 Caldecott Medal Book make the bizarre events
of the story seem perfectly natural. Only the surprised expressions of the King and Queen and a minimum of textual clues give
away the curious nature of the boy's friends. Pages of gold,
orange, red, brown, and fuchsia alternate with black on a one-
color background or black and white illustrations. The black and
white pages depict the royal couple at everyday tasks and activities: gathering flowers, dancing in the ballroom, fishing off a
pier, chasing butterflies, swinging on a swing. These peaceful
scenes provide a contrast to the vibrant hues and sometimes cha-
otic events of the surrounding pages.
   The rhyming text requires practiced reading as the rhythm is
at times awkward in its accommodation of the rhyme. Full-page
color spreads introduce the young boy's friends, and the black
lines and outlines of all the illustrations give the page the
look of the boldness of woodcuts. Short strokes and dots of
splattered ink create a fuzzy appearance, but at a distance the
lines gain definition and clarity and the compositions and colors
can be more fully appreciated.

C124   SCHEER, JULIAN. <u>Rain Makes Applesauce</u>. Illustrated by Marvin
       Bileck. New York: Holiday House, 1964, [36 pp.] 30
       illus.: color-30/illustrated title page and front matter/
       watercolor/26.6cm x 19cm
       Fantasy   Gr. K-2
   Singing teddy bears, dancing dolls, and walking houses are all
a part of the nonsense in <u>Rain Makes Applesauce</u>. On every

1965

full-page color spread, a new saying appears, always ending with
the words ". . . and rain makes applesauce." At the close of
the book, all the previous gibbering is denounced, except the
fact that rain <u>does</u> make applesauce, for it helps the apple
trees grow.

Small reminders of reality appear on nearly every other page
to reemphasize the fact that this is all just "silly talk." The
infinite detail in the drawings helps make these unbelievable
situations come to life with fantastic inventions of jelly bean
jungles, tickle trees, and lemon juice stars--all a delight to
any youngster.

The letters of the text weave in and out of the illustrations,
creating a surreal, imaginary atmosphere in the book. The hand-
lettered text is oftentimes difficult to discern from the busy
color backgrounds; as a result, legibility sometimes suffers.

No one would argue with the unusual and creative qualities of
the book, but the integration of the text into the illustrations
is not always effective and is oftentimes distracting. The creative extension of the text by the illustrations is no doubt responsible for the book's selection as an Honor Book, but the
usefulness and appeal of the book seems limited, and, in the
simplicity of its nonsensical text, demands a mature understanding.

C125   HODGES, MARGARET. <u>The Wave</u>. Illustrated by Blair Lent.
        Boston: Houghton Mifflin, 1964, 45 pp. 36 illus.:
        color-35; black and white-1/illustrated title page and
        front matter/stencil, wash, color separation, cardboard
        cuts/23.2cm x 23.5cm
        Folk Tale   Gr. 1-4

Ojiisan and his grandson, Tada, live on a mountainside of rice
fields, far above the village below. The fine reputation of this
wise and respected man makes him a source of advice and guidance
among the villagers. Celebrating their good fortune in the plentiful rice harvest one year, the villagers gather on the seashore
far below Ojiisan. A mild earthquake gently rocks the village
and mountaintop, but Ojiisan senses more serious danger.

The old man quickly sets fire to his rice fields, and the
villagers below cease their celebrating to rush up the mountainside to squelch the fire. Their anger at Ojiisan for burning
his own fields is soon quelled as the last villager struggles
to the mountaintop, just in time to see a tidal wave destroy
the village below. Years of rebuilding eventually restore the
village and its fields, and the self-sacrifice of Ojiisan is
memorialized in a temple erected in his honor.

The story, based on a Japanese folk tale from Lafcadio Hearn's
<u>Gleanings in Buddha-Fields</u>, is represented in brown, gray, gold,
and black illustrations in which the spiraling motif of the tidal
wave is ever present. A full-page spread, void of text, visually

represents the climax of the story as a gigantic wave sweeps across the pages, carrying bits and pieces of the village with it.

The watery impressions of the illustrations, Eastern garments, and Japanese architectural forms all produce an atmosphere which reflects the origins of the tale. Blair Lent's textures and unusual combinations of free flowing shapes and rigid, calculated cardboard-cutout shapes create an impression of the story's events rather than a literal interpretation. Dependent upon the manner in which the tale is presented to its audience, the story has potential for younger and more mature audiences alike.

C126 CAUDILL, REBECCA. <u>Pocketful of Cricket</u>. Illustrated by
Evaline Ness. New York: Holt, Rinehart & Winston, 1964,
[48 pp.] 42 illus.: color-42/illustrated title page and
front matter/line, wash, and color separation/26.7cm x 20.3cm
Fiction   Gr. K-2

Six-year-old Jay sets out on an August afternoon for a walk through the countryside, collecting mementos from his trek; hickory nut, fossilized rock, gray goose feather, Indian arrowhead, and speckled beans—all become part of the objects amassed in his pocket. A cricket he cups in his hands. The insect becomes his faithful pet who lives in a wire-screen cage in his bedroom. Every day Jay and his cricket spring around his bedroom, and every night Jay's cricket fiddles in the dark as the intimate friendship of child and pet develops.

Jay, reluctant to leave his pet behind when it comes time to start school, hides the insect in his pocket, and they ride the bus together. Luckily Jay has an understanding teacher who allows him to share his pet with the class, and next time he offers to bring in something less noisy to share—his speckled beans.

Alternating one- and three-color spreads display the characteristics common to the artistic style of Evaline Ness. In ochre, olive, red, and black and white, Ness's illustrations help the audience discover the natural patterns of cornstalks, hickory leaves, and rippling water. The pictures play upon these repetitive shapes to create designs within the compositions.

Shadows and background shapes build upon each other to create areas of color upon which the figures are drawn. The compositions, more confined than in other Ness works, sometimes appear secondary to the lengthy text. It is when the illustrations flow across the page and break the monotony of the book's format that word and picture interact most effectively. At these times the visuals are most characteristically and dynamically Ness.

1966

C127   ALGER, LECLAIRE [Sorche Nic Leodhas]. <u>Always Room for One</u>
        <u>More</u>. Illustrated by Nonny Hogrogian. New York: Holt,
        Rinehart & Winston, 1965, [32 pp.] 20 illus.: color-29/
        illustrated title page and front matter/chalk, wash, pen
        and ink/18.1cm x 21cm
        Folk Tale   Gr. Ps-1
    Though Lachie MacLachlan already has a wife and ten children
living in one house, he generously extends a welcome to any traveler passing by, for there is "always room for one more." Gradually a tinker, tailor, sailor, lassie, an auld wife, four peat
cutters, Piping Rury, and a shepherd lad and his dog congregate
in Lachie's house.
    There is plenty of room until Rury begins playing his bagpipes;
with everyone dancing and singing, it is not long before the entire house bursts at the seams and falls apart. But Lachie is
not dismayed; utilizing all the resources of the manpower at
hand, he has the guests construct a bigger, even better, house,
with plenty of room for one more.
    This popular Scottish song, the tune to which appears at the
back of the book, retains the original rhythm and rhyme of the
vocabulary of its heritage. The oral tradition of the work is
apparent as the text begs to be read aloud. To facilitate
understanding, the convenient glossary helps clarify some of the
unfamiliar Scottish words and expressions.
    Nonny Hogrogian's pen-and-ink illustrations, over a violet and
mossy green Scottish countryside, create an impressive and unusual interpretation of the text. Hatched and cross-hatched lines
create the Scottish garb and thatched roofs of the setting. Several figures are nothing but a series of parallel lines, which
create an expressive impression of the character's torso and its
position. The soft, smudgy backgrounds help interpret the hazy
atmosphere of heather-and-moss-covered hills, and the words can
be enhanced by the accompanying tune, an open invitation to momentarily partake in a touch of Scottish oral tradition.

C128   TRESSELT, ALVIN. <u>Hide and Seek Fog</u>. Illustrated by Roger
        Duvoisin. New York: Lothrop, Lee & Shepard, 1965, [32 pp.]
        26 illus.: color-26/illustrated endpapers, title page, and
        front matter/watercolor and gouache/24.8cm x 19.9cm
        Fiction   Gr. K-2
    A three-day fog settles in and has a variety of effects on
fishermen, vacationers, and children of this seaside area.
Lobster boats are marooned at the wharf; sailboats fold up their
sails; adults complain of ruined vacations. Only the children
enjoy the weather-induced imprisonment and manage to improvise,
playing hide-and-seek in the thick mist.

The warm rays of the sun eventually burn off the heavy cover, so the sailboats ready for a race; the lobsterman checks his supplies; and the families of vacationers return to the beach to take advantage of the favorable weather.

The impressions of this natural phenomenon are skillfully recorded in text and illustration. The gray, foggy background of the pages provides the perfect, hazy atmosphere of fog that envelops the seaside town. Shadowy, smudged shapes, with very little detail, emerge from the depths of the fog. The aquamarine of the initial full-page spread returns as the fog lifts and life resumes its normal routine.

Tresselt sensitively, almost poetically, records the fog's effects upon all ages in his text, but the appeal of the illustrations has perhaps lessened since the book's publication. The work may serve as a useful tool in elementary science lessons, but its appeal to today's audiences may be limited.

C129   ETS, MARIE HALL. Just Me. New York: Viking, 1965, 32 pp.
        28 illus.: black and white-28/illustrated title page/
        charcoal/17.8cm x 23.2cm
        Fiction   Gr. Ps-K
A small boy imitates the characteristics of different animals he encounters on a farm and in the woods in the text of this 1966 Honor Book. Prowling on all fours like a cat or strutting like a rooster, the young impersonator mimics the animals' inherent traits. A hopping rabbit, slithering snake, and contented cow offer perfect models for the little boy's imaginative imitations.

When he finally comes through the cornfield and tries to get his father's attention down at the pond, the child has to abandon all those unnatural means of locomotion; he has to run just as no one but he can. Catching up with his father, the child climbs into the boat at the pond's edge, and they motor out together across the water.

The black and white illustrations for the book are contained within oblong formats and are very similar in style to In the Forest (C32), a 1945 Honor Book, also by Ets. The figures on the pages are defined by the black backgrounds which outline the shapes in the pictures; the works almost take on the appearance of woodcuts.

Rust-colored type adds a variation to the book's format not seen in other Ets Caldecott books, but the contrasts produced by white against a darker background remain characteristically Ets. The artist captures the distinguishing traits of the animals of the story and mimics the movements of the imaginative child in a story that is not far from the truth in the creative imaginings and play of young children.

1966

C130   JACOBS, JOSEPH, ed. <u>Tom Tit Tot</u>. Illustrated by Evaline Ness.
        Charles Scribner's Sons, 1965 (OP), [32 pp.] 27 illus.:
        color-27/illustrated title page, front matter, and dedica-
        tion/woodcuts/25.5cm x 20cm
        Folk Tale   Gr. K-2
        This English folk tale, a variation of the more familiar
Rumpelstiltskin tale, finds a woman idly singing a song about
her daughter, who has single-handedly consumed five pies. When
a King overhears the singing and questions the woman, she avoids
embarrassment by saying her daughter has just spun five skeins.
The King, impressed by such a feat, marries the daughter under
the condition that she spend the last month of the year spinning
five skeins each day.
        When the final month arrives, the witless girl is rescued from
her dilemma by a black creature who offers to spin the skeins,
and, in return, the girl must guess the name of the creature or
become its companion. The girl agrees to the bargain, as it is
far more attractive than the death that awaits her if she fails
to produce the skeins.
        The month passes by, but the girl is unable to guess the crea-
ture's name, until the final night when the King dines with her
and tells her of a creature he discovered in the woods, chanting his name: Tom Tit Tot. Upon the return of the cunning impet,
the girl guesses his name and never again has to worry about her
future.
        Turquoise, brown, and olive woodcuts provide an appropriate
medium for the visual interpretation of this traditional piece
of literature. The grain of the wood is especially conducive to
the repetition of patterns so prevalent in Ness's work. The
decorative patterns of clothing, flowers, and foliage are built
upon backgrounds of large areas of color. Each full-page spread
contains a few words from the text which are carved into the composition of the woodcuts and which are incorporated at the beginning or end of the text on the page. The expressive lines of the
woodcuts direct the eye around the page, and the ghosts, small
marks that appear as a result of not removing all the wood in an
area, add an interesting effect.
        In this book Ness demonstrates her ability to adjust and adapt
her individual artistic style. The suitability of medium to text
is of extreme importance, as is the manner in which the medium
itself is handled. Color and style have helped create an original and noteworthy work of art in which the physical integration
of text and picture has embraced and strengthened the work.

1967

C131   NESS, EVALINE. <u>Sam, Bangs & Moonshine</u>. New York: Holt,
          Rinehart & Winston, 1966, [44 pp.] 32 illus.: color-32/
          illustrated title page and front matter/line and wash/
          24.8cm x 18.7cm
          Fiction   Gr. 1-3
     Samantha, Sam for short, has difficulty distinguishing between
what is real and what is imaginary--moonshine--but when she jeop-
ardizes the life of her good friend, Thomas, the difference becomes very clear to her.
     Sam is forever telling Thomas she has a baby kangaroo, so one
day she sends him off to Blue Rock to find the creature. When a
storm blows up and the tide comes in early, Thomas and Sam's cat,
Bangs, are stranded on the rock. Though Thomas is rescued by
Sam's father, Bangs is swept away. As Sam goes to bed that night,
she knows that her moonshine was responsible for Bangs's death
and almost Thomas's, but before she falls asleep, a scratching at
the window catches her attention. There is Bangs, a water-logged,
but living, mess, purring outside the glass.
     The next morning Sam is awakened by a gerbil hopping across
her bedroom floor. Off Sam runs to visit the convalescing Thomas,
to present him with Moonshine, the four-legged pet that almost
looks just like a baby kangaroo.
     Muted green and brown, with gray washes and black lines, give
the illustrations of this book the misty, foggy atmosphere of its
seaside setting. The cloudy backgrounds are conducive to Sam's
inclinations to the world of make-believe. The strong patterns
of shadows and background shapes, so characteristic of Ness's
work, are more expressive and effective in these translucent,
cool hues. Some of the work even appears to be done on wet
paper; the bleeding of lines and quick strokes produces an ex-
temporaneous and lively atmosphere.
     Though the illustrations interfere with the text in a couple
of instances, the physical integration of word and picture, extension of the text, and the reflection of the mood of the book
make this Medal winner a worthy recipient.

C132   EMBERLEY, BARBARA. <u>One Wide River to Cross</u>. Illustrated by
          Ed Emberley. Englewood Cliffs, N.J.: Prentice-Hall, 1966
          (OP), [32 pp.] 28 illus.: black on color-28/illustrated
          title page and front matter/woodcuts/19.2cm x 25.7cm
          Bible   Gr. Ps-1
     The story of Noah's Ark becomes a counting book as the animals
of the biblical story board the vessel, one by one, then two by
two. The Jordan is the river of the title, and as the rain falls
and the flood begins, the loaded ark embarks upon its journey.
When the flood recedes, the vessel finally comes to rest on the

1967

mountains of Ararat, as a rainbow fills the sky, a reassuring
symbol that the rains are over. The accompanying tune and verses,
complete with refrain, provide an added dimension to this book
of striking design and color.

Black woodcuts appear on solid backgrounds of vibrant hues:
violet, fuchsia, yellow, green, blue, and red provide the colors
on which the bold, black, stylized animals appear. Elephants,
yaks, hippos, ostriches, chickadees, alligators, and even uni-
corn, griffin, manticore, and basilisk make their appearances on
the book's pages.

The repetition of the animals, within whose shapes repeated
patterns also appear, reinforce the repetition and rhyme in the
text, which continue until the animals come in "ten by ten." As
the shapes parade in lines across the pages, they create even more
patterns of patterns, taking on the look of geometric motifs found
in North American Indian artifacts. Even the designs decorating
the sides of the floating ark contain geometric shapes and patterns that are especially apparent when the ark is wedged between
the two mountains of Ararat. This is the only page on which white
appears, and the contrast between the bold black shapes of the
woodcut, the arcing colors of the rainbow, and the white background help enhance the symbolism of the event. The simple words
of the text are complemented by these strong, bold visual counterparts. Though the intense backgrounds are sometimes overwhelming,
the book is artfully designed.

1968

C133   EMBERLEY, BARBARA. Drummer Hoff. Illustrated by Ed Emberley.
        Englewood Cliffs, N.J.: Prentice-Hall, 1967, [32 pp.]
        29 illus.: color-29/illustrated title page and front
        matter/woodcuts/19.3cm x 25.7cm
        Nursery Rhyme   Gr. Ps-1

    This cumulative story of the preparation and firing of a can-
non commences with Private Parriage bringing the carriage of the
firearm. And so the rhyming text continues, as the military personnel collect barrel, powder, rammer, and shot. When General
Border finally gives the order to fire, Drummer Hoff is responsible for the full-page explosion that follows.

    The fiery red of the explosion, on the only page without a
spot of white, produces billows of swirling gushes expelled from
the cannon. The bold designs and patterns within the shapes reinforce the repetition within the story line, as does the format
of the illustrations. With each addition to the cannon's para-
phernalia, another face, belonging to the military personnel involved, appears along the edge of the stylized grass. Large
shapes are broken down into smaller and smaller shapes and colors

within. Green, red, violet, blue, yellow, and orange provide the hues confined by the bold black lines that define the figures.

The rhyming, rhythmical text moves the story along as the procession of events moves from left to right in the book's horizontal format. The stark white of the pages provides maximum contrast between the black lines and the background. The Emberleys have combined their literary and artistic styles to create another Caldecott recipient that contributes to the originality and creativity that make children's books so versatile, alive, and fresh.

C134   LIONNI, LEO.   Frederick.   New York: Pantheon, 1967, [32 pp.]
         27 illus.:   color-27/illustrated endpapers and title page/
         mixed media: torn paper, cut paper, crayon, and chalk/
         27.5cm x 22.9cm
         Fantasy   Gr. K-2

While the members of a family of field mice diligently gather food for the winter, Frederick sits and collects rays of the sun, colors of the fields and flowers, and words of the seasons. The relatives scoff at Frederick's aesthetic activities until winter sets in and their stone wall home grows cold and dreary and gray. Food supplies have dwindled, and morale is low, so Frederick brings out the "supplies" so carefully selected in the warmer days of summer and fall.

Magically Frederick warms his companions with the imaginary rays of the sun and fills their thoughts with the bright colors of periwinkles, poppies, berries, leaves, and wheat. When the words of Frederick's own poetry astonish his relatives, their appreciation of his talents is reward enough for the shy, humble figure of Frederick, the mouse.

The torn paper shapes of the bodies of the mice, the patterned foreground and background shapes, and the corrugated look of stalks of wheat are all indicative of the variety of media Lionni employs to bring his simple, yet meaningful, texts to life. Textures and patterns abound in the compositions created by the rounded, secure shapes of the stones of the mouse hideout.

Because there is little detail in the compositions, slight variations in the shapes and positions of the eyes of the mice become very important reflections of the moods of the characters. Frederick is distinguished by his half-closed eyes, giving him a detached, remote gaze.

Lionni's subtle themes continue to find expression in his lovable creatures of the animal world, and their small size makes them endearing heroes to their faithful audiences.

C135   YASHIMA, TARO.   Seashore Story.   New York: Viking, 1967,
         [46 pp.]   36 illus.:   color-36/illustrated endpapers,
         title page, and front matter/oil pastels and watercolor/
         22.7cm x 26.8cm

1968

Fiction   Gr. 1-3
On the shores of an island at the southern tip of Japan, young
children recall the tale of Urashima, the fisherman who once rescued a wounded sea turtle. The turtle repays the kindness by
transporting the fisherman to a palace beneath the sea. Here
Urashima stays in comfort until one day he feels a longing for
his home and people. Upon his return, the fisherman finds no
home, no family--an unfamiliar village. Climbing the mountain,
Urashima opens a lacquered box, a gift of the sea people, and
instantly turns into a white-haired old man. Though the youngsters on the shore cannot fully comprehend the significance of
the tale, their teacher tries to help them understand the sacred-
ness of the family and the importance of loved ones.

Blurred impressions of human figures in pinks, greens, blues,
and grays help create the mystical atmosphere of Yashima's ancient tale. The lounging figures of the children on the shore
mimic the twirling, dancing bodies, which seem to flow with the
gentle ebb of the waves of the sea. Many illustrations are symbolic representations of the feelings of the book's characters.
Darkness overtakes the illustrations as it does Urashima's heart
when he returns to a home unfamiliar and foreboding, just as the
oval darkness into which turtle and fisherman disappear presents
a menacing omen.

Yashima's artistic style, interpreted in the soft pastel drawings, comes to life more effectively here than in his previous
Honor Books. He is able to communicate the mystery and deeply
rooted philosophy of the Japanese culture through his illustrations, and though abstract in concept and visual conception, the
book attempts an authentic presentation within its unusual,
creative approach.

C136   YOLEN, JANE. The Emperor and the Kite. Illustrated by Ed
        Young. Cleveland, Ohio: World, 1967, [32 pp.] 27 illus.:
        color-27/illustrated title page and front matter/color
        separation, cut paper, watercolor, and ink/20.3cm x 23.2cm
        Fantasy: folklike tale   Gr. K-2
Though Djeow Seow, meaning smallest one, goes virtually unnoticed by her father, the emperor, it is she, not her older
brothers or sisters, who rescues her father from his imprisonment in a high tower. Day after day, using the only means she
has, the tiny child flies her kite to the barred window of the
tower, with a basket of tea, rice, and poppyseed cakes attached.

One day, having received a message hidden in the words of an
old monk, Djeow Seow sends a sturdy rope soaring to the emperor
on the wings of her kite. Upon his escape and return to his
palace, the king expels the wicked criminals from his home, and
peace again reigns. Because Djeow Seow's kite brought food,
drink, and freedom to her father, she is never again neglected

or overlooked. Her tiny throne forever sits next to that of her father, and she comes to rule her kingdom gently and loyally in the years to come.

The stark white pages of this Honor Book provide a background which allows the striking hues and mottled outlines to stand out clearly and distinctly. The stylized patterns of robes, grass, vines, leaves, and flowers form bold outlines much like the clear, rigid lines of a woodcut. On pages lacking much illustration, the simple line of the kite string continuing off the page is enough to move the eye across the spread to the action beyond. At times only the small figure of Djeow Seow skillfully balances the stark, empty compositions.

Young concentrates and synthesizes his illustrations down to the bare minimum. There is no superfluous detail, often no background at all; only the events of importance to the theme find expression in the illustrations. This economy reinforces the simple, honest efforts of a heroine who accomplishes a task much larger, literally and symbolically, than her small stature. Just as the black shapes of the evil intruders visually reflect their character, so the innocence of the small, humble child is reflected in this tiny figure juxtaposed with and counterbalancing the enormous shapes of tower, rope, and kite.

1969

C137   RANSOME, ARTHUR. The Fool of the World and the Flying Ship: A Russian Tale. Illustrated by Uri Shulevitz. New York: Farrar, Straus & Giroux, 1968, [48 pp.] 44 illus.: color-44/illustrated endpapers and title page/pen and brush with black and colored ink/22.9cm x 26.5cm
Folk Tale   Gr. 1-3

When the Czar offers his daughter's hand in exchange for a flying ship, everyone, including the Fool of the World, sets out to find such a vessel. In his travels, the Fool meets an old man, with whom he shares his scraps of food. For his kindness, the Fool is rewarded with a flying ship and instructed to pick up everyone he sees.

With a full ship of passengers, the Fool arrives at the palace, but the Czar is not willing to give his daughter to such an ordinary peasant. The ruler devises such tasks that no man might overcome them--except, that is, the Fool and his multi-talented companions. The Swiftgoer fetches the magical water of life, aided by the Listener and the Far-shouter; the Eater consumes twelve oxen and the bread from forty ovens; the Drinker swallows forty barrels of wine. After the Moujik scatters his magic straw in the bathhouse and transforms a fagot of wood into an army, the Czar, fearing for his life, is more than happy to have the Fool marry his daughter.

1969

In this year when folk tales represent the literature of both
Medal and Honor Books, Uri Shulevitz captures the magical playful atmosphere that permeates the fantasy of the tale. He makes
the events of the Fool's trip seem commonplace and perfectly
acceptable by providing settings just realistic enough to carry
the reader over the threshold of the imagination.

The watercolor and pen-and-ink drawings of stocky, bearded,
round-cheeked individuals, farmland fields, and a domed palace
bring the ethnicity to light, while the full-page spreads of
color, with hatched and cross-hatched lines, entertain the eye.
Though the text is lengthy, Shulevitz's illustrations, rambling
from one side of the page onto the next, contain sufficient detail and variations in format to prevent a lull in the activities.
Shulevitz emphasizes the versatility of the visual and verbal
language of the picture book and preserves originality and integrity of individual artistic style.

C138 DAYRELL, ELPHINSTONE. Why the Sun and the Moon Live in the
      Sky: An African Folktale. Illustrated by Blair Lent.
      Boston: Houghton Mifflin, 1968, 28 pp. 20 illus.: color-
      20/illustrated endpapers, title page, and front matter/
      cardboard cuts/22.8cm x 22.7cm
      Folk Tale   Gr. 1-3
      This African folk tale of the sun and his wife, the moon, re-
counts the friendship of the sun and water. Theirs was a close
relationship, except for the fact that the water would never
visit the sun at his house. When the sun questions the water
regarding this, water replies that his friend's house is much
too small for the water and all his people.

The sun promptly begins to construct a house large enough for
the water and all his relatives, and when the structure is complete, and the invitations extended, the water arrives at the
house of the sun and the moon. As more and more relatives flow
into the house, the sun and the moon are forced higher and higher,
until they float out of the overflowing house and into the sky.

Although this ancient tale specifically originated in Southeast Nigeria among the Efik-Ibibio peoples, as the Note at the
close of the book indicates, the designs and symbols the artist
employs are representative of many tribes and peoples. The
tribesmen in the illustrations are masked and dressed in costumes
symbolizing the elements of nature and the creatures of the sea.

Pages dealing primarily with the water dominate in blues and
greens, while golds and browns cover the pages referring to the
sun and the moon. The geometric shapes and patterns of the masks
and costumes of the tribesmen reinforce the African origins of
the tale.

The symbolism of the story is easily grasped through the handling of the illustrations, and the attempt to explain a

phenomenon of nature in a folk tale is a common practice. The
humanization of sun, moon, and water, combined with the natural
properties of each--the sun and moon's location in the sky, the
inhabitants of the water and its flowing capabilities--help transform abstract concepts and the world view of this culture into a
meaningful and enjoyable 28-page experience.

1970

C139   STEIG, WILLIAM. <u>Sylvester and the Magic Pebble</u>. New York:
        Windmill Books/Simon & Schuster, 1969, [32 pp.]   30 illus.:
        color-30/illustrated title page/watercolor/30.3cm x 22.5cm
        Fantasy   Gr. K-2

Sylvester Duncan, a pebble-collecting donkey, one day discovers an extraordinary magic pebble. While returning home,
young Sylvester has the misfortune of encountering a lion, and
with pebble in hoof, Sylvester wishes, of all things, that he is
a rock. He is instantly granted his wish; but, since the pebble
is no longer in his possession, Sylvester has no means of returning himself to normal once the lion lumbers away.

Now Sylvester unobtrusively spends the remaining summer months,
as well as the fall and winter ones, as a rock. No one has the
slightest idea what has happened to the young donkey, until spring
arrives and his parents choose to have a picnic right on Sylvester's back. Mrs. Duncan, inadvertently placing the pebble on the
rock-table, gives her son the needed opportunity to wish he were
in his proper form. And, in such a manner, the Duncans are
happily and finally reunited.

Though the text of this Medal Book makes no mention of the
species of Sylvester, all the characters, including the Duncans,
are animals. Clean, clear watercolors create the shapes of the
characters, many of which, outlined in black, take on an air of
humor as they act and react with human emotion and mannerisms.
Their reactions to the suspense and despair of the events of the
story are clearly evident in their facial expressions, which help
heighten the humor and absurdity of the tale and, at the same
time, evoke some compassion from the audience.

The variety of full-page and single-page illustrations, sometimes with two compositions appearing on a single page, and
slight variations in text placement help avoid a monotony in the
layout of the book. The viewer seems almost to have picked up a
series of still shots from a cartoon, each illustration nearly
self-explanatory in its entirety. Steig brings the suspense and
drama of his tale to life, with skillful ease, and a touch of
humor.

1970

C140   KEATS, EZRA JACK. <u>Goggles!</u> New York: Macmillan, 1969,
           [34 pp.] 32 illus.: color-32/illustrated endpapers and
           title page/mixed media: oil, crayon, newspaper, and paper/
           20.4cm x 22.5cm
           Fiction   Gr. Ps-1
        Ezra Jack Keats presents a glimpse of the inner city in this
story of two young black boys, Peter and Archie, and a pair of
motorcycle goggles. After Peter discovers the goggles near his
hideout in a deserted lot, he has to stand up to three older boys
who decide <u>they</u> want those goggles. When the glasses slip out of
Peter's pocket during the brief encounter, Willie, his dog,
snatches them up and runs off with the prize.
        Archie and Peter rendezvous at the hideout, and, luckily,
Willie has the same idea. After sending the bullies on a wild-
goose chase to the parking lot, the boys, and Willie, run back
to Archie's house to gloat over their clever escape.
        Amid graffiti-covered walls, discarded trash, and laundry
strung from tenement windows, Keats presents a realistic slice
of life within his creative, multi-media illustrations. The suffering and dehumanization characteristics of Peter and Archie's
environment are not touched upon, and in spite of the setting,
the boys' experience has universal appeal and familiarity--there
are bullies on every street corner, begging to be outwitted.
        Keats has been careful to focus the viewer's attention on
Peter, Archie, and Willie; the setting becomes secondary to the
main characters. Brush strokes, textures, and blotches of color
contrast with the uniform floral pattern of Archie's shirt and
the plain solid red of Peter's.
        As in his 1963 Medal Book, <u>The Snowy Day</u> (C116), Keats trans-
forms an average event in the day of a young boy into a visual
experience of universal quality that has meaning for everyone.

C141   LIONNI, LEO. <u>Alexander and the Wind-Up Mouse</u>. New York:
           Pantheon, 1969, [32 pp.] 29 illus.: color-29/illustrated
           title page and front matter/mixed media/27.3cm x 23cm
           Fantasy   Gr. Ps-1
        Alexander, a real live mouse, is overcome with a desire to
become a wind-up toy like his friend, Willy, who is forever enjoying the cuddling love of the young girl who owns him. Alexander appeals to the magic lizard in the garden to transform him
into a mouse like Willy, and the reptile instructs Alexander to
bring him a purple pebble when the moon is full.
        Alexander searches and searches and finally discovers a violet
pebble next to a box of useless toys that are slated to be thrown
out. To Alexander's dismay, the wind-up mouse is in the container,
so he hurries to the garden to make his wish--that Willy become a
real live mouse. Upon his return to his home, Alexander finds a
brand new friend and roommate, a living, breathing Willy.

The small, torn-paper shape of Alexander is undoubtedly akin to Frederick of Lionni's 1968 Honor Book of the same name. Willy's form changes from a precise, mechanical, smooth shape to the fuzzy, indistinct outline of torn paper when his transformation is complete.

Various types of paper provide the range of textures in the illustrations; while some pages seem overwhelmed by the conglomerate of designs, others exhibit the control and cohesiveness usually characteristic of Lionni's creations. The artist's style, easily recognizable, quickly becomes predictable, lessening its impact, when several books are viewed in succession. But Lionni's illustrations and the themes they express, based upon simple human needs and traits--friendship, individuality, ingenuity--remain relevant to children and will continue to be so in the future.

C142   PRESTON, EDNA MITCHELL. Pop Corn and Ma Goodness. Illustrated
       by Robert Andrew Parker. New York: Viking, 1969, [36 pp.]
       15 illus.: color-15/illustrated title page and front mat-
       ter/watercolor with ink lines/20.2cm x 22.5cm
       Folk literature   Gr. K-2

Edna Mitchell Preston creates a story of nonsense by assigning two very unusual names to the main characters of her Honor Book. Pop Corn and Ma Goodness literally fall head-over-heels, crashing down a hill into one another, and end up rushing off to get married by a preacher. After building themselves a house and securing a few animals, they eventually "get them some kids" to complete their lives.

With each addition to the story, a new set of nonsense words appears to set the rhythm of the text, which, if put to music, would make a catchy tune. The recurring sounds--skippity skoppety hippetty hoppetty--and the repetitive format of the text, interspersed with the refrain, "all doon the hill," provide the elements that naturally evoke a sense of song, elements notably enhanced by reading aloud.

The pages of text, always appearing on the right and bordered with uneven pen lines, face the watercolor illustrations, which are enhanced with lines of black ink. The unusual effect of the illustrations leaves the impression that they were created quickly and spontaneously, much like the effects of the rhythmical, tongue-twisting text.

The properties of the media, the effects of watercolor on wet paper, the suggestion of shapes and shadows, take over the illustrations; in a skillful lack of control, Parker creates an incomplete look within complete, balanced compositions.

The book is for fun, and the faster it is read, the more smiles it brings. With illustrations that keep pace with the rapid succession of events in the story, the book's personality emerges, gradually enveloping the reader; the further one reads, the more naturally the nonsense flows.

1970

C143   TURKLE, BRINTON. Thy Friend, Obadiah. New York: Viking,
        1969, [40 pp.] 32 illus.: color-32/illustrated title
        page and dedication/watercolor, wash, and charcoal/
        17.2cm x 21.9cm
        Fiction: historical   Gr. Ps-2
    Nantucket Island is the home of Obadiah Starbuck, a red-headed
Quaker boy who is forever embarrassed by a seagull that constantly
follows him around and perches just outside his bedroom window.
One day Obadiah loses his temper and hurls a stone at the gull,
and the following day, when the boy is sent to buy some flour,
the gull is nowhere to be seen.
    Several days later Obadiah encounters the gull at the wharf,
his beak entangled in fishhook and line. With compassion and in
a gesture of friendship, the boy frees the gull, after realizing
their unspoken dependence upon one another. That night Obadiah
is guarded once again by his sentry--the gull perched outside his
window in the gray mist of the night.
    Through the foggy illustrations, authentic New England struc-
tures emerge from the gray winter backgrounds of this seaside
town. The warm golden glow of the interior scenes presents a
sensual contrast to the blues and grays of the hazy atmosphere
outside. In similar contrast, Obadiah's red locks are quickly
identified against the neutral backgrounds of the watercolor
illustrations. The soft lines of charcoal, defining shapes and
shadows, do not destroy the delicacy of the watercolors as they
flow from shape to shape.
    Turkle's text, honest and straightforward, finds expression in
the simple gestures of the book's main character. Obadiah's obvious dislike for the pesty gull is recorded on his face, as is
the compassion he learns to feel for the bird when he frees him
from his snare. The substance of this Honor Book makes its theme
certain to withstand the effects of time. Conservative in artistic and literary style, the work possesses a gentle understanding
of the delicate, tenuous thread that joins man to nature and man
to man.

C144   ZEMACH, HARVE. The Judge: An Untrue Tale. Illustrated by
        Margot Zemach. New York: Farrar, Straus & Giroux, 1969,
        [48 pp.] 24 illus.: color-24/illustrated title page,
        endpapers, and front matter/pen and ink and watercolor
        wash/19.9cm x 25.3cm
        Fantasy: folklike tale   Gr. K-2
    Each of five prisoners tells the tale of a scary creature,
"creeping closer day by day," and tries to warn the judge of the
impending doom. One after another, the prisoners add to the description of the horrible beast, but the judge banishes them all
to prison for their false gibberish and obvious ploys to gain
freedom.

Just as the last offender is dragged from the courtroom, the beast appears in the window behind the judge's bench. The hairy, fire-breathing, winged animal wastes no time in devouring the judge with one snap of his powerful jaws, thus ending the tale of the untrue tale.

The rhyming text, in folk-tale style, by Harve Zemach, is accompanied by Margot Zemach's watercolor and line drawings depicting the courtroom scenes. Within rectangular frames, the illustrations present the well-meaning prisoners as they try to warn the supercilious judge of the dangers lurking nearby. The ample-nosed, pink-faced, pudgy figures plead for their lives and are eventually awarded their freedom at the close of the book, in a triumph of poetic justice.

Up to the point at which the last prisoner is toted off by the court bailiffs, the illustrations reflect the text, extending it only in terms of the physical appearances of the characters. The final seven pages, however, reverse the pattern, and, with no text, the story is concluded in illustration alone.

The complacency of the honorable judge quickly disappears as the shock of seeing the beast registers on his face. It is not long before the judge is consumed on the next full-page spread, in an illustration which reaches almost to the edge of the paper. In the final scene, the group of prisoners, after regaining their freedom, appears within the rectangular frame of earlier illustrations. The humor of the inevitable ending is reflected in the illustrations of the early courtroom scenes, but the neatly designed book possesses a text which will be remembered for its humor and, at the same time, may be considered its major weakness.

<u>1971</u>

C145   HALEY, GAIL. <u>A Story, A Story: An African Tale</u>. New York: Atheneum, 1970, [36 pp.] 31 illus.: color-31/illustrated title page, dedication, and front matter/woodcuts/25.4cm x 25.7cm
Folk Tale   Gr. K-2

The 1971 Medal Book explains the origin of the traditional African "Spider Stories" of Kwakee Ananse, the spider man. In this tale of lesser creatures outwitting those of greater power and size, Ananse spins a web to the sky so that he might bring the stories of the Sky God, Nyame, down to earth.

After completing three tasks, Ananse brings Osebo, the leopard of-the-terrible-teeth; Mmboro, the hornet who-stings-like-fire; and Mmoatia, the fairy whom-men-never-see, back to Nyame in return for the stories. Ananse thus earns the golden box, which he carries with him to earth and from which he disperses his stories to all corners of the world.

1971

Heavy with African motifs, native costumes, and rich colors and patterns, the woodcuts of this Medal Book help communicate the symbolism of the story. Repeating patterns and designs cover the pages of the book, and, though abstract, they create recognizable shapes. If the basic elements of the text were memorized, the book could function effectively if the story were told, rather than read, allowing the oral origins of the tale to become more evident.

The emotional use of color and patterns draws attention to the ethnic backgrounds of the tale, but the universal elements of the story are amazing. Like the trials of Hercules and the mythical motif of Pandora's box full of intangible sorrows, Haley has brought the universality of the contents of children's books to light, as well as the traditions of a culture which commands respectable exposure in its books.

C146   SLEATOR, WILLIAM. The Angry Moon. Illustrated by Blair Lent.
        Boston: Little, Brown, Atlantic Monthly Press, 1970,
        [48 pp.] 44 illus.: color-44/illustrated title page and
        front matter/pen and ink lines with full-color acrylics/
        22.9cm x 24cm
        Legend   Gr. 1-3
        When Lapowinsa angers the moon, a rainbow appears and takes the young girl to the sky. As Lupan shoots his arrows toward the moon to retrieve Lapowinsa, he notices a chain of his arrows forms a ladder on which he climbs into the sky. Upon reaching the top he is taken by a small boy to his grandmother's house, where Lupan is given four objects to help him rescue Lapowinsa from the angered moon.

Lupan follows the sobs of Lapowinsa to the moon's home, substitutes a pine cone in her place in the smoke hole, and they begin their escape. When the pine cone eventually burns, the angry moon pursues the children. A fish eye becomes a lake to block the moon's progress, and a rose turns into a tangled thicket to slow the chase. When a stone grows into a steep mountain, the children are able to make their escape complete and return to earth to pass their story on from generation to generation.

Tlingit motifs decorate the pages of illustrations, and though not totally authentic, they help establish the atmosphere of the legend. The lines of totem poles and geometric patterns provide definition of the shapes and forms which arise from the watery backgrounds of paint and wash that spill over onto the adjoining pages. The artistic style of this Honor Book is similar to that in Lent's later 1973 Medal Book, Funny Little Woman (C153).

Violet and golds predominate in the illustrations, whose mystical qualities reflect the heavens in which Lupan and Lapowinsa temporarily dwell. The legend demonstrates for the reader the powers imparted to nature by the culture from which it comes, and the dreamlike atmosphere of the illustrations reflects the origins as well.

C147   LOBEL, ARNOLD. <u>Frog and Toad Are Friends</u>. New York: Harper & Row, 1970, 64 pp.   53 illus.:   color-53/illustrated title page and contents page/watercolor, pen and ink/21.5cm x 14.8cm
Fantasy   Gr. Ps-2

Like the 1962 Honor Book, <u>Little Bear's Visit</u> (C114), illustrated by Maurice Sendak, <u>Frog and Toad Are Friends</u> is a member of the "I-Can-Read" series. Arnold Lobel's story follows the friendship of these amphibious comrades through five chapters, which cover the range of emotional ties developed in such a relationship. In the first chapter Frog, with a little trickery involving the calendar, entices Toad to come out of hibernation and enjoy the Spring. When Frog is sick of Toad's efforts to amuse him with a story, the events become a story in themselves, which <u>Frog</u> ends up reciting to Toad.

Toad's lost button results in a massive search which turns up an overabundance of fasteners in Chapter Three, while the following section deals with Toad's self-conscious attitude toward his humorous appearance in his one-piece bathing suit. In the final chapter, Frog amuses Toad by sending him a letter, which arrives four days late, via snail delivery.

In all five chapters, Lobel demonstrates several integral elements of any friendship--sharing and enjoying companionship, concern for physical and mental well-being, helpfulness in time of need, and a desire to cheer and console. Through the muted green and brown illustrations, Lobel illustrates these mutual needs. Though the book functions as a text for children to read themselves, it would not be as effective without Lobel's endearing, lovable creatures.

The illustrations, some framed, others conforming to the spaces surrounding the text, do not overpower the pages of the book in color or in boldness of design. The muted colors, light lines of the pen, and the gray backgrounds of wash are conducive to reflecting the amiable relationship of the main characters, without distracting novice readers from their text. As in <u>Little Bear's Visit</u>, the use of animals, rather than humans, actually produces a story more relevant, and universal, to its audience of children.

C148   SENDAK, MAURICE. <u>In the Night Kitchen</u>. New York: Harper & Row, 1970, [40 pp.]   35 illus.:   color-35/illustrated title page, dedication, and front matter/watercolor, pen, and black ink/27.8cm x 21.6cm
Fantasy   Gr. K-2

1971

Mickey's dream takes him falling into the night, out of his clothes, and plops him smack into the bustle of the Night Kitchen, where a trio of "Oliver Hardy" bakers stirs him into the cake batter. Mickey, batter and all, is shoved into the oven before he comes to his senses and, garbed in a batter suit, escapes in a bread-dough airplane.

While in flight, Mickey assists the bakers by fetching some milk from the Milky Way, an oversized milk bottle. From his roost on the bottle, Mickey crows the signal of morning and slides neatly back into bed, "cakefree and dried."

Amid the backdrops of the Night Kitchen, utensils and ingredients loom like the skyline of a city. Boxes and bottles and tins of oats, yeast, salt, and coconut are transformed into windowed buildings; whisks, eggbeaters, and funnels sit atop the buildings, completing the view.

In comic-strip progression, the story smacks of the subconscious ramblings of the mind in a dream, incorporating bits and pieces of information filed deep within the brain. The airplane dangling over Mickey's bed provides the model for Mickey's bread-dough machine; a child's interpretation of the Milky Way is transformed into a giant source of milk; and when the rooster crows, night abruptly ends.

The hand-lettered text, present on all but one full page, varying in size from page to page, is contained within rectangular areas, in balloons, and contributes to the comic-strip progression, as does the horizontal or vertical division of some pages of illustration. The chanting beat of the text reflects the frenzied activity of the dream, and the detailed style so characteristic of Sendak produces environments that perfectly recreate the absurd events of the world of dreams.

<u>1972</u>

C149   HOGROGIAN, NONNY. <u>One Fine Day</u>. New York: Macmillan, 1971,
        [32 pp.] 27 illus.: color-27/illustrated endpapers, title
        page, half title, dedication page, and front matter/oils/
        20.2cm x 25.2cm
        Folk Tale   Gr. K-2
        When a fox laps up most of the milk from an old woman's pail,
she, in anger, cuts of his tail, which prompts him to embark
upon a series of requests in order to recover it. To replace
the milk, the fox has to secure some grass for the cow, but
the grass needs water, so the cumulation of events begins.

Finally a miller feels compassion for the fox and gives him some grain, which starts the animal back through the chain of demands. When he finally replaces the milk, his tail is sewn back in place, and he slinks off through the forest to rejoin his friends.

The full-page spread which ends the tale is an excellent example of physically integrating text and illustration. A single
line of text, all lowercase type, becomes an integral part of the
composition and helps create the finality of the ending, not only
as the conclusion to the sentence of the previous page, but also
in terms of the balance it creates with the elements of the composition. The rear portion of the fox, a slanted tree trunk,
and a triangular area of mossy groundcover leave a large portion
of white page, which helps emphasize and symbolize this visual
and textual statement of the end.

Throughout, word and picture are synthesized in this manner,
with careful placement of text balancing the composition. In a
similar manner, the round, golden shape of the sun often is a
counterpoint to the vibrant orange shape of the fox; sometimes
these shapes appear on opposite sides of the full-page spreads,
sometimes on the same.

Turning the pages of the book reinforces the journey of the
fox through the horizontal and linear progression of events.
Hogrogian skillfully transforms a simple tale into a picture
book of excellent design and quality.

C150   DOMANSKA, JANINA. If All the Seas Were One Sea. New York:
            Macmillan, 1971, [32 pp.] 29 illus.: color-29/illustrated
            endpapers, title page, and front matter/etchings on zinc
            with brush and ink overlays/25.4cm x 20.1cm
            Mother Goose/Nursery Rhymes   Gr. Ps-1
Janina Domanska produces a graphic and abstract visual interpretation of a repetitive nursery rhyme which builds up and then
reduces the cumulation of events. Sea, tree, ax, and man all
follow the form of the initial sentence of the book, "If all the
seas were one sea,/what a great sea that would be." Eventually,
were the great man to take the great ax and chop down the great
tree, he would most certainly create a great "splish splash" in
that enormously great sea.

The abstract representations of the author-illustrator indicate the amount of deliberate and creative planning necessary to
the production of picture books. Each full-page spread, which
accompanies the first clause of each sentence, is divided into
four sections, each section representing a variation of the subject. One of four different creatures of the sea, four varieties
of stylized trees, four shapes of an ax, or four decorative
forms of the human body appear in each of the divisions. Following the variations of each subject, a full-page figure, a conglomerate of characteristics from each example, is presented to
accompany the main clause of the sentence.

The repetition of the verbal pattern in the text is reinforced
within the design of the red, green, blue, and black pictures; on
backgrounds of parallel, perpendicular, and diagonal lines, the

1972

objects reinforce the curving visual conceptions of a universal
man, sea, tree, or ax, in the abstractions. When the fruit of
the great tree ends up neatly in the stomach of the fish of the
great sea, Domanska signals the close of the book in character
with the remainder of the work. Her deliberate and well-planned
format helps make the story experience heavily dependent upon
the illustrations and demonstrates the extent to which a simple
text may be embellished.

C151   FEELINGS, MURIEL. Moja Means One: Swahili Counting Book.
           Illustrated by Tom Feelings. New York: Dial, 1971,
           [32 pp.] 20 illus.: black and white-20/illustrated title
           page and front matter/india ink, white tempera, tissue, and
           linseed oil/22.7cm x 25.4cm
           Counting Book   Gr. K-3
       A counting book from one to ten, Moja Means One also helps
contribute to the understanding and appreciation of the unique
aspects of Swahili-speaking culture. The word which represents
each number appears in enlarged, rust-colored type, accompanied
by the pronunciation in which the stressed syllable is also noted
in rust. These words indicate the objects to be counted in the
illustrations; the page which deals with the number two, for example, emphasizes the word villagers, two of which appear in the
full-page spread. Other pages deal with additional aspects of
the culture--the geographical formation of Kilimanjaro, coffee
trees, animals, clothing, fish, market stalls, instruments, and
children and their mothers.
       The inclusion of a map of the African continent provides geo-
graphical information on the location of Swahili-speaking countries and serves to familiarize the audience with the areas of
concern. The soft illustrations of Tom Feelings communicate the
values and customs mentioned in the book's introduction and
Author's Note without the graphic styles typical of many books
of Africa for children. The illustrations demand a sensitive
understanding and lure the viewer into the Swahili culture.
       The luminous black, white, though predominantly gray, pic-
tures tend to create and retain an air of mysticism regarding
African culture. The book's purpose is to foster understanding
and appreciation in descendants of African heritage; though the
text has a traditional focus, the author is quick to point out
more current aspects of African culture--thriving cities, uni-
versities, and the arts--in her Note. This information, in conjunction with the text and illustrations, helps develop appeal
to an audience much greater than to that for which it was
originally intended.

C152   RYAN, CHELI DURAN. Hildilid's Night. Illustrated by Arnold
           Lobel. New York: Macmillan, 1971, [32 pp.] 23 illus.:

black and white-20; black, white, and yellow-3/pen and ink
drawings with yellow overlays/17.7cm x 22.8cm
Fantasy: folklike tale   Gr. Ps-1

Since Hildilid, a rotund little woman who lives in the hills
near Hexham, hated anything to do with the night, she made every
attempt she could think of to chase the night away. When her
broom did not sweep the night away, she tried to stuff the darkness in a sackcloth, boil it, tie it up, sing to it, spank it,
and even spit at it, but the night persisted.

Finally Hildilid decides to ignore the darkness, and, since
she exhausted herself trying to expel the evening, she settles
into bed to ready for another battle with the night, just as the
sun rises over the hills and fills the sky with its golden rays.

Arnold Lobel's pen-and-ink illustrations for this 1972 Honor
Book are all contained within frames, with some occasionally
divided into two or three parts. Each picture is composed of a
series of short lines--horizontal, vertical, diagonal, curving--
which, depending on their proximity, create the patterns of darks
and lights that define the shapes. Where few lines appear, as in
Hildilid's face, the shape is virtually white; where the density
of lines increases, as in the blackness of the evening sky, the
darker values of the compositions are produced.

The book's design--the balance established between the text
and illustrations on the page, the horizontal emphasis, and the
careful placement of color in the three final illustrations--is
responsible for its clean appearance, reinforced by the neatly
executed illustrations contained within their strictly defined
framework. The richness Lobel is able to extract from his medium
creates illustrations as intricate as a fine piece of crewel or
tapestry. The book is a visual delight, well integrated in word
and picture, with a touch of humor that provides a neat contrast
to the exacting style of the illustrations, which in their own
way provide a seriously funny impression.

1973

C153   MOSEL, ARLENE. The Funny Little Woman. Illustrated by Blair
        Lent. New York: E. P. Dutton, 1972, [40 pp.] 36 illus.:
        color-31; black and white-5/illustrated title page and
        front matter/pen-and-ink line drawings with acrylics/
        22.7cm x 24cm
        Folk Tale   Gr. K-2

When the funny little woman follows her rice dumpling into a
hole in the earth, she embarks upon a dangerous journey along the
road of the underworld leading to the dwelling of the monstrous
oni. Because the little woman of this Japanese tale cannot sup-
press her laugh, "Tee-he-he-he," the wicked oni capture her and

1973

force her to cook for them with a magic paddle, which turns one grain of rice into hundreds.

Tiring of her job as cook, and longing for her own home, the woman takes the magic paddle and escapes across the river, until the oni discover her escape attempt and drink all the water from the river. Stuck in the mud of the river bottom, the funny little woman is so comical that the oni cannot restrain their laughter and consequently refill the river with the contents of their mouths. The funny little woman makes good her escape, returning to her home with the magic paddle, which produces enough rice for rice balls to allow her to become a very, very wealthy woman.

The spidery lines of the murky, eerie green and brown landscapes of the underworld provide a background against which the orange and gold robe and white face of the funny little woman are easily visible. Lent contains these underground landscapes within swirling oval shapes, above which appear black and white line drawings of the world of the funny little woman's home. The sinewy lines of the statues of gods and the entangling look of tree roots encompass the environment, which holds the funny little woman captive. When the woman returns to her home, the color flows again to the world of reality, leaving the now colorless underworld behind. Above ground the colors of Lent's illustrations lighten and brighten, signaling the return of the woman and the bringing of life and color back to her world.

This tale is made for humor, and Lent's interpretation is a bit more somber at times than the story calls for, sometimes ignoring the humor of the situation and the little woman's character.

C154   BAYLOR, BYRD. When Clay Sings. Illustrated by Tom Bahti. New York: Charles Scribner's Sons, 1972, [32 pp.] 27 illus.: color-27/illustrated half-title and title page/ color separation/25.4cm x 20.3cm
Information: geography   Gr. 1-3

In this children's guide to archaeology, Byrd Baylor introduces the probable reasons for the designs and patterns which might appear on pieces of Indian pottery found by Native American children as they play. When the wind discovers the song held within these pieces of clay, it carries the tune through the hills as a reminder of the traditions associated with the production of the piece.

Baylor skillfully covers the range of possible symbols that might appear upon a piece, and in doing so, she holds a mirror to the culture from which the artifacts come. Insects, animals, and reptiles are among the representations covered in the text, and they serve as a reminder that the clay was once an integral "piece of someone's life."

Utilizing authentic designs from pottery of the American Southwest, Tom Bahti lays down large areas of color as the backgrounds
upon which the designs and text appear. The text, in black, or
occasionally off-white, is neatly woven among the compositions
of the pages, while the horizontal swirling shapes of the background pull the elements of the composition together, directing
the eye from left to right. The brown, gray, black, off-white,
and sand color scheme carries with it the significance of the
colors of the earth from which the clay comes.

The stylized, geometric designs--often several different versions of one object appear--in conjunction with the text, present the world view of a culture very much in tune with nature.
The cooperative existence of man and nature becomes evident in
word and picture; grasping these concepts and understanding their
importance may be more easily accomplished by a mature audience
which is capable of recognizing and appreciating the vital differences in the culture and world-view of the Native American.

C155   BASKIN, HOSEA; BASKIN, LISA; and BASKIN, TOBIAS. Hosie's
       Alphabet. Illustrated by Leonard Baskin. New York:
       Viking, 1972, [64 pp.] 28 illus.: color-28/illustrated
       title page/colored ink and watercolor/28.6cm x 19.7cm
       Alphabet Book   Gr. 1-4
       From an armadillo to a zebra, Hosie's Alphabet records the
letters of the alphabet with a menagerie of unusual creatures
accompanied by equally unusual and striking illustrations. Characters, on the right-hand leaf of full-page spreads, except for
the whale (W) and eagle (E), which cover entire spreads, face a
text, of various typefaces, which appears in a variety of locations on the pages.

The composition and design of each page become so interesting
that it is with hopeful anticipation that each page is turned.
The full-page spread of "the imperious eagle spangled and splendid" precedes a spread whose composition, predominantly white,
contains only a small fly faced with the greatly reduced type
reading "F/A furious fly." The juxtaposition of the enormous
eagle and the minute speck of a fly heightens the impact of the
artist's rendering.

Some animals appear on entire pages of wash background, while
others are laid upon the stark white of the paper. The uncon-
trolled properties of the washes contribute to the unique representation of the subjects, a technique characteristic of Baskin's
style, which is both striking and at times grotesque.

An artist in his own right, Baskin demonstrates the link between this art form and the realms of the world of art. Though
the book probably holds more appeal for adults and fans of
Baskin's work, its contribution to the world of picture books
is rightfully acknowledged by the Newbery-Caldecott Committee.

1973

C156   GRIMM, JACOB and GRIMM, WILHELM. Snow-White and the Seven
        Dwarfs. Translated by Randall Jarrell. Illustrated by
        Nancy Ekholm Burkert. New York: Farrar, Straus & Giroux,
        1972, [32 pp.] 15 illus.: color-15/brush and colored ink/
        30.5cm x 22.8cm
        Folk Tale   Gr. Ps-2
        Randall Jarrell's translation of the Grimm Brothers' Snow-
White and the Seven Dwarfs is accompanied by full-page spreads
by Nancy Ekholm Burkert. Alternating with full spreads of text,
the illustrations depict the wicked queen's attempts to end Snow
White's life by means of bodice laces, poisonous comb, and poisonous apple. In this translation, faithful to its German origin,
the wicked queen is punished for her vanity when she is forced to
dance in a pair of red-hot, iron slippers until she drops over
dead.
        With only seven full-page spreads of illustration, Burkert
leaves much of the story to the imagination, but when the opportunity for illustration arises, the pages are full of icono-
clastic details beyond compare. Patterns woven into tapestries
and clothing, symbolic vegetation, representations of evil, and
authentic interiors fill the pages with indications of the depth
of research involved in the project.
        Text and illustrations are contained within frames which help
reinforce the medieval influences that surface in the pictures.
The fine, delicate lines of the drawings concentrate on incidents
of primary importance to the story; the selection of events taste-
fully handles the evil aspects of the tale. Scenes in which the
wicked queen conjures up the near-fatal apple and its effects on
Snow White are dominated by gloomy, dark backgrounds, while the
bright celebration of the wedding is contrasted with the darkened
stairway and the empty iron shoes, symbolic of the queen's demise.
        Burkert lifts illustration of picture books to the realm of
high art with her disciplined research and devotion to authenticity of detail and visual conception.

C157   McDERMOTT, GERALD. Anansi the Spider: A Tale from the
        Ashanti. New York: Holt, Rinehart & Winston, 1972,
        [48 pp.] 32 illus.: color-32/illustrated endpapers and
        dedication/adapted from an animated film--pre-separated
        in four colors/19.1cm x 23cm
        Folk Tale   Gr. 1-3
        One of the many adventures of Kwaku Anansi, spider to the
Ashanti people of West Africa, is the subject of this 1973 Honor
Book which is adapted from an animated film. Anansi, of this
story, is fortunate to have six sons, each of which possesses a
special talent that is of use to Anansi when he falls into trouble
on a trip far from home. See Trouble knows his father encounters
some danger, so Road Builder constructs a pathway to the location

of the accident, and the sons discover Anansi has been swallowed by a fish.

River Drinker drains the river to strand the fish; Game Skinner splits open the aquatic foe to release his father, but unfortunately Falcon snatches up Anansi. Stone Thrower's skill forces Falcon to drop the spider, who safely lands on the back of his sixth son, Cushion.

On their return from this harrowing adventure, Anansi and his sons discover a globe of light, which is entrusted to Nyame until it can be decided which son to reward for saving his father's life. When Anansi is unable to decide the most worthy recipient, Nyame settles the controversy by placing the globe in the sky, and to this day, the moon remains for all to share.

Gerald McDermott's Prologue helps explain the culture which gave rise to the tales of Anansi, and his words reflect the mature theme and symbolism which appear in the story. Like the Ashanti who weave their symbols into their silken fabrics, McDermott weaves their symbols into and throughout his illustrations for the book. His graphic representations of the spider form are evidence of the symbolism contained within the stylized figures.

Within each body of the six sons, an abstract symbol represents the individual's particular skill. Amid geometric landscapes of magenta, turquoise, emerald, and red, the black figures, readily visible, rock across the pages on angular legs.

The white text, highly visible against the brilliant backgrounds, works in and out of the illustrations, adding balance to the compositions on the pages.

Because of the original medium of the tale, the book could well function without a text; accompanied only by the words of an artful storyteller, the illustrations communicate the tale, and though not as artistically cohesive and consistent as the author-illustrator's later Medal winner, Arrow to the Sun (C161, 1975), the work demonstrates the range of possibilities that this art form offers.

1974

C158   ZEMACH, HARVE. Duffy and the Devil. Illustrated by Margot
        Zemach. New York: Farrar, Straus & Giroux, 1973, [40 pp.]
        35 illus.: color-illustrated half-title and front mat-
        ter/watercolor and pen and ink/26.4cm x 21.6cm
        Folk Tale   Gr. 1-3
        In this Cornish tale, retold by Harve Zemach, Duffy becomes
an assistant to Squire Lovel's housekeeper, Old Jone. When
Duffy makes a three-year pact with the devil to cover up her
ineptitude at weaving and knitting, she agrees to go away with

1974

the creature if she cannot guess his name within the time span. The devil produces such fine articles of clothing that Squire Lovel admires the woman's talents and eventually decides to marry Duffy.

As the three years quickly pass, Duffy confesses her arrangement to Old Jone, who proceeds to get the devil drunk enough, down in the fuggy-hole, to reveal his name in the presence of Squire Lovel. After the Squire recounts this odd experience to his wife, Duffy is able to tell the devil his name. As instantly as Tarraway, the devil, disappears, so do the articles of clothing he crafted, leaving the squire without wardrobe and allowing Duffy to conveniently vow never to weave or knit again.

The riddle motif of this Cornish tale, which also appears in versions of Rumpelstiltskin and Tom Tit Tot (C130), is handled more lightly in the text and illustrations of this 1974 Medal Book. The simple gullibility of Squire Lovel emanates from his trusting face. The words of the text would lead the audience to believe that Lady Duffy Lovel, dressed in silks and red-heeled shoes, is indeed a light-footed, elegant dancer; but as the illustrations indicate, she and two similarly stocky women are anything but svelte. In drawings in a style similar to that of The Judge (C144), a 1970 Honor Book, Margot Zemach's figures exude an aura of corpulence in their pudgy pink faces and bodies, which definitely make their presence known on the pages.

The watercolors produce shapes defined by black outlines of squiggly, uneven character and contribute to the offbeat, unusual humor of the illustrations. That the illustrations are not confined to a definite space, as they are in The Judge, allows them to flow with the medium, across the pages, eliciting a giddy sort of response that is reflected in the characters and their every action.

C159   JEFFERS, SUSAN. Three Jovial Huntsmen. Scarsdale, N.Y.:
        Bradbury, 1973, [32 pp.] 26 illus.: color-26/illustrated
        title page/pen and ink with wash overlays in red, blue,
        black, and yellow oils/27.4cm x 20.4cm
        Mother Goose/Nursery Rhymes   Gr. Ps-1
    When the three jovial huntsmen set out on St. David's day, they anticipate an excursion rich with the rewards of the sport. As they amble through woods full of deer, opposum, raccoons, ducks, and foxes, all that the simple men see, in their nearsighted vision, are objects appearing to be what they are not.

    A ship, upon closer inspection, is only a rock; a porcupine, merely a pincushion holding pins inserted backwards. The two fuzzy ears of a hare are more properly identified in the illustrations as the tails of skunks by the white stripe covering the back of the bodies and by the clouds of an odorous protection emitted in the direction of the hunters. Thus ends the expedition for the three jovial huntsmen.

The humor of this Mother Goose rhyme is appropriately captured in Jeffers's fine line drawings, which resemble puzzles with hidden objects; the illustrations reveal the animals that go unseen by the unattending sportsmen; woven into the lines that define roots, weeds, flowers, and undergrowth, animals peer out at the audience and at the hunters, in silent mockery.

There careful studies of nature and the natural habitats of the forest provide the backgrounds from which the animals emerge. Their presence, obvious to the undoubtedly delighted audience, goes unnoticed by the men, who are more intent on conjuring up their own visions than taking note of the opportunities before their noses.

The illustration on the jacket, which accompanies some copies of the book, succinctly captures the essence of the tale's humor as the three men gaze across the terrain from a rock ledge; a plethora of bear, quail, fox, rabbit, groundhog, and squirrel peer out from the rock formations below; the animals are unquestionably unthreatened by the presence of the huntsmen.

Jeffers's style capitalizes on the tale's humor by providing the appropriate natural environments from which her animals emerge, unseen by their human predators.

C160　MACAULAY, DAVID. Cathedral: The Story of Its Construction.
　　　　Boston: Houghton Mifflin, 1973, 80 pp. 73 illus.: black
　　　　and white-73/illustrated title page and front matter/pen
　　　　and ink/30.2cm x 22.7cm
　　　　Information: architecture and history　　　　Gr. 3-up

In thirteenth-century France, the people of the imaginary city of Chutreaux want to build the longest, widest, and tallest cathedral in the country. Within this context David Macaulay weaves together a story of a time and people in history and a wealth of technical information regarding the actual erection of such a monumental structure.

As the cathedral grows in Macaulay's accurate black and white illustrations, so does the reader's knowledge regarding the social structures of the society of 1252, as well as the medieval institutions of the guilds of the time.

After eighty-two years of planning and construction, the Gothic cathedral is completed. With flying buttresses, stained-glass windows, vaulted ceilings, and gargoyled downspouts, the reader is overwhelmed and awed by the technology and accomplishment of erecting such a structure.

Macaulay's illustrations and his text make this book of information very consumable, as well as of interest to adults and older children. The preface, introduction, and glossary provide even more information, which helps the reader understand the process and terminology involved. The illustrations reflect the accuracy and painstaking detail that contribute to the creation

of one of these architectural feats or equally to the production
of such an informative book for young readers.

1975

C161   McDERMOTT, GERALD. <u>Arrow to the Sun</u>. New York: Viking,
            1974, [44 pp.] 34 illus.: color-34/illustrated endpapers,
            title page, dedication, and front matter/gouache and ink/
            24cm x 27.8cm
            Folk Tale   Gr. 1-3
    Gerald McDermott, adapter and illustrator of this Pueblo Indian
tale, catches the eye of many readers with the graphics of his
Medal Book, <u>Arrow to the Sun</u>. The story retells the quest of a
Pueblo boy to find his unknown father, via the Road of Life.
After much interrogation and searching by the Boy, Arrow Maker
sends him to the sun, transformed as an arrow, and the child is
faced with overcoming the four chambers of ceremony to prove he
is the offspring of the Lord of the Sun. After proving his courage, Boy returns to earth to celebrate the Dance of Life among
his people.
    The text of this tale remains simple and direct, with few
superfluous words; the illustrations are direct as well; bold,
vibrant hues of golds, yellows, oranges, browns, magenta, green,
and turquoise contrast against the starkness of black backgrounds.
McDermott deftly leads the reader's eye from text to illustration,
from illustration to text, with strong geometrics and diagonals,
intensifying and emphasizing the points he feels important. Although the designs of the pages sometimes become very elaborate
within themselves, they manage to retain the simplicity of the
Pueblo motifs.
    McDermott brings a new look to children's books with <u>Arrow to
the Sun</u> and creates an original method of handling the retelling
of a folk tale. By retaining the simplicity of the language as
well as the purity of Indian geometrics and color, he combines
them in a unique style to create a powerful vision of Pueblo
custom and legend. The book is truly an impressive work and
beautiful to hold and experience, and many times it can, and
does, function without text. It seems nearly impossible to
create a text which is as powerful as the illustrations in this
book, so McDermott complements it by a culmination of color, word,
and spirit in the ancient Pueblo ceremony--the Dance of Life.

C162   FEELINGS, MURIEL. <u>Jambo Means Hello: Swahili Alphabet Book</u>.
            Illustrated by Tom Feelings. New York: Dial, 1974,
            [60 pp.] 48 illus.: black and white-48/illustrated title
            page and front matter/india ink, white tempera, tissue, and
            linseed oil/22.7cm x 25.2cm

1975

Alphabet Book   Gr. 1-3
    A companion to <u>Moja Means One: Swahili Counting Book</u> (C151),
a 1972 Honor Book, <u>Jambo Means Hello</u> introduces this twenty-four-
letter alphabet in a format and with illustrations identical to
its predecessor's. Each letter is represented by a word beginning
with the corresponding symbol, and the explanation that follows
describes the word's significance to the African countries in
which Swahili is spoken.
    The words introduced appear in bold, olive green type, as
does the syllable of stress which is indicated in the pronunciation below the entry. The descriptive text presents information
on a wide range of culturally significant facts: the relationships of families, practiced customs, religious beliefs, economic factors, educational methods, wild and domesticated animals,
leisure activities, and the concept of beauty. Though each entry
can only briefly present the information, the book's purpose is
served by imparting even this small portion to its audience.
    The illustrations of Tom Feelings possess the same opaque
luminosity of those in <u>Moja Means One</u>. The dignity of the
Swahili-speaking peoples is communicated in the black and white
illustrations, which project a very calm, indistinct atmosphere
through the many values of gray, black, and white.
    The Introduction and Map of Africa help classify the work as
more than a mere alphabet book; the work is also rightfully a
book of information, and through the illustrations, as much information, if not more, reaches the audience. Although the book's
intended audience is "children whose ancestry belongs to Africa,"
other audiences will enjoy it as well.

1976

C163   AARDEMA, VERNA. <u>Why Mosquitoes Buzz in People's Ears</u>.
            Illustrated by Leo Dillon and Diane Dillon. New York:
            Dial, 1975, [32 pp.] 27 illus.: color-27/illustrated
            title page and front matter/watercolor (with airbrush),
            pastels, india ink, vellum and frisket masks/24.9cm x
            25.1cm
            Folk Tale   Gr. 1-3
    When the iguana pokes sticks into his ears so he will not
have to listen to the nonsense of the mosquito, he starts a
chain reaction that has serious results. The python misconstrues
the iguana's self-imposed deafness as a plot to do him some harm,
so he slithers down the rabbit's hole, which sends the hare skit-
tering across the clearing. Seeing this, the crow sounds an
alarm, which rousts the monkey, who accidentally falls on the
owl's nest, killing an owlet.

1976

In her grief, mother owl refuses to signal the end of night
with her hoot, so King Lion calls a meeting to uncover the reason for the extended nightfall. After tracing through the
events, the king discovers the real culprit--the mosquito. The
insect seeks cover to hide from the council and to this day buzzes
in people's ear to say "Zeee! Is everyone still angry at me?"
The pest invariably gets his answer--a quick slap, "Kpao!"

Leo and Diane Dillon's visual interpretation of this West
African tale helps reflect the story's origin in its masklike
figures comprised of series of shapes which combine to create
the abstract, though recognizable and unified, characters. The
cutout effect of the figures is achieved just so--by cutting
shapes from vellum and frisket masks. Like ceremonial masks,
the shapes of fuchsia, greens, and blues create patterns within
patterns and shapes within shapes.

The illustrations accompanied by the black backgrounds of the
ever-present night offer rich contrasts which are heightened by
the blue areas surrounding the shapes of the animals. The
Dillons' originality in their creative interpretation of this
story demonstrates their skill in translating their subjects in
a manner which apparently reflects the culture from which it
comes; by adding their own conceptions and style, the artists
produce a truly distinguished picture book for children, and
one equally appealing to adults.

C164   De PAOLA, TOMIE. Strega Nona. Englewood Cliffs, N.J.:
         Prentice-Hall, 1975, [36 pp.] 30 illus.: color-30/
         illustrated endpapers, title page, and dedication/water-
         color and charcoal/27.8cm x 21.5cm
         Folk Tale   Gr. K-3

Strega Nona and her magical pasta pot provide some problems
for Big Anthony when he decides to generate the noodle-producing
cauldron one day when "Grandmother Witch" goes off to the neighboring town. Though Big Anthony is certain he has the proper
words to coax the pot into production, he is unaware of the proper
process by which to terminate the overflowing waves of pasta.

After the townspeople have their fill of pasta, Big Anthony
is certain he has halted the magical pot's activities, until the
pasta begins flowing out of doors and windows, down into the
village. Luckily Strega Nona returns in time to throw three
kisses to the pot and end the threat of a spaghetti flood, but
poor Big Anthony pays for his folly by picking up his fork and
consuming every noodle but the one laced through the tongs of
his utensil.

Tomie de Paola's retelling of this old tale is the perfect
vehicle through which he can share his humor in both word and
picture. In illustrations that leak out of their frames here
and there like the overflowing pasta, the humor of Big Anthony's

folly and ensuing punishment is succinctly expressed by his en-
gorged figure propped against the house, inside which Strega
Nona comfortably snoozes.

The outlines, shapes, and figures of the characters are
modeled with wash and charcoal to add dimension to their
flat, almost decorative forms. Dividing the frames into two,
three, or four sections keeps the book's format interesting and
allows for the changing positions of the text. These divisions
also allow for the addition of more detail to the visual language
of the book through the series of smaller illustrations and reflect the illustrator's theatrical interests in their setlike
appearance. De Paola's humor should reach every household and
funnybone, just as every kitchen should experience the conven-
ience of such a pasta machine.

C165   BAYLOR, BYRD. The Desert Is Theirs. Illustrated by Peter
        Parnall. New York: Charles Scribner's Sons, 1975,
        [32 pp.] 26 illus.: color-26/illustrated title page,
        dedication, and front matter/pen and ink with full color
        washes/25.3cm x 20.3cm
        Information: geography   Gr. 1-3

Baylor presents the creatures and people who live in the
desert in her inimitable prose that flows like the poetry of
words of the oral tradition. Her style communicates the religious relationship of man and earth in the Papago Indian culture.
There is an existence, with plants, animals, and insects, of
sharing with the earth, not taking from it. Such has it been
since the earth's creation.

The amazing adaptations of the desert inhabitants demonstrate
the power the earth has over its temporary guests. The plants
and animals conform more easily to the constant sun and scarce
water supply than does man, who would do well to mimic their ways.

The creeping, crawling landscapes of the desert dwarf the inhabitants, man and beast, and the brilliant sun, in one stylized
form or another, is a constant reminder of the environment's heat.
Animals burrowed underneath enormous boulders and rock formations
demonstrate at least one way to deal with desert life. Vertical
columns of text fit naturally into the yellows, golds, blues, and
greens of the illustrations, which point and direct the eye from
text to picture and picture to text. Parnall's representations
of the terrain paint a desert unknown in these visual forms and
present an original interpretation of the information Baylor
provides as a voice of the Papago Indians.

The world-view, culture, and life-style presented in this
Honor Book are undoubtedly new to most, and represent the widen-
ing horizons and demand on picture books for children. Baylor's
sensitive text and Parnall's unique, clean-lined illustrations
demand much from their intended audience.

1977

<u>1977</u>

C166   MUSGROVE, MARGARET. <u>Ashanti to Zulu: African Traditions</u>.
        Illustrated by Leo Dillon and Diane Dillon. New York:
        Dial, 1976, [32 pp.] 27 illus.: color-27/illustrated
        half-title and title page/pastels, watercolor, acrylics/
        31.5cm x 25.2cm
        Information: geography   Gr. 2-6
    Traditions and customs of twenty-six peoples, from A to Z--
Ashanti to Zulu--are covered in this informative book of the
English alphabet. As the text provides insights into the culture of these people, so do the full-color illustrations. Each
picture is careful to include a man, woman, child, animal, dwelling, and artifact representative of each different group.
    The vast research on the part of the author and illustrators
creates a book whose usefulness extends into many disciplines.
The integrity of the artwork upholds the book's attempt to present accurate facts concerning cultures little known to the
readers of picture books. The introductory information reiter-
ates the informative thrust of the work, and the map on the
final page helps geographically place the peoples in the readers'
minds.
    The careful, accurate renderings which accompany each vignette
provide interesting contrast to the artists' Medal winner of the
previous year. The crisp, flat designs of <u>Why Mosquitoes Buzz
in People's Ears</u> (C163) are replaced by the subdued colors and
modeled shapes of a style more realistic than the Dillons' other
work.
    Though not without the Dillons' characteristic use of repeti-
tive patterns and stylistic simplification of shapes, these illustrations wash away the stereotypes of the African continent.
Contained within frames and bordered by the surrounding gray
tone of the pages, the illustrations and text look like photographs of some ancient manuscript. The book's format and design
are both impressive and reflect the symbolism of the Kano knots
embellishing each corner of the illustrations. The endless
search for the truth of the African people has at least, in
part, been satisfied by the joint efforts of the author and
the illustrators.

C167   GOFFSTEIN, M. B. <u>Fish for Supper</u>. New York: Dial, 1976,
        [32 pp.] 19 illus.: black and white-19/illustrated title
        page, dedication, and front matter/pen and ink/15.1cm x
        17.7cm
        Fiction   Gr. Ps-1
    This small, simple book recounts the daily routine of Grand-
mother as she rises at five o'clock and downs a simple breakfast
so she can hurry out to the lake to spend her day. Laden with

bait and fishing gear, she rows out upon the lake to catch her
evening meal.

After landing a variety of fish, she takes her catch home and
prepares a simple meal before she retires to ready for another
five-o'clock excursion. Thus the story ends, leaving the impression that Grandmother is still adhering to her daily routine,
somewhere, upon some unknown lake.

The simple text of Goffstein's book is accompanied by illustrations of equal simplicity. Each drawing, contained within
frames of equal size, is a triumph in economy of line; not a
superfluous mark appears in the clean, neat illustrations of
this small book. Only Grandmother's coal black hair and the
window-eyes of the boathouse deviate from the minimal pattern
of lines which create the perfect visual complement to the text.

With slight variations in the placement of the text or in the
shifting of the elements of the composition, Goffstein adds emphasis to her words. The type, on the same page as the illustration, sometimes facing it on the adjoining page, or sometimes
in both locations, especially adds emphasis and balance when it
appears opposite the illustrations. The drawing which shows
Grandmother settled in to fish all day is balanced by the words
of the text on the opposite page: "and stayed on the lake all
day."

Pages such as the one depicting the boathouse demonstrate the
author-illustrator's skill in communicating with a minimum of
line. The text is unembellished, as are the illustrations, and
Goffstein has produced a sensitive statement through her reduc-
tion of word and line.

C168   HOGROGIAN, NONNY. The Contest. New York: Greenwillow, 1976,
        [32 pp.] 22 illus.: color-13; black and white-9/illus-
        trated endpapers, title page, and front matter/black and
        white line drawings and colored pencil/25.3cm x 25.1cm
        Folk Tale   Gr. 1-3

In a province neighboring their own, a robber who works by
night, Hrahad, and one who works by day, Hmayag, discover they
have more in common than their occupation. Since they find they
are both engaged to the same woman, they decide to have a contest to determine who shall wed the charming Ehleezah. The day
robber displays his expertise by stealing jewels from an old
man's bundle on three separate occasions, replacing them twice.

Not to be outdone, Hrahad creeps into the palace of the
Ishkhan and dines on a roasted chicken without getting caught.
Both men, realizing their mutual talents and the prospects of a
profitable future, agree to abandon their deceiving fiancée and
look forward to their future in a new province. They abandon
Ehleezah, but she is not alone; she, too, has discovered a new
future, and a new lover.

1977

Nonny Hogrogian's color and black and white drawings create a suitable atmosphere for this Armenian tale. The woven borders that frame several of the full-color illustrations create the appearance of hanging tapestries or decorative rugs carefully produced by hand. Their crayonlike texture leaves a rich look on the pages, while the simple black and white line drawings interspersed throughout provide a neat contrast.

At a distance the full-color pages become more distinct and lose their hazy quality; the shapes grow crisp and defined. The characteristic of the medium is translated into small strokes which look like short stitches in a piece of handwork.

The small black and white drawings help progress the less important events of the text, moving the story along between full-color illustrations. The final page of the book, on which no text appears, silently spells out Ehleezah's reaction to her abandonment--entranced by her new love, who is singing to her with stringed accompaniment, she has already forgotten her two former lovers.

C169   McDERMOTT, BEVERLY BRODSKY. The Golem: A Jewish Legend.
        Philadelphia: J. B. Lippincott, 1976, [48 pp.] 38 illus.:
        color-38/illustrated endpapers, title page, frontispiece,
        and front matter/gouache, watercolor, dye, and ink/30.4cm
        x 22.7cm
        Legend   Gr. 1-4
Rabbi Yehuda Lev experiences an ominous dream which begins this Jewish legend of the Golem. In the dream, an angry mob is attacking the ghetto of the Jews in Prague so Rabbi Lev molds the Golem from the sacred clay to protect his people.

When the events of the dream finally come to pass, the Golem rises up to defeat the mob, but in doing so begins a violent rampage himself. As his master, the Rabbi must return the Golem to the dust from which he came. After the monstrous creature shatters into bits, the Rabbi returns the sacred clay to the confines of the synagogue attic.

Laden with cabbalistic symbols of the Jewish faith and letters of the Hebrew alphabet, McDermott's illustrations create a shadowy mysticism that creeps among the streets and alleys of the Jewish ghetto. The dark, forboding pages, dominated by black, signal the doom and destruction of the Golem; the contrasts of the colors and their black surroundings create the luminosity of a stained-glass window and are sometimes violent in contrast.

Almost cubistic in appearance, the facades of buildings and ghetto streets reflect the havoc that reigns as the Golem unleashes his power. The emotional impact of the colors of the illustrations, in the sweeping strokes and expressive wanderings of the media, helps heighten the power of the book's religious significance. Though the book's appeal to children will probably remain limited, it is not an easily forgotten experience.

C170   BAYLOR, BYRD. <u>Hawk, I'm Your Brother</u>. Illustrated by Peter
        Parnall. New York: Charles Scribner's Sons, 1976,
        [48 pp.] 41 illus.: black and white-41/illustrated
        title page, dedication, and front matter/pen and ink/
        25.4cm x 20.2cm
        Fiction   Gr. 2-4
    More than anything else, Rudy Soto wants to fly, not like any
ordinary bird, but like the hawk. He spends long hours observing
the flight of the bird and feels a kinship to the winged glider.
So entranced is Rudy by the magic of flight that he steals a baby
redtail hawk from its nest in the Santos Mountains. Through this
young hawk Rudy hopes to learn the secrets of flying.
    Housed in a cage and bound by a string on his leg, the hawk
resents his captivity, so Rudy reluctantly frees the bird. With
the bird's freedom Rudy gains the spirit of the hawk as he soars
overhead; as they fly together in spirit, they can be heard calling to one another, as brother to brother.
    This collaboration of Baylor and Parnall has resulted in a
book similar in format and style to their 1976 Honor Book, <u>The
Desert Is Theirs</u> (C165). In fine, sharp lines, Parnall etches
the drawings across the pages in only black and white, in contrast to the brilliant colors of <u>The Desert Is Theirs</u>.
    The conceptual abstraction of Baylor's text demands some ma-
ture and sophisticated analysis and may require some explanation.
The text is careful not to condone Rudy's nest-robbing activities,
and the subsequent freeing of the bird nearly reconciles the act.
    The positioning of the text takes on added significance as it
is incorporated as an integral element of the compositions. The
columns of text reinforce the vertical heights of the hawk's
flight and mimic the rise and fall of the mountain terrain. The
hatched and cross-hatched drawings retain the purity and simplicity of the relationship developed between boy and bird.
    Though illustrations and text are of notable quality, the
book's appeal may finally rest in the eyes of adults and middle-
grade audiences, those capable of and receptive to the sensitive
understanding so integral to Baylor's and Parnall's work.

C171   STEIG, WILLIAM. <u>The Amazing Bone</u>. New York: Farrar, Straus
        & Giroux, 1976, [32 pp.] 28 illus.: color-28/illustrated
        half-title and title page/watercolor/27.2cm x 22cm
        Fantasy   Gr. K-2
    A magical item, as innocently discovered as was Sylvester's
magic pebble, in Steig's 1977 Medal Book (C139), leads to a tale
of suspense and anxiety when Pearl, a young pig, and a talking
bone face certain death at the jaws of a fox. The bone, found
among a bed of violets in the forest, is successful in warding
off three robbers by pretending to be a lion and a snake, the
shapes of which appear in green line drawings in the backgrounds

1977

of the illustrations, but the skeletal fragment is unable to outwit the perceptive and hungry fox.

Pitiful Pearl awaits her death, none too bravely, and just as
the fox prepares to stuff this tasty morsel onto his stove, the
bone rattles off a stream of nonsense words that reduce the fox
to mouse-size. And so, as in <u>Sylvester and the Magic Pebble</u>
(C139), a happy ending prevails; Pearl returns home with her
talking bone, which supplies continual companionship and music
for both Pearl and her family.

In watercolor illustrations of outlined shapes, in the style
of Steig's 1970 Medal Book, the animal characters of this tale
assist the author-illustrator in presenting the human emotions
which provide the story's universal appeal. The audience can
easily sense the euphoria Pearl experiences as she strolls along
the water and chats with her newfound companion, who is tucked
inside her opened pocketbook. The impressionistic environment,
dabs of light spring hues and vibrant violets, reinforces Pearl's
attitudes and communicates them to the audience.

As the innocent piglet is confronted by the sharp-toothed fox,
the wickedness of the fox's intent is contrasted by Pearl's hor-
rified expression, as well as by the innocent activity of the
mother bird feeding her babies in a tree of the background.

Steig, in his inimitable cartoonlike style, has produced a
tale of the young overpowering the grips of Fate, with a little
magic and a little luck.

<u>1978</u>

C172   SPIER, PETER. <u>Noah's Ark</u>. Garden City, N.Y.: Doubleday,
         1977, [48 pp.] 39 illus.: color-39/illustrated endpapers,
         half-title page, and front matter/watercolor and pen and
         ink/20cm x 26.1cm
         Bible   Gr. Ps-2

The Dutch poem of the seventeenth century, translated by Peter
Spier, appears on the first, and only, major page of text in this
1978 Medal Book. What follows is a series of illustrations depicting the boarding of the ark, the ensuing flood, the eventual
cessation of rain, and the return of the ark to land.

In full-page spreads and pages divided into two, three, or
four sections, Spier's humor infiltrates the solemn conditions
that surround the ark's purpose and journey. Spier juxtaposes
scenes of the interior of the ark--feeding, cleaning, and tending the passengers--with illustrations of the mounting sea of
water outside the vessel. As the population increases within
the ark, so does the prevailing orderly disorder, until the dove
returns with an olive branch, symbolizing the end of the flood.

The watercolor and pen-and-ink illustrations captivate the
audience in the same way in which other of Spier's works have
done. Minute details escape the eye at first glance, but upon
closer study, the humor and delight of Spier's interpretation
become more evident. Details such as the inconspicuous pair of
snails, typically last to board and last to leave, attest to the
artist's characteristic attention to detail.

This is a picture book which holds up after many, many "readings" and is the closest example of a wordless picture book to
receive a Caldecott Medal to this point. The story is as timeless as the rainbow which arcs across the final pages, spreading
hope for the kingdom of man and animal.

C173   MACAULAY, DAVID. Castle. Boston: Houghton Mifflin, 1977,
          80 pp. 72 illus.: black and white-72/illustrated title
          page and front matter/pen and ink/30.4cm x 22.9cm
          Information: architecture and history   Gr. 3 up
When King Edward I of England appoints Kevin le Strange Lord
of the imaginary Aberwyvern, the new Lord begins the enormous
undertaking of constructing a castle and town to aid in the conquest of Wales between 1277 and 1305. Though the events and
characters of the story which comprise this 1978 Honor Book are
fabricated, they grow out of enormous amounts of research and
fact concerning this period in history and the actual techniques
necessary to construct this economic and military complex.

Strategically located at the mouth of the Wyvern River, the
fortification gradually emerges from an outcropping of limestone,
and after five years of labor, the self-sufficient town and
castle are complete. Detailed information concerning the workers, tools, floor plans, weapons, and current techniques of warfare are all woven into the story and accompanying pen-and-ink
illustrations. A preface and glossary also contribute to the
factual basis from which the book grows, and help clarify the
book's intent to its audience of older readers.

Similar in format and detail to the 1974 Honor Book Cathedral
(C160), Castle is heavily dependent upon the black and white illustrations as an aid to understanding the complex construction
of the fortress and town. The hatched and cross-hatched drawings
help emphasize the relative sophistication of techniques of the
time which gave rise to such monumental architectural structures.

Macaulay imparts more information to his audiences than a dry
recounting of the construction of a castle. A plethora of information reveals the social, economic, and political structures
of the time and provides a view of contemporary strategies of
warfare. Since the primary purpose of the structure lies in
its defense and fortification, it is only fitting that the
audience be given proof of that fact. After an actual battle
ensues, the strength of the castle prevails, the enemy is

1978

repelled, as history comes to life in this consumable and memorable book.

C174   ZEMACH, MARGOT.   It Could Always Be Worse.   New York: Farrar,
            Straus & Giroux, 1976, [32 pp.]   22 illus.:   color-22/
            illustrated front matter/watercolor and ink/22.8cm x 25.5cm
            Folk Tale   Gr. K-2
    This Yiddish folk tale recounts the plight of a poor man who
lives in an overcrowded hut with his mother, his wife, and his
six children.   The unfortunate man, unable to tolerate his noisy,
cramped living conditions, appeals to his local Rabbi for help.
At the Rabbi's insistence, the man increases the inhabitants of
the hut with chickens, a rooster and a goose, and a goat and a
cow, which only makes conditions more insufferable.
    But the wisdom of the Rabbi's words becomes evident when he
finally instructs the man to remove the animals from the premises,
an act that miraculously restores the household to a relative
calm.   The irony in the relief the man obtains from the simple
solution becomes the object of humor, as the audience and Rabbi
share the knowledge that the man's suffering is only relative to
that with which it is compared.
    Margot Zemach's text, in parts not as flowing as the texts on
which she collaborated with Harve Zemach, is accompanied by watercolor illustrations depicting the overcrowded conditions of
squawking animals and rambunctious humans.   In full- and single-
page spreads, the author-illustrator contrasts the pandemonium of
the hut's interior with the calm of the world outside.   Human
and animal figures sprawl across the pages of interior scenes,
while the illustrations of the hut's exterior contain little activity other than falling snow or the old man carrying out the
Rabbi's instructions.   The humorous twist of this tale, characteristic of Zemach works, whether original or retellings, and
the illustrations are a representative sample of the literary
and artistic style that varies little from the Zemach's first
Caldecott Honor Book in 1970, The Judge: An Untrue Tale (C144).

1979

C175   GOBLE, PAUL.   The Girl Who Loved Wild Horses.   Scarsdale,
            N.Y.:   Bradbury, 1978, [32 pp.]   27 illus.:   color-27/
            illustrated half-title page, title page, dedication page,
            and front matter/full color pen and ink and watercolor/
            25.3cm x 20cm
            Fantasy   Gr. 1-3
    A Native American girl enjoys a secret communication with the
horses of her tribe and spends many hours in their company.   After
a storm blows up and the young girl clings to the back of a

frightened horse, she finds herself in an unfamiliar setting, to which she is welcomed by a magnificent, spotted stallion.

The tribe, searching for the missing child for more than a year, discovers her, but the stallion intercedes, preventing the rescuers from recovering the child. Only after the stallion stumbles, giving the tribesmen a momentary advantage, does the girl return to her tribe; her sadness is only relieved when she is permitted to live with the stallion and return once a year to her tribe, bearing a beautiful spotted colt. This cycle continues until one year the girl never returns. Only a beautiful mare, traveling by the side of the stallion, explains her disappearance and transformation in the final illustration.

Paul Goble's illustrations for this 1979 Medal Book contain the stylized shapes of animals, which are similar to those of prehistoric cave paintings. The simplicity of the art of the cave painters, however, is absent in the overabundant patterns which repeat throughout the compositions of these illustrations. Though the bold hues of these full-color pages reflect the story's content, they also serve to create disharmony rather than cohesiveness of composition, often distracting the eye in several directions at once.

The dramatic style which Goble employs helps heighten the suspense of the story at times, especially as the black, stormy sky swirls over the stark white of the pages, but the drama begins to lose its effect page after page. Perhaps the most successful full-page spread is that in which the darkness of night dominates. With only a spattering of circular stars, the tinted golden moon, and the figures of horses and rider, the picture seems serene in comparison to the remainder of the book.

Words to Native American songs from the Navaho and Oglala Sioux tribes find inclusion at the book's close and help authenticate and reinforce the importance of the horse to the peoples in the story. Though Goble's work is nothing less than creative and skillful, it may be too powerful, visually, to appeal to most children.

C176   CREWS, DONALD. Freight Train. New York: Greenwillow, 1978, [24 pp.] 21 illus.: color-21/half-tone separations with black line drawings/20.2cm x 25.1cm
        Information: science   Gr. Ps-1

The journey of a colorful freight train is the basis for the simple text of the 1979 Honor Book by Donald Crews. Each of the cars of the train is identified by type and color; primary and secondary hues and black provide the colors of the train's components, which traverse the countryside, through tunnels, by cities, and over trestles.

As the freight train emerges from the blackness of night into daylight, it continues its journey onto the final page, where an

empty track, a trail of smoke, and the concluding word all indicate that the iron horse is, indeed, "gone." The extremely
limited text helps accent and dramatize the effects of the
illustrations, which depict cars in motion, their colors blending like smudged pastels.

The graphic qualities of the train and the stylized land- and
cityscapes attract the eye to and focus attention on the illustrations; the horizontal format of the book and the motif of the
speeding train and billowing smoke help emphasize the progression
in the action of the text and locomotive as well.

The design of this book is attractive, and the visualization
of movement is appropriately handled through the choice of technique and media. While the work capitalizes upon a familiar object of childhood experiences, it also provides a convenient tool
for aiding color identification and developing spatial concepts
so important in the growth of young children.

C177   BAYLOR, BYRD. The Way To Start A Day. Illustrated by Peter
        Parnall. New York: Charles Scribner's Sons, 1978, [32 pp.]
        27 illus.: color-27/illustrated title page, dedication page,
        and front matter/full color washes and pen and ink/25.4cm
        x 20.2cm
        Information: geography   Gr. 1-4

Byrd Baylor's text for this 1979 Honor Book, which originally
appeared in McCall's Magazine, covers customs and traditions
associated with greeting the sun of each new dawn. From the
world over--Peru, Mexico, the Congo, China, Egypt, Japan, and
the states of New Mexico and Arizona--the rituals come, some encouraging songs of praise or gifts to the sun.

The choice of words in the text underlines the religious significance of many of the traditions--blessings, offerings, and
temples are words used throughout, and the religious importance
of the sun in certain cultures, their dependence and worship of
it, also reinforces the religious intensity of the text. Baylor
has demonstrated this universal custom for her audience and en-
courages readers to create their own special ceremony for making
this one-day cycle of the sun meaningful.

The stylized and symbolic abstractions of Peter Parnall's
characteristic style serve the text well in the third Honor Book
this partnership has produced. The dominance of ochre, golds,
and yellows reflect the book's theme, while the colorful bands
of pinks, violets, and reds that sweep across the sky at dawn and
dusk easily communicate the visual effects of this daily cycle.

The far-reaching, creeping lines that create the formations of
rock and the predominantly circular shapes encompass the compositions, visually pulling together, unifying, the varied traditions
of the text. Within the compositions, too, the vertical columns
of text, another earmark of the work produced by these two

artists, become elements of the pages' layouts and demonstrate
the excellent, integrated design of this work.

1980

C178   HALL, DONALD. Ox-Cart Man. Illustrated by Barbara Cooney.
        New York: Viking, 1979, [40 pp.] 26 illus.: color-26/
        illustrated title page and front matter/opaque paint/
        20.7cm x 26.5cm
        Fiction: historical   Gr. K-3
    The 1980 Medal Book is a quiet story of the life of a
nineteenth-century New England family. After they pack up their
ox-cart with articles raised and made on their own farm, the family sends the Ox-Cart Man off to Portsmouth Market in New Hampshire
to sell the goods and purchase some items to make their lives more
enjoyable. Wool, shawls, mittens, candles, shingles, birch brooms,
vegetables, and maple sugar--all are sold at the market; even the
ox and cart find new owners.
    With business completed, the Ox-Cart Man journeys home again
to renew the cycle of New England life. Through the seasons of
the coming year, the family again prepares for the next trip to
the market. Just as the family produces their contributions, so
do the animals and land on which the family's livelihood depends.
    Plenty of space surrounds the text of the pages, giving the
book a rich look and contributing to the unrushed, calm tempo of
the text. Subtle differences in the spacing between the lines
of the text facilitate the flow of reading, while the illustrations harmoniously mimic the characters' quiet, complacent acceptance of their Early American life-style.
    Barbara Cooney's intentionally primitive style captures well
the atmosphere of this 1980 Medal Book. In a style reminiscent
of tole paintings on wood, the shapes, buildings, and landscapes
communicate the simple existence of nineteenth-century New England families. Even the winter scene of the collection of maple
sap, though reminiscent of Brueghel's painting Winter/Return of
the Hunters, retains an air of simple wholesomeness.
    The changing seasons and accompanying color schemes add vari-
ety to the book, as does the changing format of the illustrations.
Horizontal spreads accentuate the Ox-Cart Man's journey to and
from the marketplace, while the final illustration, within its
smaller rectangular frame, symbolizes the end of the story, but
not necessarily the end of the cycle of life.
    An appreciation by children of the artistic style of the book
and its story will be judged with the passage of time. The style
undoubtedly holds appeal for adults in word and picture--an appeal
which could easily be transferred to younger audiences with the
proper approach and guidance.

1980

C179   ISADORA, RACHEL. <u>Ben's Trumpet</u>. New York: Greenwillow,
        1979, [36 pp.] 29 illus.: black and white-29/illustrated
        endpapers, title page, and front matter/pen and ink/20.1cm
        x 24.6cm
        Fiction   Gr. K-2
        Though Ben, a young black child, only plays an invisible
trumpet, he isn't discouraged from pursuing his favorite pastime.
The pianist, saxophonist, trombonist, drummer, and trumpeter, all
of the Zig Zag Jazz Club, provide Ben with all the incentive he
needs, as he sits on the fire escape or the stoop and listens as
the rhythmical beat of their music fills the air.
        Because of his imaginary trumpet playing, Ben suffers through
the unresponsiveness of his family and the ridicule of his peers.
But his perseverance is rewarded when he has the opportunity to
try out a real instrument with the only person who recognizes his
potential--the trumpeter from the Zig Zag Club.
        The swinging, throbbing beat of Isadora's illustrations accu-
rately reflect the pulsating rhythm of the jazz sounds that permeate Ben's world. The black and white illustrations are full
of a variety of styles which change as quickly as the turn of
the page. Hatched and cross-hatched lines create a parquet
effect on the pages on which this technique is utilized.
        Contour drawings and silhouettes on other pages create only a
momentary impression of the Jazz Club musicians as they produce
their sounds. The art deco of the 1920s surfaces in the decorative designs, which become integral parts of the compositions,
integral only for their visual impact, whether it be to mimic the
sway of the trumpeter's walk or to visualize the aural effects of
the music on Ben. Compositions interspersed with zig zag lines
of sound waves and nearly vertical lines of the music's beat also
appear throughout the book.
        The music of Ben's trumpet reverberates in the visual images
of this Honor Book; the diversity of styles creates a disjointed
effect, not unlike the musical patterns of jazz itself, but at
times the pages seem overwhelming, often outweighing the points
they are meant to communicate.

C180   SHULEVITZ, URI. <u>The Treasure</u>. New York: Farrar, Straus &
        Giroux, 1978, [32 pp.] 19 illus.: color-19/illustrated
        title page/full-color ink and pen and ink/22.9cm x 20.2cm
        Folk Tale   Gr. 1-3
        A recurring dream finally convinces Isaac to seek a treasure
under the bridge near the Royal Palace, so this poor man embarks
upon the long journey to the capital city. Traveling mostly on
foot, Isaac makes his way through forests and mountains to reach
the city. Here he finds no treasure; but, instead, a palace guard
tells the poor man of his dream, of a treasure buried under a
stove in the house of a man named Isaac.

The peasant journeys home to discover the treasure, exactly as the guard described. With the money, Isaac builds a house of prayer, complete with an inscription in one corner: "Sometimes one must travel far to discover what is near."

In rich, clear colors, Uri Shulevitz paints this familiar tale, told in the Chassidic tradition. All contained within rectangular shapes, the illustrations depict the thick forests and steep mountains of Isaac's journey. Ample space surrounds the illustrations, giving the book a rich look and sufficiently emphasizing the artwork and accompanying text.

Precise black hatched and cross-hatched lines give definition to the shapes of the landscapes, architecture, and figures, but it is the color which makes the illustrations memorable. The clear, cool azure of sky and water penetrates nearly every illustration, drawing the eye with its magnetic powers.

Shulevitz has demonstrated his skill in a former Caldecott Medal winner (C137) and his ability to set the mood of his stories so precisely in tune with the text remains a dominant feature and earmark of his work.

C181   VAN ALLSBURG, CHRIS. The Garden of Abdul Gasazi. Boston: Houghton Mifflin, 1979, [32 pp.] 14 illus.: black and white-14/illustrated title page/pencil/24.3cm x 30.3cm
        Fantasy   Gr. 1-3

When Alan Mitz dog-sits for Miss Hester's pet, the boy has his hands full keeping the canine in line. On his afternoon walk, Fritz, the dog, bolts through the doorway of a garden--a garden strictly forbidden to dogs. Alan, chasing the runaway animal, follows the tracks to the palatial home of Abdul Gasazi, retired magician.

Alan politely inquires about the missing pet, to which Gasazi the Great responds by showing the child the dog, now transformed, so the magician says, into a duck. As Alan and his charge begin their trip home, a gust of wind carries off the boy's hat, and the duck, too, takes flight, capturing the cap in his bill as he goes.

Returning to Miss Hester's empty-handed, Alan is relieved to find Fritz safely enjoying his dinner. Miss Hester reassures the guilt-ridden boy, and after he leaves, the mysterious discovery of Alan's hat, by Fritz, leaves the audience to ponder whether or not Gasazi did use a little magic to his advantage.

The detail and precision of Van Allsburg's illustrations are skillfully produced by the value changes in his black and white illustrations. The visual results of pencil on paper provide pages of surface quality so interesting it is difficult not to linger over every inch of illustration. The crisp lines become even more so when the pictures are viewed at a distance, and the work takes on a photographic quality in its patterns of light and dark.

1980

The illustrations, faced with a text enclosed within a leaf motif border, often employ a definite light source to emphasize the shadows in the illustrations and heighten the dramatic effects of the compositions. Van Allsburg has created a unique visual presentation which convincingly sets the stage for the mystery which surrounds the book's ending.

<u>1981</u>

C182   LOBEL, ARNOLD.   <u>Fables</u>.   New York: Harper & Row, 1980, 41 pp.
         20 illus.:   color-20/illustrated front matter and contents
         page/watercolor, wash, and ink/29.2cm x 20.5cm
         Fantasy   Gr. K up
      Arnold Lobel's first Caldecott Medal Book consists of twenty modern fables, each complete with a timely moral.   The characters in each scenario are traditionally anthropomorphic, and the stories, all listed in the Contents, offer some warnings based on simple observations of human nature.   An illustration of a baboon wielding a holely umbrella accompanies the cautionary moral that advice from friends is sometimes good and sometimes bad, much like the weather.
      The format, humor, and concepts of this Medal Book are somewhat dependent upon an exposure to the original, traditional form of the fable, but the honesty beneath the humorous facades of the morals needs no further explanation to the audience, child or adult.   Lobel successfully holds a mirror up to human behaviors which transcend all time frames and societies; the audience cannot help but engage in a bit of self-examination after reading these stories.
      The rich watercolors accompanying each fable exist within rectangular frames, the borders of which are sometimes violated by the extension of tails, antennae, or frogs' legs onto the white of the surrounding page.   The illustrations themselves mean nothing without the text, but Lobel's choice of animals-- crab, lobster, rhinoceros, camel, and others--affords him the opportunity to create characters as ingeniously funny and as pathetically human as the morals they accompany.
      Lobel's artistic style in this book varies considerably from his Honor Books of 1971 (<u>Frog and Toad Are Friends</u> [C147]) and 1972 (<u>Hildilid's Night</u> [C152]).   He easily demonstrates the range of his talents in these rich, painterly, full-bodied illustrations. The text and illustrations of this Medal Book will not be quickly forgotten by audiences of any age.

C183   BANG, MOLLY.   <u>The Grey Lady and the Strawberry Snatcher</u>.
         New York: Four Winds, 1980, [48 pp.]   45 illus.:   color-
         45/illustrated front matter and title page/opaque paint
         and watercolor/20.2cm x 20cm

Fiction   Gr. 1-3

All grey, except for face, hands, and a quart of luscious strawberries she carries, the main character of this wordless picture
book remains the intended victim of the thief who stalks her from
the produce store, down sidewalks of brick, and through the entangling growth of a swamp. At every turn the Grey Lady evades the
chartreuse-caped marauder, but he persists in his quest, on foot
and on skateboard, for a strawberry.

As the victim disappears into the marshy swamp, she eludes
the cobalt-skinned Snatcher by blending into the grey backgrounds
and trees of her surroundings. It is not until the Snatcher discovers a patch of blackberries that the Grey Lady is safe; she
continues home to share her fruit with the baby, the children,
and the elderly of her extended family, while the Snatcher removes his violet hat and indulges in the sweet taste of fresh,
ripe blackberries.

Bang incorporates the suspense of this totally wordless book
into the unique juxtaposition of colors, as well as into the
foreboding expressionism of the trees of the swamp. The red-
lined, chartreuse cape of the Snatcher, he of cobalt skin, and
the violet hat possess an iridescence against the grey backgrounds
and shapes. Negative areas become important shapes in the compositions as they envelop the Grey Lady and mask her from the
Snatcher's view. Only face, hands, and strawberries are discernible at times, giving a hint to the whereabouts of the woman, and
at one point only her reflection in the swamp serves as an indication of her presence.

As the pursuance proceeds, the figures progress across the
full-page spreads, and the continual movement of the characters
from left to right recreates the sequence and necessity of escape,
as well as the dimension of passing time. Bang's innovative techniques will no doubt encourage the extension of these principles
by other picturebook artists; the effectiveness of the work depends solely on the absence of text. The book stimulates an internal, silent dialogue with the viewer, and, unlike many
wordless books, the spoken word disrupts the spell of the story--
its silent fear and suspense.

C184   CREWS, DONALD. Truck. New York: Greenwillow, 1980, [32 pp.]
        31 illus.: color-31/illustrated title page/4-color half-
        tone separation with black line drawings/20.2cm x 25cm
        Fiction   Gr. Ps-1

The journey of a shipment of tricycles in a semi-tractor
trailer offers the basic storyline for this wordless Honor Book.
This visual experience is only interspersed with words appearing
on traffic signs along the route and on vehicles--speed limit, one
way, stop, livestock, Bakery.

1981

The rig, identifiable by its red color and bold white letters
which spell the word "TRUCKING," travels through town, and in
and out of a tunnel, until it eventually meanders onto an express-
way. The run includes a stop, for food and fuel, at an all-
night diner, as well as the inconvenience of foul weather--rain
and fog. The trek concludes, eleven showing on the clock, as the
semi backs up to a loading dock, the final page revealing the
tricycles, except one, stacked outside the trailer, ready for
distribution.

The progression of Crews's truck, across page and terrain, is
accomplished through graphics reminiscent of the style of the
author-artist's 1979 Honor Book, Freight Train (C176), though
without the simplicity of composition, color and form. The pages
are full of fleeting glimpses of city streets, bumper-to-bumper
traffic, and an intertwining interchange. These busy foregrounds
lie against the simple contour drawings of the skylines in the
background; the flatness of the foreground shapes themselves
takes on an abbreviated simplicity which demands the viewer's
attention.

As the truck proceeds through the day and into evening, the
black background of the night emphasizes the glaring neon signs
of the truck stop; Crews records with visual accuracy the lighted
oasis which appears out of nowhere on long nights of travel. The
author-artist integrates the familiar experiences of our automobile-
dependent society into this Honor Book and offers young readers the
opportunity to accompany the journey of the tricycles with their
own verbal records. Just as Freight Train capitalizes upon a common object of childhood, Truck, too, offers another means of con-
veyance which traverses the country, this time to deliver the
vehicles which enable most children to become active participants
in the mobility of our society.

C185   LOW, JOSEPH. Mice Twice. New York: Atheneum, 1980, [32 pp.]
          27 illus.: color-27/illustrated half-title, title page, and
          dedication/watercolor, wash, and pen and ink/22.8cm x 17.5cm
          Fantasy   Gr. Ps-1
       Joseph Low, author and illustrator of this Honor Book, begins
a succession of "social" encounters when Cat invites Mouse to
supper. When Mouse obtains permission to bring along a guest,
Cat's appetite increases at the thought of "mice twice." With
only the intention of consuming two mice for his supper, the
feline is unpleasantly surprised when his guest appears on his
doorstep with Dog.

Reciprocating invitations ensue, but the situation finally resolves itself on the last visit. Mouse and Dog return to Cat's
home with yet another friend, Wasp, and a few stings later Cat
and friend, Lion, quickly vacate the premises, never to be of
bother to Mouse again.

The element of surprise which accompanies each invitation and the increasing physical size of the guests is reminiscent of the 1965 Medal Book May I Bring A Friend? (C123). What is not so distinctive, however, in this 1981 Honor Book is the visual presentation. Though the yellows and reds of the watercolors and the grays of the wash are defined with lines of spontaneity and expression, the illustrations are at odds with the humor and levity of the text.

The limited color scheme and the predominance of gray washes are responsible for the absence of vibrancy of which the medium is capable. Though individual pages work well in color and composition, others contribute to a rather haphazard, disjointed format. In comparison to other Honor Books of the year, Low's book lacks the distinction that normally characterizes the Caldecott choices; only with the passage of time will the lasting qualities of the book become evident.

C186   PLUME, ILSE. The Bremen-town Musicians. Garden City, N.Y.:
       Doubleday, 1980, [32 pp.] 15 illus.: color-15/illustrated
       title page and dedication/color pencil/20.2cm x 26.3cm
       Folk Tale   Gr. K-2

In this retelling of a German folk tale, four animals, all too old to be of use to their owners, join forces and proceed on a journey to Bremen-town to become a part of a band of street musicians. After the donkey, dog, cat, and rooster find themselves an uncomfortable resting place to spend the night, they notice a lighted house in the distance and decide to investigate.

After peering in the window and realizing a band of robbers occupy the premises, the animal troupe devises a method of vacating the hideaway; they all begin to make "music," the sound of which, almost demonic in nature, frightens the robbers away. The musicians quickly make themselves at home, and, except for scaring off a returning robber sent to investigate what creature had driven the bandits from their home, the animals live contentedly, with never a thought of continuing their journey to Bremen-town.

Ilse Plume's illustrations for this tale appear in rectangular formats, one picture on the right, facing a page of text on the left. The yellow bands of color, which appear above and below each segment of text, pick up the glowing yellows and ochres of the facing illustrations, creating visual harmony between text and picture, even though a physical separation of the two exists.

Though the shapes and figures of the compositions have a decorative flatness to them, the surfaces of the pages are rich in quality and texture. The soft patterns of light and dark enrich the illustrations; the subtle modeling of forms is often not recognizable until some distance comes between eye and work.

Enormous variety exists in the artist's handling of the trees, which infiltrate the landscape of the countryside, but these

1981

leafless trunks also serve as a constant reminder, in many cases, of the rigidity of shape and form in the compositions of the pages. Plume's visual impression retains the simplicity and primitive qualities of the lithographic work of the d'Aulaires, and the style appropriately captures the simple origins of the literature.

Appendix A

Note: Complete bibliographic citations appear with the annotations.
The Honor Books follow the Medal Books, and prior to 1964 the Honor
Books are arranged according to the number of votes received. After
1964 the Honor Books are listed alphabetically by author for the Newbery works and by illustrator for the Caldecott books.

THE NEWBERY BOOKS

1922

The Story of Mankind. By Hendrik Willem Van Loon.   N1
The Great Quest. By Charles B. Hawes.   N2
Cedric the Forester. By Bernard G. Marshall.   N3
The Old Tobacco Shop. By William Bowen.   N4
The Golden Fleece and the Heroes Who Lived before Achilles.   By
    Padraic Colum.   N5
The Windy Hill. By Cornelia Meigs.   N6

1923

The Voyages of Dr. Dolittle. By Hugh Lofting.   N7
No record of Honor Books

1924

The Dark Frigate. By Charles B. Hawes.   N8
No record of Honor Books

1925

Tales from Silver Lands. By Charles Finger.   N9
Nicholas. By Anne Carroll Moore.   N10
The Dream Coach. By Anne and Dillwyn Parrish.   N11

1926

Shen of the Sea. By Arthur Bowie Chrisman. N12
The Voyagers. By Padraic Colum. N13

1927

Smoky, the Cowhorse. By Will James. N14
No record of Honor Books

1928

Gay-Neck. By Dhan Gopal Mukerji. N15
The Wondersmith and His Son. By Ella Young. N16
Downright Dencey. By Caroline Dale Snedeker. N17

1929

The Trumpeter of Krakow. By Eric P. Kelly. N18
The Pigtail of Ah Lee Ben Loo. By John Bennett. N19
Millions of Cats. By Wanda Gág. N20
The Boy Who Was. By Grace T. Hallock. N21
Clearing Weather. By Cornelia Meigs. N22
The Runaway Papoose. By Grace Moon. N23
Tod of the Fens. By Elinor Whitney. N24

1930

Hitty. By Rachel Field. N25
A Daughter of the Seine. By Jeanette Eaton. N26
Pran of Albania. By Elizabeth Cleveland Miller. N27
Jumping-Off Place. By Marian Hurd McNeely. N28
The Tangle-Coated Horse. By Ella Young. N29
Vaino. By Julia Davis Adams. N30
Little Blacknose. By Hildegarde Hoyt Swift. N31

1931

The Cat Who Went to Heaven. By Elizabeth Coatsworth. N32
Floating Island. By Anne Parrish. N33
The Dark Star of Itza. By Alida Sims Malkus. N34
Queer Person. By Ralph Hubbard. N35
Mountains Are Free. By Julia Davis Adams. N36
Spice and the Devil's Cave. By Agnes D. Hewes. N37
Meggy MacIntosh. By Elizabeth Janet Gray. N38
Garram the Hunter. By Herbert Best. N39
Ood-Le-Uk, the Wanderer. By Alice Alison Lide and Margaret
   Alison Johansen. N40

Appendix A

1932

Waterless Mountain. By Laura Adams Armer. N41
The Fairy Circus. By Dorothy P. Lathrop. N42
Calico Bush. By Rachel Field. N43
Boy of the South Seas. By Eunice Tietjens. N44
Out of the Flame. By Eloise Lownsbery. N45
Jane's Island. By Marjorie Hill Allee. N46
The Truce of the Wolf. By Mary Gould Davis. N47

1933

Young Fu of the Upper Yangtze. By Elizabeth Foreman Lewis. N48
Swift Rivers. By Cornelia Meigs. N49
The Railroad to Freedom. By Hildegarde Hoyt Swift. N50
Children of the Soil. By Nora Burglon. N51

1934

Invincible Louisa. By Cornelia Meigs. N52
The Forgotten Daughter. By Caroline Dale Snedeker. N53
Swords of Steel. By Elsie Singmaster. N54
The ABC Bunny. By Wanda Gág. N55
The Winged Girl of Knossos. By Allena Best [Erick Berry]. N56
New Land. By Sarah L. Schmidt. N57
The Big Tree of Bunlahy. By Padraic Colum. N58
Glory of the Seas. By Agnes D. Hewes. N59
The Apprentice of Florence. By Anne Kyle. N60

1935

Dobry. By Monica Shannon. N61
The Pageant of Chinese History. By Elizabeth Seeger. N62
Davy Crockett. By Constance Rourke. N63
A Day on Skates. By Hilda Van Stockum. N64

1936

Caddie Woodlawn. By Carol Ryrie Brink. N65
Honk: The Moose. By Phil Stong. N66
The Good Master. By Kate Seredy. N67
Young Walter Scott. By Elizabeth Janet Gray. N68
All Sail Set. By Armstrong Sperry. N69

1937

Roller Skates. By Ruth Sawyer. N70
Phebe Fairchild. By Lois Lenski. N71
Whistler's Van. By Idwal Jones. N72
The Golden Basket. By Ludwig Bemelmans. N73
Winterbound. By Margery Bianco. N74

Appendix A

Audubon. By Constance Rourke. N75
The Codfish Musket. By Agnes D. Hewes. N76

1938

The White Stag. By Kate Seredy. N77
Pecos Bill. By James Cloyd Bowman. N78
Bright Island. By Mabel L. Robinson. N79
On the Banks of Plum Creek. By Laura Ingalls Wilder. N80.

1939

Thimble Summer. By Elizabeth Enright. N81
Nino. By Valenti Angelo. N82
Mr. Popper's Penguins. By Richard and Florence Atwater. N83
"Hello, the Boat!" By Phyllis Crawford. N84
Leader by Destiny. By Jeanette Eaton. N85
Penn. By Elizabeth Janet Gray. N86

1940

Daniel Boone. By James Daugherty. N87
The Singing Tree. By Kate Seredy. N88
Runner of the Mountain Tops. By Mabel L. Robinson. N89
By the Shores of Silver Lake. By Laura Ingalls Wilder. N90
Boy with a Pack. By Stephen W. Meader. N91

1941

Call It Courage. By Armstrong Sperry. N92
Blue Willow. By Doris Gates. N93
Young Mac of Fort Vancouver. By Mary Jane Carr. N94
The Long Winter. By Laura Ingalls Wilder. N95
Nansen. By Anna Gertrude Hall. N96

1942

The Matchlock Gun. By Walter D. Edmonds. N97
Little Town on the Prairie. By Laura Ingalls Wilder. N98
George Washington's World. By Genevieve Foster. N99
Indian Captive. By Lois Lenski. N100
Down Ryton Water. By Eva Rose Gaggin. N101

1943

Adam of the Road. By Elizabeth Janet Gray. N102
The Middle Moffat. By Eleanor Estes. N103
"Have You Seen Tom Thumb?" By Mabel Leigh Hunt. N104

1944

Johnny Tremain. By Esther Forbes. N105
These Happy Golden Years. By Laura Ingalls Wilder. N106
Fog Magic. By Julia L. Sauer. N107
Rufus M. By Eleanor Estes. N108
Mountain Born. By Elizabeth Yates. N109

1945

Rabbit Hill. By Robert Lawson. N110
The Hundred Dresses. By Eleanor Estes. N111
The Silver Pencil. By Alice Dalgliesh. N112
Abraham Lincoln's World. By Genevieve Foster. N113
Lone Journey. By Jeanette Eaton. N114

1946

Strawberry Girl. By Lois Lenski. N115
Justin Morgan Had a Horse. By Marguerite Henry. N116
The Moved-Outers. By Florence Crannell Means. N117
Bhimsa, the Dancing Bear. By Christine Weston. N118
New Found World. By Katherine B. Shippen. N119

1947

Miss Hickory. By Carolyn Sherwin Bailey. N120
The Wonderful Year. By Nancy Barnes. N121
The Big Tree. By Mary and Conrad Buff. N122
The Heavenly Tenants. By William Maxwell. N123
The Avion My Uncle Flew. By Darwin Teilhet [Cyrus Fisher]. N124
The Hidden Treasure of Glaston. By Eleanor Jewett. N125

1948

The Twenty-One Balloons. By William Pène du Bois. N126
Pancakes-Paris. By Claire Huchet Bishop. N127
Li Lun, Lad of Courage. By Carolyn Treffinger. N128
The Quaint and Curious Quest of Johnny Longfoot. By Catherine
     Besterman. N129
The Cow-Tail Switch. By Harold Courlander and George Herzog.
     N130
Misty of Chincoteague. By Marguerite Henry. N131

1949

King of the Wind. By Marguerite Henry. N132
Seabird. By Holling C. Holling. N133
Daughter of the Mountains. By Louise Rankin. N134
My Father's Dragon. By Ruth Stiles Gannett. N135
The Story of the Negro. By Arna Bontemps. N136

Appendix A

1950

The Door in the Wall. By Marguerite de Angeli. N137
Tree of Freedom. By Rebecca Caudill. N138
The Blue Cat of Castle Town. By Catherine Cate Coblentz. N139
Kildee House. By Rutherford Montgomery. N140
George Washington. By Genevieve Foster. N141
Song of the Pines. By Walter and Marion Havighurst. N142

1951

Amos Fortune, Free Man. By Elizabeth Yates. N143
Better Known as Johnny Appleseed. By Mabel Leigh Hunt. N144
Gandhi. By Jeanette Eaton. N145
Abraham Lincoln. By Clara Ingram Judson. N146
The Story of Appleby Capple. By Anne Parrish. N147

1952

Ginger Pye. By Eleanor Estes. N148
Americans before Columbus. By Elizabeth Chesley Baity. N149
Minn of the Mississippi. By Holling C. Holling. N150
The Defender. By Nicholas Kalashnikoff. N151
The Light at Tern Rock. By Julia L. Sauer. N152
The Apple and the Arrow. By Mary and Conrad Buff. N153

1953

Secret of the Andes. By Ann Nolan Clark. N154
Charlotte's Web. By E. B. White. N155
Moccasin Trail. By Eloise McGraw. N156
Red Sails to Capri. By Ann Weil. N157
The Bears on Hemlock Mountain. By Alice Dalgliesh. N158
Birthdays of Freedom. By Genevieve Foster. N159

1954

And Now Miguel. By Joseph Krumgold. N160
All-Alone. By Claire Huchet Bishop. N161
Shadrach. By Meindert de Jong. N162
Hurry Home, Candy. By Meindert de Jong. N163
Theodore Roosevelt. By Clara Ingram Judson. N164
Magic Maize. By Mary and Conrad Buff. N165

1955

The Wheel on the School. By Meindert de Jong. N166
The Courage of Sarah Noble. By Alice Dalgliesh. N167
Banner in the Sky. By James Ramsey Ullman. N168

Appendix A

1956

Carry On, Mr. Bowditch. By Jean Lee Latham. N169
The Secret River. By Marjorie Kinnan Rawlings. N170
The Golden Name Day. By Jennie Lindquist. N171
Men, Microscopes, and Living Things. By Katherine B. Shippen.
  N172

1957

Miracles on Maple Hill. By Virginia Sorensen. N173
Old Yeller. By Fred Gipson. N174
The House of Sixty Fathers. By Meindert de Jong. N175
Mr. Justice Holmes. By Clara Ingram Judson. N176
The Corn Grows Ripe. By Dorothy Rhoads. N177
The Black Fox of Lorne. By Marguerite de Angeli. N178

1958

Rifles for Watie. By Harold Keith. N179
The Horsecatcher. By Mari Sandoz. N180
Gone-Away Lake. By Elizabeth Enright. N181
The Great Wheel. By Robert Lawson. N182
Tom Paine. By Leo Gurko. N183

1959

The Witch of Blackbird Pond. By Elizabeth George Speare. N184
The Family under the Bridge. By Natalie Carlson. N185
Along Came a Dog. By Meindert de Jong. N186
Chúcaro. By Francis Kalnay. N187
The Perilous Road. By William O. Steele. N188

1960

Onion John. By Joseph Krumgold. N189
My Side of the Mountain. By Jean George. N190
America Is Born. By Gerald Johnson. N191
The Gammage Cup. By Carol Kendall. N192

1961

Island of the Blue Dolphins. By Scott O'Dell. N193
America Moves Forward. By Gerald Johnson. N194
Old Ramon. By Jack Shaefer. N195
The Cricket in Times Square. By George Thompson [George Selden].
  N196

Appendix A

1962

The Bronze Bow. By Elizabeth George Speare. N197
Frontier Living. By Edwin Tunis. N198
The Golden Goblet. By Eloise Jarvis McGraw. N199
Belling the Tiger. By Mary Stolz. N200

1963

A Wrinkle in Time. By Madeleine L'Engle. N201
Thistle and Thyme. By Leclaire Alger [Sorche Nic Leodhas].
   N202
Men of Athens. By Olivia Coolidge. N203

1964

It's Like This, Cat. By Emily Neville. N204
Rascal. By Sterling North. N205
The Loner. By Ester Wier. N206

1965

Shadow of a Bull. By Maia Wojciechowska. N207
Across Five Aprils. By Irene Hunt. N208

1966

I, Juan de Pareja. By Elizabeth Borton de Treviño. N209
The Black Cauldron. By Lloyd Alexander. N210
The Animal Family. By Randall Jarrell. N211
The Noonday Friends. By Mary Stolz. N212

1967

Up a Road Slowly. By Irene Hunt. N213
The King's Fifth. By Scott O'Dell. N214
Zlateh the Goat. By Isaac Bashevis Singer. N215
The Jazz Man. By Mary Hays Weik. N216

1968

From the Mixed-Up Files of Mrs. Basil E. Frankweiler. By Elaine
   Konigsburg. N217
Jennifer, Hecate, MacBeth, William McKinley, and Me, Elizabeth.
   By Elaine Konigsburg. N218
The Black Pearl. By Scott O'Dell. N219
The Fearsome Inn. By Isaac Bashevis Singer. N220
The Egypt Game. By Zilpha K. Snyder. N221

Appendix A

Appendix A

1976

The Grey King. By Susan Cooper. N250
The Hundred Penny Box. By Sharon Bell Mathis. N251
Dragonwings. By Laurence Yep. N252

1977

Roll of Thunder, Hear My Cry. By Mildred D. Taylor. N253
A String in the Harp. By Nancy Bond. N254
Abel's Island. By William Steig. N255

1978

The Bridge to Terabithia. By Katherine Paterson. N256
Ramona and Her Father. By Beverly Cleary. N257
Anpao. By Jamake Highwater. N258

1979

The Westing Game. By Ellen Raskin. N259
The Great Gilly Hopkins. By Katherine Paterson. N260

1980

A Gathering of Days. By Joan Blos. N261
The Road from Home. By David Kherdian. N262

1981

Jacob Have I Loved. By Katherine Paterson. N263
The Fledgling. By Jane Langton. N264
A Ring of Endless Light. By Madeleine L'Engle. N265

THE CALDECOTT BOOKS

Note: Illustrators' names appear first, if different from those of
the authors. Where one name appears, it can be assumed that the
illustrator is also the author.

1938

Animals of the Bible. Illustrated by Dorothy P. Lathrop. By
    Helen Dean Fish. C1
Seven Simeons: A Russian Tale. By Boris Artzybasheff. C2
Four and Twenty Blackbirds. Illustrated by Robert Lawson. By
    Helen Dean Fish. C3

Appendix A

1939

<u>Mei Li</u>. By Thomas Handforth. C4
<u>The Forest Pool</u>. By Laura Adams Armer. C5
<u>Wee Gillis</u>. Illustrated by Robert Lawson. By Munro Leaf. C6
<u>Snow-White and the Seven Dwarfs</u>. Illustrated by Wanda Gág. By the Brothers Grimm. C7
<u>Barkis</u>. By Clare Turlay Newberry. C8
<u>Andy and the Lion</u>. By James Daugherty. C9

1940

<u>Abraham Lincoln</u>. By Ingri and Edgar d'Aulaire. C10
<u>Cock-a-doodle-Doo . . .</u> By Berta and Elmer Hader. C11
<u>Madeline</u>. By Ludwig Bemelmans. C12
<u>The Ageless Story</u>. By Lauren Ford. C13

1941

<u>They Were Strong and Good</u>. By Robert Lawson. C14
<u>April's Kittens</u>. By Claire Turlay Newberry. C15

1942

<u>Make Way for Ducklings</u>. By Robert McCloskey. C16
<u>An American ABC</u>. By Maud and Miska Petersham. C17
<u>In My Mother's House</u>. Illustrated by Velino Herrera. By Ann Nolan Clark. C18
<u>Paddle-to-the-Sea</u>. By Holling C. Holling. C19
<u>Nothing At All</u>. By Wanda Gág. C20

1943

<u>The Little House</u>. By Virginia Lee Burton. C21
<u>Dash & Dart</u>. By Mary and Conrad Buff. C22
<u>Marshmallow</u>. By Clare Turlay Newberry. C23

1944

<u>Many Moons</u>. Illustrated by Louis Slobodkin. By James Thurber. C24
<u>Small Rain: Verses from the Bible</u>. Illustrated by Elizabeth Orton Jones. By Jessie Orton Jones. C25
<u>Pierre Pidgeon</u>. Illustrated by Arnold E. Bare. By Lee Kingman. C26
<u>The Mighty Hunter</u>. By Berta and Elmer Hader. C27
<u>A Child's Good Night Book</u>. Illustrated by Jean Charlot. By Margaret Wise Brown. C28
<u>Good-Luck Horse</u>. Illustrated by Plato Chan. By Chih-Yi Chan. C29

1945

Prayer for a Child. Illustrated by Elizabeth Orton Jones. By
    Rachel Field. C30
Mother Goose. Illustrated by Tasha Tudor. C31
In the Forest. By Marie Hall Ets. C32
Yonie Wondernose. By Marguerite de Angeli. C33
The Christmas Anna Angel. Illustrated by Kate Seredy. By Ruth
    Sawyer. C34

1946

The Rooster Crows. Illustrated by Maud and Miska Petersham.
    C35
Little Lost Lamb. Illustrated by Leonard Weisgard. By Margaret
    Wise Brown [Golden MacDonald]. C36
Sing Mother Goose. Illustrated by Marjorie Torrey. Music by
    Opal Wheeler. C37
My Mother Is the Most Beautiful Woman in the World. Illustrated
    by Ruth Gannett. By Becky Reyher. C38
You Can Write Chinese. By Kurt Wiese. C39

1947

The Little Island. Illustrated by Leonard Weisgard. By Margaret
    Wise Brown [Golden MacDonald]. C40
Rain Drop Splash. Illustrated by Leonard Weisgard. By Alvin
    Tresselt. C41
Boats on the River. Illustrated by Jay Hyde Barnum. By Marjorie
    Flack. C42
Timothy Turtle. Illustrated by Tony Palazzo. By Al Graham.
    C43
Pedro, the Angel of Olvera Street. By Leo Politi. C44
Sing in Praise: A Collection of the Best Loved Hymns. Illus-
    trated by Marjorie Torrey. By Opal Wheeler. C45

1948

White Snow, Bright Snow. Illustrated by Roger Duvoisin. By
    Alvin Tresselt. C46
Stone Soup. Illustrated by Marcia Brown. C47
McElligot's Pool. By Theodor Seuss Geisel [Dr. Seuss]. C48
Bambino, the Clown. By Georges Schreiber. C49
Roger and the Fox. Illustrated by Hildegard Woodward. By
    Lavinia Davis. C50
Song of Robin Hood. Illustrated by Virginia Lee Burton. By
    Anne Malcolmson. C51

Appendix A

1949

The Big Snow. By Berta and Elmer Hader. C52
Blueberries for Sal. By Robert McCloskey. C53
All Around the Town. Illustrated by Helen Stone. By Phyllis
   McGinley. C54
Juanita. By Leo Politi. C55
Fish in the Air. By Kurt Wiese. C56

1950

Song of the Swallows. By Leo Politi. C57
America's Ethan Allen. Illustrated by Lynd Ward. By Stewart
   Holbrook. C58
The Wild Birthday Cake. Illustrated by Hildegard Woodward.
   By Lavinia Davis. C59
The Happy Day. Illustrated by Marc Simont. By Ruth Krauss.
   C60
Bartholomew and the Oobleck. Theodor Seuss Geisel [Dr. Seuss].
   C61
Henry Fisherman. By Marcia Brown. C62

1951

The Egg Tree. By Katherine Milhous. C63
Dick Whittington and His Cat. By Marcia Brown. C64
The Two Reds. Illustrated by Nicolas Mordvinoff [Nicolas].
   By William Lipkind [Will]. C65
If I Ran the Zoo. By Theodor Seuss Geisel [Dr. Seuss]. C66
The Most Wonderful Doll in the World. Illustrated by Helen
   Stone. By Phyllis McGinley. C67
T-Bone, the Baby-Sitter. By Clare Turlay Newberry. C68

1952

Finders Keepers. Illustrated by Nicolas Mordvinoff [Nicolas].
   By William Lipkind [Will]. C69
Mr. T.W. Anthony Woo. By Marie Hall Ets. C70
Skipper John's Cook. By Marcia Brown. C71
All Falling Down. Illustrated by Margaret Bloy Graham. By Gene
   Zion. C72
Bear Party. By William Pène du Bois. C73
Feather Mountain. By Elizabeth Olds. C74

1953

The Biggest Bear. By Lynd Ward. C75
Puss in Boots. Illustrated by Marcia Brown. By Charles Perrault.
   C76
One Morning in Maine. By Robert McCloskey. C77
Ape in a Cape: An Alphabet of Odd Animals. By Fritz Eichenberg.
   C78

The Storm Book. Illustrated by Margaret Bloy Graham. By
Charlotte Zolotow. C79
Five Little Monkeys. By Juliet Kepes. C80

1954

Madeline's Rescue. By Ludwig Bemelmans. C81
Journey Cake, Ho! Illustrated by Robert McCloskey. By Ruth
Sawyer. C82
When Will the World Be Mine? Illustrated by Jean Charlot. By
Miriam Schlein. C83
The Steadfast Tin Soldier. Illustrated by Marcia Brown. By
Hans Christian Andersen. C84
A Very Special House. Illustrated by Maurice Sendak. By Ruth
Krauss. C85
Green Eyes. By A. Birnbaum. C86

1955

Cinderella, or the Little Glass Slipper. Illustrated by Marcia
Brown. By Charles Perrault. C87
Book of Nursery and Mother Goose Rhymes. Illustrated by
Marguerite de Angeli. C88
Wheel on the Chimney. Illustrated by Tibor Gergely. By Margaret
Wise Brown. C89
The Thanksgiving Story. Illustrated by Helen Sewell. By Alice
Dalgliesh. C90

1956

Frog Went A-Courtin'. Illustrated by Feodor Rojankovsky. By
John Langstaff. C91
Play with Me. By Marie Hall Ets. C92
Crow Boy. By Taro Yashima. C93

1957

A Tree Is Nice. Illustrated by Marc Simont. By Janice Udry.
C94
Mister Penny's Race Horse. By Marie Hall Ets. C95
1 Is One. By Tasha Tudor. C96
Anatole. Illustrated by Paul Galdone. By Eve Titus. C97
Gillespie and the Guards. Illustrated by James Daugherty. By
Benjamin Elkin. C98
Lion. By William Pène du Bois. C99

1958

Time of Wonder. By Robert McCloskey. C100
Fly High, Fly Low. By Don Freeman. C101
Anatole and the Cat. Illustrated by Paul Galdone. By Eve Titus.
C102

Appendix A

1959

Chanticleer and the Fox. Illustrated by Barbara Cooney. By
　Geoffrey Chaucer. C103
The House That Jack Built ("La Maison que Jacques a Bâtie"). By
　Antonio Frasconi. C104
What Do You Say, Dear? Illustrated by Maurice Sendak. By
　Sesyle Joslin. C105
Umbrella. By Taro Yashima. C106

1960

Nine Days to Christmas. Illustrated by Marie Hall Ets. By Marie
　Hall Ets and Aurora Labastida. C107
Houses from the Sea. Illustrated by Adrienne Adams. By Alice
　Goudey. C108
The Moon Jumpers. Illustrated by Maurice Sendak. By Janice
　Udry. C109

1961

Baboushka and the Three Kings. Illustrated by Nicolas Sidjakov.
　By Ruth Robbins. C110
Inch by Inch. By Leo Lionni. C111

1962

Once a Mouse. Illustrated by Marcia Brown. C112
The Fox Went Out on a Chilly Night: An Old Song. Illustrated
　by Peter Spier. C113
Little Bear's Visit. Illustrated by Maurice Sendak. By Else
　Minarik. C114
The Day We Saw the Sun Come Up. Illustrated by Adrienne Adams.
　By Alice Goudey. C115

1963

The Snowy Day. By Ezra Jack Keats. C116
The Sun Is a Golden Earring. Illustrated by Bernarda Bryson.
　By Natalia Belting. C117
Mr. Rabbit and the Lovely Present. Illustrated by Maurice Sendak.
　By Charlotte Zolotow. C118

1964

Where the Wild Things Are. By Maurice Sendak. C119
Swimmy. By Leo Lionni. C120
All in the Morning Early. Illustrated by Evaline Ness. By
　Leclaire Alger [Sorche Nic Leodhas]. C121
Mother Goose and Nursery Rhymes. Illustrated by Philip Reed.
　C122

Appendix A

1965

May I Bring a Friend? Illustrated by Beni Montresor. By
  Beatrice Schenk de Regniers. C123
Rain Makes Applesauce. Illustrated by Marvin Bileck. By Julian
  Scheer. C124
The Wave. Illustrated by Blair Lent. By Margaret Hodges. C125
A Pocketful of Cricket. Illustrated by Evaline Ness. By Rebecca
  Caudill. C126

1966

Always Room for One More. Illustrated by Nonny Hogrogian. By
  Leclaire Alger [Sorche Nic Leodhas]. C127
Hide and Seek Fog. Illustrated by Roger Duvoisin. By Alvin
  Tresselt. C128
Just Me. By Marie Hall Ets. C129
Tom Tit Tot. Illustrated by Evaline Ness. By Joseph Jacobs.
  C130

1967

Sam, Bangs & Moonshine. By Evaline Ness. C131
One Wide River to Cross. Illustrated by Ed Emberley. By Barbara
  Emberley. C132

1968

Drummer Hoff. Illustrated by Ed Emberley. By Barbara Emberley.
  C133
Frederick. By Leo Lionni. C134
Seashore Story. By Taro Yashima. C135
The Emperor and the Kite. Illustrated by Ed Young. By Jane
  Yolen. C136

1969

The Fool of the World and the Flying Ship. Illustrated by Uri
  Shulevitz. By Arthur Ransome. C137
Why the Sun and the Moon Live in the Sky. Illustrated by Blair
  Lent. By Elphinstone Dayrell. C138

1970

Sylvester and the Magic Pebble. By William Steig. C139
Goggles! By Ezra Jack Keats. C140
Alexander and the Wind-Up Mouse. By Leo Lionni. C141
Pop Corn and Ma Goodness. Illustrated by Robert Andrew Parker.
  By Edna Mitchell Preston. C142
Thy Friend, Obadiah. By Brinton Turkle. C143
The Judge: An Untrue Tale. Illustrated by Margot Zemach. By
  Harve Zemach. C144

Appendix A

Appendix A

Appendix B

Terms

1. The Medal shall be awarded annually to the author of the most
    distinguished contribution to American literature for children
    published in the United States during the preceding year.
    There are no limitations as to the character of the book con-
    sidered except that it be original work.

2. The Award is restricted to authors who are citizens or resi-
    dents of the United States.

3. The committee in its deliberations is to consider only the
    books eligible for the Award as specified in the terms.

Definitions

1. "Contribution to American literature" indicates the text of a
    book. It also implies that the Committee shall consider all
    forms of writing--fiction, non-fiction and poetry. Reprints
    and compilations are not eligible.

2. A "Contribution to American literature for children" shall be
    a book for which children are a potential audience. The book
    displays respect for children's understandings, abilities,
    and appreciations. Children are defined as persons of ages
    up to and including fourteen, and books for this entire age
    range are to be considered.

3. "Distinguished" is defined as:
    --marked by eminence and distinction: noted for signifi-
       cant achievement

*Adopted, by the ALSC Board, January 1978.

--marked by excellence in quality
--marked by conspicuous excellence or eminence
--individually distinct

4. "Author" may include co-authors. The author may be awarded the medal posthumously.

5. In defining the term, "original work," the committee will consider books that are traditional in origin, if the book is the result of original research and the retelling and interpretation are the writer's own.

6. "American literature published in the United States" means that books originally published in other countries are not eligible.

7. "Published . . . during the preceding year" means that the book has a publication date in that year, was available for purchase in that year, and has a copyright date no later than that year. A book might have a copyright date prior to the year under consideration but, for various reasons, was not published until the year under consideration.

8. "Resident" specifies that the author has established and maintained residence in the United States as distinct from being a casual or occasional visitor.

9. The term "only books eligible for the Award," specifies that the committee is not to consider the entire body of the work of an author or whether the author has previously won the award. The committee's decision is to be made following deliberations about the books of the specified calendar year.

Criteria

1. In identifying distinguished writing in a book for children:
   a. Committee members need to consider:
      Interpretation of the theme or concept
      Presentation of information including accuracy, clarity and
         organization
      Development of plot
      Delineation of characters
      Delineation of setting
      Appropriateness of style
Note: Because the literary qualities to be considered will vary depending on content, the committee need not expect to find excellence in each of the named elements. The book should, however, have distinguished qualities in all of the elements pertinent to it.
   b. Committee members must consider excellence of presentation
         for a child audience.

2. Each book is to be considered as a contribution to literature. The committee is to make its decision primarily on the text. Other aspects of a book are to be considered only if they distract from the text. Such other aspects might include illustrations, overall design of the book, etc.
Note: The committee should keep in mind that the award is for literary quality and quality of presentation for children. The award is not for didactic intent or for popularity.

CALDECOTT AWARD: TERMS, DEFINITIONS, AND CRITERIA*

Terms

1. The Medal shall be awarded annually to the artist of the most distinguished American picture book for children published in the United States during the preceding year. There are no limitations as to the character of the picture book except that the illustrations be original work.

2. The Award is restricted to artists who are citizens or residents of the United States.

3. The committee in its deliberations is to consider only the books eligible for the Award, as specified in the terms.

Definitions

1. A "picture book for children" as distingushed from other books with illustrations is one that essentially provides the child with a visual experience. A picture book has a collective unity of story-line, theme, or concept, developed through the series of pictures of which the book is comprised.

2. A "picture book for children" is one for which children are a potential audience. The book displays respect for children's understandings, abilities, and appreciations. Children are defined as persons of ages up to and including fourteen and picture books for this entire age range are to be considered.

3. "Distinguished" is defined as:
    --marked by eminence and distinction: noted for significant achievement
    --marked by excellence in quality
    --marked by conspicuous excellence or eminence
    --individually distinct

*Adopted, by the ALSC Board, January 1978.

4. The "artist" is the illustrator or co-illustrators. The artist may be awarded the Medal posthumously.

5. "Original work" means that illustrations reprinted or compiled from other sources are not eligible.

6. "American picture book published in the United States," specifies that books originally published in other countries are not eligible.

7. "Published . . . in the preceding year" means that the book has a publication date in that year, was available for purchase in that year, and has a copyright date no later than that year. A book might have a copyright date prior to the year under consideration but, for various reasons, was not published until the year under consideration.

8. "Resident," specifies that the artist has established and maintained residence in the United States as distinct from being a casual or occasional visitor.

9. The term "only the books eligible for the Award," specifies that the committee is not to consider the entire body of the work by an artist or whether the artist has previously won the award. The committee's decision is to be made following deliberation about the picture books of the specified calendar year.

<u>Criteria</u>

1. In identifying a distinguished picture book for children:
    a. Committee members need to consider:
       Excellence of execution in the artistic technique employed.
       Excellence of pictorial interpretation of story, theme,
          or concept;
          of appropriateness of style of illustration to the
             story, theme, or concept;
          of delineation of plot, theme, characters, setting,
             mood, or information through the pictures.
    b. Committee members must consider excellence of presentation
       in recognition of a child audience.

2. The only limitation to graphic form is that the form must be one which may be used in a picture book (e.g., motion picture photography is not at present possible, though still photography is).

3. Each book is to be considered as a picture book. The committee is to make its decision primarily on the illustrations, but other components of a book are to be considered especially

when they make a book less effective as a children's picture book.   Such other components might include the written text, the overall design of the book, etc.

Note: The committee should keep in mind that the award is for distinguished illustrations in a picture book and for excellence of pictorial presentation for children.   The award is not for didactic intent, or for popularity.

Appendix C

THE NEWBERY BOOKS:
A SUMMARY OF DISTRIBUTION BY TYPE OF LITERATURE

	1922–1931	1932–1941	1942–1951	1952–1961	1962–1971	1972–1981	TOTAL
Traditional Literature	5	4	3	0	3	1	16
Fantasy	10	3	7	4	9	9	42
Biography and Other Books of Information	3	11	14	11	5	2	46
Historical Fiction	13	19	11	12	4	7	66
Realistic Fiction Set in Other Lands	3	11	6	10	2	0	32
Realistic Animal Stories	2	1	4	2	1	1	11
Fiction About Regions and Minorities	2	2	3	5	5	6	23
Other Realistic Fiction Set in the United States	2	5	3	5	7	7	29
Total by Decade/ Out of Print	40/29	56/35	51/25	49/14	36/6	33/0	265/109

Appendix D

THE CALDECOTT BOOKS:
A SUMMARY OF DISTRIBUTION BY TYPE OF LITERATURE

	1938–1941	1942–1951	1952–1961	1962–1971	1972–1981	TOTAL
Traditional Literature	5	9	7	15	16	52
Fantasy	1	15	16	13	6	51
Biography	2	1	0	0	0	3
Books of Information	0	6	5	1	7	19
ABC/123	0	2	2	0	3	7
Historical Fiction	0	0	1	1	1	3
Realistic Fiction Set in Other Lands	4	2	5	1	0	12
Realistic Animal Stories	3	7	1	0	0	11
Fiction About Regions and Minorities	0	5	0	0	2	7
Other Realistic Fiction Set in the United States	0	6	6	6	3	21
Total by Decade/ Out of Print	15/4	53/24	43/9	37/5	38/0	186/42

Author, Illustrator, Title Index

Subject Index

Copyediting directed by Michael Sims
Designed and produced by Diane Dillon
Camera-ready copy typed by Jan Pinette
    on an IBM Selectric
Printed on 60# Bookmark, an acid-free paper,
    and bound by Braun-Brumfield, Inc.
    of Ann Arbor, Michigan.